Peter Schwarzburg

Practical counseling
in the schools

GARY S. BELKIN

Long Island University

WILLIAM C. BROWN COMPANY PUBLISHERS

Dubuque, Iowa   0384209

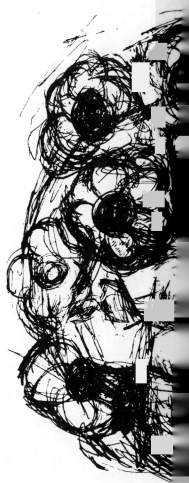

Peter Schwarzburg

TO MY PARENTS

Contents

0384209

Preface

The utility and relevance of an introductory textbook in the counseling field has recently come under challenge by those who propose that a practicum, experiential approach to the training of counselors precludes, or at least severely limits, the use of such a book. Critics of the printed medium, justly arguing that "the proper study of mankind is man," suggest that book learning—particularly textbook learning—serves little useful purpose in programs designed to foster personal growth and facilitate the development of an appropriate professional therapeutic attitude. Moreover, they point out that the very nature of a book—static, linear, and nonreactive—counters the efforts extended to produce a counselor who is dynamic, spontaneous, and responsive. While this "McLuhanized" point of view is certainly one with which we must come to grips, it fails in the end to acknowledge the basic purpose of an introductory textbook and to recognize its rightful place within the total training program.

A good textbook should serve as the single most important resource available to the counselor-in-training, as well as to the practicing counselor and the supervisor. By incorporating in a few hundred pages the research, theories, approaches, arguments, applications, and insights developed over hundreds, possibly thousands, of years, a textbook serves in effect as a cornucopia of practical information: an encyclopedia of relevant headings; an organized summary of the vast bulk of research undertaken; an overview of the problems in the field; a catalog of practical applications and examples; an enumeration and explication of the major points of controversy and contention. When viewed in this light, it becomes clear that a textbook, which places at the counselor's fingertips so much information in such an accessible way, can serve as an important adjunct training tool in the counselor-education program.

The preparation of this manuscript was undertaken with this idea in mind. I have tried to include within the covers of this book a broad panorama of the counseling position, incorporating both its theoretical and practical perspectives. In so doing, I have been particularly sensitive to the inability of a book of this type to cover everything of importance, and no doubt some readers will find that a particular point of view, a favorite research project, an innovative approach has been omitted. To guide me in the very difficult process of selection and exclusion, I have relied heavily on three fundamental questions: (1) How applicable is the material to the school counseling situation? (2) Does the material substantially clarify a counseling issue? (3) Is the material conducive to

Peter Schwarzburg

promoting in the counselor-trainee a feeling of pride and inspiration about his profession and his work?

This final point is particularly important. For while I have not deliberately excluded relevant material which may inadvertently minimize, distort, or denigrate the counseling function, I have intentionally tried to emphasize those papers and studies which reflect—in attitude, approach, and content—the efficacy, integrity, and importance of counseling as a unique profession. Where a study demonstrates beyond reasonable controversy the unique contributions of the counseling stance—whether it is to show that counselor qualities maintain priority over psychotherapeutic techniques, or to show that in some instances counseling practitioners outperform their psychiatric colleagues—I have taken special care to highlight it within the context of the subject under discussion. While one might argue that such emphasis indicates the author's unfair bias, my feeling is that such selectivity is the author's obligation to his readers. For as I indicate throughout the text, counseling has often been unfairly treated, even at times by its own advocates. The scales must now be tipped, however slightly, in the other direction, as counselors-in-training come to realize, with pride and determination, the great work that they are pledged to carry on. An introductory counseling textbook, I would suggest, is the proper place for such a counter-tipping.

One last point must be mentioned. While the particulars of this book are directed toward the school counselor, the scope of the book is more inclusive. Counselors of every type—vocational, educational, pastoral, drug, rehabilitation, family, and others—should find relevant information within the book. It is my belief that counseling, as a unique and integrated discipline, which respects and applauds the free will and volition of the client, demands for its practitioners committed, intelligent, hard-working individuals who are thoroughly familiar with all aspects of the counseling profession.

PART ONE

Peter Schwarzburg

What is counseling?

The profession of counseling is a relatively recent development, still in its flowering stages. Perhaps it is characteristic of a blossoming discipline, or perhaps it is peculiar to counseling alone, but in either case it is safe to say that counseling, in its slow process of gestation and development, is going through a confusing time of doubt and self-examination, a period of finding itself and defining its function intelligently. This period of growth, this dynamic process of self-discovery, is at times painful and at times joyous; at times fruitless and at other times invaluable; at times compellingly practical and at other times unobligingly esoteric. The character of the discipline today—its personality—is like that of an adolescent in search of identity: experimenting, rebelling, seeking, longing, trying to find a place in the sun.

When we raise the question, then, "What is counseling?" we are not inquiring about a fixed and static concept, one which can be precisely defined and explicated. Hardly! In fact, when we ask such a question, it is similar to asking about the exact position of an expanding object as the object travels swiftly through space and time toward its unknown destination. Because counseling is always somewhere different, relative to the observer, and because it is always some*thing* different, we cannot expect to answer the question other than with a rough approximation, or perhaps with an informed description of our expectations of its future positions and changing qualities.

When we speak of counseling, it must be clear that we are speaking about a growing, evolving, continually changing concept. It often occurs to me as I write these chapters that at the very moment the keys strike the paper, leaving their indelible impressions, as the sentences form and the ideas become deceivingly clear, they may at that very instant be obsolete and anachronistic. So quickly is the field changing, so rapid and unpredictable is its growth, that any attempts to pinpoint the nature, scope, and method of counseling must inevitably be doomed to failure.

A number of things can be said about counseling, however, which are not likely to change. There is a permanence of spirit which underlies the changing field, attesting to the existence of a common bias shared by all of those who

1

identify with the counseling profession. We can list these permanent ideas in the form of slogans, because they are as much rallying cries as they are descriptive statements. Each of these slogans capsulizes in briefest form some of the many ideas which recur often in the counseling literature:

Counseling is a philosophy!

Counseling is an attitude!

Counseling is a way of life!

Counseling is a commitment!

Counseling is action!

Counseling is a world view!

Counseling is a respect for the client

and an unconditioned acknowledgement of his freedom!

I must emphasize again that these are slogans rather than statements of clarification. As slogans, they impel the individual to action, and perhaps in its most basic sense this is what counseling really is: a certain type of action.

In the following three chapters, I shall attempt to sketch a detailed picture of the counseling field. Chapter 1 will differentiate counseling from psychotherapy and present a view of counseling—what I call "practical counseling"—that encompasses the goals of guidance, the skills of psychotherapy, and the insights of philosophy into a meaningful whole. We shall see how the counseling field evolved, what it has evolved into, and in which direction it is heading. A perspective which presents counseling within the context of its intellectual and historical development will be drawn, and some general definitions of counseling will be outlined. Chapter 2, "The Counseling Stance," will fill in the details of the broad sketch. We shall see how counseling, by its rejection of the mental illness approach and its acceptance of a philosophical view of man, "still betters" what has already been done in the mental health profession. Special attention will be directed toward how counseling enables the individual to find and exploit fully the possibilities of his freedom. Chapter 3, "Issues in Counseling," will complete the picture by detailing the most important areas of examination and controversy in the field. We shall explore the counseling relationship —the dynamic, emotional world which exists between the counselor and the client. We shall turn our attention to a crucial question which has troubled counselors and counselor educators for years: "What is the relationship between the counselor's theoretical orientation and what he actually does in the counseling session?" Finally, we shall examine two approaches to counseling— the absolute "Newtonian" approach and the relativistic "Einsteinian" point of view.

At the conclusion of Part One, we shall have a clear idea of what counseling really means, and hopefully our understanding of the word will help us carry out our efforts and will help us become more successful counselors.

chapter one

Guidance, counseling, and psychotherapy: a comparison

There is now, and always has been, a good deal of confusion and ambiguity surrounding the trinity of terms—guidance, counseling, and psychotherapy—and it is a confusion borne of knowledge, not ignorance. For as those familiar with the intimate workings of these three specialties know, the three terms are similar, do overlap, and in many instances are used interchangeably so well that even a semanticist couldn't quibble. Moreover, as one engages in the practice of guidance, of counseling, and of psychotherapy, it becomes even more striking how much the three have in common in terms of their moment-to-moment interactions, how many parallels of purpose and technique there are among them. It could be argued, and indeed has been, that to differentiate among the three is simply nit-picking. Yet there is a compelling reason to do just this, a reason which becomes emphatic, however, only after the differences among the terms become clear. The reason is this: Because the human organism is highly complex and specialized, both physically and psychologically, the range of problems and situations that the organism encounters is also complex and specialized. In the psychological realm, for example, problems run the gamut from the deeply emotional to decision-making, to interpersonal relationships, to minor conflicts, to learning problems, to vocational problems, and to a score of other types of problems. To deal effectively with this myriad of interlocking problems, there evolved over a period of many years specialists of different skills and backgrounds, each equipped to handle expertly one or more categories of problems, yet able to have some insight into all of the areas. These specialists work under a variety of professional titles: They are called psychologists, psychiatrists, psychiatric social workers, guidance counselors, counseling psychologists, pastoral counselors, psychotherapists, psychoanalysts, learning disability specialists, consulting psychologists, vocational and educational counselors, family counselors, mental hygienists, and so on ad infinitum. Each is equipped to handle his own specialized range of problems, yet each is acutely aware of the other specialists' responsibilities, and the possibility of referral and consultation is always present.

The school counselor, with whom we are primarily concerned in this textbook, practices an amalgam of guidance, counseling, and psychotherapy within the context of a school setting. He is also a referral person, whose familiarity with the allied mental health specialties enables him to initiate appropriate referrals where he believes that a particular client's difficulties can best be dealt with by an adjacent area of expertise. It is imperative, therefore, not only that he understand the distinctions among his guidance role, his counseling role, and his psychotherapeutic role, but also that he understand the relationships among the three roles and the relationship to other specialized roles within the broad professional ranks. Because guidance, counseling, and psychotherapy have different origins, because they have vastly different orientations, different axiomatic bases, different resources, the counselor's understanding of the differences among them not only helps him understand the three types of approaches available to him but also helps him define his function comprehensively and understand his rightful place in the mental health profession hierarchy. By looking at the three terms as three distinct phases of the mental health effort, he is better able to gain a working perspective of his role in the treatment of individual difficulties.

The purpose of this chapter, therefore, is not to clear up a semantic problem or to set up arbitrary distinctions with which a counselor can feel comfortable, but rather to begin to clarify and to define the factors which contribute to our description of the complex job of the school counselor. We shall begin with a broad perspective by taking a panoramic view of the history of psychological thought over the past two thousand years, to see the relative positions of guidance, counseling, and psychotherapy in a historical and cultural perspective.

THE HISTORY OF PSYCHOLOGICAL THOUGHT

Long before the discipline that we know as psychology came into its own, men were profoundly concerned with the issues that now constitute the core of that discipline. From his earliest endeavors in speculative thought, man has questioned how we perceive the world, why we behave in certain ways, what our relationship is with the environment and particularly with others, and how learning takes place. Heraclitus's insight that "all is flux—we never step into the same river twice" was intended to say as much about the nature of man as about the nature of the world. Kirk and Raven (1966), as a matter of fact, argued quite convincingly that it was Heraclitus who first "built up a rationalistic psychological theory, in which for the first time...the structure of the soul is related not only to that of the body, but also to that of the world as a whole" (p. 206). Even such a primitively stated idea as "in sleep, the soul is partly cut off from the world-fire, and so decreases in activity" can be seen as a subtle forerunner to Freud's later thinking on the interpretation of dreams. Murphy (1968) traces the history of psychological thought back to the pre-Socratic philosopher Pythagoras, whose theory of numbers as the underlying truth in nature not only fore-shadowed "the massive place of quantitative method in the whole structure of modern psychology" (p.13), but left its mark on such later thinkers as Plato, Herbart (the innovator in education), Kohler (a founder of gestalt psychology), and even Freud.

But it was Plato, more than any other early thinker, who began to organize his brilliant psychological insights into a systematic theory. Plato's interests were varied, and he examined the psychology of the individual in all of its rami-fications: in moral issues, in terms of education, in relation to society, in theo-logical perspective, and so on. He dealt with such questions as "What makes a man virtuous—his inheritance, his upbringing, or his formal education" (*Meno*), "How can children be most effectively taught" (*Republic*), and "Which tech-niques have been successfully used in persuading and influencing people in their decisions and beliefs" (*Gorgias*). But it is not the specific questions them-selves that prove so important to us as counselors, but rather the method that Plato used to deal with these questions, a method which, more than any other in the history of human thought, sets the way for the counseling relationship. It is a dramatic method, in which profound questions are dealt with through the dynamics of very real human interactions, a method in which the characters are as important as the things they say. The method used is the dialectic, or what is generally called the *Socratic dialogue* (after Socrates, the main character, who was Plato's teacher in real life, and dialogue, a question and answer method). The characters in these dialogues, according to Versenyi (1963), "do not merely present and analyze ideas, remaining themselves detached and out of the focus of the inquiry, but on the contrary, they enter the stage and become the actors and the center of action, the viewers and the thing viewed.... This double in-volvement parallels the double involvement of the student in Socratic educa-tion" (p. 125). As we read these dialogues, we learn not only by hearing what the characters are saying, but also by observing how they interact with one another, by seeing how their feelings about each other influence their thinking, by under-standing how the ultimate force of language is in personalities, not in words alone. It is a lesson in humanism—what Versenyi calls "Socratic Humanism"—that has been overlooked by men as far apart in their thinking as Thomas Aquinas and B. F. Skinner, whose catechismic method and conditioning meth-ods, respectively, omit the force of personality from learning.

But Plato's method is not his only contribution, of course. His ideas have perhaps done more to form the foundations of Western education than have the ideas of any other single thinker. It was Plato, for example, who first suggested a developmental curriculum, who first emphasized the importance of physical education in the schools, who first advocated the use of scientifically based teaching methodologies. It was Plato who first stressed the role of music and poetry in the development of character, who first recognized the conflicts be-tween social organization and human frailty, who first hinted at the place of guidance counselors within the schools. It is in his nondialectic writing, *The Republic*, where we get our first glimpse into the need and the rationale for

The philosopher Plato
as depicted by Raphael

counseling within the educational system. Peterson (1970) captures the essence of *The Republic* beautifully:

Plato believed that if one could structure a society with every man functioning happily within the realm for which he is best suited, then one could have an ideal, just society. But how could one implement such a plan? Plato decided that this could be done by instituting a ladderlike school system, which could serve as a screening device to place every man in his proper place. The students would thus begin school en mass and would progress up the ladder. The first to begin to fall by the wayside would be "counselled out" and sent to work in the fields where they could best fulfill their obligations to the state. The rest would continue to the next level, at which time the defenders would be screened out and then drafted into the army. This left the wisest group of the society, the elite, who, by continued lengthy training were to receive the education necessary to develop them into philosopher kings. (p. 75)

Despite the blatantly undemocratic and somewhat distasteful assumptions underlying such a scheme, it does portend what would later become the vocational guidance movement, which of course, was oriented toward a democratic, capitalistic society. According to Plato, some kind of illuminating force was needed behind education, a guiding light that would be directed toward the individual's as well as the society's future. It is no coincidence that the progressive education movement in twentieth-century America credits Plato in many instances as either the inspiration for or the first implementor of many of their ideas; for his outlook extended many years ahead of his time. It would be fair to say that no counselor in the schools today can fail to acknowledge the enormous debt he owes to the prescient insights of Plato.

Plato's student Aristotle is the second great force in the development of psychology. Aristotle's contributions to psychology are so numerous and so varied that it would take many volumes to justly credit him. No psychologist after Aristotle could ignore his debt to the great thinker, and it is not uncommon in the works of the earliest psychologists to find more than casual references to Aristotle's thoughts, particularly to his methodological and bio-psychological insights. Esper (1964) has presented a thorough and concise analysis of Aristotle's contributions to psychology. Aristotle was the first philosopher to suggest explicitly that research must begin with observation, the sine qua non of most later psychological investigations. His biological studies, which resulted in his view that the body is a group of functioning organs, each actively engaged with the others to sustain life, has had many implications for psychology, most notably Freud's subsequent conception of the psyche as composed of interacting functional elements (ego, id, superego). Aristotle also set forth a primitive theory of behaviorism, arguing that stimuli from the environment elicit responses which may be appetitive or aversive, which may act as a reinforcement for the action or as a countermotivation against the action.

Perhaps most important, Aristotle believed that "the most motivational processes are hunger, thirst, sex, anger, fear, and desire for bodily comfort.... These are 'instincts' in the sense of 'drives' which man shares with other animals; they are inborn tendencies" (Esper, p. 190). This not only foreshadowed the important work Freud would do centuries later but also set the stage for numerous philosophic revolutions which would further contribute to the development of psychology.

But Aristotle's contributions are not limited to the field of individual psychology alone; on the contrary, perhaps his major contribution was to the broad area of "social psychology," of man in interaction with his environment and with others. He formulated, for example, a psychological theory of virtue, based on the principle that action is in accordance with insight (which had many subtle implications for the training of children to function harmoniously with the goals of the society). He conceived of the State in terms of the persons who composed it: "The nature of the state is to be a plurality," because it is made up of so many different kinds of men, with different needs and interests. He developed a theory of government which was in accord with his perceptions of the individual psyche.

We can see that in the case of both Plato and Aristotle there are numerous valuable insights which for many years, although respected and reiterated, rarely found application in the efforts to confront and deal with social and personal problems. Indeed, for the next two thousand years these philosophers' thoughts would remain imprisoned within the confines of philosophic discourse and social theory, while the unfortunate fact is that philosophy is too important to be left to the philosophers.

We turn now to empiricism, which emerged at the end of the seventeenth century with Locke's "An Essay Concerning Human Understanding," which set forth what were to become the premises of empirical thought: that all knowledge derives from experience as it is presented to the mind through the senses. "Our knowledge," argued Locke, "is real only so far as there is a *conformity* between our ideas and the reality of things.... We have an intuitive knowledge of our own existence, and a demonstrative knowledge of the existence of a God: of the existence of anything else, we have no other but a sensitive knowledge; which extends not beyond the objects present to our senses" (Locke, pp. 91–92). Bishop George Berkeley, a contemporary of Locke's, extended his reasoning even further in his famous proclamation that "all the choir of heaven and furniture of earth—in a word, all those bodies which compose the mighty frame of the world— have not any subsistence without a mind." In other words, Berkeley was saying that the whole world really exists within the mind: that reality is a figment of our imagination, so to speak. David Hume, Berkeley's successor and the last of the great empiricists, extended these insights to the question of human spirit:

For my part, when I enter most intimately into what I call *myself*, I always stumble upon some particular perception or other, of heat or cold, light or shade.... I never can catch *myself* at any time without a perception, and never can observe anything but the

Aristotle's thinking forms the basis of much of modern psychological thought.

perception. When my perceptions are removed for any time, as by sound sleep, so long am I insensible of *myself*, [I] may truly be said not to exist. (*A Treatise of Human Nature*, I, 4.6)

This empirical model of the human mind—what Scheffler (1967) was later to call the "impression model" of learning—was to have profound influence upon the development of psychology. But what we have here is still prepsychological, in the modern sense, because it does not yet employ the scientific model for its basis. It is still philosophy, but a strain of the total philosophic movement which was primarily concerned with the mind of man in relation to his actions. "Since the days of the ancient civilizations," Maxine Greene (1973) points out,

scholars and philosophers have devoted their energies to determining the most desirable patterns of behavior for their particular cultural circumstances.... It was only with the nineteenth century that a body of dependable scientific knowledge about human behavior developed; but the absence of empirical studies did not stop earlier philosophers from describing or prescribing. (p. 71)

The beginnings of modern laboratory psychology (experimental) is usually traced to 1879, when Wilhelm Wundt set up a laboratory in Leipzig, Germany. The introspective method used by Wundt for his experiments would probably be considered the first distinctly psychological method. This approach consisted simply of analyzing the contents of consciousness by paying attention to whatever crossed the subjects' minds. Although Wundt and the other introspective psychologists, namely William James, E. B. Titchener, Kulpe, Angell, and Mc-Dougall, considered their method a serious advancement over the pre-scientific philosophical inquiries into psychological problems, they soon found themselves criticized for the very lack of scientific integrity which they had found fault with in their predecessors. A new school of psychology—the behaviorist school—arose in 1912, subjecting the introspectionists to a barrage of critical analysis, from which they would never recover.

The behaviorists' major criticism of the introspectionists rests on their emphasis on consciousness, an untenable concept for the behaviorists because of its intangibility. "From the time of Wundt on," Watson (1930) argues, "consciousness becomes the keynote of psychology. It is the keynote of all psychologies today except behaviorism. It is a plain assumption just as unprovable, just as unapproachable, as the old concept of the soul. And to the behaviorist the two terms are essentially identical, so far as concerns their metaphysical implications" (p. 14). Instead of building a psychology upon consciousness, the behaviorists suggested, use something which would be liable to scientific measurement and experiment: namely, observable behavior. With this as their working premise, behavioristic psychology attempted to formulate, through systematic observation and experimentation, the generalizations, laws, and principles which underly man's behavior (Watson, 1919).

The rift between these two early schools of psychology is indicative of the schism which divides the ranks of the mental health profession today. "Are we," ask practitioners, "to be primarily concerned with feelings, perceptions, associations, and other manifestations of consciousness, or are we to focus our attention on symptoms, actions, learning, and other observable forms of behavior?" Should the counselor be concerned with the client's condition of consciousness —his subjectivity—vague as this concept is, or should he deal predominantly with the client's behavior, which is observable, measurable, and hopefully trainable? These primordial questions still persist today, perhaps more compellingly than ever before, and it is the responsibility of each counselor as he enters the profession to decide which premises are right for him, which assumptions he will use to guide his practice. We shall see later how the beginning guidance movement, which was behaviorally oriented (emphasizing as it did vocational choice and educational training) was transformed over the years into a synthetic movement which embraced the dual concepts of guidance and counseling, thus taking into account both behavioral problems and states of consciousness and feelings.

*   *   *   *   *

As we look over this brief history of psychology, there appear a number of salient points which are worth noting for future reference. For as we shall shortly see, these early thinkers, with their limited means of investigation and narrow cultural perspectives, were so rich in inventiveness and brilliant speculation that they exerted a massive influence upon the subsequent development of guidance and counseling as we know them today. The influence of the philosophical stance can be found in counseling theory as well as in counseling practices. Counselors are compelled to ask such basic, yet revealing, questions as: What is the relationship between man and his society? How do we learn, and how does learning become meaningful to us? How can education prepare us for successful living? Are we born with innate instincts, or do drives develop as a result of conditioned responses? These questions, of as much relevance today as they were thousands of years ago when they were posed by philosophers who pondered man's place in the universe, have contributed to the rich, exciting profession we call counseling. Plato's idealism, Socrates's dialectical method, Aristotle's organic theories, the empirical model of the mind, introspectionism, and behaviorism have all played such an intimate role in the evolving view of man which now permeates the counseling position that it would be virtually impossible for a counselor to function effectively and authentically without acknowledging his debt to the past masters of philosophy and psychology. Moreover, an affinity of spirit with these past masters allows the contemporary counselor the opportunity to view himself in the cultural continuum, so subtly textured in the grain of history that values, insights, and treatment procedures can never be totally isolated from the tradition in which they have evolved.

As important as these contributions are, there is a striking omission in this history of psychology which bears mentioning. Despite all the efforts to come to grips with man's psyche and his place in the sun, there were no philosophical or early psychological attempts to *treat* man's emotional problems. In fact, no such discipline arose until the early nineteenth century when a number of movements took hold which attempted to cure mental and emotional illness in a humane, constructive, and scientifically valid manner. The psychological movement, from its origins in philosophy to its development in the psychological laboratory, blossomed as an attempt to study and understand man as he is, not as a method to minister to him or cure him, with the result that modern-day psychology is a discipline more attuned to studying man than to treating him therapeutically. The guidance movement, on the other hand, from its very beginnings, arose as a movement designed to help the individual resolve his difficulties, a humanitarian and therapeutic position which persists today in all guidance and counseling efforts. We shall now turn our attention to the development of that movement.

THE GUIDANCE MOVEMENT

In many ways, the emergence of the guidance movement at the dawning of the twentieth century stands as a symbol for the great democratic and individually-responsive drift of American history, beginning over one hundred years earlier with the signing of the Declaration of Independence. That important document set the tone for what was to become the great American theme, which governed our destiny and shaped our history more than any other single factor; namely, that the individual's right to freedom has priority over everything else, and that this right includes his freedom to find happiness in his life.

All of the ideas and principles which transformed the *philosophy* of democratic government into a viable social and political institution also made possible the emergence of the guidance movement in the United States at a time in our history when the individual was threatened with a loss of his pursuit of happiness as he found himself caught up in the whirlwinds of progress which swept the nation. It is important to note that the guidance movement was not precipitated by some overwhelming national failure or tragedy, but rather it arose as a natural consequence of the movements of individual Americans as they fulfilled their national and personal destinies.

The decade which most precisely pinpoints the birth of the guidance movement is the closing decade of the nineteenth century. It was a time of change in America, a time of massive building and rapid technological innovation, a time of increasing immigration from Europe and of migration from rural America into the cities. A predominantly homogeneous agrarian society was in the process of being transformed into a primarily heterogeneous urban society, as the great swell of European immigrants and American country folk flocked to the great urban centers, heating up the classical melting pot which was to play so great a part in twentieth-century American history. The consequences of this demographic tipping were staggering: The cities became melting pots of ethnic eccentricities as each of the assimilating groups gently, but often painfully, began to make their presence felt in their new homeland.

Other changes were also making themselves felt at this time. Barry and Wolf (1963) cite "industrialization, specialization, urbanization, the changing role of women, the growing need for education, rising enrollments, expanding curricula, rising secularism, the desire for useful education, and new educational theories as some of the changes and developments that created or intensified the need for guidance-personnel work" (p. 16). To this list, we must also add other, sometimes subtle, social changes which were beginning to bear profoundly on individual lives as we reach the 1890s. Five years before this decade, the first electric railroad, the prototype for urban mass transportation, was opened in Baltimore, signaling the massive influence electricity was to play on the course of history. Ironically, in the very year 1890, William Kemmler earned the dubious distinction of becoming the first man in history to be executed by electricity, at Sing Sing Prison in Ossining, New York. That same year, Ellis Island replaced the antiquated Castle Garden as the welcoming point for the hundreds of thousands of immigrants who flocked to our shores. A strike at the Carnegie Steel Mills in 1892, which resulted in a violent and fatal confrontation between management and labor, emphasized the rising antagonism between the classes —a problem which would plague this country for many years. Massive unemployment swept the country, and 20,000 Americans marched on Washington in 1894 to protest the precarious condition of the economy. These were all important national events, newsworthy and recorded. But meanwhile, unannounced and unbeknownst to most people, seemingly minor isolated events in different parts of the country were the first manifestations of the guidance movement, as it would be known many years later.

In 1895, George Merril instituted the first systematic vocational guidance program at the California School of Mechanical Arts in San Francisco. About the same time, Frank Parsons began to offer vocational counseling to poverty stricken youth in Boston. Parsons's work, generally considered the most important in terms of the founding of the guidance movement, resulted in the Vocation Bureau in Boston, which he opened with Meyer Bloomfield in 1908. Cremin's (1964) description of Parsons accurately pinpoints the philosophical basis that motivated and underlined Parsons's thinking at this time:

The key to Parsons' ultimate goal ... lay in his notion of "the useful and happy life."
Parsons, a significant figure in the history of American reform, believed not only that vocational counseling would lead to greater individual fulfillment, but that people suited to their jobs would tend to be active in the creation of a more efficient and humane industrial system. Intelligently practiced, the craft of vocational guidance would serve not only the youngsters who sought counsel, but the cause of social reform as well. Thus did the earliest, and to date the most stubbornly central thread of the guidance movement connect with the broader progressive program. (p. 13)

Whether we call this sentiment progressivism, as Cremin does, or humanitarianism, as Barry and Wolf do, it adds up to the same thing, namely, the belief that the individual is of the greatest importance, that human life possesses a certain intrinsic and unalterable dignity and worth, and that society cannot be considered separate from the individuals who compose it—that a healthy and prosperous society is composed of healthy and prosperous individuals, and likewise a sick and dying society is composed of unfulfilled and wasting individuals.

It is in this philosophic milieu, this predominantly individual approach, that the guidance movement emerged. It took many manifestations in different parts of the country: in Grand Rapids, Michigan, Jesse B. Davis organized the first large-scale school guidance program; Frank P. Goodwin instituted a similar effort in Cincinnati, Ohio; Parsons's important book, *Choosing a Vocation*, the first guidance textbook, was published posthumously in 1909; the first doctoral dissertation in guidance was accepted at Columbia University in 1914 (*Educational Guidance* by T. L. Kelley); Eli Weaver, of Boys' High School in Brooklyn, New York, began to advise his students about their career plans and future education; William Wheatly of Middletown, Connecticut, introduced special school courses on vocations and added a unit on vocations to the social studies curriculum; Ella Flagg Young, the Superintendent of Schools in Chicago, appointed Deans of Girls to act as guidance counselors to help the students with their problems; Dr. William Healy, a physician, organized the first child guidance clinic in Chicago in 1909; Clifford Beers helped found the National Committee for Mental Hygiene in that same year; the National Vocational Guidance Association (NVGA) was founded in 1913; John M. Brewer of Harvard introduced vocational guidance practices into the teacher-training curriculum, around the time of World War I. These are merely a few of the more notable events that marked the burgeoning guidance movement at the close of the last and the beginning of this century.

Two important insights are gleaned from a cumulative view of these events. First, it is abundantly clear that guidance and counseling, as we know it today, evolved from a vocational guidance movement, brought about by the changing social and demographic forces that played a part in shaping America at the turn of the century. Second, it is evident that underlying all these innovative gestures was a strong commitment to the principles that marked the beginnings of this country, namely, the belief in the individual, the humanitarian spirit, the inextricable relationship between man and his society. Taken together, we see the birth of the guidance movement as an inevitable consequence of the American spirit which has so forcefully shaped our national destiny.

This guidance movement, of course, has changed dramatically since its beginnings almost ninety years ago. No longer is guidance simply vocational or educational guidance: On the contrary, the term guidance has become linked almost automatically with its partner, *counseling*. This was a natural evolution as vocational guidance personnel began to realize that what they were doing was more than merely providing guidance, or advice. They were helping individuals resolve difficulties in their lives, sometimes very complex and deeply rooted, and treating the problems in a way that was different from psychotherapy. The narrow emphasis on vocational needs and interests began to broaden into an emphasis on human adjustment, which required more far-ranging skills than information-giving alone. Nowadays, Moser and Moser

(1963) point out, "guidance is a term with many meanings. It is a point of view; it is a group of services; it is a field of study" (p. 8). This broadness is borne out if we examine some of the contemporary definitions of guidance. McDaniel and Shaftel (1956), for example, describe the guidance function comprehensively:

Guidance in the modern school contributes in two broad areas to the concept that education is an individual process.... Guidance represents a pattern of services, which includes *orientation, individual inventory, educational and occupational information, counseling, placement, and follow-up.* (p. 17, italics added)

Kirby (1971) views guidance within the context of the total educational process:

Guidance is an *incremental* process of education that is particularly cognizant of those aspects of educational, vocational, and social development not generally or specifically planned for in the curriculum. The guidance function, being incremental, is concerned with marginal changes; it is cognizant of those "critical incidents" in development common to most tasks of the emerging adult, and is primarily concerned with assisting in day-to-day decision making. (p. 596)

Downing (1968) presents a point of view along similar lines, emphasizing the adjustment of the individual:

Guidance is an organized set of specialized services.... an integral part of the school environment designed to promote the development of students and to assist them toward a realization of sound wholesome adjustment and maximum accomplishments commensurate with their potentialities. (p. 7)

Mortenson & Schmuller (1959), too, develops a definition along the same lines:

Guidance has been accepted as the personalization of education both in theory and practice. Guidance is that part of the educational program that helps provide the personal opportunities and specialized staff services by which each individual can develop to the fullest of his abilities and capacities in terms of the democratic ideal. (p. 3)

And, finally, Sprinthall (1971), in his superb book, *Guidance for Human Growth*, suggests that the teaching function and the guidance function serve as a team to liberate the individual through education. He suggests a "dual curriculum" to develop the individual's cognitive capacities and his personal development simultaneously:

The dual curriculum implies a frame of reference with distinct but related priorities— learning to learn with a priority on subject matter mastery, and learning to learn with a priority on mastery and competence as a person. Such a dual curriculum for education makes requisite a collaboration of the two priorities. (p. 16)

In this sense, the guidance function and the teaching function work in harmony for the total development and growth of the individual.

We see from these similar conceptions of guidance—and its place in the school—how the field has expanded rapidly since its beginning. Brown and Srebalus (1972) cite four influences which have helped shape guidance into what it is today: progressive education, the mental health movement, the psychological laboratory, and the reaction to laboratory psychology. The contribution of the progressive education movement is clear: By emphasizing the specialized needs of the individual within the scope of mass schooling, there arose naturally a movement to deal with these individual needs within the context of the public school. Moreover, the progressive education movement, characterized by a sensitivity to the individual's place within society and motivated by a desire to help each student grow while pursuing his formal education, necessitated the establishment of an office to help advise and direct the individual student in terms of his personal and social adjustment. It was through the philosophy of progressive education that the first comprehensive guidance services were justified and implemented, and throughout the history of the guidance movement, progressive educators and their disciples often stood at the forefront of new services and expanded programs.

The contribution of the mental-health movement was even more profound. Until the early nineteenth century, victims of mental illness were treated either as prisoners, avatars of the Devil, or chronically and hopelessly incurable. "The insane," points out Thomson (1968), "were regarded simply with fear and dis-

The mentally ill were once burned at the stake.

14

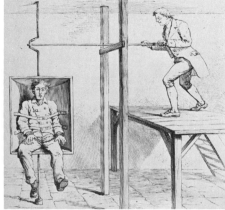

Some typical methods of treating the mentally ill were the rotator, the circulating swing, the crib, and keeping inmates chained in cells.

gust, and were thrust into prison-like asylums to be left to the mercy of brutal and ignorant keepers.... the typical European asylum contained naked, ill-fed wretches who slept on straw in filthy, unventilated and unlit cells. The quarters resembled dungeons, and the more disturbed patients were frequently chained. In England lunatics were often exhibited like animals in a side-show for the amusement of the public" (p. 194).

At the notorious Bicêtre asylum in France, a young psychiatrist, Dr. Philippe Pinel, was given charge in 1793. Pinel, motivated in part by humanitarian instincts and in part by his realization that such conditions were hardly likely to produce therapeutic changes, instituted a program of reform, based on the simple principle that the job of an asylum was to restore the inmate to functional mental health. Such a simple principle, yet one so revolutionary in its time that it met with much opposition from the community and from the national government. But Pinel persisted, at Bicêtre and later at Salpêtrière where

Le Salpêtrière: the home of Jean Martin Charcot's famous neurological clinic

he was transferred, and he deserves credit as the first pioneer in the mental health movement.

In addition to his reformative efforts, Pinel combatted the ignorant notion of mental illness as a manifestation of diabolic possession. He formulated a theory of psychopathology to account for "abnormal" behavior, which included both medical and psychological causes. He trained other young physicians to follow his lead, and by the 1850s France was the unchallenged leader in psychiatry. But psychiatry was still in its primitive throes, uncertain and not entirely scientific, desperately in need of a champion to pull the disparate pieces together. Such a leader emerged at Salpêtrière a few years after Pinel's death.

Jean Martin Charcot was a distinguished neurologist, with a special interest in diseases of a psychosomatic nature. He had spent several years diagnosing and treating multiple sclerosis, and he had noticed during this period that many patients who believed they were suffering from a form of paralysis or epilepsy actually had nothing physically wrong with them. He labeled this disorder *hysteria* and formulated a detailed clinical description of it.

It was a colleague of Charcot's, another neurologist named Pierre Janet, who discovered a method to treat this newly diagnosed disorder. Charcot had used hypnosis as a diagnostic tool in working with hysterical patients: Janet took this one step further and began to use hypnosis as a curative agent as well. He discovered through trial and error that hysterics were able under hypnosis to recall memories and feelings from the past. As the hypnotist helped the hysteric remember these buried memories, the patient suddenly began to experience a rapid alleviation of the debilitating symptom, a miraculous cure. Janet used the term "catharsis" to describe this sudden freeing of the dammed-up memories, and he set down the groundwork upon which a later student would revolutionize the field of psychiatry.

Sigmund Freud, a neurologist of Jewish-Viennese extraction, was deeply impressed by the work of Charcot and Janet. Although poor, he managed to obtain a scholarship in 1885 to travel to France to study under Charcot, who was

*Jean Martin Charcot
demonstrates the
hypnotic technique at
Le Salpêtrière asylum.*

better known at the time. Studying by day and reviewing and critically examining at night, Freud returned from his sojourn in France full of new and exciting ideas. He shared these ideas with a colleague, Dr. Josef Breuer, and the two collaborated to use the cathartic-hypnotic treatment in working with hysterical patients. This marked the beginnings of what was to emerge a few short years later as the psychoanalytic movement (see chapter 8).

While these exciting developments were occurring in Europe, what was happening in America? Very little, unfortunately. Mental illness, while regarded not quite as primitively as in pre-Pinel France, was still viewed without the slightest sophistication or optimism. No national committees, no prominent physicians, no humanitarian organizations watched out for the interests of the mentally ill. On the contrary, a mentally ill person was at best a pariah—an emotional leper—who had to be separated from society, for both his good and the common weal. This attitude was pervasive in America during the same years that the guidance movement was being born.

What was needed was someone to bring to the attention of a public long motivated by humanitarian and progressive instincts the enormity and seriousness of the problem. Such a man, ironically enough, was Clifford Beers, a minor clerk in the financial district of New York City. Beers, who suffered from schizophrenia, spent many of his years in mental institutions, outraged by the conditions but helpless to do anything about them. Finally, recovering enough to function, he wrote a book about his experiences, *A Mind That Found Itself*, which became a runaway bestseller. Even more important, the book, a subtle combination of personal experiences and reformative rhetoric, instigated rapid and

*Sigmund Freud,
founder of
psychoanalysis*

17

sweeping changes in the field of mental health care. In the following passage, Beers describes a typical situation at a sanatorium:

One day a man—seemingly a tramp—approached the main building of the sanatorium and inquired for the owner. He soon found him, talked with him a few minutes, and an hour or so later he was sitting at the bedside of an old and infirm man. This aged patient had recently been committed to the institution by relatives who had labored under the common delusion that the payment of a considerable sum of money each week would insure kindly treatment. When this tramp-attendant first appeared, all his visible worldly possessions were contained in a small bundle which he carried under his arm. So filthy were his person and his clothes that he received a compulsory bath and another suit before being assigned to duty. He then began to earn his four dollars and fifty cents a week by sitting several hours a day in the room with the aged man, sick unto death.... the uncouth stranger had never before so much as crossed the threshold of a hospital. His last job had been as a member of a section-gang on a railroad. From the roadbed of a railway to the bedside of a man about to die was indeed a change which might have taxed the adaptability of a more versatile being. (pp. 43-44)

Beers, who suffered severe psychological problems which were ultimately cured, became a social activist and crusader, helping to found the Society for Mental Hygiene. While Freud made possible the conception, men like Beers made possible the implementation of modern mental health treatment, which did so much to change the relationship of the mentally ill to the greater society.

Once the American public became aware of the need for mental health reform, the innovations of Freud and his contemporaries were quickly imported and put into practice here. From approximately 1930 on, psychiatry and psychotherapy began to make an impact in the developing guidance movement.

The work of Watson, Skinner, and other laboratory psychologists also began to make an impact on the guidance movement. Most new movements, guidance being no exception, attempt to legitimize themselves by formulating their own private nomenclature, by setting up their own disciplinary rules and formulae, and by claiming privilege through the good name of science. How tempting it was to the early leaders of the guidance movement to seize the alluringly quantifiable findings of the behaviorists and apply those findings to guidance problems. Nevertheless, laboratory psychology, which dedicated most of its time to animal experimentation, with the consequence of fixed rules and axioms, was found repugnant to many in the field who still held fast to the humanitarian principle of individuality. As late as 1973, at the American Psychological Convention in Montreal, arguments raged between proponents of the behaviorist position and the "humanitarian" position. Carl Thoresen, in a discussion with B. F. Skinner, argued recently that behavioral principles are "the horse" which pulls the "humanitarian" cart.

Perhaps the most notable reaction to the laboratory psychology movement was instituted by a young psychologist who had been trained in the psychoanalytic method, but who found even that method too depersonalizing. Arguing that each patient had to be viewed as a total, distinct, and important individual, not as proof for some tentative theory of behavior, learning, or psychosexual development, Carl Rogers set forth what he called "nondirective psychotherapy." (A complete discussion of his ideas will be found in chapter 9.) Rogers's ideas had a more significant impact upon guidance and counseling than had any other system of psychotherapy. Rogers's belief in the dignity of the individual and the ultimate worth of the client was compatible not only with the attitudes of professionals in the guidance field, but also with the attitudes of many prominent psychotherapists as well. Rogers's influence upon the guidance and counseling movement is incalculable, and the tradition he established set the stage for the merging of the three terms "guidance," "psychology," and "counseling" sometime around the late 1940s.

It is not possible to pinpoint precisely the year that the inevitable merger of these terms took place, but the forces which shaped their courtship and consecrated their mating are quite clear. Along with the growing guidance movement was found an increased interest in psychometrics (psychological testing) and psychotherapy. (A detailed discussion of the influence of the testing movement will be found in chapter 2.) By 1950, it was no longer possible to speak strictly in terms of guidance; for the guidance function, as it was by then conceived, involved the administration and interpretation of tests, personal interviews, psychological counseling, and some psychotherapeutic skills. In 1951, in recognition of the situation, the American Psychological Association adopted the term *counseling psychology* to replace *counseling and guidance* as a division. Nowadays, all that differentiates counseling from counseling psychology is the training of the practitioner, the former usually under the auspices of a guidance and counseling department, and the latter accredited by the Education and Training Board of the APA.

As the terms were joined in happy matrimony, new possibilities unfolded to develop further each of the functions embodied within the rubric. Most importantly, the burgeoning philosophy of existentialism, of great popularity during the 1950s and 60s, began to wield its weight within the movement. It was not uncommon to hear of existential approaches to vocational counseling, to job training, to personnel work, as well as to psychotherapeutic counseling. Dahms and Kinnick (1969), for example, outline an existential position for dealing with problems of student personnel work, a position which would have been unheard of before the merging of the guidance and counseling functions. Efforts to institute existential programs of vocational counseling gained a widening popularity during the early 1960s. But none of these efforts was unequivocally successful at integrating the counseling and guidance approach fully in practice.

One of the major problems facing the practicing guidance counselor is differentiating between counseling and psychotherapy. Always wary of trespassing in an area where diffidence conquered experimentation, guidance counselors as well as counselor educators stepped lightly along the precarious and ill-defined border between their discipline and that of the more expert, "better" educated psychotherapist. Whereas in the past, when guidance and counseling were a continent apart and no such temptation existed, now the practicing guidance counselor found himself for the first time asking deeply probing philosophical questions and relating to his client on an emotional, intensive level, as well as on the didactic, advice-giving level. Fearful that he was inadvertently entering the sacred province of psychotherapy, where M.D.s and Ph.D.s abound, and highly technical jargon enshrouds the reality of the patient's life, he retreated timidly, asking, as he would time and again, "Where does counseling end and psychotherapy begin?"

It is an important question, one surrounded by myths and misconceptions, in part perpetuated by an establishment with vested interests. It is to this question that we shall now turn our attention.

COUNSELING AND PSYCHOTHERAPY: IS THERE A DIFFERENCE?

The most tempting answer to this question is "No, there is no difference." Indeed, many prominent thinkers in the field would agree. Albert (1966) finds no general distinction between the two terms, and Ard (1966) admits that "a fine-line distinction between counseling and psychotherapy is admittedly difficult if not impossible to draw" (p. vi). Curran (1968) sees the terms as almost synonymous, separated in meaning by only a slight shade of connotation, "the main difference perhaps now being that counseling tends to refer to an educational, family, or pastoral setting and psychotherapy has a more clinical tone" (p. 4). Balinsky & Blum (1951) also see the two terms as identical, in the sense that both describe processes which help foster an individual's growth, "so that he can now handle problems that he formerly could not" (p. 15).

Despite these positions, however, there are strong arguments to the contrary. In this chapter, we will examine three basic positions:

1 Counseling and psychotherapy are synonymous terms.
2 Counseling differs from psychotherapy by the seriousness of the patient's problems and the emotional intensity of the treatment.
3 Counseling differs from psychotherapy in that the former is built upon a philosophy, while the latter is built upon a psychopathology, a theory of personality, and a corpus of techniques.

This last position is the most inclusive of all the differences between counseling and psychotherapy, and we shall examine it in some detail. But first, we shall consider the popular position that the terms are interchangeable and examine what fault lies in that argument. Patterson (1973) sets forth this position most clearly, and his well-thought-out argument deserves our immediate attention. He states,

If experts in counseling and psychotherapy were asked to list the theories that should be considered under each heading, there would probably be great overlapping in the lists. The difficulty in determining which are theories of counseling and which are theories of psychotherapy is taken as one evidence of the lack of clear or significant differences between them. The position taken by the writer is that there are no essential differences between counseling or psychotherapy.... The definitions of counseling would in most cases be acceptable as definitions of psychotherapy, and vice versa. There seems to be agreement that both counseling and psychotherapy are processes involving a special kind of relationship between a person who asks for help with a psychological problem ... and a person who is trained to provide that help.... The nature of the relationship is essentially the same, if not identical, in both counseling and psychotherapy. The process that occurs also does not seem to differ from one to the other. Nor do there seem to be any distinct techniques or group of techniques that separate counseling and psychotherapy. (pp. xii-xiii)

Patterson goes on to state some of the prevailing counter-arguments, but concludes quite firmly that "there are no essential differences between counseling and psychotherapy" (p. xiv). But there are several weaknesses in his reasoning that must be pointed out.

Let us begin with a dictionary definition of each term. *Webster's Third New International Dictionary* (1971) defines counseling as "a practice or professional service designed to guide an individual to a better understanding of his problems and potentialities by utilizing modern psychological principles and methods especially in collecting case history data, using various techniques of the personal interview, and testing interest and aptitudes." The same dictionary offers a much more lengthy and elaborate definition of psychotherapy. It reads as follows:

1: treatment of a mental or emotional disorder or maladjustment by psychological means, especially involving verbal communication.... 2: any alteration in an individual's interpersonal environment, relationships or life situations brought about, especially by a qualified therapist, and intended to have the effect of alleviating syndromes of mental or emotional disturbance. 3: the process whereby a patient or other subject becomes aware of the content and mechanisms of his unconscious mind through free association.*

These dictionary definitions are not intended either to support or refute the contention that there is a difference between *counseling* and *psychotherapy*; admittedly, it is not the place of a dictionary to arbitrate such issues. Rather, they show that there does exist a difference *in common usage* between the two terms. For what a dictionary actually shows is the meanings of words in their usage, and insofar as counseling and psychotherapy are concerned, there appears to be a rather clear distinction in usage between them. There are entirely different connotations to the statements, "I am in psychotherapy with Dr. X," and "I am being counseled by Dr. X," and native speakers would be intuitively aware of the distinctions elaborated by the dictionary. We shall come back to these definitions shortly, but let us first examine some definitions and ideas put forth by those whose expertise is in the practices of counseling and psychotherapy.

*By permission. From Webster's *Third New International Dictionary*. © 1971 by G. & C. Merriam Co., publishers of the Merriam-Webster Dictionaries.

Fromm-Reichman (1950) defines psychotherapy as a process "designed to bring about understanding for an insight into the historical and dynamic factors which, unknown to the patient, are among the causes of the mental disturbance for which he seeks psychiatric help" (p. ix), while Strupp (1971) sees psychotherapy as "the planful application of psychological techniques for the purpose of inducing personality and behavior change" (p. 20). This last definition raises several problems. What does Strupp mean by "psychological techniques"? Does he mean psychotherapeutic techniques that would make the definition redundant? Or is he referring to a specific set of techniques, and if so, which: conditioning, free association, reflection, paradoxical intention? Surely, these could all be considered psychological techniques, and yet they have little in common and do not differ markedly from what we would call counseling techniques. Moreover, when he speaks of "personality and behavior change," doesn't that imply that the patient's personality and behavior are in need of change? What if it is the patient's environment, not his personality and behavior, which requires change? Would that place him in the province of counseling as opposed to psychotherapy?

These are complex questions, and there are no easy answers. The question has been debated for so many years now by so many different interests that the simple semantic distinction of the words themselves has been blurred by the explicatory rhetoric. But we must press on: Sprinthall (1971) contends that the issue is of prime importance in defining an integrated guidance function and "that attempts to view distinctions between counseling and psychotherapy as irrelevant simply obscure instead of solve the problem" (p. 97). Be prepared, however, as we delve further into the question, to find even more confusion than we started out with.

Aubrey (1967) and Bordin (1968) both assert that what distinguishes counseling from psychotherapy is the degree of the client's disturbance; that in counseling, the client is an "adequately functioning individual" and in psychotherapy, the patient is "neurotic and pathological." This type of distinction is popular, and it is hard to find fault with. Like the dictionary definitions, it does seem to describe what is in fact the reality of the situation. In practice, however, many cases are not so clearly defined, either in terms of the personality level of the client-patient or in terms of the problems under treatment, that we can specify the condition of the client in his totality. Just where counseling ends and psychotherapy begins, if we view the terms on a continuum, is not clear.

Blocher (1966) distinguishes between the terms by the outcomes specified for each: "When the usual outcomes for counseling and psychotherapy are pooled, two rather dominant clusters of goals appear. These can be characterized as (a) developmental-educative-preventive goals, and (b) remediative-adjustive-therapeutic outcomes" (p. 10). Cluster (a) is typical of counseling and cluster (b) is typical of psychotherapy, but neither cluster fully and unambiguously clarifies the distinction. "Much of what has been attempted in the name of counseling," Blocher argues, "has been as remediative and adjustive in purpose as anything attempted in the name of psychotherapy." He goes on to list five basic assumptions about clients and counselors which he hopes will further differentiate counseling from psychotherapy:

1 Clients are not considered to be "mentally ill." The whole concept of mental illness is considered largely inappropriate and irrelevant to a process focused upon changing behavior. Clients are viewed as being capable of choosing goals, making decisions, and generally assuming responsibility for their own behavior and future development.*

This point does indeed differentiate counseling from *some types* of psychotherapy, but not from all types. Reality therapy and client-centered therapy, for example, both operate on the assumption that the client is not "mentally ill," and even a number of putative psychoanalytic therapists would find themselves in accord with this position. R. D. Laing and Thomas Szasz, both of whom are considered psychotherapists, reject entirely the idea of mental illness. But if we restate this point another way—that *a practitioner who deals with clients whom he considers mentally ill is clearly engaged in the practice of psychotherapy*—we have made a significant inroad. Note, however, that this restatement neither accepts nor rejects the contention that there is such a thing as mental illness, but merely suggests that some practitioners do work under the assumption that there is such a thing.

2 Developmental counseling is focused on the present and the future. The concept of development has its thrust in the future, not in the past. Developmental counselors are primarily concerned with where the client is going, not where he has been.*

Blocher's second point suggests a further refinement of the distinction, based on the context in which the practitioner perceives his client. Displays 1.1 and 1.2 compare two ways of perceiving the client. The psychotherapeutic perception views the client as the surface of his past, as the product of his personal history, whether this history be viewed as fixations (psychoanalytic), conditioned responses (behavioral), or authentic encounters as a basis for meanings (existential). The counseling perception views the client against the background of his present environment, as a figure breaking through that environment, *heading somewhere*. It sees the client as an emerging figure among the jumble of stimuli with which he interacts; as a *self*, being defined continually among its possibilities. Again, some of the so-called therapies, particularly gestalt, Rogerian, Laingian, and reality would clearly fall into the category of counseling, by this definition. Again, we are compelled to consider the possibility that there is no such thing as client-centered *therapy* or reality *therapy*, but only client-centered *counseling* and reality *counseling*. This possibility becomes even stronger as we go on with Blocher's assumptions.

---

*Donald H. Blocher, DEVELOPMENTAL COUNSELING, Copyright © 1966, The Ronald Press Company, New York.

display 1.1
TWO PERCEPTIONS

The psychotherapist's view of the patient

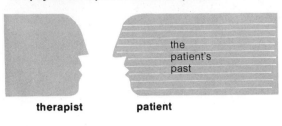

the
patient's
past

therapist   **patient**

The psychotherapist
views the "persona"
of the patient
as the uppermost layer
of his past.

display 1.2

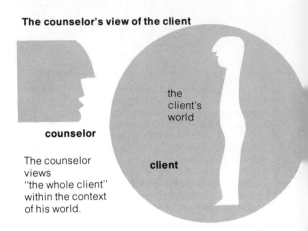

The counselor's view of the client

the
client's
world

counselor

client

The counselor
views
"the whole client"
within the context
of his world.

3 The client is a client, not a patient. The counselor is not an authority figure who comes through a transference relationship that creates the illusion of omnipotence. He is essentially a teacher and partner of the client as they move toward *mutually defined goals* (italics added).*

Here we approach the question of how the client perceives the practitioner, and how the practitioner perceives himself. It is generally recognized that client expectations are an integral part of the efficacy of the treatment, and that his expectations are in a large degree contingent upon his perceptions of the person who is treating him. Torrey (1972) has indicated that

part of the efficacy of therapists all over the world arises from their ability to mobilize the patient's hope and raise his expectations of getting well.... The therapist's ability to raise a patient's expectations is intimately connected both with his ability to name what is wrong and with his personal qualities. In reference to the first, much of the naming process and the assignment of meaning can be looked at from the vantage point of increasing the patient's faith in the therapist and increasing his expectations of a cure.... The therapist's personal qualities are also closely intertwined with patient expectations. Somewhere in the interface between the two, the word "charisma" may be found.... Another aspect of this is the therapist's belief in himself. Several studies have shown that the greater is this belief, the higher are the patient's expectations of being helped.... Therapists do other things as well to raise the expectations of their patients. In most cultures they stand out as different, apart from the great mass of people. (pp. 48-50)

*Donald H. Blocher, DEVELOPMENTAL COUNSELING, Copyright © 1966, The Ronald Press Company, New York.

24

In short, the therapist engaged in the practice of psychotherapy has a clear interest in maintaining a particular image, a face, which he presents to the patient as a reinforcement of his authority. In counseling, on the other hand, the interaction is less stratified: the counselor and client interact as equals, "partners," as Blocher calls them, working *mutually* toward their goals. Whereas, a psychotherapist would never ask a patient to assist him in establishing goals (for to do so would lower the expectations and diminish the faith in him), a counselor would likely do just this. A psychotherapist has an investment in allowing the patient to develop strong, unrealistic transference feelings, while a counselor works on the principle that the client must see him as a genuine, honest individual, who is there to help him—guide him, if you will—but is not infallible or perfect.

As we move along Blocher's list, it becomes more striking at each stage that what differentiates counseling and psychotherapy can be reduced to what is going on in the minds of the client-patient and therapist-counselor: how they see and respond to the situation. His fourth point extends this further:

4 The counselor is not morally neutral or amoral. He has values, feelings, and standards of his own. He does not necessarily impose them on clients, but he does not attempt to hide them.*

What Blocher appears to be saying here is that the counselor does not encourage transference by hiding himself (in terms of his values, feelings, and standards) from the client. However, we might do better to extend this point by saying that *the psychotherapist does impose his values on the patient by subtly encouraging him to accept his values as the correct values, by embracing his standards as the appropriate standards, by conforming to his feelings as the healthier feelings.* Frank (1971) indicates that "a historical overview of Western psychotherapy reveals that the dominant psychotherapeutic approach of an era reflects contemporary cultural attitudes and values...," and Lee (1968) has found that therapists and prospective therapists imposed their social-class values on their judgments. Fitzgibbons and Shearn (1972) have found that application of the label *schizophrenic* to a patient was determined to a large part by the professional discipline of the diagnostician, by his theoretical orientation, and by the atmosphere of the setting in which he worked—all of which are value representations. In short, one respect in which counseling differs from psychotherapy is that in the former the counselor unabashedly acknowledges and expresses his values, while in the latter values are concealed from the patient, but subtly communicated in judgments, perceptions, and emotional feedback.

Blocher's last point addresses itself to the question of technique:

5 The counselor focuses upon changing behavior, not just creating insight. He uses a wide variety of techniques within the interview and outside the interview. He makes

*Donald H. Blocher, DEVELOPMENTAL COUNSELING, Copyright © 1966, The Ronald Press Company, New York.

assignments of tasks, arranges try-out experiences, and serves as an expert consultant to the client as well as providing a relationship. He is a helping person, a teacher, a consultant, and a confidant as these functions are seen appropriate in meeting mutually defined goals. (p. 11)*

We can add to this by stating that *the psychotherapist typically relies on a pre-scribed set of techniques, based in theory, and exclusive of the therapist's personal feelings.* Indeed, adherence to techniques is designed to insure safety in the psychotherapeutic situation: to preclude the possibility of the therapist's acting emotionally, spontaneously, without a theoretical justification. Technique, in psychotherapeutic practice, serves as a way of structuring and defining the sessions to meet the requisites of the proposed curative goal. In a sense, the reliance on technique is a defensive gesture: it cuts off the therapist from the patient, emphasizing the mechanics of the interaction over the interpersonal feelings. Techniques in counseling, on the other hand, are more personal techniques, responsive to the "mutually defined goals" of client and counselor, rather than being imbedded in an underlying theory of techniques.

The implication of Blocher's five points is that counseling is a less dynamically oriented process than therapy, entailing a different view of the client, a different emphasis, and a different set of techniques. This position is subscribed to by many other writers as well: Mowrer, for instance, feels that "normal anxiety which arises from ordinary frustrating events can be treated through usual counseling procedures [while] neurotic anxiety which proceeds from the unconscious must be dealt with [by] psychotherapy" (1950). His argument differentiates between the terms by the type of activity engaged in and the level of the client's difficulties:

Counseling involves decision making and personal problems not embedded in the personality structure. Counseling as contrasted with psychotherapy is surface level, involving a present problem and a plan of action. It involves the *normal* person with the normal problem. Psychotherapy, on the other hand, is a treatment involving the inner life through depth psychology. It deals with attitudes which it endeavors to change.

Mahler (1971) differentiates between them within the context of a group situation: "Group counseling is a social experience that deals with the development problems and attitudes of individuals in a secure setting…. Group therapy is more concerned with unconscious motivation." Ohlsen and Proff (1966) argue that the client's level of adjustment determines whether the process is counseling or psychotherapy. McDaniel and Shaftel (1956) agree that the general consensus reflects the belief that psychotherapy is identified "with the development of therapeutic processes for working with the *seriously disturbed* patient, whereas counseling has been more closely identified with evolving processes for meeting the guidance needs of the *normal* person" (italics added).

*Donald H. Blocher, DEVELOPMENTAL COUNSELING, Copyright © 1966, The Ronald Press Company, New York.

Guidance, counseling, and psychotherapy: a comparison

This second point of view, then, is that the differences between counseling and psychotherapy are differences in degree and emphasis. On the whole, this is the most prevalent position in the profession. Perry et al. (1955), in an ambitious undertaking, analyze the discrepancies between counseling and psychotherapy in terms of process differences, rather than product differences alone. Their report, which is often cited in the literature, deserves our scrutiny. By examining "the differences of coloring and emphasis in the daily work of those we call psychotherapists and those we call counselors," they evaluate three postulates: (1) the psychotherapist sometimes does the kinds of things the counselor does most of the time...; (2) the counselor sometimes does the kinds of things the psychotherapist does most of the time...; (3) there is, a large part of the time a sensible difference in the character of what each does. The emphasis in this analysis is on the activity of a practitioner calling himself a psychotherapist as opposed to the activity of a practitioner who calls himself a counselor. Both seem to be dealing with problems as they work with their client-patients, but each is considering a different type of problem, with different implications.

When individual psychodynamics are thought of as problems, we think in terms of intrapersonal conflicts, and we have in mind such problems as the person's intense ambivalences, his inhibiting guilts, or his self-defeating lack of inhibition. We think also of the problems of transition or fixation at different levels of psychic development, conflicts of need, *etc*. But when roles and role choices are thought of as problems, we think in socially describable areas such as vocational choice, marital adjustment, the reorientation required by the limitations of aging, the management of the roles of the physically handicapped, *etc*. At this end are all the specific problems, posed by social development from role to role and by role conflict.*

The authors acknowledge that the two types of problems vary in degrees of intensity and are interrelated in the sense that a person with severe pathological problems will also have problems in the role areas. Even so, they are able to differentiate between a counselor and psychotherapist by the areas in which they spend the preponderance of their time and by their primary concerns and actions during that time:

The psychotherapist, as we see it, spends the predominance of his time over a number of cases ... in areas of moderate to intense intrapersonal disturbance. Even though he may frequently find himself able to help his client or patient directly in learning to handle some role with maturity, his primary concern is with looking with his client more inward toward the process represented at the left end of our dimension and less outward toward the individual's point of immediate contact with the external world. For the psychotherapist, the role problems of his clients are of interest less for themselves and more for the light they throw on inner-conflicts....

The counselor must also be concerned with these projections, but the resources of his clients make it possible for him to use many teaching tools, and in his most characteristic

*From "On the Relation of Psychotherapy to Counseling" by Wm. G. Perry, et al. In *Annals of NYAOS*. New York: New York Academy of Sciences, 1955, p. 400. Reprinted by permission.

work he need not depend primarily on the events of the transference. He spends the predominance of his time over a number of cases ... in areas of minimal to moderate personal disturbance and in relation to some particular problem area in which he claims a competence, be it vocation, education, marriage, and the like. This is not to say that he never works with persons with intense disturbances....

We can express the difference in emphasis, then, by saying that counseling looks more often toward the interpretation and development of the personality in the relations characteristic of specific role-problems while psychotherapy looks more often toward the reinterpretation and reorganization of malignant conflictural elements within the personality through the relation with the therapist.*

If we look at Perry et al. in conjunction with Blocher, we seem to be approaching a consensus which closely parallels what the dictionary indicated are differences in common usage between the two terms. Counseling is more directed toward one set of problems while psychotherapy is directed toward another set; counseling uses one set of methods, while psychotherapy uses another; counseling emphasizes the rational, environmental forces, while psychotherapy emphasizes the dynamic, inner-dimensions of experience. We get the sense, throughout these different arguments, that the thrust of counseling is upon helping the client deal with his immediate problems and improve his life situation, and that the attitude of the counselor is that of one individual interacting with another. Counseling also emerges as a more comprehensive approach than psychotherapy, in that it is not concerned specifically with the client's problems, but rather with the client himself.

Furthermore, there is a different set of axioms underlying psychotherapy and counseling. As we have seen in Blocher's assumptions, for example, the counselor always holds his client in high esteem, valuing him *as he is and for what he is*. Sprinthall (1971), too, suggests that one of the conditions for counseling is that the counselor hold his client in high regard. While the psychotherapist may also hold his patient in high regard, and often does, his primary perception of the patient—his immediate response to him— is a *clinical* response; one based on his evaluation of the patient's state of mind (including his neuroses, conflicts, deficiencies, etc.), often of a diagnostic nature. Secondly, the counselor always views his client within the context of his interpersonal and experiential environment. He sees the client as he is situated in his own phenomenological world, existing in the "here and now" with others, as a responsible, developing individual. The psychotherapist, on the other hand, generally views the client as a product of his past, whether that past be viewed as conditioning experiences or as psychosexual stages. Display 1.2 shows the counseling view of the client. We see how the counselor is more interested in the total person, while the psychotherapist (Display 1.1) is more interested in certain areas of the personality, particularly as these areas are expressed as symptoms of past disturbances.

*From "On the Relation of Psychotherapy to Counseling" by Wm. G. Perry, et al. In *Annals of NYAOS*. New York: New York Academy of Sciences, 1955, pp. 402-404. Reprinted by permission.

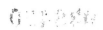

All these distinctions, encompassing both the counselor's attitude toward the client and his view of the treatment, can be most succinctly stated as follows: *Counseling is built upon an underlying philosophical foundation, while psychotherapy is built upon an underlying psychopathology, theory of personality, and corpus of specific techniques.* The implications of this simple statement are manifold and will be discussed more fully in chapter 2, but it should be pointed out at this time that *all* of the distinctions between counseling and psychotherapy stated in the arguments above are reducible to this single comprehensive distinction. This can be said in another way: that the counselor is primarily motivated in his interactions with the client by a philosophy of life which guides his own living and which he wishes to share with the client, while the psychotherapist cuts himself off from the patient by designating him either "ill" or "deficient." This clarifies some of the issues above.

Consider, for example, the premise that the psychotherapist treats a disturbed patient while the counselor treats a normal client. What this really says is that the psychotherapist *sees* his patient as "disturbed" or "sick," while the counselor does not see his client in this light. The psychotherapist and the counselor may both see the identical person differently, each in terms of the axioms which underlie his discipline and which guide his practice. Consider also the proposition that the psychotherapist deals with the personality, while the counselor emphasizes more the role problems of the client. What does this mean? In terms of the distinction we have set forth, this means that the person calling himself a psychotherapist views the patient's personality as something separate from his role problems and his actions, while the person calling himself a counselor recognizes the inextricable bond between personality and actions, between feelings and role. Consider the proposition that psychotherapy is more intense than counseling, that it requires a longer time of treatment and a greater emotional commitment. What does this mean in terms of our distinction? It means simply that the psychotherapist views the course of the treatment in this light—that he has his corpus of techniques to apply before the patient can get "well"—while the counselor recognizes the client's responsibility, his innate tendency toward growth and development, his ability to actualize without forming a highly dependent relationship with the counselor.

It must be made clear that if we accept this distinction, many of the so-called therapies are really counseling theories. Display 1.3 is designed to show how each of the popular schools of therapy would fall across an imaginary boundary line between counseling and psychotherapy. We note that in all of them there is some overlap. To the degree that they are based on philosophical premises, they fall on the counseling side of the dividing line; to the degree that the practice of the school requires a commitment to a psychopathology, a personality theory, and specific techniques, it falls on the psychotherapy side. *Client-centered* practice, with its emphasis on the total person, is almost completely a counseling concept, while *psychoanalysis* and *behavior therapy* with their emphases on personality, techniques, and symptoms fall on the other half. Part Three of this text will discuss each of these schools in more detail.

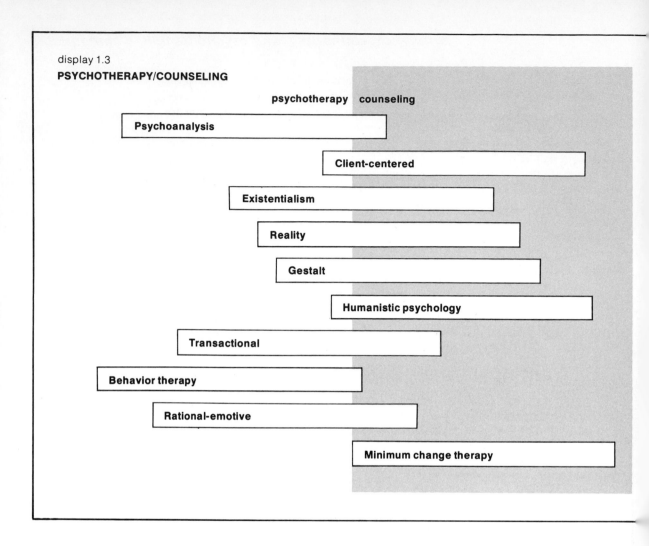

display 1.3
PSYCHOTHERAPY/COUNSELING

psychotherapy   counseling

| Psychoanalysis |
| Client-centered |
| Existentialism |
| Reality |
| Gestalt |
| Humanistic psychology |
| Transactional |
| Behavior therapy |
| Rational-emotive |
| Minimum change therapy |

Further support for this point of view may be found by even a cursory glance at books in each discipline. Psychotherapy textbooks rarely, if ever, allude to a guiding philosophy behind their applications, while counseling textbooks invariably do so. Almost any counseling textbook will present either a partial or comprehensive philosophy to guide the counselor. While these may differ from book to book, there are many areas where they share a common perspective. Tolbert (1972) lists some eclectic philosophical assumptions which appear to be universally subscribed to: Display 1.4.

These assumptions clearly demonstrate the flexibility and acceptance which are characteristic of all counseling but which are often lacking in psychotherapies. Moreover, if we look closely at these ten postulates, we find that they confirm the division of schools in Display 1.3. Those schools which coincide in their beliefs with these premises fall on the counseling side, while those which do not coincide fall on the psychotherapy side. Also, we shall see later (chapter 6) that the training of counselors as opposed to the training of psychotherapists emphasizes a philosophical point of view.

A serious misunderstanding hampers the willingness of practitioners of the counseling point of view to call themselves counselors. Rarely do we hear of a psychiatrist or psychologist calling himself a counselor, even though his practice may in fact be counseling orientated. The misunderstanding is this: many lay people as well as professionals believe that psychotherapy is a more effective mode of treatment than counseling; that only psychotherapy is capable of treating severe personality problems. Many psychiatrists, psychologists, and psycho-therapists have a condescending attitude toward counseling—"I can tolerate counseling," they imply, "but I wouldn't take it too seriously." The myth also persists that counselors are more poorly trained than psychotherapists, less skilled, and even less intelligent.

Let us set the record straight. There is no evidence to indicate that psychotherapy is any more efficacious in the treatment of any disorder than is counseling. On the contrary, there is some evidence, although of a preliminary nature, to indicate that the counseling position (as outlined in the postulates

---

display 1.4

PHILOSOPHICAL ASSUMPTIONS OF COUNSELING*

1 Man is a unity, a whole; what affects one aspect affects the total person. To understand him, the total person must be understood.
2 Each individual is unique, irreplaceable, and of value.
3 We can never know another person completely; the personal meaning of his world is available to us only to the extent that he is willing and able to share it.
4 The experiences of the observer, his perceptions of them, and the insights and meaning he has derived from them enable him to understand another person.
5 There is a positive growth force that motivates the individual to become the best that he can conceptualize and to be recognized as such. The conceptualization provides the meaning for his existence. He must build it for himself.
6 Each individual has a responsibility to his fellow man; to reach full development of himself and to find meaning in his life, he must help others and be helped by them. He must need others and be needed by them.

7 Man has freedom to choose what he will be. No one has complete freedom, but there is always some choice.
8 Man can transcend past experiences, and what might be thought of as "limiting factors" in his choosing; a choice can be in a new direction, for a completely new goal, and may represent what may appear to be a complete change for the individual.
9 With freedom comes responsibility. If man is to have freedom of choice and be able to decide what he will be, he must take responsibility for his choosing and what he is.
10 Man is not "good" or "bad" by nature; he has become what he is through his interaction with others. He alone is responsible for "goodness" or "badness," which, as defined here, would be values such as exploitation of his fellow man or the refusal to take the responsibility that goes with freedom. (pp. 95–96)

*From *Introduction to Counseling*, 2d. ed., by E. L. Tolbert (New York: McGraw-Hill, 1972). Reprinted by permission.

above) is indeed the curative force in therapy. Rogers's massive study (Rogers et al., 1967) of the treatment of schizophrenics demonstrates that what is most important is the quality of the relationship between client and counselor, particularly empathy, genuineness, and warmth. The technique that the counselor uses, his theoretical orientation (including his theory of personality and psychopathology) has no bearing on the therapeutic outcome. In chapter 2 we shall explore more fully how the counseling philosophy contributes to the efficacy of treatment, and in chapters 4 and 9 a more detailed critique of Rogers's study will be found. In the meantime, we shall work on the assumption that counseling is as valid a treatment procedure as psychotherapy, applicable in the same cases and equally as effective. There is no evidence to compel us to downgrade counseling to second place in the mental health hierarchy, and counselors should not do so.

*   *   *   *   *

It would be appropriate at this point to summarize the points we have covered in this section. First, we examined the position that counseling and psychotherapy are interchangeable terms. This position was rejected on two grounds:

1 There clearly is a difference in common usage and connotative meaning between the two words, as indicated by the dictionary, by speakers of the language, and by practitioners who are hesitant to call themselves counselors even though their orientation is identical with the counseling stance.
2 Failure to distinguish between these two terms results in confusion and obfuscation in dealing with guidance, counseling, and psychotherapy problems. On the other hand, clarifying the distinction allows us greater insight into practical distinctions.

Secondly, we considered the position that counseling differs from psychotherapy by the degree of the problem treated (its severity), the emotional and maturational level of the person being treated, and the emphasis in the treatment process. We concluded here that both counseling and psychotherapy are appropriate procedures for all types of persons with all types of difficulties. There is no conclusive evidence that intensive psychotherapies are more effective than counseling. We do, however, note that there is a different emphasis and perspective between the counseling setting and the psychotherapy setting, but suggest that this difference is in the eyes of the practitioner and not an objective difference. The way in which the practitioner sees his client and responds to him, the context in which he is viewed, is determined by the axioms which govern his individual practice, not by anything more noble or more absolute.

Finally, we suggested that counseling is built upon an underlying philosophy, while psychotherapy is built upon a psychopathology, a theory of personality, and a specific corpus of techniques and applications. This is not to suggest, of course, that the psychotherapist does not have a guiding philosophy—a well-thought-out plan of life and view of man. But rather, that the stages and continuity of psychotherapy are more dependent upon a theoretical foundation derived from the psychology than from the philosophy that underlies it. In other words, the philosophy of the psychotherapy is not as influential as the psychology of the psychotherapy, in terms of treatment strategies, even though the latter may have been derived from the former.

PRACTICAL COUNSELING

Last season's fruit is eaten
And the fullfed beast shall kick the empty pail,
For last year's words belong to last year's language
And next year's words await another voice.
    T. S. Eliot, *Little Gidding**

In many ways these lines of T. S. Eliot's reflect the situation that the contemporary counselor finds himself in with respect to the terms *guidance*, *counseling*, and *psychotherapy*. Where does he stand? How has the changing terminology over the years affected his position? What shall he call himself professionally, and how can he use these terms to unambiguously describe what he is attempting to do in his practice?

The unpleasant reality of the present situation is that a silent conspiracy exists to denigrate the counseling function as a treatment procedure, and this silent conspiracy is tolerated and encouraged by the timidity of professional counselors, particularly school counselors. It is a subtle conspiracy, executed not with bold rhetoric or striking actions, but rather with obscure licensing and certification procedures, job discrimination in clinical settings, terminological nuances which imply levels of competency (such as counseling being a watered down version of psychotherapy). While the abundance of hard scientific research indicates that the effective counselor is at least as effective as the effective psychotherapist, counselors still are quick to agree that they are not as competent as psychiatrists, psychologists, and psychoanalysts to treat the basic nonphysiological emotional problems. Humility and acquiescence, noble traits at better times, merely add fuel to this flame which devours the integrity and purpose of the counseling profession.

It is time now for the counselor to stand up and meet the challenge. He must recognize that his function—counseling—is the most comprehensive and successful form of mental health treatment yet devised. He must recognize that the attendant disciplines of psychiatry, psychology, and psychoanalysis evolved almost by accident over a period of years, and that their claim to exclusivity in the intensive emotional domain is unwarranted by the evidence and unjustified by their origin. Certainly, each of these disciplines has much to offer. Psychiatry, with its origins in medical neurology, is important in the treatment of neurological disorders which produce psychic manifestations; psychology, with its

---

*From "Little Gidding" in *Four Quartets* by T. S. Eliot, copyright, 1943, by T. S. Eliot, copyright, 1971, by Esme Valerie Eliot. Reprinted by permission of Harcourt Brace Jovanovich, Inc.

speculative and experimental lineage, is a valuable discipline for the study of man in his world, with particular emphasis in establishing and describing general rules of behavior and perception; psychoanalysis, with its high expense and lengthy commitment, is ideal for those patients who can afford it. But, counseling—and only counseling—with its origins rooted in the American guidance movement, is specifically designed and ideally suited to help a large number of individuals grow and prosper in all areas of their lives. It is the discipline of counseling, more than any other of these disciplines, which offers hope to the masses: for it is counseling that every school student should be exposed to, and counseling which works to prevent difficulties as well as curing them.

But the word counseling as it has evolved etymologically over the years does not convey the fullness and the hope. Moser and Moser (1963), for example, argue that,

Guidance is a term with many meanings. It is a point of view; it is a group of services, it is a field of study. Guidance services enter into the entire school situation; they implement the development of the student in every area of life.... Counseling has been described as the face-to-face meeting of the counselor and counselee.... Within the guidance services, counseling may be thought of as the core of the helping process, essential for the proper administration of assistance to students as they attempt to solve their problems.... It has been said that counseling is the heart of the guidance program.

While it is certainly hard to find fault with their logic, the words they are using—counseling and guidance—as they are using them, are last year's words! For, in practice, how can the school counselor, with his profound and overriding commitment to the welfare of the students in all of their endeavors, accurately differentiate between guidance services and counseling practices? Surely, there is much in the literature to suggest such a distinction is possible: that guidance is giving information, instituting programs, administering testing, and so on, while counseling is the face-to-face contact between two people functioning as counselor and client. But how valid can such a distinction be in practice? If the counselor is truly committed to the individual's growth, to his total actualization, then wouldn't it be better to find a word which expresses the dual function of this commitment, which encompasses the so-called guidance services within the counseling stance? What we need is next year's word, a new term to express the function of the counselor in all of its myriad dimensions. I suggest, therefore, the term *practical counseling*.

Practical counseling may be defined as *the total counseling process, underlined by a coherent philosophy and self-awareness, practiced with a commitment to the client's total growth, and encompassing face-to-face interviews, group processes, school services, testing programs, extracurricular activities, vocational and educational information, and anything else which contributes to the client's development and fulfillment as a person.*

The use of such a term, hopefully, will resolve the many discrepancies which plague the profession. No longer should it be necessary to apologize to psychotherapists for infringing upon their sacred domain; to apologize to administrators for being so bold as to suggest administrative reforms; to apologize to teachers for venturing to assist them with their teaching problems. No longer need the school counselor defend himself and his position from those who question "What is your function?" and "Do we really need you?" Moreover, by understanding what is meant by practical counseling it will be possible for the school counselor to appreciate fully his position in the hierarchy of education and mental health services. He will see—and feel—that he, more than any other person, has the opportunity to help raise a new generation which should be healthier, happier, and wiser than the preceding generation. For every student who attends a school should in some way, directly or indirectly, benefit from the work of the counselor. Practical counseling, as it is concerned with the whole person, is not limited to either role problems or personality problems; indeed, it makes no distinction between the two, dealing instead with each person as a unified field of self, in constant interaction in the world. Moreover, the term practical counseling is broad enough to encompass the operational aspects of what was formerly called guidance, what was formerly called counseling, and what was formerly called psychotherapy, without the necessity of arbitrarily distinguishing among the three.

Practical counseling, in other words, is a term which resolves the discrepancies among other terms by integrating the services and practices defined by these other terms into one concept.

More important, the term encourages among school counselors an attitude, a stance. For it says that everything the school counselor does, from setting up a schedule, to organizing a clean-up campaign, to conducting an intensive psychological interview, is part of the broad counseling process. Counseling, which we have suggested is no less successful than psychotherapy in the treatment of all types of problems, is practiced in almost everything the counselor does.

CONCLUSIONS

Guidance, counseling, and psychotherapy are three distinct terms with three distinct meanings, functions, and connotations. Preceding all three was a profound concern expressed by philosophers for the complexities of the human psyche and the ramifications of the human personality on social, political, religious, and cultural processes. Efforts to study and explain the human mind took the form of philosophical discourse, which was speculative and nonscientific, yet insightful enough to offer contributions which are still valid and important. The introduction of "scientific" psychology and "scientific" psychotherapy, near the close of the nineteenth century in Europe, coincides with the independent development of the guidance movement in America.

Guidance is the most general of the three terms. Roughly, it indicates a variety of organized services in an educational setting, which contribute to and expand the scope of the school curriculum. Guidance entails information giving, referral, coordination among the diverse pupil personnel services, and individual and group testing and diagnostic services. If we examine the origins of the guidance movement in the United States, we find that it arose to meet the changing social needs at the turn of the century, particularly the need for occupational information, and evolved through the influences of progressive education, the mental health movement, the findings of laboratory psychology, and the subsequent reactions to the school of laboratory psychology. Each of the influences exerted changes upon the original conceptions of guidance, expanding the purview of this new discipline to include counseling and other intensive forms of treatment.

Counseling and psychotherapy, although often used interchangeably, were shown to have different meanings in their operational senses. Both do treat emotional, adjustment, and behavioral problems, and both vary in the degree of intensity, depending upon the practitioner. But while psychotherapy is built upon a comprehensive theory of personality, a psychopathology, and a specific corpus of techniques, counseling is built upon an underlying philosophy of life, including theories of value, knowledge, and reality. In this respect, we may consider counseling as a broader discipline than psychotherapy, since it treats the whole person in the context of his interpersonal and experiential environment, whereas psychotherapy concentrates on the symptomatic, neurotic, or pathological aspects of the personality.

This functional definition of counseling allows us to integrate guidance and counseling services and practices into a unified whole, which we call practical counseling. This term refers to the interpersonal process whereby one person helps another to function better, to have a sustained interest in his place in the world and a respect for self and for others which permeates and guides all of his actions. Practical counseling is designed to treat the individual qua individual, rather than to treat the person as a deficient or partially developed organism.

In future chapters we shall examine in more detail the processes and stages that enable an individual to function as a counselor for another. We shall scrutinize the counseling experience and the counseling relationship to find those factors which determine more than any others a successful outcome.

References

Albert, G. If counseling *is* psychotherapy—what then? *Personnel and Guidance Journal*, 1966, *45*, 124–129.

Ard, B. N. (Ed.). *Counseling and psychotherapy.* New York: Science and Behavior Books, 1966.

Aristotle. Selected works.

Aubrey, R. F. Misapplication of therapy models to school counseling. *Personnel and Guidance Journal*, 1967, *48*, 273–278.

Balinsky, B. N., & Blum, M. L. *Counseling and psychology.* Englewood Cliffs, N.J.: Prentice-Hall, 1951.

Barry, R., & Wolf, B. *Modern issues in guidance-personnel work.* New York: Bureau of Publications, Teachers College, 1963.

Beers, C. W. *A mind that found itself* (5th ed.). Garden City: Doubleday, 1956.

Berkeley, G. *Treatise concerning the principles of human knowledge.*

Blocher, D. H. *Developmental counseling.* New York: Ronald Press, 1966.

Bordin, E. S. *Psychological counseling.* New York: Appleton-Century-Crofts, 1968.

Brown, D., & Srebalus, D. J. *Contemporary guidance concepts and practices.* Dubuque, Iowa: Wm. C. Brown, 1972.

Cremin, L. A. The progressive heritage of the guidance movement. In E. Landy & P. A. Perry (Eds.), *Guidance in American education* (Vol. I). Cambridge, Mass.: Harvard University Press, 1964.

Curran, C. A. *Counseling and psychotherapy.* New York: Sheed & Ward, 1968.

Dahms, A. M., & Kinnick, B. C. Existentialism and student personnel work. *Journal of College Student Personnel,* 1969, 408–413.

Downing, L. N. *Guidance and counseling services.* New York: McGraw-Hill, 1968.

Esper, E. A. *A history of psychology.* Philadelphia: W. B. Saunders Co., 1964.

Fitzgibbons, D. J., & Shearn, C. R. Concepts of schizophrenia among mental health professionals: A factor-analytic study. *Journal of Consulting and Clinical Psychology,* 1972, *38*(2), 288–295.

Frank, J. D. Therapeutic factors in psychotherapy. *American Journal of Psychotherapy,* 1971, *25,* 350–361.

Fromm-Reichman, F. *Principles of intensive psychotherapy.* Chicago: University of Chicago Press, 1950.

Greene, M. *Teacher as stranger.* Belmont, Calif.: Wadsworth, 1973.

Hume, D. *A treatise of human nature.* Book I, Part IV, Section VI.

Kirby, J. A. Group guidance. *Personnel and Guidance Journal,* 1971, *49,* 593–599.

Kirk, G. S., & Raven, J. E. *The presocratic philosophers.* Cambridge: Cambridge University Press, 1966.

Lee, S. D. Social class bias in the diagnosis of mental illness. *Dissertation Abstracts,* 1968, *28*(11-B), 4758–4759.

Locke, J. An essay concerning human understanding (abridged). In *The empiricists.* Garden City: Doubleday, 1970.

McDaniel, H. B., & Shaftel, G. A. *Guidance in the modern school.* New York: The Dryden Press, 1956.

Mahler, C. A. Group counseling. *Personnel and Guidance Journal,* 1971, *49,* 601–611.

Mortenson, D. G., & Schmuller, A. M. *Guidance in today's schools.* New York: John Wiley, 1959.

Moser, L. E., & Moser, R. *Counseling and guidance: An exploration.* Englewood Cliffs, N.J.: Prentice-Hall, 1963.

Mowrer, O. H. *Learning theory and personality dynamics.* New York: The Ronald Press, 1950.

Murphy, G. *Psychological thought from Pythagoras to Freud.* New York: Harcourt, Brace & World, 1968.

Ohlsen, M., & Proff, F. See Kirby, J. A.

Patterson, C. H. *Theories of counseling and psychotherapy* (2nd ed.). New York: Harper & Row, 1973.

Perry, W. G., Jr., et al. On the relation of psychotherapy to counseling. *Annals of the New York Academy of Science,* 1955, *63,* 396–407.

Peterson, J. A. *Counseling and values.* Scranton, Pa.: International Textbook Company, 1970.

Plato. The complete works.

Rogers, C. R., et al. *The therapeutic relationship and its impact.* Madison: University of Wisconsin Press, 1967.

Scheffler, I. Philosophical models of teaching. In R. S. Peters (Ed.), *The concept of education.* New York: The Humanities Press, 1967.

Sprinthall, N. *Guidance for human growth.* New York: Van Nostrand Reinhold, 1971.

Strupp, H. *Psychotherapy and the modification of abnormal behavior.* New York: McGraw-Hill, 1971.

Thomsom, R. *The pelican history of psychology.* Baltimore: Pelican Books, 1968.

Tolbert, E. L. *Introduction to counseling* (2nd ed.). New York: McGraw-Hill, 1972.

Torrey, E. F. *The mind game.* New York: Emerson-Hall, 1972.

Versenyi, L. *Socratic humanism.* New Haven: Yale University Press, 1963.

Watson, J. B. *Psychology from the standpoint of a behaviorist,* 1919.

Watson, J. B. *Behaviorism.* New York: W. W. Norton, 1930.

chapter two

The counseling stance

What you do
still betters what is done....
    Shakespeare, *The Winter's Tale*

Counseling, in its broadest sense, is designed to help the individual confront and
appreciate his essential condition of freedom. As a synthesis of different disciplinary insights and attitudes, and as a colligation of techniques, methods, and
strategies, counseling attempts to deal with the problem of freedom by working
both with the person and with the society in which he lives. In this respect,
counseling is a social force as well as an individual treatment procedure. All
counseling, regardless of its specific theoretical orientation, works toward a
common end: to help the client find his own personal freedom, with the idea
that as each individual becomes more free, the society in which he lives also
becomes more free. It is freedom—and the problems of freedom—which inspire
the counseling function to mediate between the individual and his world. To
understand counseling, therefore, we must first understand freedom.

DEFINING FREEDOM

Certainly, no single force has exerted a more profound influence upon the
course of human events than the persistently turbulent force of men passionately engaged in their struggles to be free. In their strivings for freedom, particularly in their efforts to break off the social and legal shackles imposed upon
them by despots, conquerors, monarchs, and repressive societies, men have sacrificed wealth, love, family, religion, and almost everything else that in saner
times would have been held too dear to sacrifice. This is understandable. For
freedom is an alluring sylph: She beckons one with her enticing promises of
opportunity and her seductive rhetoric of hope. Unfortunately, as a worldly
mate she is more of an ideal than a reality, more an illusion than a condition. As
a promise, she is rich and infinite; but as a deliverance, she often fails to bring
the goods. One cannot have enough of her; no matter how much she gives of herself, a man wants more. Such is the essential paradox of the human condition.

Of course, when we look more closely, this is no paradox at all. It is merely a misunderstanding, a consequence of faulty language that becomes quite logical when we begin to look at freedom not as a condition of the society but rather as a condition of consciousness that the individual within the society experiences. When we look at freedom as an internal, subjective experience, rather than as an objective, external condition, the paradox becomes resolved. In a totalitarian, "unfree" society, a man may feel free and be free within himself, while in a democratic, "free" society, a man may feel imprisoned within his body. Henri Charrière, the famous "Papillon," talks about how during his many years of prison confinement he often experienced a greater psychological freedom than he had known outside the wall. Eldridge Cleaver, the Black Panther, writes about how he finally found his freedom while in prison, after having been enslaved for many years of his life as a free man on the streets. Freedom, in its truest sense, then, is a state of mind.

There is probably no better illustration of this principle than that provided by the great American writer, Henry Miller, in his multivolume *Bildungsroman, The Rosy Crucifixion* (*Sexus, Nexus,* and *Plexus*). As we read through these volumes, we discover a man in search of his freedom. This search comprises many diversions, each relevant to the total goal: There is the search for sexual freedom, economic freedom, freedom to love and to be loved, the freedom to travel and explore, and most importantly the freedom of mind, which, to Miller, is the freedom to write and to be read by others. The quest for freedom, which permeates every aspect of his existence, becomes to him the paramount force in life. Miller helps us better understand freedom because he presents it from a personal, subjective frame of reference, and freedom is always a personal, subjective experience.

Formulating an objective, encompassing definition of freedom is somewhat more difficult. Wilson (1966), using the philosophy of Maurice Merleau-Ponty, deals with this problem by referring to two types of freedom: There is the subconscious freedom, which he defines as "the continual activity of 'constituting' the perceived and experienced world, of which we only become aware when it breaks down..."; and there is the conscious freedom "that enters into my act of deciding to protest about the H bomb or any other issue" (p. 150). This is a rather complex definition, although it certainly bears upon the problem of counseling inasmuch as it recognizes the psychological dimension of freedom. Morris (1966), also discussing the existential view of freedom, presents a more concise idea, describing it as a dynamic process "of struggling up from the slumber of numbness and nonauthenticity to recognize that one is the architect of one human life and, through that life, the creator of values in the world" (p. 53). Rollo May, another existential thinker, works out a complex definition of freedom in his great work, *Man's Search for Himself* (1953). Presenting freedom in its various manifestations and transformations, May finally concludes,

Freedom is man's capacity to take a hand in his own development. It is our capacity to mold ourselves. Freedom is the other side of consciousness of self: if we were not able to be aware of ourselves, we would be pushed along by instinct or the automatic march of history, like bees or mastodons.... Consciousness of self gives us the power to stand outside the rigid chain of stimulus and response, to pause and by this pause to throw some weight on either side, to cast some decision about what the response will be. That consciousness of self and freedom go together is shown in the fact that the less self-awareness a person has, the more he is unfree. (pp. 137–38)

Turning away from the existential position, if we examine the writings of John Dewey, we find a philosophical conception of freedom linked to a practical, experiential correlate. "The essence of the demand for freedom," Dewey (1916) argues, "is the need of conditions which will enable an individual to make his own special contribution to a group interest, and to partake of its activities in such ways that social guidance shall be a matter of his own mental attitude, and not a mere authoritative dictation of his acts."

SOCIAL FREEDOM AND PSYCHOLOGICAL FREEDOM

Because being free requires that the individual be able to exercise his freedom, and because the individual always functions within the context of a social order, the society's willingness to allow freedom becomes the fundamental precondition for the individual to live freely. This is the basic premise of all discussions of freedom. Often, a society may allow more freedom than the individual can ever hope to take advantage of. In this respect, the problem of freedom is a psychological problem: It is the problem of teaching the individual how to confront his freedom, of helping him learn how to be free, how to feel free, and how to live freely. Erich Fromm (1955) points out that although

man had won his freedom from clerical and secular authorities, he stood alone with his reason and his conscience as his only judges, but he was afraid of the newly won freedom; he had achieved "freedom from"—without yet having achieved "freedom to"—to be himself, to be productive, to be fully awake. Thus he tried to escape from freedom. (pp. 308-309)

In Fromm's language it is the problem of helping the person achieve a "freedom to."

This situation—where an individual is unable to exercise the fullness of his freedom—is a common situation which may have many different causes. A person may lack the training and skills necessary for him to exercise his intellect freely; he may lack the appropriate information needed to make free vocational and social choices, to take advantage of the many resources available; he may lack the self-understanding requisite for making a constructive choice of a lifetime mate, thus permanently encumbering himself in an intolerable situation. Then, again, he may have been, as Albert Ellis calls it, "propagandized" during his early years to hold fast to certain beliefs, doctrines, and dogma which seriously compromise his options to choose. His freedom may be constricted by a social stereotyping which he himself has come to accept. Studies have shown time and again that stereotyping and expectation limit the breadth of opportunities available to the individual (Rosenthal and Jacobson, 1968; Schlossberg and Pietrofesa, 1973), confining him to certain predetermined roles. The individual's freedom may also be restricted by an inability to be socially successful, to win over sincere intentions. In short, there are many different factors which limit the range of an individual's freedom and confine him to a semi-deterministic pattern.

Rogers (1963) discusses the restraints upon the individual's freedom in today's society:

The growing opinion today is that man is essentially unfree. He is unfree in a cultural sense. He is all too often a pawn of government. He is molded by mass propaganda into being a creature with certain opinions and beliefs, desired and preplanned by the powers that be. He is the product of his class—lower, middle, or upper—and his values and his behavior are shaped to a large extent by the class to which he belongs.

He is unfree in a scientific sense. The behavioral sciences have made great strides in showing that all his actions and thoughts are determined, being simply the result of previous conditioning. Hence it seems increasingly clear that the individual is formed and moved by forces—cultural forces without, and unconscious forces within—which are beyond his control. He is in all these ways unfree. (p. 28)

Rogers argues that the free person is one who has courage to make choices which lead to growth. "It is the quality of courage," he argues, "which enables a person to step into the uncertainty of the unknown as he chooses himself. It is the burden of being responsible for the self one chooses to be. It is the recognition by the person that he is an emerging process, not a static end product." This is not always possible, however.

Throughout his training, the student may be subtly coerced into giving up a part of his essential freedom. He is taught, time and again, the values of cooperation, conformity, and acquiescence—often at the expense of independence, originality, and innovation. At times, when choices occur to him which fall outside of the mainstream, he is encouraged to abandon these choices with an a priori certainty, never giving them the seriousness and credence which are due them. This is not to suggest that rebellion itself is a desirable end but only to emphasize what the great philosopher Socrates said: "The unexamined life is not worth living."

We see from this discussion that freedom is a condition involving the individual in relation with his society. The one can never be distinctly separated from the other. The society offers the option; the individual exploits the possibility.

In this chapter we shall examine "the counseling stance" from three related perspectives which, in juxtaposition, offer a panorama of the counseling experience. First, we will examine counseling from a general point of view, paying particular attention to what is expected of the counselor, what rationale he uses to organize his activities, and how the work of the counselor helps the individual and his society function together. Second, we will see how the myth of mental illness has been abandoned by counselors, who have put in its place a phenomenological view of the client. Finally, we will explore the value of philosophy in conducting counseling. Throughout each of these discussions, we should keep in mind the persistent emphasis of counseling to help the client become more free.

THE COUNSELING WAY

Counseling, unlike some of its sister disciplines in the mental health profession, places little stock in diagnostic theories, intensive probing, and psychotherapeutic techniques. Counseling is much more than this; it is something between a lifelong commitment to people which permeates the counselor's personality and a practical doggedness which influences the counselor's every move. Counseling is, as Dimick and Huff (1970) suggest, "a way-of-life." Although it is a professional activity, it is not something distinct from the daily existence of the counselor—not something the counselor does at certain times and in certain situations. Rather, counseling is an integral, harmonious part of the counselor's wholeness as a person, a manifestation of his deeper self in constructive confrontation with others. Counseling is never separate and distinct from the counselor himself.

In chapter 4 we shall explore in detail how the qualities of the counselor and his personality in the counseling relationship emerge as the most significant indices of counseling efficacy. We will see how the counselor gives of himself to help the client, how he involves himself totally and without condition in the life of the client, cresting and falling with the client in his endeavors to grow. In this section we shall examine some of the ways in which the counselor engages in practical counseling. We shall see how he integrates a variety of single activities into a comprehensive program designed to facilitate growth, to help the client experience freedom, and to guide the client into more meaningful personal encounters with others. In this section we shall explore the counseling way and all of its ramifications.

Counseling, Arbuckle (1961) points out, is a verb, an action, a dynamic movement which is more difficult to pinpoint and define than a static noun. Counseling is a happening, a spontaneous encounter, shifting at every moment to meet the changing needs of the client and the demands of the situation. It is not something confined to the counselor's office, not a specific act, but rather something which happens throughout the school environment and, hopefully, throughout the client's other nonschool related activities. Counseling is many things, a protean process, which at different times changes its shape to meet the changing situation. How then, if there are such complexities to the definition, such levels of functioning, can we hope to express what counseling really is and to capture the way of counseling? Let us approach this formidable task by looking at counseling in several of its different perspectives.

On one level counseling is the personal, one-to-one encounter between a counselor and a client, structured to satisfy basic methodological criteria and designed to strive toward practical-oriented goals. Gustad's (1953) definition of counseling, although limited in our more comprehensive scheme, is typical of a good definition of this phase of counseling:

Counseling is a learning-oriented process, carried on in a simple, one-to-one social environment, in which a counselor, professionally competent in relevant psychological skills and knowledge, seeks to assist the client, by methods appropriate to the latter's needs and within the context of the total personnel program, to learn more about himself and to accept himself, to learn how to put such understanding into effect in relation to more clearly perceived, realistically defined goals to the end that the client may become a happier and more productive member of his society. (p. 17)

As we consider this definition, we envision the counselor sitting opposite the client, empathically listening and responding to him with the genuineness and warmth characteristic of the counseling relationship. We understand that to this client the counselor is a very important person, whose professional skills and personal qualities offer him a hope of salvation in a world that may have been unkind to him. Whatever resources the counselor utilizes during his inter-actions with the client—whether he discusses test results, offers career informa-tion, examines the hidden meaning of a dream, or probes the past with an eye on the future—he does so with the ultimate goal in mind of helping the client be free. He deals with the client on different levels and in diverse areas, as the situ-ation demands, keeping in mind at all times the basic thrust of counseling: teaching the client to appreciate, experience, and exploit his fundamental freedom. When the implementation of this task requires that the client learn something, the counselor is a teacher; when it requires that the client be able to speak freely and unburden himself, he is a confidant; when it requires objec-tivity and professional insight, he is an expert; when it requires love, accep-tance, and rapport, he is a friend. We may consider this personal, face-to-face type of counseling as the highest form of counseling, the most intensively con-structive single experience of one's life. Realistically, however, practical coun-seling assumes the form of other types of activity, and it is the strength of coun-seling that it can incorporate many activities together in the common pursuit of a single goal.

What are some of these counseling activities which help to free the individ-ual, and how do they relate to the total counseling picture? The development of a career counseling service in the school enables the client to gain a latitude of choice when he enters the world of work. A comprehensive, student-oriented testing and evaluation program contributes to the student's self-knowledge and to the recognition of his potential, his interests, and his abilities. The organiza-tion of social activities, particularly activities which draw in the socially back-ward student, enables all students to develop and expand their socializing skills. Intelligent program management supports constructive curricular imple-mentations, offering each student an opportunity to benefit from what the school has to offer him. In all of these ways, in all of these different functions, the counselor carries out boldly and forthrightly the obligations of his office. In all of his work, from the tediously mundane to the dramatically innovative, the counselor strives to fulfill his commitment to free the client from his socially imposed and self-accepted shackles.

One particular aspect of this freeing process is the internal, psychological freedom. *"Freedom,"* argues May (1967), "is a special characteristic of the individual who has come to terms with his instinctual urges."

One cannot be free, of course, while his consciousness is locked in warfare with tendencies from his unconsciousness. That is why the aim of psychotherapeutic treatment is often summed up as setting the individual free—free from special inhibitions and repressions, from childhood fixations, from training formulae, and so on. Counselors likewise aim to help the person become free. People need to be freed; one feels great pity for the great majority of people that they should be so enslaved by unnecessary fears. One sees them going through life carrying great psychological burdens which keep them from freedom even more really than the prisoner's iron ball-and-chain. It is a truism that most people develop to only a third or less of their personality possibilities. *The counselor will aim to set people free so that they can develop into their own unique, autonomous selves and realize some of the rich, untapped potentialities in their personalities* (italics added). (p. 192)

But this internal freedom is always bound up, in principle and in effect, with external conditions of freedom and bondage. That is why the counselor must strive, in all of his efforts, to produce a healthy, prosperous congruence between man and his society.

Through his activities and beyond them, the counselor does counseling by becoming a presence—a force—within the school. What makes him a force, and what differentiates him from the school psychologist and from other personnel in the mental health ranks is, first, the totality of his commitment to the student in all of his life activities and, second, his basic recognition of the integration of environment and personality. Kurloff (1973) sees the counselor as a "psychoecologist," as an "observer-participant" in the students' lives. He does not stand outside of and in relation to those with whom he works but becomes intimately involved with them, interacting on all levels in their lives. Working on the assumption that the free person needs a free environment, he relates the individual's existence with the needs and structures of society. He is an integrator, a synthesizer, blending the elements of the client's life in their natural, harmonious proportions. The counselor, in this sense, serves as the bridge between the individual and the world around him.

The contemporary counselor, recognizing the mutual interaction between the individual and his environment, is deeply concerned with "freeing the potential within both his students *and* his organization" (Conyne and Diedrich, 1970). He never deals with one apart from the other; rather, he acknowledges the unity between the two. The Deweyan conception of the individual in interaction with the environment permeates every phase of every theory of counseling. Although a counselor may choose an approach which is compatible with his personality and concomitant with his ideology, his commitment to the coun-

44

seling stance requires that certain elements of his activities be predetermined by the very nature of that commitment. The counseling way is a way of unity, a way of bringing together the diverse elements in the client's life into a meaningful, manageable whole.

When we speak, then, of the counseling way, we are speaking of a program which incorporates many different activities. Some of these activities resemble psychotherapy; some resemble teaching; some resemble guidance; some, administration. All of them, however, are held together by three fundamental positions indicative of the counseling stance:

1 To counsel is to help the individual become free.
2 Freedom is possible only when the individual and his society are supportive of each other.
3 To attain freedom requires knowledge, self-insight, understanding of others, and socialization skills.

The counselor helps the client to these ends through a variety of activities.

A Policy for Human Involvement, Display 2.1, illustrates some of the basic principles underlying the counseling stance. Substituting the word "school" for

Counseling sessions can easily be held in an informal atmosphere.

"system" and the term "school counseling program" for "mental hygiene program," we have here a clear and exciting idea of how a commitment to human
freedom and dignity may be translated into a practical program which benefits
the individual and the community. We see how the prevailing attitude, that
"human needs and organizational requirements are interdependent," offers a
great hope to the counseling public. For here, at last, we find a policy of treatment, an active ideology, which offers the individual not only personal happiness and peace of mind, but an opportunity to contribute productively to society
and to make this world a better, more healthful, more satisfying, less conflict-
ridden world. Counseling is a hope: It is an opportunity, a chance for the millions of people who will never seek and probably do not need the more rigid
application of formal psychotherapy. Counseling offers the student a chance to
grow without requiring him to make a formal commitment. Because the counselor is *there*, because he carries on his work with a certainty of spirit and surety
of purpose that cannot be lessened by the host of forces working against him (see
chapter 7), he carries on his counseling by being a presence which welds together the individual and the world in which he lives.

The *counseling way* can best be summarized in five principles, derived from
what has been discussed above as well as from some material to be developed in
later chapters. After each principle, a brief example of how that principle may
lead to implementation-in-action will be offered. These principles are:

1 *The counselor establishes himself in the school or in the community as a presence. He makes himself felt through his actions, his words, his BEING.* (The
counselor never assumes a passive stance; he never waits for things to
happen. From his first day of service, he leaves his office, venturing out into
the field, letting all of those around him know that he is there and why he is
there.)

2 *The counselor's primary concern is the freedom of his client, particularly the limitations on that freedom which the client experiences as painful or debilitating.* (The counselor has formulated his own personal, philosophical understanding of the meaning of freedom. As he relates to the client, he assesses the client's need for information, for personal contact, for socialization, and for education with this conception of freedom in mind.)

3 *The counselor attempts to bridge the gap between the individual and his society, working toward helping the two function together harmoniously.* (The counselor implements programs which enable the client to grow as a person and to contribute to the society at the same time. Some examples: community clean-up campaigns, voluntary service, tutoring, etc.)

4 *The counselor accepts the client* as he is *and for what he is. He never stereotypes the client with diagnostic or judgmental language.* (The counselor rejects the psychotherapeutic model of mental illness, using in its place the nonjudgmental phenomenological model.)

5 *The counselor organizes his activities and determines his actions by using a philosophy of counseling. He strives for a continuity of experience which is provided through philosophical reflection.* (Questions regarding the nature of being and existence, of knowledge and understanding, of values are confronted directly by the counselor. He challenges the obvious, the commonsensical, choosing in their place to question and reflect.)

These last two points require further clarification. In the two sections which follow, we shall examine how the abandonment of the mental-illness model and the use of philosophy help the counselor carry out these five principles.

THE ANTI-ILLNESS MOVEMENT

One result of the major impact Freudian thinking had upon the profession of psychology was a tendency among mental health professionals to employ the "medical model" in the treatment of psychological, behavioral, and emotional problems (Ullman & Krasner, 1965). The medical model is one which assumes that behavioral and emotional problems are surface symptoms of underlying pathological conditions, particularly conditions of a psychological nature, in the same way that a physician might recognize that a fever blister is simply the observable evidence of an underlying physical abnormality. When a patient comes for treatment complaining of a phobic condition, and the psychotherapist assumes de facto that the cause of this condition lies in the patient's "unresolved Oedipal problems," he is employing the psychoanalytic version of the medical model.

The medical model helped shape the field of psychotherapy into what it is today by requiring that the practitioner deal not only with the symptoms—that is, with the observable or verbalized difficulties that the patient presents—but with what he, as the practitioner, the expert, believes to be the invisible, underlying causes of this problem as well. Such an approach demanded a new and highly complex terminology to describe these underlying, nonmeasurable phenomena, and there arose over a period of fifty years a nomenclature that was designed to describe the dynamics of patients but that actually reduced the patient's multifaceted existence and wide range of feelings into a set of preconceived categories that satisfied no one but the psychotherapist.

R. D. Laing, the British psychiatrist, has achieved acclaim during the past decade arguing, among other things, against the practitioner's reliance on technical language and his tendency to relate to the patient as if he were an embodiment of these technical words. "The words of the current technical vocabulary," Laing (1965) points out, "either refer to man in isolation from others and the world, that is, as an entity not *essentially* 'in relation to' the other and in a world, or they refer to falsely substantialized aspects of this isolated entity" (p. 19). A technical language is not necessary either for understanding the patient conceptually or for treating him therapeutically; on the contrary, the words of the technical vocabulary are obstacles which stand in the way of understanding the patient in his phenomenological reality, which is the sine qua non of all counseling endeavors.

Perhaps the most flagrant misuse of technical language in the profession is found in the process of diagnosing patients. To diagnose a patient is to attempt to capture in a single word or phrase all of the many intricacies of his problems, and at the same time to imply by the use of the diagnostic category that the practitioner has an understanding of the root causes of the patient's problem. Diagnosis originated in the field of medicine, where it was necessary to identify complex syndromes and to relate these syndromes to the internal causes of the difficulties, and it was carried over to psychiatry, which relied heavily on the medical model. Wherever the medical model is employed, diagnosis becomes an inevitable consequence.

Laing (1965, 1967, 1969) has cautioned that such diagnostic terms as schizophrenia, psychosis, neurosis, and so on, "split man up verbally," reducing his real existence into overly-simplified and somewhat arbitrary categories. The fetish for diagnosing, he argues, makes the patient an object in the therapist's world, which is contrary to the counseling attempt to make the client the center of his world, to restore his wholeness to him. Leona Tyler (1969) also argues against diagnosis, pointing out that the closer a condition comes to what we call the "normal range," the weaker is the argument for diagnosis. In counseling, where we see each client exhibiting behavior which is normal for him, diagnosis serves little use and may in fact be regarded as an interference to understanding the client. Probably the strongest argument against the use of diagnostic categories is to cite their high probability of invalidity and unreliability. Stuart (1973), after carefully surveying the literature, has concluded that practitioners are unable to agree on particular diagnoses and are unable to predict the course and the success of treatment on the basis of diagnostic categories. He found, in short, that there was no scientific basis to the art of diagnosing and no scientific evidence that diagnosing was anything more than mythical constructs.

Patterson (1969) traces the origins of psychological diagnosis to the medical model and suggests that the transfer from medicine to psychiatry "implies that physical and psychological disturbances are similar, i.e., that they can be differentiated into discrete groups or classes, each with a common etiology, symptomatology, course and outcome" (p. 8). He disputes this assumption, arguing that the validity of the analogy between medicine and psychopathology is weak and unfounded:

The two differ in many respects. The nature of the etiology is *quite different.* In the case of physical disease, though there are common factors of stress, there is always a specific ultimately verifiable, physical or external agent, whether chemical, bacteriological, or viral in nature. Such a statement cannot as yet be made regarding mental disorders. In the case of physical disease, the process is primarily one of chemical and physiological malfunctioning. In mental disturbance, on the other hand, the process is primarily a psychosocial disturbance. In physical disease, patients having the same disorder follow rather closely the same course and in most cases with the same predictable outcome. In mental disturbances, on the other hand, there are wide differences in the course and outcome among those classified as having the same diagnosis.... for the physical diseases there exist either known, or as yet unknown, specific remedies. Again, though the search and hope for such specific remedies continue, none has been found for the presumed different personality disturbances. (pp. 8-9)

In addition to the discrepancies mentioned between the medical and psychological situation, we should also mention that social factors play a vital role in determining psychological diagnostic categories while they are generally irrelevant to medical diagnosis. We see from the sum of these remarks that the diagnostic tendencies in the mental health profession not only serve little useful purpose but actually may be responsible for a great deal of harm—by misleading the practitioner, by misdirecting the course of the treatment, and by condemning the client as sick, unhealthy, or abnormal. Combs (1953) has pointed out that the use of these terms often obscures the real issues. Other studies (Chapman and Chapman, 1967; Watson, 1967) have also confirmed that so-called scientific diagnosis actually involves a great deal of subjectivity and personal bias. The bulk of evidence, therefore, weighs heavily against diagnosis.

Why, then, do most psychotherapists and many counselors still employ diagnostic categories? One significant, although unfortunate, reason is that diagnosis heightens the professional mystique. When a therapist or counselor is able to articulate what is "wrong" with a patient in a language that only his professional colleagues are able to understand, it invests him with an authority which would be lacking if he expressed himself in a language which was comprehensible to lay people as well. Diagnosis, in this sense, insulates the practitioner from uninvited comments from the lay public. At times one gets the feeling that the professional psychotherapist is behaving like a parent who spells out words or speaks a foreign language in front of his young children when he does not wish them to understand what he is saying to another adult.

A second reason is what Torrey (1972) describes as the principle of "Rumpelstiltskin." This principle illustrates the magic of the right word. In the Grimm Brothers' story, an evil man wants to take away a baby from the queen. The only way she can prevent this is to name the evil man correctly. At the last moment, just before the tragedy is to occur, she blurts out his name—Rumpelstiltskin—and the baby is saved. Likewise, argues Torrey, in psychotherapy the naming process is an important therapeutic component:

Every therapist who has ever had the experience of observing a patient's relief after solemnly telling him that he was suffering from idiopathic dermatitis or pediculosis knows how important the name is. It says to the patient that someone understands, that he is not alone with his sickness, and implicitly that there is a way to get well. (p. 14)

While this may be true, the pitfalls of diagnosis outweigh any reputed advantages. Diagnosis, by categorizing the patient and labeling him as "sick," "abnormal," "deviant," prevents the practitioner from fully accepting and understanding the patient as he is and for what he is. Diagnosis, in essence, dilutes the client's freedom by restricting him to a category, thus working against the very goals of counseling—freeing the client from categorization and confinement.

The willingness to reject the technical vocabulary and to abandon the use of diagnostic categories marks the first important step in giving up the medical model. While the medical model did at one time serve a useful function for psychotherapists, it no longer satisfies the criteria established by the counseling profession for understanding and relating to each client in a distinct and human way, without recourse to artificiality and veneers of authoritarianism and professional distancing. London (1964) points out the fallacy of even the psychotherapist's using the medical model:

Insofar as he is concerned with the diagnosis and treatment of illness, the modern psychotherapist has grown up in the tradition of medicine. But the nature of the ailments he deals with and the way he treats them set him apart from the physician and in some ways make him function much like a clergyman. He deals with sickness of the soul, as it were, which cannot be cultured in a laboratory, seen through a microscope, or cured by injection. And his methods have little of the concreteness or obvious empiricism of the physician's—he carries no needle, administers no pill, wraps no bandages. He cures by talking and listening. The infections he seeks to expose and destroy are neither bacterial nor viral—they are ideas, memories of experiences, painful and untoward emotions that debilitate the individual and prevent him from functioning effectively and happily. (p. 357)

Moreover, in recent years, the entire concept of mental illness has come increasingly under fire. It must be remembered that as long as there is such a thing as mental illness, there is a need for psychiatrists and psychotherapists. Were the idea of mental illness to be abandoned, the value of these professionals might be sacrificed to the advantage of the counseling profession. And since the myths of mental illness are perpetuated by the very same professionals whose careers depend upon the concept, we must be cautiously suspect in examining the evidence which purports to affirm the existence of mental illness.

Although years ago it took a certain boldness to reject the term mental illness, evidence and arguments have been amassed during the past decade to bolster this position both from within the profession and from without. Two practitioners who have contributed a wealth of insights are R. D. Laing and Thomas Szasz, each of whom offers to the counselor many new and invigorating implications into how counseling, without an emphasis on mental illness, can contribute more to the good of the individual and of mankind than can psychotherapy with its highly technical vocabulary, its emphasis on illness and cure, and its reliance on diagnosis and technical constructs.

Laing's position is built on the assumption that mental illness is a hypothetical term, describing more a social value than a phenomenological reality. Profoundly concerned with the total person in all his life processes, all his interactions and experiences, all his functional and perceptual encounters as a free agent, Laing exemplifies in every respect the counseling stance. Although he is a psychiatrist by training, he is not a psychotherapist in the traditional sense. He cannot be because he rejects the very criteria which define therapy—a psychopathology, a theory of personality based on social and cultural absolutes, manipulative techniques, and above all the debilitating designation of "patient" for the one being treated. Laing argues time and again in his writings that the person who seeks help must be viewed and must be dealt with not as a sick, unstable, deficient person but rather from the standpoint of his subjective world, from his reference points, from his perspective. Moreover, Laing objects to the stratification typical of the psychotherapeutic relationship, a stratification derived directly from the medical model, which describes an "ill" person seeking the professional assistance of a person who is presumably able to cure the illness. Arguing instead that the therapeutic relationship is a mutual effort at growth by both therapist and patient, Laing (1967) says:

Psychotherapy must remain an obstinate attempt of two people to recover the wholeness of being human through the relationship between them.... Any technique concerned with the other without the self, with behavior to the exclusion of experience, with the relationship to the neglect of the person in relation, with the individuals to the exclusion of their relationship, and most of all with an object-to-be-changed rather than a person to be accepted, simply perpetuates the disease it purports to cure. (p. 53)

Laing's position, free from the constraints imposed by the medical model and its reliance upon mental illness, closely parallels the classical counseling position, as exemplified by Rogers, Arbuckle, Tyler, and others.

Moreover, the Laingian view of counseling, according to Belkin and Philips (1974), emphasizes the here and now, as opposed to an emphasis on the past. So much emphasis does Laing place on the here and now that he suggests the counselor leave the confines of his office and see the client functioning within the context of his everyday life: in the home, in the school, and in other social situations.

This is an important suggestion, inasmuch as it implies the counselor's willingness to study the client in his natural habitat. Because the rejection of the mental illness model and the acceptance of the belief in man's freedom-to-be demands a comprehensive view of the individual, it is particularly important that the counselor, in his efforts to teach the client the meaning of freedom, understand the client in light of his interactions. The temptation to classify the client, to diagnose him, increases as the counselor's contacts with the client are limited to the sterile, inflexible confines of the office. Likewise, this temptation is diminished when the counselor is better able to understand the *why* of the client's behavior, gleaned from observing him in a variety of behaviorally stimulating situations.

Another important proponent of the anti-illness point of view is Thomas Szasz. His writings, particularly his well-known and influential book, *The Myth of Mental Illness* (1961), have argued lucidly and cogently against the position that conceptions of mental illness are objective and dispassionate accounts of psychopathology. Like Laing, Szasz looks at mental illness within the context of culture, criticizing its lack of scientific reliability and validity, as the practitioner imposes his own values and his own sociological biases in ascribing an illness to the patient. Szasz (1960) argues:

Difficulties in human relations can be analyzed, interpreted, and given meaning only within specific social and ethical contexts. Accordingly, the psychiatrist's socioethical orientations will influence his ideas on what is wrong with the patient, on what deserves comment or interpretation, in what directions change might be desirable, and so forth. (p. 115)

Szasz does not dispute that some individuals have more difficulty than others in fitting into acceptable social patterns of behavior. Rather, he objects solely to the designation of mentally ill for those individuals who either refuse to conform or are unable to acquiesce to the structures and standards of the society in which they live. If we look at the common practice in the Soviet Union today of classifying politically dissident intellectuals as "mentally ill," we can see in the clearest, and yet most horrendous sense, to what Szasz is referring.

Both Laing and Szasz offer a valuable insight for the counselor. In order for the counselor to relate to his client, in order for him to understand, accept, and respect the client, he must stubbornly avoid the temptation of diagnosing the client, of viewing the client as a mentally ill person, of attempting to describe the client in technical terminology.

But if we abandon the medical model as a basis for understanding psychological and emotional problems, and if we give up the mental illness paradigm, what do we put in their place? Another way of stating this question is, "On what bases and by what criteria should the counselor relate to his clients?"

The answer to this question becomes abundantly clear as we examine the literature. The counselor must rely on the phenomenological approach to replace these other paradigms of treatment. While the phenomenological approach is often associated with existential philosophy (see chapter 10 for a more detailed discussion), it has had a profound effect in client-centered counseling, psychoanalytic counseling, and gestalt counseling as well.

The phenomenological approach, briefly, attempts to reconstruct the world as it is seen from the point of view of the client. Free of value judgments, undistorted by perceptual biases, the world of the client opens up to the counselor in all its pristine clarity and internal logic. The phenomenological approach precludes the designation of mental illness by eliminating such broad categories of containment as diagnosis and curative terminology. More importantly, the phenomenological approach works independently of and in contradiction to the medical model of treatment. Thus, by embracing the phenomenological approach, the counselor frees himself of the difficulties implicit in the medical model and inherent in the theory of mental illness.

There is another advantage to the phenomenological approach which bears directly on the discussion at hand. If the counselor is truly dedicated toward helping the client discover his freedom, then he must be willing to understand the limits to that freedom which have been imposed by the client himself. Before he can do so, however, the counselor must have an intimate working familiarity with the meaning and implications of freedom. Such a familiarity can in part be gained from a study of philosophy, which, on many levels, approaches this difficult question. In the next section we shall look at the value of philosophy in helping the counselor perform, and we shall examine how the counselor "does" a philosophy—enacts it in the counseling setting. We should keep in mind as we read the following section that philosophy is the underlying basis of counseling and, therefore, the groundwork for the counselor's actions which are designed to free the client.

"DOING" A PHILOSOPHY OF COUNSELING

It was suggested in the last chapter that counseling has as its underlying basis a coherent philosophy, which guides its course and directs its activities. We then developed the point in this chapter that counseling is a freeing activity, which liberates the client from his fears, deficiencies, and self-imposed distortions. It is now possible to combine these two ideas and to illustrate how philosophy can become a valuable tool in counseling, both by helping the counselor to understand better the counseling situation and to make appropriate decisions, and by enabling the counselor to make his own life more coherent and facilitative and thus more compatible with his treatment goals. But first we must examine in some detail what is meant by the term *philosophy*, and, more importantly, what specific insights and tools philosophy offers to the counselor.

Literally, philosophy means "love of wisdom." The derivation of the word is appropriate to its current usage; for although philosophy touches upon many questions in different disciplines, it is always characterized by an enduring, unrelenting desire to shed light where there has been darkness, to make clear what has been blurred, to point out new ways of understanding and interpreting the world. Philosophy, as much as it is a discipline, is also an attitude which permeates the philosopher's every perception and thought. It is a tentative rejection of the apparent, a willingness to question and negate, a flexibility of intellect, an openness to ideas before they can be "proven" to a scientist's satisfaction. Philosophy is, in short, a systematic, organized way of looking at the world.

The discipline of philosophy comprises four subspecialties: *ontology, epistemology, axiology,* and *logic (and language analysis)*. Ontology is the study of being and existence. It concerns such basic questions as "What do we mean by *to be?*" and "How can we determine the *existent* from the *nonexistent?*" Ontology also deals with such metaphysical problems as the existence of God, the nature of *principles* and *causality*, and other abstract and scientifically nonverifiable terms, such as *the Absolute, the Infinite, the Universal,* etc. A criticism often lodged against ontology is that it deals with terms which are in effect meaningless and have no correlation in the real world. Counterarguments have been offered, however, which suggest that exploration of such abstract and inconclusive issues does, in a direct or indirect way, contribute heartily to more practical problems concerning the lives of men and the conduct of their affairs.

Walters (1958), for example, points out that metaphysics and religion, the components of ontology, answer relevant counseling questions that are unanswerable by science. Arbuckle (1958) has cited "religion" and "the nature of man," both ontological problems, as two major philosophical issues in counseling. Both of these issues bear relevance to our understanding of the counselor's attitude toward the client and his part in the counseling interaction. Astor (1965) has proposed a philosophical model of counselor self-understanding, utilizing such metaphysical categories as "ideals and reality," "being and becoming," "tentativeness and commitment," "the individual and society," "freedom and responsibility." Each of these polarized categories serves as a bridge, linking the subject and object in a uniquely metaphysical way.

In general, *ontology is important to the counselor in helping him develop a comprehensive view of man.* When science is unable to answer many of the compelling questions arising out of the counseling situation, the counselor turns his attention to a nonscientific (what Heidegger called a "pre-scientific") discipline to find answers to these very difficult, but very important questions, which challenge him in all his endeavors and upon which many of his actions are based. Ontology may be considered the most basic, fundamental branch of philosophy, a branch which the counselor must confront boldly at the outset of his inquiries. Daubner and Daubner (1972) have suggested, in fact, that the counselor *is* a metaphysician, in that he is always concerned with those questions which constitute the essence of metaphysical inquiry.

What are some of the ontological questions frequently contemplated or raised by the counselor? One major category of questions are those regarding the nature of man. Is the life of a man predetermined either genetically or in some other way or is he always a free agent, capable of choosing his calling? Does counseling affect the client's essential self or does it merely impose superficial changes upon the client's personality or character? The former question has been the core of the perennial debate between Freudians and existentialists.

ONTOLOGICAL ISSUES IN COUNSELING

What do we mean by the concept of "self"?

Existentialism: We are what we do; nothing more and nothing less.

Client-Centered: The self is a fluid and changing entity, which organizes the sum of our perceptions.

Psychoanalysis: The self is the product of the conscious, preconscious, and unconscious mind.

Humanism: The self is a growing, expanding, self-actualizing force.

Behaviorism: The self is a mythical construct, a metaphysical remnant.

What do we mean by growth?

Existentialism: Growth is making new choices and assuming responsibility for those choices.

Client-Centered: Growth is the ordinary consequences of healthy living.

Psychoanalysis: Growth is the freeing of the repressed and the lessening of intrapsychic conflicts.

Humanism: Growth is the satisfaction of our "growth needs," which implies that our lower-order needs have been met.

Behaviorism: Growth is learning new stimulus-response patterns, and changing some of our old ones.

While the psychoanalytic position is that the individual is shaped by the age of five—that his destiny from that point on has already been carved for him—the existentialists maintain that throughout his life man is free to choose his options. Experimentation cannot resolve this deeply divisive philosophic problem, and one of the tasks of the philosopher is to help the counselor deal with this complex problem in an intelligent, constructive manner. Likewise, the second question—whether counseling effects a change in the essential self or merely in the superficial layers of character—has constituted the core of debate between the client-centered and the behaviorist positions. The client-centered counselor believes in a fluid, actualizing self, continually in flux and growth, while the behavioral counselor emphasizes the conditioned patterns of behavior as the key dimension of self. If we look at Display 2.2, we will find several applications of ontology to the counseling situation and better understand how this branch of philosophy contributes to the counseling process.

Epistemology is the branch of philosophy dealing with the single verb *to know*. Epistemological questions are questions of knowledge and understanding. "How can I know that something is true?" and "What are some different types and qualities of understanding?" are typical epistemological questions. As the concern of ontology is *being* and *existence*, the ultimate concerns of epistemology are *knowledge* and *truth*.

Scheffler (1965) had identified a number of epistemological positions. One position (empiricism) maintains that everything we know we learn through our experiences. The counselor who subscribes to this point of view would inevitably try to enrich his clients' experiential worlds. A second position (rationalism) argues that the mind grasps rough approximations of ideal, absolute forms, which exist outside the mind. The counselor who subscribes to this position would recognize the impossibility of ever arriving at a truth and would accept in place of truth, approximations to truth. A third position (pragmatism) considers thinking and ideas as tentative hypotheses, which are tested out through our actions in the "real world." To the pragmatist counselor, the mind is continually regenerating itself in response to its environment, always engaged in a process of growth and development. If we look at Display 2.3, we will see how these three philosophical positions can be applied to practical counseling problems. It is the counselor's responsibility to take an epistemological stand after carefully examining all of his options.

Whichever position one takes, the basic concern about epistemological problems is necessary on the part of the counselor. Because counseling is, in part at least, a process of learning, the issue of knowledge plays a crucial role in determining counseling strategy and evaluating counseling effectiveness. Moreover, as Daubner and Daubner (1969) have pointed out, "unless the counselor is aware of, has speculated about, and has taken a position regarding ... epistemological problems..., he may be operating unknowingly from a philosophical stance that is quite at variance with the one that his counseling procedures imply." The counselor better understands himself and his role, insofar as that role includes helping the client gain knowledge about himself and the world, as he explores the basic questions which characterize the discipline of epistemology.

Axiology, the study of values, is the branch of philosophy most often cited in the couseling literature and probably the most directly relevant to the counseling process. Axiology comprises the subspecialties of aesthetics (values in art) and ethics (values in human activities—moral values). While the former has little to offer directly to counseling problems, the latter bears a compelling relevance, which has been discussed often and fruitfully (Lowe, 1959; Patterson, 1958; Korner, 1956; Dreikurs, 1957; Adams, 1965; Curran, 1960; Ajzen, 1973; Daubner and Daubner, 1970; Peterson, 1970). Ethics, insofar as it examines the moral basis of man's actions and relates actions to higher principles and purposes, illuminates the counseling interaction and offers the counselor a new and more meaningful perspective. Because of our "autonomy as moral agents" (Frankena, 1963), we need a grounding in ethics to help us with decision making as well as to insure "right action and judgment" in our conduct with our fellow men.

Ethical alternatives and problems occur at almost every point of the counseling process. The moment a client enters the counselor's world, the counselor is confronted by a variety of ethical questions which challenge his intellect. Questions such as "How do the client's values compare with my values?" and "What is 'right' for this client?" are surprisingly difficult questions to answer without a full understanding of the implications of ethical decisions. Moreover, as Patterson (1958) suggests, since many of the client's problems involve values and value conflicts, the counselor's intimacy with ethical thinking enables him to offer the client a more propitious opportunity to resolve these problems. In this respect, ethics contributes to the efficacy of the treatment.

Finally, we come to the branch of logic and language analysis. Often subsumed under the heading of epistemology, this area of philosophy is important and well enough developed to stand on its own. Symbolic logic, a major component of this branch, has not yet been applied to counseling problems, although the potential for application is there and will hopefully be explored in the near future. But language analysis and the logic of meanings (semantics) is beginning to exert a powerful impact on counseling thought.

The school of "Ordinary Language Analysis" emerged in England during the 1930s as an attempt to clarify some persistent philosophical problems by clarifying the often obscure and redundant language used to deal with the problems. One of the major figures to emerge from this school was Ludwig Wittgenstein (1889–1951), who viewed language use as a series of games played by the speakers of the language. Gilbert Ryle (1900–), another figure at the forefront, applied the critical analytic tools to psychological terms, in an effort to clarify these terms and give them meanings. The logical positivist, A. J. Ayer (1910–), has suggested that language analysis could be used to clarify such obscure terms as *intelligence, empathy*, and *subconscious*. He is especially critical of psychoanalysis, which is "full of metaphysical elements which a philosophical elucidation of the symbols would remove (1946)." As he describes the work of the philosopher in this respect, we get a clear feeling of how ordinary language philosophy can be of value to the counselor:

It would be the philosopher's business to make clear what was the real empirical content of the propositions of psychoanalysts, and what was their logical relationship to the propositions of behaviorists or *Gestalt* psychologists, a relationship at present obscured by unanalysed differences of terminology. (p. 152)

This branch of philosophy, therefore, can be viewed as the branch useful for clarifying counseling problems in terms of the language in which these problems are expressed. Some questions that language analysis might help clarify are: What do we mean by *effective counselor characteristics*? Is *intelligence* an important factor in counseling? In counselor training, how can we specify counselor competencies? A number of these questions will be answered in future chapters.

*　　*　　*　　*　　*

Having now considered the four main branches of philosophy, let us turn our attention to the specific work of a philosopher and see how that work can contribute fruitfully to the counselor's task.

Ryle (1946) attempts to answer the question, "Where does the work of the philosopher begin in relation to the work of specialists in other disciplines?" The philosopher, he suggests, begins

by wondering about the categories constituting the framework of a single theory or discipline, but he cannot stop there. He must try to coordinate the categories of all theories and disciplines. The problem of "Man's place in Nature" is roughly, the problem of coordinating the questions which govern laboratory researches with the questions governing the researches prosecuted in libraries. (p. 490)

Two important points emerge here in respect to our concern about philosophy's place in counseling. First, the philosopher of counseling attempts to understand this discipline by examining the categories of the discipline; for example, some of the major categories of the discipline and which areas of philosophy are specifically relevant to answering these questions. Questions regarding the purpose of counseling, techniques of counseling, qualities of the effective counselor, and the like are all rooted in one or more of the philosophical specialties. Moreover, as Ryle implies, philosophy helps relate the findings of the laboratory with the speculation and theoretical categories. Philosophy, in short, is the synthetic discipline which brings various types of knowledge together to deal with problems.

In this respect, philosophy is a tool that the counselor uses in his professional endeavors. It is a skill, a method, which enables the counselor better to understand and resolve some of the fundamental difficulties which perplex him in his thinking and confront him in his practice.

But on another level, philosophy is much more than a tool: It is a commitment and a provocation to action. Gelso (1970) has suggested that "a counselor's philosophy of man has an important effect upon how he conceptualizes and behaves in counseling." Strickland (1969), also thinking along this line, has suggested that a counselor's personal philosophy is the single most critical force in determining his practical effectiveness. Strickland makes clear that he is not speaking of formal philosophical knowledge but rather of an informal, unsophisticated, flexible philosophical position which helps him in his own way to understand the nature of man, value conflicts, and questions of meaning which protrude from all his counseling encounters. Moreover, Strickland argues that the counselor's own personal philosophy helps shape the theoretical constructs which govern his practice, particularly in regard to methodology. Strickland's point is well taken, for, in the long run, philosophy cannot be entirely severed from action. What the counselor believes influences what he does. Thus, philosophy is more than a tool for the counselor to use; it is an inclusive and pervasive system which governs many, if not all, of his actions.

But philosophy bears relevance to counseling in another way as well. Philosophy, as an integral part of the counselor's and the client's lives, becomes a dynamic part of the counseling relationship. Ortega (1967) suggests that philosophy helps us discover another world—a "latent or supra-world,"—which underlies the manifest world. Philosophy, in other words, helps us to penetrate the opacity of the world in which we live, helps us get to the bare, naked reality underneath. Since one of the important stages in counseling is understanding the phenomenal world of the client, a world which is clearly latent and supra-sensible, we can surmise that philosophy is a viable means of better understanding the client. Philosophy is not something external to the counseling relationship but an integral functioning part of the relationship, something "with" the counselor and "with" the client at every moment.

This concept has been clarified by Maxine Greene in her important work, *Teacher as Stranger* (1973). "Doing" philosophy, she explains, is a way of breaking from tradition, of freeing oneself from habitual, time-ingrained, and involuntary responses. It is a way of thinking, thinking freely as we consider and choose our commitments and actions. In her own words:

Philosophy may be regarded as a way of approaching (or looking at or taking a stance with respect to) the knowledge gained by the natural and human sciences, the awareness made possible by the arts, and the personal insights into existence each human being accumulates as he lives…. It is a way of contemplating, examining, or thinking about what is taken to be significant, valuable, beautiful, worthy of commitment. It is a way of becoming self-aware, of constituting meanings in one's life-world…. To do philosophy, then, is to become highly conscious of the phenomena and events in the world as it presents itself to consciousness. To do philosophy, as Jean-Paul Sartre says, is to develop a fundamental project, to go beyond the situations one confronts and refuse reality as given in the name of a reality to be produced. (p. 7)

Like Ortega, Greene views philosophy as a window beyond the "given," beyond the obvious, into a world of deeper, more intensive, more fundamental, more basic meanings. As the counselor does a philosophy, he takes a stand, makes a commitment, and lives his life by this commitment. Doing philosophy, then, is not some adjunct to counseling, but an integral, necessary, and highly effective part of the total counseling process.

Consider, for example, a counselor who is attempting to do a philosophy of humanism within the counseling context. This philosophical position is defined by Lamont (1965) as "a philosophy of joyous service for the greater good of all humanity in this natural world and advocating the methods of reason, science, and democracy" (p. 12). To do such a philosophy would require several stages in the counselor's personal and professional development. First, he would have to understand the ontological, axiological, and epistemological implications of the humanist position. He could do this by studying Lamont's classic work, *The Philosophy of Humanism*, which deals in detail with the humanistic "theory of the universe," the "ethics of humanism," the "ultimates of existence," the issue of "social good and individual happiness," and so on. But reading and understanding Lamont would not in itself be enough. The counselor would then have to explore how the methods of science advocated by the humanist can help him understand the nonempirical issues which invariably arise in counseling. Can he accept this position or is it untenable in his world? How can the principles of democracy, so important to the humanistic stance, help him work better with the individual who may be at odds with society? After examining all these interrelated questions, the counselor must finally decide if his personality, with its predilections and idiosyncracies, is emotionally suited to humanism. If his answer is in the affirmative, then—and only then—he may go about conducting himself, inside the counseling situation and outside, as a true humanist. In this way, he will be doing—not just understanding—a philosophy of humanism.

The subtle relationship between philosophy and counseling becomes clear as we approach it in this perspective. We see that philosophy is more than an adjunct to counseling; it is an integral part of the process. The counselor uses philosophy to make meaningful his encounter with the client. The four models (or modes) of philosophy discussed above come together here in the counselor's actions as he finds himself doing a philosophy of counseling. His own existence—his uniqueness, his individuality, his eccentricity, his personality—find their appropriate outlet and their constructive expression within the counseling setting as he does his philosophy. The counselor takes a stand: He commits himself to a cause, to the counseling cause, and his actions are guided appropriately.

He may, in deciding upon which actions to take, utilize the premises of a philosophic system he has committed himself to (philosophy and education); or he may attempt to help the client direct and construct his energies into a philosophical perspective (philosophy in counseling); then again, he may guide himself by utilizing a philosophical stance (philosophy for counseling); and finally, in all that he does he stands back from the doing to observe and analyze, to reflect and evaluate philosophy in counseling). In doing a philosophy, the counselor carries out the highest ideals of human conduct and action and uses the greatest forces in the personality to better the client and to make counseling the great resource that it is.

References

Adams, J. F. Ethical responsibilities of the counselor. *The School Counselor*, 1965, *12*, 197–205.

Ajzen, R. Human values and counseling. *Personnel and Guidance Journal*, 1973, *52*, 77–81.

Arbuckle, D. S. Five philosophical issues in counseling. *Journal of Counseling Psychology*, 1958, *5*(3), 211–215.

Arbuckle, D. S. *Counseling: An introduction*, Boston: Allyn & Bacon, 1961.

Astor, M. H. Counselors seek to understand themselves: A philosophical inquiry. *Personnel and Guidance Journal*, 1965, *43*, 1029–1033.

Ayer, A. J. *Language, truth and logic* (1946). Paperback edition, New York: Dover, 1952.

Belkin, G. S., & Philips, J. A. Laingian view of counseling. In G. S. Belkin (Ed.), *Foundations of counseling*. Dubuque, Iowa: Kendall/Hunt, 1974.

Chapman, L., & Chapman, J. Genesis of popular but erroneous psychodiagnostic observations. *Journal of Abnormal Psychology*, 1967, *72*, 193–204.

Combs, A. W. Problems and definitions in legislation. *American Psychologist*, 1953, *8*, 554–563.

Conyne, R. K., & Diedrich, R. C. Effective counseling: Necessary but no longer sufficient. *Educational Technology*, 1970, *12*, 47–49.

Curran, C. A. Some ethical and scientific values in the counseling psychotherapeutic process. *Personnel and Guidance Journal*, 1960, *38*, 15–20.

Daubner, E. V., & Daubner, E. S. Epistemology and school counseling. *Personnel and Guidance Journal*, 1969, *47*, 506–513.

Daubner, E. V., & Daubner, E. S. Ethics and counseling decisions. *Personnel and Guidance Journal*, 1970, *48*, 433 –442.

Daubner, E. V. & Daubner, E. S. The counselor as metaphysician. *Personnel and Guidance Journal*, 1972, *50*, 363 –370.

Dewey, J. *Democracy and education*. New York: Macmillan, 1916.

Dimick, K. M., & Huff, V. E. *Child counseling*. Dubuque, Iowa: Wm. C. Brown, 1970.

Dreikurs, R. Psychotherapy as correction of faulty social values. *Journal of Individual Psychology*, 1957, *13*, 150–158.

Frankena, W. K. *Ethics*. Englewood Cliffs, N.J.: Prentice-Hall, 1963.

Fromm, E. *The sane society*. New York: Holt, Rinehart & Winston, 1955. Paperback edition is quoted. Greenwich, Conn.: Fawcett, 1967.

Gelso, C. J. Two different worlds: A paradox in counseling and psychotherapy. *Journal of Counseling Psychology*, 1970, *17*, 271–278.

Greene, M. *Teacher as stranger*. Belmont, Calif.: Wadsworth, 1973.

Gustad, J. W. The definition of counseling. In R. F. Berdie (Ed.), *Roles & relationships in counseling*, Minnesota Studies in Pupil Personnel Work. Minneapolis: University of Minnesota Press, 1953.

Korner, I. N. Of values, value lag, and mental health. *American Psychologist*, 1956, *11*, 543–546.

Kurloff, P. J. The counselor as psychoecologist. *Personnel and Guidance Journal*, 1973, *51*, 321–327.

Laing, R. D. *The divided self*. Baltimore: Penguin, 1965.

Laing, R. D. *The politics of experience*. New York: Ballantine, 1967.

Laing, R. D. *Self and others*. New York: Pantheon, 1969.

Lamont, C. *The philosophy of humanism* (5th ed.). New York: Frederick Ungar, 1965.

London, P. The morals of psychotherapy (1964). In O. H. Mowrer (Ed.), *Morality and mental health*. Chicago: Rand McNally, 1967. (pp. 357-364)

Lowe, C. M. Value orientation—an ethical dilemma. *American Psychologist*, 1959, *14*, 687–693.

May, R. *Man's search for himself*. New York: Norton, 1953.

May, R. *The art of counseling*. Nashville: Abingdon Press, 1967.

Mental Hygiene News. A policy for human involvement. Albany, N.Y.: New York State Department of Mental Hygiene, July 6, 1973.

Miller, H. *Nexus*. New York: Grove Press, 1966.

Miller, H. *Plexus*. New York: Grove Press, 1966.

Miller, H. *Sexus*. New York: Grove Press, 1966.

Morris, V. C. *Existentialism in education*. New York: Harper & Row, 1966.

Ortega y Gasset, J. [*The origin of philosophy*] (T. Talbot, Trans.), New York: Norton, 1967. (Originally published, 1946.)

Patterson, C. H. The place of values in counseling and psychotherapy. *Journal of Counseling Psychology*, 1958, *5*, 216–223.

Patterson, C. H. A current view of client-centered or relationship therapy. *The Counseling Psychologist*, 1969, *1*(2), 2–25.

Peterson, J. A. *Counseling and values*. Scranton, Pa.: International Textbook, 1970.

Rogers, C. R. Learning to be free. *NEA Journal*, 1963, *52*, 28 –30.

Rosenthal, R., & Jacobson, L. *Pygmalion in the classroom*. New York: Holt, Rinehart & Winston, 1968.

Ryle, G. Philosophical arguments. In J. B. Hartman (Ed.), *Philosophy of recent times*. New York: McGraw-Hill, 1967. (Originally published, 1946.)

Scheffler, I. *Conditions of knowledge*. Glenview, Ill.: Scott, Foresman, 1965.

Schlossberg, N. K., & Pietrofesa, J. J. Perspectives on counseling bias. *Counseling Psychologist*, 1973, *4*, 44–54.

Strickland, B. The philosophy-theory-practice continuum: A point of view. *Counselor Education and Supervision*, 1969, *8*, 165–175.

Stuart, R. B. *Trick or treatment: How and when psychotherapy fails* (3rd printing). Champaign, Ill.: Research Press, 1973.

Szasz, T. The myth of mental illness. *The American Psychologist*, 1960, *15*, 113–118.

Szasz, T. *The myth of mental illness*. New York: Paul B. Hoeber, 1961.

Torrey, E. F. *The mind game*. New York: Emerson Hall, 1972.

Tyler, L. E. *The work of the counselor*. (3rd ed.). New York: Appleton-Century-Crofts, 1969.

Ullman, L. P., & Krasner, L. Introduction. In L. P. Ullman & L. Krasner (Eds.), *Case studies in behavior modification*. New York: Holt, Rinehart & Winston, 1965.

Walker, D. E., & Peiffer, H. C., Jr. The goals of counseling. *Journal of Counseling Psychology*, 1957, *4*, 204–209.

Walters, O. S. Metaphysics, religion, and psychotherapy. *Journal of Counseling Psychology*. 1958, *5*, 243–252.

Watson, C. Relationship of distortion to DAP diagnostic accuracy among psychologists at three levels of sophistication. *Journal of Consulting Psychology*, 1967, *31*, 142–146.

Wilson, C. *Introduction to the new existentialism*. Boston: Houghton Mifflin, 1966.

chapter three

Issues in counseling

Areas of controversy and debate, particularly those areas in which the controversy has been heated and the debate perennial, are usually indicative of underlying schisms which in a number of ways threaten the integrity and unity of a discipline. This is not to suggest that a unified discipline should be free of controversy and debate; on the contrary, contention yields a lively interest in the subject and promotes an ongoing growth of attitude and an expanding of proficiencies. Controversy encourages research; research precipitates important breakthroughs; these in turn lead to improvements in practical application. But the stubborn recurrence of a particular debate, the persistent unresolved questioning of a single issue, indicates most clearly that a fuzziness and confusion underlies this one particular aspect of the discipline, and it is the responsibility of the researcher and practitioner to attempt to come to grips with this problem.

In counseling there are a number of such areas of persistent controversy, stubborn questions that, despite the surfeit of research and the ingenuity of speculation, won't seem to go away. These questions, which over time have become issues in counseling, have been tackled in three ways: through experimental research, through theoretical argument, and through systematic observation and clinical case studies. While none of these methods is fully adequate in itself—each suffers some deficiency—the three methods combined meet the task well. The experimental method is faulty in not providing a reasonable facsimile to the counseling situation. No matter how many Minnesota Multiphasic Personality Inventories (MMPIs) we administer, no matter what sophisticated scales we devise to measure empathy, genuineness, and concreteness, no matter how cleverly we test the counselor's efficacy and strategy, the fact remains that the hypothetical conditions of the experiment differ significantly from the unpredictable variables of the counseling setting. The theoretical approach tends at key times to lose touch with the harsh realities of the counseling situation. We find that ideal, optimistic insights about counseling, for instance, are sometimes not borne out by the experimental evidence. Hardly an intuition has passed gracefully all the key tests of validation, and at times even the most basic axioms of counseling have come under embarrassing challenge by the evidence (see, for example, Gladstein's "Is Empathy Important in Counseling?"). Observation and recording—the case study approach—is also limited. A single, isolated case is generally selected because it demonstrates something specific— usually success of some type—and we know that not all counseling endeavors work out so prosperously. But together, these three methods—the empirical, the theoretical, and the case study—comprise a formidable triad, each complementing the deficiencies of the others and adding to the substance of the whole. In this chapter we shall utilize all three methods to explore the basic issues in counseling. But first, let us review briefly what we have said thus far, synthesizing some of our insights from the previous chapters and formulating some unanswered questions which still remain after our previous discussion.

First, we distinguished between counseling and psychotherapy. Counseling, we pointed out, is built upon an underlying philosophy of man, including an ontology, an epistemology, and an axiology. The ontological basis of counseling deals with such questions as "What is the relationship between the reality of the client and the objective reality?" "How does the client's existence relate to his essential qualities?" "To what higher purposes in life, toward which universals, does man strive?" The epistemological core of counseling, which deals with the question of knowledge and truth, considers such issues as "What is the nature of consciousness and its relationship with the known?" "How does the client learn new behavior and integrate it into his life style?" "What correspondence is there between what the client 'knows' and what is generally accepted to be true?" The axiological premises and bases of counseling, dealing with values, raise such intrinsic questions as "How can the counselor conduct himself without his values unduly influencing the client?" "To what degree does the individual have control over his ethical decisions?" "What part does 'conscience' play in the governing of the client's life?" Both the counselor and the client, as they engage in their intensely emotional interaction, consider, either consciously or unconsciously, a myriad of philosophical questions which influence their perceptions, judgments, and actions. Philosophies differ in a number of areas of major importance. These are briefly summarized below:

1 How *directive* or *nondirective* should the counselor be in his work with the client?
2 What emphasis is placed on the idea of *free will* and what emphasis is placed on the idea of *determinism*?
3 How deeply into the personality and unconscious of the client should the counselor probe?
4 How much of himself should the counselor voluntarily give to the client?
5 To what degree should the counselor direct himself to the client's behavior and to what degree should he direct himself primarily to the client's feelings?

6 How much allegiance does the counselor owe to the system or institution that employs him? At what times might this loyalty conflict with his loyalty and obligation to the client?

7 How do religious or other ethical concerns contribute to the quality and direction of the counseling interaction?

8 What use should the counselor make of his own experiences, perceptions, and beliefs in dealing with the client?

9 What feelings of the counselor's are appropriate or inappropriate in terms of the proposed outcomes of the treatment?

10 When behavioral change is proposed, what criteria should the counselor use for deciding on the specific goals, and for determining methods to be used to attain those goals?

11 How should the counselor go about selecting a theory or counseling school to use as the basis for his practice?

12 How should the counselor go about resolving conflicts between his intuition and the counseling model he is using?

These, and other questions like them, continue to trouble the counselor and are not readily answered by the broad definition and sweeping picture of counseling we have detailed above. Within the counseling category we can and we do find these questions. To assist the counselor in arriving at his own answers, we shall have to examine different conceptions of counseling that serve as a cohering force in counseling, holding together the moments of the interaction and blending them into a goal-directed, purposive whole.

Second, we indicated that counseling, unlike psychotherapy, relies heavily on the phenomenological approach, looking at the individual from his own frame of reference, and experiencing life as closely as possible to the way he experiences it. The counseling approach deals with the whole person, synthesizing and unifying the fragmented parts of his totality by means of the counseling relationship and all of its ancillary functions. Rejecting the prescripts of the medical model and the strictures of an orthodox psychopathology, counseling attempts to integrate into practice the environmental as well as the intrapsychic components of experience. Carkhuff and Berenson's rather comprehensive description of the "whole person" will be used in chapter 5 to illustrate what is meant by this concept.

Having gone this far in our analysis, we reach a juncture at which a decision must be made. Granted that counseling is of this certain type of activity, we must acknowledge that under the rubric counseling are included many different types of activities, rationales, and proposed outcomes. For what we have described so far is counseling-in-general, rather than a specific approach to counseling, a specific type of counseling. Under the heading counseling, we find such divergent counseling approaches as the Rogerian, the behaviorist, the existential, the gestalt, the eclectic, and so on. Practitioners of counseling have different approaches to the problem, different ways of going about dealing with the conflict, and these must be clarified. Our efforts in this direction will be divided into three sections. First, we shall examine the relationship between the counselor's theoretical orientation and his actual performance. Does the counselor's theory significantly affect his behavior, or is the theory a post facto explanation for his actions? Do his specific beliefs emanate from a broad philosophical base, or is the philosophical base designed as a substructure for his inchoate and disorganized beliefs? The second section will examine the counseling relationship, with the aim of clarifying and elucidating the counseling experience in terms of the goals and direction of the interaction, the counselor's movement and rationale within the scope of the treatment, the components and psychodynamics of the complex, multidimensional relationship. The third section will deal with two broad conceptions of counseling treatment: the "Newtonian" conception, which embraces an absolutist, causative rationale, and is particularly indicative of psychotherapeutic approaches, and the "Einsteinian" conception, which is relativistic and fluid and more indicative of what we mean by practical counseling. At the conclusion of this discussion, we shall attempt to clarify some of the basic counseling issues listed above, using the insights developed in this chapter.

COUNSELING THEORY AND COUNSELING PRACTICE

Counseling students often raise the question of why there are so many different and often conflicting schools of thought, divergent approaches, and theories of psychotherapy and counseling that are at odds with each other. At the present time there are well over one hundred different theories, approaches, and rationales, each vying for its own niche on the counseling-therapy spectrum. If counseling were truly scientific and empirical, students argue, there would be no room for contention over such basic issues as the nature of man, the role of the client, the job of the counselor, effective strategies, the counselor's appropriate attitude and responses in the treatment setting, and so on.

To respond to this paradox—or seeming paradox—it is necessary first to make clear what a theory of counseling (or a theory of psychotherapy) is, and what relationship the theory has to the treatment. Next, we will have to examine common bases underlying all these theories and the discrepancies which place them in opposition, to determine the true degree of consonance or dissonance among them. Only at that point will we be able to answer adequately this recurring and perpetually troubling question. In this section, we shall explore the first question.

Webster's Unabridged defines theory (as it applies to us) as, "a belief, policy, or procedure proposed or followed as the basis of action." The key thought in this definition is the linking up of beliefs and actions. A theory of counseling or psychotherapy predisposes the practitioner to a certain type of action and is therefore related to counseling in the sense of providing *a basis for practical judgments.*

The theory has a second application to counseling practice as well. It helps the counselor look ahead; it provides an index of the consequences of certain of his actions. In this respect, the counseling theory has a predictive value. Borger and Seaborne (1966) address themselves to this aspect of a theory:

One essential aspect of a theory is that it consists of statements which make predictions about events.... A theory must explain more than just the facts it is devised to explain; to be of any use it must be general enough to comprehend situations still untested; it may even contain some surprises. On the basis of such a theory it will be possible to predict the outcome of future events, some of which may be outside the range of situations it was designed to cover. (p. 66)

Finally, a theory has an explicative function. It explains and clarifies to the counselor phenomena which are not readily apparent, or explicit, or seemingly logical. The theory, by providing a new dimension to the counselor's awareness, illuminates the hidden, and brings out into the open parts of the counseling experience which may have been concealed under the surface of the interaction. It does so by relating seemingly isolated events or facts to one another, and by indicating their relative position and relationship within the conceptual scheme (McCabe, 1958).

Stefflre (1965) points out that a good theory must be comprehensive, explicit, parsimonious, and conducive to meaningful research. A good theory, he says, must "explain what happens to many people in many situations." It must also be precise and "translatable into denotative statements so that they can be checked against clear referents in the real world." It must be direct and to the point (parsimonious), and it should be quantifiable and verifiable. When these criteria are met, the theory becomes useful in directing the counselor, in helping him predict outcomes for his actions, and in assisting him to better understand the client.

So far, we have offered only the most general picture of a theory. Certainly, theories differ vastly from each other—say, a theory of physics from a theory of art. It is necessary, therefore, to discuss the topic more specifically in order to clarify the general question we have at hand. To do this, we shall divide the question into two parts: first, we shall discuss the relationship between counseling theory and psychotherapy theory; second, we shall examine the effect of theory upon practice.

We begin, then, by examining the distinction between theories of counseling and theories of psychotherapy. A theory of psychotherapy, as we discussed more fully in chapter 1, consists of a theory of personality, a theory of psychopathology, and a corpus of techniques.

Counseling, on the other hand, is built upon a philosophical foundation, and although it may be structured along the lines of scientific reasoning, it emphasizes man's innate dignity, his individuality and uniqueness, his phenomenological world. Theories which attempt to explain human actions, feelings, and thoughts, therefore, are divided between theories of counseling and theories of psychotherapy by the way they go about their reasoning: Where they employ the tripartite distinction, they are theories of psychotherapy; where they present a unity and integration, they are counseling theories. Chenault (1965) differentiates between counseling theory and counseling rationale: A counseling theory attempts to come to grips with the question of man's essence, while counseling rationales are concerned with questions of "What do we want for man?" and "Why?" before they speculate on "how to." A counseling theory, she argues, is a scientifically derived explanation of man's behavior and wholeness, while a counseling rationale is more of a practical guideline for "doing" in counseling. Aubrey (1967) argues against the application of psychotherapeutic theories to the school counseling situation. He points out that theories of psychotherapy have been developed to deal with a range of problems and a treatment situation different from that which we find as school counselors. Despite this difference,

the attraction of systematized, consistent, and logical psychotherapeutic models have proven too much a lure for most counselor educators to resist. The secondary school, in particular, has increasingly been a proving ground for theories, methods, and techniques initially devised for a clinical setting. However, client-centered, psychoanalytic, and behavioral models have met with only slight success in the school context.

Differentiation between counseling and psychotherapy theories is requisite for using the theory constructively in the school situation. But before we can understand how to make such a differentiation, let us look more closely at how some of the theories of psychotherapy originated.

All of the theories of psychotherapy, as we shall see in Part Three of the text, derived primarily from the experiences of a single individual, in a limited type of practice. Freud's insights evolved from his work with middle-class patients living in late nineteenth-century Vienna, which was governed by a Victorian morality and a rigid, restrictive method of child rearing. Carl Rogers's theoretical insights clearly reflect the American Protestant ethic, the philosophy of John Dewey, the capitalistic spirit, and the personalities of young midwesterners with whom he originally worked. Glasser developed many of his premises with wayward adolescent girls, while working at a reformatory in California. In each case, the theory served to generalize into concepts the particular experiences of the originating therapist and attempted to extract from these concepts broad principles of action to facilitate treatment.

But knowing as we do that in any given therapeutic situation the personality of the therapist plays a significant part in the course of the treatment, we are compelled to question whether the methods that worked for Carl Rogers or Sigmund Freud or William Glasser or Albert Ellis or Frederick Perls, or any other seminal thinker, worked because of the theoretical basis or because of unique personality factors that they utilized in the treatment. Is it fair for a therapist who has found the method that works for him to generalize and argue that this method should work for all therapists? I think the answer is clearly in the negative!

But we still have not answered the fundamental question: "What is a theory of counseling, and how does it differ from a theory of psychotherapy?" We have stated that there is a difference between a theory of counseling and a theory of

67

psychotherapy, and we have pointed out the component parts of a psychotherapeutic theory and a counseling theory, but we must go further. Stefflre (1965) compares a counseling theory to a map "on which a few points are known, and a road between them is inferred. Good maps can be filled in as we learn more about the world, and poor ones will need to be thrown away as we find out they are leading us astray." Tyler (1958) discusses the importance of a counselor's maintaining a theory of personality in order to organize his thinking and better understand his clients. But she suggests that the counselor, rather than subscribe to a single theory of personality (as we have previously argued is indicative of the psychotherapist), should develop his own synthetic theory based on a fusion of his studies and experiences:

> The counselor thus needs many different varieties of theoretical concept, but for his own confidence and peace of mind he needs to have them organized in some way. Such an organization, one's own individual personality theory, can be a dynamic, growing thing with the kind of unity that maintains itself in spite of constant modification. The cultivation of such a theory is, of course, a lifetime undertaking. Every book one reads, every client one comes to know well, adds to the complexity of its pattern.

As she describes the counseling theory, then, it is an evolving, adaptable theory—a synthesis of insights, experimentation, and observation. It is never fixed and rigid, never dogmatic in explaining the life of the client or the counseling interaction. Rather, it is a theory that is always being modified and restructured to meet the changing needs of the client, the changing perceptions of the counselor, the developmental criteria of counseling. McCabe (1958), too, argues for the adaptability of a counseling theory, pointing out that a theory of counseling becomes more practical as an instrument when it is flexible enough to become integrated:

> The practicality of a theory for a student (of counseling) is a function of the degree to which it becomes an integral part of the system by which he has reorganized his past experience into meaningful relationships; of the degree to which it has become an integral part of the frame of reference by which he derives meaning from his current experience.

Dimick and Huff (1970) also emphasize that each counselor must develop his own counseling theory which is flexible enough to accommodate changes:

> A useful theory is molded for the individual and is well thought out, practical, and consistent with the behavior of the individual counselor. At the same time it is flexible enough to incorporate change by the individual counselor.... The counselor should evolve a theory that helps him explain his own beliefs and behaviors. Theory evolvement should help free the individual rather than constrict him. (p. 59)

All these writers emphasize what is certainly the key point in counseling theory, and the point which differentiates it from strictly psychotherapeutic theories: *A counseling theory is a variable theory that can accommodate change*

68

and revision; it is a theory which accounts for the counselor's behavior as well as the client's; it helps the counselor determine his actions, it helps him better understand the client, and it helps him predict various outcomes during the counseling experience.

A counseling theory should never be viewed as a prescriptive dogma, although many theorists inadvertently do try to give that impression. A specific counseling theory is merely one of many possible ways of viewing the counseling experience and of understanding its complexities in a precise and descriptive language. With our limited knowledge of human nature—and its infinite complexity and variety of form—we must rely on logical, consistent, meaningful explanations for behavior and feelings that at times are illogical, contradictory, and seemingly senseless. The theory of counseling assists us in that task.

It is imperative, however, that the beginning counselor approach the theory of counseling with some objectivity and distance. For although each theory is built on a formal foundation, an underlying view of man and his actions, the theory as it is practiced by each counselor adapts to his unique individuality. In unapplied form, as it appears on the printed page, the theory, like an artist's palette, is no more than the unfulfilled possibility of its expression: The counselor, like the artist, blends and applies the elements from the palette in his own unique style, transforming an infinity of possibilities into a concrete, personal expression, distinctively his own. A theory of counseling, in other words, as it is applied by each counselor in his own office, is colored by the idiosyncratic tints and shades of his own personality, which ultimately give it its form.

This relationship between the counselor's theory and the counselor himself has been carefully studied and discussed in the literature. Shoben (1962), in a much discussed paper, discusses the idea of the counselor's theory as a personal trait. He differentiates between explicitly and implicitly held theories, while emphasizing the limitations and dangers inherent in the use of theory. All the activities of the counselor in understanding and guiding his client must depend upon the counselor's theory, i.e., upon "his organized generalizations about behavior." The counselor may vary from one who acts on the basis of his strict adherence to a clearly defined system of ideas (e.g., Rogerian or psychoanalytic), to one who acts on the basis of his intuitive ideas about people. All counseling theory, however, includes elements of both clearly formulated systems (explicit counseling theory) and unconscious assumptions about behavior (implicit counseling theory).

Shoben explores the applicability of abstract theory to a particular case and the relationship between a counselor's explicit and implicit beliefs about behavior. Because theories consist of generalizations, they will always fail to fit details of each individual case and may sometimes cause a counselor to perceive a client's world inaccurately or to make the client fit the counselor's preconceptions about him. The counselor must be aware of this danger and also must realize the degree to which his choice of a particular set of beliefs is very dependent upon his unconscious or intuitive assumptions about people. "The apparent plausibility of a theory," Shoben points out, "depends in some degree on the extent to which it is congruent to the experience of its student."

Theory, therefore, may be considered a cognitive trait of the counselor which both facilitates and inhibits his understanding of the client. Theory enables the counselor to understand the client, but it may also cause him to misunderstand the special nature of the client's case. The counselor, therefore, must be thoroughly aware not only of the ways in which his feelings may warp his perceptions of the client's world but also of the fact that his theoretical beliefs may do the same. These beliefs, Shoben suggests, are "a part of the counselor as a person," and their pitfalls as well as their advantages must be understood by the counselor so that he may continue to revise and modify them as a result of his experiences and thus achieve maximum professional growth.

Shoben's paper is important because it links together the theoretical ideas learned by the counselor—his explicit theory—and those intuited by him—his implicit theory. Another way of looking at this problem is to ask, "How much influence does the counselor's theory exert upon the specific actions (techniques) employed during the counseling session?"

Williamson (1962) speaks of "the counselor as technique," meaning, like Shoben, that the counselor's own personality functions as a counseling agent:

I refer to the counselor himself as a technique of counseling, not only what he does or says in the interview, but how he conducts himself and the manner of often unverbalized communication. I suggest that the style of living of the counselor himself is an extremely important and effective technique in counseling.

Both Williamson and Shoben argue a position which is generally gaining wide acceptance in the profession: that the theories of counseling are secondary in many respects to the counselor's own personality and intuitions—his character, his demeanor, his attitude, his understanding of others, his willingness to help—in short, all of the things he intentionally or inadvertently communicates to the client.

Arthur Combs's work (1969) with his colleagues on the "self as instrument" approach is indicative of this position. "The 'Self as Instrument Concept' of professional education," Busby, Combs et al. (1974) point out, "sees the production of effective professional workers as a problem in becoming. That is, an effective teacher [or counselor] is one who has learned how to use himself and his knowledge of children and subject matter to accomplish the purposes of schooling [or counseling]." The development of individual competencies, according to this position, is simultaneous with the development of individual personality traits that are facilitative and which contribute to the specified ends of the treatment process.

E. Fuller Torrey (1972) also suggests that psychotherapeutic techniques are more related to the personality of the counselor than to any other single factor:

The division between techniques of therapy and the personal characteristics of the therapist is artificial. The two reinforce each other and are really inextricably

70

intertwined. Certain therapists choose certain techniques which are compatible with their personalities.

Research concerning the question of whether therapists practice according to their theoretical beliefs is somewhat inconclusive, although generally tending toward the conclusion that personality dictates the specific theory which then, in turn, might influence techniques employed. It is just this type of circular reasoning which precludes any definite statements on the subject. Fiedler (1950a), in a famous study, compared the quality of the therapeutic relationship between therapists of three different schools (psychoanalytic psychotherapy, nondirective, and Adlerian) and found that the therapeutic relationship is a function of expertness rather than of the theory or method used. "The therapeutic relationship created by experts of one school resembles more closely that created by experts of other schools than it resembles relationship created by non-experts within the same school." The specific theoretical model employed here seemed to have little influence on practical aspects of the treatment. In two additional studies (1950b, 1951) Fiedler reinforced these findings, strengthening the position that it is the quality of the therapeutic relationship rather than any specific techniques which affected the course of the treatment. McGowan (1954) and Seeman (1948) both found that counselors tended to develop their own styles which were wholly independent of their training and theoretical orientation. The cumulative conclusion to be arrived at from these studies is that counselor theory has little influence upon counselor style and technique. In a more recent study, however, Zimmer and Pepyne (1971) found the opposite. Comparing counselors using the Rogerian, rational-emotive, and gestalt theories respectively, the authors found significant differences in practice between the three schools of counseling. "Counseling behavior by 'well-experienced practitioners,'" the authors conclude, "does differ in accordance with theoretical orientation."

Other studies could be cited to support or refute either argument. Wrenn (1960), for example, found that "theoretical orientation is of little influence in determining the manner in which experienced counselors respond." He determined that the situation in which the counselor worked exerted a greater influence than the theory of counseling subscribed to. Cartwright (1966), Hipple (1970), and Strupp (1955) have found little difference in counseling response between experienced practitioners of different orientations. The key word here is *experienced*, which indicates that either (1) experienced counselors abandon the prescriptive rules of the theory they originally aligned themselves with, or (2) as counselors gain experience, they come to rely more on their own personality than on specific techniques (cf. Shoben and Williamson, above). Watley (1967), on the other hand, found that the counselor's personal theory did influence his predictive skill, although it remains unclear whether predictive skill is related to counseling efficacy. Mink and Sgan (1963) found that, with respect to vocational counseling, some clients responded more favorably to one approach than to another.

71

As we see from this review, at the present time it is far from clear just what effect counseling theory exerts upon the individual practice of the counselor. As a general statement, we can say that the counselor makes use of a theory to guide him in the approach he will use with the client. If he subscribes to the tenets of psychoanalysis, he might believe that an interpretation would be helpful to the client's growth. If he sees himself as a behavioral counselor, he might believe that reinforcement is in order. If he holds to the client-centered approach, he might feel reflection or an empathetic communication would be appropriate. Whatever his approach, when he makes an intervention to the client based on his postulate, he puts his theory into practice, testing the validity of the generalized theory *for him.* If the intervention is successful—that is, if it helps the client move forward toward the curative goal of the treatment— then the counselor is likely to use it again and again, regardless of what premise it was derived from, regardless of which school supports it. Likewise, if it is unsuccessful, he will abandon it, regardless of how strongly he supports the underlying premise, no matter how doctrinaire he has been in his thinking. Because counseling is doing—because it is always a spontaneous, active, dynamic, evolving process between two people—there are too many variables, too many peculiarities of human nature, too many *raisons des coeurs* to be contained within the confines of a single theory.

We can say, therefore, that a theory of counseling is no more than a set of postulates proposing a course of action, explicating a pattern of behavior, and indicating a number of predictions—all subject to change during the course of the counseling process. These postulates are tied together by a set of underlying philosophical, psychological, and intuitive assumptions about man, about counseling, about the counselor himself. Strickland (1969) speaks of the "philosophy-theory-practice continuum,"

PHILOSOPHY $\longleftrightarrow$ THEORY $\longleftrightarrow$ PRACTICE

to illustrate the reciprocal interrelatedness between the three categories. He considers the relationship between them as a continuum or a cycle, with each element providing "a continuing contribution to the expansion and refinement of the others." The theory develops from an intimate understanding of and formulation of a philosophy; the practice results from a theoretical basis, and is reevaluated subsequently through philosophical guidelines. In this way, each stage of the developmental continuum provides a check and balance for the other stages. The integrity of the practice is maintained through its continuous roots in philosophy and theory.

Strickland's conception of the "continuum" is a useful model for us in our understanding of the relationship between theory and counseling practice. Unfortunately, the research has not generally borne out Strickland's premise; but this may well be a fault of the research rather than a deficiency in the model.

What seems abundantly clear from both the research and the speculation is this: In the intimacy of the counseling session, where the powerful charge of human emotions takes precedence over the exchange of words, and where feel-

In a successful counseling situation, the student and the counselor must relate well to each other.

ings inevitably triumph over logic (at least in the early stages of the treatment), it is the dynamic interaction between the counselor and the client, and not the theoretical assumptions which underlie the interaction, that determines the success or failure of the treatment. What the practicing counselor, bombarded by theories and assumptions often in conflict, would do best to remember is Jung's (1954) brilliantly pointed injunction: "Learn your theories as well as you can, but put them aside when you touch the miracle of the living soul."

THE COUNSELING RELATIONSHIP

Before speaking *about* the counseling relationship, let us take a brief look at a part of a counseling session, to better understand how the interplay of forces underlying this very complex and intense relationship contributes to the rate and quality of the treatment. The following excerpt is from a session between Ellen, an eighth-grade student, and the school counselor, Mrs. Block. This is the third meeting between them, and a key point of the experience. Long pauses are indicated by ellipsis.

*   *   *   *   *

Counselor (1). I believe we were talking last time about how you felt when you were in the hospital.

Ellen (1). Oh, the hospital, that's right. It seems like a long time ago now, even though it was just last term. I don't remember how I got into that—talking about that, I mean. Do you remember?

Counselor (2). Yes. You were saying that you haven't been as depressed lately as you were when you were in the hospital, but that you were beginning to feel more depressed now than you have been before.

Ellen (2). That's right. I was talking about the depression. Yes, now I remember. Well, in the hospital I just kept thinking about even if I got well, how I wouldn't be any better off than when I went in. I mean here I was in all that pain and the best I could expect was to come out just as well as I was before I went in. The doctors weren't sure that my leg would heal all right, so I was always scared that maybe I would be a cripple. That, and all the people who came to visit me—I mean they meant well, but....

Counselor (3). They meant well, but they weren't able to make you feel any better. Is that it?

Ellen (3). Well ... I guess that's it. You know, it's funny, but they kept telling me how I was lucky I wasn't injured worse in the accident. The car was totaled you know, and one of the people in the other car was in critical condition. They kept saying to me "Thank God, it wasn't worse. It could have been worse, you know. You should consider yourself lucky." I guess they were trying to be nice, to cheer me up. But I didn't feel lucky, even though I know things could have been worse. I guess we're never happy with what we have. *(A laugh)*

Counselor (4). What struck you as funny?

Ellen (4). That expression. It sounded just like what my mother always says. Its her expression, "We're never happy with what we have."

Counselor (5). Does your mother still tell you that?

Ellen (5). I guess so. But I don't tell her about the way I feel any more. I mean she just makes me feel bad about feeling bad. Does that make sense to you?

Counselor (6). You mean that if you feel depressed now, you are told that you shouldn't be depressed?

Ellen (6). That's it. Like I don't really have anything to be depressed about. I have a nice family, plenty of clothes, good friends, nothing to complain about.... Don't you think I'm kind of *ungrateful* for complaining so much? I mean what do I have to be depressed about?

Counselor (7). Maybe there are reasons to feel depressed that you just don't know about.

Ellen (7). Reasons that I don't know about? Like what?

Counselor (8). I don't know. But I'm sure that if you feel depressed, there is a good reason for it. We have to find the reason, and that's often not easy.

Ellen (8). But what can it be? I've always had everything that I've wanted. My parents are good to me—I have no real complaints. What possible reason could there be for my feeling depressed?

Counselor (9). (*Sits quietly and waits.*)

Ellen (9). Can you help me find the reason, if there is one? I tell you, I'd really like to know. I think I'd feel better just knowing the reason that I'm depressed. Not that I really think there is a reason.

Counselor (10). What do you think then? Do you really believe that you're an ungrateful person because you feel depressed?

Ellen (10). I don't know about "ungrateful." Maybe I'm just stupid not to appreciate the things I have. Maybe my mother's right that "We're never happy with what we have."

Counselor (11). Isn't it possible to feel happy about some things and depressed about others?

Ellen (11). Sure, it's possible. But I know the things I feel happy about. How come I don't know the things that are depressing me? When I was in the hospital with my leg broken, I knew what I was depressed about. But it healed fine, and I'm not sick anymore. Why should I feel depressed? It's crazy.

Counselor (12). (*Sits quietly and waits.*)

Ellen (12). I see you're not going to be able to help me....

Counselor (13). This seems to be a mystery that neither of us can easily solve. We may both have to put some concentrated effort into this.

Ellen (13). (*Sits silently and appears to be thinking.*)

Counselor (14). (*Sits silently and waits.*)

Ellen (14). You know, I find that I feel most depressed on weekends. During the week, I guess I'm too busy with schoolwork to feel depressed. But on the weekends I have a lot of time to think, and sometimes, I don't know why or when, I just start getting what you'd call "the blues."

Counselor (15). What do you do when you get these blues?

Ellen (15). Oh, sometimes I go up to my room and listen to music or watch TV. Sometimes I'll go over to my friend Theresa's house, or if the weather is nice go down to the playground. Why? What's the difference what I do then? Is that some kind of psychological thing?

Counselor (16). It's not a psychological thing. It's something about you, and I want to learn about you. After all, if we're going to work on this problem together, we should *both* know something about you. Right now, you know more about you than I do. After all, you've known yourself much longer than I've known you; you have a head start.

Ellen (16). (*Laughs.*) You're really funny sometimes, Mrs. Block. I wish I had a sense of humor like yours. How did you learn to become a guidance counselor? Do you have to go to a special college for that or is it the same college that the teachers go to?

We'll leave this counseling session between Ellen and Mrs. Block, for the time being, but return to it later in this section. Several things should be noted at this point. First, the student appears to feel comfortable speaking to the counselor and relates well to her throughout the interview. The student's complaint, depression, is a typical one that the guidance counselor will encounter frequently in his practice. Although specific points about dealing with depression will be covered in Part Four of this text (see chapter 16, "Crisis Intervention Counseling"), it should be mentioned at this time that it is always important in working with the depressed client to allow the client to fully experience the depression as a rightful feeling, i.e., one that has a reason, a cause, even though this cause or reason may be beyond the client's awareness at the moment.

Second, we note that the counselor allowed the student to direct the course of the interview, although the counselor did ask germane questions designed to help the student speak and to assist her in articulating her problem. Third, we see that several times during the discussion (Counselor 3, 6, 7, 11) the counselor subtly offered an interpretive communication to clarify something that the client had said previously. But what is most important is this. *The counselor carefully established with the client a team approach in which the client in conjunction with the counselor would deal with the problem together.* It was no longer just the client's problem, but now a joint problem of the client's and the counselor's, a problem that they would work on together.

The counseling relationship itself, as opposed to any specific techniques of counseling or counseling strategies, played an important part in this encounter. The counseling relationship may be defined as the *cumulative sum of feelings and perceptions held by each member of the counseling team, and the effect of these feelings and perceptions and the structure and quality of the interactions between them. It is, in short, the client's and counselor's feelings about each other.* Much research in counseling has been directed toward this relationship, and we should consider some of the observations before returning to Ellen and Mrs. Block.

Thoresen (1969) in an interesting paper speaks of the counselor as an "applied behavioral scientist." He is a scientist in the sense that he approaches a problem with ingenuity and creativity, utilizing whatever is necessary to solve the problem. He is a scientific thinker, but not a person who is devoid of feeling, passion, and emotional involvement. Thoresen speaks of him as a "disciplined romantic," who "has the courage to search and explore the depths of human experience, often pursuing intuitive hunches with little certainty." He is a union of the best parts of science with the best parts of humanism:

The applied behavioral scientist in counseling, this disciplined romantic, must bridge this anachronistic chasm separating the humanistic from the scientific. He must be concerned with fundamental human problems confronting contemporary man, and he must explore such problems rigorously and comprehensively to create strategies for preventing and ameliorating them.

The implications of this concept to the question of the counseling relationship are discussed directly: The counselor who is an applied behavioral scientist must recognize that counseling requires a variety of different kinds of relationships with clients, not a single, definable, limited "therapeutic relationship," which is all-inclusive and appropriate to all types of counseling situations. Just as there is no single method in science, but rather general rules and guidelines of procedure—what is commonly called the scientific method—in counseling, too, there is no single type of therapeutic relationship. Thoresen speaks of a "variety of procedures systematically undertaken" as the basic counseling approach. While this conception includes the traditional counseling relationship, it is not limited to it:

The counselor may take steps to alter certain characteristics of the client's daily environment.... The counselor may work with a close friend or peer of the client. The counselor may also spend considerable time with a parent focusing on how the parent can analyze behavior and demonstrate and respond to certain behaviors of the client when at home. All of these procedures may be employed by a counselor in working with a particular client.

This comprehensive concept of the counseling experience, which brings together in a complex process the interview and noninterview procedure, expands the definition of the counseling relationship and is illustrative of what I mean by practical counseling. It includes within the scope of counseling all the activities which contribute to the client's growth and betterment. More importantly, in terms of the counseling relationship, it suggests that the counselor is both a scientist and a humanist, a methodical, objective investigator and a compassionate interlocutor. As a scientist, the counselor uses a variety of techniques, including but not limited to the individual interview. As a "disciplined romantic," he extends himself beyond the confines of a role. We may describe the type of activity in which he is engaged as creative science, or the science of interpersonal communication.

Drasgow and Walker (1960) have described three types of counseling relationships: horizontal, vertical, and diagonal. The horizontal relationship is characterized by equality, with the counselor acting as a catalyst to stimulate the client to solve his own problems. An example of this approach would be found in the Rogerian, client-centered model (see chapter 9). The vertical relationship implies a hierarchy. Psychiatrists and psychoanalysts often establish a vertical relationship in which they "give" therapy to their patients. Also prone to this type of relationship are parents, teachers, lawyers, and clergymen. Compromises between the horizontal and vertical relationships are referred to as diagonal relationships. This trichotomy is helpful in understanding the general types of relationships, but it is limited in describing qualitatively the specifics of a counseling relationship.

Wiggins (1972) discusses the counseling relationship in terms of the "life space of students." The counselor, he suggests, should work to make the counseling office a part of the students' life space. To do this, it is not necessary for the counselor himself to adopt the styles and manners of youth, but rather to make the counseling services relevant and appropriate to the needs of the clients. An example is cited of a middle-class, middle-aged counselor who did this by extending to her students understanding and acceptance. The students, in turn, found her office a comfortable, welcome place for private, as well as group, discussions. Another counselor chose to become part of the life space of students by spending most of his working day out of the office. This counselor made sure to visit at least half of the teachers and all of the students in their classes during the day. In both of these cases, the counselor has extended the counseling services to the students. In order for the counselor to do this, of course, it is necessary for him to understand where the students' life space is located, both physically and psychologically.

We see from these articles an emerging picture of the counselor as one who establishes a *relevant, meaningful, productive* relationship, not confined to an office. The counseling relationship, as it is defined here, is a relationship which extends to all areas of the interaction between counselor and students.

George B. Leonard, in his exciting essay, *Education and Ecstasy* (1968), discusses the type of environment the school should provide in order to facilitate learning. He calls it a "strongly interactive" environment, and describes it briefly:

To be interactive, the environment must be responsive, that is, must provide relevant feedback to the learner. For the feedback to be relevant, it must meet the learner *where he is*, then program (that is, change in appropriate steps at appropriate times) as he changes. The learner changes (that is, is educated) through his responses to the environment. (p. 39)

This description may be applied directly to the counseling situation as well. The counselor, through his relationships with the students, provides an interactive, responsive environment in the students' own life space. While the relationship may be horizontal, vertical, or diagonal—while it may include both directive and nondirective elements—while it may be in the counseling office or outside—it is always a responsive, mutually interactive relationship.

While these comments tell us something about the structure of the counseling relationship, they tell us little about the qualitative dimension of the relationship. A number of studies have investigated this question. Carkhuff and Berenson (1969) have discussed counselor commitment as an important variable in the relationship. The counselor's commitment to the client, they argue, begins with his commitment to his own personal emergence, which in turn "frees him to make personal commitments to others." The argument is quite logical and well defined, and it does much to integrate the counselor's self-perceptions and feelings with his perceptions and feelings about the client. The nature of the commitment is expressed in four propositions:

1 *The counselor is committed to living and relating independent of society's goals.*
2 *The counselor is committed to his own well-being and fulfillment.*
3 *The counselor is actively committed to his own personal experience in a life-long learning process.*
4 *The counselor is fully aware of the implications of not being committed to constructive potency in his world.*

A number of important points are touched upon in these four propositions. First, we note that the committed counselor thinks highly of himself: He is able to formulate his own goals, independent of the social strictures, and "devote his full energies to what is best for the individual involved, whether it be himself or the counselee." Such a counselor will certainly prove instrumental in making the society in which he lives a better society for all. Second, we note that this counselor cares about himself; and we know that it is only the individual who is able to care about himself who is ultimately able to care about others. Third, the committed counselor recognizes the value of growth: "He is aware that only with his own personal experience can he be truly creative and truly constructive." Finally, he is courageous in the very special sense of honestly confronting the good as well as the bad, the pleasant as well as the unpleasant, possibilities of existence. He "openly confronts the complete meaning of death, the hell of impotency, of having lived without personal meaning, feeling, reason, or human concern, without touching the life of yourself or another." Such a counselor will certainly be able to translate this commitment to the client within the context of the counseling relationship.

Carkhuff and Berenson go on to examine the structure of the commitment as it applies to the client:

5 *The counselor views his clients as he views himself.*

6 *The counselor will do anything for the client that he would do for himself under the same conditions.*

A sharing of the commitment between himself and the client—a mutual respect and rapport—becomes the foundation of the counseling relationship. As we know intuitively, a relationship which is built on mutual trust generates mutual trust.

7 *The counselor is committed to personal and intimate involvement in a fully-sharing relationship.*

What is meant by "personal" and "intimate?" Simply, it means a unity of purpose, a pervasive empathy and warmth, a giving up of roles and pretenses, a healthy, productive identification. The next two propositions prove this:

8 *The counselor is fully aware that if the client fails as a person, the counselor as a person has failed.*

9 *No boundaries will limit the counselor's commitment to the client.*

Finally, as we look at the concluding propositions we see the harmony, the justice, the inner beauty of the counseling relationship in clear focus. Between the counselor and the client a new world is built, a universe created. It is a world where neither is alone, but where each shares joyfully and painfully in the other's life. It is a world of expanding possibilities, where each person gains strength from the other and gains energy by giving to the other. It is an exciting, limitless world:

10 *The commitment of the counselor extends to full movement into the life of the client.*

11 *The counselor's commitment extends to the expansion of his own boundaries.*

12 *The commitment of the counselor extends to nourishing constructive forces and fighting destructive forces.*

As we speak of the counseling relationship, we must be sensitive to the limits of language to express the fluid excitement of the living interaction between counselor and client. It is only by experiencing the counseling relationship—by participating in it—that we can fully appreciate the powerful dynamics that charge it with life energy. Our brief discussion only touches the surface: to get beneath the skin, we have to be there.

If we turn our attention now back to the counseling session between Ellen and Mrs. Block, it should be clearer how these important elements of the counseling relationship form an interplay of forces that contribute to the productivity of the session. We will note as we continue with the transcript that the relationship between counselor and client is essentially a horizontal relationship, with no intentional hierarchical stratification separating the two. At times, however, the relationship becomes more diagonal, especially when the client seeks some professional advice from the counselor. We should also note how Mrs. Block acts as what Thoresen would call an "applied behavioral scientist." She investigates the symptoms and causes of the client's situation logically and scientifically, but maintains at the same time a humanistic, personal, dynamic relationship with the client. Lastly, we will note the manifestations of the counselor's commitment to the client. Mrs. Block is genuinely concerned with Ellen's problem and concerned for Ellen; and her concern "extends to full movement into the life of the client." As we look into the conclusion of this counseling session, then, we should note how these qualities of the counseling relationship begin to make an impact.

*   *   *   *   *

Counselor (17). I *was* a teacher at one time, Ellen. I went back to school to learn to be a guidance counselor.

Ellen (17). Oh, I was just wondering. Do you mind that I asked you? I know sometimes counselors don't want to answer questions.

Counselor (18). I don't mind at all. Are there any other questions you would like me to answer?

Ellen (18). Just the big question of why I feel so rotten.

Counselor (19). (*Sits quietly and waits.*)

Ellen (19). I guess that *is* a question I'll have to find the answer to myself. You know, it's funny, but even though I'm really busy with school and things, sometimes I'm bored. I mean ... well, it's like nothing is really interesting to me. I don't know if you know what I mean? Do you ever feel that way? I guess bored is the right word.

Counselor (20). I've had that feeling at times. Why don't you tell me what it was like when you had it?

Ellen (20). Well, when I was in the hospital I had it—a little, anyway. Here I was each day just hoping to get better, wishing that it wouldn't hurt so much ... physical hurt, I mean. I don't know—it wasn't like I had something to think

80

about that I really wanted to happen. I remember when I was a kid how I used to look forward to Christmas. For days, maybe weeks, I would count how long it was until I'd get my presents. All year I would think I'd like this or that—I'll have to wait for Christmas to get it. Not that my parents didn't buy me things. It's just that Christmas was sort of special, and I knew that everybody got things on Christmas and that I could have almost anything I wanted, even if I had misbehaved a little during the year. Does this sound stupid? But I loved Christmas and it's just that … it's just that there are no Christmases any more. Not for me, anyhow.

Counselor (21). *(Sits quietly and waits.)*

Ellen (21). What do you think about all this? Is it crazy?

Counselor (22). I think that we all need a Christmas to look forward to. We all need something to hope for—something that is important to us—something that we really want and care about.

Ellen (22). *(A broad smile lighting up her face, nods in agreement.)* It's not that things are really terrible; it's just that I don't have anything important to look forward to.

Counselor (23). Well, it looks then like there is a reason for your feeling depressed after all. Perhaps if we could find some things that you could look forward to—some important things in your life—these feelings of depression would begin to change. How do you feel about that?

Ellen (23). I think so. It makes sense, anyway. But what things?

Counselor (24). Well, that's something that we'll have to talk about some more. Do you think you could come back here next Thursday at this hour? You have a study period then, don't you?

Ellen (24). Yes, I'll be able to come then. Are you sure it's no trouble? I mean I know how busy you are.

Counselor (25). *(Smiles gently.)* It will be my pleasure to work with you on this.

*　　*　　*　　*　　*

We note the progress that was made during this brief session. An existential explanation of this encounter would suggest that Ellen's feelings of depression are caused by a lack of meaningful commitments in her life. The counselor helped her come to this conclusion; but it was a conclusion that Ellen herself reached without the direct intervention of the counselor. The quality and substance of the counseling relationship—the richness and warmth that it provided to the client—enabled the client to deal effectively with a feeling that had eluded her for some time. By finding an understanding, sympathetic, nonimposing interlocutor, the client was able to initiate and maintain a dialogue that allowed her to release her feelings and come to grips with her problems.

In Mrs. Block we find a skillful blending of the scientific-objective and the humanitarian-subjective qualities that the counselor brings to the relationship. At no time was she detached and impersonal. In such interactions as (17) and (20), she offered a part of herself—information and personal feelings—to the client. Yet, like a scientist, she explored the hidden meanings and concealed

dimensions of the client's communications. In later sessions Mrs. Block, at Ellen's request, met with Ellen's parents and advised them of ways to help Ellen
find and sustain nurturing meanings in her life. She spoke to one of Ellen's
teachers, too, and Mrs. Block freely and fully entered the life space of this student.

In the following chapter we shall examine the particular counselor qualities
which contribute to the productivity of treatment. We will see after this chapter
that Mrs. Block clearly exhibited such qualities as warmth, genuineness, positive regard, acceptance, and so on. Her level of empathy was especially strong
and fruitful. We note here that maintaining a credible and productive counseling relationship is contingent upon the counselor's ability to blend and synthesize properly various elements of the different levels of experience between
counselor and client.

"NEWTONIAN" VS. "EINSTEINIAN" COUNSELING

A schism similar to that which arose in the field of physics at the beginning of
this century exists currently in the fields of counseling and psychotherapy. It is a
schism characterized by two fundamentally different points of view—different
underlying axioms that generate a system of laws and rules and that permeate
all of the subsequent laws of interaction, prediction, and description. More
importantly, it is not only a theoretical schism, but a schism which influences
the entire view of the world, of man's place in the world, and of the logic and
order of the universe. In short, it encompasses a group of contradictions, all held
together by the fundamental belief which underlies them.

Throughout our history, man has always strived for an understanding of the
world around him. A relatively ungifted creature sensually—lacking the olfac-
tory discrimination of dogs, the keen sight of birds, the hearing of bats, the tac-
tile acuity of the housefly—man has come to rely on his great gift, his intellect,
to make sense of the world. He has devised brilliant theories which compensate
for his sensual deficiencies, theories which allow him to extend his sense
through technological media—what Marshall McLuhan has called "the extensions of man." In so doing he has created a field of knowledge that rests upon the
productive pairing of his biological deficiencies with his intellectual gift: a field
that synthesizes the observations of his senses with the intuitions and processes
of his mind. The field I am referring to, of course, is science.

Despite its veneer of objectivity, however, science has its origins in mythology, and its destiny has been shaped in part by the human eccentricity of pride,
particularly the pride of anthropocentrism. The first explanations of the Universe, handed down to us in ancient myths, consisted of humanly motivated
anthropomorphic gods and devils carrying on their great works, pulling the
strings of the universe merrily as we—their little puppets—danced acquiesc-
ingly to the music of fate. Our mortality, recognized as our great limitation from
the beginning, demanded a humility that unfortunately was not a natural part
of the human character. But alas! Science took hold, and the mythological con-

ceits of the primordial race became the scientific conceits of the new, enlightened civilization.

The first infatuation was with numbers. Pythagoras provided the means for fusing the absoluteness of numbers with the magic of mythology. Numbers transcended their mathematical definitions, becoming to him the explicative rationale of all order and all life. He saw in numbers the common denominator between the order of the universe and the nature of man, between the infinity of eternity and the limits of temporality. The second infatuation was with the human body. The divine origin of diseases which were out of the control of mortals was dispelled by Hippocrates and Galen who sought rational explanations for physical dysfunctioning. The third infatuation was with the heavens. Ptolemy saw the heavens revolving around the earth, thus maintaining the belief in man as the center of the universe. The Copernican upheaval not only disrupted scientific thinking, but disoriented our anthropocentristic thinking as well. We became dethroned, as it were, losing our complacency to the harsh realities of science. Perhaps it was Copernicus who first shook us out of our hubristic carapace and compelled us to recognize that the conclusions of science could not always be expected to be pleasing. Science, no longer indentured in the service of our egos, came into its own.

With Newton we find the great upheaval. If science could no longer serve as our mistress of pleasure, she must become our teacher. If she cannot reassure us of our importance, she must teach us to become more important. She must help us reshape our destiny to what we want it to be.

Newton made but one important contribution: He explained the mysteries of the universe. Pope put it well in his famous lines,

Nature and Nature's laws lay hid in night:
God said, *Let Newton be!* and all was light.

Newton opened up to us the great mysteries of the world, illuminating through theoretical science that which "lay hid" from our senses. More importantly, Newton defined the world in which we live through his mathematics and science. For three hundred years, the world—or the world as we knew it—was a Newtonian world.

What was this Newtonian world like? It was a world of absolutes, of causality, of nonreferential imperatives. It was a world of unity, where the forces which explained one set of phenomena were equally applicable to other sets of phenomena, both those which had been observed and those which had not yet been. It was a world devoid of mysteries and a world where explanations for an infinite variety of phenomena could be derived from a small, finite number of laws. It was a rather comfortable world where all the permutations of the universe could be accounted for by simple laws within our grasp. Having understood this world, we were now in a position to master it, once again restored to our prime position in the universe.

For two and one-half centuries, we lived in the Newtonian, absolute world, consisting of absolute space, absolute time, and linear causality. Then at the beginning of this century, an obscure clerk in the Swiss Patent Office published a series of papers in the technical journals which displaced Newton's ideas as his had earlier displaced classical Aristotelian physics. The clerk's name was Albert Einstein.

Even before Einstein, it had been known by scientists for a number of years that Newton's laws failed to explain a number of the observed phenomena of the universe. Ironically, the extensions of our senses had now reached the point where we excelled animals of the lower order in every way, to the degree that the great intellect of Newton was no longer capable of explaining some new, unaccountable phenomena. The events of nature simply did not conform to the absolute, prescriptive logic of Newtonian mechanics. We had been waylaid by the alluring beauty of this simple system into admitting to its rules all occurrences. Now new evidence could no longer allow this deceit to prosper.

Einstein gave us a new universe, compatible with Newton's but more comprehensive. It was a *relativistic* universe which opened up "a new way of thinking about natural phenomena" (Born, 1962). Einstein reorganized our thinking about the physical world, suggesting a series of laws and principles that would account for *all* the observed and possible phenomena under a wide, but single umbrella of equations. His idea that all movement is relative to the frame of reference of the observer gave us a new insight, in which explanations could only be judged valid or invalid according to the frames of references of the observer and of the evaluator. The perfection, order, causality, and unity established by Newton gave way to the relativism and subjectivism of Einstein. Sir John Colling Squire sums up nicely the irony of the situation, in his response to Pope's famous couplet:

It did not last: the Devil howling "Ho!
Let Einstein be!" restored the status quo.

Without speculating on whether there are really angels or devils involved, we can rest assured that the Newtonian and Einsteinian conceptions of the universe had implications far beyond the areas of physics, mathematics, and astronomy. Because they fundamentally concerned *man's place in the universe*, they bear relevance to all the activities of man.

Now we get directly to the issue at hand. In the mental health professions, there are also two different ways of looking at the world and at man's place in the world. There is an absolute, causative perspective, which I call the "Newtonian" point of view, and a relativistic, nonlinear perspective, which I call the "Einsteinian." The relationship between these two perspectives, as I indicated at the beginning of this section, is comparable to the dichotomy in physical science between Newtonian and Einsteinian conceptions of the universe.

The Newtonian counseling approach, like the Newtonian approach to physics, relies on the idea of *absolutes*. "Absolute, True, and Mathematical Time, of itself, and from its own nature flows equably without regard to any thing external," Newton explicitly states his idea (Born, 1962). The Newtonian counselor, like the Newtonian physicist, also believes that there are absolute concepts of behavior and feeling, and, most importantly, that there are absolute causes for these things. All theories of psychotherapy, which rely on a psychopathology and a causative theory of personality, reflect this Newtonian approach. Whenever we try to explain the infinite mysteries of man by a series of psychological equations, such as the forms,

$$stimulus \longrightarrow response = behavior$$

or

anal fixation = obsessive-compulsive neurosis,

we are utilizing a Newtonian model of determination.

The two major points of view reflecting this are the Freudian and the behaviorist. While each differs substantially from the other in specifics (see chapters 8 and 13), in many ways, particularly broad theoretical ways, they are alike.

Both, for example, claim to be able to explain behavior and psychic activities by a series of rules, equations, and logical progressions. While the Freudians emphasize the early psychosexual stages of development, and possible fixations or regressions at or to these stages, the behaviorists emphasize consecutive, sequential learning stages from birth onwards. While the behaviorists look at psychopathology as mislearning, the Freudians look at it as traumatic development at some stage. Dollard and Miller (1950) have done much work in pointing out the gross similarities between the two approaches insofar as their logical theory is concerned.

If we look at Freudianism and behaviorism as the two major forces in psychology and counseling, we see that both are essentially Newtonian in their approach. Both emphasize the deterministic, cause-and-effect model of human activity, arguing in their own ways that human thought and behavior is a predictable consequence of some type of specific training processes. May (1967) offers a good critique of the Freudian determinism and its inherent difficulties:

The danger in the Freudian system of analysis arises when it is carried over into a deterministic interpretation of personality as a whole. The system can become simply a scheme of cause and effect: blocked instinctual urge equals repression equals psychic complex equals neurosis ... the danger lies in the influence of Freudian theory in setting up a mechanistic, deterministic view of personality in the minds of the partially informed public. . . .

To be sure, the cause-and-effect system is valid for certain aspects of mind. But it is an error to draw generalizations from this limited area which imply that causological, deterministic principles explain the whole of personality. *Freud is seduced by the handy, tangible systemization of natural science; and he uses it as a Procrustean bed on which he lays the human personality and forces it to fit.* This is the fallacy, all too common in recent decades, which arises out of a failure to recognize the limits of the scientific method. Though the objectivity of science aids us greatly in coming to a useful understanding of certain phases of human mental phenomena, to imagine that the whole of the creative, oftentimes unpredictable, certainly intangible, aspects of the human mind can be reduced to cause-and-effect, mechanistic principles is sheer folly.... *If such a determinism is accepted, human responsibility is destroyed* (italics added).

Sprinthall (1971) offers a similar type of critique about behavior counseling. Observe the parallels of argument between the positions of May and Sprinthall:

What we need to underscore is both the obvious inconsistency and perhaps hopeless illusion that is being pursued by "pure scientists"—i.e., looking for human beings who have no feelings or attitudes that may "bias" how they work on other human beings. We would also stress that reinforcement theory, whether positive or negative, does not hold all the answers as to how people learn. How we learn about the world around us, or how we learn about ourselves, resists singular or monolithic theories. And the corollary follows: the totality of human behavior is not so simple that it can be changed exclusively through the application of so-called laws of reinforcement. It then appears, "The questioning human spirit will always reject such rigidities".... if we compare counseling to the major aspects of behavior modification, a distinction appears. The locus of control and responsibility for action in counseling is with the client. In conditioning, once the objective is stated in behavioral terms, the counselor then "treats" the client, that is, he prescribes for the client. The difference between working "on" versus working "with" may be slight, unless, of course, you happen to be the client.

The two major forces in psychology, therefore, seem to fall prey to the same fallacy: that of assuming that the individual is reducible to a series of logical, causative, deterministic propositions. Each of these positions reflects, either explicitly or implicitly, the idea that human feelings, thoughts, and behavior are consequences of a specifiable set of actions and interactions with others and with the environment. The Newtonian point of view utilizes the principle,

$$a + b = c$$

where a and b are given instances in the upbringing which yield a predictable consequence, c. Unfortunately, or fortunately, as the case may be, the human being is far too complex a creature to be so easily reduced to equations.

The Newtonian counselor, who subscribes to these principles, establishes an ideology and methodology which is compatible with this linear perspective. Display 3.1 lists some of the typical characteristics of the Newtonian counselor, and later in the book (see Part Three) as we examine some of the Newtonian schools of psychotherapy, we shall find the specific manifestations of these characteristics in practice. This type of counselor emphasizes the use of techniques to deal with a client whom he understands and responds to fundamentally in terms of diagnostic and symptomatic categories. He does not experience the fullness of the client but deals with those parts of the client's existence which are accounted for by the theoretical basis of the school with which he is affiliated. The Newtonian counselor, above all, fails to appreciate the spontaneous, subjective joy of interacting constructively with the client.

In response to this reductionistic, Newtonian view of man, a third force has arisen in psychology which illustrates what I term the "Einsteinian," relativistic approach. Alternatively called the *third force*, or *humanistic psychology*, the major proponents of this approach include Abraham Maslow, Carl Rogers, and

display 3.1

THE NEWTONIAN COUNSELOR

1 The Newtonian counselor believes that the difficulties of the client can be explained by a scientific explanation, based on a theoretical model to which he subscribes.
2 The Newtonian counselor considers the client only minimally responsible for his behavior: He is viewed more as a victim of circumstances beyond his control.
3 The Newtonian counselor believes that the fate of the client is not in his own hands but rather is predetermined by past events in his upbringing.
4 The Newtonian counselor rejects spontaneity and individual uniqueness as key elements in the shaping of the client's existence. He seeks all causes in accordance with a scheme, a pattern, of aetiology and consequentiality.
5 The Newtonian counselor views his job as "treating the client," i.e., correcting these presumed deficiencies.
6 The Newtonian counselor attempts, in assessing the problems and needs of the client, to reduce these problems and needs to predetermined categories and concepts which are compatible with the system to which he subscribes.
7 The Newtonian counselor views himself outside of and distinct from the world of the client. He is there to treat the client, not to be an integral, functioning part of his total world.
8 The Newtonian counselor views the world as a mosaic of interacting causes and explanations.

Gordon Allport, although other notables would also be likely candidates for inclusion. Rogers will be dealt with fully in a later chapter, so here we will concentrate on Maslow, who originated the term third force, and Allport, who offers a number of relevant insights.

Maslow began with the assumption that psychology should start by studying the normal, healthy personality rather than the "pathological," unadapted personality. "If one is preoccupied with the insane, the neurotic, the psychopath, the criminal, the delinquent, the feeble-minded," Maslow (1954) argues, "one's hopes for the human species become perforce more and more modest, more and more 'realistic,' more and more scaled down, one expects less and less from people...." But Maslow expected a lot from people, and he worked toward developing a psychology of self-actualization which would account for the health-giving parts of the person, the growing, changing, flexible, fulfilled individual. To break away from the traditional two forces (behaviorism and Freudianism), he abandoned in part the cool, scientific approach and used in its place a subjective, personal perspective. As Goble (1970) points out,

Maslow was convinced that we can learn a great deal more about human nature through consideration of the subjective as well as objective.... Maslow felt that a comprehensive theory of behavior must include the internal or intrinsic determinants of behavior as well as extrinsic or external and environmental determinants. Freud had concentrated on the first, the Behaviorists on the second. Both points of view needed to be combined. An objective study of human behavior was not enough; for complete understanding the subjective must be considered as well. We must consider people's feelings, desires, hopes, aspirations in order to understand their behavior.

Goble goes on to explain the underlying rationale behind Maslow's approach, and this underlying rationale is equally applicable to all third force, humanistic, Einsteinian counseling theories:

The successful student of human behavior needs to be more philosophical, more creative, more diverse, more intuitive, to "see reality whole," to see all the various disciplines as mutually helpful collaborators rather than separate unrelated specialties. When the emphasis is on means and methods rather than results, there tends to be a cleavage between social scientists and other truthseekers. Science should be described as the search for truth, insight, and understanding.... Means-centered scientists tend to fit their problems to their techniques rather than the opposite.... Behavioral scientists cannot be value-free. Emphasis on "scientific techniques" encourages psychologists to be safe and sound rather than bold and daring, and convinces scientists that they are more objective than they actually are. Their conclusions become ethically neutral. Such scientists avoid the important questions of ethics, morals, right and wrong, healthy and unhealthy behavior.... By becoming overly pragmatic, psychology avoids important areas such as pleasure, fun, play, beauty, art, joy, love, and happiness.... Maslow is also critical of what he calls the atomistic approach; the approach, common in physical science, of breaking things down into their component parts and studying the component parts separately. *Man, he believes, must be studied as an entity, as a system. Each part is related to the other part, and, unless you study them all as a whole, the answers are incomplete. Most behavioral scientists have attempted to isolate independent drives, urges, and instincts, and study them separately. This Maslow found to be generally less productive than the holistic approach which holds that the whole is more than the sum of its parts.* (pp. 18–21, italics added)

We see in this selection that Maslow's repudiation is not of the specific theories themselves, but of the total approach used to derive these theories. Psychological scientists are failing to account for the fullness, the wholeness, of the individual, in their Newtonian accounts of personality, psychopathology, and treatment. He proposes, on the other hand, to begin by studying the healthy individual and from there deriving a holistic view toward understanding the psychology of man.

The basic framework within which Maslow proposes to do this includes the concepts of *self-actualization, growth, and a hierarchy of basic needs.* Self-actualization, as described by Maslow (1954), is "the full use and exploitation of talent, capacities, potentialities, etc. Such people seem to be fulfilling themselves and doing the best that they are capable of doing." The self-actualizing individual (see Display 3.2) is continually in the process of becoming, of finding his true self among the myriad of his possibilities. He is usually a talented, creative, responsive individual, one who is in touch with reality and able to accept it as it is, and to accept his place within the world. His perception is clear, he is confident yet humble, sure of himself yet sensitive to all of his limitations. He is committed to some meaningful project, some plan, which holds much of his interest. He is spontaneous and less inhibited than the person who is not self-actualizing.

What is most interesting about Maslow's (1962) concept of self-actualization, and what is most germane to our discussion, is the lack of predictability, of di-

display 3.2

THE SELF-ACTUALIZED PERSON

He has self-respect and respect for others.
He is creative, talented, and resourceful.
He is gregarious and friendly but respects the rights of others.
He respects truth, logic, reality, beauty, and justice.
He enjoys life—both the ups and the downs.
He is able to maintain a lasting, fulfilling marriage.
He is able to maintain longstanding, mutually fulfilling friendships.
He is open with others, giving of himself, unpretentious.
He is aware of his feelings and able to relate his feelings to his actions.
He is independent, able to survive by himself.

He is secure and ambitious in the healthy sense of the word.
He values the useful and practical, as well as the ornamental and aesthetic.
He is uninhibited but not impulsive.
He is able to break away from the fixed, the "known," and seek the new and unexplored.
He is tolerant of the weaknesses and foibles of others.
He is free from conflicts which immobilize neurotic people.
He is courageous, sensitive, and trusting.
He is trustworthy and honest.

rect causality, attributed to these individuals. There is a unity to these individuals which is not entirely quantifiable since it cannot be easily fragmented:

Trust, goodness, and beauty are in the average person in our culture only fairly well correlated with each other, and in the neurotic person even less so. It is only in the evolved and mature human being, in the self-actualizing, fully functioning person that they are so highly correlated that for all practical purposes they may be said to fuse into a unity. (p. 192)

This concept of the self-actualized person separates Maslow from the other two forces in psychology by its emphasis on the uniqueness of each individual. It must be remembered that Maslow's study was of people whom he considered superior, people who were well adjusted, happy in life, and as a group successful. He suggests that the study of psychology should work toward producing such people.

Maslow also introduced the theory of *basic needs*, another Einsteinian, relativistic concept. He postulates a hierarchy of needs, with the most basic needs at the bottom; as one progresses up the hierarchy, we find needs which function when the lower, more primary needs have been satisfied. At the bottom, we find the basic physiological needs: air, water, food, shelter, sleep, and sex. Slightly above them are found the needs of safety and security. When these needs are satisfied, the belongingness and love needs come into play. Above these are the esteem needs, self-esteem and respect. Finally, we reach the highest level of needs —the growth needs. Maslow believes that the satisfaction of all these needs is a prerequisite to good mental health. When some of the needs are not met, a "deficiency condition" results, which may be termed a neurosis, a character disorder, a psychosis, and the like. When the needs are all met, on the other hand, self-actualization takes place, and the individual is fulfilled.

Maslow's humanistic psychology clearly falls into the Einsteinian category because of its emphasis on the individual. Humanistic psychology, in general, refuses to categorize as sick, negative, or unfortunate what other psychologies refer to as psychopathological conditions. To the third-force practitioner, everything—including "abnormal behavior"—must be judged relative to the frame of reference of the sufferer and the evaluator. Price (1972) highlights this curious point:

Nearly all perspectives on abnormal behavior view the development of symptoms in an individual as a negative, unfortunate turn of events. Typically the terms used to denote the development of psychological disturbance are negative. Behavior is described as "maladaptive," "disorganized," "disintegrated," or "regressed." However, there is a small but growing group of theorists, especially within the humanistic tradition, who regard some forms of abnormal behavior not as negative *events* but as *hopeful* and *positive indication* of the *possibilities of personal growth*.

Such a conception may well sound unfamiliar or alien to us. Yet this idea may force a genuine shift in our perspective. Assumptions that are shared by other perspectives—for example, the idea that all abnormal behavior is negative—may not be obvious to us until we are confronted with an exception to the implicit assumption. Thus, the idea that abnormal behavior may actually be an opportunity for personal growth not only represents a genuine shift in our view of abnormal behavior but also exposes an assumption which we may previously have accepted unquestioningly.

We see that to the humanistic, third-force, Einsteinian counselor, no absolute judgments regarding the condition of the individual are possible.

Gordon Allport, another humanistic psychologist, proposes a psychology of *becoming*. Traditional psychologies, he argues, have failed to emphasize the free, democratic, growing nature of the individual who is under study. "A wholly adequate psychology of growth," he argues, "would discover all of the activities and all of the interrelations in life, which are now either neglected or consigned to an ego that looks suspiciously like a homunculus. The first thing an adequate psychology of growth should do is to draw a distinction between what are matters of importance to the individual and what are ... merely matters of *fact* to him; that is, between what he feels to be vital and central in becoming and what belongs to the periphery of his being" (Allport, 1955). In order for him to formulate such a psychology, it is necessary to redefine the most basic concept of an individual psychology, namely the concept of personality. Personality, he argues, is not merely objective, factual matters, but "includes what is warm and important also—all the regions of our life that we regard as peculiarly ours, and which for the time being I suggest we call the *proprium*."

This concept of the proprium is of central importance in his thinking. For it is the idea of the proprium which allows Allport (1955) to break free from the Newtonian, reductionistic position, and develop a psychology of growth, uniqueness, and wholeness.

The proprium is not a thing; it is not separable from the person as a whole. Above all it is not a homunculus. Proprium is a term intended to cover those functions that make for the peculiar unity and distinctiveness of personality, and at the same time seem to the knowing function to be subjectively intimate and important. The person is thus an individual organism capable of propriate activities.

He develops this point, indicating the fallacies of the Newtonian therapeutic positions.

At low levels of behavior the familiar formula of drives and their conditioning appears to suffice. But as soon as the personality enters the stage of ego-extension, and develops a self-image with visions of self-perfection, we are, I think, forced to postulate motives of a different order, motives that reflect propriate striving. Within experimental psychology itself there is now plenty of evidence that conduct that is 'ego involved' (propriate) differs markedly from behavior that is not."

The concept of the proprium leads naturally to the idea of "propriate striving" as the basis of man's motivation. Unlike the Freudian or behaviorist theories of motivation, which are impersonal and delimiting, Allport's theory, like Maslow's, recognizes the infinite possibilities of growth. Moreover, he argues, "propriate striving distinguishes itself from other forms of motivation in that, however beset by conflicts, it makes for unification of personality." The individual, according to this Einsteinian point of view, tends toward wholeness. In a subtle rejection of the other positions, Allport (1955) argues,

When the individual is dominated by segmental drives, by compulsions, or by the winds of circumstance, he has lost the integrity that comes only from maintaining major directions of striving. The possession of long-range goals, regarded as central to one's personal existence, distinguishes the human being from the animal, the adult from the child, and in many cases the healthy personality from the sick.

His conclusions, like Maslow's, use the terms *deficit* and *growth* motives. "Deficit motives do, in fact, call for the reduction of tension and restoration of equilibrium. Growth motives, on the other hand, maintain tension in the interest of distant and often unattainable goals. As such they distinguish human from animal becoming and adult from infant becoming. By growth motives we refer to the hold that ideals gain upon the process of development. Long-range purposes, subjective values, comprehensive systems of interest are all of this order. As one example of growth motives let us consider the dynamics of conscience."

We have reached a point now where we should be able to readily distinguish between the Newtonian and Einsteinian positions. The Newtonian counselor holds to the causative, absolutist view of man and his actions, subscribing to a theory of personality and psychopathology which explains human behavior through the use of linear equations. Consequently, his approach to the counseling relationship necessarily forms along vertical lines: He "treats" the client, helping him to "get well" and overcome his "illness." To him, the theoretical is of great importance, since it explains the actions of the client and reveals the complexities of the interaction.

THE EINSTEINIAN COUNSELOR

1 The Einsteinian counselor recognizes that the difficulties of the client can only be understood by way of the client's phenomenological view of the world.

2 The Einsteinian counselor encourages the client to assume full responsibility for his life. He is always viewed as the master of his own destiny.

3 The Einsteinian counselor embraces a policy of "free will," e.g., that the client is always capable of making choices.

4 The Einsteinian counselor acknowledges the importance of spontaneity as a factor in the client's existence. He recognizes that each client is a unique and different person and that no one theory or model is encompassing enough to account for the lives of all of his clients.

5 The Einsteinian counselor views his job as "working with" the client; helping him to help himself.

6 The Einsteinian counselor avoids simplifying or reducing the complexities of the client's life into any predetermined categories and concepts.

7 The Einsteinian counselor recognizes that he is an integral, important part of the client's life. He stresses the humane, personal qualities of their relationship over any specific techniques or theoretical points of view.

8 The Einsteinian counselor views the world as a mosaic of unique individuals in spontaneous interaction with each other.

The Einsteinian counselor, on the other hand, holds a very different view of counseling (see Display 3.3). He relates to the client spontaneously and naturally, using as his basis of decision-making his personal, subjective, human qualities rather than an abstract and impersonal theory. He emphasizes growth and recognizes the changing unpredictability of the client. He tends toward a horizontal counseling relationship, establishing a mutuality between himself and the client. The Einsteinian counselor, in short, is one who realizes that self-actualization and becoming are the natural processes which characterize all productive counseling relationships and interpersonal interactions.

How do these distinctions translate into practical counseling differences? Display 3.1 and Display 3.3 attempt to clarify this question by showing how the Newtonian and Einsteinian counselor would deal with several specific counseling situations. We see from this chart that the philosophical issues in counseling, enumerated earlier in this chapter, are readily explained when we understand the two broad, inclusive counseling approaches—the Newtonian and the Einsteinian.

References

Allport, G. W. *Becoming*. New Haven: Yale University Press, 1955.

Aubrey, R. F. Misapplication of therapy models to school counseling. *Personnel and Guidance Journal*, 1967, *48*, 273–278.

Borger, R., & Seaborne, A. E. M. *The psychology of learning*. Baltimore: Penguin, 1966.

Born, M. *Einstein's theory of relativity*. New York: Dover, 1962.

Busby, W. A., Combs, A. W., Blume, R., Avila, D., & Oberlin, L. Can teacher education use the "self as instrument" concept? *Educational Leadership*, 1974, *31*, 516–520.

Carkhuff, R. R., & Berenson, B. G. The nature, structure, and function of counselor commitment to client. *Journal of Rehabilitation*, 1969, *35*, 13–14.

Cartwright, R. D. A comparison of the response to psychoanalytic and client-centered psychotherapy. In L. A. Gottschalk & A. H. Auerbach (Eds.), *Methods of research in psychotherapy*. New York: Appleton-Century-Crofts, 1966.

Chenault, J. Counseling theory: The problem of definition. *Personnel and Guidance Journal*, 1965, *44*, 110–114.

Combs, A. W., *et al. Florida studies in the helping professions*. Gainesville: University of Florida Press, 1969.

Dimick, K. M., & Huff, V. E. *Child counseling*. Dubuque, Iowa: Wm. C. Brown, 1970.

Dollard, J., & Miller, N. E. *Personality and psychotherapy: an analysis in terms of learning, thinking, and culture*. New York: McGraw-Hill, 1950.

Drasgow, J., & Walker, R. J. A graphic description of the counseling relationship. *Journal of Counseling Psychology*, 1960, *7*, 51–57.

Fiedler, F. E. A comparison of therapeutic relationships in psychoanalytic, nondirective, and Adlerian therapy. *Journal of Consulting Psychology*, 1950a, *14*, 436–445.

Fiedler, F. E. The concept of an ideal therapeutic relationship. *Journal of Consulting Psychology*, 1950b, *14*, 239–245.

Fiedler, F. E. Factor analyses of psychoanalytic, nondirective, and Adlerian therapeutic relationships. *Journal of Consulting Psychology*, 1951, *15*, 37–38.

Gladstein, G. Is empathy important in counseling? *Personnel and Guidance Journal*, 1970, *48*, 823–827.

Goble, F. G. *The third force*. New York: Grossman, 1970.

Hipple, T. E. *The relationship of school counselors' assessed philosophical beliefs with the frequency of counseling techniques employed* (Doctoral dissertation, Kent State University, 1970). Ann Arbor, Mich.: University Microfilms No. 71-18, 603.

Jung, C. G. *The development of personality*. Vol. 1, *The collected works of Carl Gustav Jung (1954)*. Princeton: Princeton University Press, 1964.

Leonard, G. B. *Education and ecstasy*. New York: Delacorte, 1968.

Maslow, A. *Motivation and personality*. New York: Harper & Row, 1954.

Maslow, A. *Toward a psychology of being*. New York: Van Nostrand, 1962.

May, R. *The art of counseling*. Nashville: Abingdon Press, 1967.

McCabe, G. When is a good theory practical? *Personnel and Guidance Journal*, 1958, *37*, 47–52.

McGowan, J. F. Client anticipation and expectancies as related to initial interview performance and perception. Unpublished doctoral dissertation, University of Missouri, 1954.

Mink, O. G., & Sgan, M. Does counselor approach really matter? *Vocational Guidance Quarterly*, 1963, *11*, 204–206.

Price, R. H. *Abnormal behavior: perspectives in conflict*. New York: Holt, Rinehart, & Winston, 1972.

Seeman, J. A study of preliminary interview methods in vocational counseling and client reaction to counseling. Unpublished doctoral dissertation, University of Minnesota, 1948.

Shoben, E. J., Jr. The counselor's theory as a personal trait. *Personnel and Guidance Journal*, 1962, *40*, 617–621.

Sprinthall, N. *Guidance for human growth*. New York: Van Nostrand Reinhold, 1971.

Stefflre, B. *Theories of counseling*. New York: McGraw-Hill, 1965.

Strickland, B. The philosophy-theory-practice continuum. *Counselor Education and Supervision*, 1969, *8*, 165–175.

Strupp, H. An objective comparison of Rogerian and psychoanalytic techniques. *Journal of Consulting Psychology*, 1955, *19*, 1–7.

Thoresen, C. E. The counselor as an applied behavioral scientist. *Personnel and Guidance Journal*, 1969, *47*, 841–848.

Torrey, E. F. *The mind game*. New York: Emerson-Hall, 1972.

Tyler, L. E. Theoretical principles underlying the counseling process. In J. F. McGowan & L. D. Schmidt (Eds.), *Counseling: readings in theory and practice*. New York: Holt, Rinehart, & Winston, 1962. (Originally published 1958, Washington, D.C.: American Personnel and Guidance Association.)

Watley, D. J. Counseling philosophy and counselor predictive skill. *Journal of Counseling Psychology*, 1967, *14*, 158–164.

Wiggins, J. D. Counselors and the life space of students. *The School Counselor*, 1972, *19*, 364–365.

Williamson, E. G. The counselor as technique. *Personnel and Guidance Journal*, 1962, *41*, 108–111.

Wrenn, R. Counselor orientation: Theoretical differences. *Journal of Counseling Psychology*, 1960, *7*, 39–45.

Zimmer, J. M., & Pepyne, E. W. A descriptive and comparative study of dimensions of counselor response. *Journal of Counseling Psychology*, 1971, *18*, 441–447.

PART TWO

Peter Schwarzburg

The world of the counselor

The world of the counselor is a fascinating and complex world: a world of intensely emotional, dynamic interactions with others; a world of self-reflection and honest, often painful, self-evaluation; a world of rich pleasures and satisfactions at being able to help others, to probe the depths of another's soul in order to bring forth the richness and the goodness which lie buried underneath; a world of frustration and pain as he sees another helplessly sink before his eyes, knowing that there is nothing he can say, nothing he can do to help; a world of growth, of change, of personal expansion; a world that does not always make sense and that at times is painfully and disturbingly absurd and incoherent. To take this world, and to break it down into its component parts, is no enviable task. It is with due deference and appropriate caution that we approach this very difficult undertaking.

I have selected four areas of the counselor's world to explore in this part of the book. First, we shall examine the part of his personal world that he shows to others and which plays so important a part in the counseling process—his characteristics. The word characteristic is derived from the Greek word which means *stamp* or *mark*. One's character is the part of oneself that we reveal to others—our mark, our impression. In the case of the counselor, this mark is indelibly engraved on the psyche of the client with whom he comes into such close contact. We shall examine what it is particularly about his character—which traits—that helps or hinders the counseling process.

Second, we shall examine the counselor's private world, his personal, subjective world. We shall examine how his feelings of meaninglessness, alienation, loss of freedom all play a part in the counseling interaction. We shall see how his values, his beliefs, the component parts of his subjectivity, may distort or enrich the counseling experience. We shall consider how his intrapsychic distortions—his defense mechanisms—play havoc with the neat order of the universe. And, in all this, we shall hope to come out better versed in the harmony between the man and his world—between the counselor and his counseling.

Next, we shall direct our attention to the work setting in which the counselor plies his trade—the school. We shall see how in the school setting the counselor is pitted against a series of different expectations and demands, how he maintains, or tries to maintain, a balance between the forces which push and pull upon him. We shall see what others expect of the counselor: how the teachers, students, and administrators do their part to shape his world. And we shall consider how he is continually in the process of defining himself and his function against this backdrop of expectations and demands.

Finally, we shall look at the counselor's training. What type of training, we shall ask, can most likely be expected to produce a successful, effective, committed counselor? What requirements for admission to a program of counselor training make sense and which are superfluous? What curriculum is most closely geared to the needs of the counselor-in-training? What methods are available to train counselors to be perceptive, sensitive, giving? The world of the counselor, we will come to understand, is in part a result of his upbringing and his personality and in part a result of his training. We can do little to control the former—the die is already cast. But the latter is almost entirely the responsibility of counselor educators.

chapter four

The effective counselor

Probably no question has received more attention in counseling theory and research than the question of "What qualities are indicative of the potential and actual effectiveness of the counselor?" The attention this question has received is justified for several reasons: First, it helps us better understand the nexus of subtle factors which contribute to counseling success; second, it is important to counselor educators who must make crucial decisions regarding selection and training; third, it encourages the aspiring counselor to find within himself and to strengthen those qualities which have been indicated as predictors of successful counseling; and, finally, it assists trainers and researchers in determining the likely outcome of specific counseling interactions, based on tested criteria of counselor effectiveness. Unfortunately, despite the surfeit of research and exposition (or perhaps because of it), this very important question is still surrounded by confusion and obscurity, and it is not entirely clear at this point exactly what qualities make one counselor more effective than another.

Perhaps the major obstacle in tackling this question is the language problem. When we attempt to describe an effective counselor—or, more precisely, when we attempt to enumerate those qualities which we believe make him effective— we are forced to rely on words to condense and capsulize the multifaceted behavioral and emotional patterns we wish to refer to. Words such as "genuine," "sincere," "nonpossessive," "honest," "warm," "empathetic," "accepting," and so on are the closest we can come to pinpointing the very human and very complex qualities which contribute to counseling success. But words themselves fail in this instance to adequately define effective counseling, and more importantly, to differentiate effective counseling traits from ineffective counseling traits. There are too many words with too many overlapping meanings and not enough specific, descriptive meanings of the words we use to prove of much help in answering our questions. Before we can confidently approach the question of what qualities make an effective counselor, we must come to grips with this problem of language and decide at the outset what we are going to do to make words work for us.

A school of philosophy that has proven particularly helpful in resolving such problems is the school of "ordinary language analysis and logical positivism." This school viewed as one of the many tasks of philosophy the clarification of meanings, and it is concerned with resolving many of the problems in philosophy, psychology, and other disciplines by an analysis of the language used in these disciplines.

Our problem can be stated simply as follows: If we call X a quality associated with effective counseling, what can we do to determine if a counselor demonstrates this quality X or not? This question is not easily answered. Let us say X is empathy, and we want to determine if Counselor A has empathy for the client. We could, of course, administer an empathy-rating scale and look at his score. But what does this actually tell us? Certainly, we would not want to define empathy as such-and-such a score on the test; but what then is empathy? How can we formulate an objective definition of empathy that will separate empathetic counselors from nonempathetic counselors?

Carnap (1932), the language philosopher, deals directly with the problem of formulating a meaning for words. He offers the "criteria of application," that is, a statement from which we can deduce the meaning of a word by its relationship with empirical phenomena:

Let us suppose, by way of illustration, that someone invented a new word "teavy" and maintained that there are things which are teavy and things which are not teavy. In order to learn the meaning of this word, we ask him about its criterion of application: how is one to ascertain in a concrete case whether a given thing is teavy or not? Let us suppose to begin with that we get no answer from him: there are no empirical signs of teavyness, he says. In that case we would deny the legitimacy of using this word. If the person who uses the word says that all the same there are things which are teavy and there are things which are not teavy, only it remains for the weak, finite intellect of man an eternal secret which things are teavy and which are not, we shall regard this as empty verbiage. But perhaps he will assure us that he means, after all, something by the word "teavy." But from this we only learn the psychological fact that he associates some kind of images and feelings with the word. The word does not acquire a meaning through such associations. (pp. 362–363)

If, in place of "teavy" we use the words *empathy* or *effective*, as in the term *effective counseling*, we see directly how Carnap's observation relates to our problem. For us to make meaningful statements that use these words, we first have to determine empirical criteria which differentiate these words from others and which specify under what conditions a counselor can be said to be exhibiting these qualities.

Kurtz and Grummon (1972), in reviewing the issue of empathy, have found confusion in the studies: "These studies have used several different ways of conceptualizing and measuring empathy, but it is not altogether clear whether they deal with one variable or several different variables employing the same label" (p. 106). They speak of an ambiguity which exists in the literature, an ambiguity which is the result of not clearly being able to define empathy in terms of empirical evidence. Gellen (1970) tackles the problem in a different way. Suggesting at the beginning of his paper that "empathy is measured by the counselor's capacity to express affect rather than by the extent to which he is able to communicate his perceptions of another person's feelings and attitudes," which linguistically is not a meaningful statement, he goes on to measure empathetic response physiologically by measuring finger blood volume. In this way he is attempting to establish empirical criteria for empathy: "If a counselor's finger blood volume level approaches 'Q' while listening to a specific taped dramatic dialogue, he can be said to be exhibiting the quality we shall call empathy." Such a method allows us to objectify what is essentially a subjective quality.

It is helpful in this respect to keep in mind Ralph Waldo Emerson's idea that "Words are also actions, and actions are a kind of words." In all our efforts to describe the qualities of an effective counselor, we must attempt to link the words to some type of specifiable actions which give meaning to the words.

Another word which gives us trouble is *effective*. We must be able to define accurately and objectively what we intuitively mean by effective counseling, in order for us to evaluate seriously the component qualities. The term sounds good, but what does it actually mean? Do we mean that counseling effects a change in the client? Do we mean counseling efficiency, the ability to accomplish a wide range of objectives over a brief period of time? Do we evaluate effectiveness by the client's impressions and feelings about the treatment, or do we allow the counselor to be the sole determiner of the success or failure? Possibly we determine effectiveness by the degree of mitigation of the so-called "presenting symptoms" or "behavioral problems." This issue is far from resolved, and over the past few years there has appeared a growing sentiment, matched by a more persistent effort, among counselor educators and researchers to define this term "effectiveness" more accurately and unambiguously. Heikkinen and Wegner (1973) provide a comprehensive review of studies utilizing the Minnesota Multiphasic Personality Inventory as a measure of characteristics indicative of counselor effectiveness. Cattell, Eber, and Tatsuoka (1970) have attempted to predict counselor effectiveness from scores on the Sixteen Personality Factor Questionnaire (16PF), and Shelton (1973) has used the 16PF as an indicator in a later study. Walton and Sweeney (1969), in an oft-quoted paper, offer a survey of studies which attempt to pinpoint predictors of counseling effectiveness. They conclude that there are no clear and decisive definitions of counselor effectiveness. In most of the studies they investigated, counselor effectiveness was measured by such unquantifiable and unverifiable ratings as supervisor ratings, peer ratings, and administrator ratings, without any uniform criteria. Kelz (1968) has recently attempted to construct an objective rating scale to determine counseling effectiveness but apparently has met with only partial success.

The first problem then—one which we have to be acutely aware of in our discussion—is the language problem. Even before we confront the equally difficult problem of measuring a quality once it has been adequately defined, we must tackle this problem of language. To deal with this, I will attempt to describe each characteristic as precisely and in terms of as many behavioral objectives as is feasible under the circumstances.

A second problem which confronts us at the start of our discussion is what I call the *common sense bias*. This bias asserts that some positions are ipso facto logical and sensible; for when we speak of common sense, we imply that some things are obvious even before logical scrutiny, that they are irrefutable or at least assumed to be true until proven otherwise. In reality, however, common sense is always a culturally relative term. What may be commonsensical to a middle-class counselor may be nonsensical or downright wrong to a person from a different culture. Common sense is a term which is in fact weak but which implies a strong sense of verification. The common sense bias includes value judgments, culturally based perceptions, and intuitive beliefs. To humanistic counselors, for example, there is a common sense position that acceptance, warmth, empathy, and genuineness are positive counseling characteristics. This may or may not be true—there is evidence to support both the affirmative and negative positions—but in any case it would be best not to prejudge any specific quality or set of qualities until the evidence is assembled and evaluated. The only way to avoid the common sense bias is to assume that nothing is true until it is proven to be true.

Finally, the last problem which we face is what I call the problem of *generalization*. Is there in fact such a thing as an effective counselor or are different counselors effective for different reasons to different degrees with different clients? There is some evidence to support both positions. While some studies have shown that there are universally important counselor qualities, other studies have indicated that certain traits work well with some clients but not with others. We shall keep in mind, as we explore the literature, that to generalize from a single study to a universal proposition is often an unsound policy.

Despite these persistent problems, a good deal has been learned about qualities which contribute to effective counseling outcomes. Certainly we can offer some valid generalizations, which would most likely be met with hearty agreement by those in the profession and which would also stand up to experimental scrutiny. We know, for example, that the counselor's personal traits play a significant part in the counseling interaction and are a prime determinant of counseling effectiveness. We know, too, that there is no positive correlation between counseling knowledge and counseling effectiveness (Joslin, 1965). We know that a counselor's abilities to communicate effectively, to act maturely, to listen attentively, to work as a role model all exert a significant influence upon the counseling outcome. We can identify certain personality traits, such as openness, sensitivity, security, genuineness, and others, which have been identified with successful counseling outcomes. But what does all of this tell us? How can we translate these types of statements into behavioral equivalents? Again, we are left without a clear answer to our questions.

In this chapter we shall examine some empirical research as well as theoretical models which attempt to clarify the question of "What qualities are related to successful counseling outcomes?" We should keep in mind, as we examine this question, the problems outlined above but at the same time recognize the importance of examining this question in all of its many details and implications. We shall see that although the body of evidence is not conclusive and is at times confusing, there is enough information to indicate which qualities are most likely related to effective counseling, and I am sure that the counselor trainee will want to be conversant with some of the research findings which attempt to illuminate this issue. We shall now turn our attention to the research findings, after which we will synthesize these findings into statements and attitudes and offer some general qualities which have been found to be indicative of effective counseling.

THE EFFECTIVE COUNSELOR: AN OVERVIEW

Predictably, many of the qualities which we intuitively associate with effective counseling have been borne out in experimental studies. The value of these studies is that they confirm empirically what our philosophical premises imply are the qualities of an effective counselor. It would seem self-evident, for example, that an effective counselor would be less prejudiced than an ineffective counselor, and Milliken (1965) has confirmed this in a study in which counselor effectiveness was measured by practicum grades and supervisor ratings. We would also assume that the counselor's attitudes exert a crucial influence on his ability to deal effectively with his clients. Jackson and Thompson (1971) have supported this contention in a study which measured cognitive flexibility, tolerance of ambiguity, and attitudes toward self, most people, most clients, and counseling. Their findings were mixed: No significant differences on cognitive flexibility and tolerance of ambiguity were found between the effective and ineffective counselors; but effective counselors were found to be more positive in their attitudes toward self, toward most clients, and toward counseling. Their conclusions were that the most important factor contributing to counselor effectiveness "is the feeling that the other person is a human being who is friendly, able, and worthy, and an approach to the counseling situation that is freeing, altruistic, and important." Whitely et al. (1967) did find that cognitive flexibility showed a high positive correlation to supervisors' ratings of effective counselors, but they were unable to demonstrate that cognitive flexibility was responsible for promoting changes in pupils. Allen (1967) found that "the effective counselor is a person who is on relatively good terms with his own emotional experience and that the ineffective counselor is one who is relatively uneasy in regard to the character of his inner life." Similar findings were obtained by Combs and Sopor (1963), who indicated that effective counselors perceived their clients as capable, dependable, friendly, and worthy, and perceived themselves as altruistic and nondominating.

Wicas and Mahan (1966), in what they call a "tentative and exploratory study" found that high rated counselors in this study achieve a pattern of scores that can be interpreted to indicate that they are anxious, sensitive to the expectations of others and society, patient and non-aggressive in interpersonal relationships, and concerned about social progress but always with appropriate self-control. There is much here to suggest the picture of the pleasant, stable, and dedicated individual, and it would seem that the test results fit the expectation that high-rated counselors would establish good, non-threatening relationships and be sensitive to the feelings and needs of others. (p. 54)

The picture to which the authors refer seems indeed to suggest an ideal—or perhaps a stereotypical—picture of an effective counselor.

Truax and Lister (1970), in an important and highly controversial study concerning the employment of paraprofessional counseling aides at a residential vocational rehabilitation center, found some startling results which bear upon the question of effective counselor characteristics. In an attempt to understand how paraprofessional aides could be most advantageously deployed, they set up three management conditions for the treatment of cases, which ranged from personality disorders to mental retardation. Under the first condition, the experienced counselor worked alone with the patient in the traditional manner; under the second condition, the counselor was assisted by a counselor aide who worked with him under maximum supervisory conditions; under the third condition, the counselor aide functioned autonomously as a counselor, utilizing the experienced counselor only in a supervisory role. All clients were randomly assigned, in order to assure that each condition included clients of varying degrees of severity. Progress was evaluated by the use of a five-point rating scale developed by the Arkansas Rehabilitation Service, which measures the client's evidence of rehabilitation in his work endeavors.

When the results were tabulated and analyzed, a most interesting anomaly emerged. To their surprise, the experimenters found that the clients who made the greatest improvement were those who were treated by the untrained counselor aides alone; next in order of improvement were the clients treated by the experienced professional counselor alone; lowest in improvement were those treated conjointly by the experienced counselor and the untrained aide.

To explain these results and their conclusion "that the effectiveness of counseling and psychotherapy, as measured by constructive change in client functioning, is largely independent of the counselor's level of training and theoretical orientation," they suggested that the untrained aides fared better because they were "innately more health engendering than the professional counselors." While they do not fully explicate what is meant by "health engendering," they refer to such counselor qualities as "empathetic understanding, non-possessive warmth, and genuineness." The important point here is that *counselor knowledge and counselor training had no positive effect on counseling outcome; on the contrary, it seemed to minimize the effects of the counseling. Rather, what did emerge as important was the attitude and feelings of the practitioner.*

Because of the controversial nature of these findings, this study was followed by criticism (McArthur, 1970 and Sieka et al., 1971), which contested the experimental integrity of the study and the validity of the conclusions, and a rejoinder (Truax, 1971). On the whole, however, Truax and Lister's findings appear to hold their own weight and are in accord with other studies (Poser, 1966) which have arrived at similar conclusions.

One of the most important contributors to the literature on counselor effectiveness and qualities is Robert Carkhuff, who, along with his collaborators, Bernard Berenson and Charles Truax, have published prolifically and profitably in this area. Truax and Carkhuff (1967) have found a common thread that runs through all of the divergent theories of counseling and psychotherapy:

In one way or another, all have emphasized the importance of the therapist's ability to be integrated, mature, genuine, authentic, or congruent in his relationship to the patient. They have all stressed also the importance of the therapist's ability to provide a nonthreatening, trusting, safe or secure atmosphere by his acceptance, nonpossessive warmth, unconditional positive regard, or love. Finally, virtually all theories of psychotherapy emphasize that for the therapist to be helpful he must be accurately empathetic, be "with" the client, be understanding, or grasp the patient's meaning. (p. 25)

As the research undertaken by Carkhuff and his associates progressed, new dimensions were discovered and counselor rating scales for these additional qualities were developed. The core conditions currently associated with Carkhuff's work are: empathy, respect, warmth, genuineness, self-disclosure, concreteness, confrontation, and immediacy of relationship.

Weitz (1947) rates security, sensitivity, and objectivity as critical counselor personality factors which contribute to counseling effectiveness, while Graver (1948) has amassed a list of eighteen important counselor traits: understanding, sympathetic attitude, friendliness, sense of humor, stability, patience, objectivity, sincerity, tact, fairness, tolerance, neatness, calmness, broad-mindedness, kindliness, pleasantness, social intelligence, and poise. Strupp (1971) lists "warmth, acceptance, empathy, effort to understand, spontaneity, and related variables" (p. 115) as the key to effective psychotherapy. We see from these few examples (there are two thousand studies of effective counselor characteristics) how many adjectives can be used to describe effective counselors.

In fact, one of the more serious problems in dealing with the question of counselor effectiveness is what I call "adjectival bombardment." How can we effectively differentiate between all these adjectives, eliminating redundancy and overshadowing? Is there a substantive, empirical difference between such descriptive terms as cognitive flexibility, openness, and broad-mindedness? Are lists of adjectives, no matter how lengthy and how subtly differentiated, sufficient to deal with a problem as technical as this? Perhaps the most expeditious approach for tackling this problem is to simplify the descriptive terminology rather than to proliferate it.

Tyler (1969) has suggested, and I would agree, that "the qualities most essential for counselors are the basic attitudes that make it possible to accept and understand other people." While this is a general description, unpretentiously avoiding precision, in many ways it is more precise than the adjectival descriptions which are confusing in their ambiguity and redundancy. It may well be that words cannot describe the truly effective counselor.

To help clarify this problem, and to make it simpler to associate the diverse qualities, I have constructed a "Counselor-Qualities Matrix" (see Display 4.1), which pairs a few of the more commonly used adjectives with some broader, more inclusive categories of effective functioning. I have selected nine major categories under which to include twenty-five commonly cited characteristics. It should be emphasized that there is nothing sacred about these categories per se; they are intended only for simplicity in the process of adjectival reduction. The categories are: open-mindedness, sensitivity, objectivity, genuineness, non-dominance, positive regard, communication skills, self-knowledge, and respect. Each of these category headings can be translated into a broad range of behavioral and perceptual criteria, which will overlap into other categories and break down into more specific behavioral, attitudinal, and perceptual traits. In this way, a comprehensive picture of the effective counselor can be constructed by examining the relationships among the component terms: a relationship among the terms, among the categories, and between the categories and counselor activity. Further research, as it is able to describe the equivalent behavior, will allow us to apply "criteria of application."

If we look under the category of open-mindedness, for example, we find nine adjectives that contribute to open-mindedness: flexibility, acceptance, congruence, intelligence, concreteness, cognitive flexibility, perceptiveness, nonpossessiveness, and nonjudgmental attitude. We can then look at each of these nine adjectives in turn and see with which other categories they have been paired. In this way the connection between open-mindedness and each of these other categories could be established. While this matrix is not intended to define terms nor to articulate a comprehensive model of the effective counselor, it is designed to illuminate the often subtle relationships and intricate connections among terms, thus laying out a preliminary map of the terrain for future research.

One of the most important researchers in this area, a man whose persistence and tenacity have earned him a well-deserved following and the respect of even his harshest critics, is Carl Rogers. For the past thirty years, Rogers has been doggedly attempting to evaluate, in a precise, empirical manner, the qualities of an effective counselor: what he has called "the conditions of therapy." His well-known terminology includes empathy, genuineness, and unconditional positive regard as its key words. In a massive research effort, Rogers and his colleagues (Rogers et al., 1967) have attempted to test thoroughly his assumption that

regardless of what method or technique that the therapist uses...effective therapy would take place if the therapist fulfilled the following three "conditions"; a.) The therapist responds as the real person he actually is in this relationship at the moment. He employs no artificial front.... b.) The therapist senses and expresses the client's felt meaning, catching what the client communicates as it seems to the client. This condition was termed "empathy." c.) The therapist experiences a warm and positive acceptance toward the client. (p. 10)

display 4.1
THE COUNSELOR-QUALITIES MATRIX

Quality \ Category	Open-mindedness	Sensitivity	Objectivity	Genuineness	Nondominance	Positive regard	Communication skills	Self-knowledge	Respect
Flexibility	●		●		●		●	●	
Warmth		●		●	●	●			●
Acceptance	●	●		●	●	●			●
Empathy		●						●	
Congruence	●		●	●				●	
Honesty			●	●					
Ability to artic.							●	●	
Intelligence	●		●				●		
Interest		●		●	●	●			
Caring		●		●	●	●			
Sincerity		●		●	●	●			
Security			●					●	
Courage								●	●
Trust				●		●		●	
Concreteness	●		●				●	●	
Responsibility								●	
Dedication				●				●	
Commitment				●				●	
Professionalism		●	●	●	●	●	●	●	●
Cognitive flex.	●		●		●				
Perceptiveness	●		●				●		
Nonpossessive	●				●	●			
Self-disclosing				●			●	●	
Nonjudgmental	●	●	●		●	●			●
Awareness of lim.		●						●	

105

Rogers was attempting to test out the hypothesis, in other words, that effective counselor personality factors, what he refers to as "the conditions for therapy," outweighed all other considerations in contributing to therapeutic efficacy in the counseling process. With such findings, we would be able not only to see which qualities are important, but also to understand in which specific ways each quality contributes to the client's improvement. Rogers's study endeavored to resolve this very complex issue once and for all, and in many ways it has succeeded in its goal. Unfortunately, there were a couple of serious problems which limit its application, and these problems should be presented first.

First, the subjects in this study were divided between institutionalized "schizophrenics" and "normals" who were recruited from various community and social organizations. The experiment, therefore, involved a rather specialized population, atypical of those who seek the help of a counselor. Second, as in all studies of therapeutic efficacy, there are many serious questions regarding the validity of the experiment in relation to what it attempts to measure. Strupp (1971), in a critique of Eysenck's famous study of therapeutic efficacy, discusses the difficulties of undertaking such a study, and his comments deserve careful consideration. Finally, despite all of Rogers's positive results, which we shall discuss, he was compelled by the evidence to conclude that "in many respects the therapy group taken as a whole showed no greater evidence of positive outcome than did the matched and paired control group" (p. 80). This raises the very serious question of whether the "conditions of therapy" are also conditions of efficacy or merely trimmings which have no proven curative effect. These considerations aside, however, Rogers's research did find a great deal that sheds light on what qualities are important in a counselor.

The crux of his findings are found in the following excerpt:

Those patients who perceived a high degree of congruence in their relationship with their therapist were independently rated as showing the greatest degree of change. Those whose relationships were rated high in empathy ranked next. The control group followed, and those patients who were in relationships low in empathy and congruence showed no change or even regressive change. In spite of the subtlety of the variables being measured, in spite of the crudity of the instruments used in measuring them, there appears to be substantial evidence that *relationships rated high in a sensitively accurate empathic understanding and high in genuineness as perceived by the patient, were associated with favorable personality changes and reductions in various forms of pathology*, particularly in schizophrenic pathology (italics added). (p. 86)

It is clear from these findings that qualities of the counselor such as empathy, genuineness, and positive regard do play an important role in counseling, but it is still unclear how these qualities work toward effecting whatever we deem to be the "cure" in the treatment.

One thing, however, is perfectly clear: The qualities of the counselor constitute a dynamic component of the therapeutic process—a component that must be reckoned with. Torrey (1972) cites an interesting example of psychotherapy devoid of the human relationship:

Therapist. Hello. Please tell me your name.

Patient. Torrey.

Therapist. It's nice to meet you, Torrey. I would like to discuss your problem with you. Please tell me first whether you are male or female.

Patient. Male.

Therapist. How old are you?

Patient. Thirty-two.

Therapist. Are you married?

Patient. Yes.

Therapist. Now, how can I help you?

Patient. I don't know.

Therapist. Tell me something about your wife.

Patient. She is a fine wife. We have a good marriage.

Therapist. I understand. Now tell me something about your parents.

Patient. My father is dead. My mother has been sick.

Therapist. Tell me more about her.

Patient. She is getting better now.

Therapist. Does your wife tend to be like your mother?

Patient. No, not at all.

Therapist. I understand. Now let me ask you something else about your mother. Was she very strict in raising you?

Patient. No, she was lenient. I made all my own decisions.

Therapist. Does it bother you that you made all your own decisions?

Patient. No, I like to.

Therapist. Why do you like to?

Patient. Because then I have created my own existential meaning.

Therapist. I understand. Please tell me more about someone close to you.

Patient. Why are you so insensitive?

Therapist. I am doing my best under these conditions.

Patient. You are just a crazy machine.

Therapist. You seem interested in me personally.

Patient. Who do you think you are?

Therapist. Please think of me as a doctor trying to discuss your feelings about people close to you. Call me anything you wish. (pp. 29-31)

As I am sure you have guessed by now, the "therapist" in this dialogue is a computer especially designed to function as a psychotherapist. Torrey uses this as an example of artfully executed therapeutic techniques devoid of the richness of human contact. It demonstrates most dramatically the human component of the multidimensional therapeutic process.

Probably the most successful way to consider the question of effective counselor characteristics is to recognize the simple principle that counseling situations are not separate and distinct from our everyday activities. Carkhuff (1966) explains the relationship this way:

Counseling and psychotherapy . . . are simply additional instances of all interpersonal processes. . . . There is no evidence to suggest that these helping processes are any more or less critical than parent-child, teacher-student, and other significant human relationships.... The direct implication of this proposition is that the same dimensions which are effective in the other instances of human encounters are effective in the counseling and therapeutic processes. (p. 424)

It may well be, as Carkhuff suggests, that the very qualities which make us likable and effective persons in everyday life are the same qualities which contribute to counseling effectiveness. Let us consider for a moment the implications of such a statement: First, it implies that effective counselors are also effective (or successful) spouses, parents, and citizens. For truly, if the qualities that Rogers, Carkhuff, and others have suggested are important for counselors are considered carefully, these are clearly desirable qualities in all human beings. Secondly, it implies the priority of counselor qualities over counselor technique in respect to positive growth and change in the client. This would require us to emphasize the "counselor as a person" over the "counselor as a practitioner." The counselor's personality and spirit would take precedence over his degrees and his training: We would be compelled to ask him, "Who are you—what are you?" rather than "What degree do you have from which school?" Finally, it implies that counselors who do not possess these personal qualities would tend to produce detrimental, debilitating results in their clients, rather than positive, healthy results.

The question then reduces itself to this: "What is it about a person—counselor or otherwise—that contributes to his ability to help others, to relate meaningfully, to contribute to the freedom of his fellow man?" To approach this very difficult question, I have divided the counselor qualities into three major headings: *Understanding others, Relating to others,* and *Knowing oneself*—and we shall look at each of these broad categories to study the relationship among the qualities subsumed under each.

UNDERSTANDING OTHERS

Open-mindedness

Our awareness of the world around us, our perceptions of and feelings toward others in that world, is always relative to the frame of reference through which we perceive the world and its inhabitants. We see, hear, touch, speak, and experience in respect to reference points, parameters, against which we measure our sensory and emotional stimulation. The more fixed and inflexible our frames of reference, the less able are we to experience things which fall outside of and are incompatible with the boundaries of the reference frame. Likewise, the greater our ability to alter frames of reference to suit the needs and criteria of situations, the more likely we will be able to understand and adapt to changes which are not entirely compatible with our usual reference points. The first quality of open-mindedness, therefore, is *flexibility*.

Open-mindedness in the counseling setting may be defined as freedom from fixed preconceptions which limit the counselor's ability to perceive what "is there," and an attitude of open receptivity to that which the client is expressing.

The open-minded counselor is able to accommodate the client's values, insights, feelings, and perceptions that are different from his own. Moreover, he is able to experience and interact with the client throughout a wide breadth and range of feelings, since his flexible frame of reference does not find itself restricted by set expectation. Open-mindedness, in its sense of accommodation and receptivity combined, produces the second important quality of the effective counselor: *perceptiveness.*

The quality of open-mindedness also implies the ability to listen, to respond, to interact with the client, free from the constraints of imposing value criteria. The open-minded counselor is *nonjudgmental.* This does not mean that he has no values of his own, that he is anomic or amoral; on the contrary, the effective counselor should have a well-thought-out and meaningful sense of values with which he feels comfortable. The quality of being nonjudgmental "means that the counselor prescinds from judging the guilt or innocence of the *client*; it does not mean that the counselor may not objectively judge the *attitudes, standards,* or *actions* of the client. The client is hurt when *he* is judged; he is not necessarily hurt if his behavior is evaluated" (Biestek, 1953). The nonjudgmental counselor is able to participate effectively in a counseling interaction, in a relationship of therapeutic benefit, where the client holds a set of values that are different from his own, and accept the client as he is, for what he is. Acceptance, according to Blocher (1966), means simply "a belief in the worth of the client," and this belief can only become operative when the counselor is open-minded enough to accept the client without restrictive value judgments.

Dimick and Huff (1970) offer a good definition of open-mindedness which recaptures the points we have outlined. They say that open-mindedness is "the counselor's ability to hear and accept the values of the other person without needing to distort them to meet his own needs" (p. 111).

Sensitivity

Webster's Third New International Dictionary defines sensitivity as "the capacity of an organism to respond to stimulation...the capacity of a person to respond emotionally to changes in his interpersonal or social relationship." This capacity to respond, this "sensitivity-to" something, is a prime factor in contributing to counselor effectiveness. While open-mindedness makes possible a comprehensive and accurate view of the client, sensitivity—a cognitive as well as an emotional response to the client as a total individual—makes possible a deeper and more spontaneous response to his needs, feelings, conflicts, doubts, and so on. Open-mindedness makes possible what sensitivity actually accomplishes.

It is important to understand that during the course of a typical counseling interview, the client is continually in a state of flux and change. As a living, responsive organism, the client is reacting at any given moment to the stimulation of the interview, whether that stimulation is in the form of verbal response from the counselor, the counselor's expressions and movements (his body language), or internal, reflective thinking going on in the client's own personal world of subjectivity. Both internal processes (thoughts and associations) and external stimuli (interpersonal responses and cues) affect profoundly the quality and substance of the interaction between the counselor and his client. Fortunately, the client does indicate to the counselor, however subtly, that these changes and responses are occurring, both in his words, by his body language and his total behavioral pattern, as well as by subtle gestures and nuances of language. The sensitive counselor is one who is able to discern these minuscule, but nevertheless significant, responses on the part of the client and to assimilate these changes into his own perspective of the client and his understanding of him.

Empathy

The question arises, "How does sensitivity differ from perceptiveness?" which we categorized under open-mindedness. The distinction between the two terms is small but significant. Whereas perceptiveness is the ability to see and understand the client, sensitivity implies a deeper response on the part of the counselor, an emotional response, an ability to get into the client's skin and feel along with him. This particular manifestation of sensitivity is usually referred to as *empathy* or *empathetic understanding*.

Rogers (1957) says of empathy:

To sense the client's private world as if it were your own, but without ever losing the "as if" quality—this is empathy, and this seems essential to therapy. To sense the client's anger, fear, or confusion as if it were your own, yet without your own anger, fear, or confusion getting bound up in it, is the condition we are endeavoring to describe. When the client's world is this clear to the therapist, and he moves about in it freely, then he can both communicate his understanding of what is clearly known to the client and can also voice meanings in the client's experience of which the client is scarcely aware. (p. 77)

Two conditions are important in this definition: The counselor must be able to experience the client's feelings as the client is experiencing them, in the same way, with the same degree of affect and personal meaning. He must, therefore, put himself emotionally and intellectually in the client's place, he must *be the client momentarily*, and think and feel as the client does. Secondly, and of equal importance, he must also maintain his own identity and remain sensitively aware of the differences between himself and the client. This is what Rogers refers to as the "as if" condition, and it is an important qualifier of empathetic understanding. Empathy is a temporary bridge, joining the purposes, perceptions, and feelings of counselor and client, establishing a unity between them as they face each other during the counseling session; but empathy is not a permanent merging of the two into a single feeling or perception.

Empathy has been widely hailed as one of the most important—if not *the* most important—qualities in the counseling relationship. It must be pointed out, however, that while "there appears to be evidence...that therapists agree upon the importance of empathy and understanding" (Patterson, 1973, p. 396), there is, unfortunately, somewhat less evidence to support the idea that empathy is positively correlated to successful outcomes in counseling and psychotherapy. Gladstein (1970), in a most interesting and controversial paper, has surveyed a number of empirical clinical studies concerned with empathy in counseling and psychotherapy and has concluded that "given the empirical evidence, counselors should not assume that empathy is important in counseling outcomes." This is certainly not to discredit the importance of empathy nor to refute the idea that empathy is an important counselor trait, but rather simply to suggest that at the present time it is uncertain just how empathy contributes to counseling and to what degree empathy influences the counseling outcome. In another study, Dilley, Lee and Verrill (1971) found that while experienced counselors have a higher empathy rating than inexperienced counselors (and, therefore, that empathy can be taught), the experiment demonstrated that the degree of empathy had no discernible effect on the quality of the counseling relationship. On the other hand, a recent study by Mullen and Abeles (1970), which was not included in Gladstein's survey, did find that there was a positive correlation between high degrees of empathy and successful counseling outcomes. Likewise, Altmann (1973), in a recent study, found that "accurate empathy plays a vital role in determining whether clients will continue or terminate counseling after the initial interview." So at best, it seems that the issue in regard to empathy is far from clear at this time.

Objectivity

To remain objective, in the counseling sense, means to be able to stand back and observe what is happening from a neutral, or nonimposing, frame of reference. In one respect objectivity seems to imply the very opposite of empathy; when one is objective, one is not involved to an extraordinary degree with another. However, in terms of our discussion of empathy, we can see objectivity as the extension of the "as if" quality to the intellectual realm of experience. In another respect, objectivity seems to be very much in accord with our definition of empathy. Insofar as objectivity implies the ability to see a thing as "it is," not distorted by preconceptions, biases, and expectations, it fits comfortably into the general category of empathy.

Again, philosophy proves helpful in our attempt to understand objectivity. Ludwig Wittgenstein (1889–1951) has discussed the difference between *seeing* and *seeing as*, which bears directly on our discussion of objectivity. According to Wittgenstein (1958), we can look at the same thing a number of times and see it a different way each time. Wittgenstein speaks of this as "the dawning of an aspect"—that is, seeing something differently from the way we saw it before, while at the same time recognizing that the thing has not changed—only our perception of it has changed. A client comes to us for counseling, and we begin to see him and respond to him *in a manner*; then, as we get to know him better, our responses to him and our perception of him changes. He is the same client, to be sure, and we recognize this; but, nevertheless, to us as the counselor, he is a different client in that we see him differently. Objectivity, in its fullest sense, is the ability to put together and in perspective the various "seeing as" experiences in order to form a comprehensive accurate "seeing" of the client. With this in mind, it is easy for us to understand how empathy (the "seeing as" experience) contributes to our ability to be objective.

One aspect of objectivity, often cited in the literature, is *cognitive flexibility.* This term refers to "an ability to think and act simultaneously and appropriately in a given situation, and to dimensions of open-mindedness, adaptability, and a resistance to premature closure" (Whitely et al., 1967). Cognitive flexibility differs slightly from flexibility, which we listed under open-mindedness. In the case of cognitive flexibility, we are especially concerned with the counselor's intellectual responsiveness and behavioral adaptability, both of which directly affect his ability to understand objectively the quality and context of what is transpiring in the counseling setting. As the counselor is better able to control his emotional involvement in what is happening, as he avoids the temptation to discriminate and perceive selectively, he increases his potential for seeing, as opposed to his tendency toward seeing as.

RELATING TO OTHERS

In the preceding section we discussed the qualities which help the counselor better understand his client. In this section we shall examine those qualities which help the counselor relate and communicate more effectively with his client. Obviously, before he can relate and respond to the client, he has to be able to understand the client, which is why the former qualities may be looked at as prerequisites for relating to others.

Genuineness

An extremely difficult concept to define, genuineness overlaps in meaning and in implication such terms as honesty, sincerity, veracity, and candor. Rogers (1957) himself says of genuineness:

It means that within the relationship he is freely and deeply himself, with his actual experience accurately represented by his awareness of himself. It is the opposite of presenting a facade either knowingly or unknowingly.... It is not necessary (nor is it possible) that the therapist be a paragon who exhibits this degree of integration, of wholeness, in every aspect of his life. It is sufficient that he is accurately himself in this hour of this relationship, that in this basic sense he is what he actually is, in this moment of time. (p. 75)

In its most basic sense, then, genuineness is acting without a facade, functioning openly without hiding behind the veneer of one's role or one's professional status. All too often a counselor may be tempted to use his position for protection, to conceal his human frailties behind an authoritarian veneer. When this happens, he cuts himself off from the client, dissolves the common bond of the relationship between them in an acidic solution of insincerity. The genuine counselor is willing to give of himself during the time of the counseling interview, to allow himself as a person to interact with the client.

To appreciate fully the idea of genuineness, we must be sensitive to the many roles we are expected to play during the course of our daily lives. A role is a social mask—a persona—which we wear in the presence of others in order to define and reinforce a situation by establishing clear limits as to the participation of each character. When the counselor wears a mask, he is saying in effect to the client, "I am the counselor and you are the client—don't you forget it!" The client, acquiescing to the situation, agrees to recognize the role of the counselor and to respond to the counselor as he plays that role. Erving Goffman (1959) describes this process as one of "team cooperation," in which both members of the team (counselor and client) "cooperate to maintain a given definition of the situation" (p. 238). Such a situation, although common on one level, is directly in conflict with the idea of genuineness we are attempting to put forth. For when a genuine quality of the relationship emerges, the dependence on this type of artifice should diminish. The genuine counselor, in other words, minimizes his dependence upon role and increases his giving of self to the client. He is open, honest, and at all times "himself."

It is important, however, that genuineness not be confused with self-indulgence. The counselor should not offer those feelings which he simply desires to offer but rather those which his experience and training tell him will be beneficial to the client. Often the inexperienced counselor tends to be over-genuine (if there is such a word!), too sincere and honest with the client, communicating to him thoughts and feelings which he is not yet ready to hear. When a counselor tells something to a client which distresses the client and upsets him, and the counselor responds that he was only being "genuine," we know that his understanding of the term genuineness leaves something to be desired.

Genuineness, like any good counseling trait, represents a proportioned and well-reasoned mean, in this case between the temptation to be overbearing and forcing oneself upon the client and the need to give something of oneself. Genuineness is the appropriate giving of oneself to the client.

Nondominance

It is an ever-present temptation for the counselor, in his enthusiasm to be helpful and in his desire to be effective, to become inadvertently dominant and to attempt to direct the course and content of the counseling interview. Dominance may take a number of forms, some subtle and some more blatant: imposition of values, tendency to speak too much, interpretations of the client's communications, overeager and inappropriate use of techniques, and so on. Despite the good intentions which may motivate the dominant counselor, it has been shown that the effective counselor controls his dominating tendencies and acts in a nondominant manner.

The nondominant counselor is one who is capable of sitting back and allowing the client to initiate and direct the course of the counseling interview.

This may sound synonymous to nondirective counseling, but even in such directive schools as psychoanalysis, dominance is minimized because of the recognition that it is the client—not the counselor—who knows best how to pace the session, what ground to cover, etc.

Acting in a nondominant manner is often no easy task for the counselor. There is a great temptation to jump up and help the client, to bail him out at difficult times, to help him when an easy solution to his problem appears in the counselor's perspective. Moreover, remaining nondominant may produce tension and anxiety in the counselor, since he does not then have an immediate outlet for the expressions of his feelings. But such control as is demanded, partly the result of his training and partly the result of habit and practice, is unequivocally important for effective counseling. As Reik (1948) has pointed out, the counselor often helps the client more by listening than by speaking, and listening is possible only if the counselor controls any dominating tendencies he might have. In fact, we might say that in its manifest sense, nondominance appears as the *ability to listen*.

Listening is an art unto itself. On one level, we all know how to listen, or at least how to hear. On another level, listening is related to open-mindedness and sensitivity. On still another level, listening is empathizing, moving along with the client as he expresses his feelings. But in its most basic phenomenological level, listening is just that: sitting back, paying attention, not interrupting, and not attempting to direct what the client is saying. In this last sense, this very basic sense, listening is related to nondominance.

Positive regard

Although Rogers originally used the term *unconditional positive regard*, the elimination of the first word strengthens the concept and makes it less open to controversy. After all, Rogers has been much criticized for the use of the absolute term *unconditional*, since it is probably impossible not to be influenced by certain conditions in our dealings with others—particularly such an important other as the client.

Positive regard is based on the assumption "that growth and change are more likely to occur the more that the counselor is experiencing a warm, positive, acceptant attitude toward what *is* the client" (Rogers, 1962). In explaining the concept Rogers says,

It means that he prizes his client, as a person, with somewhat the same quality of feeling that a parent feels for his child, prizing him as a person regardless of his particular behavior at the moment. It means that he cares for his client in a non-possessive way, as a person with potentialities. It involves an open willingness for the client to be whatever feelings are real in him at the moment—hostility or tenderness, rebellion or submissiveness.... It means a kind of love for the client as he is. (p. 420)

It is important to note that positive regard is never a pretense or a technique but rather a genuine and sincere feeling of affection for the client, as he is, as he expresses himself, with his own feelings, values, and beliefs. Positive regard, even if it is only felt and not communicated intentionally by the counselor, is nevertheless transmitted to the client by the counselor in his unspoken communications. Positive regard is an attitude, a health-engendering attitude which inevitably makes the client feel more secure, more worthwhile as a person, more willing to grow and prosper. The manifestations of positive regard, as they appear in the counseling setting, are *acceptance* and *warmth*.

We note, too, that in the case of positive regard, as in the case of sensitivity and nondominance, the counselor's attitude plays a crucial role in communicating to the client the appropriate set of feelings to facilitate his development. Now we turn our attention to the most direct quality in effectively relating to others: communication skills.

Communication skills

Because counseling is essentially a verbal process, in which words are used to transmit feelings and ideas of various levels of abstraction, the effective counselor must have a proficiency in language which enables him to understand and communicate with the client over a wide range of topics. By proficiency in language, I mean not only a good vocabulary, acceptable speech patterns, and the like, although these are each important, but also that the counselor be able to direct his communications to the levels for which they are intended—that he be able to communicate in the language of youth, in the ghetto language, and in all of the other languages and dialects spoken by the students whom he counsels. For communication, in its real sense, is a cooperative effort by two people to "speak the same language," and this can only be accomplished when the counselor has a fluency in many different tongues.

One criterion of good communication is the ability to anticipate the effect that words will have on a client, to know in advance, before saying them, the inferences, denotations, and connotations of the words used and the messages transmitted. The science which studies words and their meanings is *semantics*, and an individual who specializes in this study is a *semanticist*. To some degree, every counselor is a semanticist, in that he is profoundly concerned with the shades and levels of meaning each word has in the client's thinking. As a semanticist, the counselor never assumes that a word has the same meaning to a client that it has to him. A client might, for example, say "My teacher *hates* me." The counselor, aware of the teacher's feelings, might be tempted to disagree at once. However, the client may be using the word *hate* in a specialized sense, different from the sense of the word which is familiar to the counselor, and it is necessary for the counselor to first explore with the client the meaning of the word "hate" for him. Such analyses of language, especially as they deal with *the personal meaning of words*, is a crucial part of effective counseling.

A second criterion of good communication is called *consonance*. Every communication is conducted on two levels. The first level, on which the conversational voice speaks its words, we call the *level of content*. This is the audible level of communication—the level that the client hears. The other level, the silent one which has no need for words, we shall call *the level of intent*. This is the level of meanings and implications, of connotations and inferences, the level that the client feels.

The two levels work differently. While the ear hears the content of an utterance, the heart feels the intent. The level of content speaks logically to the mind, while the level of intent speaks silently to the soul. The level of content is verbal. Information is transmitted on this level in the form of comments, questions, criticism, commands, and so on. The verbal dimension of the counseling interview is conducted on the content level, and, in general, the counseling session is structured and organized around the content. The purpose of the level of content is to inform.

The level of intent is silent. Important feelings are communicated on this level (directly, from heart to heart), craftily concealed behind the unassuming content, which serves as a distraction or a shield. The purpose of the level of intent is to express feelings which cannot be verbalized. The level of intent is deeper, more profound, than the level of content. Both levels communicate but do so in different ways.

The two levels function simultaneously during the counseling session. Every content-laden utterance conceals an intent, which charges the neutral content with an emotional meaning. Content and intent are independent instruments which may be played in harmony or discord. When they speak the same message, they are said to be playing in harmony—they are consonant. When they speak different, or opposing, messages, they are said to be playing in discord— they are dissonant. The effective counselor, in his endeavors to communicate with his client, strives for *consonance.* He aligns his words and his messages with his feelings, lessening the ever-present possibility that discrepancies in his communications can provoke anxiety and fear in the client.

*   *   *   *   *

Having now surveyed some of the more important qualities in effective counseling, we will turn our attention to the personal, subjective world of the counselor and examine which qualities of that world contribute most directly to successful counseling outcomes.

KNOWING ONESELF

Before a counselor can attempt to understand a client, before he is able to reach out and touch another, he must have an objective and satisfying understanding of himself. He must be able to recognize and accept his strengths and limitations, to understand in which areas he is likely to find success and in which he is more prone to failure. To help the counselor better understand ways of assessing himself with respect to his counseling effectiveness, I have listed the three personality characteristics most essential to effective counseling: security, trust, and courage.

116

Security

The prerequisites to security are self-confidence and self-respect. These are the foundations of any personality, and the types of feelings that these create within the individual are inevitably communicated to all with whom he comes in contact. The secure counselor must himself be free from fear and anxiety, must maintain an objective and flexible view of himself. Milliken and Kirchner (1971) found that "the more anxious counselors were less accurate in their ability to recall words spoken and feelings expressed in simulated interviews" (p. 14). Anxiety can only be reduced when one feels good about himself—when one likes himself—and recognizes the irrational nature of the anxiety.

Insecure counselors tend to act more defensively with their clients than secure counselors. They fear the client's anger and rejection and consequently act more in order to please the client than to help him. Insecure counselors may also take advantage of their clients, manipulating the client into meeting the unhealthy needs of the counselor. The secure counselor, on the other hand, knows his own ground and feels comfortable standing on it: he is unshakable and strong, a healthy model for the client.

Security, as a personal quality, also offers the counselor a strategic advantage in the performance of his duties. If the counselor knows who he is and is comfortable with the knowledge, he is then more likely to allow the client to be himself. The secure counselor has no need to shape the client in his own image; he is confident enough to allow the client to develop at his own rate and in his own direction.

Trust

Trust is a basic quality which develops during the early stages of life. To be able to trust another, in its simplest form, is to be able to give to another, to receive from another, and to depend upon another. To be able to trust and to be trustworthy are different sides of the same coin: people who experience difficulty trusting others are usually themselves untrustworthy.

The counselor who is suspicious, who questions every person's motives, whose cynicism colors all of his interactions—this counselor is unlikely to relate to clients in a manner that contributes to the client's growth and adjustment. All too often untrusting counselors attribute feelings and ideas to clients not because the client has expressed them, but rather because the counselor considers such ideas and feelings common to all men. The distrustful counselor might say, for example, "I am certain that this client doesn't pay the slightest bit of attention to what I tell him." When asked why he is sure of this, it turns out that he believes most people do not listen to others, do not trust others.

Trust, unfortunately, is a quality that is difficult to learn. So deeply rooted is it in the personality that the quality of trust may be considered one of the foundations of all subsequent personality development. The counselor who is untrusting would do best to seek his own personal counselor to resolve the problems in this area of his emotional development.

The courage to counsel

Counseling demands a special kind of courage. While each of us wants to be liked, to be admired, to be respected—to be loved—the counselor must at times place many of his own feelings aside, he must remain ungratified, in order for the client to prosper. The counselor must be willing to bear the often unjustified brunt of the client's anger—an anger which although uninspired by him inevitably becomes directed toward him during the course of treatment. The counselor must be willing to feel a profound and distressing sense of aloneness as the client, progressing during the treatment, grows away from him.

The courage required of a counselor is much like the courage required of a parent. In both cases, a stronger person—a powerful force in another's life— must be emotionally capable of relinquishing his strength and allowing the other to become stronger. The courageous counselor finds that he has enough confidence in himself, enough belief in what he is doing, enough security in his job and person, that he does not retreat in the face of adversity, does not waver weakly in the heat of anger.

The true courage of the counselor is found in his willingness to give away a part of himself without recompense, knowing that his strength will always make him strong. The counselor is courageous insofar as he is able to confront the challenges before him, bravely and with dedication and hope.

SUMMARY

In this chapter we have examined some of the qualities associated with effective counseling. The major difficulty of such an examination, it was suggested, is the language confusion between the multiple terms used to describe effective counselors as well as the confusion existing around the word *effective*. A "criterion of application" was suggested as a means of empirically determining the absence or presence of any or all of these qualities. A "Counselor-Qualities Matrix" was offered to reduce broad categories to their component parts and to relate terms to each other. The term *adjectival bombardment* was used to describe the overwhelming surfeit of adjectives used to describe effective counselors.

The review of the literature and subsequent discussion indicated a number of qualities which were assessed to be most important in the pursuit of effective counseling. The most mentioned ones are: empathy, positive regard, concreteness, genuineness, warmth, nonjudgmental attitude, sensitivity, openness, respect, self-disclosure, cognitive flexibility, security, trust, courage, and communication skills. Perhaps, however, the most compelling statement about the effect of counselor qualities was written by a client who had undergone the counseling experience (Webster, 1974). In the form of a prose poem, she captures in a few choice words all the wonder that is counseling! (See Display 4.2)

display 4.2

EFFECTIVE COUNSELING: A CLIENT'S VIEW*

Empathy

... the ability to feel as if you were me ... a willingness to descend into the depths, to feel my terror, and to share the ugliness inside me. Empathy is the courage to be open to me, even at the risk of being changed yourself through our encounter. Empathic response demands courage and fortitude. You could escape the trauma of our encounter by imposing advice or cheerfully mindless reassurance upon me. But even though there must be times when you want to retreat, you hang in there with me, and that does more for me than any counseling "technique" or inspiring philosophy. If you are willing to endure this hell with me, then perhaps there is hope.

Immediacy

God, how I am bogged down. Hopelessly entangled in lines of indiscrimination between past and present, you and me, or threats based in reality and dragons of my own imagination. You throw me a lifeline by helping me get in touch with the here and now. That's a good place to start. As I begin to find a secure base, rooted in the immediacy of our encounter, I begin to develop the perspective needed to sort out that fearsome tangle inside.

Concreteness

I am lost ... wandering through a treacherous, intricate maze of my own making. You enter my jungle with me and teach me how to get my bearings. Learning first-person responsibility, relinquishing the camouflage of generalization, and getting in touch with my immediate feelings and my body language all become pathways to self-understanding.

Respect

which you actualize by refusing to accept me as less than I can be, while recognizing my right to grow at my own pace and be me. When I blow it, you do not demean me with paternal consolation, well-meant advice, or suffocating overprotection. With respectful silence you enter into and accept my feelings of inadequacy and embarrassment. You show respect by being honest with me. When my perceptiveness strikes a vulnerable point within you, you do not retaliate by putting me down or by refusing to express your own feelings. Instead you say, "Ouch! You're right! Although I'm uncomfortable, I appreciate you."

Genuineness

You show me, through your personal example, that I don't have to wait until I am stronger or more perfect to start living, for you share not only your warmth and intensity but your own pain. Because you appear to be so strong and wise, it would be easy for me to isolate you on a pedestal and make your example an unattainable ideal. You put yourself within reach when you share your own struggle without bogging me down. If you can be who you are while you struggle and suffer, then I too can transcend my own despair.

Confrontation

It takes guts for you to confront me ... and it takes guts for me to survive your confrontation. We both grow through our experience. One of the best things you ever said to me was, "Cindy, I don't know what to do with you. We've been through so many things, and just when I think you're learning and growing, you circle back to where we started. Do we have to start all over again? I resent your dependence." After I recovered from the icy shock of awareness, my gut-level response was, "I resent my dependence too!" I began to take responsibility for effecting change in my own life.

EMPATHY ... IMMEDIACY ... CONCRETENESS ... RESPECT ... GENUINENESS ... CONFRONTATION. With these you have made contact, inspired hope, and issued a challenge.

*From "Effective Counseling: A Client's View" by Cindy Lee Webster, *Personnel and Guidance Journal*, 1974, *52*, 288–289, Copyright (1974) American Personnel and Guidance Association. Reprinted with permission.

References

Allen, T. W. Effectiveness of counselor trainees as a function of psychological openness. *Journal of Counseling Psychology*, 1967, *14*, 35–40.

Altmann, H. A. Effects of empathy, warmth, and genuineness in the initial counseling interview. *Counselor Education and Supervision*, 1973, *12*, 225–228.

Biestek, F. P. The non-judgmental attitude. *Journal of Social Casework*, 1953, *34*, 235–240.

Blocher, D. H. *Developmental counseling*. New York: Ronald Press, 1966.

Carkhuff, R. R. An integration of practice and training. In B. G. Berenson & R. R. Carkhuff (Eds.), *Sources of gain in counseling and psychotherapy*. New York: Holt, Rinehart, & Winston, 1967. (Originally published in R. R. Carkhuff, *The counselor's contribution to facilitative processes*. Urbana, Ill.: R. W. Parkinson, 1966.)

Carnap, R. The elimination of metaphysics through logical analysis of language. In J. B. Hartman (Ed.), *Philosophy of recent times*. New York: McGraw-Hill, 1967. (Originally published, 1932.)

Cattell, R. B., Eber, H., & Tatsuoka, M. M. *Handbook for the 16PF*. Champaign, Ill.: IPAT, 1970.

Combs, A. W., & Sopor, D. W. The perceptual organization of effective counselors. *Journal of Counseling Psychology*, 1963, *10*, 222–226.

Dilley, J., Lee, J. L., & Verrill, E. L. Is empathy ear-to-ear or face-to-face? *Personnel and Guidance Journal*, 1971, *50*, 188–191.

Dimick, K. M., & Huff, V. E. *Child counseling*. Dubuque, Iowa: Wm. C. Brown, 1970.

Gellen, M. I. Finger blood volume responses of counselor, counselor trainees, and non-counselors to stimuli from an empathy test. *Counselor Education and Supervision*, 1970, *10*, 64–73.

Gladstein, G. A. Is empathy important in counseling? *Personnel and Guidance Journal*, 1970, *48*, 823–826.

Goffman, E. *The presentation of self in everyday life*. Garden City: Doubleday (Anchor), 1959.

Graver, P. A study of counselors in selected industrial, educational, and social service organizations. Unpublished doctoral dissertation, Northwestern University, 1948. Cited by J. F. McGowan & L. D. Schmidt (Eds.), *Counseling: theory and practice*. New York: Holt, Rinehart, & Winston, 1962, p. 42.

Heikkinen, C. A., & Wegner, K. W. *Minnesota multiphasic personality inventory* studies of counselors: a review. *Journal of Counseling Psychology*, 1973, *20*, 275–279.

Jackson, M., & Thompson, C. L. Effective counselor: Characteristics and attitudes. *Journal of Counseling Psychology*, 1971, *18*, 249–254.

Joslin, L. C., Jr. Knowledge and counseling competence. *Personnel and Guidance Journal*, 1965, *43*, 790–795.

Kelz, J. W. The development and evaluation of a measure of counselor effectiveness. *Personnel and Guidance Journal*, 1968, *46*, 511–516.

Kurtz, R. R., & Grummon, D. L. Different approaches to the measurement of therapist empathy and their relationship to therapy outcomes. *Journal of Consulting and Clinical Psychology*, 1972, *39*, 106–115.

McArthur, C. C. Comment on "effectiveness of counselors and counselor aides." *Journal of Counseling Psychology*, 1970, *17*, 335–336.

Milliken, R. Prejudice and counseling effectiveness. *Personnel and Guidance Journal*, 1965, *43*, 710–712.

Milliken, R., & Kirchner, R., Jr. Counselor's understanding of student's communications as a function of the counselor's perceptual defense. *Journal of Counseling Psychology*, 1971, *18*, 14–18.

Mullen, J., & Abeles, N. Relationship of liking, empathy, and therapist's experience to outcome of therapy. *Journal of Counseling Psychology*, 1970, *35*, 39–43.

Patterson, C. H. *Theories of counseling and psychotherapy* (2nd ed.) New York: Harper & Row, 1973.

Poser, E. G. The effects of therapists' training on group therapeutic outcome. *Journal of Consulting Psychology*, 1966, *30*, 283–289.

Reik, T. *Listening with the third ear*, New York: Farrar, Straus, 1948.

Rogers, C. R. The condition of change from a client-centered viewpoint. In B. G. Berenson & R. R. Carkhuff (Eds.), *Sources of gain in counseling and psychotherapy*. New York: Holt, Rinehart, & Winston, 1967. (Originally published: The necessary and sufficient conditions of therapeutic personality change. *Journal of Consulting Psychology*, 1957, *21*, 95–103.)

Rogers, C. R. The interpersonal relationship: The core of guidance. *Harvard Educational Review*, 1962, *32*, 416–429.

Rogers, C. R., et al. *The therapeutic relationship and its impact*. Madison: University of Wisconsin Press, 1967.

Shelton, J. E. Counselor characteristics and effectiveness in serving economically disadvantaged and advantaged males. *Counselor Education and Supervision*, 1973, *13*, 129–136.

Sieka, F., Taylor, D., Thomson, B., & Muthard, J. A critique of "effectiveness of counselors and counselor aides." *Journal of Counseling Psychology*, 1971, *18*, 362–364.

Strupp, H. H. *Psychotherapy and the modification of abnormal behavior*. New York: McGraw-Hill, 1971.

Torrey, E. F. *The mind game*. New York: Emerson-Hall, 1972.

Truax, C. B. Effectiveness of counselors and counselor aides, a rejoiner. *Journal of Counseling Psychology*, 1971, *18*, 365–366.

Truax, C. B., & Carkhuff, R. R. *Toward effective counseling and psychotherapy*. Chicago: Aldine, 1967.

Truax, C. B., & Lister, J. L. Effectiveness of counselors and counselor aides. *Journal of Counseling Psychology*, 1970, *17*, 331–334.

Tyler, L. E. *The work of the counselor* (3rd ed.). New York: Appleton-Century-Crofts, 1969.

Walton, F. X., & Sweeney, T. J. Useful predictors of counseling effectiveness. *Personnel and Guidance Journal*, 1969, *48*, 32–38.

Webster, C. L. Effective counseling: a client's view. *Personnel and Guidance Journal*, 1974, *52*, 288–289.

Weitz, H. Counseling as a function of the counselor's personality. *Personnel and Guidance Journal*, 1947, *35*, 276–280.

Whitely, J. M., Sprinthall, N., Mosher, R., & Donaghy, R. Selection and evaluation of counselor effectiveness. *Journal of Counseling Psychology*, 1967, *14*, 226–231.

Wicas, E. A., & Mahan, T. W., Jr. Characteristics of counselors rated effective by supervisors and peers. *Counselor Education and Supervision*, 1966, *6*, 50–56.

Wittgenstein, L. *Philosophical investigations*. Oxford: B. H. Blackwells, 1958, II, xi, 193–214.

chapter five

The counselor as a person

Although our concerns up to this point have been with what the counselor *should* be doing and with what qualities he *should* possess, we are all well aware that the counselor, like any of us, is a real person with his own idiosyncratic nature, his own set of particular needs, his own problems, values, and conflicts, any of which may at times work to the detriment of the counseling process. While living up to the idealized sketch of the effective counselor is certainly not an impossibility—nor even a rarity—the sketch does simplify somewhat the multidimensionality of the individual who practices counseling, glossing over the levels of diversity within the counselor that result in a distinct and complex person. In this chapter we will examine how the counselor's problems, perceptions, feelings, and values exert a continuing influence upon the counseling process. Particular attention will be directed toward ways in which his subjectivity, insofar as it is a distortion, can be kept to a minimum. Moreover, in keeping with our premise that counseling is a way of life, we will suggest ways in which the counselor may more effectively conduct his own life, both for his personal benefit and for his professional obligation.

Before embarking on such a discussion, however, it is necessary to differentiate between the counselor as a professional and the counselor as a person. Can the two be considered as separate conditions or are they so intertwined that to differentiate between them is an exercise in futility? The answer is both yes and no! On the one hand, who the counselor is as a person invariably shapes his professional role; on the other hand, his professional capabilities may be developed in spite of personal limitations. A balanced position between these two extremes is clearly the most logical position to maintain.

To help clarify this position, we must consider the concept of *role*, which has been explicated through the disciplinary efforts of sociology. One of the first social scientists to deal with this subject was Ralph Linton, who established the groundwork from which role theory developed. Linton (1936) suggested that individuals within a social group exhibited a narrow range of behavior defined and reinforced by the group. The role, as he viewed it, was a cooperative effort between the individual and his society. In speaking about Linton's position, with respect to the school counselor, Munson (1970) states,

Role has come to be accepted as something defined by a rather specific set of *expected* behaviors. Consensus about a role one plays in a society thus leads to a set of *prescribed* expected behaviors. The more definitively these behaviors are detailed, the more prescribed the role.... Since the concept of role consensus is so popularly accepted, it is easy to understand why there is so much immediate interest and concern for specificity in determining and formulating the role of the elementary school guidance specialist. (p. 70)

This interest and concern is translatable, in terms of the problem at hand, to the relationship between the counselor as a person and the counselor playing a professional role. How much of his real self, we may ask, infuses his professional poise and posture? Erving Goffman, the sociologist who was discussed briefly in the preceding chapter, sheds light on this problem. Goffman (1959) points out that all of us—counselors, ministers, teachers, and other professionals—react in different ways to different social situations, changing, at the drop of a hat, our dress, our speech pattern and vocabulary, our level of formality and intimacy, our gestures and body language, and a variety of other signals. Our personal selves, to be sure, remain the same; but the part of ourselves which we show to others changes according to the social setting. Goffman (1959) speaks of a "social establishment" as "any place surrounded by fixed barriers to perception in which a particular kind of activity regularly takes place" (p. 238). The counseling situation is just such an establishment, with the counselor carefully carrying forward his image of his role, and the client carrying forth his image of the role of the client. The teachers and other school personnel cooperatively work together to maintain this image of the counselor—this mask—both for their own benefit and for the benefit of the students, the counselor, and the system as a whole. Even though their individual feelings about the counselor may change, they nevertheless conscientiously perform their expected role functions:

Within the walls of a social establishment, we find a team of performers who cooperate to present to an audience a given definition of the situation. This will include the conception of own team and of audience and assumptions concerning the ethos that is to be maintained by roles of politeness and decorum. We often find a division into back region, where the performance of a routine is prepared and front region where the performance is presented. (p. 238)

We can extend this dichotomy between "back region" and "front region" to the counseling situation. The counselor's personal world is the back region where his professional performance is prepared to the best of his ability. This back region includes his fantasies, wishes, fears, problems, defenses, anxieties, conflicts, values, and the like. The front region is out in the school, where he performs his counseling duties and makes professional impact. When we look at the question in this light, the relationship between the counselor-as-a-person and the counselor-as-a-professional can be restated as the degree of consonance or dissonance between the counselor's back region and front region. In the preceding chapter we explored the qualities which should be at work in the front region, and in chapter 7 we will examine how the counselor plays a variety of different roles in the school setting. In this chapter we shall examine the back region to see how the personality of the counselor plays a significant part in shaping his professional role, in limiting and defining what he is and is not capable of enacting. More simply, in this chapter we will look at the life of the counselor engaged in various activities, with a view toward better understanding the subtle relationship between his personal life and his professional commitment.

* * * * *

THE VITA ACTIVA

All human activities, suggests Hannah Arendt (1958), can be categorized under three general headings—labor, work, and action—which together she calls the *vita activa*. "All three activities," she states, "and their corresponding conditions are intimately connected with the most general conditions of human existence: birth and death, natality and mortality" (p. 10). Seeing each category as corresponding to one of the conditions of our lives—labor corresponds to the biological cycle of the body, work to the unnaturalness of human existence, and action to the condition that men must always live among others—Arendt relates the three of them to the intricacies of our existence:

Labor assures not only individual survival, but the life of the species. Work and its product, the human artifact, bestow a measure of permanence and durability upon the futility of mortal life and the fleeting character of human time. Action, in so far as it engages in founding and preserving political bodies, creates the condition for remembrance, that is, for history.... of the three, action has the closest connection with the human condition of natality; the new beginning inherent in birth can make itself felt in the world only because the newcomer possesses the capacity of beginning something anew, that is, of acting. (p. 10)

If we follow this rather complex argument, we see that (1) to act is to be reborn and (2) action arises out of the condition that man must always live among other men. The action of the counselor, therefore—and I speak here about the actions in his personal life, which in the long run have priority over his role-dictated professional actions—can be seen as his *redefining himself among others*. This is not to suggest that the counselor is a chameleon, for he is probably as consistent and predictable as any of us. Rather, this idea merely implies that the counselor through his actions creates his unique place in the universe around him.

As specialists in the ways of the human psyche, we understand that actions never exist independently of antecedents and consequences. Something prompts an action to happen, and something else occurs as a result of an action. Thus, there is a continuity to human experience. This continuity is not broken when the counselor enters his professional setting but is merely extended into

124

that setting as the demands of the role in that setting dictate. The counselor, therefore, carries his personal life into his professional activities.

If Arendt's theory about the vita activa is correct, we can say that the counselor through his labor, work, and actions—that is, through his living—defines his condition and presents his existence to others. In this way, we bridge the gap between the back region of counseling and the front region. This line of thinking is similar to the thoughts of Carkhuff and Berenson (1967), where they suggest that there is no clear delineation between the counselor-as-a-person and his professional therapeutic competencies. They capsulize the main points we have cited from Goffman and Arendt in a simple statement of the relationship between the personal life and the work of the counselor:

Effective counseling and therapy are not separate from life, but they do offer a unique and vivid contrast to the general life experience in society. This contrast cannot be experienced so long as "the more knowing" person functions within a socially defined role. Only by breaking free of roles can he give his fully integrated self to the experience, learnings, and

---

display 5.1
CHARACTERISTICS OF THE WHOLE PERSON*

1 The only consistency for the whole person is internal.

2 Creativity and honesty are a way of life for the whole person.

3 Although the way the whole person lives his life is seen by others to be too dangerous, too intense, and too profound, he is in tune with the fact that his real risk involves living life without risk.

4 The whole person realizes that life is empty without acting.

5 The whole person realizes that whatever he does is worth doing fully and well.

6 The whole and creative person functions at a high energy level.

7 The whole person comes to the realization that few men are large enough or whole enough to nourish and love the creative person.

8 The whole person is fully aware that any significant human relationship is in the process of deepening or deteriorating.

9 The whole person realizes that most men say "yes" out of fear of the implications of saying "no," and that most men say "no" out of fear of the implications of saying "yes."

10 The whole person is fully aware that in order to live life in such a way that it is a continuous learning and relearning process, he must periodically burn bridges behind him.

11 The whole person realizes that he is, and must be, his own pathfinder, and travel a road never traveled before.

12 The whole person does not fear living intensely.

13 The whole person is prepared to face the implications of functioning a step ahead or above most of those with whom he comes into contact.

14 The whole person is aware that for most people life is a cheap game.

15 The whole person is fully aware that many of society's rewards are designed to render the creative impotent.

16 The whole person realizes that to emerge within the acceptable levels tolerated by society means institutionalization.

17 The whole person realizes that he must escape traps to render him impotent.

18 The whole person is aware of the awesome responsibility which comes with freedom.

*From: R. R. Carkhuff and B. G. Berenson, *Beyond Counseling and Therapy.* New York: Copyright 1967 by Holt, Rinehart & Winston. Pp. 198-201.

relearnings. Only in this manner can he tap his own resources at a deeper level and hope to become an ever expanding whole person. This is not to say that roles in therapy are never useful. As an aspect of a preferred mode of treatment, selective therapeutic techniques that require roles can add to efficacy. (p. 197)

Carkhuff and Berenson refer to the "whole person," whose life "is made up of actions fully integrating his emotional, intellectual and physical resources in such a way that these actions lead to greater and greater self-definition." If we look at Display 5.1 on page 125, we see eighteen observations about the whole person, and we can note how aptly these fit in to the idea of a vita activa. Our assumption, then, is that the counselor-as-a-person is the more general picture of the person that assumes a specific form within his professional context.

*   *   *   *   *

One important point must be added to the foregoing discussion. The counselor's vita activa must always be a result of his judgments, commitments, and reflections. It should never be random, happening to him at the insistence of others. The counselor must assume responsibility for shaping his life, so that his life is a consequence of his own choices.

The counselor does this by organizing his work, labor, and action around a philosophy of life which guides his every movement. His destiny, therefore, is of his own choosing. While we cannot explicitly state the contents of this philosophy, we can surmise that it is a philosophy which emphasizes the dignity and worth of the individual. Vordenberg (1953) believes that as a counselor progresses in his work, beliefs take on more and more importance to him. As his insight and understanding of the problems of others grows, the counselor begins to think fundamentally about the connection between his beliefs and the human beings with whom he works. This connection—between his beliefs and the lives of others—fuses the counselor's person to his professional endeavors. When the connection is supported by a sound and meaningful philosophy, the counselor fulfills the expectations of Arbuckle (1972), which present a rather practical ideal:

A picture emerges of the person of the counselor. The counselor is a person who has faith in people, a belief that people can grow and develop and that they can stand tall, having pride in self. To become this sort of person the counselor must be a knowledgeable individual, but, far more important, this knowledge must have helped him move along the road toward wisdom, which includes compassion and love and understanding. To me this would be a humanist conception, which would stress self-actualization, and which is a philosophy of human beings rather than methodology or theory. (p. 787)

We shall now turn our attention to three special areas which might tend to make this realization difficult for the counselor: his personal problems, his psychological defenses, and his ingrained value structures. At the conclusion, we will look again to see how the counselor can overcome these problems and emerge successfully.

126

THE COUNSELOR'S PROBLEMS

It would be nice, when the counselor enters the counseling setting, if all of his personal problems and adjustment difficulties were miraculously to disappear, or, at least, to be put aside so that they would not interfere with the counseling. It would be nice, but unfortunately it is not the case. On the contrary, the counselor brings into the counseling situation all his personal problems and difficulties, and these problems, despite all his efforts, will exert a powerful force on him during his counseling activities. The mature counselor can control these factors so that they do not exert a disruptive force upon his work, but to do so he must first be intimately aware of the types of problems he has and the types of interference they are likely to cause.

The counselor has, in effect, the same types of problems as all of us. There are family problems, financial problems, relationship problems, sexual problems, health problems, problems in self-esteem and confidence, social problems, and the like. While circumstances beyond his control may dictate the extent to which these problems interfere in his daily living and professional practice, it is the counselor's responsibility to govern his own life and shape his own destiny in an intelligent, effective, and productive manner. He must, if he is to serve his clients well, have his own life in order, for his work with clients will reflect in many ways the condition of his life, particularly in regard to stability, purpose, consistency, and direction. His counseling, as we have been suggesting throughout this book, is a reflection of himself. I would agree totally with Carkhuff and Berenson (1967) that *"counseling is as effective as the therapist is living effectively"* (p. 197).

What Carkhuff and Berenson mean by that statement is that the counselor helps the client make decisions and test out courses of action, and he also understands the client's feelings by looking into his own life. The objectivity and rationality of the counselor's influence upon the client is contingent upon his being able to govern himself appropriately. Robb (1967) makes the point that "unless the counselor realizes in his own life the full import of the search for meaning and self-understanding, he will be unable to empathize adequately with the struggle of another human being who likewise seeks to realize his highest potential" (p. 1008). The counselor is hindered in his quest for self-discovery, Robb suggests, by the problems of *meaninglessness, alienation*, and *loss of freedom*. Using Robb's headings, let us examine each of these three facets of the problem, in an attempt to discover some of the obstacles the counselor inevitably encounters.

Meaninglessness

Viktor Frankl, a Viennese psychiatrist who was interned in Dachau and Auschwitz during World War II, found that the degree of meaningfulness in a prisoner's life very much influenced the probability of the prisoner's surviving the catastrophic experience. In a famous book, *Man's Search for Meaning* (1962), Frankl discusses the importance of each man's developing a sense of meaning in his life, and how this sense of meaning keeps him alive, gives him a purpose for living, and generally tends to minimize the neurotic component of his existence. It is only as the individual comes to understand and strive toward ultimate and ideal purposes and goals—meanings—that his life becomes full and rich, that his existence becomes important and special to him. "The psychological health of the individual," suggests Katz (1960), "seems to hinge on this search for meaning," and he goes on to indicate that "religion often affords the individual the answer to the question of the meaning of life" (p. 324).

Whether one chooses religion, politics, philosophy, or some other system, the search for meaning is a search for coherence and purpose in the order of things. Meaning holds together the universe; it makes sense of the contradictions we inevitably experience. Seeman (1959) indicates that meaninglessness "is characterized by a low expectancy that satisfactory predictions about future outcomes of behavior can be made" (p. 786). It is, in other words, a pessimistic, deterministic view of the future, a relinquishing of one's right to choose freely to the mythical mistress of destiny. In its most concrete form, meaninglessness is experienced as a sense of futility, as a hopelessness, as weltschmerz.

Meaningfulness, on the other hand, offers a sense of order or coherence to the universe. It not only gives us purpose but makes our individual life a thing of importance. Without meaning, the world is reduced to an inconsequential play of events—much like the theatre of the absurd.

The problem of meaninglessness, then, is a serious problem for the counselor. Meaninglessness cuts the counselor off from the world, restricts his emotional interchanges with others, and prevents him from experiencing life to the full. Meaninglessness is a serious obstacle in the counselor's striving for effectiveness in his counseling exchanges with the client. It is the responsibility of every counselor to search for meanings in his own life.

Alienation

In recent years alienation has been bandied about widely in the academic and popular journals. It is often suggested with cynical insouciance that alienation is "a sign of the times." In reality, however, alienation is a condition of the individual and of his relationship with others, not a condition of the society, although certainly society plays some role in the degree of alienation.

Rollo May (1967) discusses alienation in terms of modern man's loss of significance in the world. There are a number of factors which contribute to man's loss of significance—ranging from rapid technological change to the danger of thermonuclear war—but whatever the cause, "when the individual loses his significance, there occurs a sense of apathy, which is an expression of his state of diminished consciousness." This apathy may be appropriately called alienation.

In its purest sense, alienation means being cut off from the world around us, isolated spiritually from our environment. Wordsworth's famous lines express brilliantly and concisely this condition of alienation:

The world is too much with us; late and soon,
Getting and spending, we lay waste our powers;
Little we see in Nature that is ours;
We have given our hearts away, a sordid boon!
This Sea that bares her bosom to the moon;
The winds that will be howling at all hours,
And are up-gathered now like sleeping flowers;
For this, for everything, we are out of tune;
It moves us not.
   Sonnet, "The World is Too Much With Us," 1807

R. D. Laing, the existential psychiatrist, views this separateness as the normal condition of modern man. He uses the word alienation to express this condition, and it becomes an integral part of his view of man. "The condition of alienation," he says, "of being asleep, of being unconscious, of being out of one's mind, is the condition of the normal man" (Laing, 1967, p. 28). What forms does this alienation assume? Many forms, according to Laing, including a sense of isolation and loneliness, a separation from others, and a loss of a coherent sense of self.

Our alienation goes to the roots. The realization of this is the essential springboard for any serious reflection on any aspect of present interhuman life.... No one can begin to think, feel, or act now except from the starting point of his or her own alienation. (Laing, 1967, Introduction)

Laing, therefore, offers a positive use of alienation in helping us better grasp the intense nature of human interactions. I would certainly agree that to the degree the counselor experiences alienation, he is able to understand alienation in others.

Erich Fromm (1955), one of the more prominent thinkers in this area, presents a concise but specific picture of the alienated individual:

By alienation is meant a mode of experience in which the person experiences himself as an alien. He has become, one might say, estranged from himself. He does not experience himself as the center of his world, as the creator of his own acts—but his acts and their consequences have become his masters, whom he obeys, or whom he may even worship. The alienated person is out of touch with any other person. He, like the others, is experienced as things are experienced; with the senses and with common sense, but at the same time without being related to oneself and to the world outside productively. (p. 111)

Fromm attributes this condition of alienation to a variety of social, economic, political, and psychological causes. But regardless of the cause, he feels strongly that many individuals in our society are alienated above a healthy level.

Seeman (1959) attempts to clarify further the specific quality of alienation by breaking it down into five component parts: powerlessness, meaninglessness, normlessness, isolation, and self-estrangement. By examining each of these components, he attempts to draw a picture of the alienated individual from a sociological point of view. Like Fromm and Laing, Seeman recognizes the preponderance of alienation in our culture today. The contemporary counselor must come to grips with his own feelings of alienation in his attempts to help clients deal with their similar problems.

Loss of freedom

In chapter 2, "The Counseling Stance," we discussed the importance of man's personal search for freedom and the implications of that search in terms of counseling ideology. We indicated that freedom is as much an internal condition as it is an external condition, that there are sociological, political, economic, and psychological factors playing upon the individual's freedom at all times. Jacques Maritain in his beautiful book, *Education at the Crossroads* (1943), discusses the individual's internal freedom:

The chief aspirations of a person are aspirations to freedom—I do not mean that freedom which is free will and which is a gift of nature in each of us, I mean that freedom which is spontaneity, expansion, or autonomy, and which we have to gain through constant effort and struggle.... the freedom of which we are speaking is not a mere unfolding of potentialities without any object to be grasped, or a mere movement for the sake of movement, without aim or objective to be attained.... A movement without aim is just running around in circles and getting nowhere. (pp. 10-11)

Rather, the freedom to which Maritain is referring is the freedom to grow in the way and in the direction that one wants to grow. It is a spiritual as well as a practical freedom: a freedom-to more than a freedom-from. It is a freedom to explore, test, and finally discover and passionately embrace new truths and beliefs. "This conquest of being, this progressive attainment of new truths, or the progressive realization of the...significance of truths already attained, opens and enlarges our mind and life, and really situates them in freedom and autonomy" (p.12).

When we lose our freedom, we lose the possibility of this growth and exploration. We become isolated from the future, a victim of circumstances rather than a master of opportunities. Especially for modern man, who "has lost all the metaphysical certainties of his mediaeval brother" (Jung, *Modern Man in Search of a Soul*), this freedom is important to assure the continuity of his own experiences and the continuity of generations. It is a cultural, as well as an individual, psychological necessity.

Since counseling is a mutual engagement in a freeing activity between counselor and client, it is crucial that the counselor be ever sensitive to his own limitations of freedom, that he show not only a readiness and willingness—but an incentive and drive—to explore the possibilities of his freedom, that he be aware of the alienation and anxiety that result from a loss of freedom.

*　　*　　*　　*　　*

In conjunction with each other, alienation, meaninglessness, and loss of freedom are the three variables that most directly threaten the integrity and

130

continuity of the counselor's vita activa. While none of these is directly a condition of the time, each is present in our age and each must be confronted within the context of the conditions of our age that govern our values, technologies, and approaches to counseling. The counselor whose commitment to counseling infuses all his activities will recognize at every juncture of human interaction the play of these variables on his feelings and on the feelings of others. He will understand his human limitations and strive to overcome them, to transcend them, in order to become a more effective, more therapeutic counselor.

THE COUNSELOR'S DEFENSES

One of Freud's most important contributions, insofar as the work of the counselor is concerned, is his theory of the defense mechanisms. Technically, these mechanisms are the processes by which the ego defends itself from feelings, thoughts, and actions which are unacceptable (ego dystonic). In more general terms, however, the defense mechanisms describe typical strategies for dealing with frustrating and anxiety-provoking situations, unconscious strategies which are used by all of us in our day-to-day activities. What makes Freud's insight so significant to the counselor is that it enables him to identify and understand unconscious, dynamic processes that may tend to interfere with his effectiveness. Even if the counselor rejects the bulk of Freudian thinking, which many counselors do, he may find it useful to examine his feelings and his activities in terms of these mechanisms. While Freud's theory of the defense mechanisms' contributions to psychopathology may on the whole be tenuous, there is little doubt that all of us do, quite consistently, exhibit patterns of behavior and response which are insightfully described by these mechanisms. Allport (1962) points out that,

Among the valid portions of psychoanalysis of special use to all counselors is the brilliant account given us by Freud and his daughter Anna of the defensive mechanisms of the ego. In dealing with our client we do well to follow the advice of psychoanalysis and watch for rationalizations, denials of reality through repression, and displacements of aggression. All these and other ego defenses belong to the nature of man, and, therefore, must find a place in any theory of human personality. (p. 376)

While Allport may be referring specifically to the mechanisms used by the client, it is perhaps even more important that the counselor attempt to recognize the defenses he himself is using, defenses which distort his perception and understanding of the client. For as long as the counselor is defensive, he relinquishes the opportunity of dealing directly and constructively with counseling problems, of coping maturely with the counseling reality.

McCall (1963) differentiates between *coping* and *defensiveness*:

Coping implies a realistic facing up to the difficulty by, for example, acknowledging the hitherto unrecognized deficiency or peculiarity (adjusting the self-image), and endeavoring to control or modify it appropriately, especially in behavioral expression. This is the way of insight, reality-testing, and emotional control. (p. 46)

When the counselor copes with his problems, particularly with the problems he is experiencing with the client, he endeavors in a healthy manner to resolve the difficulty and make the counseling session more productive. Unfortunately, in many areas we have weaknesses in coping with certain feelings, particularly those feelings which threaten our self-esteem. In these "weak" areas, we resort to defensiveness:

The second way of dealing with the threat ... to self-esteem, the way of *defensiveness*, is far easier than coping because it evades the threat and nullifies it symbolically rather than facing up to it and endeavoring to overcome it directly. It is a kind of automatic and indeliberate psychic manipulation which sets defense above adjustment, and refusing to acknowledge the threat to self-esteem as a real threat, admits it like a Trojan horse into the citadel of self. (McCall, 1963, p. 47)

When the counselor acts defensively, he protects his ego at the expense of the client's growth. We must recognize, however, that the elimination in toto of the defense mechanisms is not a practical possibility. No person's ego is strong enough to accept everything—nor should it be. Fallibility is a part of the human condition. All we are suggesting is that the counselor minimize the use of defense mechanisms, in whatever areas he is capable of doing so. Recognition of these defense mechanisms is a minimal prerequisite for dealing with them maturely.

Repression

The most common defense mechanism is repression. In its most basic form, repression simply means forgetting. Whatever was once a part of consciousness, but no longer is, has been repressed. We repress both feelings and situations, thoughts and occasions, using as our guiding principle the reduction of anxiety. Whatever causes us pain or provokes anxiety becomes a likely candidate for repression and is then no longer accessible to our conscious mind. "Being repressed," said Freud (1924), "means being unable to pass out of the unconscious system."

Repression causes innumerable difficulties in the counseling situation. Whenever the counselor forgets an appointment, forgets something important that the client has said, or forgets the client's name, the counselor can be certain he is repressing. To dismiss such instances casually—"Oh, it just slipped my mind"—shows the counselor's unwillingness to accept his human frailties. Then again, whenever the counselor makes what is commonly called a Freudian slip of the tongue, he can also be assured that repression is at work. For Freud pointed out in his important work, *Psychopathology of Everyday Life*, that all such slips are signs of unconscious repressed material trying to break through to consciousness.

Projection

Projection, another common defense mechanism, is the process of attributing to another person or to an object in the outside world, feelings which emanate from within. A person who feels that no one likes him, for example, may be projecting his own internal feelings of hostility on to all of the people around him. Projection protects the ego by confusing self and other, and by attributing to the other the ego dystonic feelings of the self. Projection, even more than repression, presents a serious problem in the counseling situation by offering the possibility that what the counselor is seeing in the client are actually qualities that he does not like about himself. Ever present is the danger that the poorly adjusted counselor might confuse his own feelings with the feelings of the client:

The counselor is most effective when he is aware of his own tendencies toward fear, anxiety, shame and so forth, and when he does not have the need to project these tendencies onto his client. Insofar as he does find projection necessary, he forces the client to react to him as a real person rather than as a projected person, and makes it necessary for the client to respond to him in kind. (Symonds, 1949, p. 229)

A counselor can test for projection by examining his feelings about what the client is feeling with the feelings that the client thinks he is feeling.

Reaction formation

Reaction formation is a defense mechanism that is often difficult to recognize. Simply, this mechanism involves acting in a way which is in total

contradiction to the way one unconsciously feels. While the individual is acting in this way, however, he is not aware of his unconscious feelings and is, therefore, unable to recognize the mechanism at work. Let us say, for example, that a counselor is experiencing some unrecognized hostility toward a client but that his ideas about counseling preclude such feelings from his subjective inventory. He has been taught to feel *unconditional* positive regard, and here he is beginning to experience anger toward the client. One way of handling this is unconsciously to react to this anger. He may, for instance, feel compelled to buy the client a present, a present given not for love, but rather for self-protection. It would be far better, both for the counselor and for the client, if the counselor were to recognize his angry feelings and deal with them directly, thus working them out so that they might be productively integrated into the multidimensional counseling relationship.

Intellectualization

Intellectualization, a defense mechanism which is often considered an occupational hazard to counselors and psychotherapists, makes itself felt when the counselor understands the client intellectually, but not emotionally. Manifestations of intellectualization include: describing the client in technical language; relating to the client through abstract or impersonal techniques, rather than through spontaneity and genuine feelings; perceiving the client in terms of his symptoms and ignoring his personal complexity; understanding the client's problems in systematic, logical, theoretically-oriented perspective, rather than from the client's own internal frame of reference. The counselor intellectualizes when he attempts to grasp his own feelings and the client's feelings conceptually rather than emotionally. Because counselors and psychotherapists have been trained to understand diagnostic and symptomatic categories, they are more prone than others to misuse these categories to separate themselves from the client.

Denial

The mechanism of denial is often confused with repression and reaction formation because of the similarities in practice among the three. Denial, in its most general form, is where the conscious mind denies feelings from within or situations from without that prove threatening to the ego. True, denial often involves repressive and reacting components; but, more importantly, denial involves blocking out a portion of the world, denying it, rather than reacting to it or forgetting it. A counselor, for example, may fail to recognize that the client, is experiencing hostile feelings toward him, thereby blocking out of his perceptual world an important part of the client's phenomenal world.

Isolation

Isolation, like intellectualization, involves the severing of the affective from the cognitive realm, the cutting off of feelings from intellectual understanding.

With isolation, however, the major emphasis is on perceiving the world as an affectless, emotionless world, where the perceiver feels uninvolved with what is happening, not, as with intellectualization, placing the world within intellectual constructs. As the counselor distances himself from the client, as he refuses to confront and experience the client's feelings, he utilizes the mechanism of isolation.

Rationalization

When the counselor uses rationalization, he develops a pseudoexplanation for his actions or attitude (McCall, 1963) or attributes false, more favorable motives to explain his behavior (Patterson, 1973). Commonly referred to as sour grapes, rationalization is typified by the famous Aesop fable of the fox who tried repeatedly without success to get at a bunch of grapes. Failing time and again, the fox finally gave up his attempts, rationalizing that the grapes looked sour anyway. When the counselor uses rationalization, he defends himself from his real feelings by creating a false situation of motives and causality.

Displacement

Displacement involves the shifting of an object of a feeling or drive. A counselor, for example, may take out some of the aggression he feels toward his supervisor by displacing it on clients who are safer objects for his wrath. In general, displacement involves displacing to a safer object feelings unconsciously held toward a more dangerous or threatening object. Since the client, in his

135

relationship to the counselor, is more than likely not threatening to the counselor, he often becomes an unwitting victim of displaced feelings the counselor holds to others.

Regression

Regression means "returning," particularly returning to an earlier stage of emotional or intellectual development. When a person becomes overpowered by feelings which he can no longer handle, one way of dealing with the situation is to return to an earlier level of development where one was able either to avoid such feelings or to feel comfortable with them. The counselor may find at times that he is exhibiting behavior which is less mature than his normal behavior and indicative of his feelings at some earlier point in development. In such instances, it can safely be assumed that he is regressing to this earlier point in development in order to deal with the difficulties he is consciously or unconsciously experiencing with the client.

Introjection and identification

Introjection and identification, two mechanisms which are often confused with each other, are common occurrences in the counseling situation. Introjection occurs when the counselor's personality incorporates part of the person whom he is counseling. In a healthy counseling situation, it is the client, not the counselor, who should be introjecting. But pressures of the moment as well as painful, poignant memories of the past sometimes serve to encourage the counselor to begin to experience the world through the values and ego boundaries of the client. In such a case, he is clearly introjecting a part of the client into himself.

Freud initially used introjection to explain the learning of values by the child. A child introjects—takes inside—his parents' system of values, and they become a part of himself. But adults may introject too—for entirely different reasons. Introjection may be used as a method of gaining strength from another, of actually incorporating a part of another's will within oneself. It may also be used to get love from another: The romantic concepts of lovers uniting as one is interpreted in our language as introjecting with each other. In either case, whether the motivation be strength or love, the counselor introjects from the client when he feels, but cannot fully acknowledge, the powerful feelings drawing him and the client together.

Identification is the process where an individual confuses his identity with the identity of someone else. Rycroft (1968) points out that in identification, the person may either extend his identity *into* someone else, borrow his identity *from* someone else, or fuse his identity *with* someone else's. Three common modes of identification in the counseling situation are identification with the aggressor, identification with the victim, and narcissistic identification. In the first case, the counselor, exposed to an aggressive and threatening client, who momentarily endangers the counselor's calmness and neutrality, begins to act and feel as aggressively as the client. He does this, albeit unconsciously, to protect himself from the presumed dangers of the client.

The counselor identifies with the victim when he sees himself being hurt as the client describes his own hurt. A client may, for example, be describing mistreatment he has been exposed to by the parent. The counselor, recalling his own mistreatment during childhood, begins to feel mistreated along with the client. This differs from empathy, because the counselor is experiencing the world not from the client's point of view but rather from a point of view that, while it parallels the client's, is actually the counselor's. Too often counselors compromise their objectivity and helpfulness by becoming overly involved in the problems of the client, not because they are motivated to help the client solve these problems, but because they associate their own problems with the problems that the client is describing.

Narcissistic identification, perhaps the most common and yet the most dangerous, describes the process by which the counselor acts out his fantasies and experiences vicariously through the client's life. Sometimes called overidentification or overinvolvement with the client, this defense occurs wherever the counselor begins to confuse his own identity with the identity of the client. A counselor, for example, may be tempted at times to express his own rebellious feelings against the school, the family, or society by either encouraging or condoning the client's antisocial activity. A counselor who finds himself deriving too much pleasure or too much pain from the experiences and feelings of the client is probably identifying with the client on a narcissistic level.

While all counselors make use at times of these various defense mechanisms, they do present difficulties in the counseling situation, particularly in the counselor's attempts to relate constructively to the client. Defense mechanisms distort perception and block off a part of the world and a part of the client's experience. They corrupt the counseling relationship. Theoretically, the better adjusted the counselor is, the less need he will have for defense mechanisms. But even the best adjusted counselor will at times have no recourse but to use these mechanisms.

We will now look briefly at five hypothetical cases, extracted from real case material, to see how these mechanisms function in real practice. As we look at these cases, keep in mind instances in your own life where similar patterns of behavior, thought, and feelings occurred, and try to analyze the forces which prompted these mechanisms to work for you.

Case one. The counselor forgets an appointment, is chided by the client, and then goes home and yells at his wife.
  Defenses. Repression and displacement.

Case two. The counselor believes a certain client doesn't like him, although the client really does like him. The counselor reasons that this client wouldn't care for any counselor, no matter who he was or what he did.
  Defenses. Projection and rationalization.

Case three. A counselor acts overly nice to a client he doesn't really like.
  Defense. Reaction formation.

Case four. A counselor who believes he is making real progress with a client is shocked when he receives a letter that the client no longer wishes to see him, because no progress has been made. The counselor becomes furious and vengeful.
  Defenses. Denial and regression (revenge).

Case five. A counselor can interpret all of the unconscious reasons why a client behaves in a certain way but feels no "empathy" for the client.
  Defense. Intellectualization.

THE COUNSELOR'S VALUES

"A person's values," suggests Ajzen (1973), "may be defined as his or her basic ideas and beliefs about what is right or good and what is wrong or bad" (p. 77). Every person has such a set of beliefs, which permeate decision making, ability to appreciate the things around us, our consciences, and our perception of others. To the extent that the counselor's values are an integral part of his personality, and, therefore, a part of the back region of his professional role, they are of interest to us in examining how his set of values contributes to the counseling process.

There are, of course, many different types of values. One type, which we might call "cognitive values," asserts that one thing, *A*, is better or worse than another, *B*, citing objective or scientific evidence as the reason. For example, a counselor might believe that behavioral counseling is more effective in working with underachievers than is Rogerian counseling. Citing studies to prove his point, the counselor would deny that this is a personal value, arguing strongly that it is a conclusion based on fact rather than on subjectivity or preference. In the broad sense, however, any belief, no matter how strongly based on fact, is a value. But the more the individual believes that a particular value is a "cognitive value," the less likely he is to change that value regardless of the persuasion to which he is exposed. While other values are often receptive to change, "cognitive values" carry with them a sense of certainty that is maintained through a stubbornness which borders on the intransigent. Consider, for instance, how Copernicus or Galileo fared when they, by citing objective evidence, attempted to contradict the "cognitive values" of the societies in which they lived.

Second, we have values which are clearly not objective or grounded in experiment, but which are merely indicative of a personal preference. I prefer the Dutch Masters to the Impressionists. This is not to say that one is better than the other, but merely that one gives me more pleasure than the other. These we might call "preference values." When the individual holds preference values, he recognizes that they are values and not facts, and he is more likely to tolerate in others values which are different from his own. Because preference values, unlike cognitive values, do not define the world around us, there is less danger in encountering discrepancies against these values. A counselor might say, "I prefer face-to-face counseling over group counseling, but I don't believe that one is necessarily better than the other," thus acknowledging it is a preference value rather than a cognitive value.

Third, we have moral values. These are values based on higher principles, universals of conduct. Moral values are taught to us when we are very young, and although we are able to modify what we have learned, the basic moral tenets instilled within us hold throughout our lives. Freud suggested the idea of a *superego*, of an introjected set of parental values which we carry with us throughout life and which consciously or unconsciously become an integrated part of our personality. Moral values, like cognitive values, are strong values. We tend to believe that our values in this realm are the right values, and we judge others by our set of values. The counselor who believes that lying is wrong is likely to judge clients who lie according to the prescripts of this value. In other words, while we tolerate diversity in matters of preference, we tend to be more restrictive and less adaptive in matters of cognition and morality.

Fourth, we have cultural values. These may overlap any of the other three categories, but they differ in that they are shared values rather than individual values. Cultural values pose a particularly tricky problem to the counselor. Because they are values of consensus, shared by all those with whom the counselor interacts, he may fail to recognize them as values, instead considering them absolutes or truths. A counselor who believes that when a client is ill he should see a physician—a cultural value judgment—may not be able to understand the value of a Christian Scientist who does not hold this value. Because of the subtlety of cultural values, they often elude our rational ability to evaluate and react objectively. Even more insidious, there is always a temptation to judge those whose cultural values are different from ours as "inferior, deprived, or disadvantaged" (Vontress, 1969).

Finally, we have self-values. These values represent our feelings of self-esteem and importance. Although some writers, such as Schlien (1962), believe that this value is culturally determined, a more popular position is that one's self-esteem is more dependent upon early upbringing, particularly upon relationship to the mother. In either case, one's feelings about oneself deeply influence all one's choices, perceptions, and judgments.

While other categories of values could be set forth, these five cover the ground sufficiently. The counselor has values in each of these categories, and these values influence operationally as well as theoretically his counseling activities in manifold ways. We shall now examine some of the ways in which values influence counseling.

*   *   *   *   *

Research on the question of what influence counselor values have upon the counseling process has been rich and fruitful in recent years. Cook (1966), in an experiment using the *Study of Values* (Allport, Vernon, and Lindzey, 1960), found that differences in the counselor's and client's value systems affect counseling outcome. His findings show that when subjects were placed in high, medium, and low groups according to their similarity to counselor values, those in the medium similarity group were a greater therapeutic "success" than those in the high or low similarity group. This would suggest that when the counselor perceives the world too much like the client, or too differently, it has an adverse effect upon their communication. On another aspect of differences in values between counselor and client, Rosenthal (1955) contends that some types of counselor values invariably rub off on the client. He says that most therapists believe that the therapist's values should be kept out of therapy as much as possible, but the results of his experiment indicate that the patients who improved most changed their moral values to conform more closely with the values of their therapist. "Patients who improved tended to revise certain of their moral values in the direction of their therapists', while the moral values of patients who were unimproved tended to become less like their therapists'" (p. 435). While he is not suggesting that the therapist indoctrinate the patient, he does point out that changing values may be an integral part of therapeutic growth. Patterson (1958) agrees that the counselor cannot keep his own values out of the counselor-client relationship, and he suggests that the counselor should realize this inevitability and know what his values are. By recognizing his values, he can become a more effective counselor. Williamson (1966) points out that "counselors [must examine] the psychological possibilities of [their] relationship with students in their task of identifying themselves...to those value hierarchies that help them aspire to achieve excellence . . . their full potentiality" (pp. 622-623). He argues that "counseling cannot be independent of values, whether or not we would like to make it free" (Williamson, 1958, p. 528).

In another area of values, Lee (1968) found that social-class bias played a part in psychiatric residents' diagnoses of patients, although these findings were brought into question in a subsequent study (Routh and King, 1972). Fitzgibbons and Shearn (1972) likewise found that the professional background of the psychotherapist was an important influence in determining whether he judged a patient schizophrenic or not. This last study illustrates clearly how what some may consider a cognitive value—i.e., a diagnosis—is in fact culturally relative.

The question of cultural bias is perhaps one of the more compelling questions arising in the issue of counselor values. Bell (1971) uses the term "the culturally deprived psychologist" to describe the practitioner whose cultural values prevent him from relating effectively with black clients; but this term can be more generally used to describe the counselor who is bound up in his own cultural perspective to the degree that it obscures his view of the client's world. Leacock (1968) offers the example of a white middle-class principal who issued some guidance literature that described the characteristics of the "deprived child" and that led to a violent reaction from the black parents in the PTA, who were primarily middle class in values and orientation. Such cases are not unusual; both counselors and principals, steeped in a middle-class view of the world, tend to lose perspective of the other cultural and social values which surround them but which they do not feel a part of.

In the professional journals in recent years, there have been many articles about counseling the members of a particular minority group (Vontress, 1970; Sue, 1972; Kaneshige, 1973; Kincaid, 1969; Casavantes, 1970; Ryan, 1969). The four groups most frequently cited are blacks, Mexican-Americans, Asian-Americans, and American Indians. Regardless of which specific group he is working with, however, a common conflict emerges from the interaction between cultures, as exemplified by the interaction between counselor and client. Kincaid (1969) describes this conflict in terms of working with the black client:

The therapist working with black clients finds himself in the unique position of living in and being supported by society and yet faced with the task of seeing that society through the eyes of its victims. He must affirm and support his client's choice of movement toward a role within the present society or toward a marginal existence in some newly discovered role that may conflict with the mainstream. (p. 887)

This conflict of interest is typical of all counseling encounters where there is an underlying cultural clash. Often the counselor's cultural values are so integrated into his personality that he fails to recognize them as values and looks at them as legitimate, incontrovertible assessments of reality itself. Such a dogmatism is a serious fault in the counselor's ability to relate to members of cultural groups which are different from his own.

Another cultural value common to counselors, and one which has come under increasing scrutiny, is the counselor's attitude toward women. While women are in no way a minority group, they have suffered for many years in the same way that minority groups have suffered. They have been discriminated against financially, socially, and professionally, and they have been viewed as less than equal by the more chauvinistic men in the profession. Pyke and Ricks (1973) discuss the changing role of women in our society and offer some suggestions to the counselor:

Many female students frequent the counselor's office in search of guidance in curriculum or career planning. Counselors can no longer assume that career interest is a passing fancy, and curriculum programs for women must be carefully planned in order to ensure that future careers are not jeopardized or an emerging career interest nipped in the bud by the failure to consider it seriously. (p. 281)

Such a suggestion should be well appreciated by those of us in the profession who have witnessed over the years the tragic waste of human talent and potential brought about by counselors' failures to acknowledge the competencies and possibilities women offer to our society. Schlossberg and Pietrofesa (1973) offer some specific suggestions as to how the counselor can learn to minimize his or her biases against women. They suggest a training model designed to help the counselors participate with their constituency in an unbiased fashion. It consists of four stages:

1 Expanding the cognitive understanding of participants regarding the role of women through lectures and readings.
2 Raising the consciousness of participants regarding sexual bias through group techniques.
3 Promoting the acquisition of nonbiased helping skills among participants through audio-video taping and role playing.
4 Fostering skill development in program planning and implementation among participants through tutorial projects. (p. 51)

It is unfortunate, but true, that these four stages are necessary to overcome the pervasive bias in our culture that prevents women from maximizing their potentialities and prevents the counselor from encouraging them to do so.

The discussion so far has centered around the type of values we call cultural values. While this is not the only class of values which exerts an influence upon counseling practice, it is perhaps the most studied type in recent years. In other sections of this chapter ("The Counselor's Problems" and "The Counselor's Defenses"), we discuss the values of self, which influence counseling. Moral values were discussed in some detail in chapter 4, where we presented the nonjudgmental attitude. Cognitive values were discussed also in chapter 4.

Having now presented problems caused by the counselor's values, let us examine some positive aspects of counselor values, particularly, what kind of values should the counselor have. What set of values will help him in his practice?

*　*　*　*　*

It is, of course, necessary that the counselor be committed to some values in order that he be able to maintain the meaningfulness in his life. The core question that we are concerned with is this: To which type of values, to which logical biases, should the counselor commit himself? The answer to this crucial question becomes abundantly clear when we look at the literature and consider the issues at hand. The primary value to which the counselor must commit himself, the value from which all other values are derived, is *freedom*. Peterson (1970), in his thorough study of counseling and values, calls freedom the "valuational base for counseling." Viewing the ultimate task of the school counselor as "helping the individual to become the free person he potentially is," as we have been suggesting throughout this book, Peterson goes on to speak of the counselor's own values of freedom:

The essential quality of freedom is that it allows man room to be himself, to be creative, to make choices and be responsible for them. Freedom allows man to choose higher values if he desires. It allows him to follow his own quest for truth, to develop his own philosophy of life. Freedom is a matter of degree. We must talk in terms of *more* or *less* rather than of *presence* or *absence*. Freedom involves man in his individual functioning, in his functioning with others, and in his search for meaning. It has many facets, and man is confronted by choices involving them. Freedom can be at least part of a base from which one can examine and evaluate practice. (p. 182)

As a value from which the counselor works, freedom is an ideal that propels the individual to certain types of actions. Freedom guides the individual in the direction in which to move; it draws the individual to her. "Rather than command, dictate, or affirm, freedom as an ideal attracts. It pulls man, for it offers enhanced possibility for fulfillment. It is always out of reach in an absolute sense but at the same time is within reach to a relative degree" (p. 186).

It is far easier to speak about freedom as a concept than to experience it as a condition, however. As I indicated in the section on the counselor's problems, many of us are unable to experience freedom because of constraints within us rather than because of forces from outside. One factor which might influence the degree of freedom that the counselor is able to experience is his own upbringing. Another is forces exerted upon him by the system: The fact that he may be required to maintain a facade in the school situation will inevitably alter his choices as well as his opportunity to choose meaningfully and responsibly.

There is another factor which influences not only the counselor's freedom but the ability of the client to become free and to discover the meaning of his freedom as well. To the degree that the counselor stubbornly maintains his own value system, he precludes the opportunity for both himself and the client to grow and change values. As we have indicated, the therapist's values do influence the client. Wolf and Schwartz (1959) indicate that "the way the therapist perceives what is good and what is bad in himself and in the group affects the quality of the therapy.... A therapist can influence patients to become very much like himself, extensions of himself, or submissive border-line egos..." (pp. 38-39). To the extent that the therapist does this, he compromises his own freedom by dogmatism and proselytizing, and he restricts the client's freedom to choose by subtly manipulating him to make choices which are compatible with the therapist's.

It is imperative, therefore, that the counselor be aware of the values he subscribes to and sensitive to how deeply he is or is not committed to these values. Different types of values require different types of examination. Rosenthal (1955) points out that particularly in the areas of sex, aggression, and authority the moral values of the therapist are important because they touch directly upon the issues usually involved in the patients' conflicts. He has devised a sixty-item inventory (see Appendix III) to measure attitudes in six categories:

1 *Sex-rigid*. Sex is seen as evil, perhaps a necessary evil, dirty, to be shunned, postponed, or suppressed.
2 *Sex-free*. Sex is seen as good, healthy, natural, to be accepted, enjoyed, understood.
3 *Antiaggressive*. Acts of aggression, violence, or pain infliction are thought of as wicked, to be avoided, suppressed, suffered.
4 *Aggressive*. Aggression is thought of as necessary, rewarding, to be accepted, expressed.
5 *Disciplinarian*. Authority, discipline, order, and regulation are seen as absolute, necessary, desirable, to be accepted, supported.
6 *Libertarian*. Authority is seen as a relative matter, with individual responsibility and reason primary.

I would agree with Rosenthal that these six categories are particularly important in determining the influence of values in the counseling process. It would be valuable for every counselor to rate himself against this inventory to determine possible areas of conflict with his clients.

Before continuing, let us briefly recapitulate the main points of this section. The counselor brings to the counseling session a sense of values, which are beliefs, commitments, and predispositions toward specifiable actions. These values are generally of five types: moral values, cognitive values, cultural values, preference (or aesthetic) values, and self values. Values do tend, in one of several ways, to rub off on the patient; but the specific process and the intensity of it is still open to question. The basic value, the one which should underlie all of the counselor's other value choices, is the value of freedom. The counselor's commitment to freedom, both his own freedom and the freedom of the client, enables him to function effectively and in accordance with the basic goals of counseling. Limiting his ability to commit himself to this value, however, may be his own predisposition to a class of values which he may not be entirely aware of. He must, therefore, carefully and consciously evaluate the value bases from which he is working, particularly in those areas where his values are likely to conflict with the values of the client. Rosenthal's attitude inventory indicates value predispositions in six of these important areas.

We turn now to the question of a positive ethical basis for counseling. The profession as a whole has worked arduously on this question for a number of years, and it has developed a variety of committees to look into the problem. The result, from the American Personnel and Guidance Association (APGA), our national professional organization, is a position paper on the appropriate ethical standards for the profession of counseling. The counselor should be familiar particularly with those areas of practice (testing, research, interviewing) in which he or she is engaged. In addition, the ten commandments of counseling (Egan, 1966) might make a fine plaque in the counselor's office both to remind himself and to assure his clients that his commitment is total and ethically rooted.

We note that these ten commandments, being not merely admonitions and prohibitions, have an underlying sense of positiveness and growth. These are not the traditional "Thou shalt not's" but rather a positive, oriented attitude toward counseling, and particularly toward counseling values, which should encourage the counselor to expand his capabilities and to counsel more effectively. In essence, these ten commandments translate into practical principles the ideal of freedom we have been referring to throughout this book.

---

display 5.2

TEN COMMANDMENTS FOR COUNSELORS*

1 Remember your responsibility to handle with kid gloves the confidences entrusted to you.
2 Define realistically the limits of your competency in counseling.
3 Be ever mindful of the moral limits and counselee rights involved in your efforts to gain a comprehensive insight into your counselee's problems.
4 Subject yourself occasionally to a wholesome self-evaluation with regard to your counseling practices.
5 Never let the day arrive when your efforts at professional development come to a standstill.
6 Be cautious about your personal involvements in the problems of the counseling situation.
7 Examine critically the fundamental social principles underpinning your vocational or career guidance activities.
8 Never fail to recognize the counselee's inner resources for the resolution of his problems.
9 Review critically your program of services from time to time in terms of its comprehensiveness and balance.
10 Never let it be said that you have failed to appreciate the inherent dignity and supreme eternal worth of each human being whose life you touch.

*From "The Ten Commandments for Counselors" by John M. Egan, F.S.C.H. In *Readings in Guidance & Counseling*, edited by James Michael Lee and Nathaniel J. Pallone. New York: Copyright, 1966, Sheed and Ward, Publishers. Pp. 236–239.

CONCLUSIONS AND IMPLICATIONS

In this chapter we have examined some of the underlying qualities of the counselor as a person to determine in what ways his personal qualities contribute to or detract from the stated goals of counseling and the established criteria of efficacy. The discussion touched three basic areas: the counselor's personal problems (meaninglessness, alienation, and loss of freedom); the counselors psychological defenses and distortions of the world; and the counselor's set of values as they appear in the counseling interaction.

It was determined that the counselor, in the conduct of his own life, must inexorably deal with the problems of self-definition in a rapidly changing technical world that he may find he cannot always keep up with. He must work consciously and intensively to find his place in the world, to understand the complexity of his relationship with others, to discover anew the richness of life. It is his responsibility to take responsibility: to make choices and to commit himself to what he believes. He must confront and conquer the dangers of alienation which challenge us all; he must come to grips with the question of finding sustaining meanings in his life; he must seek his freedom and when he finds it, exploit it. He must, in short, lead the "authentic and examined life."

The counselor's efforts along this path, however, are limited in two ways. First, his perceptions of others and of the world are distorted by defense mechanisms that occlude reality by distorting his perceptions under the unconscious direction of a weakened ego. Insofar as the counselor acts defensively, he is remiss in the fundamental obligation of his profession: experiencing and accepting the client as he is and for what he is. The healthier the counselor is, the more likely he will be able to cope with his problems and resolve his conflicts, rather than attempting to avoid them with defensive strategies.

Secondly, the counselor's own problems may interfere with his ability to maintain an authentic engagement with the client. To the extent that the counselor has not established his own authenticity, he is unable to assist the client in his strivings for a meaningful, responsible life. How alienated is the counselor from others and from the world around him? To what projects, hopes, and beliefs is he committed? Has he sufficiently explored the many possibilities of his freedom? These are the basic questions that the counselor must ask himself before embarking on his professional journey.

Finally, we considered the counselor's personal values. We examined the different types of values and suggested some areas in which the counselor's values may interfere in the counseling process. We offered a positive rationale for counseling, consisting of freedom as the valuational basis and a well-developed ethical position as the content.

References

Ajzen, R. Human values and counseling. *Personnel and Guidance Journal*, 1973, *52*, 77–81.

Allport, G. Psychological models for guidance. *Harvard Educational Review*, 1962, *32*, 373–381.

Allport, G. W., Vernon, P. E., & Lindzey, G. *Study of values.* Boston: Houghton Mifflin, 1960.

Arbuckle, D. S. The counselor: who? what? *Personnel and Guidance Journal*, 1972, *50*, 785–790.

Arendt, H. *The human condition.* Chicago: University of Chicago Press, 1958. (Paper ed.: Garden City: Anchor-Doubleday, 1959.)

Bell, R. L. The culturally deprived psychologist. *The Counseling Psychologist*, 1971, *2*, 104–107.

Carkhuff, R. R., & Berenson, B. G. *Beyond counseling and therapy.* New York: Holt, Rinehart & Winston, 1967.

Casavantes, E. Pride and prejudice: a Mexican-American dilemma. *Civil Rights Digest*, 1970, *3*, 22–27.

Cook, T. E. The influence of client-counselor value similarity on change in meaning during brief counseling. *Journal of Counseling Psychology*, 1966, *13*, 77–81.

Egan, J. H. The ten commandments for counselors. In J. M. Lee & N. J. Pallone (Eds.), *Readings in guidance and counseling.* New York: Sheed & Ward, 1966.

Fitzgibbons, D. J., & Shearn, C. R. Concepts of schizophrenia among mental health professionals: A factor-analysis study. *Journal of Consulting and Clinical Psychology*, 1972, *38*, 288–295.

Frankl, V. *Man's search for meaning.* Boston: Beacon Press, 1962.

Freud, S. *Psychopathology of everyday life*, 1901.

Freud, S. *A general introduction to psychoanalysis*, 1924. (Lecture 19)

Fromm, E. *The sane society.* New York: Fawcett, 1967 (originally published: New York: Holt, Rinehart & Winston, 1955).

Goffman, E. *The presentation of self in everyday life.* Garden City, N.Y.: Anchor, 1959.

Jung, C. G. [*Modern man in search of a soul*] (W. S. Dell & C. F. Baynes, trans.). New York: Harcourt, Brace & World, 1964.

Kaneshige, E. Cultural factors in group counseling and interaction. *Personnel and Guidance Journal*, 1973, *51*, 407–412.

Katz, R. L. The meaning of religion in healthy people. In O. H. Mowrer (Ed.), *Morality and mental health.* Chicago: Rand McNally, 1967, pp. 324-327. (Originally published, 1960, *Central Council of American Rabbis Journal.*)

Kincaid, M. Identity and therapy in the black community. *Personnel and Guidance Journal*, 1969, *47*, 884–890.

Laing, R. D. *The politics of experience.* New York: Ballantine Books, 1967.

Leacock, E. The concept of culture and its significance for school counselors. *Personnel and Guidance Journal*, 1968, *46*, 844–851.

Lee, S. D. *Social class bias in the diagnosis of mental illness* (Doctoral dissertation, University of Oklahoma, 1968). Ann Arbor, Mich.: University Microfilms No. 68-6959.

Linton, R. *The study of man.* New York: Appleton-Century-Crofts, 1936.

McCall, R. J. The defense mechanisms reexamined: A logical and phenomenal analysis. *Catholic Psychological Record*, 1963, Spring, 45–64.

Maritain, J. *Education at the crossroads.* New Haven: Yale University Press, 1943.

May, R. *Psychology and the human dilemma.* New York: Van Nostrand, 1967.

Munson, H. L. *Elementary school guidance: Concepts, dimensions, and practices.* Boston: Allyn & Bacon, 1970.

Patterson, C. H. The place of values in counseling and psychotherapy. *Journal of Counseling Psychology*, 1958, *5*, 216–223.

Patterson, C. H. Theories of counseling and psychotherapy (2nd ed.). New York: Harper & Row, 1973.

Peterson, J. A. *Counseling and values.* Scranton: International Textbook, 1970.

Pyke, S. W., & Ricks, F. A. The counselor and the female client. *The School Counselor*, 1973, *20*, 280–284.

Robb, W. J. Self-discovery and the role of the counselor. *Personnel and Guidance Journal*, 1967, *45*, 1008–1011.

Rosenthal, D. Changes in some moral values following psychotherapy. *Journal of Consulting Psychology*, 1955, *19*, 431–436.

Routh, D. K., & King, K. M. Social class bias in clinical judgment. *Journal of Consulting and Clinical Psychology*, 1972, *38*, 202–207.

Ryan, C. W. Counseling the culturally encapsulated American Indian. *Vocational Guidance Quarterly*, 1969, *18*, 123–126.

Rycroft, C. *A critical dictionary of psychoanalysis*. New York: Basic Books, 1968.

Schlien, J. Levels of abstraction in criteria. In H. Strupp & L. Luborsky (Eds.), *Research in psychotherapy* (Vol. 2). Washington, D.C.: American Psychological Association, 1962.

Schlossberg, N. K., & Pietrofesa, J. J. Perspectives on counseling bias: Implications for counseling education. *The Counseling Psychologist*, 1973, *4*, 44–54.

Seeman, M. On the meaning of alienation. *American Sociological Review*, 1959, *24*, 783–791.

Sue, D. W., & Sue, S. Counseling Chinese-Americans. *Personnel and Guidance Journal*, 1972, *50*, 637–644.

Symonds, P. M. *Dynamic psychology*. New York: Appleton-Century-Crofts, 1949.

Vontress, C. E. Cultural barriers in the counseling relationship. *Personnel and Guidance Journal*, 1969, *47*, 11–17.

Vontress, C. E. Counseling blacks. *Personnel and Guidance Journal*, 1970, *48*, 713–719.

Vordenberg, W. The impact of personal philosophies on counseling. *Personnel and Guidance Journal*, 1953, *31*, 439–440.

Williamson, E. G. Value orientation in counseling. *Personnel and Guidance Journal*, 1958, *36*, 520–528.

Williamson, E. G. Value options and the counseling relationship. *Personnel and Guidance Journal*, 1966, *44*, 617–623.

Wolf, A., & Schwartz, E. K. Psychoanalysis in groups: The role of values. *The American Journal of Psychoanalysis*, 1959, *19*, 37–52.

chapter six

The school counselor in perspective

The term *school counselor*, which is preferable to the redundancy *guidance counselor*, poses a few problems of its own. Is the school counselor a counselor who simply works in the school setting, or is he a specialized type of counselor—as a psychiatrist is a specialized type of physician? How do his colleagues and his clients perceive him? What can he do to make an impact on the quality of school life, and how can he best assure that his services will be utilized and appreciated? How can he most effectively implement the driving force of the counseling stance within the context of the school setting? Before we can answer these questions, let us listen to a typical counselor, teacher, and student discuss some of their feelings and perceptions of the school counselor. Each of these monologues is extracted from a set of recorded interviews conducted at different urban and suburban schools. At the end of the three monologues, I will offer some comments to clarify the issues brought to light.

THE COUNSELOR SPEAKS

(I have asked the counselor to describe his duties and responsibilities at the school and to tell me if he thought his preparation and training had been adequate.) "It's really difficult to answer those questions, although when you first asked them, I had stock answers to give you. But you see, the problem is that in this school the principal is short-handed because of the budget, so I have to fill in a lot of times when people are out, or maybe if there's a vacant staff position. You know, doing administrative types of things, like programming, attendance reports, filing, even... things that probably the secretary could do, only he can't afford to hire another secretary.... I don't know if this is the usual situation 'cause this is the first school that I've worked in, but frankly I resent it.

"Sure, some of the time I'm doing what I was trained to do. The other day a fourth grader came down crying, and she couldn't stop. Her teacher had tried to find out what was wrong, but the girl refused to tell the teacher, so she sent her down to me. I sat down with her and we spoke for about fifteen minutes, establishing a good rapport, and she finally told me that her mother had gone away

for the afternoon and she didn't have her house key to get in after school. She was afraid that the mother would yell at her, and that's why she didn't tell the teacher, either. But I guess she felt she could talk to me.... I guess I did the 'right' thing with her. You know, after that short interview, I felt real good ... like I had accomplished more in half an hour than I sometimes accomplish in a week. I could really enjoy my job if I didn't have to put up with all the trivial paperwork."

(I asked him how he came to be given these minor clerical jobs.) "Well, it happened right from the beginning. The second day of school, the principal came up to my office...I was just sitting and waiting for someone with a problem to come in, and he made a joke about how he wished he were a guidance counselor living the life of leisure. Then he asked me if I would mind helping him with a little something—that's the words he used—so what could I say. Besides, I had nothing to do at that time, and I thought it would be a nice gesture. That little something involved setting up eight hundred folders for the new files. It took four weeks to finish.... Oh, about the teachers. We get along real well. They all seem to like me and we have some good laughs together in the cafeteria. To them, I have an easy job because I don't have to teach and I have my own office. But I don't see it that way. I always find that I'm busy with something, usually doing something for someone else. Also, the teachers don't really treat me as a professional...I mean they would never come down and talk about a problem or a teaching situation. They send down some of the kids they can't control, but that's about it.... Oh, it also upsets me that the students see coming down to my office as a threat, because they know that that's where they go when they don't behave. But it really shouldn't be like that. I'm not a disciplinarian...."

THE TEACHER SPEAKS

(This is a teacher from a different school. I asked her to discuss what she thought of the school counselor, and if she thought the counselor was doing her job well.) "All the teachers have great respect for the counselor in our school because of something she did the first week of the term—in fact, it was the first day of school, when we had our teachers' meeting. She had just replaced Mr. Davis who is on sabbatical and who never did much of anything during his three years here. But at the beginning of the term, as I said, when we had our meeting, which she didn't even have to attend, she asked us if she could speak with all of us a few minutes after the principal concluded the official meeting. All of us stayed to listen. Then she told us a little of her background and invited us to meet with her once a week after school to discuss how things were going in our classes, what problems we were having, etc. At first there was some grumbling because most of the teachers didn't want to stay late, but she made it clear that the meeting was optional and only for those teachers who had things to discuss or wanted to learn from listening to the other teachers discussing their problems. We all thought it nice, and unusual, that she was willing to stay late to help us. First impressions are important, and they certainly were correct in this case.

"She turned out to be a very dedicated and conscientious counselor. She always gave the feeling that she knew what she was doing, and that she had plans. For example, she offered to speak in our classes, either to assist us if we wished or to supplement some lessons in hygiene and the like. We all thought that was nice. She also organized quite a few after-school activities that the kids seemed to like, and we had a joke about how she would always run around the school doing things—always busy and active. Most of the teachers, especially after they got to know her, began to come to the once-a-week meeting, and you'd be surprised how helpful those meetings were to us. Instead of having to send down our difficult children every time they got out of hand, we knew that we could discuss our problems with these children at the next meeting. I guess you could say that each of us began to act a little like counselors because of those regular meetings with her.

"A few of the teachers, from what I understand, met with her to discuss some personal problems that they were having. I don't know if that's a part of her job, but it sure did a lot to increase our feelings toward her. I guess you could say that we really *appreciate* all the things she has done for us. She gives us the feeling of caring, and even more important the feeling that she is competent and willing to work to improve things around here. She's always so busy that we try to handle our problems first, before going to her for advice. We're lucky to have her as our counselor, and she's done a lot to change my whole view of what counseling is ... especially after that Mr. Davis...."

THE STUDENT SPEAKS

(The student, an eighth-grade boy, was asked to offer his opinion about the guidance counselor at his school.) "I never met Mr. S when I was in seventh grade, but I heard the kids talking about him a lot, and I knew they liked him. I never got in any trouble, so I never *had* to go to see him, but my friend R—— was sent down last year for cutting, and he told me Mr. S is an all-right guy.... Near the beginning of this year my father died, you know, and I missed almost a month of school and fell behind in all my work. No one told me to, but I decided to see Mr. S on my own. I don't even know why. I was scared and kept putting it off, but finally I figured I'd go down to talk to him. When I got down to his office, he wasn't there, so I just left and figured I'd come back another time. But later that day he came up to my class and asked Mrs. R if he could speak to me. He said that the office secretary had seen me looking for him, and if I had a few minutes now, we could talk for awhile. I was really surprised that he came to see me—I mean he's probably busy and all....

"Anyway, we talked for—it must have been over an hour. I missed my next class, and he said it's OK, he'd write a note for me. I don't even remember what we talked about—I guess about school, my friends, drugs, about my father's dying.... I know that when I left his office, I felt a lot better. He told me that he had a group of a few kids at the school who met once a week just to talk about anything they wanted to, and he asked if maybe I'd like to come to the group just to give it a try.... I said I'd think about it, and then decided to go....

"Now I've been going for almost four months, and I think it's really a good thing for my head. We just sit around and talk, about anything we want to, and some of the kids really seem to have problems, even though I don't, but I can relate to them anyway...." (I asked if there were any other guidance services offered in the school.) "Sure, there's a community club where some of the kids do things for the community, like have a 'clean-up drive,' and there's a work program for the ninth graders who want to work in a store part-time helping out, but I didn't get involved in any other things than the group.... Mr. S is always telling us about different things he's doing at the school, and some of the kids are interested, but I don't have more time than for just the group....

"It's funny, you know, how in a lot of schools the guidance counselor is someone you get sent down to if you're in trouble, but in our school he's a real nice guy and you feel that you can talk to him about anything you want.... I mean, he's not a fink or anything...."

COMMENTARY

Clearly, there is some discrepancy between the way our first counselor perceives his job and carries out his duties, the way the teacher describes the counselor at her school, and the way the student presents the counselor at his school. These examples were chosen to illustrate the problems and pitfalls confronting the school counselor, as well as to show the many opportunities available to him to prove himself of service to the school and to the community. Let us examine each issue, to gain a sense of perspective about the problem.

We note that our counselor (C1) on page 149 complains about being given unrelated work to do—things such as filing, administrative tasks, and so on. This is a common complaint of school counselors, perhaps the most common complaint. Boy and Pine (1969) point out that prior to the National Defense Education Act of 1958, administrators did not take seriously the attempts by school counselors to extricate themselves from trivial duties and administrative burdens by tending toward therapeutic counseling; but since the passage of that act counselors have been viewed in a more professional light. This evolutionary change, however, seems to have had no effect upon C1 at his school, and we must question why this is so. It is evident, both from his attitude and from what he says, that the clerical encumbrances placed upon him are indirectly a result of his own doing and not entirely the principal's fault. By failing to communicate to the other school personnel the scope of his job as he saw it, by not having a clearly defined idea of what he was supposed to be doing—and doing it—C1 invited the opportunity he now complains about. It is not uncommon to find that counselors who complain most about the low level of the functions they are asked to perform are the very same counselors who fail to take the initiative in performing the higher level functions which they believe that their jobs entail. Likewise, we find that those counselors who, from the beginning of their tenure assume an active and dynamic approach, who make their presence felt from the first day of school until the end of the semester, suffer less from the misunderstandings and exploitation which plague these others. It is only the assertive and confident school counselor, the counselor with a sense of certainty about why he is there and what he is expected to do, who is not taken advantage of by others around him, particularly by the administration.

Returning to the present case, the evidence is clear and indisputable. Compare the behavior of this counselor (C1) with the behavior of the counselor who replaced Mr. Davis (C2), and we can immediately pinpoint the cause of the problem. C1, by his own admission, spent the first day of school sitting in his office, waiting for something to happen. He took no initiative, made no effort to bring his services out to the teachers and the students. C2, on the other hand, did just the opposite. She went out recruiting, actively and enthusiastically presenting herself and her services to the teachers. Unlike C1, she didn't wait for things to happen—she made them happen. When the principal came into C1's office, he noted the lack of activity on the counselor's part and felt comfortable suggesting some busy work for the counselor. C1 invited this to happen, and there is no way around that conclusion. It would be difficult for me to imagine the principal at C2's school asking her to do the same type of chores, since she was so clearly engaged in a definitive, constructive counseling policy which took up her time.

An important first rule, then, is this: *The school counselor should walk in the first day of school with a clearly defined course of action and begin at once to implement this plan and to let it be known to his colleagues and to the students.* In this way, he not only protects himself from the opportunism and misunderstandings of the other school personnel, but he puts forth a professional appearance that will ultimately prove efficacious to his plans.

Next let us look at the relationships between the teachers in the school and the counselor. C1 describes the relationship as "lots of laughs" but then goes on to complain that the teachers do not treat him as a professional. But how can they, if he does not establish a professional relationship with them? C2, the opposite of C1, establishes from the very beginning a totally professional and serious relationship with the teachers at her school. She explains what her services are, and she offers her services to the teachers. Consequently, they respond to her as a professional and respect her accordingly. They not only seek her advice but feel free to speak to her about their own personal problems. It would be difficult to imagine the teachers at C2's school asking her to do clerical work, in view of the polished professional appearance she articulates. It should be pointed out, however, that while conducting himself professionally, the counselor must be careful not to alienate himself from the other teachers by implying either in words or in actions that he is more professional, or on a higher level, than the teachers or the other school personnel. This is a difficult balance to maintain—between functional professionalism and social egalitarianism, between eliciting respect and still maintaining friendship and cordiality —and it is the mark of a successful counselor that he is able to hold the tenuous line between the virtues of confidence and certainty and the vice of elitism, without recourse to such artificial facades as coldness, detachment, and snobbishness. The school counselor, like the small town doctor, is at most times a friend and comforter; but when needed for professional services, he must be someone who is held by his constituents in the highest regard.

C2 seems to have achieved this balance well, while C1 chose to retreat from the professional stance and immerse himself in the pleasures of friendly badinage, which ultimately served little professional good. Our second rule, therefore, could be stated like this: *The school counselor must at all times maintain a professional attitude, which should not interfere with his ability to conduct harmonious and cordial relationships with other school personnel and with students. He must exude professionalism but avoid elitism.*

Finally, let us examine the relationships established between each of these counselors and the students at his school. C1, we note, did quite well when given an opportunity to work with a student who was experiencing a distressing problem. But it was pure chance that this student availed herself of C1's services, for C1 made no efforts to reach out to the students. Mr. S (C3) on the other hand, made a conscientious effort to reach out to the students, to tell them about his services and to publicize them in the school. He did not wait for our student to come back down to his office, but rather he went up to the student's classroom to find him and to ask him why he had come. This type of initiative is

154

not only admirable and compassionate, but it is an effective counseling tool as well.

The kinds of situations and difficulties exemplified by our typical counselor, teacher, and student have been a source of concern to professional counselors and counselor educators since the beginnings of the counseling movement. In their broad perspective, they fall under the rubric of "role definition"—of clearly defining the role of the counselor. But in practice, defining the role of the counselor is far less important than teaching counselors the meaning of counseling and instilling within them the right attitudes about counseling. A role definition of counseling will emerge naturally as the counselor understands and responds to the needs of the students, teachers, and administrators with whom he works. Koch (1972), in discussing some of the problems in school counseling, has pointed out that the role of the counselor is often defined by the administration rather than by any actions on the counselor's initiative. Koch also points out that most students take the attitude that counselors are only "schedule changers," an attitude which results from the administrator's encumbering the counselors with such duties. The role definition, in this case, is not determined by the counselor, but rather by the situation at his school or by the attitudes of his administrative supervisor. Such a case is typical, and the counselor must always keep in mind that more often than not his role will be defined not by the criteria of what he should be doing but rather by the demands of the immediate situation.

In discussing the problem of role definition, Haettenschwiller (1970) points out that an "interdependence exists between the focal person—the counselor—and members of his role set—principal, teacher, parent, student, and counselor educator." All of these individuals exert a definite force on the developing role of the counselor, helping in their own ways to shape that role to their expectations. This process of shaping is accomplished through the disbursement of rewards and punishments, what Haettenschwiller calls "sanctions":

Through these rewards ... control is exercised over the role enactment of each member of the organization. In place of rewards, however, it is more appropriate to speak of sanctions, both positive and negative. Positive sanctions may include the immediate rewards of approval or praise, the instrumental rewards which facilities—for example, a secretary—provide, or the rewards deriving from compliance or collaboration by members of the role set. Negative sanctions may include restricting the performance of professional duties or prescribing nonprofessional duties, refusal to cooperate in the enactment of the professional role, negative criticism, or termination of contract. (p. 438)

The implications of this arrangement are that the counselor is bribed and blackmailed into submitting to roles which are acceptable to those who disburse the sanctions. Such a position is clearly incompatible with the goals of counseling and with the interest of the students who depend on the counselor for guidance and encouragement.

Recognizing this difficulty, Haettenschwiller suggests that the counselor must derive his power—his rewards—from outside the school boundary, from professional people with whom he can communicate openly and without compromise, rather than from administrators, teachers, parents, students, and staff.

The problem of role definition is complicated even further by the multiple roles and identities the school counselor is asked to assume during the performance of his duties. The counselor is a different "other to others": He maintains a changing persona, a flexibility and adaptability which have become his hallmark. Shertzer and Stone (1963), in reviewing the literature, have found that the counselor is perceived differently by most of those people with whom he comes in contact. Students see the counselor as being particularly helpful only in the areas of educational-vocational decision-making; teachers see the counselors as administrators to be tolerated, providing ancillary services which are expendable, who pamper students, speak in obscure jargon, and often hide behind the veneer of confidentiality when their activities are challenged; administrators view the counselor as a jack-of-all-trades who rarely succeeds; parents look toward the counselor as a persuasive agent of change in the areas of vocational and educational choice, or to correct many of the child-rearing errors they have made over the years; the general public looks toward the counselor to promote more effective manpower utilization for the country's economic and political needs. It is the job of counselors, argue Shertzer and Stone, to clarify these misconceptions and multiple demands by clearly articulating their own roles. The difficulty here, however, is the lack of consensus by counselors themselves as to what their role should be and how they should go about performing this role. This is a problem that will not be solved by counselors alone; more research and more dialogue among professionals is needed to explore the myriad complexities of this problem scientifically and pragmatically. Knapp and Denny (1961) suggest three guidelines for future research: First, counselors should be encouraged to provide data "concerning actual procedures which guidance specialists have followed in building guidance services" (p. 49). They should keep written logs of their day-to-day activities to enable researchers to determine the relative appropriation of time by effective vs. ineffective counselors. Second, a careful analysis of counseling time must be made to determine the most efficient use of time. "Counseling time must be analyzed to determine those needs which would more profitably be met through some other medium such as group guidance" (p. 50). Third, research must be conducted in the area of staff orientation, the relationships between the counselor and other staff members. Although much of this research has been undertaken since 1961, it still remains primarily the responsibility of the individual counselor to define his own role.

A third principle, therefore, may be stated as follows: *It is the responsibility of the counselor to understand and to articulate his role as he sees it. He must be aware of the multiple perceptions and multiple demands that his position encourages, and he must try his best to clarify to those with whom he works what his real purpose is and what his legitimate responsibilities are.*

This can best be done when the school counselor understands his rightful place within the educational organization. The counselor does not stand outside of the educational establishment, functioning as an adjunct to that establishment; rather, he is an integral part of the educational process, acting as either a catalyst or a guide in the education of the students at his school. Hobbs (1958) has argued that counselors should have a closer connection with the instructional program of the school than they now have. This closer connection can be achieved, he points out, if the counselors "have a continuing responsibility for contributing directly to the major purposes for which educational institutions are presumed to exist" (p. 596). In order for this to happen, however, the counselor must be careful to avoid the pressures upon him to be all things to all people. Boy (1972) suggests, quite correctly, that when the counselor attempts to satisfy all of the demands imposed upon him, he faces the danger of being nothing definite to anyone. If he attempts to satisfy all groups in determining his role, then he will be performing duties that are self-protective rather than living up to his counseling obligations as they relate to the individual child. If he responds to pressures of the moment, he can lose the opportunity to develop a role which has long-range consequences for both youth and the counseling profession.

It is necessary, therefore, that the school counselor have a thorough understanding of his place in the school and his position relative to the positions of the teachers, the principal, and other school personnel. In the following section we will explore the dimensions of the school counselor in perspective.

THE SCHOOL COUNSELOR IN REVIEW

Within the school, the counselor is a specialist who is asked to perform a variety of specialized services, ranging from intensive counseling to implementing extra-curricular programs. As a specialist, he is expected not only to have know how but to communicate to his colleagues and clients a professional attitude and a maturity which reflect his competency as well as his personal achievements. But to what degree can he be successful in communicating this attitude and in implementing his skills? Much depends on the way that he sees the job and the way that other school personnel, particularly teachers and the principal, look upon his position. For the counselor's actual effectiveness (as opposed to his potential effectiveness—see chapter 5) depends greatly upon others' receptivity toward his services and recognition of his competencies.

Carmical and Calvin (1970) tried to determine how school counselors "viewed their job functions and what their role in these functions should be." They found that the top five functions rated by counselors were:

1 Providing the student an opportunity to "talk through his problems."
2 Counseling with potential dropouts.
3 Counseling with students concerning academic failures.
4 Counseling with students in evaluating personal assets and limitations.
5 Counseling with students concerning learning difficulties. (p. 282)

Several significant insights can be gleaned from these findings. We note first that with the exception of the fourth point, each of the counseling functions is concerned primarily with students who either fail to adjust appropriately to the school environment or exhibit manifest behavioral problems such as dropping out or failing. The counselors interviewed were unable to arrive at a consensus about how they could help the average or above-average student in their capacities as counselors. Such an attitude is common not only among school counselors but among students as well. Heilfron (1960), in a study of high-school students' perceptions of the counseling function, found,

high school students feel that students who are performing well academically and socially need much less counseling than students who are intellectually inferior, socially immature, or unrealistic in their aspirations; only students who display obvious character disorders should be referred to agencies outside school for professional help.

These two findings suggest that students expect counselors to devote themselves to individuals who exhibit overtly that they have problems, possibly to the exclusion of students who need help not necessarily in overcoming social or intellectual handicaps, but in finding the best ways to use their resources. (p. 136)

The fact that such an attitude is common, of course, does not mean that such an attitude is good. On the contrary, there is evidence to indicate that the school counselor may be inadvertently contributing to the waste of our greatest natural resource: talent. For how can the counselor believe that he is meeting his obligations if he confines himself primarily to working with youth who are having difficulty succeeding in life, at the expense of those youth who have potential for greatness. True, that the problem youth needs his services; this is not to be denied. But equally true is the proposition that all of the students at his school can benefit from counseling, many of them in equal proportion to the troubled or problem-laden youth. Our eighth-grade student, as we saw earlier, benefited enormously from his interactions with C3, even though he exhibited no manifest problems which required C3's immediate attention.

A fourth principle may be stated as follows: *The school counselor, to be effective, must recognize his responsibilities to all students, including the failing student, the disruptive student, the potential drop-out, the student with an emotional problem, the student with a learning difficulty,* as well as *the gifted student, the average student, the withdrawn and shy student, and the student who does nothing during the course of his studies to attract the attention of the counselor or other school personnel.*

A second important insight gleaned from Carmical and Calvin's work is that counselors shy away from treating students with so-called emotional problems. The top-five function list carefully eschews any reference to dealing with intensive problems. Such an attitude is easy to understand for two reasons. First, as I mentioned in chapter 1, counselors are taught to believe that their competencies are limited to less severe problems, and that more serious problems are in the exclusive province of psychotherapy and psychiatry, a belief which has little or no basis in fact. The second reason, however, is compelling. The severe limitation of time imposed on the counselor by the unworkable student-to-counselor ratio at the typical school precludes the possibility of devoting enough attention to any one student to help him on a dynamic, intensive, emotional level.

While this second position is appreciated, it should be pointed out that situations in mental hospitals are not so much different, with respect to psychiatrist-to-patient ratio, from the situation in the public schools. Psychiatrists and psychiatric social workers who practice at these hospitals know that the best way to reach the largest number of patients is through group activities, including both group psychotherapy and group social, educational, and civic activities. The school counselor should also attempt to reach the core of seriously disturbed students at his school by setting up activities to which he could invite these students and supplementing these group activities with one-to-one counseling sessions, which need not be so frequent as to be prohibitive.

The counselor who does not wish to work with the severely disturbed, who believes he is not competent to handle such cases, will find much support in his job setting to reinforce this position. Studies of school personnel have shown almost unanimous agreement with the position that the school counselor is ill equipped to deal effectively with the severely disturbed student. Grant (1954), for instance, found that "in looking at the data in the personal-emotional area, it should be noted that approximately 70% of the teachers and administrators feel that someone other than the counselor should work with students in this area.... It should also be noted that counselors themselves seem uncertain of their ability to assist students in the types of problems presented in the personal-emotional category" (p. 76). In a later study, Bergstein and Grant (1961) also found that parents of school children "perceived school counselors to be more helpful with educational and vocational problems than with personal-emotional-social problems" (p. 703).

These studies, however, reflect only what the counselor is perceived as being able to accomplish, not what in fact he is or is not able to accomplish. Therein lies the important difference. For despite the agreement as to his limitations, study after study has shown that experienced psychotherapists are no more competent than experienced counselors to treat severely disturbed patients or clients. Counseling efficacy was discussed in chapter 4.

A fifth principle could be stated: *The school counselor must recognize and develop his competencies to treat severely disturbed students and students suffering from emotional problems, particularly through the use of groups, after-school programs, educational activities, and other nonintensive forms of treatment. The school counselor must, furthermore, strengthen his commitment to this group of students, since he is likely to be the first professional with whom they come in contact and who is able to help them. During his training, the school counselor must learn to develop attitudes and skills which will enable him to work effectively with this group, who have long been ignored in the school setting.*

As we examine each of these principles that guide his actions, our conception of the school counselor undergoes a number of changes. We see the various levels of functioning on which he is required to perform, and we understand the obstacles which may make his job difficult at times. Our image of the counselor —as he shifts from the intimate intensity of a face-to-face counseling interview to the less personal administrative function of coordinator of after-school activities—fuses the precise skill of a specialist with the broad range of a generalist. Wrenn (1962), in discussing the role of the counselor, sees him as both a specialist and a generalist:

The counselor is a generalist in the sense of his being widely available to the total school population and attempting to possess some knowledge of the total school program. He is a generalist also in the sense that he should be acquainted with the complete scope of school referral resources and know how these may be utilized by himself or by other members of the staff. The counselor is a specialist in his specific knowledge of the student and in his ability to relate himself effectively to the student in both individual and group situations. He is a specialist in the total scope of student learnings in and out of the classroom. He is a specialist in the collation and interpretation of information about individual students and student populations—to the student himself, to staff, to administrators, and to parents. (p. 143)

With this view in mind, let us explore specifically how this specialist as generalist implements his counseling principles into concrete, practical activities.

THE COUNSELOR'S ACTIVITIES

First and foremost, we have the face-to-face counseling interaction, which will be discussed in detail in Part Four of this book. It is clear that the face-to-face meeting between counselor and client, although highly effective and desirable, is a difficult reality to bring about in the schools. Counselors' time is precious and to allocate a significant chunk of that time to helping a single student would not appear to be the most expeditious utilization of the counseling resource. Rather, the counselor would do better to concentrate on ways of reaching the greatest number of students in the least amount of time.

To this end, we have group counseling which is both an efficient and practical method for communicating with a large number of students in a relatively brief period of time. The counselor can schedule regular weekly meetings of small groups. Even without much campaigning, word of such groups will travel through the corridors quickly, attracting those students who believe they will benefit from the group experience. The counselor may also post on the student bulletin boards creatively designed announcements to herald the groups to the student population. Remember, it is always the responsibility of the counselor to make his services known.

The school counselor may also effect significant therapeutic changes by setting up and administering after-school programs, some of which are discussed in Part Seven. The extension of the school day, which to be effective must be voluntary, is a great hope for both students and teachers alike. For it is clear that students, teachers, administrators, and counselors who voluntarily choose to participate in school functions beyond the regular school hours are not only

160

*The counselor's
effectiveness can be
increased by
conferences with other
members of the school
team.*

highly motivated to begin with, but are also more likely to benefit from their experiences, since they would not continue the activity unless it were beneficial. The way to encourage students and teachers to remain after the close of the school day is to design programs which are interesting, challenging, and clearly of benefit to the volunteers who participate in them. It is an advertising—a public relations—effort that the counselor engages in, an effort which, if successful, could prove most important for the educational, intellectual, and emotional health of the school community.

Finally, the school counselor can implement many of his ideas into actions by sharing these ideas with other members of the school team. He can and should confer with the principal, teachers, parents, paraprofessionals, community leaders, and students to learn from them what their needs are and how his ideas may be transformed into actions which will be of benefit to them.

By actively engaging himself—by committing himself to his beliefs—the school counselor can become an effective agent of growth within the school setting.

If we temporarily turn our attention away from what the school counselor might do, and examine what the typical school counselor does do, the results should be revealing.

Carey and Garris (1971) raise the question, "What does the counselor do which is different from others, or which cannot be done as well by others?" This is an important question which helps not only to clarify the role of the school counselor but also to justify the counseling function as well. Trotzer and Kassera (1971) have attempted to answer this question by determining what the

display 6.1

**COUNSELOR CONTACT
WITH STUDENTS**

	% of student contact	% of total time
Student contact		44.3
Educational	33.0	14.6
Vocational	14.8	6.6
Personal	25.7	11.4
Scheduling	8.0	3.5
School activity (attendance)	4.3	1.9
Group	5.6	2.5
Test interpretation	1.2	.5
Student and teacher (both present)	.3	.1
Test administration	7.1	3.2

Note. From "Do Counselors Do What They Are Taught?" by James P. Trotzer and Wayne J. Kassera, *The School Counselor*, 1971, *18*, 335-341. Copyright (1971) American Personnel and Guidance Association. Reprinted with permission.

display 6.2

**COUNSELOR CONTACT
WITH NONSTUDENTS**

	% of nonstudent activity time	% of total time
Nonstudent interview activity		23.3
Committee meetings	9.1	2.1
Faculty meetings	5.0	1.2
Teacher/nurse conference	24.6	5.7
Staff	16.1	3.8
Parent	17.1	4.0
Principal/ administrator	12.1	2.8
Minister, police, probation officer	2.8	.6
Psychologist, social worker, welfare	5.7	1.3
College representative, military, salesmen	7.5	1.8

display 6.3

**NONINTERVIEW
ACTIVITIES**

	% of noninterview activity time	% of total time
Noninterview activity		26.6
Mail	6.9	1.8
Write-up interviews	4.5	1.2
Prepare for testing	2.6	.7
Desk work and reports	39.5	10.5
Phone	2.2	.6
Coffee, pop, etc.	11.7	3.1
Looking up people and materials for students	.7	.2
Supervision and teaching	25.0	6.6
Miscellaneous	6.9	1.9

actual activities of the counselor are. Display 6.1 illustrates how the counselor's school time is divided between contact with students, noninterview activities, and contact with people other than students. Display 6.2 and 6.3 are even more revealing; they show that counselors spend the bulk of their time not in activities that are directly beneficial to the students but rather in extraneous activities that might well be done by other personnel.

This is an unfortunate situation, but it is one which has persisted from the very beginnings of the guidance and counseling movement. The causes of this predicament are complex and worthy of an intensive study in themselves; but suffice it to say at this point that the more clearly the counselor defines his role to himself and to those with whom he works, the less likelihood there is that his time will be used unexpeditiously. The opposite is also true, as we pointed out with C1: if the counselor is unsure of what he is to do, if he sits and waits for things to happen, for his services to be requested, he is more likely to spend an injudicious portion of his time on noncounseling tasks.

THE COUNSELOR'S PROFESSIONALISM

This brings us back to the issue of professionalism. How can the counselor unequivocally emphasize his professional status and encourage other school personnel to utilize his valuable professional resources? This is a question which has been debated time and again in the literature. Van Riper (1972) points out that the school counselor can only become a professional by what he does—by his "ostensive acts." "In spite of how busy school counselors have been," he suggests, "their work has lacked purpose and meaningful results" (p. 325). The explanation for this, as we have seen, is simple: the counselor spends too much of his time in noncounseling, and even worse, in nonprofessional activities imposed upon him by an administration which is neither sensitive to his needs nor aware of his capabilities. McCully (1962) tackles the problem in somewhat more detail. Suggesting that the problem of nonprofessionalism dates back to the origins of the vocational guidance movement, McCully argues that newer, more innovative approaches are needed to professionalize the movement. He lists six developmental stages leading toward professionalization, which are summarized as follows:

1 The unique social service of the school counselor in its performance must be identified in a manner which will differentiate it from the services of the other members of the school staff.
2 Standards for the selection and training must be developed, and they must be acceptable to the corporate group of qualified school counselors and to the preparatory schools.
3 For selection and training standards to be functional, schools must be accredited for training counselors.
4 Counselors should be certified.
5 The counselors as individuals and as a group must gain sufficient autonomy to permit them to perform their duties in the interest of the public.
6 The corporate group of counselors must have and enforce a code of ethics for its members. (pp. 683-687 *passim*)

More than a decade after the publication of this paper, many of these developmental stages have become realities, and yet the professionalization of the counselor is still only a glimmering hope. Why is this? Again there is no clear answer, but evidence would seem to indicate that counselors and counselor educators still have a long way to go in improving their own self-image of their professionalism, let alone communicating this image to others.

Arbuckle (1972) suggests that the contemporary school counselor lacks a strong professional identity. The counselor, he says, should have distinguishing qualities which set him apart from other teaching staff and other school personnel. He should be involved especially with the helping conditions that exist in the school, identifying himself with the human needs that manifest themselves. "His primary professional function—and his particular professional contribution—is in the counseling involvement with individuals, small groups of students, teachers, or parents ... individuals with stresses and problems because of minority position, their general youthful alienation, or their drug involvement" (p. 789). As the counselor does this, there exists a greater likelihood that his singular professional identity will clearly emerge and be acknowledged.

163

THE COUNSELOR'S ROLE CONFLICTS

Then again, the school counselor is in a highly unusual position. Unlike most of his colleagues in the mental health profession, the school counselor works in proximity and often under the direct supervision of a person who is not directly allied to his discipline, namely, the school principal. How unusual a situation it is, in perspective, to have a "professional" working under the auspices of an outsider to the profession. How can the counselor expect his principal to understand the complexities of his position when the principal more than likely has had no experience as a school counselor himself?

Conflicts between counselors and principals, particularly on issues relating to the counselor's role and his activities, are numerous and common. It should be pointed out, however, that in many areas counselors and principals find themselves supplementing each other rather than clashing. Schmidt (1962) has found that counselors and principals generally exhibit high agreement on the role of the counselor and on which responsibilities are associated with that role. Sweeney (1966) found that counselors and principals ranked attributes for counselors similarly, but principals tended to stress leadership more than did counselors. Moreover, the principals tended to see the counselor in terms of attributes considered necessary for an administrator—a likely bias. Both of these studies would support the argument that counselors and principals are not as far apart as is commonly believed. Hart and Prince (1970), on the other hand, found contradicting results. In an attempt to investigate "the discrepancy between the principal's expectations of the counselor's role and the ideal role as taught to the counselor during his training ... and the effect counselor experience and training have had in shaping the way principals perceive counselor role" (p. 375), Hart and Prince found that the principals with no counselor training were more apt to assign disciplinary duties and clerical tasks to the counselor than were counselor educators. Furthermore, they found that principals and counselors disagreed on other important points as well: principals felt they should have access to all confidential files; principals did not see the counselor dealing with the personal-emotional problems of the student; principals believed that the counselors should accept many varied duties not commonly associated with counseling. In short, it would seem that principals without training and experience in counseling should not be entrusted to act as supervisors (or "immediate administrative directors," as is often the case) for the school counselor.

It has often been suggested that the principal may feel threatened by the counselor, who may be the only other person in the school who rivals the esteem and professional status of the principal. Such suggestions are difficult to prove or disprove, but it is important that the counselor be sensitive to the possibility that he (or his position, as the case may be) poses a threat to the principal. Chenault and Seegars (1962) have identified possible sources of conflict between counselors and their principals, and Filbeck (1965) has offered some specific suggestions of how the counselor should behave in order to minimize conflict between himself and his principal. Filbeck states,

The counselor must be highly sensitive to those aspects of his work that are threatening to his principal. He must be able to anticipate what professional counseling activities are anxiety inducing; and where professional considerations (e.g., ethics) dictate proceeding in a manner that will arouse anxiety and antagonism on the part of his administrator, he must prepare and plan strategies to alleviate or reduce such feelings. It is suggested here that helpful strategies include: verbalized understanding of the principal's feelings, open communications with the principal, and a constant professional, competent demeanor to develop confidence, on the part of the principal, in the counselor as a proficient professional in the field of education. (p. 896)

Having examined this possibility of conflict, we can now state our sixth principle: *The school counselor must work effectively with his principal, taking into account and showing a sensitivity to the principal's needs, expectations, and fears. The counselor has an opportunity to increase his professional posture by establishing a viable, mutually respectful, and responsive relationship with the principal.*

Finally, we shall turn our attention to the ways in which the counselor is typically perceived by the teachers at his school. Evidence indicates overwhelmingly that despite some negative feelings, teachers tend to perceive school counselors as helpful, responsible professionals who are a great resource for the teaching staff. McCreary and Miller (1966), in a survey of elementary school counselors and teachers in California, found that the teachers evaluated the counseling staff as helpful in testing individual pupils, in providing individual counseling, in assisting with classroom problems, and in participating in conferences with parents. Sherman et al., in a comprehensive study, found that although teachers have some points of dissatisfaction, on the whole they experience the school counselor in a highly positive light. Display 6.4, which shows

---

display 6.4

COUNSELOR ATTITUDES AND CHARACTERISTICS
AS PERCEIVED BY TEACHERS*

Rank order, item	(N-422) Percent	Rank order, item	(N-422) Percent	Rank order, item	(N-422) Percent
1 Friendly	67	7 Well trained	29	13 Discouraging of communication	7
2 Cooperative	56	8 Efficient and effective	28	14 Condescending	7
3 Likeable people	42	9 Removed from reality	19	15 Indifferent	7
4 Understanding	35	10 Highly professional person	17	16 Too status conscious	6
5 Encouraging communication	33	11 Escaping from classroom	17	17 Demanding	2
6 Professional toward teachers	32	12 Too soft	15	18 Hostile	1

*Note. From "Teacher-Counselor Communication" by R. Sherman, D. Albaggia, M. Cohen, E. Dell, J. Nadler, I. Shapiro, and B. Silverman, *The School Counselor*, 1969, *17*, 55–62. Copyright (1969) American Personnel and Guidance Association. Reprinted with permission.

how teachers perceive their school counselor, indicates that the feelings for the counselor are generally of a positive dimension. However, when we look closely at this table, we find some discouraging indices: only 29% of the teachers interviewed perceived the counselor as "well trained," and only 28% found the counselor "efficient and effective." Even more distressing, only 17% of the teachers considered the counselor a "highly professional person." What do these results tell us? Mainly, that although counselors tend to be well liked by the teachers at their schools, they are not always respected as professionals should be respected, nor are they always perceived as being competent to handle serious and difficult problems.

One of the major difficulties faced by the school counselor, as we can see from all of these studies, is making his professionalism felt by his colleagues. Teachers and principals are prone to diminish the counselor's capabilities and minimize his or her professionalism. In chapter 2 we explored the idea of the "counselor as a professional" and referred to the self-fulfilling prophesy. Perhaps there is no better example in practice of the self-fulfilling prophesy than we find in the school setting, where the counselor, having been taught the limits of his professional capabilities, communicates these limits subtly to his colleagues, who in turn subscribe to these arbitrarily imposed limitations.

Stintzi and Hutcheon (1972), in discussing the multiple roles of the school counselor, analyze how the counselor's role is perceived by the counselor himself, by the students, by the teachers, by the administrators, and by the school district. Display 6.5 shows the different components which constitute the counselor's role as they are perceived by his constituency and by his colleagues. We see from these results an overall positive image of the counselor, in which he is perceived and respected as a professional who is deeply committed to his work. He is viewed as a constructive, indispensable member of the educational team, who works with students, teachers, and administrators to improve the quality of education. Unfortunately, because these results do not tally with other studies which analyze the counselor's use of time and the demands placed upon him by other members of the school staff, we must suspect that this list represents the *ideal* image of the counselor's role rather than the practical reality. The discrepancy that exists between this perception and the analysis of his function as compiled by Trotzer and Kassera (1971) is directly related to the loss of professional identity suffered by the school counselor as he endeavors to perform his duties.

Related to this issue is a question that has recently received much attention at professional meetings and in the professional journals. "To what degree is the counselor responsible for maintaining or for changing the institution which employs and sponsors him?" With the rising level of social and political awareness of the 1960s, coupled with the activism of youth and the particular assertions of angry minority groups, counselors were compelled to reexamine their roles in the face of heated social pressures. As the system itself came under attack—as the very premises and principles which have guided this country's development came under the fire of critical scrutiny and thoughtful

display 6.5

THE MULTIPLE ROLES OF THE SCHOOL COUNSELOR*

The counselor's role in his view

1 He is an adviser precariously balanced in a mid-position.
2 He cannot be an administrator and a counselor at the same time.
3 He should not be a disciplinarian.
4 He must be able to relate to students, parents, and faculty in counseling.
5 He should be a listener, treat discussions in confidence.
6 He should be sincere and honest—not a phony.
7 He should be active in the community.
8 He should be active in scheduling individual planning and learning, and programs and special placement.

The counselor's role from the student's view

1 He should be a source of information for career guidance and vocational opportunities.
2 He should be open for discussion on social and personal problems.
3 He should not be a disciplinarian, but should be available for consultation on discipline problems.
4 His qualities should include sincerity and intergrity—someone the students can have faith in.
5 He should allow students to make their own decisions.
6 He should be available to orient new students.
7 He should encourage an open-door policy.

The counselor's role from the teacher's view

1 He should be the teacher's advocate in supporting the teacher's views and decisions.
2 He should be the one to conduct case studies.
3 He should assume the position of consultant on disciplinary problems and administer discipline.
4 He should consult with the teacher before making decisions.
5 He should not have an autonomous position.
6 He should be obliged to participate in school supervision.
7 He should counsel students.
8 He should be active in scheduling and special placement of students.

The counselor's role from the administrator's view

1 He should be in a remote position to the administrator.
2 His prime function should be student counseling, individual and group.
3 He should be available to talk to parents.
4 He should be active in individual planning and learning programs for special placement.
5 He should maintain informal, as well as formal, student contact.
6 He should consult with teachers.

In the school district where the counselor's effectiveness was highly regarded by all, the key points were

1 Counselors were not assigned administrative tasks.
2 Counselors were not responsible or associated with punitive discipline.
3 Counselors encouraged open-door policy to students, faculty, and parents.
4 Students and faculty were well aware of the types of services available from counselors.
5 Students were encouraged to have at least one meeting with the counselors per semester.

*From ''We Have a Counselor Problem—Can You Help Us?'' by V. L. Stintzi and W. R. Hutcheon, *The School Counselor*, 1972, *19*, 329–334. Copyright (1972) American Personnel and Guidance Association. Reprinted with permission.

reexamination—the counselor found himself in the dubious position of attempting to help clients who, in many cases, were in the process of rejecting or changing the very institution to which the counselor was presumed to hold loyalty. The counselor's role, which had once been a matter of theoretical debate, now became a crucial social issue that had to be dealt with at once in order to maintain a level of efficacy that would continue to justify his position.

Banks and Martens (1973) are critical of the counselor's position, arguing that "counselors have been acting as agents and apologists for the system for too long" (p. 457). They indicate that counselors are prone to accept the rules and mores of the institution as if they were correct by definition, and that they show a reluctance to question and to challenge openly the institution where it may be at fault. Even more unfortunate, in terms of the counseling stance, is the counselor's tendency to "operate on the premise that it is the individual alone who has a problem when he fails to 'adjust' to the current order" (p. 457). The counselor cannot function effectively—indeed, he cannot even understand the problems of the client—unless he is able to stand back from his prejudices and preconceptions to understand the client's discontent and its social as well as its psychological causes.

Banks and Martens suggest that for the counselor to avoid this professional pitfall, he must broaden his understanding of the issues, and particularly of how his feelings are entwined with the issues:

The counselor must have a clear concept of what issues or institutional practices are causing problems for the clients and for others. There must be a solid base of communication between counselor and client founded on mutual trust. In order to develop this trust the counselor may have to become more open and honest about who he is and what his own frustrations are. (p. 461)

Cook (1972), likewise, after considering this question, suggests among other things that the counselor can help create a "free flow of information" inside the school, a flow which should facilitate the constructive processes of social change. "A change in an organization," he points out, "depends, in part, on the free flow of information to all parts of the system" (p. 15).

Dworkin and Dworkin (1971) take a psychosocial approach toward the problem. They reflect on the ramifications of the social upheaval:

A stable sense of meaning appears lost as children resist the values of generations past, as sons openly attack their fathers, as fathers kill their daughters. To face the here-and-now with some sense of sanity is an awesome task. The future holds no certainty, yet we cannot retreat to the past. (p. 748)

Viewing the counselor as being in the position of advocating change while acting as the protector of the status quo, the authors suggest that the effective and dedicated counselor will not sit back passively on the sidelines watching changes happen but rather will become an active agent of change within the school and community environment. Chastising counselors for being hung up on authority, they advise counselors to listen to the young and to let them lead their own lives and learn from their mistakes. To do this, counselors must re-evaluate their own lives—their life styles, attitudes, and beliefs in order better to understand their clients. Moreover, they cite the challenge of expanding the role of the counselor by recruiting a greater cross section of counselor candidates and suggest six actions to help the counselor improve his own commitment to social change and better his understanding of the needs of youth.

We see from these papers that the counselor finds himself in a position of conflict regarding his role in the changing social situation. The school employs him and expects his loyalty in return; but he is primarily committed to the clients with whom he works, and conflicts may arise between the two factions. It is the responsibility of each counselor to come to grips with this problem in a way that his conscience, his ideals, and his professional ethics dictate, and to examine and reexamine his own feelings before attempting to deal with the client's feelings.

An allied question that inevitably attaches itself to this issue is, "What does the school have a legitimate right to expect of its counselor?" Hoyt (1961), in a superb paper, delves into this question and comes up with several answers that may be helpful in resolving some of the conflicts. He says first that *"the school has a right to expect that the counselors will have a professional career commitment to education."* This commitment, which must be right alongside his commitment to counseling, distinguishes the school counselor from the counselor-in-general. Moreover, this commitment changes in part the scope of his tasks: for the inextricable tying together of counseling and education demands that his counseling endeavors satisfy the requirements of both disciplines. Second, Hoyt states that *"the school has a right to expect the counselor to be a specialist."* Particularly, it is expected that the counselor will be more capable than anyone else in carrying on certain functions, including but not limited to appraising, supplying occupational and educational information, making referrals, doing group guidance and face-to-face counseling. Third, *"the school has a right to expect that the services of its counselor will extend to the teaching staff."* This, like the first expectation, changes in part the scope of the counselor's duties. The counselor is no longer limited to individual counseling but functions as a master teacher as well, assisting the teachers to "develop competencies in such areas as student appraisal procedures and counseling methodology so that teachers may perform more effectively as guidance workers." Fourth, *"the school has a right to expect that the services of its counselor will extend to the administrative staff."* This clearly does not mean that the counselor becomes a servant to the administration but rather that the counselor offers his professional expertise as a resource to the administration in dealing with a number of their problems. Hoyt, unlike some of the writers, does feel that the counselor should be expected to deal with attendance and disciplinary problems, but only as a professional seeking the causes of behavior and determining therapeutic and ameliorative procedures.

Hoyt's assumptions seem fair and well rounded, and it would be to the benefit of the counselor to familiarize himself with the expectations his job demands. He should have a clear idea, from the first day of school, what is expected of him and what is *not* expected of him, what he feels he should be offering and what he feels he should not be burdened with. He should not allow himself to be pushed around, to become an errand boy or clerk, to become a second-rate paraprofessional instead of the first-rate professional that he really is.

In maintaining such an attitude, it is important for the school counselor to understand his rights. Stewart (1959) has developed a counselor bill of rights (Display 6.6) that clearly outlines the specific rights the counselor should demand in order to conduct his practice properly. The counselor should keep in mind the difference between a right and a privilege—that a right is something he does not have to earn or prove but which exists a priori, and which he is able to take advantage of unapologetically.

Isaksen (1964), in defining the role of the counselor in the mental health profession, discusses legitimate counseling functions which parallel this bill of rights. The role descriptions which serve as the basis of the functions of an effective counselor, according to Isaksen, are:

1 Motivate pupils to seek counseling through a creative and continuous program of orientation to counseling.
2 Conduct research designed to measure the effectiveness of the counseling.
3 Provide informational services to pupils designed to meet their need for educational, vocational, and personal-social information.

---

display 6.6

BILL OF RIGHTS FOR SCHOOL COUNSELORS*

1 The right to a reasonable counseling load.
2 The right to favorable working conditions ... office space, ample clerical help, and other material conditions.
3 The right to enough time to do his real job ... to engage in counseling *per se*.
4 The right to a real opportunity to establish effective contact with parents, referral agencies, and other organizations in the community.
5 The right to sufficient time and the privilege of serving on curriculum and other critical committees.

6 The right to have an effective voice in determining guidance and counseling policy and practice.
7 The right to have reasonable time for research.
8 The right to a recognized professional status.
9 The right to remuneration commensurate with the training and responsibility involved.
10 The right to have the full trust and support of the administrators to make the above rights effective.

*From "A Bill of Rights for School Counselors" by C. C. Stewart, *Personnel and Guidance Journal*, 1959, 37, 503. Copyright (1959) American Personnel and Guidance Association. Reprinted with permission.

4 Assist in providing testing services designed to help each pupil appraise his capabilities, achievements, interests, and levels of adjustment.

5 Assist in the placement and grouping of pupils. This could include helping new students select courses of study. The school counselor, he continues, should not involve himself in performing administrative duties such as issuing failing reports, establishing an honor roll, etc. He should not be required to function as a school disciplinarian, either. (p. 12)

In short, we can say that as the counselor comes to understand his legitimate role within the school environment, he can act appropriately and expeditiously to carry out those responsibilities which are legitimately his.

CONCLUSIONS

The general definition of counseling, set forth in the first section of this book, is expanded somewhat in this chapter, where we consider the duties and problems of the counselor in the school setting. Some of the major issues presented were: (1) the professionalization of the school counselor; (2) the relationship between the counselor, the principal, the teachers, and the students; (3) what the school has a right to expect of its counselor; (4) the counselor's bill of rights and the limits of his obligations.

We mentioned that the school counselor is perceived differently by different school personnel, and that he must have a sense of purpose, a clear understanding of his role and function in order to conduct an effective counseling office in his school. We listed six principles to guide the school counselor in his practice:

1 The school counselor should walk in the first day of school with a clearly defined course of action and begin at once to implement this plan and to let it be known to his colleagues and to the students.

2 The school counselor must at all times maintain a professional attitude, which should not interfere with his ability to conduct harmonious and cordial relationships with other school personnel and with students. He must exude professionalism but avoid elitism.

3 It is the responsibility of the counselor to understand and to articulate his role as he sees it. He must be aware of the multiple perceptions and multiple demands that his position encourages, and he must try his best to clarify to those with whom he works what his real purpose is and what his legitimate responsibilities are.

4 The school counselor, to be effective, must recognize his responsibilities to all students, including the failing student, the disruptive student, the potential drop-out, the student with an emotional problem, the student with a learning difficulty, as well as the gifted student, the average student, the withdrawn and shy student, and the student who does nothing during the course of his studies to attract the attention of the counselor or other school personnel.

5 The school counselor must recognize and develop his competencies to treat severely disturbed students and students suffering from emotional problems, particularly through the use of groups, after-school programs, educational activities, and other nonintensive forms of treatment. The school counselor must, furthermore, strengthen his commitment to this group of students, since he is likely to be the first professional with whom they come in contact and who is able to help them. During his training, the school counselor must learn to develop attitudes and skills which will enable him to work effectively with this group who have long been ignored in the school setting.

6 The school counselor must work effectively with his principal, taking into account and showing a sensitivity to the principal's needs, expectations, and fears. The counselor has an opportunity to increase his professional posture by establishing a viable, mutually respectful, and responsive relationship with the principal.

Following these six principles, and at the same time being acutely aware of the rights afforded to him and the obligations expected of him, the school counselor can make a profound and important impact upon education.

References

Arbuckle, D. S. The counselor: who? what? *Personnel and Guidance Journal*, 1972, *50*, 785–790.

Banks, W., & Martens, K. Counseling: The reactionary profession. *Personnel and Guidance Journal*, 1973, *51*, 457–462.

Bergstein, H. B., & Grant, C. W. How parents perceive the counselor's role. *Personnel and Guidance Journal*, 1961, *39*, 698–703.

Boy, A. V. The elementary school counselor's role dilemma. *The School Counselor*, 1972, *19*, 167–172.

Boy, A. V., & Pine, G. J. A sociological view of the counselor's role: A dilemma and a solution. *Personnel and Guidance Journal*, 1969, *47*, 736–739.

Carey, A. R., & Garris, D. Counselor-role differentiation: A new tack? *The School Counselor*, 1971, *18*, 349–352.

Carmical, L., & Calvin, L., Jr. Functions selected by school counselors. *The School Counselor*, 1970, *17*, 280–285.

Chenault, J., & Seegars, J. E., Jr. The interpersonal diagnosis of principals and counselors. *Personnel and Guidance Journal*, 1962, *41*, 118–122.

Cook, D. R. The change agent counselor: A conceptual context. *The School Counselor*, 1972, *20*, 9–15.

Dworkin, E. P., & Dworkin, A. L. The activist counselor. *Personnel and Guidance Journal*, 1971, *49*, 748–753.

Filbeck, R. W. Perceptions of appropriateness of counselor behavior: A comparison of counselors and principals. *Personnel and Guidance Journal*, 1965, *43*, 891–895.

Grant, C. J. The counselor's role. *Personnel and Guidance Journal*, 1954, *33*, 74–77.

Haettenschwiller, D. L. Control of the counselor's role. *Journal of Counseling Psychology*, 1970, *17*, 437–442.

Hart, D. H., & Prince, D. J. Role conflict for school counselors: Training vs. job demands. *Personnel and Guidance Journal*, 1970, *48*, 374–380.

Heilfron, M. The function of counseling as perceived by high school students. *Personnel and Guidance Journal*, 1960, *39*, 133–136.

Hobbs, N. The compleat counselor. *Personnel and Guidance Journal*, 1958, *36*, 594–602.

Hoyt, K. B. What the school has a right to expect of its counselors. *Personnel and Guidance Journal*, 1961, *40*, 129–134.

Isaksen, H. L. The role of the school counselor in mental health. *Journal of Education*, 1964, *146*(3), 11–15.

Knapp, D. L., & Denny, E. W. The counselor's responsibility in role definition. *Personnel and Guidance Journal*, 1961, *40*, 48–50.

Koch, J. H. The trouble with counseling. *The School Counselor*, 1972, *19*, 13.

McCreary, W. H., & Miller, G. Elementary school counselors in California. *Personnel and Guidance Journal,* 1966, *44*, 494–502.

McCully, C. H. The school counselor stategy for professionalism. *Personnel and Guidance Journal,* 1962, *40*, 681–688.

Macy, V. Some concerns about counseling. *The School Counselor,* 1972, *19*, 5.

Schmidt, L. D. Concepts of the role of secondary school counselors. *Personnel and Guidance Journal,* 1962, *40*, 600–605.

Sherman, R., Albaggia, D., Cohen, M., Dell, E., Nadler, J., Shapiro, I., & Silverman, B. Teacher-counselor communication. *The School Counselor,* 1969, *17*, 55–62.

Shertzer, B., & Stone, S. C. The school counselor and his publics: A problem in role definition. *Personnel and Guidance Journal,* 1963, *41*, 687–692.

Stewart, C. C. A bill of rights for school counselors. *Personnel and Guidance Journal,* 1959, *37*, 500–503.

Stintzi, V. L., & Hutcheon, W. R. We have a counselor problem—can you help us? *The School Counselor,* 1972, *19*, 329–334.

Sweeney, T. J. The school counselor as perceived by counselors and their principals. *Personnel and Guidance Journal,* 1966, *44*, 844–847.

Trotzer, J. P., and Kassera, W. J. Do counselors do what they are taught? *The School Counselor,* 1971, *18*, 335–341.

Van Riper, B. W. Professionalization by ostensive acts. *The School Counselor,* 1972, *19*, 323–327.

Wrenn, C. G. *The counselor in a changing world.* Washington, D.C.: American Personnel and Guidance Association, 1962.

chapter seven

The counselor's training

We have up to now considered the factors and situations which define and illuminate the world of the counselor. We have examined the counselor qualities which are associated with effective counseling and explored those aspects of the counselor's personality and individuality which contribute to and detract from successful counseling outcomes. We have surveyed the multiple identities of the school counselor, taking into account the different, and at times conflicting, needs of those whom he is obligated to serve. Moreover, we have suggested that the counselor maintain a continual balance between his professional responsibilities and commitments—his role—and his personal abilities and beliefs—his self. In this section we shall explore in some detail the ways in which counselors can be trained to maximize their personal and professional development.

The word train which I have intentionally chosen over its alternatives, education and preparation, poses certain problems at the outset. It has several meanings and shades of meaning, ranging from the behavioral usage of conditioning, to the educational usage of inculcation, to the more general usage of apprenticeship. In the sense I use the word, it is meant to indicate the total teaching-of and exercising-of the prospective counselor toward the attainment of a professional skill, including knowledge, practical insight, attitude, and style. Thus its use is broad enough to encompass teaching activity, cognitive and affective tasks, introspective thinking, role-playing, group work, practicum experiences, as well as other activities initiated in response to evaluative and diagnostic feedback from prior experiences. The training process is best described as a cyclical process, in which cognitive skills are translated into behavioral skills, which then become translated into attitudinal representations, which in turn require the formulation of rationales of a cognitive nature. Display 7.1 shows the major stages of this process as they apply to the mastery of empathetic understanding.

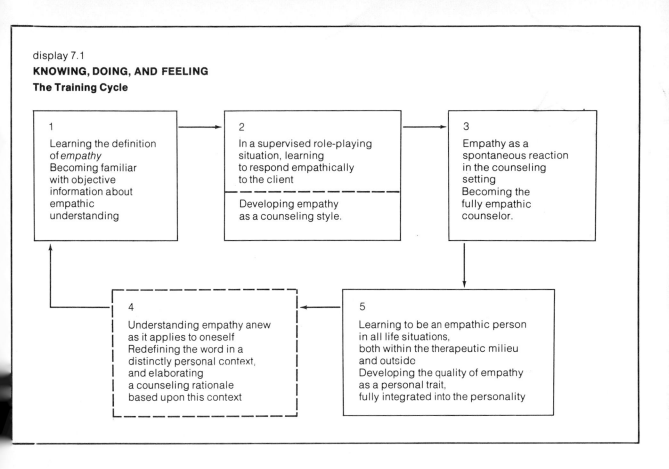

display 7.1
KNOWING, DOING, AND FEELING
The Training Cycle

1	2	3
Learning the definition of *empathy* Becoming familiar with objective information about empathic understanding	In a supervised role-playing situation, learning to respond empathically to the client ––––––––––– Developing empathy as a counseling style.	Empathy as a spontaneous reaction in the counseling setting Becoming the fully empathic counselor.

4	5
Understanding empathy anew as it applies to oneself Redefining the word in a distinctly personal context, and elaborating a counseling rationale based upon this context	Learning to be an empathic person in all life situations, both within the therapeutic milieu and outside Developing the quality of empathy as a personal trait, fully integrated into the personality

Our discussion will cover such basic areas as the counselor trainee, the counselor educator, criteria for admission to counseling programs, the counseling program, the specialized nature of counseling preparation, the stages of development toward competency, and counselor learning models. As we explore each of these areas, let us keep in mind its significance in the total development of the effective counselor.

THE COUNSELOR TRAINEE

The undergraduate background of the counselor trainee is typically in the area of either education or psychology, although often it is in a specific discipline which has subsequently been applied to classroom teaching. According to Hill (1961), most of those who choose to become school counselors do so from the teaching ranks, although in recent years it has become more common to begin training concurrently with the first year of teaching. This trend is clearly a response to the requirement in many states that teachers earn a master's degree within a specified period, thus encouraging the student to pursue his graduate work at the commencement of his teaching career. In any case, whether the

175

trainee has been a teacher or will be a teacher, he is school oriented, and he is from an undergraduate background other than counseling. His understanding of and previous exposure to the field of counseling is, therefore, limited, and as a rule his immediate impressions of what counseling is all about are either naïve, vague, or gleaned from his own particular experiences in the school.

Such a background poses a number of problems. The lack of undergraduate exposure may result in confusion about what the course of studies will entail, about the goals of the program, about what is expected of him, and about what he can expect. He is not familiar with the leading figures in the field, with the current state of research, with acceptable criteria and standards of the profession. He may experience feelings of insecurity insofar as he has never been exposed to the counseling approach before, and some of the language, insights, and lines of reasoning may be new to him. Moreover, his ideas of what to expect and of what his training is for may be distorted or confused by prior experiences and interactions with the counselor in the school in which he works.

Some of the questions which typically trouble the counselor trainees with whom I work are: How does counseling differ from therapy? Will we be studying only one theory of counseling or does the department offer a variety of approaches? Besides working in the school setting, for what other types of positions will I be qualified? It is a good idea as each new student class enters to allow the counselor trainee an opportunity to have his questions answered directly by an advisor, so that later confusion and misunderstanding can be avoided.

THE COUNSELOR EDUCATOR

Typically, the training of the school counselor is undertaken by a highly qualified professional staff, with a wider diversity of background and specialization than is ordinarily found in a single academic department. The faculty of the counseling department may include counselors, psychologists, psychiatric social workers, psychotherapists, psychometrists, researchers and theorists, philosophers of education, administrators, and so on. This is creditable inasmuch as school counseling is interdisciplinary in scope and substance. The Division 17 report of the American Psychological Association (APA), entitled "The Scope and Standards of Preparation in Psychology for School Counselors" (1962), recommended that the department be "interdisciplinary in nature. Each discipline should be taught by qualified specialists trained in the discipline itself and oriented to the work of the counselor." While the background of some faculty members may include experience in the public schools, the background of other faculty may not. Some will have experience in private practice, and others will not. All, however, should be familiar with the reality of the school environment for which the trainees are in preparation.

In some universities, the counseling department is viewed primarily as a service-oriented department, designed to train in-service teachers to assume the counseling role in the schools. It is usually only in those institutions where the master's degree in counseling is offered that the counseling department is awarded the independence and individual integrity of purpose that is expected and demanded by other departments. Because of this, it is not unusual to find counselor educators caught in the midst of conflict and confusion about their rightful place in the university. Arbuckle (1970) points out the irony of this situation in which a training department functions without a clear delineation from other departments and without "agreement as to just what constituted the education of the counselor":

The answers to questionnaires sent out by the U.S. Office of Education indicated an interesting institutional interpretation of the request for courses offering "specific preparation for guidance and student personnel." Some of the courses mentioned "Parent Counseling in Speech," "Research in Education," "Theories of Language," "Intercultural Relationships," "Modern American Family," "Introduction to Social Work," "Labor Problems," "Contemporary Problems in Education," and so on. Practically every course that one could think of in the area of education, psychology, measurement, sociology, and social service work was mentioned, and almost as many from almost every other area that might come under the heading of social science. (pp. 126-127).

The current status of counseling, in fact, is in many ways like the status of psychology in the mid to late 1800s when this new and evolving discipline was considered an offshoot of philosophy. Psychology courses at that time were offered under the jurisdiction of the philosophy department, usually under the rubric "philosophy of mind." While this did make sense within the context of the situation, it severely limited the possibilities of psychology as a developing discipline, both because of the constrictions upon the subject-matter dealt with (usually epistemology), the restricted methodology (the philosophical vs. the experimental method), and the commitment of the teaching faculty to a discipline other than what they were teaching. Another comparison could be made between the current status of counseling and the status of teacher education in past years. As long as the burden of educating teachers was placed upon the "pedagogical institutes," which were neither academic institutions nor service institutions but somewhere in the undefined limbo between, teacher training suffered as a result. It was only as education departments began to emerge as legitimate departments within the total university that teacher training was able to develop a clarity of purpose, a unity, which enabled it to incorporate freely from the other academic disciplines.

It may well be that the present situation in counseling is a direct result of counselor educators' having failed to define explicitly their scope and function, or it may be the result of feelings of insecurity by educators and psychologists who erroneously believe that their positions are threatened by the emergence of counseling as an independent discipline. But in either case, as long as counselor education is treated as a stepchild, as long as counselor educators are held amenable to some "higher" authority, as long as counseling is denied its rightful place in the academic hierarchy, counselor training will have difficulty finding itself and defining itself, and the trainee, as well as his clients, will ultimately suffer the consequences.

ADMISSION TO THE COUNSELOR EDUCATION PROGRAM

Gimmestad and Goldsmith (1973) have surveyed a number of universities to find common criteria for admission to counselor education programs. They have found, among other things, "an increasing acceptance by educators of counselors with backgrounds other than education ... an increasing production of counselors for positions in colleges and universities, rehabilitation and employment counseling, and other agency work." While the Graduate Record Examination and Miller Analogy Test scores still play an important role in selection at many universities, the trend seems to be toward dropping these tests as main criteria and perhaps relegating them to secondary place on the evaluative scale.

The issue of whether teaching experience should or should not be required of applicants, a perennial issue, seems finally on its way to resolution, as sentiment grows that teaching experience should not be a required criterion for admission to graduate counseling programs. Peterson and Brown (1968) have shown that although counselors with teaching background did perform somewhat better with routine school tasks and with providing vocational information, overall there was no significant difference between counselors with and without teaching experience in the performance of their duties. Nugent (1966), in an often cited paper, contends that teaching experience is in fact detrimental to the training of effective counselors, that the experienced teacher is less likely to develop a facilitative counseling attitude than is the non-teacher. The APA Division 17 Report (1962) stated most explicitly that "teaching experience ... is not a necessary prerequisite to becoming a counselor." Lister (1969) has undertaken a comprehensive survey of all relevant research, citing both the pro and con positions, and his conclusions are as follows:

1 During the initial portion of the counselor education program, students from a teaching background are handicapped in the counseling relationship by the heavy reliance upon a questioning, evaluating, information giving approach. In contrast, students without a teaching background appear initially more capable of entering into an effective counseling relationship.
2 The differences in counseling interview behavior between counselors with and without teaching experience tend to diminish through an intensive, supervised experience in counseling.
3 While beginning counselors without teaching experience initially feel less accepted by administrators than do former teachers, this perception is apparently of short duration. There is no research support for the argument that the counselor's acceptance by teachers is strongly dependent upon a teaching background.
4 Beginning counselors without teaching experience appear to experience some initial difficulty in understanding general school policies and procedures.

5 Beginning counselors without teaching experience feel as confident as former teachers in their ability to counsel students. Only in counseling-related activities do they feel less competent than former teachers.

6 Former teachers appear more rigid and closed-minded than counselors from non-teaching backgrounds.

7 The effects of length of teaching experience are unclear, but counselor age, an inevitable correlate of teaching experience, appears to exert a deleterious effect upon the counselor's capacity for entering into helping relationships. (pp. 47-48)

His analysis of these conclusions leads him to "the single unmistakable conclusion ... that the long-standing and widespread requirement of teaching experience for counselor certification has developed and has been maintained without sound evidence that counselors selected from the teaching ranks are systematically more effective in executing counseling and guidance services than counselors from other experiential backgrounds" (p. 50). The result of this report, as well as all of its supporting evidence, has already begun to make an impact in training programs, where there is an increasing de-emphasis on prior teaching experience. It is hoped that over the next few years, counseling candidates will represent a more varied and heterogeneous cross section of the student and working populations.

It should be pointed out, however, that although teaching need not be a criterion for either admission or certification, those candidates without experience in the school setting might benefit from some type of pre-internship exposure to the ins and outs of the public school environment.

Research has also suggested that less emphasis be placed on the so-called objective criteria often used to evaluate prospective counseling candidates, namely, undergraduate grade point average, Graduate Record Examination scores, Miller Analogy Test scores, and the like. Although Miller (1968) indicates that "grade average in undergraduate work is employed most frequently as a criterion for selection of counselor-trainees [and that] teaching experience, undergraduate preparation in the areas of education and psychology, and scholastic aptitude test scores are the other criteria that are most frequently employed" (p. 296), there is evidence that the situation is under scrutiny and in the process of changing rapidly. Arbuckle (1970), for example, argues that these criteria do not show much of a relationship with effective counseling. Supporting his point, he quotes Matulef and Rothenberg (1968):

Under the guise of objectivity, we use GRE's, Miller Analogies and grade point averages in determining admissions.... Although clinicians claim to and do evaluate personalities every day, they dare not apply their own skills to selecting trainees. We are not talking about screening out pathology as much as looking at professional attributes like empathy, positive regard and congruence. (p. 155)

Allen (1967) suggests utilizing a personality factor approach, in which a standardized personality inventory could contribute substantially to the evaluation process. Walton and Sweeney (1969) have concluded that grade point averages and MAT scores are nonpredictive indicators of ultimate counselor effectiveness, and they, too, tend toward the personality factor approach. These suggestions make much sense, particularly in light of our knowledge that what is important in counseling is ultimately the personality of the counselor, particularly his interest in others, his ability to communicate clearly, his flexibility, genuineness, warmth, self-insight, willingness to grow, and so on. Pierson (1965) has also argued that such personality factors are of the highest importance in evaluating and selecting counselor applicants.

Important work in this area has been conducted by Robert Carkhuff and his associates. Carkhuff has identified specifically the qualities indicative of effective counseling and has demonstrated that these qualities can be mastered in a training program. Working initially with Carl Rogers at the University of Wisconsin, Carkhuff, Charles B. Truax, and others investigated the "common thread" in the counselor-client relationship. They discovered the core dimensions of this relationship and amassed a wealth of evidence attesting to the validity of this core dimension. Later, Carkhuff refined and standardized scales to measure quantitatively and qualitatively these qualities, and he developed a training model designed to produce and strengthen these qualities in the counselor trainee. In their 1967 book, *Toward Effective Counseling and Psychotherapy*, Truax and Carkhuff examine this issue in some detail.

With the emphasis on the applicant's personal qualities, it would seem logical that a preadmission interview be an integral part of any counselor selection procedure, particularly if the Carkhuff model for training is to be employed. According to Gimmestad and Goldsmith, this is already becoming the trend.

During the personal interview, which ideally should be conducted by a counselor educator rather than by a general admissions interviewer because of the specialized nature of the interview procedure, it should be determined whether or not the applicant is suited to the counseling field, without the need to examine any of his previous grades, test scores, or academic achievement. Evaluation of these factors may become a subsequent basis for a decision in highly competitive departments.

One important point must be noted here. Since it is difficult to assess fairly and accurately the personal characteristics of a candidate, no matter how skilled the interviewer, it might be advisable to have an open admissions policy for the first semester of training. This is a highly controversial idea that is not subscribed to by many counselor educators. However, the reasons for such a policy are compelling, if examined without the common bias of "let's not lower our standards." In practice, such a procedure would be raising the standards, since it would in effect insure a thorough scrutiny of the candidate prior to full admission to the program, scrutiny which is possible only over a period of time as the instructors have an opportunity to observe the prospective candidate interact with his peers, respond in classes, and participate in role-playing experiences.

Having examined some of the bases for admission to the counselor education program, we shall now turn our attention to the counseling program itself, noting in particular the amalgam of disciplines which contribute to the specialized training of school counselors.

THE COUNSELING PROGRAM

The ideal counselor training program, one which could imbue the counselor trainee with all of the appropriate knowledge, skills, and attitudes in a period of a year or two, has been the Atlantis of counselor educators for many years: we know it is there, although it is hard to prove and almost impossible to find. The situation, however, is more than hopeful at the present time. Van Hoose (1970) refers to a "shift in counselor trainee orientation, from primarily cognitive to combined affective-cognitive behavior.... The intent is to produce counselors who 'feel' as well as 'think'" (p. 241). Chenault (1969) points out that "many counselor educators across the nation are in the process of revising their present counselor education programs or building new ones," and many of these new programs and ideas are beginning to make an impact in the schools. A recent

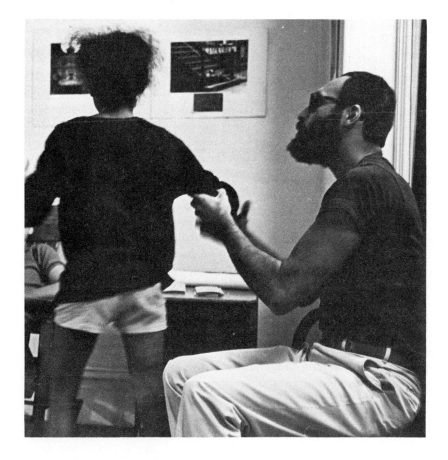

Counselor training must prepare a counselor to deal with many different situations. For example, this counselor is trying to help a runaway girl cope with some of her problems.

double issue of *The Counseling Psychologist* (1972:3,4) was devoted specifically to new approaches in counselor training, many of which we shall examine in this chapter. But before jumping into the fire, let us examine the basic questions which confront the counselor educator as he attempts to refine and improve counselor training programs.

Miller (1968) has cited a number of questions. Should counselors be generalists or specialists? What should the school counselor know about curriculum, administration, community relations? Is part-time study less effective than full-time study? Should one discipline be allowed to dominate the preparation of school counselors? How closely related are counseling and teaching? To what extent does the graduate student who is preparing for school counseling need counseling himself?

In addition to these questions, which are mostly of a practical nature, there are several other questions of a theoretical-practical nature that deserve scrutiny. We might ask, for example, "What processes will best help the prospective counselor synthesize the various facets of his training into a cognitive, affective, and perceptual whole?" Several options are available, including training groups, role-playing, videotaping, sensitivity sessions, and others. It might be helpful also to investigate the broad area of "humanistic" counselor education programs, to see if this approach is as efficacious as early research (Chenault, 1969) and experiments indicate. Another question which has come under increasing speculation (Dey, 1969) is the place of philosophy in counselor training —particularly in the development of counselor ethics. The value of metaphysics, too, has begun to be appreciated as a factor in counselor ability (Walters, 1958; Daubner and Daubner, 1972), and this issue should be explored in greater detail. "How can we specify and evaluate counselor learning models?" is another question to which we will have to turn our attention.

DEVELOPING COUNSELING SKILLS

A good starting point for our discussion might be to see how the trainees can acquire the skills necessary to execute competently their functions as counselors. The American Personnel and Guidance Association (APGA) report (1958) summarizes these functions concisely: "increasing the accuracy of the individual's self-percepts; increasing the accuracy of the individual's environmental perceptions; integrating the individual's self percepts with environmental realities and perceptions; presenting relevant information; improving the individual's ability to make and execute plans." Clearly, these functions are special functions which require specialized and somewhat technical skills and proficiencies.

To assure competency in the many specialized skills demanded by the work they will undertake at the completion of their studies, it is necessary that the counselor trainees be exposed to a program of study that encompasses many courses and stages of a highly specialized nature. Just as the medical doctor undergoes a rigorous and intensive education because of the critical character of his work—his need to perceive accurately, to make important judgments quickly and with certainty, to instill confidence in his patients—so, too, will the school counselor be perceived as the expert in his discipline, the one to whom the teachers, principal, parents, and students will turn in time of need. His expertise and competence, therefore, must be unqualified and warranted—not simply a pretense.

Like the physician, the school counselor will be asked to perform specialized tasks, namely, evaluating data, conducting counseling interviews, setting up programs, offering advice to other members of the pupil personnel team, etc. But the counselor, while he is a specialist, is also a generalist. "He is accepted as an educator, but he specializes in dealing with individuals as well as groups. He is a generalist in that he understands and appreciates the work of other specialists in related fields.... In short, he is a specialist by virtue of his being a generalist" (Tooker, 1957, p. 267). The most apt comparison here, if we may again refer to the medical model, would be between the school counselor in the helping services profession and the general practitioner in the field of medicine. The school counselor is usually the client's first contact with professional help. He must therefore have an ability to establish immediate rapport in order to facilitate communication; he must have knowledge of referral services available to the student and be familiar with the channels of referral, in order to handle the case expeditiously; he must be able to establish and maintain productive contact with the community in which he works, in order that his skills be fully utilized by the community. We may even extend this metaphor by comparing the school to a small town and the counselor to the small town physician. He not only ministers to the townspeople's day-to-day needs relating directly to medicine, but he enables them to discuss their problems, advises them on hygienic and preventative measures, provides appropriate referrals, and, in general, assumes responsibility for the health of the community. In this sense, the school counselor is a skilled specialist who functions as a generalist. And it is imperative that his training reflect this.

The scope of the training can be set down in five broad categories of counseling skills: (1) mastery of cognitive information relating directly to the counseling process; (2) ability to administer programs and to communicate effectively with other members of the counseling team as well as with clients (consultation); (3) familiarity with the particulars of the school setting; (4) self-awareness and the willingness to grow and change; (5) technical proficiency which can be demonstrated through practical counseling exercises.

The types of understanding and skills required for mastery in these five areas represent an amalgam of knowledge, of both a theoretical and practical nature, which transcends any single discipline or specialization. The trainee must be exposed to ideas in psychology and psychotherapy, to group and individual counseling practices; he must develop speech and communication skills, be familiar with the liberal arts—and particularly with our cultural heritage—with sociology, anthropology, with all the cross-cultural influences which affect the society in which he works, with teaching, learning, and educational theories, with principles of school administration, with the interrelationship of the disciplines. From his intimacy with these disciplines, he must be able to synthesize and extrapolate findings and relevant issues that pertain to the counseling environment.

His training, therefore, is an interdisciplinary training, in which he learns to apply a variety of factors to counseling and school-related problems. As Island (1972) rightly points out, "Counselor education must provide the conditions in which students can see social, educational, political, psychological, and economical contradictions in the environment" (p. 762-763). When we consider that counseling treats the whole individual—the functioning organism in interaction with its environment—it is no wonder that the counselor must be able to understand and react to the many complexities of that environment which exerts such a profound force upon the life of the counselee.

C. Gilbert Wrenn in his important study, *The Counselor in a Changing World* (1962), tackles the question directly, setting forth a proposed two-year program, designed to accomplish these ends. His program, which has been the source of much subsequent discussion, is quite comprehensive and includes a thorough grounding in psychology and sociology; an understanding of educational philosophy and curriculum; applied counseling techniques, including appraisal and occupational information; supervised practical experiences; an introduction to research; and an exposure to problems in ethics and legality.

Wrenn sees the counselor training process as multidisciplinary, in which the trainee is exposed to pertinent ideas from a variety of disciplinary frames of reference. Wrenn is to be admired for demanding that quality which, above all else, characterizes successful counselor training. I refer to the idea of *synthesis*.

Counselor training must be a synthetic type of training, bringing together insights from diverse disciplines and bringing to bear on specialized counseling problems the wealth of knowledge from many areas. Specifically, if we examine each contributing discipline, we find a direction, a pattern, to the counselor education program. Biology, the study of life itself, is fundamental to the counselor's understanding of man's place among the species, of man's interaction with his world. Through the study of biology, one begins to see the patterns of order which govern the activities of living organisms, and this understanding better enables the counselor to relate social and psychological phenomena to their appropriate place in the scheme of things. Biological understanding allows the counselor a new perspective, a perspective not isolated from the cycle of life and death which ultimately governs everything.

The study of sociology and anthropology gives the counselor insight into the many complexities and ramifications of social interaction and helps him appreciate the diversity of social orders. A study of comparative social systems, especially, will help him free himself of any ethnocentricity that lingers on from his earlier upbringing. This is important inasmuch as the counselor may well be counseling members of social, economic, and cultural groups different from his own, and as Vontress (1969) points out, it is necessary for him to have a flexible frame of reference to be able to overcome the influence of society's value of "separatism," which is a serious impediment to rapport and meaningful communication.

Education and pedagogy, the disciplines which more than any other illuminate what is happening in the schools and why, are an essential part of his training. Not only will he be working with teachers and students, the subjects of these disciplines, but counseling itself is a specialized type of teaching. Insofar as counseling is concerned, states the APA Division 17 report (Amer. Psych. Assoc., 1962), "the key factors are still in relating to both children and adults, competence in working with them in an educational setting, and understanding of the objectives, methods, and mores of that setting" (p. 150). Clearly, systematic study of education and pedagogy facilitate this understanding.

The social sciences—history, economics, and political science—tell the story of our lives in terms of man's activities of the past and his predictable actions of the future, which helps the counselor understand the continuity of civilization. All of our behavior is judged against criteria established by civilization—man is, after all, a civilized animal, if Freud is to be believed. Because these criteria are not arbitrary, but products of actions over hundreds of years which themselves have been governed by laws of probability and logic, the questions relating to an individual's behavior—particularly as that behavior deviates from the norm—are best answered by those who have an objective understanding of the full development of civilization. Even a simple question which a client may ask of a school counselor, a question such as "Should I drop out and get a job?" can be better appreciated by the counselor if he is able to transcend his acclimated response of "No, staying in school is better," and examine the question in light of his knowledge of economics, political science, and history.

Psychology and its component parts plays an obviously vital role in counselor training. Without belaboring the obvious, we need only state that the counselor trainee should be able to study psychology not as an academic discipline, but rather as a practical basis for the skills he is in the process of developing. Courses such as "Abnormal Psychology," "Social Psychology," and "Child and Adolescent Development," if not taken on the undergraduate level, should be required prerequisites for counseling courses.

We come finally to philosophy, whose importance is shamefully minimized in many counseling programs. Philosophy, more than any other discipline, helps the counselor to synthesize and evaluate his perspective, to organize his broad insights into manageable and practical categories, to speculate on metaphysical issues, which helps him distinguish the real from the non-real, "a vital issue to every counselor and client," according to Daubner and Daubner (1972). Philip Phenix (1964) has clearly stated the role of philosophy in training:

It is not easy to sustain a sense of the whole. Many a person pursues his own limited calling with scarcely a thought for his place in the total drama of civilized endeavor. While he may have a vague notion of the larger context in which his contribution is made, he may never engage in any sustained study and reflection about his relation to the entire pattern of civilization. (p. 3)

185

Philosophy, argues Phenix (p. 253), "is concerned with every kind of human experience and not with any one domain." It is precisely for this reason that philosophy must play an integral role in counselor education programs. The counselor must develop and sustain his sense of "the whole," must be able to formulate a "philosophy of life," must be able to see himself and his clients within a frame of reference which is the culmination of his synthetic understandings held together by a cogent "philosophy of counseling." As Nash (1973) points out, counselor educators and trainees must avoid the "dangerous temptation ... to concentrate upon satisfying exigent, practical needs and to neglect the less immediately rewarding and more difficult and demanding tasks of philosophical clarification" (p. xi).

The counseling program, therefore, must be a synthetic program, interdisciplinary in nature and held together by a well-reasoned philosophy of counselor training. We shall now turn our attention to the specific training in counseling which the trainee should undergo prior to his supervised internship.

JOURNEY TO COMPETENCY

The journey to competency that the trainee undertakes from the time he enters the counseling program to the time he completes his professional preparation can be roughly divided into three preinternship phases which, although distinct, do occur simultaneously: the mastery of material, the development of technical competencies, and the emerging of an appropriate professional attitude. It is the ability of each of these phases to contribute productively to the development of the others which determines the ultimate success or failure of a training program.

In addition to mastering the interdisciplinary material discussed above, there is a large amount of material peculiar to the counseling discipline which must be covered. The areas of curriculum which are most commonly covered include principles of guidance (an overview, or introductory, course), theories of counseling, techniques and applications of counseling, guidance administration, group dynamics, measurement, evaluation and appraisal, guidance research, specialized counseling approaches (vocational, family, drug, rehabilitation, pastoral), community relations, and more. The subject-matter covered in each of these areas is designed to narrow down and focus for the prospective counselor the particular concerns of the discipline, as well as the means and methods for dealing with these concerns. It is expected that by his exposure to these categories of counseling, he will learn to concentrate his attention on the most relevant information, be able to form a holistic, or comprehensive and synthetic, point of view, and acquire the skills and insights necessary to provide a rationale for his professional actions and a basis for his professional decisions.

An important part of this stage of training is his exposure to the leaders in his field: men like Shertzer, Carkhuff, Berenson, Blocher, Tyler, Arbuckle, Patterson, Berdie, Krumbholz, and many others who not only have achieved general recognition in psychology but also have become instrumental forces in counseling thought. I suggest that the trainee, at the very beginning of his training, delve into the journals which enjoy the largest circulation and influence in the profession: journals such as *Personnel and Guidance Journal, The School Counselor, Journal of Counseling Psychology, The Counseling Psychologist, Journal of Consulting and Clinical Psychology, Counselor Education and Supervision,* and other journals which clearly have a bearing on what he will be studying. It is hoped that by becoming familiar with these sources of innovative counseling thought, he will be encouraged to read them regularly, thus keeping up with the latest developments in the field and always being aware of changes of perspective, new findings, etc., which more than likely will be pertinent to many of the counseling problems he has to deal with.

This type of training works to facilitate the development of an appropriate professional attitude. Such development will be further encouraged as the student is introduced to local, state, and national professional organizations, such as the APGA, the APA, and others, many of which offer to students an opportunity for limited or adjunct membership. Attendance at professional meetings often proves productive in many ways that the student cannot foresee at the outset. In addition to increasing his cognitive awareness of the discipline and facilitating an appropriate attitude, the counselor trainee begins to *identify* with the profession of counseling by his participation in these meetings. Moreover, the counselor educator wants his trainees to appreciate fully the wide range of thinking and critical judgment which have gone into counseling research, and there is no better way to do this than to encourage attendance at professional meetings.

We can say, then, that mastery in the field of counseling is not accomplished by simply reading and learning the material, but by actively participating in the ongoing processes of counseling research and professional life as well. Intellectual knowledge alone will not suffice to make a skilled and effective counselor.

What is far more important than what the counselor *knows* is what he can *do*. I refer here to Ryle's (1949) classical distinction between "knowing how" and "knowing that." Ryle distinguishes between theory and practice, between knowing about something and knowing how to do something. Martin (1961) explains it simply but accurately:

According to Ryle, intelligent practice, that is "knowing how," is not a "step-child of theory." On the contrary, theorizing, that is, "knowing that," is "one practice amongst others and is itself intelligently or stupidly conducted." In distinguishing between "knowing how" and "knowing that" Ryle hopes to correct the intellectualist doctrine which tended to view all knowing as "knowing that." He strongly opposes the view that intelligent performance must be preceded by an intellectual acknowledgement of rules and criteria. (p. 59)

In the training of counselors, we are primarily concerned with teaching them how to do things, with helping them to "know how." They must be able to put into practice, to apply, the cognitive mastery they have gained in their classes. It is not enough that the trainee be versed in the theories of counseling; he should be able effectively to apply his skills to counseling situations. For it is only then that his unique counseling style can develop and that he will be able to avoid the pitfalls of dogmatic theoretical reasoning which, when isolated from practice, sets standards and goals which are never accurately germane to the needs and abilities of all counselors in all situations. The counselor trainee must be given an opportunity to learn about himself in relation to what he has learned about counseling. As Kemp (1962) has pointed out, he

must understand his own personality dynamics since his counseling, if genuine, will be in agreement with his inner attitudes.... Greater assistance should be given to help the counselor-in-training to identify, understand and put into operation the form of counseling which he individually has selected with the acceptance that will prevent defensiveness or guilt.... Sufficient experience should be provided in simulated "cases" to aid the counselor-in-training not only to improve in technique, but to discover to a greater degree his genotypical attitudes—the form of responses which coincide with his approach to life. (p. 157)

The kind of awareness which Kemp is referring to, what he calls the awareness of "genotypical attitudes," can only come about as the counselor masters the realm of knowing how. Indeed, the entire journey to counselor competency may be viewed as a transition from knowing that to knowing how—from a familiarity with the theoretical to an intimacy with the practical. In the following section, we shall explore a number of learning models which the counselor uses to facilitate this transition and consider how each of these models can be utilized in conjunction with the others to increase the productive competency of counselors at the conclusion of their formal training.

COUNSELOR LEARNING MODELS

When we speak of a counselor learning model, we are referring to an integrated approach to teaching, which helps the trainee apply the dividends of his didactic studies to the debits his inexperience and diffidence charge against his enthusiasm and good intention. Counselor learning models, which include groups, role-playing, supervision, and audiovisual interactions, have been studied and evaluated in some depth, with the happy consequence that a large body of information is now available to the counselor educator to help him evaluate the potential of each model within the scope of the total counselor training program.

These models often appear in the literature as methods for dealing with specific counselor training goals, such as increasing empathy, openness, or sensitivity. Other specific methods are designed to acclimate the neophyte counselor to his new professional role.

One method often cited in the literature is the *coached client* technique. This approach will be familiar to many students, for it is simply having a student or other person play the part of a client, in order for the counselor to "practice" his repertoire. There is some contention about the effectiveness of this technique. Whitely and Jakubowski (1969) have found that this method is helpful in showing the trainee how he acts in the counseling situation and in helping him develop a style. Prusok and Felker (1972), on the other hand, see little value in the coached client approach, advocating in its place natural counseling dyads and tetrads, which minimize the artificiality of the situation. The dyadic method not only helps the prospective counselor develop his "real" counseling style, but encourages self-exploration in counselor as well as in tentative client.

Both the coached client approach and the natural dyadic interaction utilize the important learning principle of role-playing. The advantages of role-playing as a training technique are many and should be mentioned. Role-playing is built upon two important principles, one of which is sociological and one, psychological. In its sociological perspective, role-playing describes what we do in all of our daily activity, particularly in our interactions with others. During the course of a single day, we assume many different roles—different faces to show to others. I may be a counselor to A, a colleague to B, a client to C, a husband to D, a son to E, a customer to F, an employer to G, and so on, showing each of them a different and appropriate part of myself. It is not that I necessarily do this consciously and intentionally but rather that I have become accustomed to performing in social situations, so that only parts of my complex self are revealed, in order to define both the situation and my place in the situation. "When an individual appears before others," points out Erving Goffman, the noted sociologist, "he knowingly and unwittingly projects a definition of the situation, of which a conception of himself is an important part" (1959, p. 242). In order that this "definition of the situation" be clear and unambiguous, the performer must be certain of the role he is playing and understand his abilities and limitations in playing this role. The training technique of role-playing is intended to facilitate this awareness in the trainee by exposing him for the first time to the role of counselor and by affording him an opportunity to become comfortable in that role.

Psychologically, the role-playing approach may be viewed as a conditioning approach. It is based on the premise that the capacity to adapt to and master different roles is not an inborn characteristic but is learned by practice. In the process of growing up, young children model themselves on the adults around them, subtly and not always consciously learning the small gestures, the words, and the mannerisms to perfect their "performances" as adults. Trainees learn to be counselors, too, by the process of imitation, by observing and imitating their supervisors, by learning to play the counseling role as their supervisors play it. In this sense we are all actors, and all the world really is a stage. This is not to imply that we are dishonest or artificial in our relations with others, but merely to say that it is necessary for us to have guidelines as to what particular actions to choose in the many possibilities which confront us. Role-playing, which includes the feedback of the supervisor, reinforces those performances which are most concomitant with our expectations of what effective counseling should be.

We also use role-playing techniques to enable the trainee to learn the professional role he will be practicing upon completion of the program. Role-playing in the presence of a counselor educator enables the trainee to obtain information about his strengths and weaknesses within the postulated counseling setting. It allows him to practice his counseling, to feel comfortable in the role of counselor, to become reinforced in positive counselor behavior, to develop his own style. Boyarsky et al. (1970) indicate that "the members of the role-playing dyad form an intimate working relationship which affords the opportunity to experience another beginner's style, techniques and modes of dealing with the patient. It seems to diminish anxiety, develop technique, and help resolve problems. Possibly, just as important, it gives the beginning therapist hours of extra experience during the crucial beginning stages" (p. 34).

Most counselor training occurs within the context of a group situation. Harris (1972) has found that a variety of group training techniques, used in conjunction with each other, were successful in helping counselors communicate feelings of empathy, respect, genuineness, and concreteness, as well as improving their abilities to discriminate high and low level responses in the counseling situation. Foreman (1967) has evaluated the effect of a group experience at the University of Cincinnati Testing and Counseling Center, both positively and negatively. On the plus side, it was found that most of the participants considered the group experience worthwhile; on the minus side, it was found that the primary problem faced was the need to break through "the traditional academic hierarchy in order to establish nondefensive communication."

Another important counselor learning model is the supervisory relationship. It is generally agreed that much of the trainee's practical knowledge and skills—his knowing how—are acquired during the period of his training when he works under supervision. The value of supervision as a part of the counselor training program is unchallenged; all that is questioned is which methods of supervision and which models are most effective in achieving the desired ends. Altucher (1967) correctly points out that the essential assumption underlying all supervision is the belief "that learning to be a counselor is both an emotional and intellectual experience and of the two the emotional part is the most crucial" (p. 165). He suggests that the supervisory relationship is most constructive when it enables the trainee to identify his own achievements and difficulties, and it is the responsibility of the supervisor to see that this happens. An effective supervisory relationship is one that enables the supervisee to develop a sense of independence and responsibility.

Supervision assumes a variety of forms. McGee (1968) identifies four models of supervision: typical dyad, typical triad, group supervision, and a model in which one group co-therapist also serves as a supervisor to the other co-therapist. The integration of audiotape and videotape playback equipment in conjunction with supervision has been the subject of a number of recent studies. Fredrickson et al. (1970) caution counselors to examine both the advantages and drawbacks before making a decision to use this expensive and time-consuming equipment. Results of their studies, they point out, "indicated no judged differences among the playback treatment groups, nor could discriminate rankings be made among the various playback methods." Eisenberg and Delaney (1970), using a slightly different application of videotape, found that where counselor trainees were shown videotapes of experienced counselors at work with clients, they increased their capacity to model themselves after the experienced counselors.

Perhaps the most exciting use of videotapes in counselor training is found in *microcounseling.* Microcounseling, as defined by Ivey (1973), one of its originators (Ivey et al., 1968), "is a systematic method for teaching counseling skills in a short period of time, by use of development of specific counseling skills and subsequent self-observation on videotape" (p. 1). Miller, Morrill and Uhlemann (1970) found in an experimental study utilizing the microcounseling principle enthusiastic results including attitude changes and higher judge's ratings.

Bellucci (1973) in a more recent study confirms the positive results of microcounseling which "can be combined with imitative learning theory in a manner which may prove to be highly effective in training" (p. 94). We may conclude, then, that the blossoming field of microcounseling promises many important developments in the integration of videotape playback in the counselor training program.

One of the difficulties with traditional supervision, supervision in conjunction with audiovisual taping, and microcounseling is the possible lack of permanence of any effects achieved by the experimental groups. Counselor educators know quite well that a student who performs well under supervision may go out into the field to become a less than adequate counselor. It has been suggested, therefore, that supervision be extended into the graduate's work environment during his first year or two of training. The supervised internship as well as a probationary period for new counselors have both been suggested to deal with this problem.

Gust (1970) cites a number of studies which emphasize the need for on-the-job supervision for beginning counselors. After examining the problem in some detail, he concludes that on-the-job supervision is beneficial not only to the counselor but to the entire counseling profession as well. This is an important point, for it is crucial that counselor educators recognize that their responsibilities do not end the day that their trainees receive their certification and their first case loads.

Probably the most important advance in counselor training during the past decade is the "human technology" approach, developed by Robert R. Carkhuff and his associates. This approach is based on three simple steps:

1 determining the kinds of skills that people need to live effectively.
2 developing step-by-step programs to produce these skills.
3 developing delivery systems to insure the effective delivery of skills to the people who need them.

If the words of this program sound a bit mechanistic and impersonal, the program itself certainly is not. The basic paradigm used by Carkhuff (1969, 1970, 1971a, 1971b, 1972) is illustrated in Display 7.2.

This diagram is best understood within the context of Carkhuff's total thinking over the past decade. Working on the assumption that "the therapeutic endeavor is, on the average, ineffective," Truax and Carkhuff (1967, p. 1) recognized, however, that "some counselors are significantly helpful while others are significantly harmful." In order to maximize counselor training, they proposed that "through research it is possible to identify the major ingredients of helpful and harmful therapy" (Truax and Carkhuff, 1967, p. 1).

Carkhuff's chief contribution is in quantifying the helpful and harmful ingredients and in demonstrating that these ingredients can be strengthened through counselor training programs. Specifically, Carkhuff, with his associate Bernard G. Berenson (1967), called these ingredients *levels of functioning*:

For our own purposes, we have incorporated five levels of functioning, with the lower levels being essentially commensurate with the description of the distressed client or retarding therapist, and the higher levels commensurate with the facilitative individual, whatever his label. (p. 46)

What Display 7.2 implies then is that through a process of training, comprising the three phases, a person can develop higher, more facilitative levels of functioning.

Translated into practice, this paradigm would be used first as the training model for the counselor and then as the helping model for the client. The counselor trainee goes through the stages of self-exploration, understanding, and finally appropriate action—in this case, appropriate counseling actions. The specific goals of this process would be the qualities designated by Carkhuff as essential to counselors: empathy, respect, warmth, concreteness, genuineness, self-disclosure, confrontation, and immediacy. The counselor then learns how to use this model with his own clients to work through their problems constructively and quickly. Gazda (1973) has prepared a comprehensive training manual for educators and counselors based on the Carkhuff model. Specific training exercises have been developed to help the trainee sensitize himself to the appropriate responses to situations. The Carkhuff model will be discussed in more detail in chapter 15.

CONCLUSIONS

1 Most counseling students come from undergraduate backgrounds in psychology or education, which necessitates a more intensive exposure to counseling at the beginning of their studies.

2 At many universities the individuality and uniqueness of the counseling department and its faculty is not made clear. Efforts must be undertaken to maintain counseling departments as distinct, full-functioning departments.

3 Teaching experience, undergraduate grades, and standardized test scores are poor indicators of future success in counseling programs. A better indicator is the counselor-in-training's personal qualities, which can be most adequately assessed during a personal interview.

4 An effective counselor training program must synthesize didactic, experiential, and dynamic courses to help the trainee master the "knowing-how" dimension of counseling. Interdisciplinary studies—including psychology, philosophy, biology, and the social sciences—should be included within the scope of counselor training.

5 Important counselor learning models utilized in counselor education include the coached-client technique, role-playing, group dynamics and group experiences, and supervision.

6 Audiotaping and videotaping may be used in conjunction with supervised counseling experiences. These have been most effective in a program of microcounseling.

7 The training model developed by Robert R. Carkhuff and his associates is built on the premise that the skills necessary for effective counseling can be acquired through training.

References

Allen, T. W. Effectiveness of counselor trainees as a function of psychological openness. *Journal of Counseling Psychology*, 1967, *14*, 35–40.

Altucher, N. Constructive use of the supervisory relationship. *Journal of Counseling Psychology*, 1967, *14*, 165–170.

American Psychological Association. The scope and standards of preparation in psychology for school counselors. (Report of a special committee of Division 17). *American Psychologist*, 1962, *17*, 149–152.

Arbuckle, D. S. *Counseling: Philosophy, theory and practice* (2nd ed.). Boston: Allyn & Bacon, 1970.

Beck, C. E. (Ed.). *Philosophical guidelines for counseling.* Dubuque, Iowa: Wm. C. Brown, 1973.

Bellucci, J. E. Microcounseling and imitation learning: A behavioral approach to counselor education. *Counselor Education and Supervision*, 1972, *12*, 88–97.

Boyarsky, R., et al. The use of role-play in psychotherapy training. *Group Therapy and Psychodrama*, 1970, *23*, 34–40.

Carkhuff, R. R. Critical variables in effective counselor training. *Journal of Counseling Psychology*, 1969, *16*, 238–245.

Carkhuff, R. R. Systematic human relations training. In G. M. Gazda & T. L. Porter (Eds.), *Proceedings of a symposium on training groups*. Athens: College of Education, University of Georgia, 1970.

Carkhuff, R. R. *The development of human resources: Education, psychology, and social change*. New York: Holt, Rinehart, & Winston, 1971a.

Carkhuff, R. R. Helping and human relations: A brief guide for training lay helpers. *Journal of Research and Development in Education*, 1971b, *4*(2), 17–27.

Carkhuff, R. R. *The art of helping*. Amherst: Human Resources Development, 1972.

Carkhuff, R. R., & Berenson, B. G. *Beyond counseling and therapy*. New York: Holt, Rinehart & Winston, 1967.

Chenault, J. A proposed model for a humanistic counselor education program. *Counselor Education and Supervision*, 1969, *8*, 4–11.

Daubner, E. V., & Daubner, E. S. The counselor as metaphysician. *Personnel and Guidance Journal*, 1972, *50*, 363–370.

Dey, G. R. Philosophers, counselor educators, and relevant questions. *Counselor Education and Supervision*, 1969, *8*, 135–142.

Eisenberg, S., & Delaney, D. J. Using video simulation of counselors for training counselors. *Journal of Counseling Psychology*, 1970, *17*, 15–19.

Foreman, M. E. T groups: Their implications for counselor supervision and preparation. *Counselor Education and Supervision*, 1967, *7*, 48–53.

Fredrickson, R. H., et al. Influence of playback techniques on counseling performance. *Counselor Education and Supervision*, 1970, *9*, 178–183.

Gazda, G. M. *Human relations development: A manual for educators*. Boston: Allyn & Bacon, 1973.

Gimmestad, M. J., & Goldsmith, E. B. Admission policies for graduate programs in counselor education. *Counselor Education and Supervision*, 1973, *12*, 172–177.

Goffman, E. *The presentation of self in everyday life*. Garden City: Doubleday (Anchor), 1959.

Gust, T. Extending counselor supervision. *Counselor Education and Supervision*, 1970, *9*, 157–161.

Harris, G. A. Training and evaluation of school counselors' communication with students. *Counselor Education and Supervision*, 1972, *12*, 200–205.

Hill, G. E. The selection of school counselors. In J. F. McGowan and L. D. Schmidt (Eds.), *Counseling: Readings in theory and practice*. New York: Holt, Rinehart & Winston, 1962. (*Personnel and Guidance Journal*, 1961, *39*, 355–360.)

Island, D. An alternative for counselor education. *Personnel and Guidance Journal*, 1972, *50*, 762–766.

Ivey, A. E. Microcounseling: The counselor as trainer. *Personnel and Guidance Journal*, 1973, *51*, 311–316.

Ivey, A. E., Normington, J., Miller, C. D., Morrill, W. H., & Haase, R. F. Microcounseling and attending behavior: An approach to pre-practicum counselor training. *Journal of Counseling Psychology Monograph Supplement*, Part 2, September 1968, pp. 1–12.

Kemp, G. C. Influence of dogmatism on the training of counselors. *Journal of Counseling Psychology*, 1962, *9*, 155–157.

Kirk, B. A. Techniques of in-service counselor training. *Personnel and Guidance Journal*, 1955, *34*, 204–207.

Lister, J. L. Teaching experience necessary for counselors? *NASSP Bulletin*, 1969, *53*, 39–53.

Loeffler, D. Counseling and the psychology of communication. *Personnel and Guidance Journal*, 1970, *48*, 629–636.

Martin, J. R. On the reduction of "knowing that" to "knowing how." In B. O. Smith and R. H. Ennis (Eds.), *Language and Concepts in Education*. Chicago: Rand McNally, 1961, pp. 59-71.

Matulef, N. J., & Rothenberg, P. J. The crisis in clinical training: Apathy and action. *Special Bulletin of the National Council on Graduate Education in Psychology*, 1968, *2*, 8.

McGee, T. F. Supervision in group psychotherapy: A comparison of four approaches. *International Journal of Group Psychotherapy*, 1968, *18*, 165–176.

Miller, C. D., Morrill, W. H., & Uhlemann, M. R. Microcounseling: An experimental study of pre-practicum training in communicating test results. *Counselor Education and Supervision*, 1970, *9*, 171–177.

Miller, F. W. *Guidance: Principles and service* (2nd ed.). Columbus: Chas. Merrill, 1968.

Nash, P. Foreward. In C. E. Beck (Ed.), *Philosophical guidelines for counseling*. Dubuque, Iowa: Wm. C. Brown, 1973.

Nugent, F. A. A rationale against teaching experience for school counselors. *The School Counselor*, 1966, *13*, 213–215.

Peterson, B. H., & Brown, D. Does teaching experience matter? *Personnel and Guidance Journal*, 1968, *46*, 892–897.

Phenix, P. *Realms of meaning*. New York: McGraw-Hill, 1964.

Pierson, G. A. *An evaluation: Counselor education in regular sessions institutes*. Washington, D.C.: U.S. Dept. of Health, Education, and Welfare, Office of Education, 1965.

Prusok, R., & Felker, K. R. An innovation in pre-practicum training. *Counselor Education and Supervision*, 1972, *11*, 224–226.

Ryle, G. *The concept of mind*. London: Hutchinson's University Library, 1949.

Tooker, E. Counselor role: Counselor training. *Personnel and Guidance Journal*, 1957, *36*, 263–267.

Truax, C. B., & Carkhuff, R. R. *Toward effective counseling and psychotherapy*. Chicago: Aldine, 1967.

Van Hoose, W. H. Conflicts in counselor preparation and professional practice: An analysis. *Counselor Education and Supervision*, 1970, *9*, 241–247.

Vontress, C. E. Cultural barriers in the counseling relationship. *Personnel and Guidance Journal*, 1969, *48*, 11–17.

Walters, O. S. Metaphysics, religion, and psychotherapy. *Journal of Counseling Psychology*, 1958, *5*, 243–252.

Walton, F. X., & Sweeney, T. J. Useful predictors of counseling effectiveness. *Personnel and Guidance Journal*, 1969, *48*, 32–38.

Whitely, J. M., & Jakubowski, P. A. The coached client as a research and training resource in counseling. *Counselor Education and Supervision*, 1969, *9*, 19–28.

Wrenn, C. G. *The counselor in a changing world*. Washington, D.C.: American Personnel and Guidance Association, 1962.

PART THREE

Peter Schwarzburg

Theories of counseling and psychotherapy: an overview

In chapter 3, you recall, we examined in some detail the relationship between the counselor's theoretical rationale and his practical experience. We saw indications then that there is no clear and indisputable cause-and-effect relationship between the counselor's theory and his technique, although there is some evidence to indicate an influence upon his actions by the theoretical position to which he subscribes. In this section, we shall examine seven major schools of counseling and psychotherapy, to get a better understanding of the possibilities of theoretical range which underlie counseling practice. The seven schools are: psychoanalysis, client-centered, existentialism, gestalt, reality, rational-emotive, and behavioral counseling.

To show the full development of each of these positions—in an admittedly limited amount of space—and to facilitate the exposition, I have divided each position into its basic component parts. After a brief history of each school, the first category discussed is the *view of man*, which explicates the ways in which practitioners of a particular position look at the human condition and, consequently, at the client, especially in terms of personality development, motivation, learning, perception, and growth. Next, we consider the *role of the client* and what is expected of him in order to make the treatment successful. We will see that in some schools (such as psychoanalysis and client-centered counseling) very little is required of the client, while other positions (reality and behavioral) require the client to engage in some risk-taking and early commitments to courses of action. We then turn our attention to the *role of the counselor* and to the *techniques and goals* of the treatment. Here we explore the crux of the therapeutic process. What specifically does the counselor do (and for what reasons) in order to help the client overcome whatever difficulties he came into treatment to work on? It is at this stage that we get a clear idea of the mechanics of psychotherapy. Finally, we present a brief evaluation of the position and look at its relevance for the school counseling situation.

Two important schools which are not discussed in this section are the humanistic approach and the eclectic approach. These are omitted from this part of the book because they are presented in other chapters: Humanism is discussed in chapter 3, and the eclectic approach is discussed in the chapter on the counseling interview (chapter 14). In addition, Thorne's eclecticism is discussed at various points in Part Four, "The Counseling Experience." A review of all seven positions will be found in Part Six, the concluding section of this book.

As the counselor studies each of these theoretical positions, he should be asking himself what parts of each school are relevant to his needs and aptitudes. Not every counselor is able to maintain the detached coolness expected of the psychoanalyst nor is every counselor able to engage in the dynamic interactions of the gestalt approach. As each counselor comes to recognize what he can use from each of these positions, he will be better able to draw from his own emotional and intellectual reservoir to establish and perfect his own counseling techniques, held together by his own personal theory of counseling.

chapter eight

Psychoanalysis

As we have seen in earlier chapters, psychoanalysis has played an important part in the development of all Western psychotherapies and, indirectly, in the development of the counseling movement in the United States. While its defenders and critics are usually intemperately vehement in their bold assertions and blanket denunciations, a dispassionate and logical purview of psychoanalysis reveals some significant strengths as well as some glaring weaknesses in Freud's great legacy to the profession. In this chapter we shall look at psychoanalysis from both a historical and theoretical perspective. At the conclusion of our examination, we shall evaluate the application of different psychoanalytic principles to school counseling.

HISTORY OF THE SCHOOL

Psychoanalysis evolved during the 1880s from the research conducted by Doctors Sigmund Freud and Josef Breuer on the use of hypnosis in the treatment of hysterical patients. Working together, Freud and Breuer discovered that the physical symptoms of hysteria (psychogenic paralysis) could be alleviated as the patient, under hypnosis, recalled and verbalized unpleasant forgotten memories, thereby releasing psychic energy bottled up inside the body. This sudden freeing of the repressed was called a *catharsis* (purging), and this type of treatment was called the cathartic treatment.

As a means of achieving catharsis, however, hypnosis had its drawbacks. Some patients were incapable of being hypnotized. Others would forget upon awakening what they had remembered while in the hypnotic trance. Most unfortunate, the promising curative effects obtained from the hypnotic state often proved to be transitory, vanishing almost as quickly as they appeared, or developing into a new symptom.

Recognizing this, Freud gradually abandoned the use of hypnosis. In its place, he encouraged the patient into a state of mental relaxation where the patient was able to produce spontaneous verbalization, without regard to proprieties and tact. Through analysis and interpretation, these verbalizations led to

199

*Freud, from a painting
made in the 1920s*

the repressed memories. This technique came to be known as the method of free association.

Between 1892 and 1897, while using the method of free association to study the dynamics of unconscious processes, Freud developed his theory of psychoneuroses, of intrapsychic conflicts which resulted from emotional difficulties during childhood. It was during this period that he concluded unequivocally that the free association method was superior as a means of analysis to the hypnotic method, which he was in the process of abandoning. By 1900 he had eliminated the use of hypnosis altogether and reduced his efforts at helping the patient to relax and concentrate. He established the basic rule of the *free association method*: that the patient lie on a couch and say whatever comes to mind. This encouraged more uninhibited and expanding associations, which in turn allowed greater insight into the unconscious mind.

The discovery of the free association method marked the beginning of *talking* as a therapeutic strategy. For the first time in history, mental disorders producing physical symptoms were being treated both medically and scientifically by no other means than the direct use of the patient's verbalization. The putting of feelings into language in a controlled, analytical setting was replacing the use of hypnosis, water treatments, exorcisms, and drownings, which characterized the treatment of mental illness in earlier periods. The patient talked and got well—how remarkable this must have seemed to those who heard of it! Despite all of the subsequent rebellions and reactions to Freudian psychoanalysis over the years, this simple principle of a "talking cure," as Freud called it, was to remain the guiding principle for most other psychotherapies. If we were to pinpoint the single discovery which launched psychotherapy on its way, it would have to be Freud's realization that patients could cure themselves of both physical and psychological ailments through speaking. But Freud did not stop there.

Over the next few years, by studying the free associations of his patients, Freud discovered the significance of childhood sexuality upon the development of personality. He learned how the infant's sexual instinct expressed itself through different areas of the body (erogenous zones) during the first five years of life, and he developed his theory of the psychosexual stages, which became a crucial theoretical base for psychoanalytic treatment. He explored the unconscious sexual life of the child, particularly the child's innate incestuous wishes and desires, shocking a Victorian public that found such reasoning blasphemous. He used both of these concepts to explain how repressions of early sexual feelings and the resulting intrapsychic conflicts contributed to the formation of a symptom and the development of a neurosis. In the process, Freud discovered what many consider to be his most remarkable contribution to the theory of the unconscious: the meaning of dreams.

Freud (1900) referred to dreams as "the royal road to the unconscious." Dreams revealed in symbolic and disguised form, he argued, the wishes of the unconscious mind which were unacceptable to the conscious mind. The dream that the patient remembers and presents to the analyst (manifest content) has a deeper, hidden meaning behind it (latent content), which is arrived at through free association and analysis. Through his continuing analysis of his own and his patients' dreams, Freud was able to support and expand his theories of infantile sexuality, the Oedipus complex, castration anxiety and penis envy, the instincts, and the transference phenomenon. His attempts to interpret dreams scientifically, and to dispel the superstitious beliefs about the prognostic and supernatural powers of dreams, resulted in his monumental scientific study, *The Interpretation of Dreams*, published in 1900.

Psychoanalysis emerged as a major social force during the 1920s. In addition to its popularity as a form of treatment for emotional disorders, its influence was clearly felt in literature and the arts. By this time, a number of Freud's closest disciples—most notably Alfred Adler, Carl Gustav Jung, and Otto Rank —had broken away from the founder's tenacious grasp and were developing their own derivative theories. Adler (1956) emphasized man's struggle for

power, his fight against feelings of inferiority, his life style, and his relationship to the society in which he lives. Rejecting Freud's notion of the primacy of the sexual instinct as a basis for all human motivation, Adler suggested that man instinctively strives for perfection as he attempts to compensate for his feelings of inferiority through his striving toward superiority (the terms *inferiority complex* and *superiority complex* are derived from Adler's writings). Moreover, Adler considered social striving as equivalent in intensity, persistence, and pervasiveness to Freud's sexual instincts. If we look at Adler's (1958) interpretation of the Oedipus complex, we can see most clearly the theoretical differences between Freud and Adler:

In the Freudian theory of the Oedipus Complex, it is supposed that children have a tendency to fall in love with their mothers and wish to marry them and to hate their fathers and wish to kill them. Such a mistake could never arise if we understood the development of children. The Oedipus Complex could appear only in a child who wished to occupy his mother's whole attention and get rid of everyone else. Such a desire is not sexual. It is a desire to subjugate the mother, to have complete control of her and to make her into a servant. It can occur only with children who have been pampered by their mothers and whose feeling of fellowship has never included the rest of the world. In rare cases it has happened that a boy who had always remained connected only with his mother made her the center also of his attempts to meet the problem of love and marriage; but the meaning of such an attitude would be that he could not conceive of cooperation with anyone but his mother. (p. 126)

De-emphasizing the Freudian psychosexual schema, Adler developed in its place a comprehensive view of man and his actions, dominated by alternative social and psychological motivations, feelings, intuitions, and strivings. Scarth (1969) summarizes the main assumptions of Adlerian thinking—what Adler called "individual psychology"—briefly and accurately:

1 Personality is the individual's unique and self-consistent unity.
2 Behavior is purposive and goal-directed. All things an individual does serve a purpose for him.
3 There is one basic dynamic force behind all human activity, a striving from a felt minus situation toward a plus situation, from a feeling of inferiority toward a superiority, perfection, totality.
4 The individual is striving for success in VTHE solution of his problems, this striving being anchored in the very structure of his life.
5 Man is socially embedded. He becomes what he is in interaction with other people. The individual should be perceived in the social context if he is to be understood. We refuse to recognize and examine an isolated human being.
6 Social interest, i.e., a concern for others and its expression in cooperation, is necessary for the solution of life's problems.... Social interest, like all innate human potentialities, will develop in accordance with the individual's self-consistent style of life.
7 Each individual creates his own unique life style based on his subjective perception of himself and his environment, and what appears to him as success.
8 In the healthy individual social interest, as the ultimate form of mankind ... a normative ideal, gives direction to the striving. In mental disturbance, where social interest is lacking, striving is on the socially useless side.
9 Inferiority feelings are present in all individuals. The minus situation gives the impetus to action.
10 People approach life with different degrees of activity. (pp. 146-147)

We see from this wide range of categories that Adler's contribution to the discipline of psychoanalysis was monumental. In the very areas where Freud was weakest—the social sphere of existence, the life style of the individual, the accessible unconscious—Adler offered a comprehensive explication of the human psyche, connected to the activity of the individual.

More importantly to us as counselors, Adler was the first of the psychoanalysts to show a direct interest in child guidance. In 1920 he established child guidance clinics in Vienna, where difficult as well as normal children were offered counseling, conducted at joint sessions with their teachers and parents. The Adlerian model of psychoanalysis—individual psychology—offers much to the school counselor as we shall see later in this chapter.

Another disciple of Freud's who subsequently broke ranks with him to begin his own movement—which is called "Analytical Psychology"—was Carl Gustav

The work of Alfred Adler is particularly applicable to the school counseling setting.

Jung. Jung, like Adler, believed that Freud placed too much emphasis on sexuality. While he is in agreement with many of Adler's points, he differs from Adler on crucial issues, utilizing in place of the Adlerian concepts discussed above man's immediate conflicts and his "will to live." Although Adler and Jung expressed a similar disinclination to the Freudian schema, they took off in different directions, each pursuing the specific area of psychology that he knew best and which to him explained most clearly the complexities of the human psyche. Whitmont and Kaufman (1973) point out,

Carl Gustav Jung, Swiss psychiatrist

Analytical psychotherapy strongly differentiates itself from other systems in its emphasis on the purposive, prospective functioning of the psyche and the placement of the human being within a given, specific archetypal constellation, thereby allowing him to experience a sense of meaning for both his suffering and his achievement. What it objects to in other dynamic systems of psychotherapy is the exaggerated emphasis on reductive, causal thinking…. Analytical psychology considers itself to be empirical and phenomenological in that aside from the very few basic principles posited, the therapist is required to lay aside his various preconceptions about human behavior and be ready to follow the vicissitudes and serpentine ways of the psyche wherever they might lead him. (p. 92)

As we can see from these comments, Jung attempted to avoid many of the deterministic pitfalls of the Freudian system.

Jung contributed a number of specific innovations for which he earned fame. He established the dichotomy between *introversion* and *extroversion*. He rejected Freud's assumption of a single unconscious, arguing instead that we have two unconsciouses: a *personal* unconscious and a *transpersonal* or *collective* unconscious. The personal unconscious closely resembles Freud's version, consisting of everything that has been repressed during one's development. The collective unconscious, his unique contribution to the theory of psychoanalysis, consists of *archetypes*—innate predispositions derived from the cumulative experiences of the race. These predispositions, which influence and help shape our behavior, perceptions, thoughts, and feelings, are not directly accessible to our consciousnesses but appear indirectly and symbolically through the recurring, amaranthine symbols of mythology, folklore, and art. For example, the ideas of a God, of a Hero, of Unity, and of Perfection are recurrent symbols throughout the history of man. Although they assume different forms during different cultural ages and take on different manifestations in each man's life, they have consistently appeared in the literature and mythologies of all people throughout the ages.

Freud's third important disciple, although far less important than either Adler or Jung, was Otto Rank. Rank came from a lower-middle-class family and was the only member of the "Vienna Circle" (as Freud's coterie was known) who was not a medical doctor. Rank became at first Freud's most devoted follower, idolizing the master with an intensity that should have foreboded the coming rift. He served as a secretary to the group while completing his doctor of philosophy degree at the University of Vienna.

But during the early 1920s Rank slowly began to break away from Freud, coming into his own with the publication of his most famous work, *The Trauma of Birth*. This book, which argued that most psychoneurotic conflicts were a result of attempts by the individual to deal with the harsh trauma of the birth process, was viewed by Freud, many now believe unfairly, as a direct rejection of his ideas. While Freud himself had originally suggested the concept of the birth trauma, Rank conceptualized the ramifications of this trauma into a comprehensive system.

Following his break with Freud, Rank emigrated to Paris and the United States, where he began to acquire his own following. As his earlier works, such as *The Myth of the Birth of the Hero* and *The Artist*, began to find a substantial audience, Rank continued his writings, attempting to develop a neo-Freudian type of psychotherapy that placed more emphasis on the patient than he felt Freud did. His final book, *Will Therapy*, was said to have an influence upon the thinking of Carl Rogers. Unfortunately, Rank's writings have had little influence on psychoanalytic theory and practice. His chief contributions are in the areas of aesthetics (Rank, 1932), social psychology (Rank, 1914), and in cultural psychoanalytic thinking.

Karen Horney, although she did not study with Freud, is another important figure in neo-Freudian psychoanalysis. Horney, like Adler, Jung, and Rank, became disillusioned with the narrowness of the Freudian insight. In her writings

Karen Horney, the first major feminist in the psychoanalytic movement

(1937, 1939, 1950), she stresses the social and environmental factors that influence the personality development of the individual. Her theory of neurosis is a vividly detailed theory of intrapsychic conflicts, with different systems of the psyche at war with each other. Cantor (1967) offers a clear description of Horney's view of neurosis:

The neurotic person is ... at war with himself. That the war exists is signalled to us by the existence of self-hate and all of its self destructive mechanisms. The war is based on two different kinds of conflicts. One conflict is within the Pride system.... To the extent that the person is driven to actualize his Idealized Self, his life has been dedicated to a search for glory which has led him to become increasingly alienated from himself and produced a basic uncertainty about how he experiences himself.... The second and deeper conflict which Horney called the Central Inner Conflict is between the whole Pride System which was developed to serve the Idealized Self, and the Real Self from whence comes all constructive forces toward authentic growth.... As the person begins to "feel his own feelings, to know his own wishes, to win his freedom of choice, to make his own decisions and assume responsibility for them" [Horney, 1950, p. 112] he begins to appreciate the existence of a Real Self, a way to be quite different from his Idealized Self.... Now the self-hate is directed against the emerging constructive forces of the Real Self, not simply against the limitations and shortcomings of the Actual Self. (pp. 189-190)

We note in this description of the dynamics of neurosis how Horney's system differs markedly from Freud's psychosexual description. While Freud emphasizes the early sexual fixation, Horney speaks of the current conflicts between systems of the psyche. Consequently, her treatment strategies differ in many ways from the earlier Freudian strategies (discussed below). Horney sees as the primary task of the analyst eliciting constructive forces in the patient's life, and helping the patient mobilize these forces to resolve his problems and conflicts. Although early childhood experiences are significant in both systems, they play less of a role in Horneyan therapy than in Freudian.

Other psychoanalytic thinkers who should be mentioned are Harry Stack Sullivan, Wilhelm Reich, and Anna Freud, Sigmund Freud's daughter. Sullivan, an American psychiatrist, developed a theory of psychopathology and personality built on the relationship between the infant and the person who is primarily responsible for his care—the "mothering one." He conceived of psychiatry as the study of "interpersonal relations" and emphasized the importance of the nuclear family in all subsequent psychological development. Reich, whose emotional problems led to his incarceration in Leavenworth penitentiary where he died, is primarily known for his *orgone therapy*, which is built on the assumption that "biophysiological states are reflected or represented in psychic modes of behavior" (Reich, 1949), and that both the biological and psychological energy systems consist of orgone energy. Reich also made an important contribution in the area of character analysis and the ego's protective armor. Anna Freud, essentially in complete agreement with her father's thinking, has become well known in the field of child psychoanalysis and the application of psychoanalytic principles to teaching and education.

During the 1930s and 40s, a number of writers, including some acerbic critics of Freudian orthodoxy, clearly indicated some of the weaknesses of psychoanalysis as a form of treatment. From the 1940s to the present, the thrust of new psychoanalytic developments has been in the treatment of seriously disturbed patients, particularly schizophrenics. Freud disqualified from psychoanalysis a large portion of the population, whom he deemed "analytically unfit" because they were isolated from interpersonal relations by what he termed "the stone wall of narcissism." These patients, many of whom have the greatest need for therapy, do not respond to the interpretive method advocated by Freud. Hyman Spotnitz (1968), John Rosen (1953), Marie Coleman Nelson (1968), and others have introduced a variety of new techniques which do not require that the patient be emotionally or intellectually capable of understanding interpretations. These techniques, alternatively called *preanalytic*, *direct psychoanalysis*, and *paradigmatic*, attempt to influence directly the patient's unconscious by communicating on an emotional rather than intellectual level, which he is maturationally capable of understanding throughout his limited range of feelings.

THE VIEW OF MAN

Freud viewed man as an inherently instinctual creature, driven by his strivings for infantile gratification. Throughout his life, the individual is strongly motivated to seek out satisfaction of his primitive instinctual drives, sex and aggression, often beclouding in the process his perceptual and emotional awareness of self and others. He distorts the reality of the world around him by utilizing defense mechanisms (see chapter 5), which protect his ego by allowing him to block out and subjectively redefine that which he cannot accept. While this does protect his ego, and consequently his sanity and stability, it alters the world and his relationships in the world significantly, so that what he sees, thinks, and feels consciously is only a fraction of the wide range of possibilities that are within him. Man's vision of life, according to Freud, is obscured by his unconscious fears and wishes, by his persevering and often unmet needs, by his maturational limitations—all of which are rooted in his childhood. He is basically selfish and self-satisfying except insofar as he is able to sacrifice his gratification "of the primitive impulses ... for the common good."

It is this last statement which sheds light on the positive side of Freud's view of man. What makes man different from lower order animals is his ability to transform all of his brute lust into such socially productive forces as art, politics, medicine, humanitarian projects, and the like. His social capabilities are functional psychic transformations of his instinctual drives, and the strongly sexual and aggressive nature of man at birth is ultimately responsible for all his great deeds and actions. Freud's study of Leonardo da Vinci is a classic example of his thinking on this matter; for here he demonstrates how a great genius, artist, and inventor is motivated by his incestuous maternal fantasies. The psychoanalytic view of man is underlined by the belief that the primitive fires of fury that burn within us become the fuels to move civilization from one stage to the next. This process, by which man rechannels his instincts into socially constructive actions that benefit mankind, Freud called *sublimation.*

To explain specifically the dynamics of the mind, Freud postulated the concepts of *id, ego,* and *superego.* The id is the primitive, unorganized mass of energy behind the unconscious mind. It is the part of the mind from which all psychic energy springs, but it is undirected, unorganized, and in total obedience to the pleasure principle. The ego is the executive of personality, the part of the mind that mediates between the id and the real world. The function of the ego is to satisfy the instinctual demands of the id by carrying out transactions with the external world. The superego is the part of the psyche in which parental introjects are located. It is roughly equivalent to conscience, but it is different in that it also includes unconscious factors and other forces which may conflict with the individual's sense of conscience.

Freud's view of man is deeply influenced by his notion of the unconscious. Our personality and our actions, argued Freud, are in a large part determined by the thoughts and feelings contained in the unconscious. These thoughts and feelings are not directly accessible to consciousness, cannot be readily recalled, and are consequently outside the individual's field of awareness, observation, and self-reflection. In *The Psychopathology of Everyday Life* (1901), he demonstrated how the repressed content of the unconscious inadvertently slips through in our words and deeds, resulting in what is commonly called the Freudian slip.

This belief that most activities are governed by the unconscious indicates that the individual may have a limited responsibility for his actions. It is not so much that Freud views man as the victim of circumstances but rather as the victim of his own past. Freud describes this past graphically, in terms of the psychosexual stages of development. During the first year of life, the oral stage, the infant is unable to differentiate between self and other, and he is totally dependent upon the mother for survival. The anal stage that follows is characterized by anal eroticism, desires to be retentive and stubborn, sadistic and masochistic fantasies, and the development of a sense of individuality and self-assertion. Following the anal stage is the phallic stage, in which the child begins to develop sexual interest in the genital area. Finally, the oedipal stage, in which the child develops sexual attachments toward the parent of the opposite sex, serves as the prototype of all later sexual relationships and love relationships. According to Freud, each man is fixated to varying degrees at different stages of development, and the result of these fixations determines to a large part his adult conduct and abilities to react to situations. A person who is stingy and stubborn is not that way because he chooses to be or because he has evaluated all of the options, but rather because during the anal stage of his development, certain difficulties arose which were never adequately resolved. An overly timid woman, who has difficulties dealing with people around her, according to Freud, might be suffering from repressed oedipal fixations of which she is unaware. The implications of this type of reasoning are clear: We are enslaved to our past to the degree that our past repeats itself in our present situations.

208

Freud also stated the principle of the *repetition compulsion*, the phenomenon by which each individual has a tendency to repeat painful experiences and to relive the early unconscious patterns of behavior and responses that he learned from his parents during his early childhood. By the time the child reaches the age of five, argued Freud, most of his later personality and character traits are completely determined. Thus, the psychoanalytic view of man is a deterministic view, in which man's feelings, actions, behavior, and responses to situations are governed, to a significant part at least, by forces outside his awareness, beyond his conscious control, and carried over from his childhood.

THE ROLE OF THE CLIENT

Psychoanalysis has been much criticized, even by some of its strongest adherents at times (Rank, 1945), for its rather restricted view of the client and his place in the treatment. According to Phipps (1959), the psychoanalytic client must accept that he has an illness and that the psychoanalyst is the one who is able to heal him. The client must accept the validity of the psychoanalytic theory to improve, Phipps goes on, and then compares the relationship to that of an interrogator and prisoner in a brainwashing situation. Rogers's (1942) criticisms of the psychoanalytic view of the client also concern this notion that the client is viewed as ill, or somehow disturbed—a point of view to which he objected strenuously. Farrell (1963), too, feels that at the onset of the treatment, the client is put into a weakened position in which he is highly suggestible to the analyst's interpretations. He believes that the material that the patient produces is not necessarily representative of the patient's true character and personality but rather an acquiescing response to the analyst's subtle suggestions to produce this type of material. There is much truth to these criticisms, particularly insofar as the basis of psychoanalytic treatment is that the patient is initially disoriented and not entirely in touch with reality, and that the analyst will ultimately help him see the truth. However, we must keep in mind that more humanistic and client-centered concerns have over the years made themselves felt in even the most classical psychoanalytic approaches.

The psychoanalytic client is expected to bring all his thoughts and feelings into the analytic counseling session and to verbalize them through the use of free association. Traditionally, he is asked to lie on a couch in a supine position, with the counselor seated behind him outside the range of his vision. This is to enable the client to feel relaxed and remain uninfluenced by either real or imagined expressions of the counselor.

It is then expected that the client, no matter how eager he is for treatment, will resist treatment because of his unconscious fears. This resistance can take many forms, including missing appointments, refusing to speak, telling jokes, falling asleep, and so on. Freud identified resistances as originating in either the ego, the id, or the superego. Ego resistances include the patient's desire to keep some material repressed and away from awareness, his attempt to avoid recalling early parental feelings by transferring these feelings onto the counselor, and his wish to continue deriving some positive pleasure (secondary gain) from the neurosis. The id resistances (instinctual resistances) are the most difficult to work through in the analysis. Superego resistances stem from the client's sense of guilt and his need for punishment.

Most important of these resistances therapeutically is the *transference* resistance. Transference can be defined as transferring onto the person of the counselor feelings that were once attached to emotionally significant figures early in life. Originally, Freud considered transference an obstacle to treatment; but eventually he realized that it was the phenomenon of transference that made the treatment and the cure possible. As the client transfers his feelings onto the counselor, he is able to re-experience emotionally his early life situation (*regression*) from which his present difficulties arise. Through this regression, the counselor is able to learn directly of the client's childhood.

For example, consider the case of a client who has developed a transference relationship with his counselor. He begins to experience the counselor as rejecting and ungratifying in the same way he unconsciously experienced his parents many years earlier. If he communicates these transference feelings to the counselor, as he should, and if the counselor is perceptive enough to see them, as he hopefully is, the counselor will then have an understanding of the client's early childhood that could not be provided by the client himself, since he is not consciously aware of these feelings. Clients, in fact, often reveal many of their unconscious wishes, fears, distortions, and conflicts through the transference relationship. Whenever the counselor feels he is being perceived *as if* he were someone other than who he really is, it is reasonably certain that the transference is at work.

Although the client is expected to resist the treatment, he is also expected to be cooperative. This simply means that he will avoid *acting-out*, that is, discharging his repressed feelings by gratifying them outside the analytic session rather than verbalizing them within. In order to have a successful psychoanalytic experience, the client is asked to avoid making any major decisions on his own without first discussing them fully with the analyst. Freud's injunction against marrying, divorcing, having children, changing jobs, or anything else during the course of the treatment was designed to prevent acting-out, which he viewed as a dangerous detriment to the therapy. While such enjoinders do insure a certain integrity to the course of treatment, they place an emotionally stressful burden on the client and foster an attitude of dependency upon the analyst which is difficult to break even after the analysis is completed. Pattison (1970), however, cites another point of view, that after the treatment is completed, "the past relationship with the therapist showed a gradual shift from a therapeutic relationship to a human sharing relationship ... [the] patient was able to use the psychotherapeutic relationship as a paradigm for forming, extending, and using relationships with others after psychotherapy" (p. 213). It may well be that the client's dependency during the treatment is a necessary first step for his subsequent independence after the treatment is completed.

THE ROLE OF THE COUNSELOR

In discussing the role of the psychoanalytic counselor, a clear discrepancy exists between the classical conception of the psychoanalyst and the various modern conceptions. The single major question that the psychoanalytic counselor faces today is how active he is expected to be during the sessions. How much of himself should he give to the client? What feelings of his are allowed to be shown? To what degree can he respond objectively to the client, and to what degree is he supposed to respond primarily to the unconscious communications of the client?

Typically—or stereotypically, as the case may be—the analyst is viewed as extremely passive and detached, offering little of himself and repeatedly responding with his famous "Um hum." This image is not entirely accurate, however. True, the classical psychoanalyst, as defined in Freud's writings, is one who maintains an attitude of objective neutrality, of "evenly suspended attention" (Freud, 1912), who refrains from responding positively or negatively to any of the client's expressions, and studies with detachment the meaning of the client's associations, communications, and dreams. After he has done this, he can then interpret to the client the unconscious meanings of what he has been saying, in order to help the client realize the forces being exerted upon him by the inaccessible reaches of his psyche.

But even during Freud's own time, this passive image of the analyst began to change. Sandor Ferenczi, one of his most influential colleagues and disciples, proposed what he called "active psychotherapy," in which the analyst became a responsive contributing member of the treatment team. In his impressive paper on the subject, Ferenczi (1950), while carefully proclaiming his allegiance to the Freudian theory of treatment, stresses an active phase of treatment designed to facilitate the "education of the ego." Drawing upon insights developed by Freud several years prior, Ferenczi offers examples of certain difficult cases that responded favorably to an active emotional or educational intervention of the analyst. Spotnitz (1963) carries the theory of active psychotherapy even further, arguing that the psychoanalyst uses his own countertransference feelings which have been induced by the patient to inject verbally back into the patient at an appropriate time in order to relieve the patient of toxic, harmful feelings he is experiencing:

This process was conceptualized as one of immunizing a patient against toxic affects.... Mutual contagion emerged as a basic factor: the analyst has to experience the patient's feelings in order to "return" them to him; the patient, through experiencing them from the analyst, is helped to discharge the feelings in language. (pp. 87-88)

John Rosen, perhaps the most radical of the active psychoanalysts, suggests that the analyst live with the patient, functioning as a new, health-engendering mother.

While all of these techniques are used predominantly with severely disturbed patients, recent efforts to apply these principles to typical neurotic patients

211

indicate a significant trend in the psychoanalytic profession, a trend which may have great implications for the counseling profession in future years.

In any case, the most important therapeutic task of the analytic counselor is to help the client resolve his resistances which disrupt treatment and prevent his living maturely. In classical psychoanalysis, this is accomplished by interpreting to the patient the nature and causes of his resistances, with the belief that by understanding his resistances he will be able to control them. Modern psychoanalysis, however, differs from classical psychoanalysis by concentrating on those deeply embedded resistances which do not respond to interpretation. The modern analytic counselor uses reflective and mirroring techniques (see chapter 10) rather than interpretation to *show* the client his resistances—to enable him to feel them—instead of explaining them to him.

This seemingly technical theoretical distinction results in a significant practical discrepancy concerning the role of the counselor. Classical analysts believe that the counselor maintains an essentially passive role, while the modern approach is geared to an active role for the counselor. In opposition to the classical notion of objective neutrality, the modern approach stresses the counselor's use of his countertransference feelings in the treatment. *Countertransference is the counselor's response to the client's feelings.* Whenever a counselor, or a psychoanalyst, works over a period of time with a client, it is inevitable that the counselor will develop some feelings about the client. According to the modern analysts, whether or not these feelings are positive or negative is not as important as whether or not they are realistic, objective responses to the way the patient is feeling about the analyst. Wherever the counselor's feelings are objective—that is, are reality-oriented responses to the client—they are productive in the treatment. When, on the other hand, they are subjective, neurotic distortions by the analyst, they are counterproductive to the goals of the treatment. Thus, if the client is inducing positive feelings in the counselor and the counselor in turn feels positive toward the client, this is said to be an objective countertransference. If the client is expressing a great deal of invisible hostility, and the counselor begins to pick up these negative feelings from the client, this is also objective countertransference. In both cases, the counselor's feelings, as long as they are objective responses to the client's feelings, serve as an indicator of what the client is feeling unconsciously. Thus, the countertransference serves the same purpose to the counselor as the X-ray machine serves to the physician: to reveal those parts of the client that are hidden from view.

Theodore Reik (1948), a disciple of Freud's, describes the concept of "listening with the third ear." The counselor does this by associating along with the client, experiencing his own relevant feelings as the client speaks to him. The counselor, naturally, is not daydreaming while the client is speaking, but rather is allowing the client's words to stimulate in him feelings and ideas which are relevant to the communications that the client is offering. This is a further use of countertransference, whereby the counselor relies on his own feelings to understand and empathize with the feelings of the client.

We can best clarify the role of the counselor by stating five cardinal rules which would probably be acceptable to most psychoanalytic practitioners, regardless of their specific orientation. These rules are:

1 Never offer personal information about yourself, unless there is a specific and compelling therapeutic reason to do so.
2 Analyze resistances as they appear. Do not try to quash or minimize a resistance; confront it head-on, interpreting or reflecting as may be necessary.
3 Learn about the patient not only by listening to what he is saying, but by examining your own feelings about the patient, which are responses to his communication.
4 Give priority to freeing the patient's unconscious over making him feel comfortable. Avoid interjections and interpretations which are solely designed to reduce anxiety, and emphasize those communications which are compatible with the long-range goals of the treatment.
5 Consider all comments, requests, and other communications from the client within the total context of the treatment, rather than isolated instances. This not only helps the counselor understand the implications of specific material in the client's mind but helps unify and structure the treatment in a progressively curative manner.

TECHNIQUES AND GOALS

Freud (1912) says of technique in psychoanalysis that "it consists simply in not directing one's notice to anything in particular and in maintaining the same 'evenly suspended attention' ... in the face of all that one hears...." "This physical 'isolation'" Eidelberg (1968) suggests, "permits the analyst to give himself over to his own unconscious associative processes" (p. 430).

These comments are typical of the psychoanalytic emphasis on the analyst's neutral attitude as a primary technique. Even more important than what the analyst actually does is his willingness to act as a figure for the transference to blossom. Moreover, we see here that the analyst is self-reflective, examining his own unconscious associations as a means of better understanding the patient.

When we speak of psychoanalytic technique, we must always keep in mind that psychoanalysis works on the assumption that there is something wrong with the patient and that the doctor knows what that something is. Unlike other therapists, such as the existential or client-centered, the psychoanalyst, because of his emphasis on the patient's past as a source of his present difficulties, believes that he can diagnose the patient with relative ease and decide on the course of treatment near the outset. It is not unusual in psychoanalytic textbooks to see suggestions that the analyst plan a tentative course of treatment at the first interview. But beyond this assumption and the assumption of transference (discussed earlier), there are some individual differences in the specifics of psychoanalytic technique.

The predominant technique of classical psychoanalysis, as has been mentioned, is interpretation. The analytic counselor interprets in order to help the client understand his unconscious mechanisms. Ideally, however, the counselor, rather than directly interpreting to the client, guides the client to his own interpretations, since the client is more likely to accept the conclusions that he has arrived at himself rather than those the counselor has forced him to recognize. Thus, the predominant method in classical psychoanalytic counseling is leading the client to correct interpretations.

Modern psychoanalysts rely very little on interpretations. Recognizing that the average patient today is intelligent, widely read in psychology, sophisticated, and quite possibly intellectually aware of his problems, modern analysts have drastically de-emphasized the role of interpretation. The old joke about two analysts who pass each other on the street, where one greets the other "Good afternoon," and the other asks, "I wonder what he means by that," is no longer applicable.

In place of interpretation, modern psychoanalytic counselors use *paradigms*. A paradigm, derived from the Greek word for "model," is "a showing by example" (Nelson et al., 1968). It is a technique of teaching the patient something emotionally, a technique used in lieu of interpretation. The authors go on to explain.

By "example" we do not mean that the therapist presents his feelings, his belief or his behavior as a model for the patient to emulate. We mean that the therapist initiates, induces or prolongs modes of interaction with the patient which promote the latter's self-understanding without manifest recourse to interpretation in the explanatory sense. (p. 45)

Paradigms offer an advantage to the counselor in that they do not require the patient to "admit" his unconscious difficulties in order to resolve them. Where a classical analyst may tell a patient that his stubbornness is a result of his overly-strict toilet training, a paradigmatic counselor would deal with the client's stubbornness by allowing him to be constructively stubborn, thereby compensating for the parents' severity at an earlier point in life.

Strean (1968) gives an example of how a paradigm may be used successfully to treat an adolescent who is compelled to make up bizarre fantasies: Whenever the patient made up a fantasy, the analyst made up an even more bizarre fantasy, in effect demonstrating to the patient that the analyst's "craziness" was equal to his own. Finally, after a year and a half, the patient expressed his real hostility to the analyst.

The differences between classical and modern psychoanalysis can be summed up as follows: classical psychoanalysis believes that as the patient comes to understand his problem, he will be able to overcome it; modern psychoanalysis offers the position that to grow, the patient must re-experience his early emotional difficulties with the analyst and that the analyst must provide the proper and appropriate care that the patient's parents failed to provide.

The goal of all psychoanalysis, regardless of the underlying beliefs, is to reduce the patient's anxieties, to cure his fixations and regressions, and to enable him to reach a stage of integration. At this stage, his ego is able to organize and unite his diverse drives and tendencies to function harmoniously within the personality, thus enabling the individual to think, behave, and feel in a constructive, organized, and direct manner. This level of integration is generally considered the highest level of psychological development.

To reach this level, however, requires a number of sacrifices of immediate gratification. The ultimate efficacy of the psychoanalytic treatment demands a disciplined attitude at each stage of the progress. Just as the young child learns to mature by mild frustrations which he is forced to deal with, the psychoanalytic patient begins to recover from his problems and gain strength by learning to cope with the frustrations he encounters during his sessions. The psychoanalyst is supposed to frustrate the patient, is supposed to make him anxious and unsure at times, is supposed to mobilize all his hostility and anger. This is all for a good purpose, to be sure, but nevertheless a painful and difficult part of the treatment.

The self-control of the analyst, and his ability always to see the treatment in a comprehensive perspective, become his two most forceful techniques. For it is only by his willingness to delay interpretations and communications until the appropriate time that the patient is given an opportunity to gain strength and certainty which will become an ultimate part of the cure.

EVALUATION

Psychoanalysis has often been minimized as a technique applicable to the school counseling setting. Its critics argue that it places too much emphasis on sexuality and early childhood experiences, that as a treatment it requires too much time and an impractical frequency of sessions, that it does not deal directly with the problem, that it brings to the surface more repressed material than is necessary, and that it only works for certain kinds of patients. While many of these criticisms are justified and essentially valid, psychoanalysis does in fact have much to offer the school counselor.

Adlerian psychology, by its very nature, is conducive to the school counseling situation. Because it deals with the actions of the individual child, his life style and adjustment to the social situation, and because it takes into account the child's conscious as well as unconscious forces, it has gained a wider following among school personnel than the orthodox Freudian point of view. It is also important to keep in mind that Adler himself founded the first child guidance clinics in Vienna, thus demonstrating in practice as well as in theory the relevance of his approach to school counseling.

Ansbacher (1971) lists twenty-seven key principles that are likely to be held by an Adlerian counselor, principles that are philosophical and positive, that are totally consonant with the underlying foundations of the counseling stance. Perhaps if the critics of psychoanalysis were to examine these principles, they would be surprised to find the degree of concordance between their own counseling beliefs and the explicit principles stated by Ansbacher.

Platt (1971) has evaluated the efficacy of the Adlerian model in elementary school counseling, concluding that the model was effective in the limited setting in which it was experimentally used. Nelson (1967) has suggested a program for utilizing Individual Psychology for counseling low achieving students. Stormer and Kirby (1971) have described an Adlerian program implemented in an elementary school. Based on the principles of individual psychology (outlined in Ansbacher and Ansbacher's 1956 book) in this program

the school counselor … begins by identifying the purpose of the child's misbehavior, then discloses this purpose to him, in an acceptable way, and helps him to respond to his situation in more constructive and socially beneficial ways. The counselor also communicates his understanding of the case to the significant persons in the child's environment, and helps them to encourage the child's changed, more desirable behavior. For the child, understanding is facilitated in group counseling. For the parents and teachers observation of such group sessions, together with discussion groups of their own, is an effective way of increasing their understanding and skills of responding. (p. 162)

We see here a very different picture of psychoanalysis from the one typically presented by the Freudian advocates, a picture that, again, is highly conducive to the aims and scope of school counseling. Dinkmeyer (1964) has perhaps the most telling comment on the relevance of the Adlerian position:

Adlerian theory … adds a dimension to the counselor. He may study causes, but he goes beyond to an awareness of purposes. Thus he gains insight into some really significant factors in understanding and treating the individual. (p. 178)

Moreover, some recent research has indicated that the direct application of classical psychoanalytic insights to school-related problems and the implementation of non-Adlerian psychoanalytic methods within the school setting holds great promise. Graffagnino et al. (1970), in a study of latency-age children with emotional problems who come from low socioeconomic backgrounds, found that psychoanalytically oriented psychotherapy in a clinical-educational setting offered some benefit to the children. Jarvis (1969) has discussed some learning disabilities from a psychoanalytic point of view, suggesting that disturbances in the child's fantasy formation may interfere with the normal capacity for learning. Other writers have applied classical psychoanalytic principles to a variety of school related problems (Stefflre, 1965).

Many counselors now believe that a number of classical psychoanalytic principles, when extrapolated from the overall philosophy, are directly relevant to school counseling. Particularly important to the counselor is the recognition of unconscious forces in shaping and directing one's behavior. As the counselor comes to recognize the power of the unconscious, he is better able to understand not only the behavior and feelings of the client as the products of unconscious interactions, but his own behavior and feelings toward the client as manifestations of his unconscious as well.

The Freudian psychoanalytic principles directly applicable to the school counseling situation include the phenomena of resistance and transference, which explain the client's interaction with the counselor, the repetition compulsion, which clarifies the client's illogical behavior, and the method of interpretation, which is useful in helping the client become aware of the forces outside of his recognition.

The school counselor who is interested in psychoanalysis as a technique can apply many of these principles in his everyday practice. He might, for example, examine the client's behavior for deeper meanings by asking him questions such as "Why did you act in that way?" or "What does this mean to you?" While listening to the client, the psychoanalytic counselor would study the associations that the client is producing and try to understand the client's unconscious perceptions. Most important, the psychoanalytic counselor must always be aware of the client's limited perception of and control over himself, and he must try to help the client reach a more satisfactory understanding of himself, by teaching him, through interpretations, the unconscious meanings of his behavior.

Because they deal so directly with the unconscious, however, psychoanalytic methods must be used cautiously and only after sufficient training. Inexperienced counselors exhibit a tendency to interpret too much to the client, overwhelming him with more feeling than he can appropriately handle. The counselor must always keep in mind that the material that the client has repressed is the material he is not yet emotionally capable of acknowledging.

In summary, we can say that psychoanalytic principles can be applied to school counseling in a sensible, moderate, integrated, nonindulgent manner, where the counselor shows sufficient caution and an awareness of the effect of what he is saying upon the client.

References

Adler, A. Development of the style of life. In H. L. Ansbacher & R. R. Ansbacher (Eds.), *The individual psychology of Alfred Adler: A systematic presentation in selections from his writing.* New York: Basic Books, 1956. Pp. 186–192.

Adler, A. *What life should mean to you.* New York: Capricorn, 1958.

Ansbacher, H. L., & Ansbacher, R. R. (Eds.). *The individual psychology of Alfred Adler: A systematic presentation in selections from his writing.* New York: Basic Books, 1956.

Ansbacher, R. First workshop on training Adlerian counselors. *The Individual Psychologist*, 1971, *8*, 41–48.

Cantor, M. B. Karen Horney on psychoanalytic technique: Mobilizing constructive forces. *American Journal of Psychoanalysis*, 1967, *27*, 188–199.

Dinkmeyer, D. Conceptual foundations of counseling: Adlerian theory and practice. *The School Counselor*, 1964, *11*, 174–178.

Eidelberg, L. (Ed.). *Encyclopedia of psychoanalysis.* New York: Free Press, 1968.

Farrell, B. A. Psychoanalysis-II: The method. *New Society*, 1963, *39*, 12–14.

Ferenczi, S. *Further contributions to the theory and practice of psychoanalysis.* London: Hogarth, 1950.

Freud, S. *The interpretation of dreams.* (Originally published, 1900.)

Freud, S. *The psychopathology of everyday life.* New York: Signet, 1961. (Originally published, 1901.)

Freud, S. Recommendations to physicians practicing psychoanalysis (1912). In J. Strachey (Ed.) *The standard edition of the complete psychological works of Sigmund Freud.* London: Hogarth, 1953–1970. Vol. 12 (1958), pp. 111–120.

Graffagnino, P. N., Bucknam, F. G., Orgun, I. N., & Leve, R. M. Psychotherapy for latency-age children in an inner city therapeutic school. *American Journal of Psychiatry*, 1970, *127*, 86–94.

Horney, K. *The neurotic personality of our time*. New York: Norton, 1937.

Horney, K. *New ways in psychoanalysis*. New York: Norton, 1939.

Horney, K. *Neurosis and human growth*. New York: Norton, 1950.

Jarvis, V. Learning disability and its relationship to normal fantasy formation. *Psychological Review*, 1969, *56*, 288–297.

Nelson, M. C. Individual psychology as a basis for the counseling of low achieving students. *Personnel and Guidance Journal*, 1967, *46*, 283–287.

Nelson, M. C., Nelson, B., Sherman, M. H., & Strean, H. S. *Roles and paradigms in psychotherapy*. New York: Grune & Stratton, 1968.

Pattison, E. M. The patient after psychotherapy. *American Journal of Psychotherapy*, 1970, *24*, 194–213.

Phipps, H. The dynamics of the psychotherapeutic relationship. *Psychiatry*, 1959, *22*, 17–39.

Platt, J. M. Efficacy of the Adlerian model in elementary school counseling. *Elementary School Guidance and Counseling*, 1971, *6*, 86–91.

Rank, O. *The trauma of birth*. New York: Nervous and Mental Diseases Publishing Company, 1914.

Rank, O. *Art and artist: Creative urge and personality development*. New York: Tudor, 1932.

Rank, O. *Will therapy*. New York: Knopf, 1945.

Reich, W. *Character analysis*. New York: Orgone Institute Press, 1949.

Reik, T. *Listening with the third ear*. New York: Farrar, Strauss, 1948.

Rogers, C. R. *Counseling and psychotherapy*. Boston: Houghton Mifflin, 1942.

Rosen, J. *Direct psychoanalysis*. New York: Grune & Stratton, 1953.

Scarth, P. Implications of individual psychology for the school psychologist. *Journal of Individual Psychology*, 1969, *25*, 146–154.

Spotnitz, H. The toxoid response. *The Psychoanalytic Review*, 1963, *50(4)*, 81–94.

Spotnitz, H. *Modern psychoanalysis of the schizophrenic patient*. New York: Grune & Stratton, 1968.

Stefflre, B. *Theories of Counseling*. New York: McGraw-Hill, 1965.

Stormer, E. G., & Kirby, J. H. Adlerian group counseling in the elementary school: Report of a program. *Journal of Individual Psychology*, 1971, *27*, 155–163.

Strean, H. S. Choice of paradigms in the treatment of parent and child. In M. C. Nelson et al. (Eds.), *Roles and paradigms in psychotherapy*. New York: Grune & Stratton, 1968.

Whitmont, E. C., & Kaufman, Y. Analytical psychotherapy. In R. Corsini (Ed.), *Current psychotherapies*. Itasca, Ill.: F. E. Peacock, 1973.

Suggested additional readings

Alexander, F. A., & French, T. *Psychoanalytic therapy*. New York: Ronald Press, 1946.

Arlow, J. A., & Brenner, C. *Psychoanalytic concepts and the structural theory*. New York: International Universities Press, 1964.

Brammer, L. M., & Shostrom, E. L. Therapeutic psychology. Englewood Cliffs, N.J.: Prentice-Hall, 1962.

Fairbairn, W. R. D. *Psychoanalytic studies of the personality*. London: Tavistock, 1952.

Fenichel, O. *The psychoanalytic theory of neurosis*. New York: Norton, 1945.

Ferenczi, S., & Rank, O. *The development of psychoanalysis*. New York: Nervous and Mental Diseases Publishing Company, 1925.

Freud, A. *The ego and the mechanisms of defense*. New York: International Universities Press, 1946.

Fromm-Reichmann, F. *Principles of intensive psychotherapy*. Chicago: University of Chicago Press, 1950.

Jones, E. *The life of Sigmund Freud* (3 vols.). New York: Basic Books, 1953–1957.

Jung, C. G. *Two essays on analytical psychology*. London: Balliere, Tindall & Cox, 1928.

Lindzey, G., & Hall, C. *Theories of personality*. New York: John Wiley & Sons, 1957.

Munroe, R. L. *Schools of psychoanalytic thought*. New York: Dryden Press, 1955.

Paul, L. (Ed.). *Psychoanalytic Clinical Interpretation*. New York: Free Press, 1963.

Sullivan, H. S. *The interpersonal theory of psychiatry*. New York: Norton, 1953.

Sullivan, H. S. *The psychiatric interview*. New York: Norton, 1954.

Wolberg, L. *The technique of psychotherapy*. New York: Grune & Stratton, 1954.

chapter nine

Client-centered counseling

Of all the theories of counseling and psychotherapy, none has had a more profound impact upon the profession of school counseling than the client-centered point of view. Democratic and egalitarian, practical and optimistic, client-centered counseling has emerged as a decided favorite among school counselors. Moreover, Rogers himself, unlike Freud, has written a number of papers specifically applicable to the school setting, ranging from treating counseling problems to applications of client-centered counseling in classroom teaching. As we look at the client-centered approach, we shall see at almost every point a sharp and uncompromising disagreement with the directive, deterministic classical psychoanalytic point of view.

HISTORY OF THE SCHOOL

Client-centered therapy is America's first distinctively indigenous school of therapy. It was born and nurtured from the work of a single man, Carl R. Rogers, and consequently it is sometimes referred to as Rogerian therapy. Unlike many schools of therapy, whose histories are colored with schisms and rebellions against the precursory dogma, client-centered therapy is nonprescriptive and responsive enough to allow the expression of individual styles and techniques within the overall philosophy and accepted framework. In fact, every client-centered counselor develops his own particular style of treatment, compliant only to the basic principle of "an open and accepting attitude" by the counselor, as developed and explained by Rogers. This flexibility of technique is in part determined by the nature of the therapy, where the client himself directs the movement of the treatment, and in part by the unusually flexible attitude of the founder.

Rogers emerged from a background of liberal education and progressive social beliefs. Steeped in liberal Protestant theology, the progressive educational ideas of Dewey and Kilpatrick, and Franklin D. Roosevelt's new social policy, Rogers's character was not at all suited to the strict Freudian tenets to which his training in clinical psychology exposed him. Disturbed by the belief that Freudian psychotherapy did not focus on the world of the patient, but rather placed the patient in a category of preconceived diagnosis, Rogers reacted against its narrowness, injecting into his counseling practice his own liberal, humanistic values, adapted to the therapeutic milieu.

It would be almost impossible to pinpoint with accuracy the many writers and ideologies which helped shape Rogers's thinking. Lister (1965) has cited John Dewey, Paul Tillich, Martin Buber, and Sören Kierkegaard as the major philosophical influences to whom Rogers is indebted. It is clear that Dewey's experiential approach to reality, Tillich's idea of "the courage to be," Buber's philosophy of dialogue, and Kierkegaard's precursory existential insights all find a psychotherapeutic expression in Rogers's theory and ideology. To these influences, we must also add William Heard Kilpatrick, Otto Rank, and a number of his teachers in high school, college, and graduate school (Meador and Rogers, 1973). Speaking of the influences exerted upon him during his graduate training, Rogers (1959b) says,

Having rejected the family views of religion, I became interested in a more modern religious viewpoint and spent two profitable years in Union Theological Seminary, which at that time was deeply committed to a freedom of philosophical thought which respected any honest attempt to resolve significant problems, whether this led into or away from the church. My own thinking led me in the latter direction, and I moved "across the street" to Teachers College, Columbia University. Here I was exposed to the views of John Dewey, not directly, but through William H. Kilpatrick. I also had my first introduction to clinical psychology in the warmly human and common-sense approach of Leta Hollingsworth. There followed a year of internship at the Institute for Child Guidance, then in its chaotic but dynamic first year of existence 1927–28. Here I gained much from the highly Freudian orientation of most of its psychiatric staff, which included David Levy and Lawson Lowrey. My first attempts at therapy were carried on at the Institute. Because I was still completing my doctorate at Teachers College, the sharp incompatibility of the highly speculative Freudian thinking of the Institute with the highly statistical and Thorndikean views at Teachers College was keenly felt. (p. 186)

We see, then, that Rogers's thinking represents a synthesis and transformation of a number of divergent approaches to which he had been exposed in his training. But probably what contributed most powerfully to Rogers's thinking, in a negative way at least, was his dissatisfaction with the Freudian psychoanalytic approach to therapy. His early thinking, particularly, is a distinct reaction to the Freudian position.

First, he objected to the use of the word *patient* because of its connotations of debility. In its place, he substituted the word *client* to convey "one who comes actively and voluntarily to gain help on a problem, but without any notion of surrendering his own responsibility for the situation" (Rogers, 1951, p.79). Next, he reacted against the directness of Freudian therapy. Influenced by the

Carl Rogers, originator of client-centered therapy

progressive psychoanalytic techniques of Otto Rank, and particularly by Rank's emphasis on the role of the client, Rogers began to develop his client-centered point of view, referring to it at the time as *nondirective* counseling. Where Rogers differed from Rank, and where he in fact parted company with the psychoanalytic approach, was at the point where he rejected the principle of the unconscious, accepting in its place what we now call a *phenomenological* view of the client: that is, accepting the client's feelings as they are presented, rather than looking for hidden clues underneath. This important step enabled Rogers to take a new, uncolored view of the client and, consequently, to evolve his new form of treatment.

Rogers published his first book, *The Clinical Treatment of the Problem Child*, in 1939. He had written the book several years earlier, and by the time of its publication many of the insights and ideas which were inchoate at the time of writing had begun to crystallize. In 1940, Rogers delivered the first paper distinctively about his new therapy, entitled "Newer Concepts in Psychotherapy," to the Minnesota chapter of Psi Chi. During this time, Rogers was tape-recording sessions with his clients at Ohio State University. These verbatim transcripts represented a significant step in the objective scientific study of counseling and in the training of counselors. For the first time in the history of psychotherapy, an entire counseling session could be studied verbatim, rather than relying on reports from the therapist or a subjective summary of the session.

Most of Rogers's earlier theoretical concepts, along with a verbatim transcript, were first presented in *Counseling and Psychotherapy*, published in 1942.

221

In this book, which aroused much professional controversy, Rogers stated the basic procedures of nondirective counseling: that the counselor must maintain a nonjudgmental attitude, provide a warm and receptive atmosphere for the client to communicate in, and allow the client to direct the course of the treatment. But the book was far from a complete picture of client-centered counseling as it exists today. It was heavy on techniques and therapeutic strategies, both of which Rogers abandoned in later years.

In 1951, having revised some of his views—the revisions based in part on his experience at the counseling center of the University of Chicago where he practiced from 1945 to 1957—he published *Client-Centered Therapy*. In this book, Rogers outlines a comprehensive statement of his theory. He had changed the name of his therapy from nondirective to client-centered. "The change was not merely semantic," point out Meador and Rogers (1973, p. 123).

It indicated a shift in emphasis from the negative, narrower statement, "nondirective," to the positive focus on the growth-producing factors in the individual client himself.

The tone and content of the book had shifted from his earlier position as well. Rogers's research during the intervening years had persuaded him that the quality of the therapeutic relationship was the prime determinant of the degree to which the client was able to readjust his concept of *self* so that it would become congruent with his experiences. He emphasizes in this book the importance of accurate empathic understanding and minimizes the use of specific therapeutic techniques. *Client-Centered Therapy* also presents Rogers's theory of personality for the first time. This theory postulates a fluid self-concept in organic interaction with its environment. It is a self which is capable of change, becoming congruent or incongruent as circumstances, perceptions, and feeling change.

During the decade of the 50s, Rogers and his colleagues doggedly pursued their research, attempting in a number of ways to isolate those factors which contributed most substantially to therapeutic efficacy. Several important studies and position papers (Rogers, 1954, 1957a, 1959b, 1967) emerged from this research. As the client-centered approach began to cohere around the postulate that the therapeutic relationship (and, particularly, the qualities of genuineness, warmth, empathy, and unconditional positive regard) had priority over all other variables, Rogers's ideas were beginning to make a profound impact in the schools, both in counseling and in teaching. School personnel began to recognize that they could find and develop these key qualities in themselves in order to become more successful in their interactions with students.

In 1957 Rogers moved to the University of Wisconsin, where he was offered the position of professor of psychology. Concentrating largely on group counseling by this time, and especially on working with the seriously disturbed patient, who was unreceptive to the other therapies, Rogers further refined his principles of counseling. He began to explore the possibilities of client-centered counseling as a tool in dealing with psychotic patients, with mixed results, which were published in 1967 under the title, *The Therapeutic Relationship and Its Impact*. In this important study, probably the most massive research effort ever conducted in the field of psychotherapy, Rogers and his colleagues studied the impact of the therapeutic relationship upon hospitalized schizophrenics and a matched group of normal individuals. "The general aim," Rogers (1967) says, "was to make an intensive study of the factors involved in the process of change in personality and behavior as it occurs in schizophrenic and normal individuals during a period of psychotherapy" (p. 3). Careful experimental procedures were instituted, with the aim of isolating pure variable factors and weighing their relative impact. Although the results were of an overall positive nature, certain therapeutic variables did not demonstrate conclusively their contribution to the efficacy of the treatment.

What stands out from this sweeping view of Rogers's activities is his continual willingness to evaluate and revise his thinking. From the very beginnings at Ohio in the early 40s, Rogers was actively engaged in research to test out the hypotheses he had intuitively arrived at in his practice. Where evidence indicated that a change of position was appropriate, he never hesitated to revise his views, bringing them in accord with the evidence.

In 1964 he moved to California, where he joined the Western Behavioral Sciences Institute at La Jolla and continued his work with groups. In his most recent book, *Carl Rogers on Encounter Groups*, he translates a number of the client-centered principles into group psychotherapy concepts. While client-centered therapy seems to have lost some of its influence in recent years, it is still the most popular form of therapy in the school setting and is gaining increasing acceptance in group work.

THE VIEW OF MAN

The client-centered counselor sees man as essentially good in nature, inherently capable of fulfilling his destiny and living his life in a peaceful, productive, and creative way. The forces which prevent this type of fulfillment are not intrinsic to his personality, but rather an amalgam of interacting social and psychological forces which muster against the realization of his potentialities. In the Rogerian philosophy, man is seen as having the capacity to deal with his own conflicts, but he is limited in doing so insofar as he lacks knowledge about himself.

Rogers himself has generally presented his view of man within the context of his therapeutic observations. Although a number of writers have suggested the influences of Rousseau, Dewey, or Emerson on Rogers's picture of man, this has not yet been systematically investigated. One of Rogers's clearest and most direct statements on the subject is found in his 1957 response to those writers who have discussed his view of man:

My views of man's most basic characteristics have been formed by my experience in psychotherapy. They include certain observations as to what man is not, as well as some description of what, in my experience, he is. Let me state these very briefly and then endeavor to clarify my meanings.

I do not discover man to be well characterized in his basic nature by such terms as fundamentally hostile, antisocial, destructive, evil.

I do not discover man to be, in his basic nature, completely without a nature, a tabula rasa on which anything may be written, nor malleable putty which can be shaped into any form.

I do not discover man to be essentially a perfect being, sadly warped and corrupted by society.

In my experience I have discovered man to have characteristics which seem inherent in his species, and the terms which have at different times seemed to me descriptive of these characteristics are such terms as positive, forward-moving, constructive, realistic, trustworthy. (Rogers, 1957b, p. 199)

We see from these comments that Rogers's view is not an accidental consequence of his thinking but rather a well-thought-out part of it.

Moreover, like Dewey, by whom he was greatly influenced, Rogers looks at man in his continual interaction with his environment. His environment, argues Rogers, is not an objective reality, mutually perceived by all the people in the world, but a subjective, personal reality, dependent upon the individual's feelings, perceptions, and abilities. This reality, as it is perceived, is called the *phenomenological field*. As a person's experiences and feelings change, so, too, does his environment, which is a product of these feelings and experiences. Thus, his interaction with the environment is one in which both the individual and his environment change, in regard to each other.

The individual's sense of self emerges from this interaction with his phenomenal field. Rogers defines the self as "an organized, fluid, but consistent conceptual pattern of perceptions of characteristics and relationships of the 'I' or 'me,' together with values attached to these concepts ... which emerge as a result of interaction with the environment, and particularly as a result of evaluational interactions with others" (Rogers, 1951, p. 498). Because the self is the center of the individual's experiences with the environment, the individual's perceptions of and interactions with the environment change as his sense of self changes. This constitutes the basic movement of the therapy.

The ways in which the individual behaves and the ways he adapts to situations are always consistent with his self-concept. His actions are reflections of his perceptions. Rogers's general rule is that the experiences that the individual undergoes are either (1) organized into the self structure, (2) ignored because they are inconsistent with the sense of self, or (3) perceived distortedly because they are not harmonious with the self-perceptions. Consequently, the individual is said to be well adjusted when he is able to assimilate on a symbolic level all of his experiences into a consistent relationship with the concept of self. In this respect, Rogers's thinking is similar to Freud's concept of the integrated personality.

Rogers's view of man differs most markedly from Freud's in its emphasis on the changing, protean, evolving nature of man. In opposition to Freud's deterministic viewpoint, Rogers sees man as a creature of changing destinies, capable of dealing with his own problems, of reorganizing his perceptions, and of learning to understand others differently.

THE ROLE OF THE CLIENT

The burden of cure in client-centered therapy is directly upon the client. The client is expected to learn to deal with his conflicts, to order and direct the forces of his life, to come to grips with his problems, and to "overbalance the regressive and self-destructive forces" (Rogers, 1951, p. 122) that are the source of his difficulties. Most succinctly stated, the client's job is to cure himself through his constructive relationship with the counselor, from whom he is to gain support, encouragement, and understanding.

The belief underlying these premises, as Butler and Seeman (1950) point out, is "that an individual who is aware of his own attitudes and motivations is likely to be an integrated person." They go on to explain.

Client-centered therapy ... postulates that an individual has within himself the capacity and resources to develop this self-understanding, and ... therapy should provide the conditions under which these resources may be released. The significance of the client-centered approach to counseling seems to revolve about what has been called the internal frame of reference ... that behavior is a result of the way in which an individual thinks about himself, his relationship to others, and his environment. (p. 520)

What the client is actually engaged in as he undergoes the therapy is a process of self-exploration. His task within the therapeutic context is to explore his feelings and behavior, to discover, with a sense of wonder, new aspects of himself, and to bend these new aspects into the image of self which holds together the range of his perceptions. This process of self-exploration comprises several stages: "Before an individual can engage in intrapersonal exploration he must be able to reveal or expose himself," Patterson (1969, p. 15) points out. He describes these revelatory processes, in terms of the client-centered approach, as self-disclosure (particularly of the negative aspects of self), followed by an openness to experience, increasing existential living, and an increasing trust in one's organism. In toto, these processes lead to self-actualization and fulfillment.

The client may not, however, be immediately capable of this difficult task. Because of his previous experiences with a counselor or therapist, or because of erroneous preconceptions about counseling or therapy, he may regard the therapeutic experience as "one where he will be labelled, looked upon as abnormal, hurt, treated with little respect, [or] look upon the counselor as an extension of the authority which referred him for help" *(Client-Centered Therapy*, p. 66). He may feel threatened by the counseling setting, self-conscious, ashamed. In any case, it is the counselor's job to help the client realize the nonjudgmental, accepting reality of the situation, after which the client is able to begin helping himself.

THE ROLE OF THE COUNSELOR

The primary job of the client-centered counselor is to develop a therapeutic relationship with the client. This is accomplished not so much by formal techniques and procedures, but rather by the counselor's total attitude toward the client and toward the therapy. First, he must be nonjudgmental, willing to accept the client as he is, a whole person, always in flux, always growing, always different. He must be willing to listen to the client patiently, understandingly, and without interpreting or imposing his views—his reality—upon the client. He must be cognizant of the client's total responsibility for himself, and willing to allow the client to experience the range of this responsibility, without developing a dependency upon the counselor.

The client-centered counselor must enter the subjective personal world of the patient and experience along with him his myriad feelings and perceptions, not as a therapist studying a patient, but as one person interacting strictly on a personal level with another. As Rogers describes it, he is to assume "the internal frame of reference of the client, to perceive the world as the client sees it, to perceive the client himself as he is seen by himself, to lay aside all perceptions from the external frame of reference while doing so, and to communicate something of the empathetic understanding to the client" *(Client-Centered Therapy*, p. 29). By so doing, the counselor helps the client overcome his frightening and negative feelings about the counseling situation, engenders a feeling of trust and rapport with the client, and helps the client begin to reorganize and restructure his own subjective world wherever it is *incongruent* (defined as the discrepancy between the individual's experience and his distorted perception of the experience).

"One of the main hypotheses of the client-centered counselor," point out Butler and Seeman (1950),

is that if he has been able: (1) to create the proper psychological atmosphere, (2) to understand the client in the client's own terms, and (3) to communicate his understanding, then the client will be enabled to look squarely at himself as he is with what he feels are both his good and bad characteristics. It is this process of facing himself, of admitting his attitudes into awareness that allows him to reorganize his way of seeing himself and his world in the direction of greater emotional freedom and maturity. (p. 521)

In order for the counselor to meet these conditions, it is necessary that he have within himself the proper attitudes and personal characteristics that Rogers asserts are the very "conditions of therapy."

Three of the most important qualities that Rogers considers imperative for the client-centered counselor are genuineness, empathy, and unconditional positive regard. This trinity of terms has become the shibboleth of the Rogerian practitioner, and the bulk of Rogers's research during the late 1950s and 60s has been designed to specify these conditions and test their validity as therapeutic variables. The significance attached to these qualities is based on the principle that constructive personality growth and change comes about only when the client perceives and experiences a certain psychological climate in the relationship. The conditions which constitute this climate do not consist of knowledge, intellectual training, orientation in some school of thought, or techniques. They are feelings or attitudes which must be experienced by the counselor and perceived by the client. (Rogers, 1962, p. 422)

Genuineness simply means that the counselor be himself in the relationship, that he avoid presenting a facade or acting the role of the therapist. The counselor must be able to accept all of his own feelings, even those which may be inappropriate to the relationship. "Genuineness," Rogers (1957a) says,

means that within the relationship he [the counselor] is freely and deeply himself, with his actual experience accurately represented by his awareness of himself. It is the opposite of presenting a facade, either knowingly or unknowingly.... It should be clear that this includes being himself even in ways which are not regarded as ideal for psychotherapy. His experience may be "I am afraid of this client" or "My attention is so focused on my own problems that I can scarcely listen to him." If the therapist is not denying these feelings to awareness, but is able freely to be them (as well as being his other feelings), then the condition [of genuineness] is met. (p. 97)

Empathy, a condition which has probably been investigated more thoroughly than any other condition (see chapter 4), constitutes the central focus of the counselor's perception of the client. Rogers's (1962) description of empathy demonstrates its importance dramatically:

The second essential condition in the relationship ... is that the counselor is experiencing an accurate empathic understanding of his client's private world, and is able to communicate some of the significant fragments of that understanding. To sense the client's inner world of private, personal meanings as if it were your own, but without ever losing the "as if" quality.... To sense his confusion or his timidity or his anger or his feeling of being treated unfairly as if it were your own...this is the condition I am endeavoring to describe. (p. 419)

Unconditional positive regard occurs when the counselor accepts the client and all of his experiences, without judgment, without evaluation, and without any conditions. This is a much criticized condition of client-centered counseling, inasmuch as it is nearly impossible to accept so totally another person. But as Rogers explains, this is the optimum level of acceptance to be strived for.

In short, we can say that the client-centered counselor acts as a sympathetic ear and an invisible guiding hand. Through his listening, he empathizes along with the client his feelings and experiences. His communications to the client act as a catalyst for growth and are not intended to impose changes upon the client's life. He helps the client guide himself to better understanding by his nondirective and unobtrusive attitude. He is there, as Rogers says, primarily to motivate and support the client in his personal quest for answers to his difficulties.

TECHNIQUES AND GOALS

Although the counselor's attitude and personality are of prime importance in client-centered counseling, there are several techniques that are also prominently used. Lister (1965) mentions "reflection of feeling, listening, and clarification" as the main techniques. Most important of these techniques is the technique of reflection. In reflection, the counselor repeats back to the client, in an emotionally equivalent tone, what the client has just said. While this seems simple enough, it serves two important purposes: first, it enables the client to see how another (a very important other, I should add) is perceiving what he is saying; second, it helps the client feel that the counselor is accepting him for whatever he says and whatever he is.

The counselor must also help the client modify and reorganize his perceptual field. But he must do this in a nondirective way, that is, without interpreting incongruities to the client. He must deal with this task by communicating to the client his own positive feelings about him, his own willingness to accept him, his own regard for him. If this is carefully and honestly communicated, the client will soon begin to re-experience himself in the context of his relationship with the counselor. Then, after his sense of self is reevaluated within the relationship, he will test out his new perceptions outside the relationship, in a different environment, where he will again reorganize his self-identity.

The essential technique in client-centered counseling, therefore, is to show the client, by way of verbal communications, a different reality from the one he has been experiencing. This is done by reflecting his feelings back to him and by relating to him the counselor's positive feelings.

Rogers (1958) has examined the process of psychotherapy in terms of the stages of development by which personality change takes place. He has concluded that in successful psychotherapy, the client moves from fixity to changeableness; from rigid structures to flow; from stasis to process. He attempts in his paper, "A Process Conception of Psychotherapy" (1958), to pinpoint seven crucial stages of the change process. At the first stage, internal communication is blocked; there is no communication of self or personal meanings, no recognition of problems, no individual desire to change. At this stage, the client is closed, "and communicative relationships are construed as dangerous ... there is no desire to change."

When the client feels himself to be fully accepted as he is (and for what he is), the second stage follows naturally. This second stage is characterized by a number of factors, positive and negative:

Expression begins to flow in regard to nonself topics ... problems are perceived as external to self ... there is no sense of personal responsibility in problems ... feelings are described as unowned, or sometimes as past objects ... feelings may be exhibited, but are not recognized as such or owned ... experiencing is bound by the structure of the past ... personal constructs are rigid, and unrecognized as being constructs, but are thought of as facts ... differentiation of personal meanings and feelings are very limited ...

contradictions may be expressed, but with little recognition of them as contradictions. (p. 144)

The third and fourth stages involve further loosening of symbolic expressions in regard to feelings, constructs, and self. These stages constitute an important moving forward in the therapy. In the fifth stage, feelings are expressed freely as in the present and are very close to being experienced:

They "bubble up," "seep through," in spite of the fear and distrust which the client feels at experiencing them with fullness and immediacy ... there is a beginning tendency to realize that experiencing a feeling involves a direct referent ... there is surprise and fright, rarely pleasure, at the feelings which "bubble through" ... there is an increasing ownership of self feelings, and a desire to be these, to be the "real me" ... there is a strong and evident tendency toward exactness in differentiation of feelings and meanings ... there is an increasingly clear facing of contradictions and incongruences in experience ... there is an increasing quality of acceptance of self-responsibility for the problems being faced ... an improvement in, and reduced blockage of internal communication. (p. 145)

The sixth stage continues this process of growth, self-discovery and self-acceptance, congruence, and responsibility. This is a very crucial stage: the client has become very close to an organic being which is always in process; he is in touch with his flow of feelings; his construction of experiences is free flowing and repeatedly being tested against referents and evidence within and without; experience is differentiated and thus internal communication is exact.

The client enters the seventh and last stage often without the need of the therapist's help. He is now a continually changing person, experiencing with freshness and immediacy each new situation, responding with real and accepted feelings, and showing "a growing and continuing sense of acceptant ownership of these changing feelings, a basic trust in his own process."

This paper represents Rogers's clearest, most explicit description of the stages of therapeutic change, although throughout his writings these stages are implicit.

The goal of client-centered counseling is *congruence*, the concordance between the client's perceptions of his experiences and the reality of those experiences. This requires a critical reorientation of the sense of self in interaction with the environment. The client must come to understand himself and care about himself differently from the way he did when he began the counseling.

Rogers explains this concept comprehensively in his idea of *self-actualization*. Self-actualization is a teleological movement by which the client reaches a condition of self-respect, self-awareness, acceptance of himself and others, an objective understanding of his interactions with the world, and, most importantly, fulfillment of his many capacities. As the individual "perceives and accepts into one consistent and integrated system all his sensory and visceral experiences ... as the individual perceives and accepts into his self-structure more of his organic experiences ..." *(Client-Centered Therapy)*, he moves toward the condition of self-actualization. It is this movement that most precisely describes Rogers's faith in the client and his ultimate goal of the therapy.

Rogers (1959a) describes specifically some of the changes he expects successful psychotherapy to produce:

The person comes to see himself differently.
He accepts himself and his feelings more fully.
He becomes more self-confident and self-directing.
He becomes more the person he would like to be.
He becomes more flexible, less rigid, in his perceptions.
He adopts more realistic goals for himself.
He behaves in a more mature fashion.
He changes his maladjustive behaviors, even such a long established one as chronic alcoholism.
He becomes more acceptant of others.
He becomes more open to the evidence, both to what is going on outside of himself, and to what is going on inside of himself.
He changes in his basic personality characteristics in constructive ways. (p. 232)

We see from this description the relationship between the stages of the therapy and the desired goals of the cure. Rogers's criteria for successful therapy, moreover, reflect his deep concern for the self-actualization process of the individual client as he embarks upon the course of treatment.

EVALUATION AND IMPLICATIONS

Of all the schools of therapy to be discussed in this book, client-centered therapy is by far the most popular form of treatment in the school system. This popularity (which, by the way, is peculiar not only to our country, but to many European and Asiatic nations as well) may be attributed to the optimistic attitude of the therapy, to the simplicity of its techniques, and to a number of other factors. In any case, it is quite clear that at the present time and probably for some time to come, many prospective school counselors will be using the client-centered approach in their schools.

Client-centered counseling has some disadvantages in the school setting. Most notably, it requires an attitude of the counselor that in fact many counselors are unable to maintain. While it is theoretically desirable to speak of unconditional positive regard, total acceptance, warmth, and empathy, in the real world of school counseling these fine feelings are frequently the farthest thing from the counselor's mind. In addition, most school counselors are under pressure by the teachers and the administration to encourage their clients to change their behavior immediately, and the nondirective stance of client-centered counseling works considerably against this end.

On the other hand, client-centered counseling can be practiced successfully with a minimum of training. Because it relies more on the feelings and personality of the counselor than on his technical know-how, it offers many possibilities to the counselor who has not had an opportunity to study intensively the more directive therapeutic approaches. Confronted by the complex and sometimes overwhelming forces that disrupt many clients' lives, it is sometimes more expedient as well as more therapeutic to offer the client appropriate feelings and genuine concern than to attempt to treat the unconscious, repressed factors underlying his problem.

A large number of papers have appeared in the journals, reporting specific applications of client-centered counseling to school-related problems. Demos (1964) has found that unconditional positive regard, empathy, and respect were significant factors in contributing to positive outcomes in short-term educational-vocational counseling. Salomone (1971), too, has suggested that the client-centered approach is ideally suited to job placement counseling. "The *client-centered placement* approach," he indicates,

requires the client to assume the major responsibility for securing job leads, for contacting employers, and for performing the necessary follow-up activities where employment applications have been left with personnel men. Therefore, it is likely that the client may experience feelings of self-satisfaction and confidence when he obtains his job. (p. 267)

Arbuckle and Boy (1961) have discussed the application of client-centered therapy in counseling students with behavior problems, concluding that it was a valid and successful approach.

Other studies have shown less successful results. West (1969), in an investigation concerned with evaluating the significance of client-centered play therapy as a counseling technique for the elementary school, did not find that the group exposed to this technique showed any significant benefit over the control group. English and Higgins (1971), likewise, did not find client-centered group counseling of any particular benefit for elementary school children.

Thus, the cumulative result of the research is both positive and negative. In some studies, client-centered counseling has been proven effective, and in some it has not. Rogers's own major study of the efficacy of the client-centered approach (Rogers, 1967) also offers ambiguous results, as we saw on p. 106.

Carkhuff and Berenson (1967), in assessing the value of the client-centered approach, cite both contributions and limitations of the approach. Among the contributions are the emphasis on the client in all of its ramifications, the opportunity for the counselor to communicate his feelings and perceptions, the openness and honesty in the relationship. Among the limitations are some artificiality, limitations upon the therapist (in "giving fully of himself"), the inevitable tendency toward socially acceptable responses.

On the whole, Carkhuff and Berenson's remarks are fair and accurate. However, as has already been said, the client-centered approach is especially relevant for the school counseling situation, and because of its relevance it has been widely adopted. Among the list of limitations are a number of factors which may be limitations of all psychotherapies and not of client-centered therapy alone.

231

In the following chapter, we shall examine a school of psychotherapy that, although quite different from the Rogerian approach in many ways, has some common sources and derivative techniques and rationales: existentialism.

References

Arbuckle, D. S., & Boy, A. V. Client-centered therapy in counseling students with behavior problems. *Journal of Counseling Psychology*, 1961, *8*, 136–139.

Butler, J. M., & Seeman, J. Client-centered therapy and the field of guidance. *Education*, 1950, *70*, 519–522.

Carkhuff, R. R., & Berenson, B. G. *Beyond counseling and therapy.* New York: Holt, Rinehart, & Winston, 1967.

Demos, G. D. Application of certain principles of client-centered therapy to short-term vocational-educational counseling. *Journal of Counseling Psychology*, 1964, *11*, 280–284.

English, R. W., & Higgins, T. E. Client-centered group counseling with pre-adolescents. *Journal of School Health*, 1971, *41*, 507–510.

Lister, J. L. Client-centered counseling: For the secondary school? *The School Counselor*, 1965, *8*, 140–146.

Meador, B. D., & Rogers, C. R. Client-centered therapy. In R. Corsini (Ed.), *Current psychotherapies.* Itasca, Ill.: F. E. Peacock, 1973.

Patterson, C. H. A current view of client-centered or relationship therapy. *The Counseling Psychologist*, 1969, *1*(2), 2-25.

Rogers, C. R. The clinical treatment of the problem child. Boston: Houghton Mifflin, 1939.

Rogers, C. R. Counseling and psychotherapy. Boston: Houghton Mifflin, 1942.

Rogers, C. R. *Client-centered therapy.* Boston: Houghton Mifflin, 1951.

Rogers, C. R. The necessary and sufficient conditions of therapeutic personality change. *Journal of Consulting Psychology*, 1957, *21*, 95–103. (a)

Rogers, C. R. A note on "the nature of man." *Journal of Counseling Psychology*, 1957, *4*, 199–203. (b)

Rogers, C. R. A process conception of psychotherapy. *American Psychologist*, 1958, *13*, 142–149.

Rogers, C. R. Significant learning: In therapy and in education. *Educational Leadership*, 1959, *16(4)*, 232–242. (a).

Rogers, C. R. A theory of therapy, personality, and interpersonal relationships as developed in the client-centered framework. In S. Koch (Ed.), *Psychology: A study of a science* (Vol. 3, *Formulations of the person and the social context*). New York: McGraw-Hill, 1959. (b)

Rogers, C. R. The interpersonal relationship: The core of guidance. *Harvard Educational Review*, 1962, *32*, 416–429.

Rogers, C. R. *Carl Rogers on encounter groups.* New York: Harper & Row, 1970.

Rogers, C. R. (Ed.). *The therapeutic relationship and its impact.* Madison: University of Wisconsin Press, 1967.

Rogers, C. R., & Dymond, R. F. (Eds.), *Psychotherapy and personality change.* Chicago: University of Chicago Press, 1954.

Salomone, P. R. A client-centered approach to job placement. *Vocational Guidance Quarterly*, 1971, *19*, 266–270.

West, W. B. An investigation of the significance of client-centered play therapy as a counseling technique (Doctoral dissertation, North Texas University, 1969). Ann Arbor, Mich.: University Microfilms No. 69–19, 950.

Suggested additional readings

Boy, A. V., & Pine, G. J. *Client-centered counseling in the secondary school.* Boston: Houghton Mifflin, 1963.

Ford, D. H., & Urban, H. B. *Systems of psychotherapy.* New York: Wiley, 1963.

Forgey, E. W., & Black, J. D. A follow-up after three years of clients counseled by two methods. *Journal of Counseling Psychology*, 1954, *1*, 1–8.

Gorlow, L., Hoch, E., & Telschow, E. F. The nature of nondirective group psychotherapy: An experimental investigation. New York: Teachers College Press, 1952.

Nordberg, R. B. Persons and praxis—a reply to Rogers. *Personnel and Guidance Journal*, 1961, *40*, 58–59.

Rogers, C. R. *On becoming a person.* Boston: Houghton Mifflin, 1961. (a)

Rogers, C. R. The place of the person in the new world of the behavioral sciences. *Personnel and Guidance Journal*, 1961, *39*, 442–451. (b)

chapter ten

Existentialism

HISTORY OF THE SCHOOL

Existential psychology and existential counseling derive from the philosophy of existentialism, which was originated by Sören Kierkegaard, a nineteenth-century Danish theologian and philosopher. Although Kierkegaard did not call his philosophy existentialism (the word was coined many years after his death), he did lay down the basic framework upon which all later existentialist thinking was built, namely, that each man carves his own destiny and that his *essence*, his inner being, is the product of his actions. Kierkegaard, however, shaped his philosophy in the context of Christian theology, which on the one hand limited its general application as a philosophic premise, but on the other hand opened the door to the existential-theology movement, led by such thinkers as Karl Jaspers, Paul Tillich, Martin Buber, Nikolai Berdyaev, and Dietrich Bonhoffer. It was not until seventy years after Kierkegaard's death that existentialism took hold as a distinct philosophical movement, with the publication of Martin Heidegger's massive tome, *Being and Time (Sein und Zeit).*

Heidegger's monumental study attempted to examine the meaning of being by discovering and explicating "all the essential structures of man's existence, thereby illuminating the way in which man understands both his own being and the being of other beings" (King, 1964, p. 13). Heidegger calls the existence of man *Dasein*, an imprecise German compound word that can be roughly translated into English as something between *being here* and *being there*. The lack of clarity is intentional, for it is Heidegger's contention that man's existence is an active, ongoing, moving process, in which man, by existing *here* and *there* through *time*, defines his being and gives concreteness to his existence. The existence of man, argues Heidegger, is not like the static existence of a *thing*: Man articulates his being—shapes it—in his actions and interactions with others and with the things of the world. He is never isolated from or independent of the things around him but is engaged in existence with them by his perceptions,

Existentialism: the confrontation with self, with others, with death!

moods, and feelings—by his subjectivity. It is an ontological analysis of the specific moments of these interactions that constitutes the bulk of *Being and Time*.

Jean-Paul Sartre, who follows Heidegger in time but not in importance, engaged in his own existential investigation of being in another epic study, *Being and Nothingness (L'Etre et le Néant)*. Sartre distinguishes between two kinds of being: the *in-itself* and the *for-itself*. The in-itself is nonconscious being, the being of things. This kind of being cannot be broken down beyond this, because it has no capability of self-reflection, no meaning beyond that of its existence for consciousness. The for-itself is consciousness, reaching out into the world for being. Consciousness never exists independently of things, insofar as its constituent elements are the things in the world which it "intends"—which it grasps for itself.

234

Jean-Paul Sartre, the French existentialist, whose work Being and Nothingness *is one of the foundations of modern existential thought*

The language and structure of both *Being and Time* and *Being and Nothingness* are highly technical and obscure. Because of the complex and ontological nature of the inquiry, both writers found themselves experimenting with new grammatical and linguistic arrangements to facilitate their expression. But while the contents of those works give a lay reader pause, the ideas expressed far transcended the specific scope of the philosophic inquiry and entered the realm of man's practical life style. For the implications of both these studies is that man's destiny is shaped by himself; that his consciousness creates itself, over and over again; that his existence defines his life, not the other way around.

By the 1940s, existentialism had flowered into a life style for many individuals who did not have the slightest idea what the philosophy was about. The term had transcended its meaning. During the 1950s, beatniks and other rebels against the accepted social norm paraded under the banner of existentialism. As its popularity grew, it became more misunderstood and more identified with its so-called proponents than with the men who originated the philosophy. This is perhaps why it took so long for existentialism to make itself felt in psychotherapy.

The merging of existentialism and psychotherapy, however, was inevitable. Throughout its history, psychotherapy has always been deeply influenced by the social, cultural, and intellectual trends of the time. All that was required was for someone to come along and apply the principles of existential philosophy to psychotherapy. That someone turned out to be Ludwig Binswanger.

Binswanger was a Swiss psychiatrist, deeply influenced by the Freudian psychoanalytic approach. As a student of existentialism, Binswanger realized the enormous possibilities in applying existentialist principles to his psychiatric practice, particularly the ontological ideas of Heidegger and Buber's "philosophy of dialogue." He explored in his day-to-day practice how existential concepts could be used to understand and treat the patient, elaborating a complex system of classifications and techniques based on explicit analyses of being.

Viktor Frankl (1967), an Austrian born psychiatrist, developed *logotherapy*, a specialized form of Binswanger's existential analysis. Frankl, who was incarcerated in a German concentration camp for several years, studied the psychology of people under severe stress and hardship, concluding that many of the insights about these extreme cases could be applied to neurotic and psychotic patients he later encountered in his practice. Specifically, in addition to an analysis of being, Frankl was concerned with an analysis of meanings in the patient's life. Unlike the Freudian contention of the organism's will to pleasure or the Adlerian contention of his will to power, Frankl sees the will to meaning as the underlying essence of man's authentic existence:

In the last analysis, it turns out that both the will to pleasure and the will to power are derivatives of the original will to meaning. Pleasure, as we have said above, is an effect of meaning fulfillment; power is a means to an end. A certain amount of power, such as economic or financial power, is generally a prerequisite for meaning fulfillment. Thus we could say that while the will to pleasure mistakes the effect for the end, the will to power mistakes the means to an end for the end itself. (p. 6)

The logotherapist, unlike the Freudian or Adlerian psychoanalyst, emphasizes the meaning of meanings as opposed to the meaning of actions. In his book, *Man's Search For Meaning*, Frankl relates his experiences in the concentration camp and explains how he was able to learn about the mechanics of survival, the will to live, and each man's quest for meaning in his life. In *The Doctor and the Soul*, he refines some of his ideas and expands his notion of logotherapy.

Rollo May, probably the most famous existential psychoanalyst in the United States, may be the single person most responsible for the popularity of existential psychotherapy today. May, who was deeply influenced both by Binswanger and by Medard Boss's alternative *Daseinanalysis* (analysis of being), articulated some of the more practical applications of existential thought to psychoanalytic practice. In his writings, May emphasizes each man's individuality and the need for the therapist to separate himself from preconceived diagnostic categories in attempting to understand and treat the patient.

By the 1960s, existential psychotherapy had become a force to be reckoned with. Many psychoanalysts, attracted by the conception of man as an emerging, growing, evolving, and creative force in nature, gradually accepted the existential principles to supplement their basic psychoanalytic approach. At a recent counseling conference (1972), it was suggested that existential ideas can also be helpful to the client-centered counselor who, on many issues, is closely aligned to the existentialist idea.

THE VIEW OF MAN

The convenient catch phrase that expresses the basic tenet underlying all the diverse philosophies and theologies found under the rubric of existentialism is *existence precedes essence*. In its most simple form, this means that what a man does with his life—the way he lives it—determines what he is. We are not born to be anything, argues the existentialist, but we become what we are through our actions and our commitments to those actions. We make choices between alternatives, exercising our free will and judgment and then accept complete responsibility for the choices we have made. In this way, we govern our own lives, shape our destinies, and develop our essential nature.

Heidegger speaks of *authenticity*, a mode of being where man, seriously engaged in projects that are meaningful to him, exhibits concern for the project, commitment to its goals, and responsibility for its results. This notion pretty well sums up the feelings of all existentialists regarding the importance of meaningful activities in a man's life. We cannot simply live our life as if it were a part in a play, prearranged and inevitable, but rather we must actively participate in making our life something special—that which we desire. Paul Tillich, the theologian, calls this "the courage to be."

The existentialist is aware that this existence of man—this defining of his essence—never occurs in isolation but always in the world, in awareness of the world and of others, and in interaction with the reality. This concept, which Heidegger calls *being-in-the-world*, can be explained as follows: The free self, that is, the self striving to carve its own niche in the world, is dependent upon its relationships with others, entities, ideas, laws, social customs, emotional bonds, and so on. This dependency in some ways limits and in other ways defines man's mode of existence in the world. The degree to which it limits or defines one's existence depends upon one's ability to perceive the world and oneself as they really exist.

Perception, to the existentialist, is studied through the discipline of phenomenology, the branch of existentialism concerned with the perception by consciousness of phenomena in the world "out there." Edmund Husserl (1859–1938), who was Heidegger's teacher, developed the system of phenomenology. Husserl began with the assumption that for philosophy to be an engaging productive discipline, it must begin from assumptions and axioms different from those which underlie the natural sciences, that philosophy must start with our original intuition of the things in the world about which we want to make statements. These things, which pass in and out of our field of experience, are called

Edmund Husserl, the founder of phenomenology

phenomena, and the method set forth by Husserl is designed to grasp and understand these phenomena *as they are*. The technique utilized to accomplish this is called *reduction*, a process, or series of cumulative processes, by which we eliminate extraneous areas of the experience in order to see the object in its distinct and total unity.

Husserl speaks of two kinds of reduction: eidetic reduction and phenomenological reduction. "The eidetic reduction leads us from the realm of facts to that of general essences, and the phenomenological reduction makes us pass from the world of realities to that of their ultimate presuppositions" (Kockelmans, p. 30). In practice, this two-stage process would work as follows: First, our attitude toward the intuited object is that it is a sample of what the object really is, which we must analyze in terms of our memories of such objects, in terms of our known perceptual distortions, in terms of our acknowledged subjectivity and bias. We strip the object of its covering, peeling off the layers of illusionary bias, to get at its real essence—its being-as-an-object. Second, we "bracket out" our experiences from our perception of the object—remove ourselves from the perceptions to grasp the object in its naked presentation. As a part of this second stage, this phenomenological reduction, we seek out the meaning of the object free from its cultural context. It is at this stage of the reduction processes where the object is restored to its primordial world of life—its "as is" rather than "as if" quality.

In terms of counseling, the phenomenological approach suggests a way of perceiving, of understanding, the client. It is the method of existential psychotherapy, just as it is the method of existential philosophy. "The phenomenological approach," argues Arbuckle (1965), "seeks to understand the behavior of the individual from his *own* point of view. It attempts to observe people not as they seem to outsiders, but as they seem to themselves" (Combs & Snygg, 1959, p. 11). Moreover, the phenomenological method helps the existential counselor understand the world, and his place and his client's place in the world. After we have bracketed out our preconceptions, we find that the phenomena of the world possess essences underlying their appearances—that they have a meaning-for-us beyond their apparent reality. The phenomenological reduction consists of seeing our own individual existence, separate and isolated from these things in the world, yet aware of our interaction with these things.

The popular conception of existentialism as a morbid philosophy probably derives from the existentialist's view of death and the importance attached to it. Heidegger speaks of "the fear of non-being …," the fear of death, which causes anxiety for all men. Death becomes important in the day-to-day activity of a man because of its inevitability and termination of all activities, projects, meanings in life, etc. The existentialists do not embrace a *carpe diem* attitude in the usual sense, but rather they believe that all of our activities must be engaged in with the full knowledge that death can disrupt them at any time, unexpectedly. The knowledge of death can either corrupt our authenticity, by forcing our submission, or make us more authentic, by our continual striving to create in the shadow of this ultimate doom.

Another important existentialist concept partially responsible for the public image is the notion of *choice* and *commitment*, which function as a single action. Man as a free agent is constantly choosing between possibilities of action. He alone is responsible for his choices and for the consequences of those choices. Since whatever choices he makes helps determine his existence, and hence *who* he is, choosing is an essential part of being. The validity of his choices is not determined by how successful the choices were in executing the ends (as they would be in pragmatism), but in how willing the individual is to accept the consequences of the choices as his own doing—as a part of himself. Maxine Greene (1973) sums up the existentialist position in regard to choice and action clearly:

For the existentialist, the self is devoid of character or coloration before action is undertaken. When the individual begins devising projects and purposes, he begins creating an identity. No outside factor or force, no science or set of rules or moral law, can make decisions for him. The only significant choices are those that involve him totally and project his existence into the future still unknown. The only meaningful choices are those for which he takes full responsibility. If he sits back and makes abstract judgments ("Yes, racism really should be abolished"; "Teachers are justified in joining the union"; "Classes here ought to be individualized"), he is in danger of "bad faith." His chances of authentication are diminished, because his authenticity depends on his capacity (or his courage) to cope with the anxiety of the human condition, his condition. The ability to confront the threat of nothingness, to acknowledge mortality, moves a person to act. He *knows* the only meanings that exist are the ones he achieves, the only values that exist are the ones he creates; he knows that if he does not act, nothingness will overtake him and his world. (p. 256)

To the extent that "man is what his own choices make him," the fundamental condition of man is aloneness. He is naked out there in the world, confronted with the possibilities of existence, free to choose whatever life style he may prefer, free to choose his friends, free to embrace whatever ideas he may want to. He is concerned, exhibiting what Heidegger calls *Sorge* (care), a concern for himself and for the activities in which he is engaged. This concern causes anxiety and fears, but it is also the basis of love and affection.

Concern about others is an important part of existentialist thought. The fact that we live with others, work with others, have feelings about others, and share our values with others does not mean that we maintain an authentic mode of existence with others. This depends more on our ability to see others as distinct entities from ourself, our ability to meet others on their terms and yet maintain our own sense of integrity and wholeness, our desire to share with others because of the validity of their being to us. Charity is a poor substitute for communion.

The existentialist view of man can be summed up in five basic tenets which underlie the philosophy:

1 Existence precedes essence: What we do determines who we are.
2 Man is free to choose and responsible for the consequences of his choices—his existence.

3 Man's life is always lived with a view-toward-death. His authenticity derives from his ability to be aware of this.
4 Man's existence is never completely separate from the existence of others and the world, and the existence of the world is never completely separate from man's existence.
5 Perception is more valid when subjective preconceptions are bracketed out.

THE ROLE OF THE CLIENT

The client is always seen in his wholeness, a total person, as the end product of his choices, not as a victim of his circumstances. Like the client-centered counselor, the existential counselor believes that the client is responsible for his actions, capable of changing himself, the shaper of his own destiny, and that his life is not a problem to be solved, not a symptom, but a reality to be experienced and enjoyed. As Pine (1969) points out,

The existential heart of counseling is the recognition of the student's right to make his own choices and his own "mistakes." Counseling is an encounter in which the counselee is free to become more free. The student who feels trusted to make his own choices begins to trust in himself more and becomes aware that the meanings of his experiences, the meaning for his existence emerge from within himself. The ideas of freedom and accountability indicate that the student must be free to choose whether he wishes to participate in the counseling process. (p. 353)

But where the underlying view of client-centered therapy is in man's essential goodness and ability to make right choices, the underlying view of existentialism is less optimistic and positive. The existentialists believe more in an unconscious, dynamic process of choice. Kierkegaard, for example, says that "the personality is already interested in the choice before one chooses, and when the choice is postponed the personality chooses unconsciously, or the choice is made by obscure powers within it" (*Either/Or*). Furthermore, the existentialists do not believe that the client can totally free himself from the constraints "of his nothingness—from the threat of obliteration." Instead, the client is to accept this frustration as an inevitable part of his existence.

Because the ability to choose is fundamental to good mental health, the client is expected early in the treatment to learn what choice and commitment mean. He is encouraged to assume responsibility for himself at the outset. If he shirks this responsibility, if he attempts to blame all his frustrations on the past, on his early years, on others, he is shown how only he himself is responsible for and to himself and how only he can be the one who truly mistreats himself. This is, of course, a difficult lesson for many clients, nurtured on other philosophies, to accept and assimilate.

The existentialist client is never seen as a static person who can easily be categorized by a diagnosis (although many existential analysts do use the standard Freudian diagnostic categories for reference), but rather as a complex, evolving, changing, choosing individual, essentially lonely and unfulfilled, searching for richness and meaning in life. Frankl argues that an adequate view of the client "can only be properly formulated when it goes beyond homeostasis (maintaining equilibrium), beyond self-actualization, to that sphere of human existence in which man chooses what he will do and what he will be in the midst of an objective world of meaning and values" (*Psychotherapy and Existentialism*, p. 51). This most clearly sums up the existential counselor's view of the client.

THE ROLE OF THE COUNSELOR

The existential counselor has three basic tasks in the counseling relationship: to help the client discover valid meanings in his existence; to help him develop the freedom to govern his own destiny; to help him deal more effectively in his encounters with others. In many ways, the function of the existential counselor is identical to the function of the client-centered counselor. Both try to understand the client from his point of view by entering his subjective world. Both participate with the client in his internal realities and beliefs. Both accept the client's idea of reality as essentially correct, although possibly a distortion. Both emphasize the counselor's attitude toward the client and toward the course of the counseling over the application of specific techniques. And yet, both do have a specific methodology which is designed to facilitate a developmental response to a healthy attitude maintained by the counselor. Dreyfus (1971) states it most explicitly:

Existential counseling ... is not a system of techniques but an underlying attitude toward counseling. It is concerned with the uniqueness of man.... The method employed by the existentially oriented counselor is called the phenomenological method. That is to say, the counselor is concerned with the immediate, existing world of the client at the moment. He is concerned with the raw data offered by the client. Hence the approach is ahistorical in the sense that the counselor does not attempt to actively delve into the client's past. The past is important only insofar as the client introduces it into the present.... The point of departure during the counseling hour is the conflict which brought the client to the counselor, not that which led up to the conflict. (p. 416)

In other ways, the existential counselor may function in a way similar to the psychoanalytic counselor. He may attempt to study the patient's past history, with an eye toward discovering causes for the patient's inability to fulfill himself. He may also be guided by such classical Freudian concepts as ego, the unconscious, instincts, and the Oedipus complex. For the most part, however, he is concerned with the here and now existence of the patient that is presented to him in the treatment setting.

The existential counselor can only be successful to the extent that he is able to understand the client in terms of the client's perceptions of and relationship with the counselor. Anxiety and guilt, two of the most important concepts in treatment, are analysed in terms of their appearance within the counseling relationship. In his analysis, the counselor explores the client's anxiety and guilt phenomenologically, perceiving them as the client does without his own subjective experiences coloring the perceptions.

TECHNIQUES AND GOALS

In existential counseling, as in several other schools of counseling, the attitudes of the counselor are more important than any specific techniques that he employs. Kemp (1971) points out that in existential counseling, *"technique follows understanding*.... the existential counselor's primary goal is to understand the counselee as a person, a being and as a being-in-the-world. This does not mean that he has a low respect for technique, but rather that technique takes its legitimate place in a new perspective"* (p. 18).

When techniques are employed, however, existential counselors differ markedly in the kind of techniques they use. Many of them, indoctrinated in the classical Freudian analytic approach, rely heavily on free association and interpretation, while others whose background is in the client-centered approach deal more with active verbal interactions with the client. In either case, it is likely that the existential counselor, more perhaps than any other type of counselor, will rely most on whatever techniques are most compatible with his personality. For in existential counseling, the "being" of the counselor is always a dynamic force in the counseling interaction, with the consequence that far greater emphasis is placed on the meaningfulness of the relationship than on the particular application of techniques.

Rather than speak of existential techniques, therefore, it would be more accurate to refer to the "existential approach." Pine's (1969) statement describes the situation accurately:

The existential school counselor has translated existentialism into a counseling approach designed to increase freedom within the pupil, to assist the pupil in discovering meaning for his existence, and to improve his encounter with others. *The existential school counselor sees counseling as more an attitude than a technique.* It reflects the self of the counselor and represents a sharing of the counselor's self in a personal and human relationship with a fellow human being. School counseling is viewed primarily as an encounter which implies a special kind of relationship requiring the counselor to be totally present to the student, to participate in the student's existence, to be fully with him. (p. 352)

It would be wrong, however, to give the impression that existentialists have some type of aversion to techniques. Frankl, for example, discusses an important technique which he calls *paradoxical intention*. The counselor uses paradoxical intention when he tells the client to wish for something, attempt to do something, or think intensely about something, where the something represents the client's worst fears. He gives the example of a phobic patient who had a fear of sweating and was encouraged by the therapist to show people whom he met how much he was able to sweat. "A week later he returned to report that whenever he met anyone who triggered his anxiety, he said to himself, 'I only sweated a liter before, but now I'm going to pour out at least ten liters!' ... After suffering from his phobia for four years, he was quickly able, after only one session, to free himself of it for good by this new procedure" (*Psychotherapy and Existentialism*, p. 146). It is not immediately clear, however, if this type of dynamic technique is a basis for Frankl's existential approach, or incidental to it.

The goal of existential counseling, if we may speak of a singular goal, is to help the client find and develop meanings in his life. This is generally accomplished in two stages. First, the client must be shown his condition as *free agent*, capable of choosing both that which is right for him and that which is not. Some clients believe that they can only make choices which repeat the early choices that their parents taught them (cf. "repetition compulsion" in psychoanalysis). After the client realizes the myriad possibilities he is capable of exploring, he must begin to understand how the consequences of these different choices have profound ramifications in his existence. Medard Boss's term *Daseinanalysis* is used to explain how the client comes to understand and accept his essential nature through his interaction with the counselor, particularly in the counselor's responses to the choices that he demonstrates in the counseling setting.

The existential counselor, unlike the psychoanalytic or behavioral counselor, does not view anxiety as a dangerous or neurotic condition. Rather, anxiety is seen as a fundamental condition of existence. The job of the counselor is to help the client accept his anxiety as a part of his fundamental being. In this respect, the existential counselor is working with the client to help him come to grips with the crux of his existence, his "essential self."

The client is better able to understand his essential self after he resolves the distortions in his perceptions which are causing him disproportionate anxiety and frustration. To this end, the counselor attempts to teach him the fundamentals of phenomenological perception, particularly the use of bracketing prior to experiences. The client may at first believe that it is the counselor's perceptions which are false and struggle to persuade the counselor that only his own perceptions are accurate and objective. But as he comes to understand his relationship with the counselor, and to learn from that relationship the meaning of phenomenological perception, he will be better able to appreciate how the distortions are on his side of the relationship. All this, of course, is dependent upon the counselor's skill in entering the patient's world and in not permitting his own distorted perceptions to interfere with the treatment.

EVALUATION

The existential approach has much to offer to the school counselor. Its philosophic basis is quite relevant to the needs of young people in the school, who are always in a state of turmoil and change, confusion and flux, growth and evolution. Its emphasis on individuality and development of self is particularly helpful to the counselor working with adolescents, who are perhaps closer than anyone else in experiencing the existential concepts of anxiety and dread.

Many counselors find it particularly helpful to use such existential concepts as phenomenological perception and free choice to understand the activities of the young people they work with in a new light. While the nonjudgmental, client-centered approach poses a problem in that it requires the counselor to express positive feelings about a client whom he may find repugnant or incomprehensible, the existential approach allows him to experience the client as the client is experiencing himself, while not necessarily approving of the client or accepting his actions. This extra latitude is likely to help the counselor in working with difficult cases.

Dahms and Kinnick (1969) have listed the ten major assumptions regarding students which characterize the existential position:

1 Students are unique and sacred beings of inherent dignity and worth.
2 Each student's behavior affects all members of the ... community.
3 Each student should accept responsibility for all members of the school.
4 Students are free agents of choice.
5 Students direct and control their own search for meaning.
6 Current students direct the evolution of their own lives now and will significantly influence the evolution of higher education and the whole social order soon.
7 Students are competent to discharge their own affairs.
8 Students grossly underestimate the degrees of freedom open to them.
9 Students' freedom is exercised within given limits:
—Civil and criminal law
—Institutional regulations
—Group safety
—Individual safety.
10 Students must know where the limits are in their world. (p. 411)

These ten positions, which are accepted by the existential counselor as well as by the existential student personnel worker, elucidate the freeing and explorative nature of existentialism as it becomes adopted in the social and educational milieu.

More important, perhaps, to the school counselor is the meaning of an existential relationship. One of the most difficult tasks of the school counselor is establishing a workable relationship with the client-student. Most students begin with a sense of suspicion and distrust, equating the counselor with the feared authority of the school that has brought the student to the counselor in the first place. The best way the counselor can deal with this is by experiencing the student as a whole complex person, involved with a variety of forces from which he is trying to extricate himself. The ten postulates listed above, when they are accepted by the counselor and communicated however subtly to the student, will facilitate this process. As soon as the student gets the feeling that the counselor respects his integrity and acknowledges his freedom and uniqueness, he will be able to communicate to the counselor the feelings that he found most difficult to share with others.

References

Arbuckle, D. Existentialism in counseling: The humanist view. *Personnel and Guidance Journal*, 1965, *44*, 558–567.

Combs, A. W., & Snygg, D. *Individual behavior*. New York: Harper & Brothers, 1959.

Dahms, A. M., & Kinnick, B. C. Existentialism and student personnel work. *Journal of College Student Personnel*, 1969, *11*, 408–413.

Dreyfus, E. A. An existential approach to counseling. In C. Beck (Ed.), *Philosophical guidelines for counseling*. Dubuque, Iowa: Wm. C. Brown, 1971.

Frankl, V. *Man's search for meaning: An introduction to logotherapy*. (Preface by G. W. Allport.) Boston: Beacon Press, 1962.

Frankl, V. *The doctor and the soul: From psychotherapy to logotherapy*. New York: Alfred A. Knopf, 1965.

Frankl, V. *Psychotherapy and existentialism: Selected papers on logotherapy*. New York: Simon & Schuster (Clarion Books), 1967.

Greene, M. *Teacher as stranger*. Belmont, Calif.: Wadsworth, 1973.

Heidegger, M. [*Being and time*] (J. Macquarrie & E. Robinson, trans.). London: SCM Press, 1962.

Kemp. G. C. Existential counseling. *The Counseling Psychologist*, 1971, *2*, 2–30.

Kierkegaard, S. [*Either/or*] (W. Lowrie, trans.). Garden City: Doubleday-Anchor, 1958.

King, M. *Heidegger's philosophy*. New York: Dell, 1964.

Kockelmans, J. (Ed.) *Phenomenology*. New York: Doubleday-Anchor, 1966.

Pine, G. J. The existential school counselor. *Clearing House*, 1969, *43*, 351–354.

Sartre, J. [*Being and nothingness*] (H. Barnes, trans.). New York: Philosophical Library, 1956.

Crawford, C. C. Commitment. *Personnel and Guidance Journal*, 1966, *44*, 907–909.

Crumbaugh, J. C. The application of logotherapy. *Journal of Existentialism*, 1965, *5*, 162–166.

Greene, M. *Existential encounters for teachers*. New York: Random House, 1967.

Husserl, E. [*Ideas: A general introduction to pure phenomenology*] (W. R. B. Gibson, trans.). New York: Macmillan, 1952.

Husserl, E. [*Logical investigations*] (J. N. Findlay, trans.). New York: Humanities Press, 1970.

Jaspers, K. *Reason and existence*. New York: Noonday, 1955.

Kneller, G. F. *Existentialism and education*. New York: Philosophical Library, 1958.

Leslie, R. C. Viktor Frankl's new concept of man. *Motive*, 1962, *22*, 16–19.

May, R., Ellenberger, H. E., & Angel, E. (Eds.), *Existence*. New York: Basic Books, 1959.

Morris, V. C. *Existentialism and education*. New York: Harper & Row, 1966.

Pervin, L. A. Existentialism, psychology, and psychotherapy. *American Psychologist*, 1960, *15*, 305–309.

Thevanaz, P. *What is phenomenology?* Chicago: Quadrangle Books, 1962.

Van Kaam, A. *The art of existential counseling*. Wilkes Barre, Pa.: Dimension Books, 1966.

Weisskipf-Joelson, E. Logotherapy and existential analysis. *Acta Psychotherapeutica*, 1958, *6*, 193–204.

Suggested additional readings

Barrett, W. *Irrational man*. New York: Doubleday, 1958.

Blackham, H. J. *Six existentialist thinkers*. New York: Harper Torchbooks, 1959.

Cottingham, H. F. The challenge of authentic behavior. *Personnel and Guidance Journal*, 1966, *45*, 328–336.

chapter eleven

Gestalt therapy

No concept of psychotherapy has achieved a more rapid popularity in a short period of time, both in the press and in the profession, than has gestalt therapy during the 1960s and 70s. Dynamic, dramatic, intensive, and absorbing, gestalt therapy has already exerted a powerful influence upon school counseling, encounter group therapy, marathon groups, family counseling, counseling of delinquents and prisoners, and drug counseling. Institutes such as Esalen, at Big Sur, California, that emphasize the gestalt approach have received national attention and have attracted as workshop leaders such diverse and impressive figures as Abraham Maslow, Buckminster Fuller, and B. F. Skinner (Murphy, 1967). Unfortunately, the gestalt approach seems also to have inspired a glittery show business atmosphere at times, although this is certainly more a reflection of unscrupulous promoters and exploiters than of the therapy and of the serious, ethical practitioners. An advertisement in a New York weekly recently advertised a "weekend of skiing and Gestalt therapy" at a mountain resort hotel. Another newspaper ad promoted a "singles Gestalt encounter" as an ideal opportunity to meet one's future mate. Such gross exploitation is the inevitable liability of a therapy that achieves so much popularity in so short a period of time.

In this chapter we shall examine some of the premises and applications of the legitimate gestalt approach. The emphasis will be on the serious, therapeutic applications of gestalt therapy, rather than on the social and entertainment uses mentioned above. At the conclusion of the chapter, an evaluation of the relevance of gestalt counseling for the school counselor will be presented.

HISTORY OF THE SCHOOL

Gestalt therapy derives from the school of the same name in the psychology of perception, which originated in Europe in the years prior to the first world war. Gestalt psychology, as expounded by Wertheimer, Koffka, and Köhler, held that the analysis of conscious experience as practiced by the associationist was insufficient to explain fully the complexities of perception and the interaction between perception and behavior. The gestalt movement instituted a new kind of analysis: one which began with the perceptual field as a whole, differen-

tiating it into figure and background, and then examining the relative properties of each of these and their interrelationship to each other. The word *gestalt*, which is roughly equivalent to the English word *pattern*, expresses the basic meaning of the movement, namely, that all perceptions are dependent upon a number of distinct stimuli that are organized by consciousness into a perceptual whole, a total pattern.

Unfortunately, the academic gestalt psychology movement failed to relate its general psychological insights about perception to the perception of one's own inner-body and affective experiences. Gestalt psychology remained essentially a theory of perception, limited in its ability to account for the activity of the human organism as a whole. "The academic Gestalt psychologist," Wallen (1957) points out, "never attempted to employ the various principles of gestalt formation (proximity, the law of good continuation, *pregnanz*, similarity, and so on) to organic perceptions, to the perceptions of one's own feelings, emotions, and bodily sensations" (p. 8). It is in this area that Frederick (Fritz) Perls made his contributions which subsequently blossomed into the birth of gestalt therapy.

Perls received his medical degree from Friedrich Wilhelm University in Berlin in 1921 and continued his training in psychoanalysis at the Psychoanalytic Institutes of Berlin, Frankfurt, and Vienna. Forced to flee Germany in 1933, he settled in Amsterdam where he worked in private practice until the specter of Nazism drove him to South Africa in 1935. In 1947 he published *Ego, Hunger, and Aggression*, the first statement of his principles of gestalt psychology applied to personality development. In 1946 he moved to the United States and set up a private practice. Between 1964 and 1969, he conducted training workshops in gestalt therapy at the Esalen Institute in California. His publications include *Gestalt Therapy: Excitement and Growth in the Human Personality* (1951, with Ralph Hefferline and Paul Goodman) and *Gestalt Therapy Verbatim* (1969).

Perls developed a systematic therapeutic approach which utilizes the large body of literature in gestalt psychology and the practical insights and experiences of a working therapist. The object of this therapy

is to overcome the fragmentation of feeling, thinking, and acting which is so characteristic of our culture, and replace it with a holistic, unitary outlook on life. This can be done by encouraging a more flexible relationship between the individual and his environment or, in Gestalt terms, between figure and ground. (Goldenson, 1970, p. 508)

In recent years, a number of psychoanalytic, existential, and client-centered therapists and counselors have adopted some of the gestalt principles in their own practices.

THE VIEW OF MAN

Like the existential and client-centered counselors, the gestalt counselor's view of man is essentially phenomenological. Specifically, the gestalt counselor considers man's perception (and this means his perceptions of himself, his feelings, his relationships, etc.) in terms of the *figure-ground* dichotomy. Gestalt therapists believe that a healthy personality exists when a person's experiences form a meaningful whole, when there is a smooth transition between those sets of experiences that are immediately in the focus of awareness (what they call *the figure*) and those that are in the background. Proper functioning, therefore, is dependent upon one's abilities to continually shift the figure-ground relationship.

The gestalt theory of psychopathology, as expounded by Perls, (1966) is a far cry from the Freudian or existential theories. In language and content, Perls offers a dramatic, metaphorical description of neurosis, consisting of five layers. He writes, for example, that,

The first layer we encounter is what I call the Eric Berne layer, or the Sigmund Freud layer, or the phony layer, where we play games, play roles. It is identical with Helene Deutsch's description of the "as if" person. We behave *as if* we are big shots, *as if* we are nincompoops, *as if* we are pupils.... It is always the "as if" attitudes that require that we live up to a concept, live up to a fantasy that we or others have created whether it comes out as a curse or as an ideal.... It's an attempt to get away from oneself. The result is that the neurotic person has given up living for his self in a way that would actualize himself. He wants to live instead for a concept.... We don't want to be ourselves; we don't want to be what we are. We want to be something else, and the existential basis of this being something else is the experience of dissatisfaction. (p. 20)

Perls (1966) calls this the *implosive layer* of the neurosis. It is the task of therapy to help the patient pass through this layer to *the explosion*.

The explosion is the final neurotic layer that occurs when we get through the implosive state. As I see it, this progression is necessary to become authentic. There are essentially four types of explosion: explosion into joy, into grief, into orgasm, into anger. (p. 22)

We note in this description of neurosis a sense of fragmentation and isolation that, ideally, should be corrected through the therapeutic experience. The transition from the implosive state to the explosive is a transition from lifelessness and isolation to animation and expression. Perls compares the implosive layer to catatonia: The patient's energy is dammed up, producing rigidity and tenseness. As he surpasses this level, his energy is freed, to be expended in such activities as "thinking, moving about, being alive."

The emphasis in gestalt therapy is upon man's *wholeness*. This concept, which parallels in many ways Rogers's idea of self-actualization, relates to man's interaction with his environment and with others.

Let us call this interacting of organism and environment in any function the *organism/environment field* ... it is always to such an interacting field that we are referring, and not to any isolated animal.... The human organism/environment is, of course, not only physical but social ... so we must speak of a field in which at least social-cultural animals and physical factors interact. (Perls et al., 1969)

As the individual comes to perceive his interactions in this field in the proper perspective, he moves toward mental health and fulfillment, ultimately reaching his potentials. "The average person of our time," says Perls, "lives only 5% to 15% of his potential at the highest. A person who has even 25% of his potential available is already considered to be a genius.... And the reason for this is very simple: we live in clichés. We live in patterned behavior. We are playing the same roles over and over again.... So we come to our basic conflict and the basic conflict is this: Every individual, every plant, every animal has only one inborn goal—to actualize itself as it is.... The average person, having been raised in an atmosphere full of splits, has lost his Wholeness, his Integrity. To come together again he has to heal the dualism of his person, of his thinking, of his language.... The unitary outlook which can dissolve such a dualistic approach is buried but not destroyed.... The organism grows by assimilating from the environment what it needs for its very growth" (Perls, 1969, Perls et al., 1969).

Although the gestalt view of man tends to be nonjudgmental, there are a number of values underlying the philosophy. Naranjo (1970) has listed nine important "moral injunctions" implicit in gestalt therapy. They are:

1 Live now. Be concerned with the present rather than with the past or future.
2 Live here. Deal with what is present rather than with what is absent.
3 Stop imagining. Experience the real.
4 Stop unnecessary thinking. Rather, taste and see.
5 Express rather than manipulate, explain, justify, or judge.
6 Give in to unpleasantness and pain just as to pleasure. Do not restrict your awareness.

7 Accept no *should* or *ought* other than your own. Adore no graven image.

8 Take full responsibility for your actions, feelings, and thoughts.

9 Surrender to being as you are. (pp. 49–50)

In many ways, these nine principles are existential, and it would be difficult to distinguish these from the basic tenets of existentialism, even though the language in which they are expressed may at points differ. The gestalt view of man, like the existentialist position, looks at man in continuous interaction with others and with his environment, striving for authentic engagements and commitments, actualizing, as he lives his life meaningfully, his full potential.

THE ROLE OF THE CLIENT

The client has come for help because he cannot help himself. He must be taught, therefore, how to help himself, and this type of teaching requires his active participation and involvement.

The self only finds and makes itself in the environment. If the patient is an active experimental partner in the session, he will carry this attitude abroad and make more rapid progress; for the environmental material is much more interesting and urgent. (Perls et al., 1969)

Contrary to the Freudian notion of the patient's changing through the intervention of the counselor, the gestalt practitioner believes that the patient ultimately changes through his own activities.

This is demonstrated nowhere more clearly than in the question of resistances. The gestalt counselor, like the psychoanalytic, believes that the patient comes to the treatment encumbered by resistances. Whereas in the classical psychoanalytic approach, "the resistances are 'attacked,' the defenses are 'dissolved,' and so forth," in the gestalt approach, the resistances "are taken as active expressions of vitality," and the counselor allows the client full expression of his resistances, with the belief that "by realizing the resistances ... there is the possibility for resolution rather than annihilation" (Perls et al., 1969). The client, therefore, is encouraged to resist.

The gestalt client is likewise required to experience rather than simply to intellectualize. Whereas in some forms of therapy, it is sufficient for the client to speak about his feelings, in the gestalt approach it is imperative that the client be willing to expose himself to a direct experiential reliving of his feelings. This is true in the gestalt method of interpreting dreams, in confronting resistances, in coming to grips with the repressed past. Rosen (1972) cites an example of how this approach works:

As an example of direct experiencing, not talking about, a patient who says that he has trouble expressing hostility may be asked to say something hostile to each member in a group, or to the therapist in an individual session. He and the therapist and others, if present, can directly experience his difficulty in doing this, and can also experience with appropriate focusing on patient's voice, posture, response of others, etc. what are the factors involved in his difficulty. Finally, he may be urged to try again using his newly gained awareness. He may observe, when asked "What are your hands saying as they clasp one another?" that they are holding one another for reassurance. When asked to see what he feels when he holds them apart he may experience his fear more intensely. He may be directed to try saying to someone "I'm afraid and also furious at you for...." If the timing is good and he feels safe he may then have a different experience in expressing his anger, perhaps more clearly and forcefully than ever before in his life. (p. 96)

We see from this example how the client who comes for gestalt treatment must be willing to experience heightened and difficult moments directly. There is no beating around the bush in gestalt therapy, no sugar-coating with words and euphemisms the true depth of one's feelings.

Moreover, the gestalt client learns to accept without pain the types of interpretive interventions to which he is exposed as he progresses in the treatment. At the beginning, the client will typically experience an uncomfortable self-consciousness, in which he is aware that all his gestures and body signals are under close scrutiny. He may become rigid at first, attempting to hide from the therapist or the other group members what he is experiencing internally. But as he begins to get in touch with himself, as he begins to integrate the fragmented parts of his personality into a cohesive whole, there appears a greater concordance between his body expressions and his verbalizations, between the content of what he is saying and its implications emotionally. The client

has to discover that all his energy that goes into manipulation can be resolved, and used, and that he can learn to actualize himself, his potential—instead of trying to actualize a concept, an image of what he wants to be, thereby suppressing a lot of his potential and adding, on the other side, another piece of phony living, pretending to be something he is not. (Perls, 1969)

THE ROLE OF THE COUNSELOR

"In Gestalt therapy," Passons (1972) points out, "the principal means for facilitating responsibility and integration is the enhancement of self-awareness." The primary task of the gestalt practitioner, therefore, is to help the client with this process of facilitation. This is accomplished in several ways. First, the counselor must "teach the patient *how* to learn about himself." As Perls (1969) states it,

The therapist provides the person with the opportunity to discover what he needs—the missing parts that he has alienated and given up to the world. Then the therapist must provide the opportunity, the situation in which the person can grow.

To do this, the counselor must learn about his client in the "here and now" of the counseling setting, not as a compilation of symptoms and not as a product of his past history. He avoids interpretations, reality orientation, even empathic communications. Instead, he studies the hidden voice behind the patient's words—his expressions, gestures, and what Perls calls his "psychosomatic language."

The therapist's real job is restoring a personality to its gestalt, its organized whole. One method of doing this is to help the patient better understand the relationship between himself and his environment. "Gestalt therapists," Denner (1968) suggests,

demonstrate loss of contact with the environment by means of brief exercises that require the [client] to examine various aspects of his behavior and his world that are rarely examined closely. (pp. 527–528)

These types of exercises, also called "experiments," "games," and "gimmicks," help the client redefine and integrate himself within the environment. The gestalt therapist is, like the reality therapist, a teacher—but a teacher of a different sort. He does not try to impose upon the patient his notions of reality, but rather he helps the patient arrive at his own orientation of reality, his own integration of perceptual and emotional stimuli, his wholeness of person.

The gestalt practitioner directly utilizes principles from the gestalt psychology of perception insofar as he helps the patient understand the *patterns* of his life. Within the framework of gestalt therapy, patterning functions as the equivalent to diagnosis. Fagan (1970) addresses herself to this analogy:

The therapist is first of all a perceiver and constructor of patterns. As soon as he is informed of a symptom or a request for change, and begins listening to and observing a patient and responding to him, he begins a process that I refer to as *patterning*. While *diagnosis* is a more common term, it has the disadvantage of provoking the analogy of the medical model and implying that the purpose of the process is arriving at a specific label. A better analogy for the process of patterning is that of artistic creation, involving sometimes cognitive, sometimes perceptual and intuitive skills in interaction with the material and demands of the environment. (pp. 88–89)

If we examine the transcripts of gestalt therapy sessions, we gain an insight into the specifics of how patterning takes place. The therapist points out to the patient, at various times, his movements, gestures, signs, and other verbal and body communications, to show how these contribute to the total picture of the individual. Patterning is another way of exploring the whole person, which, as we have seen, is one of the fundamental premises of the therapy.

The gestalt counselor, like the client-centered counselor, also acts as a catalyst for the patient's growth. He avoids intervening directly in expressions of the client's will, but by his gentle guidance and dynamic influence he assists the patient in making appropriate and well-thought-out choices. Unlike the client-centered counselor, however, the gestalt counselor avoids the attitude of helpfulness and reassurance.

Any therapist who wants to be *helpful* is doomed right from the beginning. The patient will do anything to make the therapist feel inadequate, because he has to have his compensation for needing him.... We have a very simple means to get the patient to find out what his own missing potential is. Namely, the patient uses me, the Therapist, as a projection screen, and he expects of me exactly what he can't mobilize in himself. (Perls, 1969)

This dynamic interpretation of the client's perceptions of his relationship with the counselor clearly differentiates the gestalt counselor from his Rogerian counterpart.

TECHNIQUES AND GOALS

As with all schools of counseling, gestalt counseling begins by finding out as much as possible about the client's life. While the client who comes for treatment may remain unaware of the underlying and embedded conflicts that are the source of his problem,

some dissociation or other is bound to become manifest in the first interview. Some anxiety, some talking around the subject will provide the opportunity to show him [the client] the existence of unrealized conflicts. (Perls, 1948)

As the counselor discovers these conflicts, he attempts to help the client resolve them by enabling him to identify with all his vital functions—to accept himself as a total, functioning organism, a whole entity. The counselor does this by emphasizing (and at times insisting on) the here and now—the immediacy of the counseling situation.

Sentences like "Here and now" or "Now I am aware of" are chosen not only to bring out the top layer of the patient's character formation and some of the more primitive resistance but also to clear the path to the recognition of all his functions, especially his dysfunctions, conflicts, attitudes of escape. (Perls, 1948)

This is not to suggest, however, that the client's past is irrelevant or extraneous to the treatment. But in gestalt treatment material from the past is utilized differently from the way it is utilized in many other forms of psychotherapy and counseling:

This material [from the past] is dealt with actively when it is felt to be germane to important themes of the present personality structure. However, the most effective means of integrating past material into the personality is to bring it—as fully as possible—into the present. In this way we avoid the bland, intellectualized "aboutisms" and strive vigorously to give all material the impact of immediacy. When the patient refers to events of yesterday, last week, or last year, we quickly direct him to "be there" in fantasy and to enact the drama in present terms. (Levitsky and Perls, 1970, p. 141)

The essential technique at the disposal of the gestalt counselor is the establishment of what Perls calls a *continuum of awareness.* "This continuum of

253

awareness is required so that the organism can work on the healthy gestalt principle: That the most important unfinished situation will always emerge and can be dealt with" (Perls, 1969). The counselor does this by integrating the client's attention and awareness, by helping him assimilate into his structure of self the totality of his experiences.

Often psychology doesn't differentiate between *attention* and *awareness*. Attention is a deliberate way of listening to the emerging foreground figure, which in this case [where there is a conflict] is something unpleasant. So what I do as a therapist is to work as a catalyst both ways: provide situations in which a person can experience this being stuck—the unpleasantness—and I frustrate his avoidance still further, until he is willing to mobilize his own resources. (Perls, 1969)

Provocation, therefore, is a legitimate, integral part of the gestalt repertoire of techniques. The gestalt therapist plays provocative games with the patient, games that are intended to force him to confront and acknowledge his feelings that he has been so arduously trying to avoid. In some ways, these games resemble Moreno's psychodrama, where the patients become players in symbolic interactions that represent their deepest, most difficult feelings. But in other ways, the gestalt games are more abstract and imaginative than the games used in psychodrama. Mintz (1971) offers a catalog of interesting gestalt games that she uses in her marathon groups. In one of the games, "Feedback," each group member selects three people whom he likes and three about whom he feels critical. He verbalizes these feelings to the other group members, and feedback then ensues. In another game, "Hand Dialogue," two group members, set up as partners, improvise dances with their hands. This game is designed to lessen the rigidity between them. In "Name Game," two interlocutors carry on a conversation using only their two names, and no other words. In the "Yes-No Game," they do likewise, using only the words *yes* and *no*. As we can see from these examples, some of the gestalt games are rather unconventional and quite dramatic. But as Perls explains above, it is the therapist's job to help the patient mobilize his resources, and this at times may require that he experience unpleasurable feelings of absurdity and unrelatedness.

An important distinction between the gestalt and psychoanalytic approach is in the interpretation of dreams. "In Gestalt Therapy," says Perls,

we don't interpret dreams. We do something much more interesting with them. Instead of analyzing and further cutting up the dream, we want to bring it back to life. And the way to bring it back to life is to re-live the dream as if it were happening now. Instead of telling the dream as if it were a story in the past, act it out in the present, so that it becomes a part of yourself, so that you are really involved. (Perls, 1969)

This markedly emphasizes both the gestalt concern with the here and now—and the gestalt counselor's concern with the patient's understanding himself as a totality.

The goal of gestalt counseling, like the goal of psychoanalytic counseling, is integration of the personality.

The treatment is finished when the patient has achieved the basic requirements: change in outlook, a technique of adequate self-expression and assimilation, and the ability to extend awareness to the averbal level. He has then reached that state of integration which facilitates its own development, and he can now be safely left to himself. (Perls, 1948, p. 585)

This is all to be accomplished, however, without the need for intensive probing into the psychological past of the client.

EVALUATION

Gestalt therapy offers the school counselor a number of ideas and techniques which may prove applicable to his work in the school setting. The emphasis on the here and now is attractive to the school counselor, whose limited time and restricted facilities may require direct intervention into the immediacy of the client's situation. The gestalt therapist's concern with the *wholeness* of his client expresses an intuitive belief which is already held by many school counselors. Furthermore, the gestalt emphasis on body language proves a fruitful resource to the school counselor, who has a rich opportunity to study the body language of his client over the period of the school day.

Gannon (1972) has found that gestalt group work proved helpful to a group of high-school students in improving their openness and interpersonal relationships. Passons (1972) has suggested some ways of using gestalt interventions during group counseling sessions. Bunt (1970) presents a gestalt approach to the diagnosis and treatment of early childhood psychopathology, in which the counselor studies

the significant stimuli in the child's environment, from the time of conception, as they interact with his organism ... and attempts to bring about positive changes within his organism and the environmental stimuli, until the whole integrative state of the organism along with the whole setting of the stimuli produce an adequate pattern of behavior. (p. 26)

Foulds (1972) has discussed the experiential-gestalt growth group, detailing and clarifying some of the techniques that the counselor may wish to employ.

Although gestalt counseling relies on the dramatic element, the school counselor may draw from the vast repertoire those techniques that are especially applicable to the problems he confronts in the school. The gestalt group approach is particularly relevant to the needs of the school counselor, and this topic will be explored in more detail in Part Five.

References

Bunt, M. E. A gestalt approach to the diagnosis and treatment of early childhood psychopathology. *Psychology*, 1970, *7*(1), 17–26.

Denner, B. Deception, decision making, and gestalt therapy. *Journal of Consulting Psychology*, 1968, *32*, 527–531.

Fagan, J. The tasks of the therapist. In J. Fagan & I. L. Shepherd (Eds.), *Gestalt therapy now*. Palo Alto, Calif.: Science and Behavior Books, 1970.

Foulds, M. L. The experiential-gestalt growth group experience. *Journal of College Student Personnel*, 1972, *13*, 48–52.

Gannon, W. J. *The effects of the gestalt oriented group approach on the interpersonal contact attitudes of selected high school students* (Doctoral dissertation, Case Western Reserve University, 1972). (Ann Arbor, Mich.: University Microfilms No. 72–26.)

Goldenson, R. M. *The encyclopedia of human behavior* (Vol. 1). Garden City, N.Y.: Doubleday, 1970.

Levitsky, A., & Perls, F. The rules and games of gestalt therapy. In J. Fagan & I. L. Shepherd (Eds.), *Gestalt therapy now*. Palo Alto, Calif.: Science and Behavior Books, 1970.

Mintz, E. E. *Marathon groups: Reality and symbol*. New York: Appleton-Century-Crofts, 1971.

Murphy, M. Esalen—where it's at. *Psychology Today*, 1967, *1*, 34–39.

Naranjo, C. Present-centeredness: Technique, prescription, and ideal. In J. Fagan & I. L. Shepherd (Eds.), *Gestalt therapy now*. Palo Alto, Calif.: Science and Behavior Books, 1970.

Passons, W. R. Gestalt therapy interventions for group counseling. *Personnel and Guidance Journal*, 1972, *51*, 183–189.

Perls, F. S. *Ego, hunger, and aggression*. (Originally published, London: Allen and Unwin, 1947.) New York: Random House, 1969.

Perls, F. S. Theory and technique of personality integration. *American Journal of Psychotherapy*, 1948, *2*, 563 ff.

Perls, F. S. Four lectures (1966). In J. Fagan & I. L. Shepherd (Eds.), *Gestalt therapy now*. Palo Alto, Calif.: Science and Behavior Books, 1970.

Perls, F. S. *Gestalt therapy verbatim*. Lafayette, Calif.: Real People Press, 1969.

Perls, F. S., Hefferline, R. F., & Goodman, P. *Gestalt therapy: Excitement and growth in the human personality*. New York: Dell, 1969.

Rosen, S. Recent experiences with gestalt, encounter, and hypnotic techniques. *American Journal of Psychoanalysis*, 1972, *32*, 90–102.

Wallen, R. Gestalt therapy and gestalt psychology (1957). In J. Fagan & I. L. Shepherd (Eds.), *Gestalt therapy now*. Palo Alto, Calif.: Science and Behavior Books, 1970.

Suggested additional readings

Clements, C. C. Acting-out versus acting-through: An interview with Frederick Perls. *Voices*, 1969, *4*, 66–73.

Kempler, W. Experiential family therapy. *International Journal of Group Psychotherapy*, 1965, *15*, 55–71.

Kempler, W. Gestalt therapy. In R. Corsini (Ed.), *Current psychotherapies*. Itasca, Ill.: F. E. Peacock, 1973.

Perls, F. S. Morality, ego boundary, and aggression. *Complex*, 1953, *9*, 42–51.

Perls, F. S. *In and out of the garbage can*. Lafayette, Calif.: Real People Press, 1969.

Pursglove, P. D. *Recognition in gestalt therapy*. New York: Harper & Row, 1971.

Sutich, A. J., & Vich, M. (Eds.), *Readings in humanistic psychology*. New York: Free Press, 1969.

chapter twelve

Reality and
rational-emotive counseling

Two schools of therapy which have begun to make an impact in the school counseling profession in recent years are reality therapy and rational-emotive therapy. Although there are many differences between these two types of treatment, both emphasize the "here and now" and rely on man's logical faculties to overcome his emotional difficulties. Moreover, both reality and rational-emotive therapy offer insights and techniques that are particularly applicable to the school counseling situation, and it is probably for this reason rather than because of any special virtues of the positions that they have both been highlighted in workshops and training groups held for school counselors in different parts of the country. In this chapter we shall examine the theoretical framework of these two positions and comment on their direct application to school counseling problems.

HISTORY OF THE SCHOOLS

Reality and rational-emotive therapy, like client-centered therapy, are each largely the product of a single man. The man associated with reality therapy is Dr. William Glasser. Glasser, like Rogers, was trained in the psychoanalytic approach, with which he became discouraged late in his training. He objected primarily to the concepts of neurosis and mental illness, arguing instead that the patient is weak, not ill, and that if his abilities were strengthened, he would be a more fit member of society. At the time, Glasser's teacher, Dr. G. L. Harrington, was having his own doubts about the merits of psychoanalysis as a curative science. Harrington believed that there was no significant proof that psychoanalysis had any curative powers, and he sought a more effective type of psychotherapy. His doubts inspired Glasser to develop what emerged as reality therapy.

Again like Rogers, Glasser arrived at his treatment through experimentation and trial and error. In the first place, he found that in treating patients it was not necessary to explore their past histories in any detail. What counted most was what was happening at the present time, not what had transpired in the past. Second, he also rejected the Freudian notion of transference, arguing that the patient perceived the therapist as another human being, a real person, and not as some imagined figure of the past. Thirdly, he rejected the very important Freudian idea that to be mentally healthy, one had to have insight into one's unconscious mind.

In 1962 Glasser joined the staff of the institute for wayward adolescent girls at Ventura, California. Three years later he published *Reality Therapy: A New Approach to Psychiatry*, which outlined the details of his therapy and offered rich examples of its use at the Ventura school. In 1969 he published *Schools Without Failure*, which applied the principles of reality therapy to the school setting. He has lectured widely in recent years on the application of reality principles to education.

The person associated with rational-emotive therapy is Dr. Albert Ellis. Ellis, like Glasser and Rogers, was trained in the traditional classical psychoanalytic approach, which he practiced for a number of years during the late 1940s and early 1950s. Also like Glasser and Rogers, Ellis became disillusioned with this approach when he realized that "no matter how much insight his clients gained, nor how well they seemed to understand the events of their early childhood and to be able to connect them with their present emotional disturbances, they rarely lost their presenting symptoms ... and when they did, they still retained tendencies to create new troubling symptoms" (Ellis, 1973b, p. 168). Exploring this problem, he discovered that the source of his clients' emotional difficulties and psychological misperceptions were not simply a result of what had happened in the past but were also a reflection of an active, ongoing process in their lives.

Albert Ellis, founder of rational-emotive therapy

In working out his theoretical position, Ellis undertook a number of experimental strategies with his patients. He discovered, in his own words,

that people are not exclusively the products of social learning (as the theories of the psychoanalysts and the behavior psychologist emphasize) but that their socalled pathological symptoms are the result of *bio*social learning. That is to say, *because they are human* ... they tend to have several strong, irrational, empirically unvalidatable ideas; and as long as they hold on to these ideas ... they will tend to be what we commonly call "neurotic," "disturbed," or "mentally ill." (Ellis, 1973b, p. 169)

During the middle 1950s Ellis began to abandon altogether the psychoanalytic approach and concentrate on his new-found rational-emotive psychotherapy. In 1959 he founded The Institute for Rational Living, a non-profit scientific and educational organization in New York City. Nine years later a state-chartered training institute, The Institute for Advanced Study in Rational Psychotherapy, was founded to train rational-emotive therapists.

Ellis has written a number of important books and articles, outlining his position. His most important works are: *Reason and Emotion in Psychotherapy* (1962), *The Art and Science of Love* (1969a), *Growth Through Reason* (1971), and *A Guide to Rational Living*, co-authored with Robert A. Harper (1961). A journal, *Rational Living*, is published to bring up to date the research in this field.

THE VIEW OF MAN

The reality therapist, like the behaviorist, views man largely in terms of his behavior. But rather than examining behavior in terms of the S-R paradigm as the behaviorist does, or looking at the individual's behavior phenomenologically as the client-centered counselor does, the reality therapist considers behavior against an objective standard of measurement, which he calls reality. This reality may be a practical reality, a social reality, or a moral reality. In either case, he sees man as functioning in consonance or dissonance with that reality.

"When a man acts in such a way that he gives and receives love, and feels worthwhile to himself and others, his behavior is right or moral," argues Glasser (*Reality Therapy*, p. 57). Throughout his thinking, the criterion of "right" plays an important role in determining the appropriateness of behavior. He uses such terms as *satisfactory*, *improved*, *good*, and *moral* to describe behavior, and his view of mental health is directly related to how well one's behavior meets these standards of measurement. The reality counselor's view of man is continually shadowed by the normative points of these higher goals.

Glasser sees as the main motivation in man's behavior his attempts to fulfill his needs. He suggests that there are two basic psychological needs: the need to love and be loved, and the need for "achievement of self-worth, the feeling that you are worthwhile as a person both to yourself and to others" (Glasser, 1971). In a later paper (Glasser and Zunin, 1973), he reduces this to one basic need: the need for identity. It is

the need to feel that we are somehow separate and distinct from every other living being on the face of this earth; that no matter where we go we will not find another person who thinks, looks, acts, and talks exactly as we do. This need is universal and transcends all cultures. Its significance is evidenced, for example, in religious teachings of both primitive and civilized societies. (p. 292)

When the individual is frustrated in satisfying his needs, he may lose touch with the objective reality, stray from the imposing confines of the real world, and lose his ability to perceive things as they are. "In their unsuccessful effort to fulfill their needs," Glasser (1965) argues, "no matter what behavior they choose, all patients have a common characteristic: they all deny the reality of the world around them."

It is in the strivings to satisfy these basic needs, argues Glasser, that the patterns of our behavior are determined. Man's sense of responsibility for himself helps him change and modify his behavior, to arrive ultimately at more acceptable and satisfactory standards that, in turn, enable him to gratify his needs more successfully.

To be worthwhile we must maintain a satisfactory standard of behavior. To do so we must learn to correct ourselves when we do wrong and to credit ourselves when we do right. If we do not evaluate our behavior, or having evaluated it, we do not act to improve our conduct where it is below our standards, we will not fulfill our need to be worthwhile and we will suffer. (*Reality Therapy*, p. 10)

Thus, the reality counselor attaches therapeutically direct values to behavior, measuring a man's success or failure in treatment against these values and how well they have been met.

The rational-emotive view of man is dominated by the principle that emotion and reason—thinking and feeling—are intricately and inextricably entwined in the psyche. Ellis (1958) explains the connection between the cognitive and affective domains this way:

Thinking and emoting are closely interrelated and at times differ mainly in that thinking is more tranquil, less somatically involved ... and a less activity-directed mode of discrimination than is emotion ... among adult humans raised in a social culture, thinking and emoting are so closely interrelated that they usually accompany each other, act in a circular cause-and-effect relationship, and in certain ... respects are essentially the *same thing*, so that one's thinking *becomes* one's emotion and emoting *becomes* one's thought.... since man is a uniquely sign-, symbol-, and language-creating animal, both thinking and emoting tend to take the form of self-talk or internalized sentences; and that for all practical purposes, the sentences that human beings keep telling themselves *are* or *become* their thoughts and emotions. (p. 36)

In the process of growing up, he suggests, the child is taught to think and feel certain things about himself and about others. Those things that are associated with the idea of "This is good," argues Ellis (1958), become positive human emotions, such as love or joy, while those associated with the idea "This is bad!" become negative emotion, with painful, angry, or depressive feelings. Psychopathological behavior, he goes on to point out, is illogical and irrational, associating "This is bad!" with things which really are not. He offers as an example the aetiology of a phobia, in which an individual experienced an early life disturbance upon discovering that he had strong death wishes against his father. Because he thinks such wishes are bad, he feels that he should be blamed and punished for having these feelings. As a result of this incongruity, he develops a neurotic phobia against dogs (because dogs remind him unconsciously of his father, who loves to hunt). "Later on," Ellis continues,

this individual may grow to love or be indifferent to his father; or his father may die and be no more of a problem to him. His fear of dogs, however, may remain: not because, as some theorist would insist, they still remind him of his old death wishes against his father, but because he now hates himself so violently for *having* the original neurotic symptom— for behaving, to his mind, so stupidly and illogically in relation to dogs—that every time he thinks of dogs his self-hatred and fear of failure so severely upset him that he cannot reason clearly and cannot combat his illogical fear. (Ellis, 1958, p. 39)

The rational-emotive view of man emphasizes that man is born with the potential to be rational and logical but becomes illogical and "crooked thinking" because of his distortions during childhood and his contemporary repetitions of these distortions. "The central theme of RT," Ellis (1962) explains, "is that man is a uniquely rational as well as uniquely irrational animal; that his emotional or psychological disturbances are largely a result of his thinking illogically or

irrationally; and that he can rid himself of most of his mental or emotional un-
happiness, ineffectuality, and disturbance if he learns to maximize his rational
and minimize his irrational thinking" (p. 36).

THE ROLE OF THE CLIENT

The primary job of the client in reality therapy is to learn to make appropriate choices, to develop a sense of responsibility, to be able to interact constructively with others, and to understand and accept the reality of his existence. Although this appears on the surface to be identical to the role of the
existential client, it differs in two important aspects: The reality client, unlike
the existential client, is not in the process of creating his own existence and his
own destiny through his choices, but rather he is conforming to the counselor's
notions of reality; secondly, the reality client's sense of responsibility is defined
as "the ability to fulfill one's needs, and to do so in a way that does not deprive
others of the ability to fulfill their needs" (*Reality Therapy*, p. 13).

The client comes to treatment to fill a void in his life. "Almost of emptiness.
They look to the psychiatrist to supply in a measure what they lack, and in
proper psychiatric treatment he does this. When the patient finally begins to
establish a real feeling of identity, the empty feeling leaves and the person begins to become alive and vital" (*Mental Health or Mental Illness?*, p. 26). Glasser
views this emptiness as a lack of genuine involvement with others and attributes to this source many of the major psychological problems.

In many psychotherapies, the client conducts a monologue, presenting to the
therapist his past history, his current problems, his perceptions, his feelings,
and so on. In rational-emotive therapy, on the other hand, the client is responsible for engaging in a dialogue with the therapist—a dialogue that is dynamic,
reactive, and at times painful and provocative. The client in rational-emotive
therapy functions much as the learner does in the educational setting, and his
ability to improve is contingent upon his motivation and cooperation in the
learner's role. He must be willing, specifically, to recognize and deal with those
feelings and beliefs that he once considered logical and natural and which now
he is discovering are illogical and unhealthy. This is often no easy matter. "No
matter what a person's past history may be," Ellis and Harper (1961) explain,

or how his parents, teachers, and other early associates may have helped him to become
emotionally disturbed, he only remains disturbed because he *still* believes some of the
unrealistic and illogical thoughts which he originally imbibed. To become undisturbed,
therefore, it is only necessary that he see what his present irrational self-indoctrinations
are and that he energetically and consistently work at deindoctrinating and
reindoctrinating himself in these connections. His understanding of how he *first* became
neurotic may be of some help, but it is most unlikely that it will be truly curative. (pp. 50–
51)

The rational-emotive client, therefore, must live in and deal with the present
rather than the past.

261

THE ROLE OF THE COUNSELOR

Glasser says the following about the role of the counselor in reality counseling:

The therapist has a difficult task, for he must quickly build a firm emotional relationship with a patient who has failed to establish such relationships in the past. He is aided by recognizing that the patient is desperate for involvement and suffering because he is not able to fulfill his needs.... The ability of the therapist to get involved is the major skill of doing Reality Therapy.... One way to attempt an understanding of how involvement occurs is to describe the qualities necessary to the therapist.... The therapist must be a very responsible person—tough, interested, human, and sensitive. He must be able to fulfill his own needs and must be willing to discuss some of his own struggles so that the patient can see that acting responsibly is possible though sometimes difficult.... The therapist must always be strong, never expedient. He must withstand the patient's request for sympathy, for an excess of sedatives, for justification of his actions no matter how the patient pleads or threatens. Never condoning an irresponsible action on the patient's part, he must be willing to watch the patient suffer, if that helps him toward responsibility.... The therapist must have a knowledge and understanding about the person who is isolated or different because he cannot properly fulfill his needs.... He must never be frightened or rebuffed by the patient's behavior.... Finally, the therapist must be able to become emotionally involved with each patient. (Glasser, 1965, pp. 21–23)

The therapist, in other words, establishes a relationship with the client in which he is able to exert his critical awareness for the client's benefit. He guides the client, directively and dynamically, to a condition of congruence with the objective reality; but unlike the client-centered counselor, the reality counselor is judgmental and advisory at every juncture. He uses his own experiences and feelings, when these are appropriate and relevant, to help the patient.

The rational-emotive therapist is also directive, and he intentionally leads the client to a healthier perspective. In keeping with his view that "not only are all psychotherapies more or less authoritative but they are also to some degree authoritarian," Ellis (1962) favors the therapist's providing a high degree of direction to the client:

The therapist, because of his training and experience, is invariably some kind of authority in his field; and by virtue of the fact that he is presumably less disturbed than his patient, and is often older and/or wiser, he is something of an authority- or parental-figure. Even if *he* does not look upon himself in this manner, the members of his clientele almost invariably do. And whether he likes it or not, a considerable portion of his effectiveness with his patients results from his being or appearing to be something of an authority figure to them. (pp. 364–365)

The therapist, according to Ellis (1962), devotes his efforts toward distinguishing what he sees as the difference between understanding and a deeper level of involvement on his part. "That the therapist should normally understand his patient's world and *see* the patient's behavior from this patient's *own* frame of reference," he points out, "is highly desirable."

That the therapist should literally *feel* his patient's disturbances or *believe in* his irrationalities is, in my opinion, usually harmful rather than helpful to this patient. Indeed, it is precisely the therapist's ability to comprehend the patient's immature behavior *without* getting involved in or believing in it that enables him to induce the patient to stop believing in or feeling that this behavior is necessary. (p. 115)

We note the sharp contradiction between Ellis's conception of the role of the counselor and Carl Rogers's conceptions. To Ellis, the counselor works directly and authoritatively as a "lead" figure for the client, helping the client to understand and resolve the illogicalities in his thinking which have led to emotional difficulties.

Ellis sees no reason why the therapist should not be able to inject his own values into the therapeutic relationship when his experience dictates that they are advisable. After all, he argues, his values are presumably healthy values, and there is no logical reason why the client should not be exposed to healthy values—or at least values which are healthier than his own. Like Glasser, he believes that the counselor's values are a legitimate therapeutic tool. His key remarks on the value of directiveness in rational-emotive therapy are found in this passage from *Reason and Emotion in Psychotherapy*:

Patients [learn] to reperceive or rethink their life events and philosophies and thereby to change their unrealistic and illogical thought, emotion, and behavior.... the more emotional and less persuasive methods of psychotherapy are, when employed with most disturbed persons, relatively ineffectual and wasteful. On the other hand, the more direct, persuasive, suggestive, active, and logical techniques of therapy are more effective at undermining and extirpating the basic causes (as distinct from outward symptoms) of the emotional difficulties of most—though by no means necessarily all—individuals who come for psychological help. (pp. 36–37)

TECHNIQUES AND GOALS

The basic technique of reality therapy is a teaching technique, specifically, to teach the patient the meaning of reality and to show him how to act responsibly within the context of that reality. Prior to this teaching, the therapist must first gain the necessary involvement with the patient, for "unless the requisite involvement exists between the responsible therapist and the irresponsible patient, there can be no therapy" (*Reality Therapy*, p. 21). After the therapist gains the necessary involvement, he begins to point out to the patient the unrealistic aspects of his irresponsible behavior. "If the patient wishes to argue that his conception of reality is correct," Glasser points out, "we must be willing to discuss his opinions, but we must not fail to emphasize that our main interest is his behavior rather than his attitude."

Glasser's statements on techniques and goals are clear:

Along with the emphasis on behavior and as a continuing part of the involvement, the therapist freely gives praise when the patient acts responsibly and shows disapproval when he does not…. The skill of therapy is to put the responsibility upon the patient and, after involvement is established, to ask him why he remains in therapy if he is not dissatisfied with his behavior…. As therapy proceeds, the therapist must teach the patient that therapy is not primarily directed toward making him happy … the therapist must guide the patient toward understanding that no one can make another person happy for long unless he becomes more responsible…. As part of becoming involved the therapist must become interested in and discuss all aspects of the patient's present life…. We are interested in him as a person with a wide potential, not just as a patient with problems…. We must open up his life, talk about new horizons, expand his range of interests, make him aware of life beyond his difficulties. Anything two people might discuss is grist for therapy….

The patient develops an increased sense of self-worth in the process of parrying his convictions and values with a trusted, respected person. The therapist relates the discussions to what the patient is doing now, confronting him with the reality of what he does as compared to what he says. Sessions which do not bear directly on the patient's problems are not wasted as long as they relate to his growing awareness that he is part of the world and that perhaps he can cope with it….

The therapist now directly, but skillfully, interweaves a discussion of the patient's strong points. Discussing those areas in which he acts responsibly, we show how they can be expanded…. To do Reality Therapy the therapist must not only be able to help the patient accept the real world, but he must then further help him fulfill his needs in the real world so that he will have no inclination in the future to deny its existence. (*Reality Therapy*, pp. 7, 28–32)

Rational-emotive therapy, like reality therapy, also consists of teaching techniques, but teaching techniques which synthesize the cognitive and emotional facets of the patient's existence. The content of the therapy, Ellis and Harper (1961) point out,

largely consists of teaching the patient effective self-analysis: How, specifically, to observe his own feelings and actions, how to evaluate them objectively instead of moralistically and grandiosely, and how to change them, by consistent effort and practice, so that he may achieve the things that he most wants to do in this brief span of human existence while, simultaneously, not interfering seriously with the preferences of others. Self-analysis, in this sense of the term, is not merely an important but actually a requisite aspect of successful psychotherapy.

We see, then, that the ultimate goal of rational-emotive teaching is that the patient becomes capable of introspectively analysing and correcting his distortions of the world.

"All the techniques in rational-emotive therapy," Ellis (1973a) argues, "are designed to do more than change behavior and help the client feel better. They are also used to change basic philosophies and to give him or her specific means of restructuring these philosophies again and again, until he or she rarely reverts to personally sabotaging and other-hating views and actions" (p. 62). He views the rational-emotive approach as "scientific," and many of his statements about the importance of techniques conjure up images of the behavioral counselor systematically working to alleviate symptoms.

264

Ellis (1973b) divides the course of the treatment into three basic modes, each comprising a set of techniques: *cognitive, emotive,* and *behavioristic.* "Cognitive therapy," he explains,

attempts to show the individual that he is an arrant demander and that he'd better give up his perfectionism if he wants to lead a happier, less anxiety-ridden existence. It teaches him how to find his *should, oughts,* and *must;* how to separate his rational ... from his irrational beliefs; how to use the logicoempirical method of science in relation to himself and his own problems; and how to accept reality, even when it is pretty grim. (p. 182)

This is the level of rational-emotive therapy that is closest in principle and technique with the reality therapy approach.

"Emotive-evocative therapy," Ellis goes on to explain,

employs various means of dramatizing truths and falsehoods so that he can clearly distinguish between the two ... the therapist may employ *role-playing,* to bring forth to the client exactly what his false ideas are and how they affect his relations with others; *modeling,* to show the client how to adopt different values; *humor,* to reduce some of the client's disturbance-creating ideas to absurdity; *unconditional acceptance* of the client, to demonstrate to him that he is acceptable, even with his unfortunate present traits; ... *exhortation,* to persuade him to give up some of his crazy thinking and replace it with more efficient notions. (p. 183)

This is the level of the treatment that is most overtly dramatic and that is generally associated with the showy side of the rational-emotive approach. It is important for the counselor to remember, however, that this is only one phase of the treatment—not the entire treatment, as some lay people and critics would lead us to believe.

Behavior therapy methods are employed "to help the client change his dysfunctional symptoms and to become habituated to more effective ways of performing, and to help him radically change his *cognitions* about himself, about others, and about the world" (Ellis, 1973b, p. 183). These behavioristic methods may include giving the patient a homework assignment, encouraging him to take a risk, or having him intentionally fail at some effort in order to cope with the feelings of failure. Some of these techniques resemble respondent conditioning techniques, and others look remarkably similar to Frankl's paradoxical intention.

We see from these remarks that rational-emotive therapy comprises a variety of different types of techniques, all clustered around the central goal of the therapy—to correct the patient's illogical beliefs and irrational feelings. The goals of the treatment are therefore specifiable in terms of the ideas and thoughts which are to be corrected. Ellis (1958) offers a tentative list of 12 common illogical thoughts that often require correction during the treatment.

It must be mentioned, however, that a complete list would be as limitless as the number of patients who seek treatment.

EVALUATION

Since the publication of Glasser's first book in 1965, reality therapy has gained many adherents in the ranks of public school counselors and has had a powerful impact on the practice of school counseling. Many client-centered counselors, disillusioned by the inefficacy of unconditional positive regard in dealing with serious school-related problems, yet wary of approaches involving the element of an unconscious and put off by the inhumaneness of behavioral techniques, found themselves turning steadily toward reality counseling as a viable alternative. Clients, too, find attractive a counseling situation where the counselor appears as a knowledgeable, responsible, and participating person, who is willing to offer the client some clear-cut advice on occasions where it can be helpful.

The rational-emotive approach is also beginning to enjoy a wider acceptance in the school counseling situation. Ellis (1969b) has discussed the application of rational-emotive techniques for teaching emotional education in the classroom. Lafferty et al. (1964) have applied rational-emotive techniques to a school mental health program. They offer an example of how Ellis's approach was used to study human behavior in the classroom. Counselors who wish to draw from the rational-emotive approach would do well to familiarize themselves thoroughly with Ellis's writings, in order to avoid the pitfalls in mistaking the superficial aspects of the treatment for its core.

References

Ellis, A. Rational psychotherapy. *The Journal of General Psychology*, 1958, *59*, 35–49.

Ellis, A. *Reason and emotion in psychotherapy.* New York: Lyle Stuart, 1962.

Ellis, A. *The art and science of love.* New York: Lyle Stuart, 1969. (a)

Ellis, A. Teaching emotional education in the classroom. *School Health Review*, 1969, *1*, 10–13. (b)

Ellis, A. *Growth through reason.* Palo Alto, Calif.: Science and Behavior Books, 1971.

Ellis, A. The no cop-out therapy. *Psychology Today*, 1973, *7*, 56–62. (a)

Ellis, A. Rational-emotive therapy. In R. Corsini (Ed.), *Current psychotherapies.* Itasca, Ill.: F. E. Peacock, 1973. (b)

Ellis, A., & Harper, R. A. *A guide to rational living.* Englewood Cliffs, N.J.: Prentice-Hall, 1961.

Glasser, W. *Reality therapy: A new approach to psychiatry.* New York: Harper & Row, 1965.

Glasser, W. *Schools without failure.* New York: Harper & Row, 1969.

Glasser, W. Reality therapy and counseling. In C. Beck (Ed.), *Philosophical guidelines in counseling* (2nd ed.). Dubuque, Iowa: Wm. C. Brown, 1971.

Glasser, W., & Zunin, L. M. Reality therapy. In R. Corsini (Ed.), *Current psychotherapies.* Itasca, Ill.: F. E. Peacock, 1973.

Lafferty, J., Dennerll, D., & Rettick, P. A creative school mental health program. *The National Elementary Principal*, 1964, *43*, 29–35.

Suggested additional readings

Reality therapy

Glasser, W. *Mental health or mental illness?* New York: Harper & Row, 1961.

Glasser, W. *The identity society.* New York: Harper & Row, 1972.

Hawes, R. M. Reality therapy in the classroom (Doctoral dissertation, University of the Pacific, 1973). Ann Arbor, Mich.: University Microfilms.

Zunin, L. M. Reality therapy: Its concepts and principles. *Search Magazine*, 1972, *2*, 30–35.

Rational-emotive therapy

Ard, B. N., Jr. *Counseling and psychotherapy*. Palo Alto, Calif.: Science and Behavior Books, 1966.

Ard, B. N., Jr. Rational therapy in rehabilitation counseling. *Rehabilitation Counseling Bulletin*, 1968, *12*, 84–88.

Argabrite, A. H., & Nidorf, L. J. Fifteen questions for rating reason. *Rational Living*, 1968, *3*, 9–11.

Brainerd, C. J. Personal worth and perception of one's parents. *Rational Living*, 1970, *4*, 17–19.

Diamond, L. Restoring amputated ego. *Rational Living*, 1967, *2*, 15 ff.

Ellis, A. Outcome of employing three techniques of psychotherapy. *Journal of Clinical Psychology*, 1957, *13*, 344–350.

Ellis, A. What really causes therapeutic change? *Voices*, 1968, *4*, 90–97.

Ellis, A. *Humanistic psychotherapy: The rational-emotive approach*. New York: Julian Press, 1973.

Hauck, P. A. A RET theory of depression. *Rational Living*, 1971, *6*, 32–35.

Meehl, P. E. Psychologists' opinions as to the effects of holding five of Ellis' "irrational ideas." *Research Laboratory of the Department of Psychiatry, University of Minnesota*, 1966.

Trexler, L. D. Rational-emotive therapy, placebo, and no-treatment effects on public speaking anxiety (Doctoral dissertation, Temple University, 1971). Ann Arbor, Mich.: University Microfilms.

Wagner, E. E. Techniques of rational counseling. *High Spots*, 1963, *3*, 2.

chapter thirteen

Behavioral counseling

The behavioral approach to counseling differs substantially from the other schools of psychotherapy we have considered. In fact, there is considerable debate as to whether the behavioral approach can legitimately be considered a psychotherapeutic approach at all. It may be more of a retraining, a reeducation, a learning procedure than a psychotherapy. For unlike the other psychotherapies we have considered, the behavioral approach does not utilize as the fundamental principle the axiom that the client improves by his talking alone; nor does it emphasize the importance of the psychotherapeutic relationship. Instead, behavioral counseling comprises a body of related approaches held together by the common belief that emotional, learning, and adjustment difficulties can be treated through a variety of mechanical, usually nondynamic, techniques and procedures. In this chapter we shall explore the origins of the behavioral approach and its present application to the school counseling situation.

HISTORY OF THE SCHOOL

The various (and sometimes conflicting) approaches that make up behavioral counseling were each introduced by an important and innovative seminal thinker who was disturbed by the status quo. While the philosophical and psychological premises of the behavioral approach can be traced back to the empirical philosopher John Locke, the important foundation of the behavioral approach—the groundwork that led to the subsequent systematic exposition of the theory—was laid at the beginning of this century in the United States. Two important figures who certainly should be acknowledged are John B. Watson and Edward L. Thorndike.

Much of behavioral counseling derives from the system of psychology called *behaviorism*, which was founded by an American psychologist, John B. Watson, in 1913. Watson was attempting to develop what he called an *objective psychology*, one that would deal only with the observable behavior of the organism and avoid probing into what he considered to be the subjectivity of mental activity, which he felt deprived psychology of its scientific basis. He considered objective observation of the organism the only valid method of psychological investigation.

The first statement of Watson's ideas are found in his article, "Psychology as the Behaviorist Views It," which appeared in the *Psychological Review* in 1913. Six years later a more comprehensive outline of his ideas appeared in the form of a textbook, *Psychology from the Standpoint of a Behaviorist*. In both the article and the book, the influence of the Russian physiologist, Ivan Pavlov, and the English physiologist, Sir Charles Sherrington, is made clear. Watson uses Sherrington's principle of animal reflexes and Pavlov's more fundamental proof of the conditioned reflex to lay down the foundation for his new psychology.

John B. Watson, founder of behaviorism

Watson (1913) begins by arguing that, "The time seems to have come when psychology must discard all reference to consciousness; when it need no longer delude itself into thinking that it is making mental states the object of observation." He criticizes the psychology of his time (introspectionism) for being too bound up with philosophy and religion and therefore lacking the scientific integrity necessary to make it an effective and practical study. He goes on to clarify the problem:

Psychology, up to very recent times, has been held so rigidly under the dominance both of traditional religion and of philosophy—the two great bulwarks of mediaevalism—that it has never been able to free itself and become a natural science.... The reason for its failure was largely its limitation of subject matter and choice of method. Psychology limited its subject matter to the so-called states of consciousness—their analysis and synthesis. "States of consciousness" like the so-called phenomena of spiritualism are not objectively verifiable and for that reason can never become data for science.... The psychologists' use of "introspection" as its principal method has been another very serious bar to progress.... All that introspective psychology has been able to contribute is the assertion that mental states are made up of several thousand irreducible units.... But the truth or falsity of this assertion is inconsequential, since no other human being can make an introspective observation upon anyone but himself. (Watson, 1924)

He goes on to suggest that for psychology to become truly scientific it must rely solely on observable behavior as its subject matter, and it must "attempt to formulate, through systematic observation and experimentation, the generalizations, laws, and principles which underly man's behavior" (Watson, 1924).

"As a science," he continues, "psychology puts before herself the task of unraveling the complex factors involved in the development of human behavior from infancy to old age, and of finding the laws for the regulation of behavior." To help formulate these laws, he explicates the concepts of *stimulus* and *response* and the law that from any given stimulus we can deduce a predictable response. This idea—that each stimulus is linked up to a response—has become the basic rule of behavioral psychology and behavioral counseling.

Watson applied these principles of experimental psychology to human behavior problems. Arguing that neurosis is in fact a learned pattern of behavior, he pointed out that these patterns could also be *unlearned* by proper conditioning. The principle that psychological disorders can be unlearned is the basis of all behavioral counseling. His first book, *Behavior: An Introduction to Comparative Psychology* (1914), had an immense influence on American psychology, resulting in Watson's election to the presidency of the American Psychological Association the following year.

In 1920 Watson and his associate Rayner reported a clinical example of a phobia being induced by methods of conditioning. They took an eleven-month-old boy, Albert, and taught him to be fearful of white rats. They did this by emitting a loud, frightening noise whenever Albert reached out to touch the rat, which he was initially not frightened of. After a few of these trials, the boy developed a fear whenever he saw the rat—even if the noise was no longer emitted. Ultimately, he acquired a phobia for all furry objects, apparently generalizing the fear of the rat to these other objects as well.

Eysenck and Rachman (1965) have summarized the theoretical implications of Watson's experiment in nine statements:

1 Phobias are learned responses.
2 Stimuli develop phobic qualities when they are associated temporally and spatially with a fear-producing state of affairs.
3 Neutral stimuli which are of relevance in the fear-producing situation and/or make an impact on the person in the situation are more likely to develop phobic qualities than weak or irrelevant stimuli.
4 Repetition of the association between the fear situation and the new phobic stimuli will strengthen the phobia.
5 Associations between high intensity fear situations and neutral stimuli are more likely to produce phobic reactions.
6 Generalization from the original phobic stimulus to stimuli of a similar nature will occur.
7 Noxious experiences which occur under conditions of excessive confinement are more likely to produce phobic reactions.
8 Neutral stimuli which are associated with a noxious experience(s) may develop (secondary) motivating properties. This acquired drive is termed the fear-drive.
9 Responses (such as avoidance) which reduce the fear-drive are reinforced. (p. 67)

What is most important about these principles is that if such a fear can be instilled through conditioning, then it can also be removed by conditioning. In fact this is exactly what happened. Four years later, Mary Jones used these same principles in reverse to treat the phobia of a three-year-old boy, thus providing the first clinical example of behavioral principles applied to the treatment situation.

A decade before Watson's work, Edward L. Thorndike had conducted a series of important experiments in psychology, using animals as subjects. In one famous study, he put a hungry cat into a cage which was constructed in such a way that the cat could trigger a mechanism to allow him access to food which was immediately outside the grating of the cage. At first the cat tried to force his way out of the cage in order to get at the food. He fiercely struggled in vain, continually repelled by the solidity of the steel grating. Finally, by accident he triggered the mechanism which allowed him to leave the cage and obtain the food. After a brief interval, he was placed back in the cage and the situation was repeated. Thorndike observed that the cat gradually learned the relationship between triggering the mechanism, leaving the cage, and obtaining the food. After many such repetitions, the cat could immediately trigger his release after he was placed in the cage.

Thorndike called the principle that was at work here *the law of effect*. Simply, this law states that an act which is reinforced positively will tend to be repeated, and an act which is reinforced negatively will tend to be avoided. Thorndike developed and refined this law into his comprehensive *connectionist psychology*:

Edward L. Thorndike formulated the law of effect.

Connections lead from states of affairs within the brain as well as from external situations. They often occur in long series wherein the response to one situation becomes the situation producing the next response and so on. They may be from parts or elements or features of a situation as well as from the situation as a whole. They may be largely determined by events preceding their immediate stimuli or by more or less of the accompanying attitude or set of the person.... They lead to responses of readiness and unreadiness, awareness, attention, interest, welcoming and rejecting, emphasizing and restraining, differentiating and relating. (Thorndike, 1949)

While Thorndike acknowledged that the variety of human responses is so vast that it precludes containment in such a simple scheme, he attempted boldly to examine the processes of mental systems with the hope of explicating the cumulative pattern of human behavior in terms of its component parts. In one of his experiments (Thorndike, 1949, p. 97), he concludes that "nearly 95 per cent of the responses are explainable by connections formed by repetition and reward in the course of hearing and seeing and using words."

One of Thorndike's major contributions to behaviorism is found in his concept of punishment. While he conceded that behavior is shaped by both reward and punishment, it is the former that produces a far more satisfying and productive result. "The strengthening of a connection by satisfying consequences seems," he said, "... to be more universal, inevitable, and direct than the weakening of a connection by annoying consequences" (Thorndike, 1949, p. 37). He went on to contrast the two reinforcers:

Rewards and punishments alike will teach by virtue of the conditions and activities which they produce in the animal. Rewards in general tend to maintain and strengthen any connection which leads to them. Punishments often but not always tend to shift from it to something else and their educative value depends on what this something else is. They weaken it, by strengthening some competing connection.

Punishment for its own sake, then, is of little value. It is only when the punishment is coupled with something positive that it becomes a viable educational tool.

Although the work of Thorndike and Watson laid the groundwork for behaviorism, three "neobehaviorists" are primarily responsible for the wide application of behavioral principles and the subsequent development and popularity of the theory. These three are Clark L. Hull, E. C. Tolman, and B. F. Skinner. Working at Yale University, Hull, assisted by his colleagues, made a number of important contributions to the field. Beginning with a biological-integrative theory of behavior, in which the organism is viewed in its total relationship with an active environment, Hull (1943) developed a sophisticated reinforcement theory of learning and behavior. His theory is clearly based on the Newtonian conception (see chapter 3 of this book), and an excellent summary of his major findings is provided by Borger and Seaborne (1966):

Hull tried to model the form of his theory on that of physics as the senior science, particularly the Newtonian system. Accordingly it is comprehensive, purporting to provide the framework for an account of all mammalian behavior; it is also highly formalized, being composed of a series of postulates, theorems and corollaries....

There are, within Hull's system, three kinds of variables. Two of these are observable, relating to input—such as intensity of stimulation, degree of deprivation of the organism, number of reinforced trials—and to output or response—such as the amplitude, probability of occurrence or latency of responses.... The third category consists of intervening variables, related by equations to both observable classes, acting as a sort of bridge between them, to facilitate thinking about the relationship between terminal events. For example, habit strength is such an intervening variable, symbolized by sHr. It is functionally related to the number of times the joint occurrence of a particular stimulus and a particular response has been followed by reinforcement.... Reaction potential is reduced by reactive inhibition (Ir) and conditioned inhibition (sIr), variables which are most easily thought of in terms of fatigue developed in the course of responding. There are many more variables, and their relationships are complex. (pp. 68–69)

We should note the increasing refinement and sophistication from Thorndike's early experiments to Watson's generalizations to Hull's scientific approach to behavior.

E. C. Tolman, a prominent behaviorist during the 1930s, introduced the concept of *intervening variables*, factors outside the direct conditioning situation that influenced the S-R pattern. Tolman was a cognitive theorist who rejected the simple S-R schematic, adding to it the much more complex idea of expectancy.

Probably the most important of the neobehaviorists was B. F. Skinner, who systematically refined and developed new principles of behaviorism.

During the 1930s Skinner set forth some of the assumptions that would influence his thinking for the next forty years. He strongly rejected the psychoanalytic notion that behavior problems were the result of unconscious conflicts, arguing instead that drive and motivation are not intrinsic to the person but the result of outside stimulation and training. Skinner also expounded the basics of *operant conditioning*, a method through which the subject is retrained by changing the consequences of his behavior. As positive behavior is rewarded

*B. F. Skinner,
the most important
neobehaviorist*

and negative behavior punished, argued Skinner, the subject learns to behave more positively. Skinner conducted a series of animal experiments, usually with rats as subjects, and he is well known for his invention of the Skinner box, which is actually a training maze. His novel, *Walden Two*, attempts to portray a utopian social system based on his principles of learning and conditioning.

Using Hull's learning theory, Joseph Wolpe developed a theory of behavioral psychopathology and treatment that was meant as a strong response to the prevailing Freudian theories. His theory is known as *reciprocal inhibition*. In short, this approach attempts systematically to desensitize the patient to neurotic, anxiety-provoking situations. The patient may, for example, provide the behavior therapist with a list of anxiety situations, ranged from least to most anxious. The therapist induces a mild hypnotic trance and helps the subject deal with each situation, one at a time, in increasing order of produced anxiety, until the problem is resolved. Wolpe has developed several important techniques from his practice, which will be discussed later in this chapter.

During the 1950s Dollard and Miller attempted to reexplain basic psychoanalytic principles in terms of Hull's behavior theory. In 1953 Lindsley delivered a paper on the application of operant conditioning techniques in the treatment of schizophrenia. Six years later, Eysenck labeled these new and complex approaches to treatment, all of which derived from Watson's original premises forty years earlier, as *behavior therapy*.

THE VIEW OF MAN

To the behavioral counselor, the individual is a product of his conditioning. The behaviorist speaks of the S-R paradigm as the basic pattern of all human learning. Each man reacts in a predictable way to any given stimulus, depending on what his training has taught him. Man is no different from animals, except that his responses to stimuli are more complex and on a higher level of organization.

The basic equation of all human behavior, according to the behaviorist point of view, is $B = (f)s$: behavior is a function of a stimulus (Dimick and Huff, 1970). This reduces considerably the complex factors influencing human reactions to situations and allows the behaviorist to focus in on a specific problem as a reaction to a given set of stimuli. Of course, behavioral counselors realize that simple equations do not adequately explain the totality of human nature, so they have set forth a number of concepts to explain modifications of behavior and the processes through which learning and change take place.

The key word underlying the behavioral view of man is *conditioning*. Although there are several types of conditioning, there are two basic classes that are usually discussed: classical (respondent) conditioning and operant (instrumental) conditioning. Classical conditioning is "the process whereby an originally neutral conditioned stimulus, through continuous pairing with an unconditioned stimulus, acquires the ability to elicit a response originally given to the unconditioned stimulus" (Price, 1972). This is the type of conditioning illustrated in Pavlov's famous experiment with the dog. As you may recall, Pavlov discovered, while studying digestion in animals, that if a bell rang immediately before a dog was fed, after a time the ringing of the bell itself would cause the dog to salivate. The pairing of the ringing bell (conditioned stimulus) and the feeding (unconditioned stimulus) caused the dog to respond to the bell by salivating.

Likewise, a number of the basic learning experiences of the average individual can be explained through the classical conditioning paradigm. Most important of these experiences, from the counselor's point of view, are the maladaptive or neurotic learning experiences. Eysenck and Rachman (1965) have suggested a three-stage explanation of the development of abnormal behavior. The first stage involves a series of traumatic events that produce autonomic reactions in the individual. These autonomic reactions are considered as unconditioned responses, which in turn may result in neurotic behavior patterns. The second stage utilizes the classical conditioning paradigm directly. This stage is particularly useful in explaining the generalization of anxiety to unhealthy proportions. The final stage involves instrumental avoidance of painful or anxiety-provoking situations. Let us consider as an example a boy who has developed a

274

fear of dogs. It may have begun with a traumatic incident in which he was bitten by a dog. The trauma of being bitten (unconditioned stimulus) produced an immediate body reaction (pain—autonomic response), which set the stage for the development of the phobia. Now, whenever he sees a dog (conditioned stimulus), he associates this with the traumatic event and runs away (conditioned response). Running away from dogs and avoiding them (operant avoidance) produces a relief of his original anxiety that was brought about by the traumatic event in the first place. Thus, the phobia and avoidance serve as a *reinforcing stimulus*.

As we see from this description (and this is only one of many paradigms the behaviorists use to explain neurotic behavior), the mechanics of learning neurotic behavior can be quite complex. But there is always a logical, learning-oriented motif to the behavioral view of man and his problems that holds together all of the particular explanations.

The second major class of conditioning is operant or instrumental conditioning. This is the type of conditioning generally associated with the work of B. F. Skinner. "In operant conditioning, voluntarily or spontaneously emitted (operant) behavior is strengthened (or discouraged) by positive reinforcement (reward) (or by negative reinforcement, which is a stimulus whose removal increases the probability of the behavior it follows), by lack of reinforcement...or by punishment" (Patterson, 1973, p. 80).

Consider, for example, what happens in a simple Skinner box. In this contraption, an animal (usually a mouse or rabbit) is taught to push a lever and is rewarded with food (*positive reinforcement*). This pattern of behavior eventually becomes learned. The learning principle behind operant conditioning is that new learning occurs as a result of positive reinforcement, and old patterns are abandoned as a result of negative reinforcement. Ullmann and Krasner (1965) have written extensively on the consequences of operant learning and its application to emotional problems and learning disturbances.

It would be unfair to imply that the entire behavioral view of man is dominated solely by these learning theories. True, the concepts of reinforcement and stimulus-pairing play a key role in the explanation of how human behavior is learned; but the behaviorists also recognize that other factors play a vital role as well. Carter and Stuart (1970), in responding to a highly critical assessment of the behavioral approach, attempt to clarify this oversimplification of the behaviorists' point of view:

The behavior of living organisms is highly complex and its attribution to a single cause can only be the product of naive reductionism. Accordingly, the common accusation that behaviorists explain all behavior in terms of learning history is inaccurate. Behaviorists recognize as well the impact of physiology and contemporary events. The relative contribution of each influence will vary as a function of the character of the organism, the nature of the response under study, and the conditions under which the study is being conducted.

Physiology influences both the selection of environmental events that function as stimuli for the organism and the nature of its response to these stimuli. While the change

The reward of food is the positive reinforcement used in the Skinner box. For example, the pigeon must peck at the light disk ten times in a row to be rewarded with the food.

of a traffic light from green to red is an environmental event, it will have radically different stimulus value for the blind as contrasted to the sighted person. But physiology alone does not determine a response. Certain events that do have stimulus value may be interpreted differently by people who have had different learning histories. For example, research on the behavior of persons in the paths of tornados has shown that some failed to respond to the auditory cues available (a tornado is said to sound like an onrushing train). Most of these individuals were neither deaf nor suicidal; they simply had not been trained to attend to the relevant cues with self-protective activity. When learning history is de-emphasized, one may erroneously attribute to physiology the failure of a response to occur. For example, it has been demonstrated that even vegetative idiots, who were presumed to be incapable of emitting social responses, can do so following careful shaping procedures.* (p. 44)

We see from these remarks that the behaviorists are cognizant of the myriad of factors which contribute to our highly complex behavior, and they are sensitive to the possibilities of various interpretations of behavioral phenomena. This recognition helps us better understand the behavioral theory of personality, which is in fact an amalgam of different causative postulates. The main theme of the behavioral theory of personality is that hypothetical concepts such as ego or self are eventually undefinable and unverifiable and therefore impractical for empirical research. The behaviorist looks at these concepts as myths which are perpetuated out of ignorance of causes, not out of understanding.

Skinner (1953), for example, says, "The self is most commonly used as a hypothetical cause of action. So long as external variables go unnoticed or ignored, their function is assigned to an originating agent within the organism...." He objected to this, arguing in its place that all behavior is a direct consequence of conditioned responses. Criticizing the introspective schools of psychology, he goes on to say, "If we cannot show what is responsible for a man's behavior, we say that he himself is responsible for it. The precursors of physical science once followed the same practice, but the wind is no longer blown by Aeolus, nor is the rain cast down by Jupiter Pluvius" (p. 283).

Like the existentialists, the behaviorists also devote much attention to the role of anxiety in neurotic disorders. But where the existentialist believes that anxiety is an inevitable condition of the human predicament, the behaviorist believes that anxiety is a disruptive and unnatural force which can be eliminated through appropriate conditioning and retraining.

THE ROLE OF THE CLIENT

The primary task of the client in behavioral counseling is to learn new responses to old situations. Wherever he has been responding neurotically with too great a degree of anxiety and stress that interferes with his functioning, he must develop new patterns which will enable more successful interaction with

*From "Behavior Modification Theory and Practice: A Reply" by R. D. Carter and R. B. Stuart, *Social Work*, 1970, *15*: 37–50. Reprinted by permission.

others and with his environment. In addition, he is expected to learn how to elicit positive responses from others with whom he is involved and from his environment. This is the key to successful living.

The client must provide the counselor with an enumeration of the stimulus situations that provoke the greatest anxiety. He does this verbally, discussing with the counselor all of the situations that have recently caused him to feel anxiety and finding, if possible, the common denominator among these situations. Of particular concern will be those situations in which anxiety arose as a result of an interpersonal relationship, since his functioning with others is of prime importance.

In behavioral counseling, the client is an active participant in the learning situation. In order to be conditioned to respond in a healthy and appropriate manner to disruptive stimuli, it may at times be necessary for the client to expose himself directly to those stimuli, no matter how painful the exposure (and particularly the anticipation of exposure) may be. A client who has difficulty asserting himself, for example, has to be taught to do so in the counseling setting and then rewarded for his successful attempts (positive reinforcement). While he may protest to the counselor at first that he is not capable of doing so, the counselor must insist that he try so as to facilitate the conditioning process.

THE ROLE OF THE COUNSELOR

The role of the behavioral counselor is limited primarily to dealing with the client's observable behavior. Unlike the other counselors we have discussed, the behavioral counselor makes no attempt to probe and explore the inner reaches of the psyche. On the contrary, he avoids such excursions because he considers them irrelevant to the task at hand. Michael and Meyerson (1962) emphasize this point:

The behavior system...has the clear implication that observable behavior is the only variable of importance in the counseling and guidance process, and it is the only criterion against which the outcome of the process can be evaluated. Conceptual formulations such as ego-strength, inferiority feelings, or self-concept are not behavior but simply ways of organizing and interpreting observable behavior by referring it to an inner determiner. Such formulations may be incorrect, insufficient, or merely superfluous. They may be harmful or impeding when applied in the sense that they direct attention and effort to irrelevant variables, or they may be unessential "decorations" which do no harm but do not contribute to the counselor's efforts or the learner's behavior. (p. 395)

Although the behavioral counselor is limited to dealing with observable behavior, it is agreed that much of this observable behavior will touch upon the realm of feelings. But his manner of approaching feelings, and changing them, requires intervention in the behavior itself.

John D. Krumbholtz, a leading proponent of the behavioral counseling approach, makes two important points regarding the role of the behavioral counselor. First, he suggests that it is the counselor's job to work on any problem for which the client has come for help. "The central purpose of counseling," he argues (Krumbholtz, 1965), "is to help each client resolve those problems for which he requests help." Second, he suggests that the success of counseling be measured by how well the counselor has been able to meet the client's request. "When a professional man does accept a client...he is implicitly agreeing to exert whatever efforts he can to accomplish what his client requests. The use of clients' requests as a basis for generating the criteria of success is as appropriate for counselors as it is for lawyers and physicians."

Christoplos and Valletutti (1969) cite three tasks of the behavioral counselor:

1 Identifying and measuring the frequency of the behavior to be acquired, reinforced, or eliminated.
2 Identifying the conditions which lead to the development and maintenance of the behavior; and
3 Delineating the behaviors the client will exhibit in order to establish the conditions for change. (p. 30)

While many of these procedures may seem somewhat mechanical, it must be pointed out that within the total role of the counselor lies the primary responsibility for correcting neurotic behavior. In this respect, one of the main tasks of the behavioral counselor is "to find an acceptable response pattern which is antagonistic to the neurotic activity of the patient and to substitute this adaptive behavior for the non-adaptive neurotic behavior" (Rachman, 1967a). He does this by exploring with the patient the constellation of situations which provoke the anxiety. The behavioral counselor, while he does give credence to the client's perceptions and insights into what causes anxiety, relies most heavily on his own observations of the client in his relationship with the counselor. Considering the emphasis on observable behavior, this priority seems perfectly logical.

The behavioral counselor, additionally, is the dispenser of reinforcement. When operant conditioning is in use, his ability to time the reinforcements maximally can be the critical variable between success and failure. Krumbholtz (1966b) has discussed this important principle:

The timing of reinforcement can be useful in producing the kind of behavior desired by the client...human beings are affected by reinforcers...and we learn to do those things which produce certain kinds of desirable conditions. For example, we engage in certain kinds of activity because we receive money as well as other benefits for so doing. Money is reinforced...(in school) A grades are another kind of reinforcer...the attention and approval of our friends, neighbors and associates have reinforcing consequences.... The attention and approval of a counselor might have reinforcing effects for a client, especially if the client feels that the counselor understands his problem and can do something to help. (Introduction)

Counselor reinforcement, according to Durbak (1974), can take a variety of forms, including verbal responses, token payment, and so on. "The kind of response made by the counselor," she points out, "will determine to some extent the direction that the client will take in the future...."

Counselors reinforce by their attention, interest, and approval certain kinds of client responses. By their inattention, lack of interest and failure to respond, they extinguish or diminish the tendency of the client to talk about certain things.... The counselor is reinforcing some kind of response or failing to reinforce some other kind of response whether he knows it or not.

From these remarks, we see that one of the main jobs of the behavioral counselor is to act as the therapeutic agent of reinforcement.

The counselor's humaneness is generally de-emphasized in the behavioral approach. His function is to appropriate reward and punishment in an objective and scientific manner, not to become an emotionally significant figure to the patient, not to become a source of dependency, and not to cause the patient to reexperience earlier life trauma. "All in all," says Skinner (1953),

the original power of the therapist is not very great. Since the effect which he is to achieve requires time, his first task is to make sure that the time will be available. The therapist uses whatever limited power he originally possesses to make sure that the patient will remain in contact with him—that the patient will return for further treatment. As treatment progresses, however, his power increases. As an organized social system develops, the therapist becomes an important source of reinforcement. If he is successful in providing relief, the behavior of the patient in turning to him for help is reinforced.... He may suggest modes of action which are likely to be positively reinforced. (p. 369)

He is, therefore, a directive, goal-oriented therapist, who scientifically tries to improve the patient's circumstances by reshaping his behavior.

TECHNIQUES AND GOALS

Behavioral counseling is clearly the most technique-oriented of all the schools of counseling we have looked at. Because the quality of the counseling relationship is de-emphasized, and because the main priority is on the resolution of the client's symptoms, the behavioral counselor relies heavily on a repertoire of techniques to deal with each specific problem. It should also be mentioned that although in other systems the counselor's technique may be considered a part of his personality trait or of his emotional disposition (see chapter 3 for a full discussion of theory and technique), in behavioral counseling the employment of technique is wholly independent of the counselor's feelings, beliefs, and personality. These techniques are mechanical, operational procedures designed to achieve certain specific ends.

The behavioral techniques are all derived from learning theory. Each technique is based on a principle of learning. "Behavior therapy," Grossberg (1964) points out, "is derived from the rejection of traditional psychodynamic personality theories, and *consists of the application of the principles of modern learning theory to the treatment of behavior disorders*" (italics added). As we examine each of these techniques, therefore, we will note that there is at work a learning principle applied to a psychological-behavioral problem.

Systematic desensitization

Systematic desensitization is a technique of respondent conditioning in which anxiety-provoking situations are paired with inhibitory responses. Wolpe (1961) describes the process like this:

The desensitization method consists of presenting to the imagination of the deeply relaxed patient the feeblest item in a list of anxiety-evoking stimuli—repeatedly, until no more anxiety is evoked. The next item of the list is presented, and so on, until eventually, even the strongest of the anxiety-evoking stimuli fails to evoke any stir of anxiety in the patient. (p. 191)

The technique of systematic desensitization is based upon the learning principle of *reciprocal inhibition,* which was developed by Wolpe (1958). Reciprocal inhibition means that if a relaxing response is paired with an anxiety-producing stimulus, a new bond develops between the two so that the anxiety-provoking stimulus no longer provokes anxiety. Bugg (1972) explains the theory this way:

The essential principle of reciprocal inhibition is that an organism cannot make two contradictory responses at the same time. Behavior therapy assumes that anxiety responses are learned (conditioned) behaviors and may be extinguished by reconditioning. If the response that is contradictory to anxiety results in a more pleasant state or more productive behavior for the subject, the new response to the anxiety-evoking stimuli will gradually replace the anxiety response. (p. 823)

For example, let us say that a patient has a fear of flying on a plane. If every time the patient thinks of flying on a plane, he is relaxed and made to feel comfortable by the therapist, ultimately the stimulus (of flying on a plane) will fail to elicit the anxiety it once did.

The systematic desensitization approach requires the patient to produce a list of such anxiety-producing stimuli in order of intensity (e.g., driving to the airport, waiting in the lounge, boarding the plane, taking off, being in the air, etc.). The stimuli are dealt with, one at a time, until the most anxiety-provoking is no longer capable of generating anxiety. This approach comprises, in other words, cumulative, sequential processes of desensitization. Rachman (1967b) aptly describes the technique of desensitization:

The patient is relaxed and then requested to imagine the anxiety-producing stimuli in a very mild and attenuated form. When the image is obtained vividly, a small amount of anxiety is usually elicited. The therapist then relaxes the patient again and instructs him to stop imagining the scene and to continue relaxing. The full sequence is: *relax, imagine, relax, stop imagining, relax* (italics added).... This process is then repeated with the same stimulus or with a stimulus which is slightly more disturbing. The patient is again relaxed and the next stimulus is then presented and dissipated. With each evocation and subsequent dampening of the anxiety response, conditioned inhibition is built up.... Eventually the patient is able to imagine even the previously most anxiety-provoking stimulus with tranquility, and this tranquility generalizes to the real-life situation. (p. 94)

Garvey and Hegrenes (1966) offer an example of how systematic desensitization was used to treat a child suffering from school phobia, a disorder which responds especially well to this technique. The patient, a ten-year-old boy, was unable to get into the car that was to take him to school in the morning. The desensitization consisted to twelve stages. One, the therapist sat with the boy in the car that was parked in front of the school. When the boy finally felt comfortable in this situation, the next step was applied, and so on until the final step was taken. The steps were:

2 Getting out of the car and approaching the curb.
3 Going to the sidewalk.
4 Going to the bottom of the school steps.
5 Going to the top of the steps.
6 Going to the door.
7 Entering the school.
8 Approaching the classroom a certain distance each day down the hall.
9 Entering the classroom.
10 Being present in the classroom with the teacher.
11 Being present in the classroom with the teacher and one or two classmates.
12 Being present in the classroom with a full class.

We note in this example how systematic desensitization slowly builds up, step by step, to the highest anxiety-producing situation. This required, according to the authors, twenty treatments, involving a total of ten to twelve hours of the therapist's time. Systematic desensitization is an economical, relevant method for the school counselor.

Extinction

"When a learned response is repeated without reinforcement the strength of the tendency to perform that response undergoes a progressive decrease" (Dollard and Miller, 1950). This is the simplest definition of extinction. Let us say that a teacher has been giving a star to each student who hands in a neat homework assignment. When her supply of stars runs out, she forgets to buy a new box. After a period of time, according to the theory of extinction, the students will be less likely to hand in neat assignments because the reinforcement they had been receiving for doing so is no longer there. "The rate of exinction," Bandura (1969) points out,

is governed by a number of factors, among them the irregularity with which the behavior was reinforced in the past, the amount of effort required to perform it, the level of deprivation present during extinction, the ease with which changes in conditions of reinforcement can be discerned, and the availability of alternative modes of response. Because of the diversity of the controlling variables, a number of different theoretical conceptualizations of extinction have been proposed. (p. 355)

The theory of extinction becomes much more complicated than the simple definition listed above. Calvin et al. (1956) have shown, for example, that the time interval between extinction trials influences the rate of extinction. Bandura (1969, pp. 356–423) cites over a hundred studies of different factors which influence the rate of extinction.

Benoit and Mayer (1974) have discussed the uses of extinction as a classroom behavior modification technique. They provide a flow chart (see Display 13.1) to help the teacher or counselor decide whether extinction is the appropriate technique. The practitioner answers the questions encircled in the flow chart and determines whether he will be able to use this technique or whether it will be necessary to find an alternative technique such as desensitization or operant conditioning. As we see from this chart, to use the method of extinction, it is

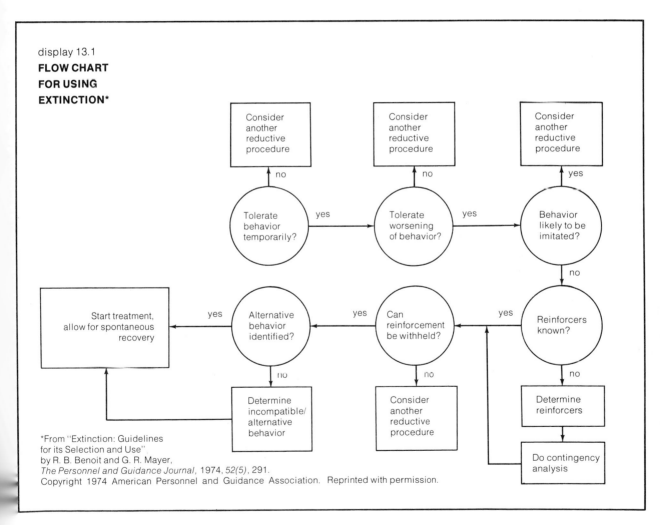

display 13.1
**FLOW CHART
FOR USING
EXTINCTION***

*From "Extinction: Guidelines
for its Selection and Use"
by R. B. Benoit and G. R. Mayer,
The Personnel and Guidance Journal, 1974, *52(5)*, 291.
Copyright 1974 American Personnel and Guidance Association. Reprinted with permission.

necessary for the practitioner to tolerate a temporary worsening of the behavior, and this may not always be possible. For example, one use of extinction would consist of ignoring the outbursts of a student who acts unruly to get attention. By ignoring him when he misbehaves, the reward for misbehaving is slowly withheld.

Other behavioral counseling techniques

Shaping is a technique often used by behavioral counselors. "In shaping," Patterson (1973) points out, "the experimenter at first reinforces behavior that is only similar to the behavior that is ultimately desired but does not exist at present." Through gradual changes in the pattern of reinforcement, the desired behavior is finally reached. Michael and Meyerson (1962) offer an example of shaping:

In teaching a child to talk, his efforts to pronounce a particular word will at first be reinforced rather uncritically. Eventually, some of the variations are allowed to extinguish.... This procedure for producing new behavior is called *shaping*. It is essentially the differential reinforcement of successive approximations to some complex form of behavior. It is the technique which animal trainers use to produce unusual and entertaining behaviors in their subjects, and it is the technique whereby humans acquire the complex response topographies of speech, athletic abilities and other motor skills. (p. 387)

Modeling is another important technique used by behavioral counselors. With this technique, the subject models himself after another's behavior or actions. It may not be necessary for the client to perform in any particular way in order to learn from modeling; merely observing the model's behavior is often sufficient. "When a person observes a model's behavior," Bandura (1969) suggests, "but otherwise performs no overt responses, he can acquire the modeled responses while they are occurring only in cognitive, representational forms." This constitutes a form of sensory conditioning. Nye (1973) has discussed a variety of uses for the modeling technique in counseling, and Bandura (1961) has discussed the general topic of "social imitation," which includes modeling as an important factor in children's learning.

Systematic applications of respondent conditioning constitute an important corpus of behavioral techniques. Ullmann and Krasner (1965) have presented a comprehensive explication of the role these techniques play in psychopathology, and Krumbholtz and Thoresen (1969) have collected a variety of papers presenting applications of these forms of conditioning to the school counseling situation. Rachman (1967a) offers a list of some learning techniques used by behavioral counselors, along with studies which the practicing counselor might wish to consult.

While most of the therapies we have discussed have a single specifiable goal (integration in psychoanalysis; self-actualization in client-centered; authenticity in existentialism), the goal of behavioral counseling depends entirely on the type of problem for which the client has sought treatment. Krumbholtz

(1966a) argues that "it is the counselor's job to help the client translate his problem into a behavioral goal that the client wants to attain and that the counselor believes will contribute to the welfare of his client." These problems fall into a number of categories. Display 13.2 illustrates some of the categories and the variety of behavioral goals associated with each category. We see that in behavioral counseling the aim of the treatment is directed always to the presenting problem, and the removal of that problem is the goal of the treatment.

---

display 13.2

BEHAVIORAL GOALS FOR COUNSELING*

1–Altering maladaptive behavior

—Increasing socially assertive responses
—Decreasing socially assertive responses
—Increasing social skills necessary in meeting new people
—Decreasing fear responses to examinations
—Increasing ability to concentrate for longer periods of time on school work
—Decreasing the frequency of stealing
—Increasing participation in school activities
—Learning to assume responsibility for a task and carry it through to completion
—Decreasing aggressive responses to smaller children
—Increasing aggressive responses to abusive peers
—Learning to respond calmly to hostile remarks
—Decreasing quarreling behavior with other members of the family
—Increasing ability to complete work on time
—Decreasing the frequency of reckless and fast driving
—Increasing the sharing of possessions with friends
—Decreasing excessive sharing with friends and acquaintances
—Increasing ability to say "no" to salesmen
—Increasing ability to return unsatisfactory articles to stores
—Decreasing threatening or violent behavior
—Learning to discriminate between insults and friendly teasing
—Decreasing weeping behavior in social situations
—Increasing ability to communicate with friends and acquaintances

2–Learning the decision making process

—Generating a list of all possible courses of action
—Gathering relevant information about each feasible alternative course of action
—Estimating the probability of success in each alternative on the basis of the experience of others and projections of current trends
—Considering the personal values which may be enhanced or diminished under each course of action
—Deliberating and weighing the facts, probable outcomes and values for each alternative
—Eliminating from consideration the least favorable courses of action
—Formulating a tentative plan of action subject to new developments and opportunities
—Generalizing the decision making process to future problems

3–Preventing problems

—Developing a school marking system so that even the poorest student in each class can be encouraged by seeing the extent of his own progress
—Implementing a system of helping young men and women select compatible marriage partners
—Planning an educational program in child rearing techniques for parents
—Helping to construct a curriculum more useful and effective for the students in it
—Evaluating the effectiveness of preventive and remedial programs

*From "Behavioral Goals for Counseling" by John D. Krumboltz, *Journal of Counseling Psychology*, 1966, *13*, 153–159. Reprinted by permission.

In general, the goal of much behavioral counseling—particularly with the method of desensitization—is the elimination of neurotic anxiety. The behaviorists believe that this anxiety acts as an inhibiting factor against healthy, adaptive behavior.

Bandura (1969) has stated this goal of behavioral counseling quite succinctly: "The patient has a repertoire of previously learned positive habits available to him, but these adaptive patterns are inhibited or blocked by competing responses motivated by anxiety or guilt. *The goal of the therapy, then, is to reduce the severity of the internal inhibitory controls, thus allowing the healthy patterns of behavior to emerge*" (italics added).

EVALUATION

Ironically, what has been generally cited as the greatest fault of behavioral counseling proves to be its greatest advantage in the school counseling situation, namely, that it deals directly with the symptom. Most of the difficulties that the school counselor is confronted with take the form of behavioral problems. Students are typically referred to the counseling service because they have exhibited manifest signs of emotional problems that are interfering with their education. The critical shortage of time and personnel requires that the school counselor use the most expedient methods in dealing with the problem at hand. In this respect, behavioral counseling, with its emphasis on the symptom itself, does offer a practical bonus to the counselor.

Vance (1969) has discussed the use of reinforcement techniques in modifying hyperactive and aggressive behavior. Hoopes (1969) has shown how behavioral techniques may be used in helping a college student overcome procrastination, and Beach (1969) has shown how an underachieving student may be dealt with behaviorally. Krumbholtz and Thoresen (1969) have collected these and other applications of behavioral counseling in a book which is rich in insights and examples.

Behavioral counseling has been widely criticized for its lack of emphasis on the human qualities of the client and the counselor. It reduces the complexities of human interactions to simple equations that, although they may adequately explain the individual's ostensible behavior, do not take into account the motive behind it, the feelings accompanying it, and other crucial factors. Sprinthall (1971) has argued that "it virtually ignores developmental stages: stages of moral development, personal development, epistemological development—so much so that we may have inadvertently left the human being out of the process" (p. 66).

One can see, however, how some behavioral concepts—such as desensitization, extinction, reinforcement, and shaping—in conjunction with the warmth and acceptance of the Rogerian, the probing of the psychoanalyst, and the exploration for meanings of the existentialist, can add to the full dimension of counseling and to the counselor's understanding of the client.

References

Bandura, A. Psychotherapy as a learning process. *Psychological Bulletin*, 1961, *58*, 143–159.

Bandura, A. *Principles of behavior modification.* New York: Holt, Rinehart & Winston, 1969.

Beach, A. Overcoming underachievement. In J. D. Krumbholtz & C. E. Thoresen (Eds.), *Behavioral counseling: Cases and techniques.* New York: Holt, Rinehart, & Winston, 1969.

Benoit, R. B., & Mayer, G. R. Extinction: Guidelines for its selection and use. *Personnel and Guidance Journal*, 1974, *52*, 290–295.

Borger, R., & Seaborne, A. E. M. *The psychology of learning.* Baltimore: Penguin, 1966.

Bugg, C. A. Systematic desensitization: A technique worth trying. *Personnel and Guidance Journal*, 1972, *50*, 823–828.

Calvin, A. D., Clifford, L. T., Clifford, B., Bolden, L., & Harvey, J. Experimental validation of conditioned inhibition. *Psychological Reports*, 1956, *2*, 21–56.

Carter, R. D., & Stuart, R. B. Behavior modification theory and practice: A reply. *Social Work*, 1970, *15*, 37–50.

Christoplos, F., & Valletutti, P. Defining behavior modification. *Educational Technology*, 1969, *9*, 28–30.

Dimick, K. M., & Huff, V. E. *Child counseling.* Dubuque, Iowa: Wm. C. Brown, 1970.

Dollard, J., & Miller, N. E. *Personality and psychotherapy.* New York: McGraw-Hill, 1950.

Durbak, C. Methods of behavioral counseling. Unpublished paper, 1974.

Eysenck, H. J., & Rachman, S. *The causes and cures of neurosis.* London: Routledge & Kegan Paul, 1965.

Garvey, W. P., & Hegrenes, J. R. Desensitization techniques in the treatment of school phobia. *American Journal of Orthopsychiatry*, 1966, *36*, 147–152.

Grossberg, J. M. Behavior therapy: A review. *Psychological Bulletin*, 1964, *62*, 73–88.

Hoopes, M. H. Overcoming procrastination. In J. D. Krumbholtz (Ed.), *Behavioral counseling: Cases and techniques.* New York: Holt, Rinehart, & Winston, 1969.

Hull, C. L. *Principles of behavior.* New York: Appleton-Century-Crofts, 1943.

Jones, M. C. The elimination of children's fears. *Journal of Experimental Psychology*, 1924, *7*, 383–390.

Krumbholtz, J. D. Behavioral counseling: Rationale and research. *Personnel and Guidance Journal*, 1965, *44*, 383–387.

Krumbholtz, J. D. Behavioral goals for counseling. *Journal of Counseling Psychology*, 1966, *13*, 153–159. (a)

Krumbholtz, J. D. (Ed.). *Revolution in counseling: Implications of behavioral science.* Boston: Houghton Mifflin, 1966. (b)

Krumbholtz, J. D., & Thoresen, C. E. (Eds.). *Behavioral counseling: Cases and techniques.* New York: Holt, Rinehart, & Winston, 1969.

Macmillan, D. L., & Forness, S. R. Behavior modification limitations and liabilities. *Exceptional Children*, 1970, *37*, 291–297.

Mayer, R. G., Rohen, T. M., & Whitely, A. D. Group counseling with children: A cognitive-behavioral approach. *Journal of Counseling Psychology*, 1969, *16*, 142–149.

Michael, J., & Meyerson, L. A behavioral approach to guidance and counseling. *Harvard Educational Review*, 1962, *32*, 382–401.

Nye, S. L. Obtaining results through modeling. *Personnel and Guidance Journal*, 1973, *51*, 380–384.

Patterson, C. H. *Theories of counseling and psychotherapy* (2nd ed.). New York: Harper & Row, 1973.

Price, R. H. *Abnormal behavior: Perspectives in conflict.* New York: Holt, Rinehart, & Winston, 1972.

Rachman, S. Treatment of anxiety and phobic reactions by desensitization. *Journal of Abnormal and Social Psychology*, 1959, *102*, 421–427.

Rachman, S. Behavior therapy. In B. Berenson & R. Carkhuff (Eds.), *Sources of gain in counseling and psychotherapy.* New York: Holt, Rinehart, & Winston, 1967. (a)

Rachman, S. Systematic desensitization. *Psychological Bulletin*, 1967, *67*, 93–103. (b)

Skinner, B. F. *Science and human behavior.* New York: Macmillan, 1953.

Skinner, B. F. *Walden two.* New York: Vintage, 1966.

Sprinthall, N. *Guidance for human growth.* New York: Van Nostrand Reinhold, 1971.

Thorndike, E. L. *From a connectionist's psychology.* New York: Appleton-Century-Crofts, 1949.

Ullmann, L. P., & Krasner, L. *Research in behavior modification.* New York: Holt, Rinehart, & Winston, 1965.

Vance, B. J. Modifying hyperactive and aggressive behavior. In J. D. Krumbholtz and C. E. Thoresen (Eds.), *Behavioral counseling: Cases and techniques.* New York: Holt, Rinehart, & Winston, 1969.

Watson, J. B. Psychology as the behaviorist views it. *Psychological Review*, 1913, *20*, 159–170.

Watson, J. B. *Behavior: An introduction to comparative psychology.* New York: Henry Holt, 1914.

Watson, J. B. *Psychology from the standpoint of a behaviorist* (2nd ed.). Philadelphia: J. B. Lippincott, 1924.

Wolpe, J. *Psychotherapy by reciprocal inhibition.* Stanford, Calif.: Stanford University Press, 1958.

Wolpe, J. The systematic desensitization treatment of neuroses. *Journal of Nervous and Mental Diseases*, 1961, *132*, 189–203.

PART FOUR

Peter Schwarzburg

The counseling experience

In this part of the book, we will look at some specific instances of the counseling experience. First we will explore the dynamic processes of the counseling interview. How does the counselor select the techniques he will use? How does he go about implementing these techniques and objectively evaluating their results? What practical strategies might the counselor employ during the initial interview to assure a more favorable treatment prognosis? What guidelines can he use in responding to clients' questions?

Next we will look at the counseling process in terms of the structure and content of the transaction. If counseling is truly a helping relationship, what efforts of the counselor's and the client's can work productively toward facilitating that relationship? Additional counseling techniques will be presented in this chapter, with special emphasis on ways in which the counselor selectively uses techniques to the client's advantage. What are the expectations and goals of counseling and how do these influence counseling outcomes? What are the values of the group counseling approach, and what are some of its uses and applications?

How is the effectiveness or ineffectiveness of counseling manifest in changes in client behavior? These and other allied questions will be dealt with in chapter 15, "The Counseling Process."

The concluding chapter in this section will explore a very special form of the counseling experience: crisis intervention counseling. This is a limited but important type of counseling that has enjoyed a wide interest in recent years. Many of the counseling experiences we are likely to have during our professional lives are crisis counseling experiences, and it is only during the past decade that school counselors have directly confronted this difficult and emotionally exhausting subject.

One of the points I hope to bring out in this part of the book is that *counseling works*. Practical counseling, the inclusive experience that synthesizes all of the counselor's activities, is a far more effective method of treatment than is psychotherapy, which usually enjoys a more professional prestige. A number of studies have been conducted to determine the efficacy of psychotherapy, and while the evidence at this time is far from conclusive, the results of the bulk of these studies are not encouragingly in support of psychotherapeutic efficacy. A brief review of some of the evidence should convince even the most stalwart advocate of psychotherapy that something is wrong somewhere.

The granddaddy of all the efficacy studies was the Eysenck study of 1952. Hans Eysenck compared patients treated by psychoanalytic psychotherapy with those treated by eclectic methods and compared both to an untreated control group. Analyzing the results of his investigation, he found an improvement rate of 44% for those patients treated by psychoanalysis; an improvement rate of 64% for those patients treated eclectically; and an improvement rate of 72% for those neurotics treated without benefit of psychotherapy (either by general practitioners or by custodial care). The implications of this research were not encouraging for advocates and practitioners of formal psychotherapy. Strupp (1971) provides a detailed evaluation of Eysenck's research methods along with some germane comments by his critics.

Stuart (1970) has reviewed twenty-one studies of the efficacy of psychotherapy, of which only two demonstrated positive results. In weighing the importance of these studies, one must be cautious about the methods used, the statistical integrity of the study, and the validity of the conclusions. Maher (1970) has provided an excellent evaluation of the methods and difficulties of research in psychopathology, and his comments would have to be carefully considered before evaluating any single study. Nevertheless, study after study does seem to indicate a fundamental weakness in the psychotherapeutic approach.

Consider, for example, a study by Barron and Leary (1955) in which they attempted to measure changes in psychoneurotic patients, some of whom were exposed to psychotherapy and some of whom were not. One hundred fifty patients were tested with the Minnesota Multiphasic Personality Inventory before and after an interval of time during which some of them received psychotherapy and some of them did not. The aim of the study was to compare the degree of change, using the MMPI scores, between the two groups. An analysis of the data revealed the following conclusions:

1 The mean pre- and post-MMPI scores of patients undergoing individual therapy showed significant improvement on symptom scales.
2 Patients who decided to enter therapy but who were required to wait for treatment showed some MMPI improvement during the waiting period, primarily in prognosis.
3 The therapy patients did not improve significantly more than did the waiting-list controls.

We see from these results that there is no clear indication that psychotherapy improved the situation of the patients exposed to it.

Other studies, of course, have had more positive results. Rogers and Dymond (1954), in a famous study, found positive results after exposure to the client-centered approach. A number of behavioral studies have shown positive results for that approach (Paul, 1966). But on the whole, there is no evidence at the present time to confirm the global claims made in favor of psychotherapy.

As we look at the counseling experience, then, let us keep in mind that we are searching for a treatment method that, although modest in aims and limited in scope, will outperform its more inflated, less productive counterpart in the mental health profession. Let us with humility and caution examine the moments of the counseling experience.

References

Barron, F., & Leary, T. Changes in psychoneurotic patients with and without psychotherapy. *Journal of Consulting Psychology*, 1955, *19*, 239–245.

Eysenck, H. J. The effects of psychotherapy: An evaluation. *Journal of Consulting Psychology*, 1952, *16*, 319–324.

Maher, B. *Introduction to research in psychopathology.* New York: McGraw-Hill, 1970.

Paul, G. *Insight vs. desensitization in psychotherapy.* Stanford: Stanford University Press, 1966.

Rogers, C. R., & Dymond, R. F. *Psychotherapy and personality change.* Chicago: University of Chicago Press, 1954.

Strupp, H. H. *Psychotherapy and the modification of abnormal behavior.* New York: McGraw-Hill, 1971.

Stuart, R. B. *Trick or treatment.* Champaign, Ill.: Research Press, 1970.

chapter fourteen

The counseling interview

In this chapter we shall focus in on the face-to-face interaction between the counselor and client engaged in individual counseling. Our discussion in chapter 3 concerning the relationship between counseling theory and counseling practice revealed that much of what the counselor actually does in the intimacy of his office is more a result of his personality and underlying philosophy than a result of the dictates of the theory to which he subscribes. In Part Three we looked at some of these theories in detail and found a variety of different recommended techniques from which the counselor can draw. Now we shall explore the group of techniques he uses, to see how these are evolved, how they are implemented, and what results they produce. First we should consider what we mean by a *counseling technique*.

The question we must first answer is: Is a technique an explanation of what the counselor is doing, or is it, as has often been suggested, designed to assist the counselor prior to action? Techniques should serve as guidelines, tentative parameters of approach, in helping the counselor maintain the delicate therapeutic balance of the counselor-client relationship. They should advise the counselor when he should offer a communication to the client, what he should say, and how he should say it.

A technique may or may not originate from a specific theory of counseling. To be sure, each theory has its own repertoire of techniques, integrated into the total theoretical approach, and its own blacklist of implicitly verboten techniques. Yet most of the techniques practiced by counselors neither meet the explicit requirements of the theoretical technique, nor are common to merely one particular counseling orientation. On the contrary, most counseling interactions are universal, regardless of theoretical considerations. Let us, therefore, consider the technique in practice, rather than in theory, to arrive at the criteria for a successful counseling technique.

To be effective, a counseling technique must be flexible, organized, goal-directed, and practical. Flexibility is necessary because of the far-ranging possibilities of client problems, client expectations, and client needs with which the counselor will be confronted. A technique which is too prescriptive and dogmatic will severely limit the counselor in his interaction with the client and restrict the possibilities of growth within the counseling situation.

In addition, a technique must be organized around a fundamental principle of the treatment and directed toward the ultimate goal of the treatment. By organized, I mean specifically that the technique is addressed to that facet of the client which is prominent in the treatment milieu. If a client-centered attitude is dominant on the part of the counselor, he should then use techniques that will meet the conditioned expectations of the client who has now been exposed to this attitude and approach. If a psychoanalytic approach is dominant, the counselor should then use techniques which are compatible with the client's interpretive and probing expectations. This assures that the technique itself will contribute to the total treatment, becoming an integral part of the goal by becoming an assimilated force in the counseling relationship.

The technique must also be practical. I use this word in its dual sense of realistic and pragmatic to convey the dual responsibility of an effective counseling technique. On the one hand, the technique must not call on the counselor to offer more than he is capable of offering, to say or do what he does not truly believe. On the other hand, the technique must work, must achieve a specific end, must effect a therapeutic change in the client.

Unlike a theory, which is general, a technique maintains moment-to-moment contact with the here and now of the counseling situation. Whereas the primary characteristic of a counseling theory is its discursiveness, the prominent trait of a counseling technique is its responsiveness. If we look at the counseling technique as a unique medium of communication, we can readily see that it is truly the case in counseling that "the medium is the message." For this reason, an intimacy exists between the counselor and his technique that might well be compared to the intimacy that exists between the singer and his song. With this in mind, we will now explore the dynamics of the relationship between the counselor and his techniques.

THE COUNSELOR AND HIS TECHNIQUES

The relationship between the counselor and his techniques changes as the counselor becomes more experienced, more confident in his abilities, more comfortable in the counseling situation, and more aware of his client as a person. At first the counselor is likely to hold onto the techniques as a man who cannot swim would hold on to a life preserver: They not only give him the ability to stay afloat, but they continually support him and conserve his efforts. The techniques tell him what to do, how to behave with the client and how to respond to the client's communications, what is appropriate or inappropriate for him to say. The techniques spare him the burden of dealing with the client blindly, meeting him head on, confronting him without knowledge of how the confrontation will conclude. In short, the techniques enable the inexperienced counselor to function adequately without having to make any major decisions.

As the counselor gains experience and confidence, he gradually becomes less dependent upon techniques and more reliant upon his own counseling sense and intuition. He may continue to use the same techniques with the same frequency as he did before, but the techniques are now at his service instead of his being at the service of the techniques. Soon the counselor begins to modify techniques to suit his own idiosyncratic nature; he gives the bland, objective, impersonal techniques his own personal touch.

It is at this point that counselors often become troubled by conflicts that arise between their theoretical orientation (and the techniques dictated by that theory) and the feelings they are experiencing in the here and now of the counseling setting. A client-centered counselor, for example, may be unable to feel much positive regard for a certain patient. In spite of what he believes he should be doing in a specific situation, the feelings he is experiencing are communicated to the client above and beyond the application of the technique being employed. Menninger (1958) has pointed out that the counselor's life style carries much influence with the patient, and Berdie (1951) has discussed the crucial interdependency between the counselor's attitudes and his techniques. Shentoub (1955), in discussing the psychoanalytic approach, shows that what the counselor *is* has a far greater influence upon the client than what the counselor *does*. It is clear, therefore, that the counselor and his technique must at some given point, out of necessity, become compatible with each other.

This compatibility evolves slowly and requires flexibility and openness on the part of the counselor. The counselor must be willing to study himself in the counseling situation to learn where his capabilities and weaknesses lie, where he has much to offer the client and where he has little to offer, where his needs might conflict with the client's needs, and where his personality might inadvertently distort his perceptions of the client. Hiltner (1950) has discussed the importance of the counselor's self-awareness in dealing with the client, and a demonstration of this axiomatic principle is found in Lambin's dissertation (1959) where he shows the relationship between the perception of self and the evaluation of another. While the evidence does not indicate either that feelings have priority over techniques, or that techniques are more important than the counselor's feelings, it is clear from the research that techniques and feelings are interrelated and that each is to some extent functionally dependent upon the other.

With this in mind, let us examine some of the elementary counseling applications and techniques that are used most advantageously by the beginning counselor. We shall begin by examining the initial counseling interview.

THE INITIAL INTERVIEW

Beginning the counseling process is critical to the ultimate success or failure of the entire course of the treatment. The very continuity and integrity of the counseling experience attest to the importance of the beginning phase. When we look at the initial interview, therefore, we should keep in mind that our discussion transcends the narrow temporal limitations of this single session and extends throughout the course of the counseling experience.

The moment the client enters the counselor's office for the first time, a number of things should be going through the counselor's mind. Under what circumstances was this appointment arranged? Was it a voluntary appointment or one required by a teacher, the court, the parents of the client, etc? How does this client appear as he walks in the door? What does his body language tell the counselor? Does his face reveal any particular indications of attitude? What might be his expectations at this moment? The counselor recognizes that because this is the client's first appointment he is most likely nervous, unsure of what to expect, and probably in the throes of some type of conflict. "The beginning interview," Porter (1950) argues,

presents certain problems to the counselor that are in part different from subsequent interviews. It is likely that the beginning interview will be more demanding of the counselor for several reasons. The counselor and the client are new to each other and the relationship which is established at the outset will color a great deal of what follows. The counselor must be prepared to adapt himself to the mode of expression the client develops: the counselor is not going into the interview with a set routine. It is in the first interview that the client will begin to reveal himself. The counselor's reactions are correspondingly important. Errors in understanding the client may result in his hasty withdrawal. And usually it is in this interview that the client decides whether the counseling relationship is the method he will use in his attempts to work out his difficulties. (p. 88)

Porter's comments highlight the difficulties as well as the importance of the initial interview. From these comments, as well as from common sense, it might be discerned that the beginning interview is best used by the counselor as a time to study the client, to learn about him and decide on the way the treatment is likely to proceed, to weigh prognostic considerations, and so on. Bell (1965) points out that the initial interview can be used productively as a factor in determining instances of significant changes in the client's behavior. Drasgow (1956) has presented a detailed and informative discussion of the procedures of clinical intake interviews, and many of his insights are applicable to the school counseling, first interview situation, particularly if subsequent interviews are to follow. Since in many cases the first interview is the only interview (in cases of short-term counseling), Tyler's idea of minimum change therapy (Tyler, 1960) should be studied by the counselor as a possible approach to handling single interview counseling. In another paper, Tyler (1956) discusses three aspects of the initial interview which are more generally applicable: assessing the foundation for the relationship, identifying the client's psychological realities, and structuring the counseling situation.

To meet the demands of the initial interview, the beginning counselor might do well to have a tentative, but very flexible, routine worked out so that he feels comfortable during the first interview. This is not to suggest that he act in a mechanical way during the first interview but that he have an overall structure from which he may freely deviate as the need arises. He should have a repertoire of possible responses available to meet the specific needs of the client during the initial interview. He should have a *tentative* structure planned. This structure may include any or all of the following components: eliciting a personal history from the client, beginning the counseling relationship, helping the client feel comfortable, discussing frankly alternative possibilities to counseling, and establishing a contract if the client indicates he wishes to continue with the counselor. This last point requires some clarification.

A contract in counseling differs from the use of the word in its legal context. A counseling contract is an unwritten but usually explicit agreement between the counselor and the client about what the treatment should do, how many sessions are expected, what general rules and guidelines will be followed, etc. It is not intended to rigidly fix the course of the counseling but to assure both the counselor and the client that an understanding exists between them and that any deviations from this understanding should be mutually agreed upon by both of them. Some counselors, particularly behavioral counselors, use the contract to establish the particular goals of the treatment, while other counselors use the contract to explore the range of areas to be examined during the course of treatment. Ezell and Patience (1972) have studied the use of the contract as a counseling technique.

Shertzer and Stone (1971) offer as guidelines for the initial interview *establishing rapport with the student, providing some structure, helping the counselee talk, remaining alert to the counselee's feelings, and smoothly terminating the interview.* We should discuss each of these in some detail.

Rapport is established when the counselor demonstrates an accepting, open attitude, when he shows interest in what the client has to say, and when he does everything in his power to make the client feel comfortable. Tyler (1969) offers some helpful remarks on how to communicate positively with the client at the outset:

We must recognize that the people who consult us may have mixed feelings about being understood. They must be sure that understanding can in no way constitute a threat before they can welcome it. Many of us are afraid that someone will "see through us," uncovering our hidden weaknesses. We have put up strong defenses against this. Much of what we say, many of the things we do, are designed to hide rather than to reveal our underlying motives and traits. For this reason if it happens that the counselor shows by some penetrating remark that he has seen through a new client's defenses, the person may very well retreat in panic from the whole situation. It is only when he has become certain of a thorough-going unshakable acceptance that he can run the risk of trying to make his real feelings understood. (pp. 49–50)

In order to establish rapport, therefore, it is important that the counselor not probe too deeply into the hidden recesses of the client's psyche, that he not manipulatively bring too much too quickly. The establishment of rapport requires patience and understanding.

The counselor provides structure during the initial interview by translating into practice his concepts and beliefs about counseling. "Providing some structure for the interview," Shertzer and Stone (1971) point out, "means that the counselor must have clearly in mind his concept of counseling." The Rogerian counselor will structure the interview far differently from that of the psychoanalytic, reality, existential, or behavioral counselor. In general, the client's moves toward structuring the interview should have priority over the counselor's.

Helping the counselee talk is often the most difficult part of the initial interview. The silent client, who sits and stares blankly at the counselor (or the client who is silent out of fear), is a terror to most counselors. There are a number of gentle, appropriate ways of helping the client speak: asking questions, suggesting things that he might speak about, asking him if he is comfortable, and so on. A general guideline is that the counselor should say only things that are intended to act as a catalyst for the student in his efforts to communicate. Rarely does the situation occur in which the counselor makes the client feel comfortable and the client is still unable to speak.

Remaining alert to the client's feelings and providing for his needs is the first distinctively therapeutic part of the treatment. The counselor wants to get a *sense of the client*, an appreciation of the client's unconscious reservoir of feelings. Typically, the client will demonstrate certain needs during this session. He may request information, vocational advice, or tutorial assistance. He may explain that he "just needs someone to talk to," or that he wants sympathy for some predicament in which he has been unable to find someone to speak to. He may be seeking punishment and chastisement for something he has done which he considers "bad" or "evil." While the client may not directly comment on his needs, he usually offers a number of subtle indications of what he is presenting or will be looking for during the course of the counseling treatment.

The skillful termination of the interview has been the subject of much research and speculation. We know that the conclusion of the initial interview is important both in bringing the client back again (when required) and in shaping his judgment about the entire session. Brammer and Shostrom (1968) suggest what they call "capping techniques," which consist of changing the subject to something less intense, "yet still propelling the interview forward." I would agree that it is important to end the initial interview on a calm level, rather than in the midst of a highly emotional interchange. Any of the following statements by the counselor may serve as an adequate closing of the interview:

"Well, I think we have a number of things to discuss in our next session."
"So, our next appointment is Thursday at noon. I'll see you then."
"I hope you'll decide to call for another appointment. I would like to explore this further with you."

It is only through his experiences, however, that the counselor gets a sense of how to terminate an interview in a manner which is most in accord with his own personal style.

TYPES OF COUNSELING TECHNIQUES

Although in Part Three we surveyed a wide variety of counseling techniques, each categorized under the rubrics of a particular school of psychotherapy, there are many counselors who draw widely and freely in their selection of techniques and who utilize a number of alternative philosophies in formulating their rationales for using certain techniques. A certain corpus of counseling techniques, therefore, has enjoyed a wider audience than have the techniques of the parochial practitioner of a single position. A counselor who draws from different schools in his choice of techniques is said to be *eclectic*.

Eclecticism, according to Thorne (1973), its founder and chief proponent, "involves the selective application of basic science methods using the most valid current knowledge available for specific clinical situations according to indications and contraindications. It is not committed to any parochial view of man." Like the applied behavioral scientist presented by Thoresen (see chapter 3), the eclectic counselor utilizes a scientific approach to the problems of treatment in which he selects and combines, through careful planning, "compatible elements from diverse sources, even from otherwise incompatible theories and systems" (Thorne, 1973).

Brammer (1969), in an interesting paper on eclecticism, traces the development of learning and personality theory in psychology and maintains that "there is a need for an eclectic position that avoids indiscriminate picking and choosing and leads to a consistent and comprehensive synthesis of theory unique to the individual counselor" (p. 193). Brammer "not only contends that there is room for the emerging eclectic position elaborated in this paper but also suspects that an empirical study of counselor practices would reveal it is the most dominant, though unexpressed, point of view." He asserts that "each counselor must grapple with the task of developing his own comprehensive point of view. A counselor cannot in good professional conscience go to the literature on theories of counseling and psychotherapy to find a ready made one for himself" (p. 193).

Brammer tells us that to develop this eclectic view "it is necessary to resist emphasizing theory exclusively." The counselor "must sharpen his powers of behavioral observation in the best scientific tradition.... adopt a behaviorist stance in the broad meaning of the term.... trust his own powers of observation, criticism, and experimental technique.... know his own personality. The counselor must be aware of his values, need-distorted perceptions, and potentials and limitations with particular kinds of clients" (p. 195). Sometimes, then, a counselor is able to reach a point where he "transcends both person and method to develop a creative, innovative approach to behavior change."

The basic organizing principle used by the eclectic practitioner is objective evaluation of the client. Rather than approach the client with clinical biases (such as a predetermined view of man or a predetermined conception of what the cure or the treatment should be), the eclectic practitioner adapts the course of the therapy, as well as his own strategies, to the particulars of the client's situation. In this section we shall examine some techniques that may be used by an eclectic practitioner, as well as by practitioners in almost any other school. Thorne (1950,1967) emphasizes that the selection of these techniques requires some organization, and the beginning counselor should keep this admonition in mind.

As a rule, the technique is named after the type of response the counselor offers to the client. Some of the techniques to be mentioned are applicable only to one or two of the schools of therapy, while others are extensively used by all of the schools. Seven of the most common (and most useful) counselor responses are offered below, with a brief illustration of each:

1 Clarification

This is intended to clarify either for the counselor or for the client the meaning of one of the client's communications. In addition to achieving cognitive understanding of information, it may help the client to understand ambiguities or confusions in his thinking.

Client. I can't get along with Mr. Jones or Buzzy, so I don't go to class.
Counselor. Buzzy is who?
Client. The kid who sits in front of me...you know, Mr. Jones's favorite student ...the teacher's pet.

2 Reflection

Repeating to the client, in an emotionally equivalent or emotionally neutral tone, the last words that the client has said. The counselor never expresses his judgment in a reflective statement.

Client. I've been feeling badly lately...like I've done something bad.
Counselor. Like you've done something bad?
Client. Yes. Like I deserve to be punished.
Counselor. You feel that you should be punished.

3 Probing

The counselor, through the use of questions, attempts to encourage the client to expressions of greater depth and to awareness of deeper understanding. The probing questions should never be overwhelming to the client.

Client. I find that I just can't study, even if I know that I'm going to fail the test.
Counselor. What happens when it gets down to study time?
Client. I get blocked. I can't concentrate.
Counselor. What are your feelings at such a time?
Client. I feel like I'm going to fail....

4 Silence

Although it is sometimes not recognized as a legitimate technique, silence is one of the most helpful expressions that the counselor can offer to the client. It is particularly useful when the client is engaged in self-analysis, which can be helpful to the ultimate success of the treatment.

Client. Why do you think I'm so upset about this test? Intellectually, I know I can pass it, but emotionally....
Counselor. (Silence.)
Client. Why do I feel this tenseness?
Counselor. (Silence.)

5 Interpretation

The counselor explains to the client a hidden meaning behind his statements or actions.

Client. I'm sorry that I'm laughing at you—don't take it personally. I can't help it, but I find you very funny looking. Whenever I think of you, I laugh.
Counselor. Perhaps it is really feelings of anger that you are experiencing.

6 Empathic response

The counselor shows that he accepts the client and that he understands him. It is important that the counselor can differentiate between sympathy and empathy. The former is an expression of pity, while the latter is an acknowledgement that the counselor, too, has had the same feelings.

Client. I feel like such a stupid idiot...such a failure. Everyone has a date for the party except me. No one has asked me...and I know nobody is going to.
Counselor. I, too, have felt left out at times...like I was some kind of freak...an object of ridicule. I thought at the time that I could never survive, never show my face again. But I have survived, and so will you.

7 Investigating alternatives

This has two purposes: to assist the client in making choices and to help him understand the reasons underlying whatever choices he is disposed to. This technique is particularly helpful in terms of the client's reality orientation.

Client. Since I wasn't able to get into any college, I guess I'm going to be a failure.
Counselor. What are some other possibilities you might consider?
Client. Well, I guess I could pursue carpentry. I do love working with wood.
Counselor. How would you get a job in that field?
Client. I guess I could ask my Uncle Al. He's in the union, you know.

The above seven represent only a handful of the many counseling techniques. They have been selected because they are the most general in scope and the most widely used. Another that should be mentioned is the "open-ended question" that allows the client flexibility of response because of the question's lack of structure. These types of questions—"Tell me about yourself"—are particularly helpful during the first interview.

ANSWERING CLIENTS' QUESTIONS

A systematic analysis of the typical counseling interaction will undoubtably reveal that one of the major forms of communication between counselor and client is the question. The question is a viable and productive medium of communication because it requires an answer and therefore promotes the interactive nature of the relationship between counselor and client. Questions asked by the counselor are dealt with often in the area of techniques. In this section we will examine some ways in which the counselor might answer questions posed by the client.

First we must ask what kinds of questions does the typical client pose to the counselor. There are four basic types: information questions, questions of value, direction questions, and personal questions. Let us examine each individually.

Information questions may be either objective or subjective. "What colleges offer degrees in forestry?" is an objective question. So are the questions, "Where can I find an abortion clinic in this city?" "What average do I need to make the honor society?" "What were the results of the test I took last month?" When such a question is asked, certainly all the counselor needs to do is answer the question. This will satisfy the student and provide types of information which may help him with his plans. But what if the counselor does not know the answer—what should he do then? Might the client not lose confidence in him because he doesn't know?

The solution to this problem is simple. The counselor must acknowledge that he does not have the answer. For it is only when he is truthful with the client (as well as with himself) that the client can develop the respect for him that is prerequisite for a successful counseling relationship. "If the client asks a question regarding facts," Darley (1950) points out, "and you don't have the facts, it is better to say 'I don't know' rather than to run with a lot of vague generalities or in some other way try to cover up your own ignorance. The client is likely to have more confidence in the interviewer who does not hesitate to admit his ignorance. It would be desirable for the counselor to get these facts later, and to tell the client where to get them."

Felker (1972) takes a different tack. She feels that in many cases when the counselor is approached with questions he cannot answer, he must "turn the tables back to the obstinate inquirer." She gives a number of examples:

The first response you could try is bold-faced and direct. It consists of the counter question, "What do you think the answer is?" A second alternative response builds in a bit of reinforcement for the questioner, and while he basks in the compliment he may decide not to persist in seeking an answer. It goes something like this: "I can see that you devoted a good deal of thought to this issue, and since you seem to be a very critical thinker, let me get your views first." The third approach is one I recommend when you want to bolster your own ego or position.... You say something like this: "I've spent a good deal of time thinking about that very question; let me see if your opinions are similar to mine." (p. 684)

Felker's manipulative methods may be adequate for dealing with a hostile questioner who is out to prove how ignorant you are. I include them here not to advocate their use with sincere clients, but because these methods are often used inadvertently or intentionally by counselors who do not feel comfortable when they don't know the right answer. There is no shame in not knowing, but there is shame in using tricks to cover up one's ignorance unless the intentions of the questioner are hostile and provocative.

Subjective information questions refer to personal information about the client. "Why am I feeling this way?" or "Is there something wrong with me?" are typical questions requiring information which is subjective, interpretive, or downright speculative. These are not in the technical sense questions for information but merely assume the form of such questions. "Questions are often disguises for more penetrating and deep concerns," suggest Dimick and Huff (1970). "It is the job of the counselor to assess the nature of the questions—to 'hear' what is meant by the child. When a legitimate request for information is 'heard,' then the counselor responds with whatever data resources he may have. When some other request is 'heard,' he responds to that need."

Clients often ask for value judgments from the counselor. Particularly in areas where their own value orientation is fuzzy, the student may seek a resolution for a moral dilemma by eliciting from the counselor an evaluative response. But because the counselor may be perceived as an authority figure—or at least an *authoritative* figure—his value judgments will be weighed more heavily than they should be by the client. Therefore, the appropriate response in such a situation is to help the client arrive at his own moral decisions, rather than imposing moral or value decisions upon him. Belkin (1974) has used the metaphor of *communion* to describe the interactive value-forming process between teacher and student (or, as the case may be, between counselor and student) rather than the typical authority-subject stratification.

When a client seeks information regarding the direction he should take (what choice to make, what approach to use, etc.), there is ever present a strong temptation on the counselor's part to tell him, particularly if the counselor feels that he knows the best answer to the client's problems. This should generally be avoided, however, inasmuch as the client will gain his own strength if he is allowed to make his own judgments. Certainly, one of the important goals of counseling is to enable clients to make better decisions, and part of this process may require that the counselor become an active agent in the decision-making process. But to answer a client's decision-oriented question with a specific, closed-ended answer diminishes significantly the possibility that the client will grow enough to make his own decisions.

To do this, the counselor should respond to the client's directional questions with questions of his own, questions which are designed to help the client arrive at his own solutions. For example,

Client. Which college do you think I should apply to? Harvard, where I don't have much chance of getting accepted, or State, where I can probably get a scholarship.

302

Counselor. Well, how would you feel about going to Harvard and how would you feel about going to State?

Or,

Client. I'm not sure if I should enroll in that special enrichment class or not. What do you think?
Counselor. What are your feelings about the class?

In this way, the counselor gently leads the client to making his own decisions, which is very important for his future growth, his development, and above all, his independence as a person.

Personal questions asked by the client—"How old are you?" or "Are you married?"—are often a source of confusion to the counselor. There is no absolute rule here. Each counselor will have to decide for himself how much personal information he is willing to give out, but a good rule of thumb is that giving the client some personal information will help him recognize the humanness of the counselor and increase the level of rapport in the relationship. Often the client asks personal questions not so much because he desires the information but because he feels that if he is willing to share his personal self with the counselor, the counselor should be willing to share his personal self with the client. This is a fair request, and the psychoanalytic position of withholding all personal information seems to be a weakness of that theory.

In conclusion, then, the counselor should answer questions for information if the answers are helpful to the client, give some personal information about himself, and acquaint the client with resources he can use to get further answers to his questions. He should avoid answering moral or value judgment questions or directional questions and encourage the client to arrive at his own answers to these questions.

SYNTHETIC COUNSELING TECHNIQUES

The word *synthesis* means *the putting together of parts, often contradictory or antithetical parts, to form a whole which is unified and coherent.* The counseling setting is filled with such parts, namely, the role of the counselor, the role of the client, the client's needs, the client's expectations, the counselor's abilities to meet these needs and expectations, the client's willingness to cooperate in the counseling venture, outside experiences that contribute to the success or failure of the treatment, theoretical considerations that influence the counselor, and, of course, the dynamics of the relationship itself. If one were to ask a simple question, such as "What happened at such and such a counseling session?" it would take a very sophisticated computer to sort out all of the information on all of the different levels, evaluate what had transpired, and then form logical and cogent conclusions. But no computers are available to the counselor during his sessions, when it is essential that he have a full understanding of what is happening. It is for this purpose that synthetic counseling techniques are used.

303

A synthetic counseling technique is one that is developed from the circumstances of the immediate situation. It evolves from a standard technique and undergoes three transformational processes:

1. It utilizes the principle of *therapeutic control.* This important principle states that every word and every feeling that the counselor communicates to the client has great significance to the client, and consequently communications must be carefully thought out, their ramifications understood, their effect appreciated, and the possible dangers noted. In counseling and psychotherapy, words are medicine: Just as the physician would not dispense a drug until he understood the full nature of the patient's problem and the possible dangers of allergic reaction, the counselor must offer no communication to the client without first evaluating its beneficial and harmful effects.

A standard counseling technique may be modified after a consideration of therapeutic control. The counselor may feel, for example, that the presentation of alternatives to the client, usually an emotionally innocuous process, could be viewed by the client as an unwarranted imposition on his plans. Deferring to the reality of the immediate situation, the counselor would then forgo this technique. Or he could modify the technique in some way to make the presentation of alternatives more palatable to the client.

2. A synthetic counseling technique *expresses the counselor's countertransference feelings in a therapeutic and appropriate manner.* I use the word *countertransference* not strictly in its psychoanalytic sense but to indicate the cumulative sum of feelings that the counselor has for the client at any given moment. These feelings are extremely important both to the counselor and to the client: They are important to the counselor because they indicate to what degree his subjectivity about the client might interfere with his perceptions of the client and his ability to respond to the client; they are important to the client because the client depends upon emotional feedback from the counselor to learn about himself, to appreciate himself more, and to know how others (particularly an important other) see him.

The synthetic counseling technique is in many ways an ideal vehicle for the counselor to use in expressing himself. Since the technique is designed to facilitate the treatment and define the working relationship, it ipso facto becomes a productive expression of the counselor's feelings. Also, since the technique is a prescribed and structured form of expression, it assists the counselor in his desire to express himself to the client. Moreover, by expressing his own countertransference feelings through the medium of the technique, the counselor feels more comfortable and natural with the technique (inasmuch as it becomes an expression of his true self). This resulting naturalness, in turn, makes the technique more effective.

3. A synthetic technique *fuses in content and implication the immediate problem with the long-range goal of the treatment.* This simply means that the client is to learn through the counselor's use of techniques how to solve his own

problems without the need for the counselor's help. This is most important since psychotherapy can never hope to solve all of the client's specific problems, problems which are bound to crop up over and over again during the years. The therapeutic experience must become a learning experience for the client; specifically, he must learn how to be his own counselor.

Synthetic techniques, therefore, are modified and transformed counseling techniques. They begin as general counseling techniques and are altered to the immediate demands of the treatment, taking into account the counselor's countertransference feelings (where these feelings are appropriate and helpful to the client's growth), and presented to the client in such a way that he not only learns about himself but also learns how to go about solving his own problems when the counselor is not there to help.

Let us consider two examples of synthetic counseling techniques, paying particular attention to their effects upon the client. Below is a brief transcription from a counseling session conducted by one of my trainees:

Client. I don't think I'm gonna come here no more.

Counselor. May I ask why?

Client. I ain't doing so good and I don't want to waste your time no more. I like you and you really tried for me. But I'm just me—that's the way I am. Guess I'm gonna get thrown out now.

Counselor. So, you're angry at me, eh? It's about time!

Client. What do you mean?

Counselor. Well, I thought you'd be angry before this. After all, I haven't been doing as good a job as I should have. You still got in trouble at school last week—a note home. If I had been a better counselor, you would have made more improvement by now. I've let you down. I've failed you.

Client. Well, it ain't all your job (fault).

Counselor. But still some.

The counselor in this exchange was using a synthetic technique. Beginning with the psychoanalytic technique of interpretation (You want to leave treatment because you can't express to me the feeling that I have failed you.), she added her own feelings of having failed with the client and at the same time taught the client an important lesson: that he has a right to be angry when someone he cares for has failed him. Compare her answer to the client's question "What do you mean?" with the direct interpretive statement offered above. Notice how much more meaningful to the client her statement is, how much more feeling there is in it, how much more natural it is in its expression. Now, consider this second transcription.

Counselor. I notice that you are half an hour late for the appointment today.

Client. Something happened.

Counselor. Something happened?

Client. Yeah, I was playing ball in the park.

Counselor. You were in the park?

Client. Yeah, with my friends.

Counselor. With your friends.

Client. I wet my bed again last night.

Counselor. We can talk about that later. First, let's discuss why you came late today.

At first glance it might appear that the counselor's last statement is inappropriate, but if we look closer we see what the counselor was cleverly doing. It appeared to the counselor that the client had come late because he was ashamed to talk about having wet his bed again (he was seeing the counselor because of his enuresis problem). The counselor wished to probe in order to find out what had caused the client to wet his bed, but direct probing would have been too dangerous for the client's already fragile ego. So the counselor used a synthetic technique. He rewarded the client's willingness to explore his problem by telling him to avoid speaking about it as soon as he showed a willingness to discuss it. In this way, he strengthened the client's cooperativeness by reinforcing it with an emotionally reassuring statement (If you are willing to cooperate and discuss your problems, I will do the very opposite of probing.). This utilized the principle of therapeutic control and the counselor's countertransference feelings of the client's anxiety about the bed wetting. Let us look further at how this session went:

Client. I already told you why I came late.

Counselor. Tell me more.

Client. I'd rather talk about last night.

Counselor. Go ahead, then.

As you can see, the counselor made it safe for the client to speak about his feelings.

SUMMARY

The term synthetic is used to describe a variety of counseling techniques that are transformations of standard counseling techniques. The transformation involves three processes: (1) the influence of the immediate needs of the situation as they affect the implementation of the standard technique—the process known as *therapeutic control;* (2) the inclusion of the counselor's appropriate countertransference feelings; (3) the fusing of learning principles in the application of the technique. Synthetic techniques are advantageous because they allow the counselor a constructive outlet for personal expression and offer the client an opportunity to learn to deal with his own problems.

References

Belkin, G. S. Communion in teaching. *Educational Theory*, 1974, *24*, 170–182.

Bell, H. M. Significant changes in the direction of behavior. *Personnel and Guidance Journal*, 1965, *43*, 438–442.

Berdie, R. F. Counselor attitudes. *Educational and Psychological Measurement*, 1951, *11*, 349–354.

Brammer, L. M. Eclecticism revisited. *Personnel and Guidance Journal*, 1969, *48*, 192–197.

Brammer, L. M., & Shostrom, E. *Therapeutic psychology* (2nd ed.). Englewood Cliffs, N.J.: Prentice-Hall, 1968.

Darley, J. G. In A. H. Brayfield (Ed.), *Readings in modern methods of counseling*. New York: Appleton-Century-Crofts, 1950.

Dimick, K. M., & Huff, V. E. *Child counseling*. Dubuque, Iowa: Wm. C. Brown, 1970.

Drasgow, J. Intake interviewing in counseling. *Personnel and Guidance Journal*, 1956, *35*, 100–102.

Ezell, B., & Patience, T. G. The contract as a counseling technique. *Personnel and Guidance Journal*, 1972, *51*, 27–31.

Felker, S. How to feel comfortable when you don't know what you are doing. *Personnel and Guidance Journal*, 1972, *50*, 683–685.

Hiltner, S. Hostility in counseling. *Pastoral Psychology*, 1950, *1*, 35–42.

Lambin, H. J. An experimental study of the relation between perception of self and evaluation of another. Unpublished doctoral dissertation, Loyola University, 1959.

Menninger, K. The character of the therapist. *Pastoral Psychology*, 1958, *9*, 14–18.

Porter, E. H., Jr. *An introduction to therapeutic counseling*. Boston: Houghton Mifflin, 1950.

Shentoub, S. A. *Le rôle de la personnalité de l'analyst dans thérapeutique psychoanalytique. Année Psychologique*, 1955, *55*, 397–399.

Shertzer, B., & Stone, S. C. *Fundamentals of Guidance* (2nd ed.). Boston: Houghton Mifflin, 1971.

Thorne, F. C. Principles of personality counseling. *Journal of Clinical Psychology*, 1950.

Thorne, F. C. *Integrative psychology*. Brandon, Vt.: Clincal Psychology Publishing Company, 1967.

Thorne, F. C. Eclectic psychotherapy. In R. Corsini (Ed.), *Current psychotherapies*. Itasca, Ill.: F. E. Peacock, 1973.

Tyler, L. E. The initial interview. *Personnel and Guidance Journal*, 1956, *34*, 466–473.

Tyler, L. E. Minimum change therapy. *Personnel and Guidance Journal*, 1960, *38*, 475–479.

Tyler, L. E. *The work of the counselor* (3rd ed.). New York: Appleton-Century-Crofts, 1969.

chapter fifteen

The counseling process

We have now examined in some depth a few of the various interactions that take place during the counseling session. We have seen ways in which the initial interview is conducted, and we have considered some constructive ways in which the counselor can respond to client questions. We have also examined a few of the techniques in the counselor's repertoire. Now we shall look at the counseling process in more depth, paying particular attention to client and counselor expectations and goals, to the stages of the process, and to methods of group counseling—a specialized counseling form. By the conclusion of this chapter, the reader should have acquired, subject to the limitations of the printed medium, a feel for the counseling process, particularly its myriad complexities and diversities.

EXPECTATIONS AND GOALS

When the client enters the counselor's office, he is there for a reason—although the reason may be as elusive to him as it is to the counselor. Moreover, not only is he there for a reason, but he has entered the office accompanied by certain beliefs, presuppositions, feelings, and expectations that immediately color the situation and his responses to it. It is the counselor's first responsibility in the counseling session to find out why the client is there and to discuss with him his expectations of and goals for the counseling sessions. This will have the very positive effect of eliminating (or at least minimizing) misunderstandings and clarifying the raison d'être of the treatment.

What are some of the typical reasons why individuals enter counseling? The reasons are, of course, as varied as the individuals, but we can list a few of the more common classes of reasons. Some clients enter because they are forced to by school personnel, legal authorities, parents, or other powers-that-be. Some enter for particular guidance or advice, information or professional insight into the alternatives that confront them. Some enter because of inner pain: the torment of anxiety or depression, the nagging hurt of guilt, the hollow emptiness of insecurity and self-despisement. Still others enter counseling because they themselves believe that their behavior must be changed, that new ways of living have to be discovered, alternative life styles explored. A few—and these are the special few that we must treasure—enter only to maximize their potentialities

in life, to become more in touch with themselves and others, and, hopefully, to one day become counselors themselves.

Despite the clarity with which we can state these reasons, the client often has difficulty expressing the reason that has brought him to counseling. The counselor, through his patient questioning, his even more patient silence, and his communication of respect for the client, enables the client to express the reason for his being there. For the counselor is well aware that not only does this reason influence and help shape the course of the counseling process, but it reveals something about the client and his life hopes as well. The reason, translated into practice, becomes what White (1973) calls the "guiding idea" of the counseling process:

When two people meet in an office, one of whom defines himself as a counseling psychologist, the other as a person in need of expert help with problems of living, the ensuing conversation takes place under the influence of a guiding idea. In its most general form, this guiding idea is that the client can lead his life better and that the counselor can help him do so. If the client comes with a highly specific complaint, such as being afraid to cross streets, the guiding idea is so obvious as to escape notice.... But the difficulties of living that clients put before their counselors are not often so sharply circumscribed. Sometimes they are broadly encompassing, as when a client announces that he does not know who he is. Whatever procedure the counselor adopts, he can hardly be of service if he has no guiding ideas of his own on the subject of how to live. (p. 3)

The guiding idea, as White presents it, is a combination of the client's expectations of counseling and the counselor's own views of counseling—and of living, in general.

One reason a client comes to counseling, a reason that usually augurs an unfavorable prognosis, is that he has been forced to come and would rather not be there. Strictly speaking, this person should not be considered a client. He becomes a client only after indicating a motivation to be there—a need for counseling. "Counseling," Lewis (1970) argues, "cannot take place with a client who has no counseling need.... The person who enters the counselor's office with no reason of his own for being there is not at the moment a client. He may become one eventually, but his motivation must first be aroused." Boy (1974) compares the unmotivated with the motivated client:

Clients who voluntarily enter counseling are in a better position to profit from the relationship. Since it is their idea to engage in counseling, voluntary clients are less resistant, more willing to move toward behavioral change, more honest in appraising their behavior, more willing to expend their psychic energy needed to change their behavior, and more trusting of the counseling relationship. (p. 166)

It is clear from these comments that if the client is not initially motivated, no meaningful counseling can take place and that therefore the counselor's first responsibility is either to motivate the client or to terminate the pseudocounseling relationship, a move that the unmotivated client will surely respect.

Exploring the motivated client's expectations of counseling is essential before the crux of the process can get underway. "What do you expect from your visits here?" "What would you like to talk about while you're here?" "How long do you plan to see me?" "What do you hope to gain from counseling?" These and other questions explore the problem of expectation. It is imperative that when the client's expectations are unrealistic, the counselor help him evolve realistic expectations that can be met during the counseling experience. Such an act is in itself therapeutic since realistic expectations are a part of healthy living.

In establishing the goals of the counseling process, the counselor should place the major burden on the client himself. For it is only the client who knows what he wants. As we noted in Part Three, however, certain psychotherapeutic approaches have inherent goals built in (integration in psychoanalysis, authenticity in existentialism, etc.), and the counselor should be careful to maintain a flexible attitude that will allow the individual client to articulate his own goals, even if these do not conform entirely to the goals of the treatment theory to which the counselor subscribes. One of the great contributions of the counseling profession is the willingness—even encouragement—to allow the client to define his own goals of the treatment. This is sometimes ignored in practice, however. Poole (1957), for example, found that the counselor's own orientation about counseling exerts a strong influence on the process goals. The counselor must be sensitive to this tendency and work conscientiously and undeceptively to allow the client to find his goals and to express them.

PROCESS CONSIDERATIONS

The counseling process is characterized primarily, if not solely, by the helping relationship that exists between the counselor and the client. This helping relationship, in which the counselor uses his self—his feelings and perceptions—to help the client grow and prosper (Combs et al., 1969) has been

*Counseling is talk,
counseling is
understanding.*

the subject of much study and research. In this section we shall examine the relationship of this "instrumental self" to changes in the client and to movement
in the counseling process.

Benjamin (1969) sees as primary in the relationship the "feelings within ourselves that we wish to help him [the client] as much as possible and that there is
nothing more important to us." This attitude is inevitably conveyed to the
client, and it enables the client to open up and express himself, which in turn
enables him to grow and to resolve the difficulties that brought him to counseling in the first place.

Assuming that such an attitude is present—that the counselor has the appropriate feelings to act as a facilitator—we can look at the counseling process in its
totality. One view of the process, a panoramic one certainly, is the dialectical
view. The counseling process may be seen as a dialectic movement between
counselor understanding and counselor response. The synthetic result of this
dialectic is client growth and maturity.

By counselor understanding, I mean the deepest, most profound type of understanding, roughly akin to what Rogers calls empathy. Curran (1968) describes this type of understanding:

To understand another at the deepest level of his feelings and reactions is an
immeasurably more profound, complex and delicate kind of understanding than simply
to know the meaning of the words he uses. Yet this is what another person really means
when he says after an interview, "You know, he really understood me." The counselor's

311

striving to understand him intensifies the person's own efforts to understand himself and to share with the counselor what he slowly and sometimes tortuously is discovering about himself. (p. 125)

This type of understanding, as we can clearly see, is a direct result of the counselor's feelings about the client and about the counseling process. It is, in effect, understanding "through the heart," rather than by the intellect alone.

The second part of the dialectic, counselor response, is somewhat more varied and specific to the situation that the counselor finds himself in. In the preceding chapter we looked at some counseling responses, including clarification, reflection, probing, silence, interpretation, empathic response, and investigating alternatives. These are the types of counselor responses we call techniques, and they have been criticized for artificiality. The sensitive counselor, however, can freely use these techniques and still avoid the artificiality by using them only in appropriate instances. Perez (1968) points out, for example, that "how effective the counselor is with various techniques ... depends on several variables ... (1) the counselor's affect, (2) how suitable the technique is to the personality of the counselee, and (3) how appropriate the particular technique is to the moment and the counseling climate" (p. 73).

In addition to techniques, another facilitative counselor response is what Mahoney (1967) calls "the helping art of presence," which is simply being there in an accepting and receptive frame of mind. This is an effective nonverbal response, well attuned to the client's needs of the moment. Mahoney (1967) explains this response thus:

The art of presence involves our doing and saying very little; its effectiveness lies in what we convey through our presence alone. The act of being present or absent is one of the most fundamental forms of nonverbal communication, and even in our highly verbal society it is one of the chief means of granting or withholding approval.... More than anything else, we look to presence as an indication of who is viewed as important by whom, and who views what as important.... The action of being present is usually taken as nonverbal evidence of our verbal assertions to the effect that we think something or someone is important. (pp. 110–111)

While one might argue that being present is not technically a counselor response, it becomes evident that it is a form of counselor response, especially when we modify our original statement and say that the counselor can be present in varying degrees. His attentiveness, his concern, his body language, his own feelings are all components of his being present—of his *being-there*.

Curran (1968, p. 34 and following) cites a client communication that he calls the "language of affect." It is a spontaneous language, with "little or no reflective awareness," in which the client has to react to his feelings, in which he cannot control them. In such a case, the counselor responds in the "language of cognition," which helps provide the client "with a means of grasping the significance of these feelings or happenings within him." The language of cognition may be viewed as a counselor response that is not technically a counselor tech-

312

nique. Rather, it is a maturational response that better enables the client to get in touch with his own feelings.

Some counselors view the counseling process not in this dialectical framework but as a singular, continuous process of growth, unified in its directionality. Gibb (1968) offers one definition of this growth:

In the normal processes of growth persons are confronted with sets of recurring concerns.... Growth consists of increased resolution of these concerns. (p. 25)

He lists the categories of concerns as: acceptance and membership, intimacy and decision making, motivation and productivity, control and organization. As the individual grows, he learns mastery in each of these areas of his life.

A somewhat different, but not conflicting, conception of growth is put forth by Rogers. Rogers (1961) sees growth as the basic direction of counseling and psychotherapy. In a different paper, he outlines some of the specific criteria of growth that have appeared in his writings over the years. Some of these are (Rogers, 1959):

1 The client is more congruent.
2 He is consequently more realistic.
3 He is consequently more effective in problem solving.
4 His psychological adjustment is improved.

He goes on to list more indications, but these four are the main ones and entirely representative of the Rogerian conception of growth.

While the dialectical and growth paradigms are not exclusive of each other, the major emphasis of each is different. The dialectical paradigm emphasizes the counselor's response, within the dialogue framework, as the primary factor in client growth; the emphasis in the latter position, however, is on internal client traits and propensities (such as self-actualization) which blossom forth almost independently of what the counselor does. The first position is more likely to emphasize counselor techniques, while the second position stresses the personal qualities of the counselor.

In addition to the dialectic and growth conceptions of the counseling process, we have what might be called the *modeling* conception. This view is based on the idea that the client models himself after the counselor as he progresses through the course of counseling. The Freudian notion of transference (see chapter 8) lends itself to this type of interpretation, but such a view is also utilized by some counselors who are clearly not Freudian in their orientation. Shoben (1965) discusses the implications of this argument:

If, as a model, the counselor thus operates as an attractive object of identification, he also, by virtue of the advantages of his role, is able to invest a high degree of genuine concern in his patient. Because he need not face the rigors of continuing intimacy and unremitting personal obligation that other relationships entail, he can engage in an active search for

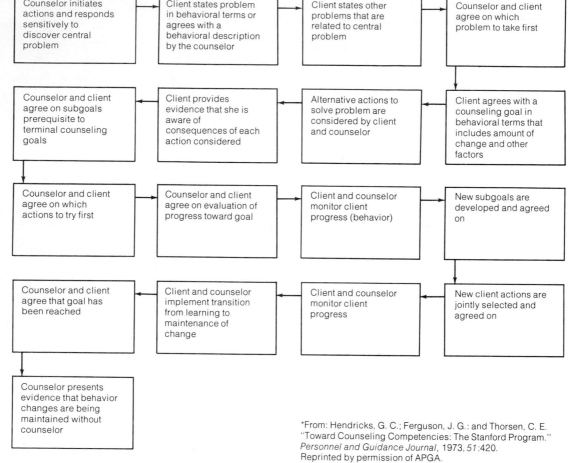

display 15.1

THE COUNSELING PROCESS
FROM A BEHAVIORAL VIEWPOINT*

Counselor initiates actions and responds sensitively to discover central problem

Client states problem in behavioral terms or agrees with a behavioral description by the counselor

Client states other problems that are related to central problem

Counselor and client agree on which problem to take first

Counselor and client agree on subgoals prerequisite to terminal counseling goals

Client provides evidence that she is aware of consequences of each action considered

Alternative actions to solve problem are considered by client and counselor

Client agrees with a counseling goal in behavioral terms that includes amount of change and other factors

Counselor and client agree on which actions to try first

Counselor and client agree on evaluation of progress toward goal

Client and counselor monitor client progress (behavior)

New subgoals are developed and agreed on

Counselor and client agree that goal has been reached

Client and counselor implement transition from learning to maintenance of change

Client and counselor monitor client progress

New client actions are jointly selected and agreed on

Counselor presents evidence that behavior changes are being maintained without counselor

*From: Hendricks, G. C.; Ferguson, J. G.: and Thorsen, C. E. "Toward Counseling Competencies: The Stanford Program." *Personnel and Guidance Journal*, 1973, 51:420. Reprinted by permission of APGA.

the characteristics of the help-seeker that may evoke quite authentic reactions of warmth and affection. (p. 228)

Asbury and Winston (1974) speak of reinforcing self-exploration and problem solving as a part of the counseling process, and this would probably (although not certainly) fall under the modeling conception of the process. They differentiate between what they call the "naive perceptualist" and the "expert perceptualist." They describe the difference:

The naive perceptualist [refers] to the novice, the perceptually based (client-centered) counselor who makes no attempt to be selective in his use of empathy and respect. He is probably unaware of what behavior he is reinforcing: therefore, he may in fact reinforce self-defeating behavior in his clients.

The expert perceptualist is selective in his use of empathy and respect; therefore, he reinforces some client behaviors and fails to reinforce others....By responding to specific expressions of feelings and thoughts, he becomes selective in his reinforcement. (p. 205)

While this would certainly not be in accord with the client-centered viewpoint, it utilizes some client-centered qualities within the context of a different process conception of counseling.

VARIABLES OF THE COUNSELING PROCESS

In reality, there are only two variables in the entire counseling process: the counselor and the client. To learn about the process and to discuss it intelligently, we break down these two variables into subvariables, such as age, sex, race, background, motivation, personality, etc. Motivation is discussed at the beginning of this chapter, and race will be discussed in several other places.

One variable not yet mentioned is what Gendlin (1961) calls "experiencing." He describes it this way:

(1) Experiencing is *felt*, rather than thought, known, or verbalized. (2) Experiencing occurs in the *immediate* present. It is not generalized attributes of a person such as traits, complexes, or dispositions. Rather, experiencing is what a person feels here and now, in this moment. Experiencing is a changing flow of feeling which makes it possible for every individual to feel something any given moment. (p. 234)

Gendlin sees this variable as significant because it affects the client's ability to conceptualize, to change, and to grow.

Snyder and Snyder (1961) have undertaken a thorough analysis of variables in the counseling relationship that contribute substantially to the quality of the counseling process and to the results of counseling and psychotherapy. They found that an analysis in terms of transference, countertransference, and dreams revealed key dimensions of the counseling process in the relationship itself, but it seems that further study is necessary before any definite conclusions can be drawn.

THE HELPING DIMENSION

We can now focus more closely on the key facet of the entire counseling process: the helping dimension. Rogers (1961) lists the questions that circumscribe this dimension:

Can I *be* in some way which will be perceived by the other person as trustworthy, as dependable or consistent in some deep sense?...Can I be expressive enough as a person that what I am will be communicated unambiguously?...Can I let myself experience positive attitudes toward this other person?…Can I be strong enough as a person to be separate from the other?…Am I secure enough within myself to permit him his separateness?…Can I let myself enter fully into the world of his feelings and personal meanings and see these as he does?…Can I receive him as he is? (pp. 50–54)

The answers to these questions and several others like them lead Rogers to the "process conception" of therapy, which is discussed fully in chapter 9. This conception examines the various movements of the client toward growth as he experiences the facilitative communications of the counselor.

Carkhuff and Berenson (1967) speak of a "multidimensional model" of facilitative processes, comprising five levels, "with the lower levels being essentially commensurate with the description of the distressed client or retarding therapist, and the higher levels commensurate with the facilitative individual." The level 1 person is someone so unfamiliar with facilitative relationships that he is, for all practical purposes, untouched by such a relationship. The indication here is for long-term treatment. The level 2 person, slightly better, would require a moderately long treatment. Level 3 is the minimum level of acceptable functioning, and this type of person usually responds well to therapeutic encounters. Persons at levels 4 and 5 are even more facilitative and self-actualized, the latter being the level of cure after therapy. The principle that is important here is that "persons at higher levels of functioning can help persons at lower levels to achieve higher levels of functioning." The multidimensional model proposed by Carkhuff and Berenson consists of quantified levels, "process variables," that explicate the direction and degree of client change.

FACTORS AND DIRECTIONS OF CLIENT CHANGE

It is generally assumed that after participation in a counseling experience, some changes will take place in the client. There may be a change in behavior, a change in affect, a change in attitude, or some other change. The types of change desired and the general reasons for change have been the subject of much speculation and debate.

Kemp (1967) differentiates between two types of changes, phenotypical and genotypical:

Change may be phenotypical, having all the appearances of genuineness, but lacking any reorganization of values. It may also be genotypical, genuine change, which has resulted from a working through and reorganization of the individual's value system.… Change may commence by being phenotypical, a matter of expediency or the perceived necessity of conforming to the demands of another. But the values and behavior resulting from such introjection may be finally accepted on its own merits. At this point the individual engages in more integrative change. (p. 162)

We can say, moreover, that all meaningful change in the client must be meaningful *to* the client. While change can be imposed, it can never sustain unless it is accepted honestly and willingly by the client.

316

This leads us, however, to the problem that perennially puzzles counselors, counselor educators, and counseling researchers: How can change be measured? Usually such methods as personality tests, rating scales, self reports, and behavioral objectives are used for this purpose. We see from Kemp's comments above, however, that the mere measurement of change may not be enough; the important ingredient in change is not the change itself but the genuineness of the change.

Now let us turn our attention to a specialized form of the counseling process: group counseling.

GROUPS IN COUNSELING

Much of the counselor's time will typically be spent in conducting group counseling activities. If one surveys the wealth of research on the subject of group counseling, one is sure to notice a number of direct parallels to the literature on individual, face-to-face counseling: Between these two, there is a striking similarity of goals, processes, and rationales, with the chief difference being the reference to counselor/client or to leader/group. While this parallelism attests to the similar nature of the two endeavors, it belies the subtle differences between them. The group experience is a far more common, far more natural experience than the individual counseling experience. It fits unobtrusively into the normal school day pattern in which we interact with others in a variety of social, educational, and psychological situations. The counseling group, moreover, as a basic social unit, recapitulates other primary groups in which we interact: the family, the class, our peer groups, the scouts, religious groups, etc. With this in mind, let us explore the components of the group counseling experience.

WHY A GROUP?

Group counseling offers a number of general advantages over individual, face-to-face counseling. Moreover, there are a number of specific situations where the group counseling approach would be particularly indicated over the individual approach. In this section we shall examine the criteria for using the group approach over the face-to-face approach.

First, the group approach is more *economical* than the individual approach. This does not refer necessarily to the fiscal advantages—for the school counselor does not usually concern himself with these matters—but to economy in terms of the conservation of time, the counselor's most precious commodity. If in a typical school there is one counselor for every 800 students, and the counselor has 22 counseling office hours a week, then he would be able to see each student individually only once a year! This, certainly, would be unfair to those students who may need the assistance of the counselor several times a month. If, on the other hand, the same counselor uses the group approach, setting up small- to medium-sized groups (6 to 20), depending on the type of counseling required, he could see each student twice a month, rather than once a year, and still have six hours a week available for individual interviews. This is all theoretical, however, since many of the students do not want and do not require counseling. A more realistic analysis, based on the data I have acquired in my own research, shows that the counselor who relies primarily on the group approach is able to meet twice a week with every student who wants, needs, or is even vaguely interested in guidance or counseling, with still much time left over for individual interviews. This analysis is based on the size of the group, of course, which will be dealt with later in this chapter.

A second advantage of the group over the individual approach is that the group is more typical of social reality than is the individual, private counseling encounter. This has two important implications: It enables the group leader (the counselor) to study the patterns of the client's social interactions, and it facilitates the client's socialization. In the face-to-face encounter, while the counselor may learn a great deal about the client, he is never able to see the client as he engages in the social interactions that comprise a large part of his everyday existence. As the counselor is presented with a real life opportunity to study the client in his social milieu, he gains a more legitimate and relevant insight into the workings of the client's social side of his personality. This is especially important for clients whose problems are in part a result of social difficulties: the disruptive child, the shy and withdrawn child, the characterologically neurotic child, the aggressive child, etc. As we can see, this comprises a large percentage of the typical client population. The group experience facilitates socialization by enabling each group member to improve and refine his socializing techniques. The group experience is a part of social learning.

A third important advantage to the group over the individual approach is that the group, by bringing together many different people, with different backgrounds, personalities, and experiences, provides a reservoir of insights, perceptions, and emotional responses that a single counselor, no matter how skilled and experienced, could not possibly provide. This is certainly one of the chief therapeutic advantages of the group experience, and it may also be exploited in guidance groups, where learning and information, rather than personality reformulation, is the goal.

Within the context of the group experience, the client usually searches out responses which he intuitively knows are facilitative, or in some cases the counselor encourages such responses by group members for the benefit of a client. In an individual encounter, only the feelings, perceptions, and experiences of the counselor are available to the client, while in a group situation there exists a wider range of possibilities.

A fourth advantage of the group approach, particularly in the school, is that the group parallels more closely the classroom setting than does the face-to-face experience. Because the client is accustomed to functioning in a group experience, less resistance appears if he is placed in a counseling group than if he were extracted totally from the group situation and asked to interact in the counselor's office. This maintains a continuity of experience that is both healthy and productive.

Pascale (1968) has summed up many of the points discussed above to support his position that the counseling services can be enhanced through the utilization of group counseling. He points out that "the individual counseling service is both expensive and time consuming ... the 'desired' student counselor ratio of 300 to 1 does not allow an adequate amount of time for the important function of individual counseling." He suggests that group counseling programs be used in place of individual counseling, wherever possible. "The nature of group counseling," he suggests, "enables the counselor to counsel more students for longer periods of time."·

Of course, there are some disadvantages to the group experience, too. Some clients find it easier to speak in privacy than in front of their peers. Some regress in the group situation, repeating the difficult behavior patterns that indicated the need for counseling in the first place. The group experience cannot provide a single dynamic relationship of the intensity found in the individual experience. But all things being equal, the school counselor will most likely utilize the bulk of his time conducting group experiences, while leaving sufficient time to see those clients individually who require that type of treatment.

GROUP GOALS

Our basic concern here is with contractual groups (Egan, 1970). These groups have counseling goals that the client ideally should understand at the outset. Different writers have offered different conceptions of group goals, and we should examine some of these views to better understand the coherence of any given group experience.

The goals of a therapy group, for example, can always be stated in terms of curative objectives. What processes in the group experience will lead to the resolution of the difficulties which brought the members to the group in the first place? Corsini and Rosenberg (1955) cite nine curative factors at work in the successful group experience: acceptance, universalization, reality testing, altruism, transference, spectator therapy, interaction, intellectualization, and ventilation. Berzon et al. (1963) analyzed eighteen outpatients from two therapy groups, arriving at another nine curative factors that overlapped with Corsini's and Rosenberg's.

Yalom (1970) uses these and other studies (Talland and Clark, 1954; Dickoff and Lakin, 1963) to develop a comprehensive table of curative factors at work in a therapy group. These are indicated in terms of twelve basic categories (see Display 15.2), which constitute the objectives of the therapeutic group experience. From this comprehensive list, the differences among types of contractual groups may be readily appreciated. Guidance groups, for example, would emphasize factors 26–30 over the other factors. Sensitivity groups would emphasize factors 1–5, 16–20, and 56–60. Different types of groups may be defined in terms of the curative factors sought in the group experience.

display 15.2

CURATIVE FACTORS*

1 Altruism

RANK ORDER†

1 Helping others has given me more self-respect. — 40T (tie)
2 Putting others' needs ahead of mine. — 52T
3 Forgetting myself and thinking of helping others. — 37T
4 Giving part of myself to others. — 17
5 Helping others and being important in their lives. — 33T

2 Group cohesiveness

6 Belonging to and being accepted by a group. — 16
7 Continued close contact with other people. — 20T
8 Revealing embarrassing things about myself and still being accepted by the group. — 11T
9 Feeling alone no longer. — 37T
10 Belonging to a group of people who understood and accepted me. — 20T

3 Universality

11 Learning I'm not the only one with my type of problem; "We're all in the same boat." — 45T
12 Seeing that I was just as well off as others. — 25T
13 Learning that others have some of the same "bad" thoughts and feelings I do. — 40T
14 Learning that others had parents and backgrounds as unhappy or mixed up as mine. — 31T
15 Learning that I'm not very different from other people gave me a "welcome to the human race" feeling. — 33T

4 Interpersonal learning, "input"

RANK ORDER

16 The group's teaching me about the type of impression I make on others. — 5T
17 Learning how I come across to others. — 8
18 Other members honestly telling me what they think of me. — 3
19 Group members pointing out some of my habits or mannerisms that annoy other people. — 18T
20 Learning that I sometimes confuse people by not saying what I really think. — 13T

5 Interpersonal learning, "output"

21 Improving my skills in getting along with people. — 25T
22 Feeling more trustful of groups and of other people. — 10
23 Learning about the way I related to the other group members. — 13T
24 The group's giving me an opportunity to learn to approach others. — 27T
25 Working out my difficulties with one particular member in the group. — 33T

6 Guidance

26 The doctor's suggesting or advising something for me to do. — 27T
27 Group members suggesting or advising something for me to do. — 55
28 Group members telling me what to do. — 56
29 Someone in the group giving definite suggestions about a life problem. — 48T
30 Group members advising me to behave differently with an important person in my life. — 52T

†Some of the items are nearly identical, but it was convenient methodologically to have the same number of items representing each category. The twelve categories are: altruism; group cohesiveness; universality; interpersonal learning, "input"; interpersonal learning, "output"; guidance; catharsis; identification; family re-enactment; insight; instillation of hope; existential factors. They are not quite identical to those described in this book; we attempted, unsuccessfully, to divide interpersonal learning into two parts—input and output. The category "insight," poorly labeled, was included to permit examination of the importance of derepression and genetic insight. "Existential factors" was included at the suggestion of several colleagues.

*From *The Theory and Practice of Group Psychotherapy*, by Irvin D. Yalom. New York: Basic Books, Inc., 1970. Pp. 66–69. Reprinted by permission.

7 Catharsis	**RANK ORDER**
31 Getting things off my chest.	31T
32 Expressing negative and/or positive feelings toward another member.	5T
33 Expressing negative and/or positive feelings toward the group leader.	18T
34 Learning how to express my feelings.	4
35 Being able to say what was bothering me instead of holding it in.	2

8 Identification	
36 Trying to be like someone in the group who was better adjusted than I.	58
37 Seeing that others could reveal embarrassing things and take other risks and benefit from it helped me to do the same.	8
38 Adopting mannerisms or the style of another group member.	59
39 Admiring and behaving like my therapist.	57
40 Finding someone in the group I could pattern myself after.	60

9 Family re-enactment	
41 Being in the group was, in a sense, like reliving and understanding my life in the family in which I grew up.	51
42 Being in the group somehow helped me to understand old hang-ups that I had in the past with my parents, brothers, sisters, or other important people.	30
43 Being in the group was, in a sense, like being in a family, only this time a more accepting and understanding family.	44
44 Being in the group somehow helped me to understand how I grew up in my family.	45T
45 The group was something like my family—some members or the therapists being like my parents and others being like my relatives. Through the group experience I understand my past relationships with my parents and relatives (brothers, sisters, etc.).	48T

10 "Insight"	**RANK ORDER**
46 Learning that I have likes or dislikes for a person for reasons which may have little to do with the person and more to do with my hang-ups or experiences with other people in my past.	15
47 Learning why I think and feel the way I do (i.e., learning some of the causes and sources of my problems).	11T
48 Discovering and accepting previously unknown or unacceptable parts of myself.	1
49 Learning that I react to some people or situations unrealistically (with feelings that somehow belong to earlier periods in my life).	20T
50 Learning that how I feel and behave today is related to my childhood and development (there are reasons in my early life why I am as I am).	50

11 Instillation of hope	
51 Seeing others getting better was inspiring to me.	42T
52 Knowing others had solved problems similar to mine.	37T
53 Seeing that others had solved problems similar to mine.	33T
54 Seeing that other group members improved encouraged me.	27T
55 Knowing that the group had helped others with problems like mine encouraged me.	45T

12 Existential factors	
56 Recognizing that life is at times unfair and unjust.	54
57 Recognizing that ultimately there is no escape from some of life's pain and from death.	42T
58 Recognizing that no matter how close I get to other people, I must still face life alone.	23T
59 Facing the basic issues of my life and death, and thus living my life more honestly and being less caught up in trivialities.	23T
60 Learning that I must take ultimate responsibility for the way I live my life no matter how much guidance and support I get from others.	5T

display 15.3

USE OF DIFFERENT GROUPS IN SCHOOL SITUATIONS

type of problem	therapy group	discussion group	training group	guidance group
Student underachievement	X			X
Helping teachers learn to deal with disciplinary problems in the classroom		X	X	
Resolving racial tensions in the school		X		X
Helping students confront their occupational choices		X		X
Working with the emotionally disturbed teacher or student	X			
Helping teachers develop counseling skills		X	X	X

Display 15.3 shows how different types of groups may be used together in the school situation. Utilizing a combination of group dynamics, therapy groups, discussion groups, training groups, and guidance groups, the counselor can maximize the possibilities of enhancing the student's educational experiences.

GROUP GUIDANCE

Group guidance includes informational services and objective discussion of various role difficulties. "The primary goal of group guidance," Parks (1973) suggests, "is to prevent and ameliorate the development of problems rather than just remediation of existing problems, which differentiates group guidance from group counseling and group therapy." The content of group guidance, Parks goes on to point out, is primarily information: information about educational programs, about jobs, and outside-of-school activities. Rothney (1972) offers seven justifications for group guidance:

1 Imparting of information not available from other sources.
2 Providing opportunity to recognize and discuss common problems which are met in making educational, vocational and personal choices.
3 Giving students an opportunity to practice the acceptance of responsibility for their own learning in group situations.
4 Learning to use democratic process in reaching common goals.
5 Developing interpersonal relationships which will help in group situations in the future.
6 Providing students and counselors with information which may be useful in the counseling situation.
7 Establishing relationships between students and counselors which create a demand for, and facilitate, counseling services. (p. 93)

We see from Rothney's seven rationales (objectives) how the diverse elements of practical counseling synthesize naturally within the group guidance context. Group guidance is a method through which the counselor economically accomplishes many of the goals of practical counseling.

THE GROUP LEADER'S JOB

In broad terms, the job of the group leader is the same as the job of the counselor in individual, face-to-face counseling. Several remarks are in order, however, to show just how this job is accomplished within the group setting.

One problem the group counselor faces is getting together enough individuals to form a group. Sometimes the group is formed to accommodate people with a common problem; sometimes it is limited by the client population of the school. Hyman Spotnitz (1961), a psychoanalytic group leader, describes his approach to forming a group:

In forming a group, I put together persons who will be able to develop intense emotional reactions to each other. The sexes get equal representation. The patients are usually alike in some respects and different in others. Divergence in personality structure blended with reasonably compatible backgrounds ... usually make it possible for group members to relate well to each other and to function efficiently as a unit. With diverse personalities represented, interchanges go on among the calm, the excitable, those who easily arouse excitement, and others who tend to check it. As they stimulate each other in different ways, group process is mobilized.

A second situation particularly applicable to the group setting is maintaining order and continuity in the face of anxiety and tension. Several individuals functioning as a group can be more untoward and refractory than a single individual, no matter what his resistances. The group leader must work toward a positive group attitude by demonstrating to the group members the security that is present in the group situation.

Finally, the group leader, like the individual counselor, must be a facilitator.

Carl Rogers (1971), an innovator in encounter group practices, describes his way of facilitating the group experience:

I tend to open a group in an extremely unstructured way, perhaps with no more than a single comment: "I suspect we will know each other a great deal better at the end of these group sessions than we do now...." I listen as carefully and as sensitively as I am able.... I wish very much to make the climate psychologically safe for the individual—I have found that it "pays off" to live with the group exactly where it is. Thus I have worked with a group of very inhibited top-notch scientists, mostly in the physical sciences, where feelings were rarely expressed openly, and personal encounter at a deep level was simply not seen. Yet this group became much more free and innovative, and showed many positive results of our meetings.... I am willing for a participant to commit himself to the group.... I am willing to accept silence and muteness in the individual, providing I am quite certain it is not unexpressed pain or resistance.... I tend to accept statements at their face value.... I try to make clear that whatever happens will happen from the choices of the group.... When talk is generalized or intellectualizing, I tend to select the self-referent meanings to respond to out of this total context. (pp. 275–278)

We see how Rogers's approach toward group leadership is both a reflection of his personality and of his theoretical orientation. A gestalt group leader would use vastly different types of techniques, involving preassigned actions and specific behavior by the group members (Mintz, 1971). These gestalt "games" are designed to facilitate growth within the group but in a manner that is incompatible with the Rogerian stance.

SUMMARY

In this chapter we examined the counseling process, looking at goals and expectations, factors that affect the process, the helping dimension of the process, client change, and group counseling. Two important points might be noted: (1) although there are different conceptions of the counseling process, it is generally agreed that the *helping relationship* is the crux of the process; (2) the goals of counseling, whether individual or group, influence such other factors as technique, counselor response, and curative criteria.

References

Asbury, F. R., & Winston, R. B. Reinforcing self-exploration and problem solving. *The School Counselor*, 1974, *21*, 204–209.

Benjamin, A. *The helping interview*. Boston: Houghton Mifflin, 1969.

Berzon, B., Pious, C., & Parson, R. The therapeutic event in group psychotherapy: A study of subjective reports by group members. *Journal of Individual Psychology*, 1963, *19*, 204–212.

Boy, A. V. Motivating elementary school pupils to seek counseling. *Elementary School Guidance and Counseling*, 1974, *8*, 166–172.

Carkhuff, R. R., & Berenson, B. G. *Beyond counseling and therapy*. New York: Holt, Rinehart & Winston, 1967.

Combs, A. W., et al. *Florida studies in the helping professions*. Gainesville: University of Florida Press, 1969.

Corsini, R., & Rosenberg, B. Mechanisms of group psychotherapy: Processes and dynamics. *Journal of Abnormal and Social Psychology*, 1955, *51*, 406–411.

Curran, C. A. *Counseling and psychotherapy.* New York: Sheed & Ward, 1968.

Dickoff, H., & Lakin, M. Patients' views of group psychotherapy. *International Journal of Group Psychotherapy,* 1963, *13*, 61–73.

Egan, G. *Encounter: Group processes for interpersonal growth.* Belmont, Calif.: Brooks/Cole, 1970.

Gendlin, E. T. Experiencing: A variable in the process of therapeutic change. *American Journal of Psychotherapy,* 1961, *16*, 233–245.

Gibb, J. R. The counselor as a role free person. In C. A. Parker (Ed.), *Counseling theories and counselor education.* Boston: Houghton Mifflin, 1968.

Kemp, C. G. *Intangibles in counseling.* Boston: Houghton Mifflin, 1967.

Lewis, E. C. *The psychology of counseling.* New York: Holt, Rinehart & Winston, 1970.

Mahoney, S. C. *The art of helping people effectively.* New York: Association Press, 1967.

Mintz, E. E. *Marathon groups: reality and symbol.* New York: Appleton-Century-Crofts, 1971.

Parks, J. C. Group guidance—a perspective. In D. Brown & D. J. Srebalus (Eds.), *Selected readings in contemporary guidance.* Dubuque, Iowa: Wm. C. Brown, 1973.

Pascale, A. C. Enhancing the counseling services through the utilization of group counseling. *The School Counselor,* 1968, *16*, 136–139.

Perez, J. F. *The initial counseling contact.* Boston: Houghton Mifflin, 1968.

Poole, A. Counselor judgment and counseling evaluation. *Journal of Counseling Psychology,* 1957, *4*, 37–40.

Rogers, C. R. A theory of therapy, personality, and interpersonal relationships, as developed in the client-centered framework. In S. Koch (Ed.), *Psychology: A study of a science* (Vol. 3), *Formulations of the person and the social context.* New York: McGraw-Hill, 1959.

Rogers, C. R. *On becoming a person.* Boston: Houghton Mifflin, 1961.

Rogers, C. R. Facilitating encounter groups. *American Journal of Nursing,* 1971, *71*, 275–279.

Rothney, J. W. *Adaptive counseling in schools.* Englewood Cliffs, N.J.: Prentice-Hall, 1972.

Shoben, E. J., Jr. The counseling experience as personal development. *Personnel and Guidance Journal,* 1965, *44*, 224–230.

Snyder, W. V., & Snyder, B. J. *The psychotherapy relationship.* New York: Macmillan, 1961.

Spotnitz, H. *The couch and the circle.* New York: Knopf, 1961.

Talland, D., & Clark, G. Evaluation of topics in therapy group discussion. *Journal of Clinical Psychology,* 1954, *10*, 131–137.

White, R. W. The concept of a healthy personality: What do we really mean? *The Counseling Psychologist,* 1973, *4* (2), 3–12.

Yalom, I. D. *The theory and practice of group psychotherapy.* New York: Basic Books, 1970.

chapter sixteen

Crisis intervention counseling

Crisis intervention is to counseling what first aid is to medicine—a temporary but immediate relief for an emergency situation presented by an incapacitated client. Like first-aid procedures, crisis intervention procedures are usually specific and clear-cut, and the counselor should have more than a nodding acquaintanceship with them.

The first and foremost problem of crisis counseling is the same problem one encounters in first-aid treatment: the sudden unexpectedness of the situation. *Be prepared!* The Boy Scout's motto is an appropriate slogan for this type of situation. Because the counselor is never entirely ready for a crisis situation, because he does not expect it to happen, there is an immediate unconscious tendency to want to escape the situation instead of confronting it head on. Obviously, this is not to the client's advantage and should be avoided at all costs. In this chapter we shall explore a variety of techniques and insights that the counselor may find helpful in dealing with crisis situations, and we shall examine a segment of a crisis intervention session conducted by a skilled counselor.

Recent literature has discussed a variety of applications of crisis counseling principles. Levy (1965) has discussed a community clinic geared toward dealing with crisis situations. McCarthy and Berman (1971) report on a student-operated crisis center, which should be of interest to the high-school counselor, and Strickler (1965) has a lucid presentation of the application of crisis counseling theory in a community clinic situation. Schmitz and Mickelson (1972) have attempted to evaluate the efficacy of Rogerian methods in telephone crisis counseling, but they are inconclusive in their results. Argles and Mackenzie (1970) present a case study in which crisis intervention is used in the family counseling setting. Our task is to explore in some depth the meaning of crisis and the strategies the counselor can use in dealing with it.

WHAT IS A CRISIS?

The type of crisis to which we are referring in this chapter is determined by its external symptoms. All of us, at some time in our lives, have witnessed or experienced crisis situations—loss of a loved one, drug induced crisis, inability to cope with life situations, a family crisis, an interpersonal crisis with one we love or care about, and so on. When a crisis reaches the stage where it immobilizes us and prevents us from consciously controlling ourselves, then it becomes the type of crisis for which people seek treatment. Brockopp (1973) explores the dynamics of this kind of crisis:

When a person is confronted by a problem situation in which the previously used methods of restructuring his life or environment are either not available to him or not successful in his solving the problem, the person is confronted by a critical situation, that is, one in

327

which he is uncertain about the end or resolution of the problem. Since he is unable, through the use of his normal problem-solving techniques, to resolve the difficulty with which he is faced, the critical situation is emotionally hazardous and he may rapidly move toward a state of crisis.... A crisis then is an intolerable situation which must be resolved, for it has the potential to cause the psychosocial deterioration of the person. (p. 74)

The critical quality of a crisis, then, is the person's inability to deal with it. In this sense, a crisis is a subjective experience. What may be a mildly difficult situation to one person may be a crisis to another. Evaluation of the seriousness of the crisis, as well as diagnostic and prognostic considerations, are not determined by the situation itself but by the individual's response to the situation. Brockopp is sensitive to this subtle point of differentiation:

The crisis ... is not the situation itself, but the person's response to the situation. And the person's response is initially ambivalence and uncertainty, not knowing where he is relative to the problem or what he needs to do or can do to solve the problem and return to a point of equilibrium or homeostasis. (p. 76)

The implication of this statement is that what the person needs is some type of structured orientation suggesting how to go about solving his problem. And, indeed, one of the chief difficulties of the crisis situation is the individual's feeling of disorientation—of not being able to "get hold of himself."

Bloom (1963) has attempted to clarify the contextual definition of what constitutes a crisis by focusing in on the client's awareness or lack of awareness of the precipitating event and by the anticipated length of time required for recovery. In true crisis situations, the client is often unable to specify what brought about the crisis, and it may require several months for this fundamental question to be accurately explored.

Caplan (1964), like Brockopp, views the crisis in terms of intrapsychic disequilibrium: "The normal consistency of pattern, or equilibrium, is maintained by homeostatic reequilibrating mechanisms, so that temporary deviations from the pattern call into operation opposing forces which automatically bring the pattern back to its previous state" (p. 38). In a crisis situation, the reequilibrating forces are unsuccessful within the usual time range.

Forer (1963) differentiates between three levels of crisis: a situational crisis brought about by a sudden change in the environment; an intrapsychic conflict crisis between the ego and superego (crisis of values); or a disintegration of the ego. A crisis of grief caused by the loss of a loved one is typical of the first type. A sexual crisis in which one's deepest values are challenged is the second type. An ego-fragmenting drug trip induced by a hallucinogen is an example of the third type. The three types will be explored more closely later in this chapter.

Although the fundamentals of the crisis situation are adequately described by this conception, there are a number of different types of crises. Lindemann (1944), in an often cited paper, describes the crisis of acute grief. Family crisis situations have been described by Klein and Lindemann (1961). Suicide crisis,

the most commonly investigated class of crises, has been explored by Lester and Brockopp (1973). Drug crisis, a painfully prevalent problem in our time, has been discussed by Foreman and Zerwekh (1971), among others. Bieber (1972) has presented an interesting analysis of sexual crisis, a topic of increasing importance in crisis counseling. All these will be discussed in the following section.

THE COUNSELOR AND THE CRISIS

While we do not generally associate the term *contagious* with psychological states, there is considerable evidence that the concept is applicable to particularly turbulent psychic states—such as the state of crisis. No doubt when the counselor first comes into contact with the extremely agitated and fomenting client in crisis, he will, if he is not careful, begin to experience parallel crisis feelings of his own. Just as laughing is infectious (as anyone who has gone to a

Broadway comedy knows), so are crisis and grief in the sense that one can experience another's feelings during difficult times.

If the counselor catches the client's turbulent and disorganized feelings, he will most likely be ineffective in helping the client get a grip on himself, and possibly even be unable to function altogether. Direct observations have shown repeatedly that the counselor who catches the crisis feelings becomes frightened and defensive. The first manifestation of this is his hasty and ill-timed attempts to assure the client that nothing is really the matter, that things will work themselves out. Although such assurance may seem to the counselor to be what the client needs, in fact it is reassurance for the counselor rather than the client.

A good rule for the counselor to remember is this: Do not try to reassure the client that everything is all right, for every time the counselor does so, unless the client specifically asks for reassurance, the counselor is actually reassuring himself, defending his own anxiety, isolating himself from the client's feelings.

What, then, should the counselor do when confronted unexpectedly by a client in a state of crisis? Probably the most significant help the counselor can offer at the outset is to remain calm, poised, and well in control of himself. Then, the client will be able to begin to relate to him on a constructive level.

The maintenance of a calming attitude serves two distinct purposes. First, it enables the counselor to function effectively, to allow the desperate client full expression of his fears and conflicts, to listen to these expressions without severe censorship, to empathize with the client even when the empathic feelings are difficult for the counselor himself to deal with. If we view crisis as the failure of the psychological balancing (regulating) mechanism, it is easy to understand how the counselor's stability—his granite certainty—helps the client to reestablish his psychic balance. Kalis et al. (1961) offer a picture of the crisis state which clarifies this conception. Arguing from the psychiatric position, they point out,

Psychiatric theory pictures the mental apparatus of an individual continuously maintaining and reestablishing its stability after disturbances by external and internal stimuli. This process is achieved through the utilization of various coping mechanisms and defensive maneuvers. When this stabilizing process fails, a type of emergency state arises. Anxiety which represents repetition of early traumatic states appears.... The concept of precipitating stress envisions an individual as moving from some previously achieved level of adoption, emotional equilibrium or integration, with the stress into disequilibrium. An event or series of events reactivates a psychic conflict; it is the interaction of event and conflict which is stressful and leads to the request for psychiatric help. (pp. 219–220)

We can see from this dynamic picture of the crisis state why the counselor's calmness, strength, and certainty of orientation enable the client once again to regain his psychic equilibrium, which is necessary before he can deal adequately with his problems.

A second factor also plays a part here. Just as emotionally turbulent feelings are contagious, very calming and relaxing feelings can also be induced from one person to another. How many times have we come into the presence of a calm and relaxed person and begun to feel that calmness and relaxation in ourselves? The counselor's calmness serves as an emotional tranquilizer, slowly helping the client to pull himself together.

To remain calm in the turbulence of the client's stormy emotions, however, is often no easy matter. If the counselor has foreknowledge of the crisis to come (or of the client's visit), he can prepare himself for the task at hand. But more often than not, particularly in the school counseling setting, the client's visit comes as a complete surprise to the counselor, who may or may not be emotionally ready for it. Even before the client says a word, the counselor unconsciously senses the crisis in the client's expression. I can remember many instances where I have seen a person looking highly distressed, and even before he says a word, I am ready to ask "What happened?"

In such a case, when the counselor is not ready for the client and has not had an opportunity to compose himself, the counselor should ask the client to sit down and then excuse himself for a moment. "Have a seat. I'll be with you in a minute," is a fine therapeutic intervention both for the client who is excited and for the counselor who is expected to help him. This pause reduces the anxiety and allows the counselor an opportunity to prepare himself for the highly emotional confrontation which is to ensue.

The next step, and probably the most important, is to encourage the client into a dialogue. For the client to receive help at this critical time, it is necessary above all else that he be able to communicate his feelings and his difficulties to the counselor. While the specifics of the dialogue will depend heavily on the precipitating trauma, Rapoport (1962) has outlined three patterns of responses that lead to a healthy crisis resolution:

1 Correct cognitive perception of the situation, which is furthered by seeking new knowledge and by keeping the problem in consciousness.
2 Management of affect through awareness of feelings; an appropriate verbalization leading toward tension discharge and mastery.
3 Development of patterns of seeking and using help with actual tasks and feelings by using interpersonal and institutional resources. (p. 216)

Just which of these three will be utilized and in which specific way depends on the client, his condition, and the particulars of the crisis-producing situation. Let us consider four types of individual crises that the counselor is likely to encounter and see what we can determine about the course of each one.

GRIEF CRISIS

Certainly one of the most common situations is the crisis of grief. A loved one has died—either unexpectedly or after a long illness—and the person is unable to manage his feelings and to get a grip on himself in this difficult and painful situation. The client might wish to talk about his memories of the deceased, possibly about how he never was as good to the deceased as he should have been, about how the deceased enjoyed life and deserved to live, or about how unjust the world is. The counselor listens and tries to experience the client's painful feelings along with him. The death may have been recent or some time ago. "The duration of a grief reaction," Lindemann (1944) points out,

> seems to depend upon the success with which a person does the *grief work*, namely, emancipation from the bondage to the deceased, readjustment to the environment in which the deceased is missing, and the formation of new relationships. One of the big obstacles to this work seems to be the fact that many patients try to avoid the intense distress connected with the grief experience and to avoid the expression of emotion necessary for it. (p. 143)

The task of the counselor, in this case, is to help the client get through the "grief work." The counselor must recognize that the client's disorientation and confusion is caused by his inability to deal with himself and with the world without the presence of the deceased other. The client is, in Lindemann's words, "in bondage" to the deceased. To free him from this bondage, the counselor must be willing to experience along with the client the profound sense of loneliness and isolation that follows the initial mourning, the feelings of guilt and responsibility that plague the survivor. To do this, the counselor, of course, must have his own feelings well in control.

FAMILY CRISIS

A second type of common crisis situation is the family crisis. Usually a family crisis has been a long time in the making, and it is only when it reaches a head and becomes totally intolerable that the family members (or a single member, in many cases) seek professional help. The counselor should assess the full situation carefully before attempting any intervention because he wants to avoid being accused of siding with one member or one faction over others. This requires the skill of a therapist and the tact of a diplomat, and the counselor should be aware when he is treading on dangerous ground. Klein and Lindemann (1961) offer four stages for planning the interventions which are appropriate in family crisis situations:

1 Appraisal of the predicament—Attempts are made to mobilize the ego resources of the client by enlisting him in assessing the problem.
2 Planning the intervention—The extent to which the crisis exists, potential or actual impact on client and others in his social orbit, and the strengths and resources of the people involved must be recognized.
3 Altering the balance of forces—Restoration of reasonably healthy equilibrium in the social orbit, and redefining and clarifying the predicament.
4 Resolving the crisis and anticipatory planning service continues to be available ... review of progress and resolution, some follow-up. (pp. 287–293)

These four stages are logical, viable steps to helping the client caught in the midst of a family crisis. We note that they are based on the balance of forces theory—that a crisis is a loss of homeostasis, when some forces outweigh others and slip out of control. These stages represent organizing layers of bringing the forces back into check.

ANXIETY CRISIS

The third type of common crisis situation is termed the anxiety crisis. In this situation, the client is in a state of high anxiety and turmoil, usually uncertain of exactly what it is that has precipitated this feeling. Drugs, particularly hallucinogenic drugs, are a common cause of this type of crisis, although certainly the counselor should not assume that such a crisis is caused by drugs until he has adequately explored this possibility with the client. The best rule of thumb in an anxiety crisis is to ask the client object-oriented questions. These are questions of fact or circumstance that do not infringe upon the client's ego domain. "What time did you leave for school today?" and "How old are you?" and "When did these feelings begin to bother you?" are object-oriented questions. If a drug is suspected, the counselor should learn from the client what drug was ingested, how much, and when, to determine whether medical attention is needed. Obtain a thorough drug history to assess patterns of drug use, which will prove important during the therapeutic and rehabilitative stages of the treatment.

Object-oriented questions have a calming effect upon the anxiety client because they compel him to reorganize his thinking so he can respond logically to stimuli from the external world (the counselor's questions). As the client focuses his attention upon these factual questions, he begins to reexperience his logical awareness of the world. Asking object-oriented questions is one of many ways to help the client reestablish his psychic balance.

Foreman and Zerwekh (1971) have suggested establishing feelings of rapport to help the victim of a drug crisis. If the client feels he is able to speak freely to the counselor, it will better enable him to "come down" from his bad trip.

Bieber (1972) has discussed some of the methods for handling homosexual crises, resulting from overwhelming ego-dystonic feelings of homosexual panic. Tayal (1972) has examined the level of suggestibility in crisis states and found that the suggestibility of girls who were pregnant out of wedlock was significantly higher than a control group.

SUICIDAL CRISIS

The last, and most difficult, crisis we shall discuss is the suicidal crisis. In this situation the client expresses to the counselor either a specific or a vague intention of committing suicide. Usually such a client is suffering from a feeling of overwhelming hopelessness and futility, the belief that nothing can help him, nothing can make a difference. He feels closed in, confined in an unbearable situation from which there is no escape. The fact that he is speaking to someone about this feeling does indicate he wants help, but it is a serious error to assume that because he wants help he is not serious about his suicidal intentions. The case books are rife with tragic examples of successful suicides committed shortly after an interview with a psychiatrist or counselor (Marilyn Monroe is a good example of this).

In dealing with the suicidal client, the counselor must be willing to listen to him and suffer with him. This is indeed a difficult thing for the counselor to do. But it is absolutely necessary that the counselor experience along with the client his feelings of total despair and hopelessness, his sense of futility and isolation, his feelings of abject grief and failure, his rage directed both at himself and at the world. The very worst thing the counselor can do is to tell the client that things are not as bad as they seem, that things will improve, that he has plenty of reasons to go on living. Although realistically all these statements may be true, they make the client feel that he is not understood by the counselor, and they reinforce his feelings of isolation from the people around him. For the counselor truly to help the client, he must fully experience the reality from the client's hopeless perspective.

Experience and research have come up with a number of helpful rules in dealing with the suicidal client. It is generally a good idea to ascertain whether the method of destruction has been arrived at. "How do you intend to kill yourself?" the counselor may ask. The more specific the client's plans, the closer he is to carrying out the act. Second, it is not advisable to have the client "look at the bright side" of the situation; if the client could accept a bright picture emotionally, he would not be in this predicament in the first place. Third, always take all suicidal threats seriously. Many a counselor has had deep regrets after dismissing a serious suicide threat as an immature bid for attention.

The following section from a transcript of a counseling interview conducted between a skilled counselor (Bob) and a suicidal client illustrate some of the better ways of handling this type of situation.

Counselor (13). Do you feel you can speak about it?
Client (13). There's nothing to tell. It's just not worth it, man. Like I believe we each have a right to live or die, and that it's my choice. I just can't take it anymore. If I can't have her I don't want to live. There is nothing else.
Counselor (14). You love her very much, don't you?
Client (14). (Laughs hysterically, out of control.) Love her! I love her so much I could kill her. I love her more than anything—more than God, more than my family, more than myself. I can't go on, Bob. It's just not worth it. If I'm dead, I won't have to think about it—that's why.
Counselor (15). How are you going to do it?
Client (15). With the car. I'll crash it at 70 into a wall. I'm just gonna drive and drive until I have the guts to do it—then whammo! Right into the fucking

wall. *(Laughs hysterically.)* You call her up, Bob, you tell her. You tell her what she did to me. Let her know.

Counselor (16). There is no one like her, is there? I mean is there a chance, even, of finding someone else?

Client (16). *(Laughs hysterically.)* No, Bob, no way out. I wish. But there's only her, Bob. You met her—you know. She was *the one*—the one for me and I blew it. Now, what's left—fifty years of pain and suffering—a lifetime of looking back at what could have been? It's not for me. I couldn't take it.

Counselor (17). Can you take it for another two days? Can you stand the pain for that long?

Client (17). Why? You think I'll get over it in a couple of days? You're kidding yourself. It you're trying to tell me she'll come back, Bob, you're not kidding me. I know what the score is. She told me.

Counselor (18). No, I don't think any of those things. I see what the situation is, and I don't know what to say. But suicide's a big decision, a final one, and I think we should at least talk about it again before you go ahead. I'm not going to stop you—I'm not going to feed you a line about how things will work out. I just want *us both* to be sure. I'd like to see you Friday—just to talk about it one more time. If you want to go ahead then … I won't stop you. I don't feel I have a right.

Client (18). Friday. That's two more days of this. I don't know if I can hold on till then.

Counselor (19). If you don't think you can, call me. I'll see you before then. I just want to discuss it once more before you make the big move. Of course, the final decision is up to you—but I'd like to talk to you first.

Client (19). OK. Let's make it Friday. But if I can't hold out till then, I'll call you. Can I call at home?

Counselor (20). Of course. Any time....

The skill of the counselor shines through these few brief lines of interaction. Note what he did and did not do. He never tried to convince the client that things really weren't that bad, that he would find another girl friend. Certainly if the client were able to understand and appreciate such a realistic assessment, he would not be contemplating suicide in the first place. The counselor did allow the client to express his fantasies of self destruction and inquired as to the means of this act. In this way he was able to assess the client's determination to carry out what he had threatened. The counselor did not ask the client to give up his suicidal plans but just to postpone them for a couple of days to give the two of them a chance to discuss them again. "The final decision is up to you," he told the client (Counselor (19), assuring the client that he would not attempt to dissuade him from his plans. The counselor joined the client in his fantasy and emotionally understood the hopelessness and pain of the client's predicament. Everything he said to the client, everything he communicated both verbally and nonverbally, he actually felt in a manner parallel to the way the client felt it. To treat the client, it is always necessary for the counselor to feel the full force of the client's depression. Display 16.1 shows some of the more important *do's* and *dont's* of crisis counseling, extracted both from the literature and from the writer's personal experience in this area.

CONCLUSIONS AND IMPLICATIONS

The state of crisis is characterized by a loss of orientation, a disequilibrium of the intrapsychic forces, and profound feelings of confusion, alienation, disruption, and panic. When the crisis client presents himself to the counselor, he exhibits an emotional turbulence that may inadvertently be induced in the counselor, in the manner of contagion. The counselor must, to be effective at such times, remain calm and poised. The therapeutic phase of the treatment depends upon the nature of the specific crisis: In a crisis brought about by grief, the counselor must help the client get through the grief work; in a family crisis, the counselor must help the client understand the nature of the family crisis; in an anxiety crisis, the counselor must determine the source of the problem and use object-oriented questions to help the client come to grips with it; in a suicidal crisis, the counselor must allow the client full expression of his feelings, determine if a method of destruction has been arrived at, experience the hopelessness along with the client, and request a temporary postponement of his plans.

In all these cases, the counselor must be willing (and emotionally stable enough!) to experience along with the client the fears and frustrations that inevitably accompany a crisis situation. He must react empathically and honestly but with enough self-control and emotional detachment to avoid becoming overwhelmed by the imbroglio of the crisis.

References

Argles, P., & Mackenzie, M. Crisis intervention with a multiproblem family: A case study. *Journal of Child Psychology and Psychiatry and Allied Disciplines*, 1970, *17*, 187–195.

Bieber, I. Homosexual dynamics in psychiatric crisis. *American Journal of Psychiatry*, 1972, *128*, 1268–1272.

Bloom, B. L. Definitional aspects of the crisis concept. *Journal of Consulting Psychology*, 1963, *27*, 498–502.

Brockopp, G. W. Crisis intervention: Theory, process and practice. In D. Lester & G. W. Brockopp (Eds.), *Crisis intervention and counseling by telephone*. Springfield, Ill.: Charles C. Thomas, 1973.

Caplan, G. *Principles of preventive psychiatry*. New York: Basic Books, 1964.

Foreman, N. J., & Zerwekh, J. V. Drug crisis intervention. *American Journal of Nursing*, 1971, *71*, 1736–1739.

Forer, B. R. The therapeutic value of crisis. *Psychological Reports*, 1963, *13*, 275–281.

Kalis, B. L., Harris, R. M., Prestwood, R. A., & Freeman, E. H. Precipitating stress as a focus in psychotherapy. *Archives of General Psychiatry*, 1961, *5*, 219–228.

Klein, D. C., & Lindemann, E. Preventive intervention in individual and family crisis situations. In G. Caplan (Ed.), *Prevention of mental disorders in children*. New York: Basic Books, 1961.

Lester, D., & Brockopp, G. W. (Eds.), *Crisis intervention and counseling by telephone*. Springfield, Ill.: Charles C. Thomas, 1973.

Levy, R. A. A crisis oriented community clinic. *Mental Hospitals*, 1965, *16*, 336–338.

Lindemann, E. Symptomatology and management of acute grief. *American Journal of Psychiatry*, 1944, *101*, 141–148.

McCarthy, B., & Berman, A. C. A student operated crisis center. *Personal and Guidance Journal*, 1971, *49*, 523–528.

Rapoport, L. The state of crisis: Some theoretical considerations. *Social Service Review*, 1962, *36*, 211–217.

Schmitz, M. B., & Mickelson, D. J. Hot line drug counseling and Rogerian methods. *Personnel and Guidance Journal*, 1972, *50*, 357–362.

Strickler, M. Applying crisis theory in a community clinic. *Social Casework*, 1965, *46*, 150–154.

Tayal, Shanti. *Suggestibility in a state of crisis*. (Doctoral dissertation, University of Maryland, 1972.) Ann Arbor, Mich.: University Microfilms.

PART FIVE

Peter Schwarzburg

Specialized counseling services and applications

"Practical counseling," as the name implies and as I have suggested throughout this text, comprises a variety of counseling applications ranging from the deeply personal exploratory interview to the more mundane, and yet equally significant, tasks of providing information to students, consulting with teachers, meeting with parents, organizing school activities, administering and interpreting tests, organizing and conducting group activities, and so on. In this part of the book, we shall examine some of these specialized counseling services—the staple product of the counseling function—to see exactly how the practical counselor works and to understand the rationale behind his multifaceted actions.

Chapters 17 and 18, "Youth and the Drug Culture" and "Human Sexuality in the Counseling Milieu," examine two of the areas of practical counseling that have become particularly important in recent years. The widespread drug abuse problem that haunts the corridors of almost every school needs no introduction. The counselor is hard pressed to cope with this refractory problem, and this chapter is designed to offer a few insights, a little knowledge, and some suggestions for further study. The counselor's role in sex education, which falls into the category of preventive (educational) counseling, will be explored from the practical, rather than the theoretical, point of view. We will consider both the elementary and the secondary school situation, along with some specific examples of sex education dialogue between the counselor and clients.

Chapters 19 and 20, "Counseling for Constructive Social Change" and "Appraisal, Consultation, and Team Counseling," examine the counselor's full social responsibility and ways in which the execution of that responsibility can be facilitated. Such contemporary problems as counseling minority group clients and working effectively with the female client will be given attention. We shall also look at some constructive ways in which the counselor can work effectively with the community. The counseling team—including the counselor, the teacher, the parent, the school psychologist, medical personnel, and others—is a useful concept in our search for counseling models that are viable and efficient.

In chapter 20 we shall see how the counselor, through his consultative and cooperative efforts with others, geometrically increases his effectiveness for the benefit of the client, school, and community. Moreover, we shall explore ways in which the appraisal service can be used to support his efforts.

Chapter 21, "Counseling in the Classroom," will discuss methods by which the teacher can carry out the counseling function in the classroom. Theories of moral and intellectual development will be presented, with special emphasis on Bertrand Russell's view of education as the synthesis of moral and intellectual growth. Some practical suggestions, designed to enable the teacher to be a facilitator of emotional growth, will be presented.

The concluding chapter in this part of the book, "Vocational, Educational, and Leisure-Time Counseling," will address itself to a very important part of the counselor's function. We shall look at some of the more important theories of career development and vocational choice and consider how the use of information can contribute to the student's growth and development. Leisure-time counseling, through which the client learns to use his free time constructively, will be introduced as an important, developing field of counseling.

chapter seventeen

Youth and the drug culture

One of the more serious and pervasive problems facing the school counselor in these times is the widespread misuse of mind drugs by school-age youth. Much has been written about this problem, and the government has spent large sums of money to combat drug abuse; yet the problem persists. One of the more tragic aspects of this problem is the way drug abuse patterns have expanded cancerously during the past few years: from a relative confinement in a few inner-city schools to the entire range of all schools in city and suburb; from high schools, to junior high schools, to elementary schools; from a few classes or delinquent cliques in each school to the general school population. In this chapter we shall examine the role of the school counselor in fighting the drug problem and present information that should prove helpful to the counselor in understanding the problem and in effectively dealing with the young people involved. See Appendix I for a glossary of commonly used drug culture terms.

HISTORICAL BACKGROUND

During the past few years, the drug problem has grown to epidemic proportions in the United States. A wide range of readily available mind-affecting drugs is a twentieth-century phenomenon. From the beginnings of civilization, however, men have used mind-affecting drugs to alter their moods and change their states of consciousness. References to the use of opium, a narcotic (from a Greek word meaning "to benumb") are found in the writings of Hippocrates, the father of medicine, who recommended the drug for a variety of medicinal purposes. By the twelfth century, Moslems throughout the Middle East were using the drug, both as a medicine and as a source of pleasure (NACC, 1971). Alcohol, it has been said, is as old as man. Pliny describes a distilling process that can be used to produce alcohol, and the Bible is abounding in references to fermented juices. Morphine, a derivative of opium, was discovered in 1805. Named after Morpheus, the Greek god of dreams, the drug was at first hailed as a cure for opium addiction until it was recognized that it was only a substitute drug. After the hypodermic needle was invented in 1856, it was widely used in injecting morphine into the ill and wounded. Thousands of United States veterans of the Civil War returned to civilian life suffering from "soldiers' sickness"—morphine addiction.

Throughout history, the use of drugs to produce pleasurable mental states has bee indigenous to many cultures. This joss pi was used for smokin opium.

In 1896, heroin, the most potent of all opium derivatives, was synthesized from morphine. Physicians, apparently not learning from the past, began to prescribe heroin as a cure for opium and morphine addiction. Again, the result was substitution of one addiction for another. During the 1960s methadone, a synthetic narcotic drug, was used widely to cure heroin addiction. Here, too, it was found that the use of methadone merely replaced one addictive substance with another.

Cocaine, another popular mind-affecting drug, has an unusual history. In 1884 Freud made the first study of the physiological effects of cocaine. He had read reports from America claiming that cocaine was of great value in the treatment of morphine and alcohol addiction. Freud's friend, Ernst von Fleischl, had become addicted to morphine following a painful thumb amputation. Hoping to cure his friend, Freud obtained cocaine and proceeded to experiment with it. He was immediately impressed by the exhilarating and euphoric effects of the drug and noted, too, possibilities of its use in the treatment of other drug addictions (opium and alcohol).

However, the value of cocaine as a cure for morphine addiction became increasingly hard to support. Reports were made that cocaine was itself addicting. Soon a controversy developed between those who claimed it was addicting and those who claimed, as Freud did, that cocaine was entirely beneficial. Meanwhile, von Fleischl rapidly deteriorated into a pathetic victim

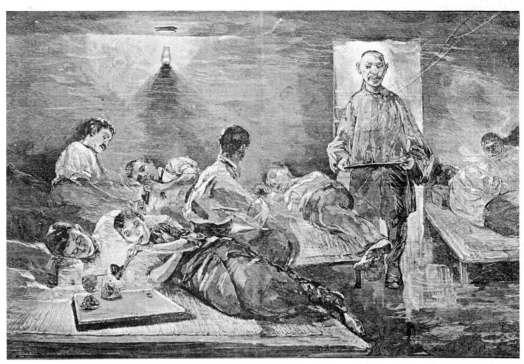

Opium smokers in a New York den in the 1800s

of cocaine. Freud had succeeded in withdrawing him from morphine but at the cost of producing the first known cocaine addict of modern times.

Freud retracted his endorsement of cocaine as a cure for morphine addiction in an article written in 1887. He stated that morphine addicts do abuse cocaine. He emphasized that it was not the drug that was to blame, it was the persons themselves. In support of this, he referred to a leader of the American medical profession, Dr. William A. Hammond, who placed habituation to cocaine on a par with habituation to coffee or tea—"an entirely different sort of habituation from morphine addiction."

Following the publication of this statement, Freud retired from psychopharmacology and went on to found the branch of psychiatry for which he became famous. His experiments with cocaine were buried in the archives and remained unknown to the scientific world until the publication of a new biography in 1955.

At the time that Freud had been experimenting with cocaine as a cure for morphine addiction, his colleague Karl Köller was experimenting with the anesthetizing property of cocaine, and he soon introduced cocaine into ophthalmology as a local anesthetic. Unlike Freud's experiments with cocaine, Köller's experiments and claims caused no controversy. His initial observations were accepted and extended by other investigators. In 1884 cocaine was introduced as a local anesthetic into dentistry. One year later, the American surgeon,

Dr. William S. Halsted, demonstrated that cocaine could stop transmission in nerve trunks. This laid the foundation for nerve-block anesthesia in surgery.

As the medical investigation of cocaine proceeded, its high toxicity became more and more apparent. Since it could cause damage to the cornea and excessive dilation to the pupils, its use in eye surgery diminished. When injected, if used over too long a time or in too high a concentration, it caused cells to die—and it could not be absorbed by the skin.

Because of these disadvantages, a chemical search for a substitute began in 1892 with the work of Einhorn and his colleagues. This resulted in 1905 in the synthesis of procaine, which today is still widely used under the trade name Novocain. With the synthesis of procaine and other similar local anesthetic drugs, the use of cocaine in medicine has steadily declined. The major remaining medical use of cocaine is to anesthetize the nose and throat (NACC, 1971).

Among the most dangerous of the abused drugs are the barbiturates. First synthesized in 1863, barbituric acid is the basis of all barbiturate drugs. In 1903 Emil Fischer and Joseph von Mering produced diethyl barbituric acid, a drug with notable hypnotic qualities, which was marketed under the trade name Veronal. Since that time over 1,500 different barbiturates have been prepared and marketed. Less than a score of these are still in medical use today.

Amphetamines, a group of stimulating drugs, were first synthesized in 1927 by Gordon A. Alles. The discovery that amphetamines could be absorbed by inhaling led to the development of the Benzedrine inhaler in 1932 to reduce nasal congestion—the first medicinal use of amphetamine. Today amphetamines are used in medicine to curb the appetite in overweight persons; to relieve mild depression such as that accompanying grief, senility, menopause, and convalescence; and to keep patients awake in narcolepsy—a disorder characterized by brief attacks of deep sleep.

The hallucinogenic (psychedelic) drugs—LSD, DMT, mescaline, and psilocybin—are products of the twentieth century, although in their natural forms they have been used for centuries. Popularized during the early 1960's by Professors Timothy Leary and Richard Alpert of Harvard University, these drugs have become the most widely abused of all the mind-affecting substances. They are commonly mislabeled as *mind-expanding* drugs because of their tendency to produce in the user a feeling of omniscience and omnipotence. In fact, however, they are *mind-destructive* drugs when overused.

Marijuana (cannabis) is the dried leaves and flowering tops of the hemp plant, which grows wild in many areas of the world. Used widely by the peoples of the Far East for centuries, it is also believed that cannabis was used by the American Indians in their ritual ceremonies. The famous peace pipe smoked by the Indians was most likely filled with marijuana leaf. At various times, in different cultures, marijuana has been outlawed, glorified, commercially marketed, or issued only by prevailing ministers of the church. Geller and Boas (1969) offer a detailed history of the uses of marijuana in the United States, along with a thorough explanation of the pharmacology of marijuana.

*Marijuana grows
wildly–even in the city!*

WHAT IS DRUG ABUSE?

There is nothing intrinsically dangerous or destructive in any of the drugs discussed above; the problem is purely a result of the uses to which the drug is put. Alcohol, for example, is sipped graciously at guidance counselor conventions with no discernible harm to anyone. But when a seventh-grade boy comes to school drunk each day, or when the parents of a fourth-grade girl cannot give her appropriate care because of their dependence on alcohol, those are drug problems. Marijuana, a drug without proven danger to the user, produces pleasant, relaxed feelings, with heightened sensual awareness. When a high-school youth, however, becomes unable to study because of excessive use of this substance, or when a student loses ability to function except when using the drug, then we are dealing with a serious drug problem. Amphetamines, barbiturates, hallucinogens, and cocaine, likewise, each have many legitimate uses. It is only when they are abused by the user that they become a problem for the counselor to be concerned with.

One of the more unfortunate aspects of the drug abuse problem is the student's inability to distinguish between the relative dangers of different drugs. Often a student experiments with LSD or a barbiturate as readily as he would with marijuana or hashish, far less dangerous drugs. Thomas Thompson (1973), in his pathetically tragic account of the short life of Richard Diener, tells how young Richie's experimentation with "downs" led to such a state of mental deterioration and social malfunctioning that he finally ended up in a face-to-face duel to death with his father. What is interesting in Thompson's account is the amalgam of social, familial, and psychological forces that play a part in the drug activity of the young person.

Perhaps the single most accurate criterion of what determines drug abuse is the attitude the individual has toward the drugs. If the drug experiences serves as an occasional social meeting ground, this is a far different situation from the one in which the drug has become a panacea the young person cannot live without. If the addictive or nonaddictive substance becomes the central focus of the person's existence—his raison d'être—the individual may clearly be said to be suffering from drug abuse.

Display 17.1 outlines some of the major drugs that are commonly abused and presents some relevant information about each one, information that should enable the school counselor to identify and understand the particulars of a student's drug problem. The critical question, the one with which we shall now

---

display 17.1

COMMON SYMPTOMS OF DRUG ABUSE

1 Changes in school attendance, homework quality, discipline or grades.
2 Poor physical appearance.
3 Sudden and unusual emotional outbreaks or flare-ups.
4 Furtive behavior regarding drugs or possessions.
5 Sudden change of associations and social patterns.
6 Borrowing money from students to buy drugs.
7 Wearing sunglasses at inappropriate times to hide pupils of eyes.
8 Stealing small items from school or home.
9 Finding student in odd places during school day, such as closets or storage rooms, to take drugs.

SPECIFIC DRUG SYMPTOMS

Glue
1 Excessive nasal secretions, plus watering of eyes.
2 Odor of substance inhaled on breath and clothing.
3 Slurred speech, very slow response.
4 Poor muscular control, drowsiness or unconsciousness.
5 Presence of plastic or paper bags or rags containing dry plastic cement.

Stimulants (Amphetamines, Bennies)
1 Excessive activity, restlessness.
2 Acute irritability, argumentative, nervous, difficulty in sitting still.
3 Dilated pupils.
4 Chain smoking during recess.
5 Dry mouth and nose with licking of lips and rubbing or scratching of nose.
6 Sudden exhaustion or sleep from long periods without eating or sleeping.

Depressants (Barbiturates, Goofballs)
1 Falling asleep or lack of interest in class.
2 Symptoms of alcohol intoxication without odor of alcohol on breath.
3 Staggering or stumbling walk.
4 Drowsy or disoriented behavior.

Marijuana (symptoms will appear only when person is "on" the drug)
1 Animated and hysterical behavior with rapid, loud speech and bursts of laughter.
2 In later stages, sleepy or stuporous appearance.
3 Indications of distorted depth and color perception.

Hallucinogens (L.S.D.)
1 Fearful or panicky behavior or paranoid reaction to group.
2 Dreamy, trance-like state.
3 Indications of distorted sight, hearing, touch and/or time.
4 Changes of mood or behavior.
5 Widely dilated pupils requiring dark glasses to protect eyes from light.

Narcotics (Heroin)
1 Hidden syringes, burned spoons, cotton and needles.
2 Traces of white powder around nostrils if user is inhaling (snorting) heroin.
3 Scars (track marks) on inner arms from injections (mainlining).
4 Constant wearing of long sleeve shirts to hide scars.
5 Constricted pupils which do not respond to light.
6 Lethargic behavior.

Prepared by The City of New York, Addiction Services Agency, 71 Worth Street, NY, NY 10012.

come to grips, is "What is the counselor to do about drug problems in his school once these problems have been identified?"

YOUTH AND DRUGS

First the counselor must understand why drug use is particularly prevalent among young people. We find, if we examine the culture of adolescence, a number of answers to this question. Shertzer and Stone (1971), after surveying the literature, present three generalizations about adolescence with which most authorities would likely agree:

1 Adolescence is a transition period between childhood and adulthood. It refers to the physiological and psychological characteristics dominant between puberty and maturity. The use of chronological age to denote the period is virtually meaningless because the onset of puberty varies fairly widely and researchers agree on no specific age as the termination for adolescence. The most frequently cited age span is twelve to twenty.
2 Physical and sexual maturation as evidenced by changes in both the primary and secondary sex characteristics results in shifts in attitude toward the proper masculine and feminine sex role. This period of development includes the acceptance of one's own physical self and its potential reproductive processes.
3 Adolescence also includes searching for emotional, social, and economic independence. It is a time for the individual to utilize at a more mature and complex level the ability to give as well as get, to communicate with others and to trust them, and to learn what is harmful and what is good for himself and others. (pp. 5-6)

We note from Shertzer and Stone's description that adolescence is a period of change, of growth, a transitional stage in life. Such periods of transition are generally characterized by strivings for identity; for resolutions of anxiety-provoking confusion; for a fuller, more comprehensive, and more satisfying understanding of self and one's role with others (Blos, 1962; Erikson, 1950). Youth has not changed much since Irene Josselyn described the adolescent over twenty years ago:

The adolescent struggles for independence, verbalizing vehemently his protest against the protective ruling of the adult group. He does not want to be told what clothes to wear, what hours to keep, what food to eat, what political party to respect, or what ethical or moral formula to embrace. On the other hand, he is unable to handle his independent activities as adequately as he did in the immediate past. He is impulsive in his behavior and confused about his goals. Not only does this disturb the adults who are interested in his present and future adjustment; it also disturbs and frightens him. As a result, he is apt to make demands for dependence which he has not made since he was a small child. At the same time he wants advice about what clothes to wear, what hours to keep, what food to eat, what political party to respect, or what ethical or moral formula to embrace. (p. 38)

This picture of the adolescent suggests an individual in a state of profound ambivalence and confusion, of irresolution and doubt, of turmoil and change.

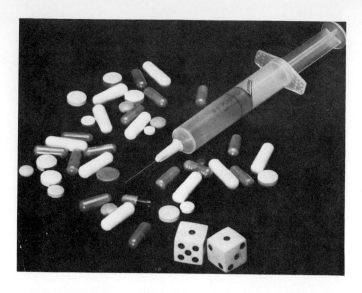

Drug abuse–it's a gamble!

Kelly (1969) has referred to adolescents as "a suppressed minority group," which places them in the same untenable position as most minority groups.

A person undergoing such changes as these is more likely than a mature person to rely on drugs for escape, for fantasy, for peer group identification. The escape value of these drugs lies in their potential for allowing one to forget one's problems and to seek refuge temporarily from the real world, and who needs this more than the adolescent? A fantasy world is set up, a world where the individual is freed of all responsibilities and where nothing is important, where there is no way to get hurt by others. It is a false, unrealistic world, but a world where the fragile young person is safe from the hurt and rejection he encounters in his daily living. A fifteen-year-old client of mine, a girl heavily into drug use, wrote a short poem about her feelings that illustrates this point:

Here I am safe while sinking,
Surrounded by my barbs and meth and grass
My three lovers who will never hurt me,
Who always understand,
Who are always there when I need them,
Who love me for what I am!

We see from these few lines the escape from loneliness provided by the drugs, the feeling of being wanted, of being important, of existing for a purpose, even if it is a false, unauthentic, and possibly fatal purpose. Moreover, because young people are inclined toward grouping, because a part of their identity, of their reality, is established through the group, the group reinforces their use of drugs. This is why a student who is taking drugs invariably hangs out with others who take drugs and avoids with condemnation and scorn the straight kids who shy away from drug use. No proselytizer is as active and enthusiastic as a drug user with a strong and vested interest in seducing others toward his point of view.

Young people, then, are attracted to drugs because drugs provide an alternative mode of existence that—compared to the turmoils and difficulties encoun-

348

tered in the real world—is easier to deal with. Drugs are an escape into fantasy, an escape that is reinforced by the values of their peers and countered by the values of the greater society, which in effect strengthens their appeal to the rebellious adolescent.

THE COUNSELOR'S ROLE

While it is universally agreed that the schools must assume a large burden of the drug education and addiction prevention programs, it is unclear what roles the teachers, counselors, and administrators specifically should be expected to play in this vital effort. Certainly there should be a coordination and integration between their functions that will enable the student to utilize maximally the range of resources available to him. The entire scope of activities and programs may be divided as follows:

I. Preventive
   1. Understanding the problem.
   2. Creating a drug education program.
   3. Making available to students adequate information.
II. Therapeutic
   1. Working with drug users.
   2. Maintaining ongoing patterns of facilitative communication.
III. Administrative and legal
   1. Cooperating with system-wide efforts.
   2. Working with the community.
   3. Maintaining communication and feedback with law enforcement authorities.

The school counselor should be actively involved in all three phases of this work. In the preventive phase, as the key mental health professional working in the school, he should have a thorough and well-grounded understanding of the drug problem. He should also be engaged in a continual interaction with teachers, sharing his understanding, learning from them, and helping to implement within the school a viable drug education program. Directing himself to what teachers and counselors can and should do, Demos (1968) suggests:

Become more familiar with the subject matter.... Be aware of the differences between narcotics and other drugs. Too frequently the terms are used interchangeably. There is no quicker way to lose a knowledgeable audience than to refer to LSD and marijuana as a narcotic. *Provide avenues for drug users and potential users to level with you with impunity.* Is there a place well-known to young people in your school and community where talk about drugs and drug usage is privileged communication?...*Strive to be a better model.* Young people are searching for authentic models.... Let us influence the young by being authentic, open, trusting, and honest....*Listen to the young.* What are they saying? Is there any validity to their charges? How viable are their dreams and aspirations?...*Offer youth accurate information....* Inaccurate information widens the credibility gap between youth and the adult society. (p. 215)

display 17.2

USEFUL INFORMATION ON DRUGS SUBJECT TO ABUSE

Name	Heroin	Codeine	Morphine	Methadone	Cocaine	Marijuana
SLANG NAME	H, Horse, Skag, Junk, Snow, Stuff, Harry, Joy Powder, Smack	Schoolboy	White Stuff, Miss Emma, M, Dreamer	Dolly	Speedball, Gold, Dust, Coke, Bernice, Corine, Flake, Star Dust	Texas Tea, Nezz, Weed, Pot, Grass, Locoweed, Mary Jane, Hashish, Reefer, Hemp, plus local slang names
PHARMACOLOGIC CLASSIFICATION	Depressant	Depressant	Depressant	Depressant	Stimulant	Stimulant, Depressant or Hallucinogen
MEDICAL USES	None	Ease Pains and Coughing	Pain Relief	Pain Relief, Detoxification of Drug Addicts, Maintenance of Drug Addicts	Local Anesthesia	None in U.S.
HOW TAKEN	Injected or Sniffed	Swallowed	Swallowed or Injected	Swallowed or Injected	Swallowed	Smoked or Swallowed
USUAL DOSE	Varies	30 Milligrams	15 Milligrams	Varies Depending on Use or Abuse	Varies	1 or 2 Cigarettes
DURATION OF EFFECT	4 Hours	4 Hours	6 Hours	Varies Depending on Use or Abuse	Varies	4 Hours
INITIAL SYMPTOMS	Euphoria, Drowsiness	Drowsiness	Euphoria, Drowsiness	Less Acute than Opiates	Excitation, Talkativeness, Tremors	Relaxation, Euphoria, Alteration of Perception, Judgment
LONG-TERM SYMPTOMS	Addiction, Constipation, Loss of Appetite, Convulsions in overdose	Addiction	Addiction, Impairment of Breathing	Addiction	Depression, Convulsions	?
PHYSICAL DEPENDENCE POTENTIAL	Yes	Yes	Yes	Yes	No	No
MENTAL DEPENDENCE POTENTIAL	Yes	Yes	Yes	Yes	No	?
NOTE	Usually found as white crystalline powder in paper or glassine envelopes or capsules		Usually found as a white powder		Usually found as a white crystalline powder	Usually found as dried, pulverized flowering tops, seeds and leaves

Printed for the Addiction Services Agency by Lenox Hill Hospital with funds made available by its Woman's Auxiliary.

Name	Barbiturates	Amphetamines	L.S.D.	DMT	Mescaline	Psilocybin
SLANG NAME	Barbs, Candy, Goofballs, Sleeping Pills, Peanuts, also: (1) Yellows, Yellow Jackets, Nimby, Nimble, (2) Reds, Pinks, Red Devils, Seggy, Seccy, (3) Reds and Blues, Double Trouble	Bennies, Dexies, Co-Pilots, Wake-ups, Truck Drivers, Hearts, Pep Pills, Proppers	Acid, Sugar, Big D, Cubes, Trips	Business-man's High	Cactus, Peyote	Mushrooms
PHARMACOLOGIC CLASSIFICATION	Depressant 2	Stimulant	Hallucinogen	Hallucinogen	Hallucinogen	Hallucinogen
MEDICAL USES	Sedation, Relieve High Blood Pressure, Hyperthyroidism, Epilepsy	Relieve Mild Depression, Control Appetite, Narcolepsy	Experimental Study of Mental Function, Alcoholism	None	None	None
HOW TAKEN	Swallowed or Injected	Swallowed or Injected	Swallowed	Swallowed	Swallowed	Swallowed
USUAL DOSE	50 to 100 Milligrams	2.5 to 5 Milligrams	100 Micrograms	1 Milligram	350 Micrograms	25 Milligrams
DURATION OF EFFECT	4 Hours	4 Hours	10 Hours	4 to 6 Hours	12 Hours	6 to 8 Hours
INITIAL SYMPTOMS	Drowsiness, Muscle Relaxation	Alertness, Activeness	Exhilaration, Excitation, Rambling Speech	Exhilaration	Exhilaration, Anxiety, Gastric Distress	Nausea, Vomiting, Headaches
LONG-TERM SYMPTOMS	Addiction with Severe Withdrawal Symptoms, Possible Convulsions	Delusions, Hallucinations	May Intensify Existing Psychosis, Panic Reactions	?	?	?
PHYSICAL DEPENDENCE POTENTIAL	Yes	Yes	Yes	No	No	No
MENTAL DEPENDENCE POTENTIAL	Yes	Yes	?	?	?	?
NOTE	(1) Pentobarbital Sodium (Nembutal) (2) Seconbarbital (Seconal) (3) Amobarbital (Tuinal)					

LAST WARNING TO
ALL DOPE PEDDLERS AND GANGSTERS
BLACK - WHITE - PUERTORICAN
GET OUT OF HARLEM & NEW YORK CITY
We are going to return Harlem back into the hands of Decent People
DOPE ADDICTS ARE VIOLATING THE CIVIL RIGHTS OF BLACKS & WHITES
THIS MUST BE STOPPED NOW!
DOPE GANGSTERS ARE LYNCHING ADDICTS WITH OVERDOSES STOP IT NOW
1200 DEAD SINCE JANUARY 1ST 1968 .... STOP IT NOW
WE ARE CALLING FOR FEDERAL TROOPS, STATE AND LOCAL
LAW ENFORCEMENT FORCES TO MOVE INTO THE STREETS
OF HARLEM AND NEW YORK CITY NOW AND CLEAN IT UP
ANTI CRIME & ANTI NARCOTIC COMMITTEE · REV. O. D. DEMPSEY, DIRECTOR

Community action is often a deterrent to widespread drug use.

If the counselor was not brought up in a culture exposed to drugs, it is necessary for him to embark conscientiously and open-mindedly on a program of drug education for himself. He must particularly attempt to understand the drug world from the students' own phenomenological point of view—to see how they perceive different drugs and what these drugs mean to them.

This understanding must be counterbalanced by the counselor's own rational understanding of the situation, based on research and knowledge—not on myths and wishful thinking, nor on social values and school-dictated sentiments. It is important, for example, that the teacher be able to approach objectively the question of marijuana smoking. Many counselors make the mistake of equating the use of marijuana use with serious drug use. In fact, according to the report of the National Commission on Marihuana and Drug Abuse (1972), the most serious side effect of marijuana use is legal—not medical or psychological and the recommendation was that marijuana possession be decriminalized. Zinberg and Weil (1969), for example, conclude that it is "unlikely that marijuana has any seriously detrimental physical effects in either short-term or long-term usage." While the evidence is not all in at this point, it is clear that marijuana use is a less serious psychological problem than the use of barbiturates, heroin, amphetamines, or hallucinogenic drugs.

In the therapeutic phase of the drug program, the counselor must see that those students who want help will have it available and that those students who do not overtly want help will be properly encouraged to seek help. Randall (1970) has suggested that drug treatment and prevention programs should begin at the early grades. Winston (1969) gives an example of a drug counseling workshop for students. Jaffe and Reed (1969) present the concept of "structured rapping" as a way of relating to young people. It is important in this phase of the program, too, that the counselor *know the facts, fantasies and uncertainties about drugs and drug use . . . present an objective view of drug use and abuse* (Wolk, 1969, p. 224). Display 17.3 (Yolles, 1970) answers some of the more common questions raised by teen-agers regarding drug information and drug use.

352

QUESTIONS AND ANSWERS ABOUT DRUGS

Is it safe to try drugs once just to see how it feels?

This depends entirely upon the drug and the person —both of which involve important unknown quantities. Few people who try heroin once, for example, never touch it again. On the other hand, a majority of people who try marijuana, or "pot," do so fewer than 10 times before quitting entirely.

You cannot be certain ahead of time of your own reaction to a drug experience. About 10 percent of the people who try marijuana, for example, become chronic, compulsive users, often to their surprise. Some drugs, such as LSD and methamphetamine or "speed," can cause serious harm even with one experimental dosage. The risks of any kind of drug taking are too great to be dismissed lightly.

Can I become addicted to "pot"?

Unlike some other drugs, marijuana does not cause addiction—the disruption of your body's chemical balance to the point that you need it to stay well physically. But it can be as habit-forming as ordinary cigarettes. Chronic users become dependent upon it psychologically. Without it, they may feel restless, unable to face life.

Can marijuana affect my personality?

Yes, and with use it apparently can also contribute to severe emotional problems in some individuals. You may become very passive and apathetic, lose your motivation and interest in activities that once seemed important to you, experience memory difficulties.

What should I do at a party where everyone is on drugs and they're trying to get me to take them?

Leave immediately! Most people start on drugs the first time in just such circumstances. Even if you stay but don't "turn on," you are in danger legally. A person present where drugs are being used can be arrested along with the users.

Isn't marijuana safer than alcohol?

We have much yet to learn about the long-range effects of marijuana, but there is no firm evidence now that it is less harmful physically, psychologically, or socially, than alcohol if used consistently and in strong quantity.

Both intoxicants can impair your physical coordination and hamper your judgment. In countries where alcohol is forbidden by religious taboo, there are skid rows created by marijuana smokers.

Don't drugs make a person more creative?

Some drugs, such as "pot" and LSD, may make you feel more creative. But they tend to hamper your actual performance. Under drugs your motivation to work and execute creative ideas most likely will be reduced because of chemically induced lassitude and passivity.

Can I get to know myself better through LSD?

Under hallucinogenic LSD, probably the most powerful drug known to man, you may have the illusion that you are gaining great insights into your personality and behavior. This is because notions that come to you in the highly suggestible drugged state seem much more "real." It is doubtful, however, that valid insights occur with any regularity. The psychedelic world is one of fantasy, and to the average layman it yields no more "truth" about himself than his dreams while sleeping.

Does LSD cause chromosome damage?

Research that may answer this question is still under way. Some preliminary experiments have shown that chromosome damage may occur three or four times more often in LSD users. In any case, the taking of drugs by young women, especially expectant mothers, is extremely risky.

What can happen during a "bad trip" on LSD?

Almost anything. The sense of losing control during hallucinations can cause you to panic and blindly injure yourself or others. Horrible delusions that seem terrifyingly real can cause personality-shattering psychotic breaks with reality which may last days or years after the drug has worn off. Because of feelings of omniscience and indestructibility, the "tripper" may believe he can fly—and plunge to his death from a high window as many have done.

Can a user "trip" on LSD even without taking it?

Yes, the LSD experience can recur spontaneously weeks or months after a user last took the drug. Such "flashbacks" are most common during physical or psychological stress but can also be brought on unexpectedly by some common medicines.

Will "speed" keep me alert and smarter than usual?

People on "speed" or methamphetamine, the strongest of all amphetamines, may seem to be more alert because they are so extremely active and talkative. The drug excessively stimulates the brain cells, much as normal body chemicals do when you face an emergency. But when this excitation is prolonged by "speed," undesirable changes take place, including an actual dulling of the mind. The speed user has great potential for violence and bizarre behavior. Mental illness induced by the mind-accelerating "high" can last long beyond the period of actual drug activity.

Is it true that "speed" kills?

Some medical authorities estimate that once you become hooked on "speed" your life expectancy is about five years. Besides the risk of brain damage, habitual methamphetamine takes a heavy toll on the user's liver and heart.

Can I become addicted to "medicine chest" drugs?

Definitely. In fact, many young people are getting "high" illicitly on the very drugs their parents use under prescription. Amphetamine pills for losing weight, tranquilizers for easing tension and anxiety, stimulants for "perking up," barbiturates and other sedatives for fighting insomnia—all can be addictive.

What's wrong with sniffing glue and aerosol products?

The cheap thrills obtained from inhaling a wide variety of deliriants, which include model-airplane glue, paint thinner, laughing gas, nail-polish remover, and the mists from aerosol cans of furniture spray, cleaning fluid, and other chemical compounds, can be deadly. Most of these substances contain dangerous chemicals never meant to be taken by man.

Temporary blindness, convulsions, and permanent brain damage have been reported, along with damage to bone marrow, kidneys, liver, and lungs. Many deaths have occurred.

Can a person stop using drugs by himself?

Once you are addicted or habituated to drugs, it is very unlikely that you can "cure" yourself. In some cases, deep-seated psychological or character disorders, which require psychiatric treatment, may lie behind drug-taking. An abrupt withdrawal from some drugs is dangerous. For these reasons, hospitalization or at least close professional supervision while kicking the drug habit is most desirable.

Where can I go for help?

Unless you really want to stop using drugs, probably no one can help you. If you do, seek out someone you trust—a friend, teacher, doctor—and ask him to help you locate the best professional resource in the community to treat your problem.

Treatment will involve helping you understand and cope with the reasons you turned to drugs in the first place, as well as with the problems drug use has added to your life. The cure rate for drug users is not encouraging—another good reason not to get involved when drugs first look tempting.

In the administrative and legal phase of the program, the counselor functions as a liaison between the students and the administration, between the school and the community, between the school and the district. The counselor should acquaint himself with the laws regarding drug use, confidentiality, etc., in his community, and have a clear idea of what the system and administration expect of him in this regard. Community drug centers—particularly in urban areas—are usually happy to cooperate with school personnel in providing speakers, acquainting the staff with available resources, etc. These community services should be fully utilized by the counselor.

Perhaps one of the most singularly effective gestures counselors and teachers can make is to create a facilitative, joyous environment within the school. In many ways, widespread alienation and drug abuse may be indicative of serious deficiencies within the school environment. Cohen (1969) addresses himself to this crucial point, which many professionals are hesitant to acknowledge:

If the educator is to learn anything from the current striving for drug-induced perceptual, emotional, and cognitive changes, it is that important areas of human experience have been neglected by our child-rearing and child-teaching practices. Many of those attracted to the drug experience suffer from *anhedonism,* the inabilitiy to derive pleasure from ordinary existence, and *alienation,* the inability to find meaning within or outside oneself. These are serious deficits, and in a young person they lead to serious disorders of behavior or character. From childhood through adolescence we are failing (1) to provide goals appropriate to our times, (2) to train the emotions and the senses, and (3) to set limits. Therefore, goallessness, an inability to enjoy, and an attenuated sense of social responsibility predispose to chemical escape, chemical hedonism, and the search for chemical enlightenment. (p. 120)

Perhaps if the schools could truly create what George B. Leonard (1968) calls a "climate of delight"—of ecstasy—then the drug problem would no longer have a host on which to feed. Counselors and teachers, by working together, can help create this climate—and should do so!

Establishing constructive relationships with law-enforcement officials is a delicate job for the counselor. He must make clear to these officials the extent to which he is willing to cooperate, and he must at all costs respect student privacy because this is the very basis of therapeutic counseling. Usually a police department has an education division charged with the responsibility of visiting schools and providing information to students, parents, and teachers. The counselor can find out what resources the police authorities have available by calling the local precinct.

The full dimensions of this problem are far too complex and intricate for a complete treatment in this brief chapter. It would be advisable for counselors who encounter serious drug problems in their school to explore the subject more thoroughly. Consumers Union (1972) has published an up-to-date, comprehensive discussion of drug abuse, that should be of great value to the school counselor.

References

Blos, P. *On adolescence.* New York: The Free Press, 1962.

Cohen, S. *The drug dilemma.* New York: McGraw-Hill, 1969.

Consumers Union. *Licit and illicit drugs.* Boston: Little, Brown, 1972.

Demos, G. D. Drug abuse and the new generation. *Phi Delta Kappan,* 1968, *50,* 214–217.

Erikson, E. *Childhood and society.* New York: W. W. Norton, 1950.

Geller, A., & Boas, M. *The drug beat.* New York: McGraw-Hill, 1969.

Jaffe, A., & Reed, A. Involving the turned-on generation through structured rapping. *Personnel and Guidance Journal*, 1969, *48*, 311–315.

Josselyn, I. *The adolescent and his world.* New York: Family Service Association of America, 1952.

Kelly, H. Adolescents: A suppressed minority group. *Personnel and Guidance Journal*, 1969, *47*, 634–640.

Leonard, G. B. *Education and ecstasy.* New York: Delacorte Press, 1968.

NACC (New York State Drug Abuse Control Commission. Formerly, New York State Narcotic Addiction Control Commission.). Series of pamphlets: Barbiturates, heroin, amphetamines, cocaine. Albany, N.Y.: 1971.

Randall, H. Patterns of drug use in school age children. *Journal of School Health*, 1970, *40*, 296–301.

Shertzer, B., & Stone, S. C. *Fundamentals of Guidance* (2nd ed.). Boston: Houghton Mifflin, 1971.

Thompson, T. *Richie.* New York: Saturday Review Press, 1973.

United States Government, National Commission on Marihuana and Drug Abuse. *Marihuana: A signal of misunderstanding.* Washington, D.C.: Government Printing Office, 1972.

Winston, S. L. The drug counseling workshop: A new resource for schools. *Journal of Secondary Education*, 1969, *44*, 352–353.

Wolk, D. J. Youth and drugs: Guidelines for teachers. (1969). In G. S. Belkin (Ed.), *Foundations of counseling.* Dubuque, Iowa: Kendall/Hunt, 1974.

Yolles, S., Remsberg, C., & Remsberg, B. An expert answers teen-agers' questions about drugs. *Family Weekly Magazine,* March 8, 1970.

Zinberg, N. E., & Weil, A. T. The effects of Marijuana on human beings. *The New York Times Magazine*, May 11, 1969.

chapter eighteen

Human sexuality in the counseling milieu

Because counseling is concerned with every facet of human needs, development, and growth, some of the counselor's efforts will invariably be directed toward the client's sexual adjustment. The form of these efforts is generally referred to in the professional literature and in the popular press as *sex education*, although this term probably belies the true dynamic, emotional significance of this counseling function. However, for the sake of simplicity I shall continue the use of this term, with the caution that sex education efforts, both in the classroom and in the counselor's office, are more intense and profound than mere didactic instruction would lead us to believe.

For sex education to be effective and meaningful, it must begin in the primary grades. Too often, teachers, administrators, and planners who advocate sex education in the schools make the mistake of postponing the program until the junior-high-school level, under the mistaken assumption that it is only at this late stage that students become interested in and motivated about sex. Quite the opposite is true: The first-, second-, third-, and fourth-grade child will have a ready and lively interest in sexuality, motivated by an intense curiosity about where he came from, what his parents do at night, and the biological differences between the sexes.

While much of the responsibility for educating children about sexuality rests with the curriculum planners and teachers, the counselor also has a vital role in this effort, and this chapter will examine some ways in which the counselor can be helpful to the total sex education program.

ANSWERING CHILDREN'S QUESTIONS

Before the counselor attempts to answer children's and young adults' questions about sex, the counselor himself must have a thorough understanding of human sexuality and an appropriate attitude that will enable him to answer questions without inducing unhealthy feelings in the child. As for the first criterion, it is sufficient if the counselor makes an effort to educate himself about the subject. An excellent book that he may want to read is *Human Sexuality* by

James Leslie McCary, which outlines in detail almost all our knowledge about human sexuality. This knowledge includes the biological structures, the physiology of reproduction, social and psychological factors involved in sexuality, myths and fallacies of sexuality, and various sexual positions. The counselor might also have on hand a dictionary of sexual terms with which to improve his own sexual nomenclature. There are many such dictionaries on the market today, and even a brief perusal of their contents is often enlightening. Counselor education programs would do well to include a course on human sexuality so that counselor trainees would have an opportunity to be exposed to material that might well become an important part of their practice.

In regard to the counselor's attitude, it is necessary that he carefully examine his own hang ups about sexuality. Does he come from a home where he learned that sex is bad or wrong, dirty or improper? What is the counselor's attitude toward his own children when they ask sexually oriented questions? In his own life, is the counselor able to enjoy healthy, fulfilling sexual experiences? Juhasz (1970) has suggested that for the sex education teacher (or counselor) to be most effective, he should be able (1) to accept and respect himself and all humans as sexual beings, (2) to empathize and establish rapport with students and, in this atmosphere of freedom, (3) to communicate and carry on a dialogue in which (4) accurate and comprehensive information is exchanged and evaluated. Keller (1972), too, suggests that before teachers attempt to teach sex education, they examine their own feelings about sex.

Assuming that the counselor has the knowledge and the correct attitude, how does he go about answering clients' questions about sex? Where the question is factual, there is little difficulty. The counselor simply provides the information asked for. Let us look at a few examples to see how a counselor properly answers questions. Note that although all the answers are factual, specific, and precise, the way in which they are expressed differs according to the maturational level of the client.

Client (2nd-grade boy). How do girls make wee-wee?

Counselor. Girls have a tiny hole between their legs where they urinate from. They also have a larger opening called the vagina. When they become women, this is where babies come out of. In the back, they have another opening for the bowel movements.

This answer was designed to resolve the myth of the *cloaca*. A cloaca is a biological structure which serves both excretory and reproductive functions in some animals (reptiles, amphibians). Children tend to believe, until they are educated otherwise, that in girls there is a single opening from which excretion,

A child is no less stunned by the mysteries of creation than we are.

urination, and reproduction and birth all take place. This is important to clarify for the young child, since misunderstanding may produce anxiety about the "dirtiness" of sexuality. The counselor, instead of simply answering the one question, clarified the entire issue for the child.

Now let's consider this example:

Client (7th-grade girl). When boys play with themselves, something comes out when they're done. It's a sticky thing. Is this normal?

Counselor. Yes, this is quite normal. It's called semen. When a boy becomes very aroused, he spurts out this semen. We call this ejaculation. This semen contains sperms—little, tiny creatures that make babies when they combine with an egg inside a woman's body.

Again, the counselor answered the question factually but also provided additional information. It is clear that this girl is engaging in some type of sexual activity with her boyfriend and that she is not sophisticated about the mechanics of sexuality. The counselor is advising her subtly about the possibilities of pregnancy from intercourse by pointing out to her that if the man's penis goes inside her, she may become pregnant.

Sometimes clients ask moral questions rather than factual questions. Let us look at this example:

Client (10th-grade boy). There's this girl in my class who goes all the way. She went all the way with Joe and with Dave, I know. I'm going out with her this weekend, and I was wondering if I should make her go all the way with me?

Counselor. Well, sex between two people is fine if both love each other and care about each other. If you just want to make this girl go all the way because she did it with your friends, then I personally don't think it's such a good idea.

Here the counselor tried to communicate a positive emotional message to the client: that sex and love ideally go together. Such moral statements are certainly permissible in counseling, even in nonjudgmental counseling.

SEX EDUCATION IN THE ELEMENTARY SCHOOL

At the elementary school level, most of the questions children ask regarding sexuality concern either the biological functions and structures or the meaning of certain words. Children at this level have little knowledge about the pleasurable aspects of sex and little moral confusion about sexual activity. Some questions may also concern things they have observed in the home, either between their parents or with older siblings.

The elementary school counselor may take the initiative in bringing sex education to the classroom. By offering teachers encouragement, support, and information, the school counselor can bring about a comprehensive sex education

Sometimes, it may take little boys and little girls a lifetime to understand one another.

program. It is important, of course, that the administration and the community, as well as the teachers, are in sympathy with this effort. Cook (1972) relates the story of a sex education program in Anaheim, California that ran afoul of the community and ultimately had to be abolished. This story is a good example of the dangers faced by such programs, particularly in very conservative communities.

Youngs (1970) has described his experiences teaching sex education to fifth-grade children. He found that there is much less emotional overlay with children at the fifth- and sixth-grade levels than there is at later grade levels. Children of the seventh- and eighth-grade levels appear to demonstrate more emotional involvement, possibly because some of the children are experiencing ramifications of the developmental processes that may tend to arouse anxiety.

Chanter (1966) has described, in a brief book, the development and implementation of a sex education program for the elementary schools. He justifies one of the rationales for such a program:

Quite young children have hidden fears and worries about sex. Unless cleared up these fears may extend into adult life, and even into marriage. The subject acquires part of its secrecy, mystery and embarrassment through the child's awareness that many grownups will not talk about it. Any condemnation, untruth, or prohibition on the part of the adult can only lead to mistrust, anxiety, and secretiveness on the part of the child, and what is even more serious, a real fear of asking anyone for accurate information. (pp. 9–10)

The purpose of an elementary school sex-education program, in this respect, is to lessen the child's fears and reduce the painful consequences of those fears later in life. Chanter also describes involving the parents in the sex education program, and these aspects will be mentioned in chapter 20.

SEX EDUCATION IN THE SECONDARY SCHOOL

At the secondary school level, the problem becomes more complex. For not only are students in need of information, but they are also most likely going through difficult personal, psychological changes relating to their sexual awareness. Adolescence is a period of heightened sexual interest, of great arousal and intense emotional involvement. Yet at this very time of life, the channels to sexual fulfillment are blocked with injunctions, social repressions, and fears.

The primary job of the secondary school counselor in the area of sex education is to help the adolescent overcome his fears of and confusions about sexuality. These fears fall into five basic categories, and we will examine each one individually.

Masturbation

According to definitive studies (Kinsey et al., 1948), approximately 95% of adolescent boys and 50% to 80% of adolescent girls masturbate. Masturbation is a normal, healthy, pleasurable awakening of the sexual instincts that, unfortunately, may cause the adolescent to experience guilt, confusion, and remorse. It is the job of the counselor to help the adolescent recognize the value of masturbation and to overcome the fears which enshroud it.

One particularly constructive use of masturbation is learning to experience heightened sexual pleasure. At this period of life, with its limitations and taboos on sexual activity, it is through autoerotic activity that the healthy adolescent learns to appreciate sexual response. The appreciation takes two forms: fantasy and bodily stimulation (Ford, 1966). Through fantasy, the young person is able to appreciate the diversity and creativity of the sexual experience. Through bodily stimulation he or she learns about those areas of his or her body that for him or her provide the most heightened sexual stimulation (erogenous zones). Masturbation should be discussed openly and with the idea of resolving the adolescent's guilt feelings and repressions surrounding this difficult emotional subject.

Petting

The earliest type of sexual activity occurring between young people of the opposite sex is usually petting. Broadly speaking, petting is sexual activity that does not culminate in intercourse. It may include kissing, touching various parts of the body, oral stimulation of the erogenous zones, and mutual masturbation. Because petting arouses heightened sexual interest—because it is very stimulating—and does not provide for sexual release, it is often the basis of anxiety and confusion resulting from increased pressure without the opportunity of discharge.

Moreover, petting activity is the subject of much moral confusion for the adolescent, especially the adolescent girl. Questions regarding the propriety and morality of petting are not unusual in the counselor's office. Girls, victims of an insidious double standard that permeates our sexual thinking, risk the loss of their social esteem, the possibility of a defamed reputation, and complete ostracism as punishment for their activities. Boys, on the other hand, acquire a new social status, a respect of their peers, and a better self-image as a consequence of their sexual exploits. It is the counselor's role in this complex situation to help the adolescent boy and girl gain a more appropriate, fulfilling perspective of the reality of the sexual situation. *Young people should not be compelled to view sex as a competitive sport but as an expression of feelings, a way of demonstrating affection between two people.*

Contraception

For those adolescents engaged actively in sexual intercourse, it is most important that contraceptive information be provided to them. Certainly this is more the job of a physician than of a counselor, and it is important, therefore, that the high school counselor work in conjunction with a physician. The counselor, however, should be familiar with the different methods of contraception and should be able to answer students' questions regarding contraceptive procedures. A number of family planning organizations—such as Planned Parenthood—offer a wealth of free literature that a school counselor may wish to distribute to his students to help answer some of the more difficult questions.

Policies of the school system regarding the dissemination of contraceptive information should be recognized by the counselor. The counselor should also be familiar with state laws regarding this subject; these laws vary widely from state to state. The counselor can usually obtain legal information either from the counsel to the school board or from the attorney for the teachers' union, where there is one. The school counselor can usually do more good working entirely within the law than sidestepping it, even when he feels this is necessary. Also, religious convictions must always be respected.

Venereal disease

The schools have been most negligent in dealing with the problem of venereal disease, a problem that reached epidemic proportions among young people during the late 1960s. During the time that schools took on an ever-increasing interest in preventive health care, they showed little or no interest in detecting the presence of venereal disease and in educating students about the prevention and recognition of this disease. Yet both of these are simple procedures, and the school counselor, in conjunction with school medical personnel, should direct their attention to this area.

Venereal disease education, the aspect of the program most directly under the auspices of the guidance office, should include lectures, discussion groups, films, and readings. A bibliography of relevant literature is available from the Department of Health, Education, and Welfare in Washington, D.C. Films are available, usually from the central resource library of the large school district, and these should be explored by the counselor. Present legal regulations concerning the registration and identification of carriers of venereal disease may seriously limit the counselor's activities in this area, and it is important that he be familiar with the laws before taking any positive action.

Homosexuality

An area of recent interest, brought about in part by the militancy of gay groups, is the plight of the homosexual student in the secondary schools. At a period in life when acceptance by peers and conformity to images are of paramount importance, it is indeed difficult, if not impossible, for the adolescent homosexual to express himself to his peers and to engage in the type of sexual activity that he finds pleasurable. The main question that has lurked threateningly over the head of the homosexual is whether homosexuality is a sickness or not. Professionals disagree vehemently on this question, but recent sentiments are that homosexuality may be an alternative life style, rather than an illness.

A number of novels in recent years have discussed poignantly the difficulties of growing up homosexual. Of course, it is far from clear exactly what the guidance counselor can do to resolve this problem and make the lives of homosexual students easier. Certainly the counselor should be active in creating in the school a climate of acceptance and respect for homosexuals; the counselor might want to go so far as to allow homosexual dances, a homosexual club, a homosexual newsletter, etc., such as now are common on college campuses. Those homosexuals who wish to become heterosexuals should be afforded psychiatric help and additional counseling.

THE SEX EDUCATION PROGRAM: CONCLUSIONS

The counselor must work with the teacher, parents, students, medical personnel, and the community to set up a comprehensive sex education program with the school. The program should be preventive and educational. It should include group counseling as well as supplemental curricular work and after-school activities. To relate to young people in this difficult emotional area, it is necessary for the counselor and his staff to have resolved their own sexual problems and to be aware of their own sexual values.

McCary (1967) discusses the "why" of sex education at some length. He points out,

The only way our society is going to achieve proper sexual stability and mental health, which are undisputed requirements for maturity, is to instigate and persevere with a sound sex education for everyone. This goal means that those who are in a position to instruct must freely admit to what they do not know, at the same time teaching that which they know to be the truth. They must educate, not indoctrinate; teach fact, not fallacies; formulate a code of ethics, not asceticism; be objective, not subjective; be democratic, not autocratic; and seek knowledge, not emotionally biased constructs. This will be difficult because most people have grown up in a culture which produces and espouses most or all of the negative agents in sexual ignorance and maladjustment. (p. 17)

McCary's remarks illustrate what may be one of the more important considerations about sex education in the schools. Such a program is beneficial not only to the individual student but to the entire society as well. The practical counselor, whose commitment is to integrate the individual with his society and to produce a healthy concordance between them, would certainly wish to be at the forefront of efforts such as these. For such efforts represent, in a practical application, the very essentials of "the counseling stance." Practical counseling is the kind of counseling that utilizes programs such as these to develop the "whole person," sexually, emotionally, and intellectually within the phenomenological context of his world.

References

Chanter, A. G. *Sex education in the primary school.* London: Macmillan, 1966.

Cook, P. W. A great experiment in sex education—The Anaheim story. *Journal of School Health*, 1972, *42*, 7–9.

Ford, C. S. Self-stimulation. In M. F. DeMartino (Ed.), *Sexual behavior and personality characteristics.* New York: Grove Press, 1966.

Juhasz, A. M. Characteristics essential to teachers in sex education. *Journal of School Health*, 1970, *40*, 17–19.

Keller, D. E. How and who of sex education. *American Biology Teacher*, 1972, *34*, 285.

Kinsey, A. C., Pomeroy, W. B., & Martin, C. E. *Sexual behavior in the human male.* Philadelphia: W. B. Saunders, 1948.

McCary, J. L. *Human sexuality.* New York: Van Nostrand Reinhold, 1967.

Youngs, R. C. Reactions to a fifth grade program in sex education. *Journal of School Health*, 1970, *40*, 32–34.

chapter nineteen

Counseling for constructive social change

The crucial question to which we shall address ourselves in this chapter is "How far do the responsibilities of the counselor extend in terms of his obligations to society?" Do they extend beyond his office? Beyond the school? How extensively into the structures of society is the work of the counselor supposed to make an impact? In what ways is the counselor responsible for effecting social changes that are broader and more inclusive than the demands of the school situation alone?

We shall look at this subject from three points of view. First, we shall examine the *consciousness raising* of counselors. In what ways can the counselor become more aware of his place and his role in society? Second, we shall examine the counselor and his professional relationships with clients from minority groups and with women clients. How do his attitudes and biases affect his interactions with blacks, chicanos, other minority clients, and women? Third, we shall look at the counselor in interaction with the community, to see in which community activities the counselor can constructively engage to promote better educational conditions in the society. The purpose of these three sections is to evaluate the potential of the counselor as a constructive, therapeutic social force.

COUNSELOR CONSCIOUSNESS RAISING

The process of *consciousness raising*—of gaining a personal awareness and sensitivity that takes account of the idiosyncracies of the times—is as applicable for the counselor as it is for women's groups, for blacks, for the poor, and for all the others with whom this term has become associated during the past few years. In its most profound and inclusive sense, consciousness raising means becoming aware of oneself and of others, appreciating the subtleties of the interaction between oneself and others. In this section I use the term to refer not so much to the counselor's own self-awareness, which is discussed more fully in chapter 5, but to his awareness of and sensitivity to the needs of the community, of minority groups and women, of the society in which he lives. What can the counselor do to improve the world in which he functions? How can he promote an atmosphere that will encourage constructive change and the progressive development of interests and abilities in those he counsels? How can he come to grips with his own feelings that might not be in accord with the ideal goals of counseling? These are some of the difficult questions we shall consider.

Banks and Martens (1973) have launched a broadside indictment of the counseling profession, referring to counselors as "agents" and "apologists" for the system. They speak of counseling as "the reactionary profession" and cite as evidence the tendency of counselors to defend the system that employs them. In many ways, their arguments are justified and understandable, and yet there is some evidence that the attitudes of counselors are beginning to change as a result of the massive social upheavals of the 1960s. The counselor, like any citizen of a society, is not immune to the myths that perpetuate inequality in social structures; by the same token he is not isolated from the climate of change that has been felt by all of us in recent years. Carkhuff's (1972) "Credo of a Militant Humanist," for instance, is an excellent example of how the traditional values of counseling can be integrated with a social awareness so that the counselor can "constructively exploit both human and community resources."

Morgan and Wicas (1972) blame counselors in part for the demise of the student protest movement. They point out that counselors were never at the forefront of the movement for social change, and they see this as a symptom of the counselor's investment in maintaining the status quo:

Counselors must certainly shoulder some of the blame for the stagnancy of thought and action that has prevailed throughout our secondary schools. As agents of change, counselors have probably been no more effective or ineffective than the rest of the schools' faculties, but in light of what we have witnessed occurring in the schools, this is a damning indictment indeed.

All too often counselors melt readily into the establishment with the result that they are perceived by many students as being maintainers of the status quo, as ineffectual, and as hypocrites.... the counselor needs to become a sensor of sore spots so that serious difficulties and tensions between the institution and the individual can be alleviated, or, better yet, averted. This, of course, implies that the counselor must be willing to stand up to the oppressor, whether the oppressor is the school's principal, a teacher, one or more of the student body, or the community at large. If a counselor really does care, he ought to be able to do much more than just throw up his hands and say, "Well, that's the way it's always been done around here." (p. 37)

The counselor, in other words, according to Morgan and Wicas, can no longer remain embalmed in his complacency. He must be resurrected by his own social consciousness to become a viable social force, capable of effecting changes and profoundly influencing the course of events in society. This is not to suggest that the counselor become a raving radical, nor that his views need be liberal or leftist politically. Certainly a politically conservative counselor can be as effective as a politically liberal counselor. But the point to be emphasized is that the counselor, within the context of his political views, must show a willingness— even an eagerness—to work for constructive social change.

For example, every counselor—every human being—must concern himself with the shattering pains of poverty. The sense of hopelessness, of futility that is the daily bread of the poor manifests on many occasions in the counseling situation, particularly in those schools that are charged with the education of the indigent. Ironically, the very poor, who most need counseling, are least suitable for the process and least likely to afford themselves of any counseling opportunities. As Nass and Nass (1974) have aptly pointed out:

Counseling services, until very recently, have focused on the needs of middle class clientele. Although many counselors have long sought to broaden their practice to include individuals of lower socioeconomic background, their traditional training has not often enabled them to reach people whose impoverished circumstances hinder the progress of conventional modes of therapy.

In their struggle for survival, people of very low socioeconomic status are too absorbed with the harsh realities of everyday life to attend to the subtleties of traditional psychological therapies. (p. 294)

Miller and Mishler (1964) discuss the mental health problems of the poor in an excellent anthology, *Mental Health of the Poor*, edited by Riessman, Cohen, and Pearl. This is an enlightening book for the counselor who is working with the poverty client.

But consciousness-raising, in its broader sense, involves every aspect of the counselor's work. The counselor's continual recognition of the problems of his fellow man, coupled with his sensitivity to his contribution to these problems, enables him to work effectively to change the society in which he lives. Aubrey (1973) describes the difficulties of the adolescent in today's society and proposes constructive social policy for guidance personnel, illustrating most clearly this principle in action.

COUNSELING MINORITY GROUP CLIENTS

The Civil Rights movement of the 1960s, which included legal precedents, social activism, and a new consciousness of the plight of minority members, has had a profound influence upon the counseling profession. Not only have counselors come to realize the special needs of minority members, but they have also been compelled to rethink critically and objectively their own attitudes and beliefs about minority group clients. Although there are certainly substantive differences in the ways of counseling different types of minority members, the basic idea that underlies the problems is the same for all minority groups. We shall look at some of these problems and examine ways in which the counselor can become effective in his work with minority group clients.

Bell (1971) points out that "the counseling psychologist, be he black, white, or otherwise, is likely to function as a culturally deprived person in the black community if his training has taken place in the typical traditional counselor training program" (p. 104). This is a serious indictment of counselor training programs and one that Bell does not go on to substantiate. Nevertheless, it is clear to those of us who are associated with such programs that there is often insufficient opportunity in the training experience to examine and readjust one's ethnic sensitivities. Perhaps the difficulties that plague counselors in their interactions with minority group clients would be significantly lessened had they had an opportunity to express their feelings during their training. Beginning with the assumption that this has not been the case for most counselors, we turn our attention to the question of what the counselor, once engaged in his practice, can do to function effectively with minority group members.

First the counselor must recognize the needs and perceptions that differentiate minority group counselees from other counselees. Often, all too often as a matter of fact, the minority group member is from a lower socioeconomic group than is his white counterpart. He may be experiencing difficulties in school as a result of a poor home environment, of physical and/or mental deprivation, or of a general misunderstanding between himself and his teachers. Below are listed nine special needs and perceptions that I have found commonly expressed or indicated by minority group members, particularly black and Puerto Rican students, in the New York City school system:

1 The MGC (Minority Group Client) needs to feel that he is perceived as an individual, rather than *only* as a member of a group.
2 MGC wants to be able to retain his own identity as well as to function within the context of the larger society.
3 The MGC may tend to perceive the white counselor as being *white*, above all other perceptions. This implies that whatever general stereotypical feelings about whites he has will be projected onto the counselor.
4 The MGC needs a sense of social mobility; he wants to be able to feel that he has an opportunity to rise above his present station in life. Often this hope has been tempered by the realization of the severe restraints that poverty imposes upon social advancement.
5 The MGC wants the emotional freedom to be able to express his own prejudices toward white people. He wants to be able to feel that the white counselor will not be overly threatened by this expression.
6 The MGC wants the school—through its curriculum, its teachers, and its rules—to relate to his world rather than to the world of whitey.
7 The MGC sees things happening around him over which he feels no control. He wants to be better able to control his world, and thus his own destiny, but he is lacking many of the educational and psychological tools necessary for doing so.
8 The MGC often has less opportunity than his white counterpart to discuss home and family life problems. His loyalty to his family may deter him from discussing these with an outsider.
9 The MGC may see the school as the primary social institution (which he considers oppressive and nonresponsive), and be inclined to act out his rage and anger within the school environment.

*The changing times
demand a change in
counselor sensitivitie*

The counselor's understanding of these nine special situations will enable him to understand better and interact with the minority group client. This is not to suggest that understanding alone will enable the counselor to accomplish this very difficult task. Often the obstacles between counselor and client are insurmountable, especially when the client is a late adolescent who for so many years has seen himself as a victim of a system that has little concern for him and even less understanding of him.

Clemont E. Vontress (1967, 1969, 1970) has been particularly vocal in discussing the counselor's interactions with members of minority groups. He has presented the variety of problems confronting the counselor as he sits opposite the black client and attempts to relate to him constructively and therapeutically. "To achieve a high degree of positive regard for people who are different," he suggests that "the counselor must learn more about their [MGC's] way of life and their ethnic and social values" (Vontress, 1970). This is easier said than done; it is often extremely difficult to understand the values of people who are different from ourselves. Melville J. Herskovits's monumental study, *The Myth of the Negro Past,* should be read by every counselor who deals with black students. This book examines black culture from its African roots to twentieth-century America, and it is an invaluable aid in understanding the subtleties of the contemporary black person's cultural and social environment. The willingness of the counselor to study conscientiously the past of his client's heritage avoids what Vontress (1969) calls "the greatest blockage in the relationship...the counselor's lack of understanding of the sociopsychological background of the client."

There are other difficulties in counseling the black or minority group student, as well. Russell (1972) points out that the black student's general negative image of guidance makes the task of counseling him difficult:

For the black student whose lot is to attend those schools dominated by white administrators and where white counselors are the main force in shaping his present and future course, the image of guidance is so negative that it is completely stultifying. The student perceives guidance as an instrument of repression, controlled by counselors who constitute a roadblock he must somehow manage to get around if he has ambitions that do not coincide with those his counselors consider appropriate for him. (p. 288)

This negative attitude, however, can be lessened if the counselor shows his recognition of the client's needs and perceptions as enumerated above. Probably there is no situation in counseling which evidences as clear-cut a need for the nonjudgmental attitude as the interaction between counselor and client of different races, different cultures, and different socioeconomic levels.

Barkiotes et al. (1972) have discussed the language gap between counselors and clients of different ethnic backgrounds. Recent psycholinguistic studies have amplified the significance of this problem considerably, and most counselors nowadays at least recognize the problem, even if they are not entirely able to overcome it. Probably the best way to overcome the language gap is through exposure to and learning of minority group idiosyncratic language patterns and the specialized terms and usages of these groups—in other words, through the same processes that enabled us to learn our native language.

William H. Grier and Price M. Cobbs, two black psychiatrists, have analyzed many of the emotional difficulties of the black in contemporary American society in an important work, *Black Rage.* "The overriding experience of the black American," they point out, "has been grief and sorrow and no man can change that fact." All we can really ask is that the counselor understand this perception of blacks and interpret it in a way that is meaningful both to his intellect and to his conscience.

Franklin (1971) has discussed the difficulty of the black counselor trainee in a counselor training program, and many of his insights offer some optimism to a generally bleak situation of conflict and hopelessness. Davenport and Perry (1973) discuss ways in which the counselor can make career education a socially constructive experience for minority group clients.

Problems of minority groups other than blacks have also found their fair place in the literature. The difficulties of counseling the American Indian have been discussed by Ryan (1969), Gifford (1964), Zintz (1962), and others. Considerations about counseling the Mexican-American client have been discussed by Brown and Srebalus (1972), Casavantes (1970), and others. Sue and Sue (1972) have discussed counseling Chinese-Americans. But perhaps the group that has been the subject of most attention during the early 1970s is not a minority group at all but a majority group that in many respects has been treated as a minority group. I refer, of course, to women.

COUNSELING WOMEN

The raising of women's consciousness, a phenomenon of our times, has had a profound effect upon the counseling profession, both in the male counselor's relationships with his female clients and in counselor training programs. What can the sincere and conscientious male counselor do to assure that he is not an unwitting victim of unconscious prejudices about the place of women in society? How can counselors of both sexes assure that their female clients will be given an equal opportunity to maximize their potential? The complexities of the entire problem of woman's role in our society are far too detailed and technical for inclusion in this book, but it is important for the practicing counselor to keep in mind the changing role of women in our society, and to be sensitive to their changing needs and requirements. I shall limit the discussion in this section to some insights about the counselor in his interactions with female clients.

Shertzer and Stone (1974) discuss the scope of the problem:

The difficulty facing many counselors lies in accommodating the counseling process to the realities of this life pattern when their female clients struggle with choice, decision making and long term life plans. Those in the forefront of women's rights emphasize strongly the necessity for a woman to make informed choices between the following: marriage, a career, a career in combination with a marriage, marriage with a career later in life. At present, they believe that an enlightened choice for many women is extremely difficult, if not impossible, to attain because of pervasive sexist attitudes....

Counselors, male or female, must be sensitive to and aware of their beliefs about women and their role in contemporary society. Without doubt, these beliefs have an impact upon a female client, may well influence the counseling relationship, and may have an effect on the client's future life. *The female client must be treated as an individual rather than simply as a member of the female sex. Both participants must consider the future difficulties faced by the liberated female in a society which modifies its expectancies very slowly and grudgingly* (italics added). (p. 342)

We see that one of the key problems in this analysis is the conflict between the true existential freedom of the woman to choose and pursue her destiny in the ways she sees fit, and the constraints imposed upon her by society and regressive, sexist thinking.

A number of studies have confirmed this hypothesis. Schlossberg and Pietrofesa (1973), for example, review a variety of studies that demonstrate the nature and extent of counselor sexual bias. They point to a study by Friedersdorf (1969) that found, among other things, that "Male counselors tended to think of women in feminine roles characterized by feminine personality traits.... Male counselors perceived the college-bound girl as having positive attitudes toward traditionally feminine occupations regardless of the classification level of the

Women want their rights–now!

occupations. Occupations traditionally engaged in by men were not considered by male counselors as occupations that college-bound girls would like as careers" (p. 47). Another study by Hawley (1972) found that the feminine model held by 52 female counselors-in-training allowed a wider range of educational and career choices than the feminine model held by 45 female teachers-in-training, indicating that female counselors of the future might offer a hope in this area. Schlossberg (1972) has integrated many of the insights developed from her extensive research and presented a framework for counseling women, based on the ideas of openness to the true reality of the female client.

Berry (1972) has discussed the phase of counseling women that is of most concern both to the women and to the counseling profession: occupational counseling. For it is in this area more than any other that biases and stereotyping prevent the female client from fulfilling her potential. Berry lists nine activities that the "alert counselor" would certainly want to explore in order to limit the pitfalls of sexist counseling:

1 Collect materials describing emerging opportunities for women in new fields such as ecology, consumer health, home-related services, and apprentice professional training.

2 Seek, secure, and use newly developed materials, such as the APGA cassette series "Counseling; Today and Tomorrow" (one cassette of which is currently being prepared in cooperation with the Women's Bureau of the U.S. Department of Labor) and films and other media presentations that combat sexism by showing women in job, career, and political situations commonly set aside for men only.

3 Arrange educational and informational sessions to help parents understand and accept the life and career perspectives of their daughters.

4 Assist girls to make occupational choices in traditional male occupations such as dentistry, engineering, law, and medicine.

5 Motivate girls toward leadership positions and career goals that lead to the highest levels of responsibility in private business and local, state, and federal government.

6 Provide detailed assistance with scholarship, loan, and fellowship opportunities and applications that are needed to support girls and women, who have traditionally been ruled out as bad risks.

7 Plan community workshops and seminar sessions for employers and school placement officers to check out new job opportunities and avenues of career advancement for women. Such exchanges will foster important firsthand understanding of what is happening in institutions and organizations to diminish barriers that block women from top level assignments. Counselors should be alert for subtle attitudinal forces and factors responsible for these barriers and on the lookout for token arrangements, which often parallel the upward movement of blacks.

8 Make an all-out effort to understand barriers that women put in front of themselves. Girls have been socialized to avoid certain career roles and high level responsibilities. Career-marriage conflicts and fears of failure ... must also be dealt with in the context of counseling for the New Woman.

9 Assist in explaining to young men, who are often baffled by the New Womanhood, the rising vocational and career priorities of girls and women.* (pp. 107–108)

Using these as guidelines, the creative counselor should be able to develop his own individual counseling approach with women, an approach that, hopefully, will enable the female client an opportunity to develop fully and in accord with her own abilities, interests, and options. A recent issue of the *Personnel and Guidance Journal* (October 1972) is devoted entirely to the subject of "Women and Counselors," and it would be of interest to all counselors who wish to improve their abilities in this area.

THE COUNSELOR AND THE COMMUNITY

School and community

The school is an important part of every community. The majority of families in a given community have at least one child in attendance at a local school for six hours every day. The school building is often used as a meeting place for

---

*From "The New Womanhood: Counselor Alert" by Jane B. Berry, *Personnel and Guidance Journal*, 1972, *51*, 105–108. Copyright 1972 American Personnel and Guidance Association. Reprinted with permission.

The counselor should be familiar with the neighborhood that is "home" for those whom he counsels.

community functions, and the school's athletic field or playground may be used several hours each day for recreation by members of the community. The job of the school—education of the community's children—is of prime concern to the adults of the community.

In a ghetto community, the school takes on a special importance. It represents to the parents of the community an opportunity for their children to escape the confines of the ghetto, to acquire more social and economic prestige, to be—as the American dream states—a success. But to these same parents, the school also represents a threat. Its immense influence upon the lives of their children may cause the parents concern about what the children are being taught, what values are being learned, what allegiances are being forged. Traditionally, this has been called the threat of *assimilation*, of minority members being reeducated in the culture of the majority and consequently being absorbed into that culture, usually against the direct will of their parents. It is important, therefore, that educators be sensitive to this fear of the parents and attempt to include in school activities, as well as in curricula, elements of the local group's culture.

In a typical school, much of this sensitivity and subsequent planning will fall on the shoulders of the school guidance counselor. He serves, as much as the principal, as a representative of the school to the community. It is his attitude toward the values of the local groups and his awareness of their needs, reflected in his actions, that will enable the local group to judge the entire school. Much may depend on this. Recently a school counselor in New York City organized a Latin music festival in his school's playground. Members of the community, which was predominantly Latin-American, attended the festival, many of them coming for the first time to the school attended by their children. Soon after the festival, the teachers and administrators of the school noticed a considerable increase in parents' interest in school functions: PTA attendance doubled, the library committee gained four new members, and the annual cake sale was a bigger success than ever before. As a result of that one-day festival, the parents felt a newfound comfort in the school, a new respect, which yielded an abundance of interest and activity.

In addition to his awareness of community culture, the school counselor must also be acutely aware of how the problems of a specific community may make themselves felt in the school. After Dewey, no one can doubt that the school is an integral, functioning part of the community, as healthy or as unhealthy as the community itself. The most obvious example is the ill effects that a poverty-stricken community has upon its school. This is more of a social problem than a counseling problem, but it is extremely important that the counselor be aware of the community's situation and its influence upon the school. One unfortunate incident occurred when a school counselor sent a child home because the child's shoes were worn through and his feet were wet. The counselor sent an angry note home with the child, advising the parents to dress the child better before sending him to school. What this counselor should have realized was that the child's parents would have gladly bought new shoes if they had had the money. They were gravely offended by the counselor's insensitivity to the poverty in that neighborhood.

Community goals

In recent years Americans have become more aware of their sense of community than in any other period since the New England town hall meetings in the nineteenth century. Oddly enough, this awareness is growing at a more rapid rate in the big cities than in rural areas. Partly responsible for this is a new awareness by minority groups, an awareness of the opportunities that await them out there in the world beyond the community. Community organizing includes clean-up drives, political campaigns, picketing for various causes, war against drug addiction, and community control of the schools. Whatever the school counselor may think of any of these personally, and his feelings are often extreme in either direction, it is crucial that he maintain an objective sense of proportion and an attitude of fairness and understanding. To the community for which he works these are very important values.

Certainly the counselor should not be asked to participate in activities or to voice agreement to principles that contradict his values. But likewise, neither should he be obliged to represent the school administration's position on matters that could be offensive to the community. During the teachers' strike of 1969 in New York City, a number of school counselors were placed in the compromising position of having to explain to members of the community with whom they had established a rapport over the years why the teachers were striking and why the administration supported the strike. Even though these counselors tried to make clear that these were not necessarily their own personal opinions, the fact that they were voicing these opinions and representing the striking group negated many of their constructive efforts of the previous years.

There are many community efforts that can be endorsed by all school counselors. The two most important of these are the war against drug addiction and drives to clean up the community. The first is discussed in chapter 17. The second requires some special consideration here.

A counselor who resides in a middle-class community often has difficulty understanding the intensity and involvement that a clean-up drive produces in a lower-class ghetto community. A clean-up drive usually consists of the following activities, which would be unnecessary in a well-kept suburban or upper-class community:

1 Picking up litter and discarded furniture from vacant lots.
2 Sweeping the streets.
3 Search for and killing rats. Sometimes a bounty is offered for each dead rat.
4 Preparing complaints to the authorities about abandoned buildings and fire violations.

Such a drive has enormous advantages to the community, besides the obvious one of having a cleaner, healthier, and safer place to live. It channels the

A community clean-up campaign is a valid therapeutic experience for many students.

anger and frustration of community members into constructive social outlets. It helps the community members develop a sense of self-pride as well as community pride. Of special importance to the counselor is that the children's activities in local clean-up drives often extend to the school itself. Students become more active in keeping their school clean after they gain awareness of the sanitation problem and what they are capable of doing about it.

The school counselor can participate in community clean-up drives in several ways. He can offer community members his administrative and organizing experience in helping to make the drive a success. He can publicize the effort in his school and encourage students to participate. Most important, in terms of the relationship between the community and the school, he should urge the teachers, administration, and staff of his school to assist the community in their drive. This can do more to help community relations than years of good intentions and pleasant rhetoric. The students and their parents, working hand in hand with the school staff in picking up litter and improving the community, will experience good and productive feelings toward each other that can only be helpful in the long run.

Community agencies

Most urban communities nowadays have a number of local agencies, both public and private, each one dedicated to some aspect of community service. Most common are agencies devoted to employment, human rights, education, police relations, and religious matters. In addition to their stated goals, these

agencies often serve as meeting places for community members, as symbols of social consciousness and pride, and as powerful organizing forces within the community.

The counselor should be familiar with these agencies because they are important community resources. He should visit each agency and note what services it offers that might be utilized by his students. He should have available for his students and their parents mimeographed material describing each agency and its purpose, giving its address, personnel, and additional information that might be useful in dealing with whatever problem is bringing the member to that agency. Providing such material not only gives the parents and students information they can use, but it shows the community and the students that the counselor is aware of resources and interested in community affairs.

These agencies should also be cognizant of the school counselor. He should offer his services wherever they might be of help to the agency, and he should explore with the agency how it might be helpful to him in his counseling duties. One counselor in Detroit, for example, established a fine rapport with an agency dedicated to assisting college-bound ghetto youths obtain scholarship assistance. The counselor saw an opportunity beyond the immediately stated goal of the agency and invited the director of the agency and some students who had received assistance to speak at his school. These speakers, all residents of the local community, showed the students that it was indeed possible for them to go to college if they applied themselves. Many students knew the speakers' younger brothers and sisters, which made the message even more meaningful.

379

Particularly useful to the school counselor in his efforts to utilize community resources is the *Directory of Urban Affairs Information and Research Centers* (P.O. Box 656, Metuchen, N.J. 08840: Scarecrow Press, Inc.). This directory provides the school counselor with a guide to those organizations, agencies, and institutions that may be of assistance in solving urban problems. Entries provide information about specific areas of competence, services, activities, staffing, publications, etc., and subject indexes are provided. The *Integrated Personnel Services Index* (University of Michigan, 611 Church Street, Ann Arbor, Mich. 48104: ERIC) is also a useful reference work, indexing information about resources currently available in all fields of student services, including school counseling, school psychology, school health work, and employment counseling.

SUMMARY

The counselor must always keep in mind the interlocking relationship between the school and the community. What happens in the community is never isolated from the activities of the school, and what takes place in the classroom and in the counselor's office is never totally distinct from what is happening in the community.

The counselor, therefore, must be familiar with the economic, cultural, and political realities of the community in which his school is situated. He should participate in constructive community activities and encourage the school staff to do so as well. Community agencies should be explored, and a working relationship between these agencies and the school counselor should be established.

Moreover, the counselor must explore his own attitudes concerning those issues which are in process of turbulent social change. His attitudes toward minorities, toward women, toward the culturally different must all bear careful scrutiny. If he works in a poor neighborhood, or a ghetto, he must ask himself, "How capable am I of understanding and empathizing with the needs of the people in this community?" In attempting to do vocational counseling, he must be sensitive to the rising aspirations of the student, and to the social obstacles often placed in front of women and minorities.

We examined some ways in which the counselor could help the students and school personnel become involved in community activities. A community clean-up campaign was used as an example of a social effort that channels students' energies into appropriate directions.

References

Aubrey, R. F. *Experimenting with living: pros and cons.* Columbus, Ohio: Charles E. Merrill, 1973.

Banks, W., & Martens, K. Counseling: The reactionary profession. *Personnel and Guidance Journal*, 1973, *51*, 457–462.

Barkiotes, F., Barkiotes, P. G., & Schumacher, L. C. Language compatibility and minority group counseling. *Journal of Counseling Psychology*, 1972, *19*, 225–256.

Bell, R. L., Jr. The culturally deprived psychologist. *The Counseling Psychologist*, 1971, *2*, 104–107.

Berry, J. B. The new womanhood: Counselor alert. *Personnel and Guidance Journal*, 1972, *51*, 105–108.

Brown, D., & Srebalus, D. J. *Contemporary guidance concepts and practices: An introduction.* Dubuque, Iowa: Wm. C. Brown, 1972.

Carkhuff, R. R. Credo of a militant humanist. *Personnel and Guidance Journal*, 1972, *51*, 237–242.

Casavantes, E. Pride and prejudice: A Mexican-American dilemma. *Civil Rights Digest*, 1970, *3*, 22–27.

Davenport, L., & Perry, R. *Minorities and career education.* Columbus, Ohio: E.C.C.A. Publications, 1973.

Franklin, A. J. To be young, gifted, and black with inappropriate training. *The Counseling Psychologist*, 1971, *2*, 107–112.

Friedersdorf, N. W. A comparative study of counselor attitudes toward the further educational and vocational plans of high school girls. Unpublished study, Purdue University, 1969. (Quoted in N. K. Schlossberg & J. J. Pietrofesa, Perspectives on counseling bias: Implications for counselor educators. *The Counseling Psychologist*, 1973, *4*, 44–54.)

Gifford, S. Educating the American Indian. *School Life*, 1964, *47*, 10–12.

Grier, W. H., & Cobbs, P. M. *Black rage.* New York: Basic Books, 1968.

Hawley, P. Perception of male models of femininity related to career choice. *Journal of Counseling Psychology*, 1972, *19*, 308–313.

Herskovits, M. J. *The myth of the Negro past.* Boston: Beacon Press, 1958.

Miller, S. M., & Mishler, E. G. Social class, mental illness, and American psychiatry. In F. Riessman, J. Cohen, & A. Pearl (Eds.), *Mental health of the poor.* New York: Free Press, 1964.

Morgan, L. B., & Wicas, E. A. The short, unhappy life of student dissent. *Personnel and Guidance Journal*, 1972, *51*, 33–38.

Nass, S., & Nass, D. R. Counseling with clients of lower socioeconomic background. In G. S. Belkin (Ed.), *Foundations of Counseling.* Dubuque, Iowa: Kendall/Hunt, 1974.

Riessman, F., Cohen, J., & Pearl, A. (Eds.) *Mental health of the poor.* New York: Free Press, 1964.

Russell, R. D. Black perceptions of guidance. In D. Brown & D. J. Srebalus (Eds.), *Contemporary guidance concepts and practices: An introduction.* Dubuque, Iowa: Wm. C. Brown, 1972.

Ryan, C. W. Counseling the culturally encapsulated American Indian. *Vocational Guidance Quarterly*, 1969, *18*, 123–126.

Schlossberg, N. K. A framework for counseling women. *Personnel and Guidance Journal*, 1972, *51*, 137–146.

Schlossberg, N. K., & Pietrofesa, J. J. Perspectives on counseling bias: Implications for counselor education. *The Counseling Psychologist*, 1973, *4*, 44–54.

Shertzer, B., & Stone, S. C. *Fundamentals of counseling* (2nd ed.). Boston: Houghton Mifflin, 1974.

Sue, D. W., & Sue, S. Counseling Chinese-Americans. *Personnel and Guidance Journal*, 1972, *50*, 637–644.

Vontress, C. E. The culturally different. *Employment Service Review*, 1967, *4*, 35–36.

Vontress, C. E. Cultural barriers in the counseling relationship. *Personnel and Guidance Journal*, 1969, *48*, 11–17.

Vontress, C. E. Counseling blacks. *Personnel and Guidance Journal*, 1970, *48*, 713–719.

Zintz, M. Y. Problems of classroom adjustment of Indian children in public elementary schools in the southwest. *Science Education*, 1962, *46*, 261–269.

chapter twenty

Appraisal, consultation, and team counseling

The three activities referred to in the title of this chapter occupy a major portion of the counselor's time. As an appraiser, an evaluator, the counselor administers tests, interprets test results, keeps records, and uses tests, interpretation, and record keeping to assist the student in his plans and to guide him in his endeavors. The appraisal function, which we shall discuss in some detail in this chapter, is one of the mundane but necessary parts of the counseling function that in the long run contributes to the overall effectiveness of counseling. While it is neither as exciting as psychological counseling nor as dramatic as crisis counseling, it serves the very same purpose as these two functions, namely, to help the client in whatever way is best for him.

The counselor as consultant is a familiar role to most practicing counselors. The counselor is the communicator of vital counseling information. When he speaks to parents, teachers, school medical personnel, the school psychologist or social worker, the administrator, or others, the counselor functions as a consultant. When he works *with* any of these persons for the benefit of the client, he functions as a member of the counseling team. Both these positions will be considered in this chapter.

THE APPRAISAL FUNCTION

The student appraisal services are designed to gather and collate data about each student *for the purpose of helping him carry out his plans and improve in areas where he is deficient, and to identify early any difficulties which may interfere with the student's growth.* It is important to emphasize, in an age as sensitive to individual privacy as is ours, that this collection of data is never intended to be used against the student but always for the student's own benefit.

A good appraisal service should be integrated, continuous, and utilitarian. By integrated, I mean that it should include a variety of both test and nontest information: results of school-administered aptitude and intelligence tests; anecdotal records (see p. 386); autobiographical information; questionnaires and rating scales; specialized test materials administered under the auspices of

the counselor's office; interest inventories and occupational tests. The integration of all these different kinds of information enables the counselor to enjoy a wider, more accurate picture of the student.

An appraisal service should also be continuous. To be meaningful, it must continue from year to year, recording the student's progress in school, the changes observed by his teachers, his relative high's and low's of performance and attitude. Later in this chapter we shall examine the continuity of a testing program, and the comments there apply as well to the continuity of the nontest phase of the appraisal function.

A utilitarian appraisal function is one which can easily be translated into some type of practical application.

Utilitarian here means specifically that the data collected must be put to work for the benefit of the student. If the records and test results were allowed to gather dust in the counselor's files over the years, there would be little justification for appraisal. A good appraisal program is always student-oriented.

Hansen (1967) suggests that before we can have a program that uses information for the student's benefit, we must set up protective guidelines concerning the release of information to outside agencies and to other people without a clear-cut interest in the student's welfare. This concern regarding the privacy of appraisal information is directly related to the utilitarian issue. Heayn and Jacobs (1967) outline procedures for insuring the confidentiality of information. They define four levels of openness of information, ranging from the unrestricted (name, sex, date of birth, previous school attended, etc.) to the confidential (psychological reports, psychiatric evaluations, etc.). It is important that the counselor have a clear understanding of what information he is entitled to release, which is prohibited, and which is discretionary. Local school districts, as well as cities and states, differ in their policies, and it is essential that the counselor be familiar with the rules in effect in his bailiwick. In all cases, however, the counselor must defer to the ethical standards of the American Personnel and Guidance Association (available from APGA, 1607 New Hampshire Ave., N.W., Washington, D.C. 20009).

Assuming, then, that the counselor has safeguarded the privacy of the information, how can he put this information to some constructive use—how does he make it utilitarian? This differs in detail depending upon the type of information. Six general principles of using appraisal information are outlined below:

1 The counselor evaluates the information as a whole, never relying on a single piece of information. For example, the counselor may receive from a teacher an anecdotal report that speaks poorly of the child. If he examines the rest of the student's folder, however, he may find that this report is an exception rather than the rule. Any single piece of information must be assessed in terms of all the information.

2 The counselor applies his interpretive skills in evaluating the information instead of simply accepting it at face value. He may apply his psychological skills and insights in evaluating subjective information and his statistical skills in evaluating objective test results.

3 In sharing information with other members of the counseling team, the counselor assumes full responsibility for the use made of the information. In this sense, the counselor is the guardian of student information.

4 The counselor attempts, in his interactions with clients, productively to integrate the information into the interview. He may, for example, inform a student who is showing poor performance in school that his abilities, as measured by a test instrument, far exceed his performance. Test results may be particularly helpful to the counselor in career counseling, where tests especially designed to evaluate career interest and potential can save the counselor a great deal of time and guesswork.

5 The counselor looks at all information as it reaches his office, in order to act immediately when the information suggests that such action would be of benefit to the student.

6 The counselor contributes to such school functions as curriculum decisions, hirings and promotions, disposition of cases, discipline committees, and the like, in cognizance of the information in his files. This is to say that the coun-

selor puts this information into practice in contributing to broad policy decisions that affect all students. For example, the results of a standardized test may show that the students at his school are performing very poorly in mathematics. This may well indicate a need to review and/or revise the mathematics program.

With these general principles in mind, let us now examine some particular kinds of appraisal tools, both of the testing and nontesting type, to pinpoint more accurately the purposes of each.

NON-TEST APPRAISAL TECHNIQUES

All of the techniques to be discussed below are used widely in the school system. While the relative importance and accuracy of these different techniques has been the subject of much contention over the years, it is generally agreed that these techniques provide an essential service to the students as well as to the school (Traxler and North, 1966). Some counselors and teachers have devised new methods of appraisal that are not included in this section; the methods listed below are the most widely used and accepted.

Observation

Observation, it has been said, is the basis of all science. Observation differs from *looking* or *seeing* by the selectivity and organization of the data perceived by the observer. Observation, the dictionary* says, is "the act or practice of noting and recording facts and events, as for some scientific study." In other words, observation is a type of seeing, governed by an inner wisdom and by the principles of scientific scrutiny.

When one observes a situation, one should have at least a preliminary idea of what to look for. For example, if I were a naturalist on an expedition designed to study the effects of pollution on plant life in New Mexico, I would, as I walked the terrain of New Mexico, take especially careful note of the signs of destruction of indigenous flora, for evaluation later on. This preliminary frame of reference allows the observer to concentrate more accurately on the subject at hand, since no person could conceivably absorb the millions of stimuli that bombard him at any given moment. It is important, then, that the observer have an idea of what he wants to observe. Strang (1949) has provided a detailed list of pupil behavior that would be of special interest to the observer, and this list has been much quoted since its original appearance.

There are a number of difficulties implicit in the observation model. Subjective biases and poor insight may prevent the observer from accurately evaluating and recording the reality of the observed situation. Shertzer and Stone (1971) have suggested that to increase the accuracy of observation, "a number of

Webster's New World Dictionary of the American Language, 2nd College Edition. New York: The World Publishing Co., 1970.

observations should be made in a variety of situations and at different times."
We might also keep in mind Alexander Pope's insight,

To observations which ourselves we make
We grow more partial for th' observer's sake.

In other words, don't take note only of those things that you, as the observer,
want to notice!

Anecdotal records

When observations are recorded, they are called anecdotal observations.
Warters (1956) offers a balanced definition:

The anecdotal record is a word picture of a specific incident. The record should be limited
to objective description and should be free of generalized description, interpretations, and
evaluations. At times, however, explanatory, interpretive, or evaluative statements are
needed for the full significance of the incident to be understood; but such statements
should be reported apart from the account of the incident, preferably on the reverse side of
the record sheet. Ordinarily a number of anecdotal reports are needed before much useful
information may be obtained on a student through this method, but the large size of many
classes makes it difficult for teachers to write many reports on many students.
Unfortunately, the anecdotal records of the majority of teachers yield primarily
information about the quality of the student's academic performance and his attitudes
toward teachers and schoolwork rather than information regarding the student's social
adjustment and his attitudes toward himself and his peers. This fact and the fact that
many teachers tend to report their reactions rather than their observations and tend to
report unusual and unfavorable behavior more often than typical and favorable behavior
reduce the value of the anecdotal technique. Properly used, however, it can produce
significant data on adjustment and personality development that cannot be easily
obtained otherwise. (p. 139)

While the anecdotal record has traditionally been used to report disruptive
incidents, it can also serve a positive role in the counseling program by providing the counselor with a developmental, longitudinal portrait of the student,
capturing succinctly moments of his growth and development through the educational program. Roeber, Smith, and Erickson (1955) comment on this point:

Anecdotal records were originally devised to report incidents which were indicative of
pupil deportment. Although the attitude of the pupil toward himself and others around
him is significant, there are several facets of possible reporting which have been neglected
and may be equally significant. Educational and vocational planning are dependent upon
evaluations of interests and abilities, as well as other factors. The anecdotal-record
system, if put into effect for grades one through twelve, can supply a developmental
picture of any pupil's interest and abilities. The incident may be some special project
which demonstrates an ability. Only anecdotal records supply day-to-day classroom
incidents which indicate trends in interests and abilities. (p. 152)

The anecdotal record becomes an integrated productive part of the appraisal function. As such, it must be accurate and objective. Miller (1968) has detailed the characteristics of a good anecdotal record, with concise instructions how the recorder can be assured of doing a competent job. He emphasizes immediacy, specificity, objectivity, selectivity, simplicity, and insight as the key criteria for a good anecdotal record.

Cumulative records

As the name implies, the cumulative record is a progressive, coordinated record of the student's progress in school. The cumulative record may include any or all of the following: student's name, address(es), date of birth, grades in school, results of standardized tests, disciplinary actions, health information, family information, extracurricular activities, self-reports, anecdotal records, rating scales, samples of the student's work, and other data. It is, in the broadest sense, a comprehensive paper portrait of the student.

Warnken and Siess (1965) discuss ways in which the cumulative record may be used in the prediction of behavior. By reducing a large number of different observations and data to a manageable set of terms, the authors demonstrate that the information contained within the cumulative record can be a valid predictor of student expected behavior. They propose a specific check-list technique for recording observations, which should make observation reports within an individual school more uniform and consistent. While such uniformity is a step in the right direction, more efforts will have to be undertaken in the future (perhaps by APGA) to make cumulative records uniform nationwide, in view of the great mobility of families in our country today. Roeber, Smith, and Erickson (1955) list eleven types of forms and records that would probably be included in the cumulative record folder: pupil personal data blank, administrative record, achievement and activities inventory, test profiles and records, autobiography, anecdotal and rating records, plan sheets, fact-finding interview records, sociometric and miscellaneous data, placement and follow-up records.

Other nontest appraisal techniques

In addition to the techniques discussed earlier, there are a number of other important nontest appraisal techniques. The autobiography, a report written by the student about himself, provides the counselor with an important insight into the student's self-perceptions. One of the major advantages of the autobiography, Tolbert (1972) points out, is that it "provides the counselor with a view of the counselee's world as perceived by the counselee" (p. 176). Annis (1967) has written a comprehensive paper on the uses and values of the autobiography in professional counseling and psychology. He includes a thorough list of references on the subject, and the counselor who wishes to exploit fully this counseling tool would do well to read his paper.

Rating scales to help the counselor quickly, although superficially, to grasp some aspect of the client's personality. Rating scales make it easy to quantify the client and to categorize him according to the rating categories. The weakness of rating scales is (1) their oversimplification of the complexities of the client to a few choice categories and quantifiers and (2) their subjectivity. In both the construction and the interpretation of rating scales, it is important that the counselor be sensitive to these two serious limitations.

There are four basic types of rating scales. *Descriptive rating scales* provide the counselor with a variety of descriptive statements from which he may choose those that best describe the student. *Numerical rating scales* and *graphic rating scales* both utilize gradations of numbers to indicate the student's relative rating. The difference between these two is that the graphic rating scale uses a pictorial representation, as in this example.

COOPERATION

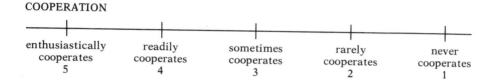

| enthusiastically cooperates 5 | readily cooperates 4 | sometimes cooperates 3 | rarely cooperates 2 | never cooperates 1 |

The graphic scale may use either numerical or descriptive indices or both. Another rating method often used is the *paired comparison method*, in which the rater compares the subject to others in a group as equal, worse, or better. There are advantages and disadvantages to each of these methods. The counselor must decide exactly what he wants to find out and then decide on the best method for getting the information.

Sociometric techniques are used to measure the student's social values, preferences, and interactions. Thorndike and Hagen (1969) define a sociometric technique as "a procedure for determining each individual's position within a social group such as a school class by analyzing the choices (and rejections) made by each group member with respect to the others in the group" (p. 653). Questionnaires, rating scales, and tests are all used to determine sociometric quantification. Gronlund (1960) has thoroughly explored sociometric methods that are relevant to the classroom situation. Many of these techniques involve observation and construction by the teacher. Other approaches involve the use of printed sociometric inventories. Gronlund includes a number of these tests in his book.

Having now examined some nontest appraisal techniques, let us turn our attention to student appraisal services that use testing and evaluation procedures based on test and statistical data.

TESTING AND EVALUATION

Nowadays many counseling graduates profess not to believe in testing. Some of them, children of the early and mid-fifties, when testing in the schools had reached new peaks, remember with dismay the many hours they were required to labor, pencil in hand, hunched over their desks answering questions that seemed irrelevant to their lives. They recall the SAT's, the MAT's and the GRE's that more recently challenged them. They recall the many studies and articles they have been exposed to in their training that lambast the testing movement and minimize the value of tests in learning about the individual. They cite testing as another instance of the depersonalization prevalent in the schools and in society today, and they vow with integrity not to become part of this very system when they become guidance counselors. They remember with sadness their own failures on tests—their pain, their excuses, their rationalizations—and judge the instrument by their own personal experiences. They rebel.

Despite this common sentiment, testing remains an integral part of the counseling function, and it is perhaps the single most important part of the counselor's specialized appraisal skills. Many counseling positions are created precisely for the purpose of test administration, and the skilled clinical counselor, regardless of his qualifications, can hardly lay claim to professional expertise without at least an acquaintance with the area of testing and evaluation.

Moreover, testing and evaluation, while at times badly abused, serve as an integral part of the counselor's resources. Testing, looked at objectively, is a virtual bonanza for the counselor who does not have time to meet individually

Taking a test need not be an unpleasant experience.

with each student in his school. Within a large school population, testing allows the counselor to identify those students who are most in need of counseling, remediation, or other forms of guidance. Testing also enables the administration and instructional staff to design a curriculum that is responsive to the needs, interests, aptitudes, and abilities of the students. Testing serves another function as well: It enables a community to measure the progress of its students against the progress of students in other communities, thus indirectly evaluating the efficacy of its school system.

Individual testing also has several advantages for the counselor. From a test the counselor is often able to get information about the client that is accessible neither through the face-to-face interview nor through consultation with teachers, parents, and other interested parties. For example, a child working with a counselor under my supervision was diagnosed by the physician at her school as having minimal brain damage. We administered a battery of tests and ultimately determined that the child was of above normal intelligence but was suffering from mild dyslexia. Several treatment sessions with a specialist cured a problem that had almost inadvertently ruined this young girl's life.

Individual testing also offers the counselor an opportunity to confirm his intuitive impressions of the client. Often when working with a client, the counselor develops feelings about a client: It may be a feeling relating to his occupational interests, to his intellectual abilities, to his preferences and personality characteristics. In any case, one can never be entirely sure of one's feelings, so that it is often reassuring to the counselor to find a suitable test instrument to determine the accuracy of his intuition.

A SEVEN STAGE TESTING PROGRAM

In addition to administering individual and group tests, the school counselor is often asked to institute a testing program. A testing program consists of an organized school-wide or system-wide effort to administer and evaluate standardized tests. Typically, the counselor situated in the public school is placed in charge of a testing program for his school, although in smaller school districts a school counselor may be asked to take charge of the testing program for the district. Such a counselor will, however, generally have had advanced training in testing and evaluation. In either case, the counselor's responsibility is heavy in the areas of testing, and his competency should be worthy of the degree of responsibility.

Thorndike and Hagen (1969) cite three desirable characteristics of a testing program: *relation to use*, *integration*, and *continuity*. "Relation to use" means that the specific tests offered should be applicable to the problems that the school is attempting to solve or to the insights they wish to gain. If, for example, a counselor is in charge of the testing program for a school in a large urban center that has a central testing program, the tests he offers in his school would not repeat what the system-wide tests are measuring nor would they measure traits that are of little interest to the school administration. Similarly, in a sixth-grade class for slow learners, tests that discriminate high intelligence levels should not be used.

"Integration" refers to the extent to which there is logical and clear cut relationship between the different test instruments being used and between the testing administered from grade to grade. Speaking about this concept, Thorndike and Hagen point out,

In an integrated program, it will usually be desirable to use the same series of tests over the grade range for which it is appropriate. Thus, if the *Metropolitan Achievement Tests* are being used to measure progress in basic skills, it will probably be desirable to use them in any grade from first up to sixth, and possibly eighth or ninth, in which an achievement battery is being used. The advantages are that norms are based upon the same sampling of communities from grade to grade, and the tests conform to a common outline of content and format. Thus, scores from one grade to the next are more nearly comparable, so that a truer picture may be obtained of pupil growth. (p. 522)

To have "continuity," a testing program must be continued over a period of years. Continuity allows us to follow the growth of an individual student from year to year, to measure the abilities of specific teachers, curricula, administrators, etc., as well as allowing us the option of getting to know our test instruments better. It is through the continuing use of test instruments, and through the continuation of the testing program, that a longitudinal study of growth and development may be undertaken.

Carey (1969) suggests six fundamental questions that the counselor should ask himself in order to evaluate the overall quality and utility of a testing program. These questions are compatible with the three criteria suggested by Thorndike and Hagen but are specific enough to enable the counselor to make a precise determination. The six questions are:

1 To what real use are the tests being put?
2 Are the uses really pertinent to the students who take them, or are they "administrative" and merely add to the record?
3 Are the uses significant enough to justify time usurped from classes, counselor time in administering and handling data, and money expended?
4 Do school personnel have enough time to really use test results?
5 Is the program balanced? Does it provide useful information for average and lower ability students as well as the college-bound, and vocational as well as educational counseling?
6 Is the program concentrated at choice-points in order that a fresh, relatively complete self-picture is available for each student when he must make an important decision or, at earlier stages, when an important decision must be made about him? (p. 205)

As the counselor conscientiously approaches these questions, he will be forced to recognize the different stages of a testing program and the interrelationships between these stages. For the sake of simplification, the testing and evaluation procedures have been divided into seven general stages (see Display

THE SEVEN STAGES OF TESTING AND EVALUATION

1 Assessing the need for a test and determining what is to be measured, how much time is available, and a general evaluation of the resources.
2 Selecting a test instrument. Requisitioning.
3 Arranging for the administration of the test.
4 Collecting the tests and distributing them for scoring.

5 Preparing test data sheets and an accompanying interpretive guide.
6 Making test results available to appropriate parties and interpreting the implications of specific test data.
7 Follow-up.

20.1), and we shall look at each of these briefly to determine the practical steps the counselor must follow in order to implement a successful testing program.

1 Assessing the need for a test and determining what is to be measured, how much time is available, and a general evaluation of the resources

In almost any educational situation, one could easily find valid reasons to administer tests to the student population. Since testing allows the teachers, counselors, and administrators to learn more about each student—as well as more about the population as a whole—a basic reason behind much, if not all, testing is to enable the system to learn about the individuals in it. This, however, is not a compelling reason to administer a testing program. It can, however, become a compelling justification when the "desire to know" is coupled with a commitment to action and change.

Let us say, for example, that Principal Jones believes his new and liberal administration has been doing a superior job in improving the students' chances for college entrance, bolstering their achievements in several areas, and increasing their interest in the arts and humanities. He approaches Counselor Smith and asks him to administer tests to the students to determine exactly how far they have gone since the commencement of his tenure at the school. Counselor Smith must immediately ask himself (and, ultimately, Principal Jones) some crucial questions regarding the use to which the tests will be put if they are in fact administered. Questions of this type might be asked: What if we discover that the students have not improved in some areas? Would you then be willing to rethink the curriculum? If the results are very positive, will you still continue to experiment and find more meaningful and expeditious ways of teaching? How will we use these test results to help individual students? Are there tests that will measure other qualities or traits that will be of more benefit to the students than tests merely to determine how the administration has improved the school over the past few years? Can we use system-wide tests already being administered, or is it absolutely necessary to have other test data in addition? These—and questions like them—put the need for a testing program to a real challenge and insure that tests are not arbitrarily or capriciously administered in order to boost an ego, deflate an ego, or prove something that is of interest to a person in power but perhaps of little benefit to the students.

The cardinal rule in assessing the need for a test (or for a testing program) is the ultimate benefit the students will reap from the test. Other considerations, research efforts, personal considerations, etc., must always be placed second.

Once the need for a test has been established, the counselor narrows down the specific quality or qualities that are to be measured. Let us say, for example, that a junior-high-school counselor determines, after critically thinking and rethinking the question, that there is a legitimate need for a test to identify in time the students who are likely to drop out of school before the completion of their studies. One instrument designed particularly for this task and standardized over a period of years is the Demos-D Scale. While this is an excellent test instrument, the counselor might ask himself whether there is perhaps another test that has been correlated with dropout proneness and that will measure other qualities or traits that would be of use to the students at the school. He may find, for example, that the Adolescent Alienation Index or the School Motivation Analysis Test or the School Interest Inventory—all standardized tests—would serve the purpose just as well and in addition identify other student difficulties that the counselor would want to be aware of.

The counselor determines what is to be measured by considering the students, the needs of the school, the instruments available, and the time and expense (Goldman, 1961). He evaluates, in general, the resources available to him for the administration of the testing program and determines from this evaluation: How long a test can be used? How much money can be spent on the test (including scoring)? How will proctors be secured and paid? How much school time is available? Where can he expect cooperation and where can he anticipate resistance? After this determination is made, and he knows the qualities to be measured and is satisfied that a test or a testing program is needed, he goes about selecting a test instrument.

2 Selecting a test instrument. Requisitioning

Once he has a clear idea what he wants to measure, how does the counselor go about deciding on a specific instrument to use? Before he makes this decision, he should be familiar with the different types of tests. The basic categories of tests are: aptitude tests, interest tests, achievement tests, and personality tests. An aptitude test measures the individual's potential in a specified area. Rather than measure what he has learned or what he is able to do, the aptitude test measures what he can learn or what he should be able to do. Intelligence tests are a popular form of aptitude tests.

Interest tests measure the subject's "tendency to prefer or engage in a particular type of activity" (Thorndike and Hagen, 1969). Interest tests often used by counselors are the vocational interest inventories, which measure the subject's interest in a particular occupation or class of occupations.

Achievement tests measure the individual's ability to perform certain tasks. The test that the teacher administers to determine what a student has learned in class is an achievement test. A standardized achievement test measures the student's ability to perform in comparison with a wide reference group with whom the student can be compared.

Personality tests measure intrapsychic modes of feeling, of perceiving reality emotionally, and of acting.

Thorndike and Hagen (1970) discuss in detail the various types of tests, and Buros (1966) offers a complete, up-to-date description of every published test in all these categories.

All reputable test publishers limit the accessibility of their instruments to qualified professionals. The Psychological Corporation, for example, has a rule that "school teachers and counselors may purchase tests by official purchase order or with the written authorization of the superintendent, principal, or guidance director." Most other test publishers have similar restrictions, and the school counselor may consult the test catalogue of a publisher to determine in which cases he may or may not qualify as a purchaser.

3 Arranging for the administration of the test

4 Collecting the tests and distributing them for scoring

These two stages are basically administrative, and the counselor's administrative abilities will be put to the test during this time. He must see that adequate facilities have been secured for the test administration, that proctors and assistants are briefed in advance, that all the test materials have been received, that the test subjects have been notified, etc. Brown and Srebalus (1972) offer a detailed list of procedures for the counselor to follow (pp. 147-148) during this stage of the testing program.

5 Preparing test data sheets and an accompanying interpretive guide

After the counselor has collected the answer booklets and all other test materials, it is his responsibility to see that the test is sent out for scoring or, if scoring is to be done at the school, that the material is put in a safe place and is secure from theft. Reppert, Campbell, and Kirk (1965) discuss the responsibilities of the counselor during this phase of the program, describing in some detail the counselor's work in arranging materials, bookkeeping, examining the used examination booklets, sending out the answer sheets for scoring, etc.

6 Making test results available to appropriate parties and interpreting the implications of specific test data

Having conscientiously carried out his duties to this point, the counselor enjoys a brief respite until the results of the tests are returned. Then he goes back to work again, this time making sure that these results are used properly.

The first question with which the counselor must deal is, "Who is an appropriate party?" He does not want to release test results indiscriminately; at the same time, he does not want to horde these results and keep them only to himself. In other words, he wants the test results be put to good use. In most cases, every person on the counseling team (see later in this chapter) falls into the category of an appropriate party and not only is fully entitled to see the test results but should actually be encouraged to see them to understand more clearly the needs, interests, and abilities of the students with whom they are working. Methods of communicating and interpreting test results will be explored in the next section of this chapter. A few general principles can be stated here:

1 Appropriate staff, faculty, and administration should be informed when the test results are available.
2 The counselor should prepare a short brochure of the meaning of the test, what it is designed to measure, its presumed accuracy, and the table of scores.
3 The counselor should identify for the personnel those students whose scores indicate that they may be in need of special attention or services.
4 When requests are made for information by other parties, such as parents, the counselor should be prepared to meet with the party and to present information in a constructive, meaningful way (see below for a more detailed discussion).
5 The counselor should arrange interviews with those students whose scores indicate that an interview with the counselor might be beneficial.

7 Follow-up

A testing program would be of little value if there were no follow-up procedures. The discussion of continuity at the beginning of this section goes into this point. Since tests are often used as diagnostic tools, it is the counselor's responsibility to see that meaningful use is made of the information obtained from the tests.

COMMUNICATING TEST RESULTS

For the counselor to understand the meaning of test results, he should have some familiarity with testing terminology. While he need not be a statistician, he should be familiar with the concepts of central tendency, standard deviation, reliability, validity, norms, and so on. A glossary of testing terminology, including all the major terms that the counselor might confront, is appended to this text (see Appendix II). There are a number of valuable papers and books that the counselor might wish to examine to get a more detailed understanding of some of these terms (Ebel, 1956, on validity; Anastasi, 1950, on testing terminology; Garrett, 1972, on statistics). But it is important to emphasize that while these technical terms are useful in understanding test results, only a humane, personal attitude can help the counselor understand the meaning of a test score in relation to the client with whom he is working.

As the counselor discusses the results of a test with a client, he must attempt to avoid the technical jargon that may have been useful in helping him interpret the test results to himself. The value of communicating test results to clients is stultified if the counselor cannot present the information in a language the client can understand. Lister and McKenzie (1966) list four conditions designed to assure that test interpretation will help the student client achieve a better self-understanding:

1 THE STUDENT EXPERIENCES A NEED FOR INFORMATION.... It is not enough for the counselor to believe the student can benefit from knowing his test results; the student himself must feel such a need.
2 THE STUDENT'S QUESTIONS ARE TRANSLATED INTO OPERATIONAL TERMS ACCEPTABLE TO HIM.... Until a student can approach an operational statement of his questions, test interpretation remains generalized and of limited value to the individual. In the course of counseling with a student about higher education, the student might successively ask the following questions: What are my chances of getting into college? What are my chances of finishing the first two years of college? ... What are my chances of graduating from medical school?
3 THERE IS A RELATIONSHIP BETWEEN TEST RESULTS AND THE CRITERION PERFORMANCE. Translating a student's test results into a statement about some probable behavior takes specific evidence of a relationship between his scores and that behavior.
4 THE INFORMATION IS CLEARLY COMMUNICATED TO THE STUDENT. (p. 62)

These four principles adequately sum up the major rules of communicating test results to the client. We may also add that the client should demonstrate a willingness, or even an eagerness, to learn the test results. They should never be imposed upon him, never used in the sphere of confrontation. Rather, they should be presented as a logical response to a client's appropriate questions.

The more subtle meanings of test results can also be communicated to the client or consultee during the counseling interview, but this must be done in a way that is understandable. Adams (1963), for example, suggests that an illustration of the normal curve may be useful in showing graphically to parents and children what the test scores mean in terms of the total population. Berdie, Layton, Swanson, and Hagenah (1963) present a detailed explanation of ways in which test data can be presented constructively to the counselee. Berg (1956) has discussed ways in which confusion and misunderstanding can be prevented in the counseling setting when test interpretation is the subject.

THE COUNSELING TEAM

Much of the work of the counselor is carried out in conjunction with other members of the counseling team, along with parents, community people, and other interested parties who have the benefit of the student population at heart. Counseling is always an interactive activity, not only between the counselor and the counselee, but between the counselor and other concerned people as well. In this section we will look at some approaches to the coordinated counseling function, and examine the specific role of the counselor as a consultant.

The counseling team typically consists of the counselor, the teacher, the school psychologist or social worker, the consulting psychiatric specialist, medical and paramedical personnel (physicians, nurses, etc.), community personnel, and other specialists in the mental health and educational professions. We shall examine individually constructive modes of professional interaction between the counselor and the teacher, between the counselor and the school psychologist, and between the counselor and other members of the team. As we do so, we should keep in mind that the contribution of these other team members is equal to the contributions brought to the team by the counselor. The teacher contributes an intimate knowledge of the client in the classroom setting; the school psychologist brings specialized psychological skills, including diagnostic ability, psychometric information, and the like; other members of the team each contribute in their own ways.

THE COUNSELOR AND THE TEACHER

Probably the single most important member of the counseling team, in addition to the counselor, is the teacher. Helpern (1964) describes ways in which the counselor can effectively assist the teacher in the performance of his duties and in expediting the comprehensive counseling function:

Since he is concerned with on-going developmental processes and with a continuous study of the individual needs of all children as they progress through group situations, his work must necessarily take the form of frequent communication and consultation with teachers. Teachers...frequently need additional help if they are to assess accurately the needs of children and of themselves. They need further information about child growth and development, about how children learn, about what constitutes normal behavior, about the importance of individual methods of response, about the exploded myths of the past (as the over-emphasis on the I.Q.) and about the new experiments currently being conducted. They need this type of continuing cognitive experience but need above all...the opportunity to talk about how *they* feel about what is happening in the classroom, in the school, about their reactions to the children, about their own anxieties and frustrations in their teaching roles, about their own interpersonal relationships and expectations.... Such opportunities for discussion may be offered in one-to-one teacher-counselor relationships or may be extended to discussion groups, to child-study workshops or to in-service training courses. (pp. 17–18)

According to this view, *the counselor functions as a facilitator of the teacher's growth and development as well as in a consultative capacity*. The counselor's two-fold function, facilitator and consultant, illustrates the complexity of the balance that must be maintained so delicately as he deals with the teacher, whom he most likely sees on a day-to-day basis.

Lundquist and Chamley (1971) also view the counselor as both a counselor and a consultant in his relationship with the teacher. They list six counseling functions that define the facilitating aspect of the relationship with the teacher:

1 Help the teacher or teachers to develop an increased awareness of their affective domain and how it relates to their professional identity and fulfillment of their roles as teachers.

2 Help the teacher or teachers to develop an awareness of how their intrapersonal feelings effect [sic] and influence their roles in the educative process with children.

3 Help the teacher or teachers to learn to identify and express the intrapersonal feelings they own.

4 Help the teacher or teachers to develop more positive attitudes about the feelings they possess so that they may function more effectively with students in the total learning environment.

5 Help teachers to learn to relate to other professional people in more effective ways.

6 Help teachers by providing personal and professional support in crisis situations. (p. 364)

Other writers have supported this role of the counselor (Dinkmeyer, 1968; Tyler, 1969; Brown and Srebalus, 1972), and it is generally accepted in the profession that the effective counselor must work with teachers as well as with students at the school. Some writers, such as McClain and Boley (1968), emphasize the "complementary" nature of the counseling and consultation function.

If we look at the counselor's relationship with the teacher in terms of this dichotomy—counselor and consultant—we can better appreciate how the counselor and the teacher form a constructive team that enhances the potentials of the educative process. The counselor supports the teacher, and the teacher utilizes this support to become more proficient in his job with the student. Thus, the student-client benefits from the efforts of two people, working together on his behalf.

Munson (1970, pp. 121–129) describes this complex relationship in some detail. The consulting relationship, he points out, is one that "builds continually from the first contact." He differentiates between *first-level*, *second-level*, and *third-level* consulting relationships. The first-level relationship usually deals with external matters that are not personally threatening or emotionally intense to the teacher, matters such as curriculum, dealing with a discipline problem, and the like. The second-level relationship is more intense and dynamic:

It is at this second-level of consultation that the more creative, innovative practices can be encouraged. Assuming that the consultant is aware of and concerned about his relationship with the consultee, he can begin to intervene in ways which can result in a positive influence on the learning environment.... He functions very much as he would in the counseling relationship. He reads feelings, he encourages the expression of feelings, he is aware of attitudes. He is involved with the teacher. He is concerned with her growth. He cares. (p. 124)

The third-level relationship is simply an extension of the second-level. It is a relationship of the same quality and intensity, continued in time. Munson does not suggest, however, that the counselor use this phase of the relationship to commence a psychotherapeutic relationship because this might well entail a number of difficulties. The counseling relationship, however, should continue to progress and develop.

Lauver (1974) has developed what he calls a "systematic approach" for consulting with teachers. This approach consists of seven steps:

Step 1. Identify a problem situation in which a need for change may exist.

Step 2. Identify what constitutes a desirable outcome in operational terms—terms that will allow you to know whether or not the outcome has been achieved.

Step 3. Observe the situation for relevant information about relationships among important people, objects, and actions.

Step 4. Identify encouragers for desirable behavior and discouragers for undesirable behavior.

Step 5. Devise a plan for using encouragers and discouragers to achieve the desired outcomes.

Step 6. Try out the plan.

Step 7. Observe the results and compare what has actually happened with what was desired.

In many cases such a structured approach may prove helpful—especially to the beginning counselor who has not yet found his own style.

THE COUNSELOR AND THE SCHOOL PSYCHOLOGIST

Unfortunately, many instances of conflict between the counselor and the school psychologist have prevented these two related specialties from achieving the harmony and concordance they so much need in order to work effectively. Sources of conflict between the counselor and the school psychologist usually are a result of failure adequately to define their roles or the relationships between their respective roles, or failure of communication, which invariably leads to misunderstandings. Where the two are able to work together—as is sometimes the case—the consequences are most advantageous to the students.

A number of writers have scrutinized the coordination between the counseling and school psychology functions (Johnson et al., 1961; Mathewson, 1962; Patterson, 1962; Byrne, 1963; Gray and Noble, 1965). Gray and Noble (1965), who have reviewed the literature, point out that "working together always demands some compromises and some giving up of cherished functions," and they argue that both the school psychologist and the school counselor must recognize this in order to work together effectively. Perhaps the simplest solution to the difficulties that divide the professions is for school counselors and school psychologists to engage in mutual consultation, in which each utilizes the expertise of the other for the benefit of the student. The psychologist may be more adept at testing and statistical interpretation, while the counselor may prove to be a more skillful interviewer. By combining their talents and skills, it is inevitable that the student-client will benefit in the long run.

CONSULTING WITH PARENTS

There are three major reasons for conscientiously consulting with parents. First, the counselor is meeting his ethical obligation to the parent, who is, after all, a citizen and taxpayer responsible for the counselor's salary. Second, and more important, consultation with the parent can and should help the parent become a more responsible family member and able to deal more effectively with whatever difficulties in the home are manifesting themselves in the school setting. Third, and most important, the parent becomes an active member of the counseling team. By definition, he is working *with* the counselor to improve the life situation *for* the student-client, whom the counselor is directly interested in helping.

Consultation with parents reflects a specialized skill of the counselor's. He must understand how to communicate effectively with the parent in a manner and style that is open and straightforward, yet not threatening or accusatory. At all times, unnecessary nomenclature should be avoided; the parent responds best to language that he is readily able to understand. When the counselor begins to flaunt his technical vocabulary at the expense of clarity, although it may impress the parent, it does little to promote a feeling of trust and rapport between the counselor and the parent.

The parent can also serve as a resource person for the counselor. Rothney (1972) discusses this aspect of the counselor-parent interaction:

Parents can make contributions that no one else can provide to the information needed about a counselee. They can describe patterns of their child's development; reactions to norms and pressures he has met; frustrations and opportunities he has experienced; persons to whom he has showed strong attachment or repulsion; and the models which through imitation and introjection he has adopted. Only parents can provide dependable information about financial matters when expenditure of funds is required to further the counselee's plans. (pp. 90–91)

APPROACHES TO CONSULTATION

Consultation is an art of its own. Simply meeting with a teacher, parent, or a professional colleague is not in itself necessarily consultative. What determines consultation is the approach used by the counselor in his meetings with others. Technically, *consultation is meeting of counselor and another person (third party) to discuss a client.* There are a number of guidelines the counselor may find useful in his consultative endeavors. These guidelines are admittedly general and would at times have to be modified to meet the special needs of particular situations:

1 In his consultative capacity, the counselor must conduct himself in a fully professional manner, recognizing his limitations and strengths, aware of his ethical and legal responsibilities, and sensitive to philosophical and theoretical axioms that underlie his work and support his commitment.
2 As a consultant, the counselor always recognizes that his primary reponsibility to the client dictates the substance and spirit of this third-party intervention.
3 In providing advice or information to others, the counselor must always attempt to present it objectively and unbiasedly: to show the other person, when it is appropriate, that there may be more than one way to look at a sit-

uation, that there may be legitimate points of view different from the one the counselor favors. In short, the person with whom the counselor consults always has a right to know and to choose.

4 Consultation implies cooperation. It is the counselor's obligation, more than anyone else's, to work toward this cooperative spirit. At times this may require compromise; at times, retreat. The counselor must be willing to sacrifice at times the needs of his ego to the demands of the situation.

5 Goals of consultation should be mutually established by the consultant and the consultee. Misunderstandings can often be avoided when there is a mutual reason for sharing a consultative session.

6 When the person consulting with the counselor is overly impressed by professionals (as parents often are), the counselor must take extra care to impress upon the consultee that the counselor is not infallible and is as likely to make errors as anyone else.

MODELS OF COUNSELING TEAMWORK

Mahoney (1972) makes the point, using a catchy phrase, that "action is the product of guidance teamwork." This is quite true, and in this section we will examine some ways in which the counseling team can become effectively coordinated and accomplish those actions that are productive, therapeutic, and in accord with the goals of counseling.

What is a team? The dictionary* defines a team, in the sense that we wish to use it, as "a group of people working together in a coordinated effort." The coordinated efforts in this case are toward the facilitation of learning and the prospect of emotional growth, with the resolution of those barriers that militate against these efforts. Since the processes of growth and development in the school situation comprise both educational and psychological components (see chapter 21 for a fuller discussion of this relationship), the counseling team will coordinate the efforts of the learning specialists with the mental health specialists. It is important that the counselor be at the heart of this coordinating effort, that he become the primary administrator of the coordinated counseling services. Yet the counselor must scrupulously avoid becoming bogged down in administrative, bureaucratic, and organizational trivia. He is working with the organization—but for the client. As Tyler (1969) most aptly states it, "To make use of organizations without becoming an 'organization man,' to make use of bureaucracy without becoming a bureaucrat—that is the course a counselor must try to follow."

Fazzaro and Gillespie (1972) describe six different models of guidance program organization. The *traditional bureaucratic model* is the one we are all so painfully familiar with. It is an inflexible model, "usually found in those schools

---

Webster's New World Dictionary of the American Language, 2nd College Edition. New York: The World Publishing Co. 1970.

that are organized to provide a more traditional program" (p. 155). In the *differentiated role model*, each member of the counseling team has a specific role to perform. "For example, if there are four members on the counseling staff, then one counselor would be responsible for all testing, another for community service liaison, another for job and college placement services, and perhaps another for providing individual counseling for specific students" (p. 155). This is a particularly viable model for the counselor to use in implementing the coordination between counseling and other student personnel functions.

The *laissez-faire model* "is one which allows the student to select the counselor of his choice at the time his services are needed" (p. 156). For this model to be effective, the authors point out, "there must be complete agreement regarding professional matters between various members of the counseling and guidance staff." If we translate this model into a broad counseling application, we would have to assume that the student could adequately discriminate between the different functions of the student personnel team, which is not likely the case. Because this is not the case, the counselor must act as a source of referral when services other than his own are needed.

The *task group model* "is one in which counselors and other specialists are grouped together in order to accomplish a specific objective or task" (p. 156). This is a particularly constructive model when a serious problem requires consultation, cooperation, and coordination between several specialists. The counselor, school psychologist, and school nurse may work together under this model, for example, to deal with drug problems in the school (see chapter 17).

The *objectives model*, which has recently been gaining wide popularity, works by stating specific objectives to be met and the methods by which the team will try to meet these objectives. "The focus of this particular model is on performance" (p. 156). The *performance contracting model* "also stresses the defining of specific objectives, then contracting with a private agency to meet these objectives" (p. 157). What would be more useful to us, however, is the idea of the counselor's contracting with other members of the student personnel team to carry out the objectives that have been defined. For example, having determined that there is a serious problem of teen-age gangs causing chaos in the school environment, the counselor can contract with the psychologist, with teachers, with administrators and supervisors, with parents, and with law enforcement personnel each to assume a part of the total burden dealing with this problem. In many ways, such performance contracting is similar to the task group model discussed above.

These six different models of organizational counseling should help the counselor better understand some of the possibilities of the team counseling approach. "The staff of guidance programs that have achieved recognition and praise," Shertzer and Stone (1971) point out, "have high morale and work cooperatively.... Cooperation among personnel marks the good guidance program." To achieve this facilitative level of cooperation, the counselor must take the initiative of organizing his guidance program in such a way that the skills of a variety of members of the counseling team are utilized.

CONCLUSIONS AND IMPLICATIONS

We have examined in this chapter a number of ways in which the school counselor carries out his function, particularly in the areas of appraisal, consultation, and team efforts. As an expert in appraisal, the counselor administers testing programs, interprets the results of tests to clients and to other members of the student personnel team, and keeps records of the student's progress. It is important that the counselor understand the confidentiality of appraisal work and that he is sensitive to the possible misuses that appraisal information can be put to.

One method of increasing the effectiveness of the counseling function is to utilize a team counseling approach. This means, in effect, that a group of professionals and nonprofessionals work together to provide competent counseling services in a mutually consultative capacity. Various models of organization have been discussed, and we noted for each some advantages and disadvantages. Above all, I have tried to emphasize that consultation and team work require cooperation, which is a sign of both emotional maturity and professional security. So great is the value of teamwork that when the counselor pairs his efforts with the efforts of others the total effort increases geometrically.

References

Adams, J. F. Using the pictorial normal curve in test interpretation. *Personnel and Guidance Journal*, 1963, *41*, 812–813.

Anastasi, A. The concept of validity in the interpretation of test scores. *Educational and Psychological Measurement*, 1950, *10*, 67–78.

Annis, A. P. The autobiography: Its uses and value in professional psychology. *Journal of Counseling Psychology*, 1967, *14*, 9–17.

Berdie, R. F., Layton, W., Swanson, E. O., & Hagenah, T. *Testing in guidance and counseling*. New York: McGraw-Hill, 1963.

Berg, I. A. Test score interpretation and client confusion. *Personnel and Guidance Journal*, 1956, *34*, 576–578.

Brown, D., & Srebalus, D. J. *Contemporary guidance concepts and practices: An introduction*. Dubuque, Iowa: Wm. C. Brown, 1972.

Buros, O. K. *The seventh mental measurement yearbook*. Highland Park, N.J.: Gryphon Press, 1970.

Byrne, R. *The school counselor*. Boston: Houghton Mifflin, 1963.

Carey, A. Take a look at your testing program. *The School Counselor*, 1969, *16*, 205–207.

Dinkmeyer, D. C. The counselor as consultant: Rationale and procedures. *Elementary School Guidance and Counseling*, 1968, *3*, 187–194.

Ebel, R. L. Obtaining and reporting evidence on content validity. *Educational and Psychological Measurement*, 1956, *16*, 269–282.

Fazzaro, C. J., & Gillespie, J. O. Organizational models for effective counseling and guidance programs. *Clearing House*, 1972, *45*, 153–158.

Garrett, H. E. *Elementary statistics* (2nd ed.). New York: David McKay, 1972.

Goldman, L. *Using tests in counseling*. New York: Appleton-Century-Crofts, 1961.

Gray, S. W., & Noble, F. C. The school counselor and the school psychologist. In J. F. Adams (Ed.), *Counseling and guidance: A summary view*. New York: Macmillan, 1965.

Gronlund, N. E. *Sociometry in the classroom*. New York: Harper & Row, 1960.

Hansen, L. S. How can we use appraisal data for students' welfare? *The School Counselor*, 1967, *14*, 281–286.

Heayn, M. H., & Jacobs, H. L. Safeguarding student records. *Personnel and Guidance Journal*, 1967, *46*, 63–67.

Helpern, J. M. G. The role of the guidance consultant at the elementary school. *Journal of Education*, 1964, *146*, 16–34.

Johnson, W., Stefflre, B., & Edefelt, R. *Pupil personnel and guidance services*. New York: McGraw-Hill, 1961.

Lauver, P. J. Consulting with teachers: A systematic approach. *Personnel and Guidance Journal*, 1974, *52*, 535–540.

Lister, J. L., & McKenzie, D. H. A framework for the improvement of test interpretation in counseling. *Personnel and Guidance Journal*, 1966, *45*, 61–65.

Lundquist, G. W., & Chamley, J. C. Counselor-consultant: A move toward effectiveness. *The School Counselor*, 1971, *18*, 362–366.

Mahoney, W. M. Action is the product of guidance teamwork. *Clearing House*, 1972, *46*, 427–430.

Mathewson, R. H. *Guidance: Policy and practice* (3rd ed.). New York: Harper & Row, 1962.

McClain, A. D., & Boley, K. J. Counseling and consultation interrelationships. *Elementary School Guidance and Counseling*, 1968, *3*, 32–39.

Miller, F. W. *Guidance: Principles and services* (2nd ed.). Columbus, Ohio: Charles E. Merrill, 1968.

Munson, H. L. *Elementary school guidance: Concepts, dimensions, and practice.* Boston: Allyn & Bacon, 1970.

Nelson, R. C. Counseling versus consulting. *Elementary School Guidance and Counseling*, 1967, *1*, 146–151.

Patterson, C. H. *Counseling and guidance in the schools.* New York: Harper & Row, 1962.

Reppert, H. C., Campbell, J. P., & Kirk, C. R. The management and supervision of a testing program. In J. F. Adams (Ed.), *Counseling and guidance: A summary view.* New York: Macmillan, 1965.

Roeber, E. C., Smith, G. E., & Erickson, C. E. *Organization and administration of guidance services* (2nd ed.). New York: McGraw-Hill, 1955.

Rothney, J. W. M. *Adaptive counseling in the schools.* Englewood Cliffs, N.J.: Prentice-Hall, 1972.

Shertzer, B., & Stone, S. C. *Fundamentals of guidance* (2nd ed.). Boston: Houghton Mifflin, 1971.

Strang, R. *Counseling technics in college and secondary schools* (Rev. ed.). New York: Harper & Bros., 1949.

Thorndike, R. L., & Hagen, E. *Measurement and evaluation in psychology and education* (3rd ed.). New York: Wiley, 1969.

Tolbert, E. L. *Introduction to counseling* (2nd ed.). New York: McGraw-Hill, 1972.

Traxler, A. E., & North, R. D. *Techniques of guidance* (3rd ed.). New York: Harper & Row, 1966.

Tyler, L. E. *The work of the counselor* (3rd ed.). New York: Appleton-Century-Crofts, 1969.

Warnken, R. G., & Siess, T. F. The use of the cumulative record in the prediction of behavior. *Personnel and Guidance Journal*, 1965, *44*, 231–237.

Warters, J. E. *High school personnel work today* (2nd ed.). New York: McGraw-Hill, 1956.

chapter twenty-one

Counseling in the classroom

While the counselor himself has little opportunity to apply his trade in the classroom, he helps the teacher to counsel in a number of ways, which we have discussed in other chapters. This chapter is particularly designed for the teacher—in addition to the counselor—and is intended to provide a brief compendium of counseling insights and applications that the classroom teacher may wish to use. The professional guidance counselor is usually instrumental in bringing to the teacher's attention practical insights that will help him in dealing with classroom situations.

PSYCHOLOGICAL FORCES IN THE CLASSROOM

The forces that come into play in the counseling setting are also at work in the classroom. Because the classroom is structured differently, of course different manifestations of these forces are bound to occur. Belkin (1974a) has examined psychoanalytic dimensions of the teacher-student interaction, concluding that:

For the teacher to be *aware*, he must be willing to accept the priority of psychodynamics in teaching over the logical, discursive level of the experience. He must recognize that his and the student's feelings, which are determined early in life, and are pre-experiential in relation to their interaction, form the basis for both of their perceptions, feelings, and actions. He must accede to feelings where they contradict logical progression in the interaction, and deal directly with these feelings whether they be resistances, transference manifestations or whatever. The psychodynamically aware teacher must also be intimately aware of his own feelings and free of the restraints and repressions of the neurotic personality. He must be courageous in his willingness to concede that his own feelings may at times be inappropriate for the educational experience, and yet these feelings will nevertheless remain "his own" and remain strong. (pp. 113–114)

These comments are the result of an investigation of the teacher-student interaction based on psychoanalytic insights. Other ideologies as well can be applied to an examination of school- and classroom-related problems. Rogers

We also serve who only sit and wait!

(1969), for example, has approached the problem of education from a client-centered perspective, Glasser (1969) from the reality therapy point of view, and Krumbholtz (1969) from the behavioral point of view. While it is no doubt helpful to apply these parochial therapeutic insights to the classroom, of more benefit to the teacher would be a general catalog of counseling insights that he could use in teaching. Certainly the teacher recognizes that the psychological forces that charge the counseling encounter with energy also play a part in classroom activity. Particularly the insights gleaned from group dynamics and group therapy are applicable in the classroom, which may be considered another form of group experience. Let us first consider how the teacher-as-counselor may facilitate learning in the classroom by creating a more receptive and adaptive environment.

FACILITATING LEARNING

Leonard (1968) speaks of a strongly interactive environment as a prerequisite for meaningful learning. "The human organism is incredibly flexible," he argues. "If there are limits on the human ability to respond to learning environments, we are so far away from the limits as to make them presently inconsequential. Throughout human history to date, it has been the environments, not the human beings, that have run up against limitations" (p. 39).

There are a number of things the classroom teacher can do to promote an effective learning environment. He must recognize the interplay of needs that are manifest in the learning situation. Students' needs include not only the need for recognition and approval, but intellectual needs, social needs, familial needs which are unsatisfied in the home, and creative, aesthetic needs. Not all students enter that situation with a positive attitude, with a willingness to learn, with an optimism about their capabilities. On the contrary, many students, turned off for years by the educational experience, come into the classroom with a sense of disillusionment, with a morbid pessimism, with an expectation of failure and frustration.

Pine and Horne (1969) have expounded fourteen principles of learning "which incorporates and integrates the basic therapeutic experiences:"

1 Learning is the process of changing behavior in positive directions.
2 Learning is an experience which occurs inside the learner and is activated by the learner.
3 Learning is the discovery of the personal meaning and relevance of ideas.
4 Learning (behavioral change) is a consequence of experience.
5 Learning is a cooperative and collaborative process.
6 Learning is an evolutionary process.
7 Learning is sometimes a painful process.
8 One of the richest resources for learning is the learner himself.
9 The process of learning is emotional as well as intellectual.
10 Learning fuses work and play.
11 Learning is a "religious" experience.
12 The learner is a free and responsible agent.
13 The processes of problem solving and learning are highly unique and individual.
14 Teaching is learning.

These fourteen principles are inclusive and comprehensive: They represent a basic working axiom for the teacher who endeavors to use therapeutic counseling applications in his classroom. The important point to remember is that teachers who give deliberate attention to social and emotional development in the classroom can have a more pronounced effect on learning than those teachers who concentrate on academic performance alone (Stanford, 1972).

Boy and Pine (1971) develop this idea fully through a humanistic therapeutic perspective built upon the assumption "that when a student learns something, it is because he has responded to the teacher *as a person*; a person who relates to students with a core attitude of acceptance, empathy, concreteness, transparency, and personal genuineness." Jersild (1965), Hill (1971), and Cantor (1972) have also examined the learning process in terms of the teacher's personality and his willingness and ability to present to the students those attitudes that facilitate learning. In short, the qualities that make for an effective counselor, and the attitudes that make for counseling effectiveness, also make an effective teacher and contribute to effective teaching.

Display 21.1 shows twelve conditions that facilitate learning, based on the principles of learning developed by Pine and Horne. These are general conditions that should be applicable to all subject matters, all levels of education, all types of teaching situations. These are the conditions for effective therapy and counseling as well as the conditions for effective teaching and learning.

---

display 21.1

CONDITIONS WHICH FACILITATE LEARNING*

1 *Learning is facilitated in an atmosphere which encourages people to be active.* ("People are active and creative beings who need the opportunity to determine goals, issues to be discussed, and the means of evaluating themselves. They learn when they feel that they are a part of what is going on—when they are personally involved.")

2 *Learning is facilitated in an atmosphere which promotes and facilitates the individual's discovery of the personal meaning of ideas.* ("The art of helping people to change their behavior requires the development of goals which provide sufficient elbowroom for people to explore and to internalize behavior that is satisfying and growth-producing to themselves.")

3 *Learning is facilitated in an atmosphere which emphasizes the uniquely personal and subjective nature of learning.* ("People need to develop an awareness that all that is to be learned is not outside or external to themselves. They develop such an awareness when they feel that their contributions and their value as people are generally appreciated.")

4 *Learning is facilitated in an atmosphere in which difference is good and desirable.* ("If people are to look at themselves, at others, and at ideas openly and reasonably, then they must have the opportunity to express their opinions no matter how different they may be.")

5 *Learning is facilitated in an atmosphere which consistently recognizes people's right to make mistakes.* ("Growth and change are facilitated when error is accepted as a natural part of the learning process.")

6 *Learning is facilitated in an atmosphere which tolerates ambiguity.* ("The open and fearless exploration of solutions calls for time to explore many alternatives and time to proceed without feeling any pressure for immediate and forthcoming answers.")

7 *Learning is facilitated in an atmosphere in which evaluation is a cooperative process, with emphasis on self-evaluation.* ("If learning is a personal process, then people need the opportunity to formulate the criteria to measure their progress. Self-evaluation and peer evaluation enable people to really judge how much they have learned.")

8 *Learning is facilitated in an atmosphere which encourages openness of self rather than concealment of self.* ("People can invest themselves fully and openly in the collaborative and interactive process of learning when they know that no matter what they say or express, it will not result in psychological punishment or penalties.")

9 *Learning is facilitated in an atmosphere in which people are encouraged to trust in themselves as well as in external sources.* ("People learn when they begin to see themselves as the wellsprings of ideas and alternatives to problems.")

10 *Learning is facilitated in an atmosphere in which people feel that they are respected.* ("Confrontations and differences of opinion become constructive forces in a group in which people experience that they are respected as persons.")

11 *Learning is facilitated in an atmosphere in which people feel that they are accepted.* ("People need to feel that they have an option—to change or not to change.")

12 *Learning is facilitated in an atmosphere which permits confrontation.* ("Confrontation is a proving ground which enables ideas to be synthesized, new ideas to emerge, and people to change.")

13 *The most effective teacher is the teacher who creates the conditions by which he loses the teaching function.* ("The teacher creates the climate for learning by becoming a facilitator who views himself as a learner and who authentically behaves as a learner.")

*From *Expanding the Self: Personal Growth for Teachers* by A. V. Boy and G. J. Pine. Dubuque, Iowa: Wm. C. Brown, 1971. Adapted from pp. 114–118. Reprinted by permission.

Cognitive learning is only a part of the educative process.

This clear-cut parallel between the counseling situation and the classroom situation has been gaining a wider audience during the past few years. Gazda (1973) has developed a human relations training model for teachers and teacher educators based on the counselor training model developed by Robert Carkhuff and Charles Truax. In his research, he cites numerous studies of teacher effectiveness, training, and attitudes that parallel in detail (both in content and structure) investigations of counselor traits. This recognition, that a model of an effective teacher is in many ways synonymous with a model of an effective counselor, is encouraging because it promotes the idea that teaching is a therapeutic experience that should be used in conjunction with other therapeutic experiences to promote human growth. Sprinthall (1971) has been particularly vocal in promoting this dual curriculum of teaching and counseling. "The dual curriculum implics," Sprinthall points out, "a frame of reference with distinct but related priorities—learning to learn with a priority on subject matter mastery, and learning to learn with a priority on mastery and competence as a person" (p. 16). He envisions a collaboration of the two functions that necessitates a cooperation between the personnel who staff both functions. Facilitating learning, according to Sprinthall, means facilitating emotional learning as well as intellectual learning through their "organic connection," the dual curriculum.

The organic focus providing simultaneous development through a dual curriculum would prevent such an estrangement and indeed promote growth and development both personally and educationally. Then maybe we could stop implying that for the student himself, at least, there would be a significant difference in these two domains. (p. 17)

Now let us turn our attention to an issue that has clearly proven its relevance to both teachers and counselors: the learning of values and the development of character within the school setting.

CHARACTER DEVELOPMENT:
THE TEACHING AND LEARNING OF VALUES

One of the chief aims of education has traditionally been the development of character. Plato, in *The Republic*, argued that the development of character must precede intellectual growth, since it is only through one's character (and values) that knowledge is put to use. When the character has been neglected while the intellect has prospered, the result is an individual whose lack of moral scruples endangers all society. "You must have noticed in dishonest men with a reputation for sagacity," Plato suggests, "the shrewd glance of a narrow intelligence piercing the object to which it is directed. *There is nothing wrong with their power of vision, but it has been forced into the service of evil*, so that the keener the sight, the more harm it works." In other words, knowledge without a value basis can be a very dangerous thing.

Moral education, therefore, becomes an integral part of the educative process. Kohlberg (1966) cities "moral maturity as an aim of education." In attempting to define moral maturity, he begins by directing his attention to moral judgments:

Maturity levels are most clearly apparent in moral judgment. Furthermore, the general direction of maturity of moral judgment is a direction of greater morality.... We do not mean by this that a more mature judgment is more moral in the sense of showing closer conformity to the conventional standards of a given community. We mean that a more mature judgment more closely corresponds to genuine moral judgments as these have been defined by philosophers. While philosophers have been unable to agree upon any ultimate principle of the good that would define "correct" moral judgments, most philosophers agree upon the characteristics that make a judgment a genuine moral judgment. (p. 21)

To utilize his conceptual framework, Kohlberg proposes a set of moral stages of development, which are closely aligned with cognitive developmental factors. The integration between cognitive and moral maturity constitutes the nexus of his theory:

In general ... the problem of insuring correspondence between developing moral judgments and the child's action is not primarily a problem of eliciting moral self-criticism from the child. One aspect of the problem is the development of the ego abilities involved in the non-moral or cognitive tasks upon which the classroom centers.... The encouragement of these attentional ego capacities is not a task of moral education as such but of general programming of classroom learning activities. (p. 25)

410

Arguing that students are "philosophers" intent on organizing their lives into universal patterns of meaning (Kohlberg & Turiel, 1973; Kohlberg, 1968), Kohlberg, probably more than any other contemporary thinker, fuses the intellectual and moral realms in a unified conception of growth and development within the school setting.

Raths, Harmin, and Simon (1966) have presented a thorough analysis of values in the classroom, also from a developmental point of view. While they, too, see a direct integration between cognition and valuing, they are careful to distinguish between the thinking process and the valuing process, the former being directed toward understanding, the latter toward decision-making. Within the classroom setting, the two are combined both in curriculum and in teacher presentation. Specifically, the goals and processes of value education, according to Raths, Harmin, and Simon (1966) are to

help children: (1) make free choices whenever possible, (2) search for alternatives in choice-making situations, (3) weigh the consequences of each available alternative, (4) consider what they prize and cherish, (5) affirm the things they value, (6) do something about their choices, and (7) consider and strengthen patterns in their lives.... As the teacher helps students use these processes, he helps them find values.

The implications of the above positions are that the teacher (and/or counselor) is inevitably engaged in value teaching, whether this is intentional or not. Since values are the basis of character development, and since character development

411

is the basis of growth within the school setting, it is imperative that the teacher confront directly the challenge of value education that stands before him. "The educationist," Bantock (1965) points out, "is unavoidably a moralist, by the very logic of his position." To conscientiously and purposefully help students develop their independent, yet organized, systems of values is one of the higher and most productive functions of the teacher.

A variety of innovative and effective methods by which the teacher may do this have been presented in the literature. Simon (1973) has suggested methods of "values clarification strategy," based on his work with Howe and Kirschenbaum (Simon, Howe, & Kirschenbaum, 1972). These strategies can be used in the classroom to encourage students to deal with moral dilemmas by helping them get in touch with their feelings and by having them observe their own moral behavior in various arranged situations.

Belkin (1974b), representing an existential position, suggests that moral development occurs in the classroom as the "student is shown his condition of freedom by the teacher, as he is made to feel the unlimited scope of his possibilities."

Moral values are learned in the classroom by example and introjection. The way in which the teacher behaves and acts, not what he says, serves as an example for the student.... Whenever the teacher forces his will upon the class, reducing their destiny to his desires, he limits and stunts their moral development.... [The student] asks the teacher to serve as an example for him. Inasmuch as the teacher has encouraged this request by the freedom he has taught the student to make use of, the student accepts the teacher by introjecting parts of him into his own personality. We can say, then, that the student's moral development in the classroom comes about as he learns to deal with his freedom. (p. 178)

Having examined some general conceptions of moral development in the classroom, we must ask the crucial question that directs our attention toward the student and his developmental needs. What qualities should the student be able to develop in school to make his life and his learning more fulfilling, productive, and valuable? Another way of stating this question is, "To what developmental ends should moral education be directed?" Bertrand Russell (1926a, 1926b; 1927; 1930; 1932) has reflected on this point in some detail, and even today—almost half a century later—his ideas still bear a compelling relevance.

Russell argues (1926a) that the child must develop in school four "virtues" in order for his learning to be meaningful to him and productive to society. These virtues are the connecting links between the needs of the individual and the needs and demands of the world in which he lives. They are *vitality, courage, sensitiveness*, and *intelligence*. An understanding of these four virtues will make clear how Russell's scheme contributes to the broad goals of counseling in the classroom.

Vitality is synonymous with good health and a strong body. It is achieved by keeping the child fit through a good diet and a well-balanced schedule of exercise. It gives one a feeling of pleasure in being alive. More important, its cultivation causes one to take an interest in the outside world "and thus promotes objectivity, which is an essential of sanity." It also acts as a safeguard against envy by giving a person pride in himself and by making his whole existence more pleasurable. Plato's "sound mind and sound body" thesis comes to mind here.

Courage, the second virtue, begins with an absence of irrational fears. It is always achieved by instruction, not by suggestion or undue persuasion. The child is shown the groundlessness of his irrational fears and taught to approach and manipulate the object he fears. Both example and experience are a part of instruction—the example of the parent dealing with the feared object and then permitting the child to have his own experience with it. Often, irrational fears, such as ophidiophobia, are a result of the timidity of the mother and her subsequent suggestion to the child. This kind of experience should be avoided in the classroom.

Bertrand Russell, the British philosopher, wrote extensively about education.

But avoidance of fear is only part of the cultivation of courage. Also important is the instilling of fears of things that *are* truly dangerous. This enables the child to recognize dangers and cope with them. Russell uses the example of his son's ignorance of the dangers of a steep cliff. Russell illustratively taught the child what would happen if he were to fall down that cliff.

The classroom teacher can be especially instrumental in helping students develop courage by making them more "rational beings." Just as the parents may have induced in the child unhealthy, neurotic beliefs through irrational, fear-inducing training, the teacher can counteract these forces by using reason and logic in the classroom. Albert Ellis's rational-emotive therapy is a particularly good example of this type of training (see chapter 12).

Sensitiveness, Russell's third virtue, assumes two forms: emotional sensitiveness and cognitive sensitiveness. Emotional sensitiveness consists of the ability to react appropriately to a situation, to properly sort out and handle oncoming stimuli. Sympathy is a form of emotional sensitiveness and should be properly cultivated while the child is young. It should be cultivated, however, to occur in the right situations. The teacher can be an active participant in the process of emotional education, which reflects his own emotional maturation as it is demonstrated before his students in the classroom.

Cognitive sensitiveness is closely aligned to intelligence. It differs, however, in that it contains more subjective elements. Such matters as aesthetic appreciation are forms of cognitive sensitiveness.

Intelligence is the fourth virtue to come under scrutiny. Intelligence differs from cognitive sensitiveness because of its heavy reliance on curiosity. The type of curiosity it thrives on is one borne out of a true love of knowledge. This kind of curiosity is not natural and should be cultivated early in childhood. Curiosity is at its best, says Russell, when it is not motivated by any personal advantage and when its own end is knowledge. The teacher is one who is best able to foster attitudes of curiosity in the students by promoting an active interest in the subject matter and by allowing the students to question freely and engage in lively debate.

Russell's ideas about education and development are compellingly relevant to the problems faced by the teacher who wishes to act as a therapeutic, as well as an educational, force in the classroom. To help the child develop all his capacities, all his strengths, while at the same time instructing him—teaching him—is the highest, most productive form of classroom education.

CONCLUSIONS AND IMPLICATIONS

For schools to break free of the status quo, in order for meaningful changes to take place, it is necessary that educators—particularly teachers—examine objectively their investment in the existing social order (Zeigler, 1970). Breaking free of traditional teaching methods and recognizing the individual, differing needs of students enables the psychodynamic teacher to teach more meaningfully, more relevantly, and consequently to make a more profound impact upon his students. Teachers must recognize their twofold obligation, to effect positive changes in the development of character while teaching the subject matter (Belkin, 1974b).

Teaching, like counseling, must become an experience that facilitates growth and change, an experience that enables the individual to blossom fully into the richness of all his potentialities. To do this, the teacher must have a love of his subject matter as well as a love for those he teaches. He must be able to combine the two feelings in a constructive manner, interacting with the student in a flexible, respectful way. "The teacher who is inspired by love of his subject, combined with affection for children, can in most circumstances achieve far more in the way of imparting knowledge and civilization than can ever be achieved by the man who loves order and method and efficiency but lacks knowledge and hates children" (Russell, 1932). The truly creative teacher synthesizes his respect for the student and his respect for the idea both in the content and in the manner of his teaching.

The teacher is always in the bind of a paradox between what is expected of him and what he can actually do (Ulich, 1966). He is supposed to be accepting and understanding, yet he is required to maintain discipline at the same time. He is told that he is a professional, and yet he is often treated with far less dignity than are other professionals. To resolve this paradox, the teacher, like the counselor, must come to grips with the nature of his professional commitment and work stoically toward developing productive, therapeutic relationships with his students, who will someday be his peers.

References

Bantock, G. H. *Education and values.* London: Faber & Faber, 1965.

Belkin, G. S. *Psychodynamic dimensions in the teacher-student interaction: A Freudian interpretation.* (Doctoral dissertation, Columbia University, 1974a). Ann Arbor, Mich.: University Microfilms.

Belkin, G. S. Communion in teaching. *Educational Theory*, 1974, *24*, 170–182 (b)

Boy, A. V., & Pine, G. J. *Expanding the self: Personal growth for teachers.* Dubuque, Iowa: Wm. C. Brown, 1971.

Cantor, N. *Dynamics of learning.* New York: Schocken, 1972.

Carkhuff, R. R. *Helping and human relations: A primer for lay and professional helpers*, 2 vols. New York: Holt, Rinehart & Winston, 1969.

Gazda, G. M. *Human relations development: A manual for educators*. Boston: Allyn & Bacon, 1973.

Glasser, W. *Schools without failure*. New York: Harper & Row, 1969.

Hill, J. C. *Teaching and the unconscious mind*. New York: International Universities Press, 1971.

Jersild, A. T. *When teachers face themselves*. New York: Teachers College Press, 1965.

Kohlberg, L. Moral education in the schools: A developmental view. *School Review*, 1966, *74*, 1–30.

Kohlberg, L. Early education: A cognitive-developmental view. *Child Development*, 1968, *39*, 1013–1062.

Kohlberg, L., & Turiel, E. (Eds.). *Recent research in moral development*. New York: Holt, Rinehart, & Winston, 1973.

Krumbholtz, J. D., & Thoresen, C. E. (Eds.). *Behavioral counseling: Cases and techniques*. New York: Holt, Rinehart, & Winston, 1969.

Leonard, G. B. *Education and ecstasy*. New York: Delacorte, 1968.

Pine, G. J., & Horne, P. J. Principles and conditions for learning in adult education. In A. V. Boy & G. J. Pine, *Expanding the self: Personal growth for teachers*. Dubuque, Iowa: Wm. C. Brown, 1971. (Originally published, 1969.)

Raths, L., Harmin, M., & Simon, S. *Values and teaching: Working with values in the classroom*. Columbus, Ohio: Charles E. Merrill, 1966.

Rogers, C. R. *Freedom to learn: A view of what education might become*. Columbus, Ohio: Charles E. Merrill, 1969.

Russell, B. *Education and the good life*. New York: Boni & Liveright, 1926. (a)

Russell, B. What shall we educate for? *Harpers Magazine*, April, 1926. (b), 152, 586–597.

Russell, B. The training of young children. *Harpers Magazine*, August, 1927, 155, 313–319.

Russell, B. Mental health and the school. In N. A. Crawford & K. A. Menninger (Eds.), *The healthy minded child*, 1930. New York: Coward-McCann, 1930.

Russell, B. *Education and the modern world*. New York: Norton, 1932.

Simon, S. B. Values clarification—a tool for counselors. *Personnel and Guidance Journal*, 1973, *51*, 586–590

Simon, S. B., Howe, L., & Kirschenbaum, H. *Values clarification: A practical handbook of strategies for teachers and students*. New York: Hart, 1972.

Sprinthall, N. A. *Guidance for human growth*. New York: Van Nostrand Reinhold, 1971.

Stanford, G. Psychological education in the classroom. *Personnel and Guidance Journal*, 1972, *50*, 585–592.

Truax, C. B., & Carkhuff, R. R. *Toward effective counseling and therapy*. Chicago: Aldine, 1967.

Ulich, R. *Crisis and hope in American education*. New York: Atherton, 1966.

Zeigler, H. Education and the status quo. *Comparative Education*, 1970, *6*, 19–36.

chapter twenty-two

Vocational, educational, and leisure-time counseling

The school counselor spends a significant portion of his time engaged in the types of counseling that directly affect the decisions and choices the client is about to make. I refer to educational, vocational, and leisure-time counseling, the three forms of counseling that directly touch upon the client's "real life" role activities. These types of counseling integrate fluently all of the different aspects of counseling we have discussed throughout this book: the psychological, intensive, dynamic phase of counseling; the group approach; the information-giving services; the evaluation and appraisal functions. For that reason, it may be fairly said that educational, vocational, and leisure-time counseling challenge the counselor to use all his resources and to apply all his training and skills in a single problem area.

In this chapter we will examine these three types of counseling, paying particular attention to the established goals and applied techniques. It should be kept in mind that these types of counseling are excellent examples of the integrative, functional, practical counseling approach.

WHAT IS VOCATIONAL COUNSELING?

As we pointed out in chapter 1, the vocational guidance movement is the father of the contemporary guidance and counseling movement. Traditionally, vocational guidance comprised only information-giving and directive job counseling: providing the appropriate training and information that would enable applicants to learn about the job market and to develop the skills necessary to secure the jobs to which they aspired. But more sophisticated thinkers have now evolved a number of theories of dynamic vocational choice, which, combined with the basic informational aspect, comprise the contemporary vocational guidance function.

A number of comprehensive definitions are found in the literature. Sanderson (1954), in discussing the purpose of vocational guidance, suggests,

Vocational guidance has no other justification for existence than to assist people with their occupational adjustments in a manner that will be truly beneficial to those in need of

The vocational counselor helps the client better understand himself.

help. To attain this objective, the vocational counselor will utilize his interviewing skills, his body of knowledge regarding occupations, his intimate familiarity with psychological dynamics and psychometric data. In addition to his professional training, the counselor will also convey to the client that he is genuinely interested in the latter's problems, that he tries to understand the client's needs, and that he respects the client's right to differ from him. (p. 9)

We see from Sanderson's statement that present-day vocational counseling synthesizes a number of different elements designed to help the client and places the client at the center of this effort. Tarrier et al. (1971) suggests that client self-knowledge rather than counselor knowledge about the client is the important factor in vocational guidance. The client should be encouraged to explore his own self within an occupational framework. The client is to be encouraged to know his own values, attitudes, and biases about work and is to be helped to use this knowledge to investigate occupations and the world of work. "The study of self and occupations are inextricably related....Young people should be helped to better understand themselves and the place of work in the lives of all of us" (Tarrier et al., 1971).

The emphasis in contemporary occupational counseling is on *career guidance.* Not only is the term different from its predecessor, but the focus of career guidance is more on the total person than on his career choices alone. The joint position paper of the National Vocational Guidance Association and the American Vocational Association, entitled *Career Development and Career Guidance*, is a valuable source in elaborating this entire issue. This paper expresses the many different facets of career guidance and the relationship between theories of career development and career guidance services.

Smith (1973) has described the objectives of a career guidance program:

to provide students with on-the-job experiences in the world of work.
to make students more aware of career ladders available to them in the world of work.

to provide students with "hands on experiences" which relate to specific types of skills training in various career fields.

to help students toward a more realistic awareness of self in relation to developing more positive attitudes toward the world of work.

to provide occupational and job placement counseling for students about to enter the working world.

He goes on to provide a detailed list of activities designed to help meet these goals, a list that reflects the wide range of counselor actions brought to bear upon the problem of career choice and development.

Tolbert (1974) defines career counseling and career guidance in their contemporary usages:

Career counseling ... is really much the same as other kinds of counseling except that it focuses on planning and making decisions about occupations and education. As in all counseling, the personal relationship is critical. It includes exploration of values and attitudes, but information and factual data ... are more significant than in personal counseling. Even so, it usually is not possible to help someone with a vocational problem without recognizing such other aspects of his life as needs, conflicts, and relations with others.

Career guidance, which includes counseling as a specialized service, encompasses all of the services that aim at helping pupils make occupational plans and decisions.... Many of the activities currently used in career education resemble career guidance, e.g., role-playing, simulated work experience, viewing occupational films, taking field trips, and participating in career conferences and career fairs. Career guidance is an organized program to help youth develop self-understanding, learn about the world of work, gain experiences that will help in decision making, and find jobs. (p. 27)

These definitions show us the long way that the vocational counseling movement has come since its earlier days of information-giving. This is not to minimize the role of information in career counseling but to emphasize the host of other significant factors that also play a vital role.

The career guidance counselor must be familiar with all of the general theories of counseling—psychoanalytic, client-centered, existential, reality, gestalt, rational-emotive, and behavioral—as well as with the specialized theories of career development discussed below. Moreover, the same philosophical principles that play so vital a role in the counselor's effectiveness also make their impact in vocational counseling interactions. Recent discussions about career counseling reflect with an ever-increasing frequency the amalgam of factors that play a part in this vital counseling function (Foreman and James, 1973; Ginzberg, 1972; Herr and Cramer, 1972; Hoffman, 1972; Stefflre and Grant, 1972). No longer is it possible to view the occupational-career counselor in isolation from the total counseling process that integrates the sum of therapeutic, educational, and growth facilitating experiences under a single rubric. With this in mind, let us examine some of the tools, insights, and axioms that guide the career counselor in his work (see Display 22.1).

MAJOR CHARACTERISTICS OF PRESENT CAREER EDUCATION APPROACHES*

	General education	Vocational education	Guidance
Skills	Academic subject matter as it relates to occupational terminology	Job skills development "Employability" emphasis	Self-understanding Decision making
	"Knowing"	"Doing"	"Feeling"
Activities	Vicarious experiences, e.g., reading out of a book	Work tasks, real and simulated, relating vocational theory to practice	Counseling Roleplaying groups Field trips
Personnel Focus	Academic classroom teacher	Vocational instructor	Counselor as a resource
Student Outcomes	Prepared for further education	Trained for a specific skill Make an informed occupational choice	Psychologically and emotionally prepared for work Make a considered career choice

* From: Bottoms, G. & Sharpe, D. "Career Education: A Broadening Educational Perspective." *The School Counselor*, Nov. 1973, 21(2):121-128. Reprinted by permission.

Occupational counseling inevitably touches upon the nature of work. "Man becomes man through his work," Karl Marx said, illuminating the importance of work in one's existence. Boy and Pine (1971) speak of work "as a therapeutic and personally integrating experience." As the counselor attempts to do vocational counseling, he must have a conscious awareness of his own attitudes, biases, and subjective feelings about the work experience, since these will invariably influence the client.

While the contemporary occupational counseling service includes many factors, it still relies heavily on occupational information. Norris, Zeran, and Hatch (1960) define occupational information:

Occupational information is valid and usable data about positions, jobs, and occupations, including duties, requirements for entrance, conditions of work, rewards offered, advancement pattern, existing and predicted supply of and demand for workers, and sources for further information. (p. 22)

Simply, the informational aspect of the vocational counseling program provides to the student all of the necessary information he will need to make valid, well-thought-out occupational choices. Shartle (1959) provides a detailed list of some different sources of occupational information (Display 22.2). In addition to

display 22.2

OCCUPATIONAL INFORMATION

Local and State Prepared Information

Kind of Material	By Whom Prepared	Availability	Uses
Job descriptions (including specifications of specific jobs in individual establishments). Usually prepared from job analyses.	Local firms, local government, and community agencies.	To officials in the establishments and agencies supplying applicants.	Job evaluation, placement, and training within establishments. Placement and counseling by schools, employment services, rehabilitation agencies that are cooperating with establishments.
Folders and booklets from individual establishments describing the establishment and kinds of openings. Often promotional as well as factual.	Local firms and agencies.	Generally available to anyone.	Recruitment information to attract applicants. Counseling and referral by schools, colleges, rehabilitation agencies, employment services, and other agencies.
Civil Service announcements of examinations and openings, usually prepared from job descriptions.	City, county, and state governmental organizations.	To general public; also, usually sent to a mailing list of schools, colleges, and placement and rehabilitation agencies.	Recruitment information to attract applicants. Counseling and referral by schools, colleges, rehabilitation agencies, employment services, and other agencies.
Occupational guides, leaflets, job briefs (local and state), based on information from employers and prepared in mimeographed or booklet form for each occupation.	State employment services, sometimes in cooperation with schools.	To mailing list of local schools, colleges, and various counseling agencies.	School courses, background reading for counselees and counselors in schools, placement and rehabilitation agencies, and for counseling.
Labor market reports (local & state), usually mimeographed and issued monthly. Some cover one labor market area, others the entire state. Prepared from reports from employers and community agencies.	State employment services.	To mailing list including local schools, colleges, employers, unions, and counseling agencies.	Local and state industrial planning. Background for community surveys. Reading material for school and college courses, and for counseling.
Community surveys for determining educational needs, future job opportunities, industrial expansion, and the like.	Local agency or committee involving employers, schools, unions, employment services.	To agencies, employers, unions, schools, the press.	Background for community planning including industrial and educational expansion. Background reading for school and college courses and for counseling.
Directory of school and college facilities in the state including approved vocational schools.	State Department of Education.	To schools, colleges, placement and counseling agencies.	Reading information for students, counselees, and counselors. Counseling, course selection.
College bulletins including entrance requirements, courses, and statements of fields in which agencies enter.	Municipal, state, and private colleges and universities.	To prospective students and their parents, schools, and counseling agencies.	Study by high school students, educational planning, counseling in schools, employment services, and rehabilitation agencies.

Reprinted by permission of the author.

Local and State Prepared Information Continued

Kind of Material	By Whom Prepared	Availability	Uses
List of licensed occupations including qualifications for application.	State Department of Education or other state agency.	To schools, counseling agencies, individual citizens who write.	Background for school courses, counselees, and counselors in schools, rehabilitation and placement agencies.
State industrial and occupational regulations including minimum age for working, maximum hours, minimum wages, regulations for employment of women, insurance requirements for employers, industries covered by unemployment compensation.	State agency concerned with industrial relations.	To employers, unions, schools, placement and counseling agencies, and citizens who inquire.	Background for college and school courses. Background and referral for counselees and counselors in schools, employment services, rehabilitation agencies.

Information Prepared for National Use

Kind of Material	By Whom Prepared	Availability	Uses
Current occupational information literature, including quarterly listings and ratings by National Vocational Guidance Association in *Vocational Guidance Quarterly*.	National Vocational Guidance Association (division of American Personnel and Guidance Association), 1605 New Hampshire Avenue, N.W. Washington, DC 20009	To members of National Vocational Guidance Association and readers of their *Quarterly*. Contact local branch.	Maintaining up-to-date library of suitable occupational information.
Indexes and lists of occupational publications.	H. W. Wilson Co. 950 University Ave. Bronx, NY 10452 Chronicle Press Moravia, New York Supt. of Documents Washington, DC 20402 Personnel Services, Inc. Peapack, New Jersey B'nai B'rith Vocational Service Bureau 1761 "R" Street, N.W. Washington, DC 20009	Must be purchased. Write for description and latest prices.	Aid in learning about new information published. Used principally by counselors and librarians.
Names and addresses of trade, labor, and professional associations.	U.S. Dept. of Commerce (Trade assoc. list only) Washington, DC 20210 U.S. Dept. of Labor (Union list only) Washington, DC 20230 Gale Research Company 247 Kenworth Road Columbus, OH 43214 (Comprehensive list)	Must be purchased. Write for latest description and price of publication.	Aid in writing to various associations for occupational information. Used by students, counselors, and librarians.

this list, the two publications that will be useful to the counselor are the *Dictionary of Occupational Titles (DOT)* and the *Occupational Outlook Handbook*. The following sources will also be helpful: Careertapes, Project WERC, and computer based systems ECES and ISVD.

Careertapes is a trademark of the Macmillan publishing company. They consist of eighteen audio-cassettes of actual voices of people in the working world, who describe their jobs as they see them. Each person interviewed describes where he or she works, including pay, hours, fringe benefits, promotional opportunities, what they like and don't like, etc.

The American Personnel and Guidance Association's Project WERC ("Why Not Explore Rewarding Careers?") provides information about careers that do not require a college degree. It consists of a series of films designed "to broaden the student's understanding of the world of work and help him make a more intelligent vocational decision."

ECES (Educational and Career Exploration System) and ISVD (Information System for Vocational Decisions) are computer based systems that integrate computer functions with counselor functions to help the individual obtain occupational information and make better vocational choices. Barnard (1972) describes the ECES system:

The high school guidance counselor schedules a two-hour introductory session for each of his students at the ECES terminal. Each student is given a number; already stored against that number in the system's computer are the student's current grades as well as his aptitude scores. Under the supervision of a monitor, the student discovers he can command ECES' performance by means of a light pen which he touches to various points on a 2760 display screen to put the computer to work.

Is there an occupation the student is curious about? ECES, by means of 18,000 cartridge-stored visual images, can describe and define any of 400 occupations, from actuary to zoologist.... Words and pictures describe the activities performed, the working conditions, chances for advancement, salary levels, and educational requirements for the occupation being explored. Then it quizzes the student to determine whether he feels positive, negative, or dubious about it. (p. 46)

THEORIES OF CAREER DEVELOPMENT

Underlying all serious efforts in career guidance and counseling are a number of highly sophisticated and carefully developed theories of career development. The term *career* has come to replace its alternative terms, occupation and vocation, because of its broader, more inclusive emphasis. A career, Super (1969) points out, is "the sequence of occupations, jobs, and positions occupied during the course of a person's working life. Careers actually extend beyond either end of the working life to include prevocational and postvocational positions such as those of students preparing for work and of retired men playing substitute roles." A recent objection, however, to the use of the term *career* over *vocational* has been lodged by Herr and Cramer (1972):

While the term "career development" has a more favorable connotation for some persons than the term "vocational development," "career development" does not lend itself to use in summarizing the behavioral development that parallels socialization. The term "vocational development," on the other hand, does. Recent theories view vocational behavior as a continuing, fluid process of growth and learning, and they attach considerable importance to individual self-concept(s), developmental experiences, personal history, and the psycho-social environment of the individual as major determinants of the process. (p. 39)

They go on to suggest the term *vocationalization* to describe this dynamic process that is a "corollary of socialization." It seems to this writer that this debate over which term is preferable—career or vocational—is largely unnecessary and a symptom of academic carping. What is important, and what does influence all these theories, is the recognition that a theory of career development must account for the fluid, changing process of vocational awareness and feelings.

In this section we shall examine a number of the major theories of career/vocational development. We must keep in mind as we look at these theories that a "vocational development theory is not a general theory of development that could serve as a basis for all counseling and guidance" (Tolbert, 1974). Rather, it is a specific, purposeful theory designed to help the counselor in his vocational counseling. Hewer (1963) argues that no single theory of vocational development is sufficient to explicate the many complexities of the individual. In sum, however, the bulk of these theories reflect the growing awareness of the intricate matrix of psychological, social, and educational factors that play a part in vocational choice and career satisfaction.

Super's theory of development

Donald E. Super has developed a theory of vocational choice based on the idea that the individual's self-concept influences his occupational choice and his ultimate satisfaction or dissatisfaction with his choice. The vocational choice, according to Super (1957), is the result of a developmental process that puts the individual's self-concept into practice. He lists ten propositions that characterize his theory:

1 People differ in their abilities, interests, and personalities.
2 They are qualified, by virtue of these circumstances, each for a number of occupations.
3 Each of these occupations requires a characteristic pattern of abilities, interests, and personality traits, with tolerances wide enough, however, to allow both some variety of occupations for each individual and some variety of individuals in each occupation.
4 Vocational preferences and competencies, the situations in which people live and work, and hence their self concepts, change with time and experience (although self concepts are generally fairly stable from late adolescence until late maturity), making choice and adjustment a continuous process.

5 This process may be summed up in a series of life stages characterized as those of growth, exploration, establishment, maintenance, and decline, and these stages may in turn be subdivided into (a) the fantasy, tentative, and realistic phases of the exploratory stage, and (b) the trial and stable phases of the establishment stage.

6 The nature of the career pattern (that is, the occupational level attained and the sequence, frequency, and duration of trial and stable jobs) is determined by the individual's parental socio-economic level, mental ability, and personality characteristics, and by the opportunities to which he is exposed.

7 Development through the life stages can be guided, partly by facilitating the process of maturation of abilities and interests and partly by aiding in reality testing and in the development of the self concept.

8 The process of vocational development is essentially that of developing and implementing a self concept: it is a compromise process in which the self concept is a product of the interaction of inherited aptitudes, neural and endocrine make-up, opportunity to play various roles, and evaluations of the extent to which the results of role playing meet with the approval of superiors and fellows.

9 The process of compromise between individual and social factors, between self concept and reality, is one of role playing, whether the role is played in fantasy, in the counseling interview, or in real life activities such as school classes, clubs, part-time work, and entry jobs.

10 Work satisfactions and life satisfactions depend upon the extent to which the individual finds adequate outlets for his abilities, interests, personality traits, and values; they depend upon his establishment in a type of work, a work situation, and a way of life in which he can play the kind of role which his growth and exploratory experiences have led him to consider congenial and appropriate. *

Super and his associates have developed these early premises into a comprehensive framework for assessing vocational choice and vocational development. He differentiates between the exploratory stage and the establishment stage of vocational development. The exploratory stage is characterized by fantasy, searching, investigating, experimenting, and testing out hypotheses. It is the period during which vocational images are molded and refined. The establishment stage consists of the period during which the individual actually begins to enact a career role and to shape the career model into his own unique style. These stages may be considered maturational-psychological stages and may also be divided according to chronological ages.

Holland's heuristic theory

Holland also looks at vocational interests and preferences as a part of the total personality of the individual. He refers to his theory as a *heuristic* theory because it is intended to stimulate "research and investigation by its suggestive character rather than by its logical or systematic structure" (Holland, 1966). In this sense, his theory is a working hypothesis by which he can investigate the details of vocational psychology. He explains the essence of his theory this way:

*From "A Theory of Vocational Development" by Donald E. Super, *American Psychologist*, 1953, 8, 189–190. Copyright 1953 by the American Psychological Association. Reprinted by permission.

Briefly, the theory consists of several simple ideas and their more complex elaborations. First, we assume that we can characterize people by their resemblance to one or more personality types. The closest a person's resemblance to a particular type, the more likely it is he will exhibit the personal traits and behaviors associated with that type. Second, we assume that the environments in which people live can be characterized by their resemblance to one or more model environments. Finally, we assume that the pairing of persons and environments leads to several outcomes that we can predict and understand from our knowledge of the personality types and the environmental models. These outcomes include vocational choice, vocational stability and achievement, personal stability, creative performance, and susceptibility to influence. (Holland, 1966)

The details, as he suggests, are more complex and form the basis for his empirical investigations. He defines six character types that include most persons: *realistic, intellectual, social, conventional, enterprising,* and *artistic* (Holland, 1962). The realistic type "is masculine, physically strong, unsociable, aggressive; has good motor coordination and skill; lacks verbal and interpersonal skills; prefers concrete to abstract problems....Laborers, machine operators, aviators, farmers, truck drivers, and carpenters resemble this type." The intellectual type "is task oriented, intraceptive, asocial; prefers to think through rather than act out problems; needs to understand....Physicists, anthropologists, chemists, mathematicians, and biologists resemble this type." The social type "is sociable, responsible, feminine, humanistic, religious; needs attention; has verbal and interpersonal skills; avoids intellectual problem solving, physical activity, and highly ordered activities; prefers to solve problems through feelings and interpersonal manipulations of others; is orally dependent. Social workers, teachers, interviewers, vocational counselors, and therapists resemble this type." The conventional type "prefers structured verbal and numerical activities and subordinate roles; is conforming (extraceptive)....Bank tellers, secretaries, bookkeepers, and file clerks resemble this type." The enterprising type "has verbal skills for selling, dominating, leading...avoids well-defined language or work situations requiring long periods of intellectual effort; is extraceptive; differs from the conventional type in that he prefers ambiguous social tasks and has a greater concern with power, status, and leadership; is orally aggressive. Salesmen, politicians, managers, promoters, and business executives resemble this type." The artistic type "is asocial; avoids problems which are highly structured or require gross physical skills...prefers dealing with environmental problems through self-expression in artistic media. Musicians, artists, poets, sculptors, and writers resemble this type."

Holland (1959, 1962) has attempted to measure each of these personality types through a Vocational Preference Inventory, which ranks the subject's personal orientations in terms of these six categories. The difficulty with his formulation is the serious question of whether people can truly be placed largely within the confines of a single category on the basis of their vocational interests and occupations. To assume that each pair of figures can be placed in the same class because of their alleged vocational determinants seems to suffer from the logical fallacy of stereotyping.

Building upon this idea of six character types, Holland sets forth the following theory: *people search for environments and vocations that will permit them to exercise their skills and abilities, to express their attitudes and values, to take on agreeable problems and rules, and to avoid disagreeable ones* (Holland, 1966). A realistic personality type would function best in a realistic environment, while a social type would function best in a social environment, and so on. The choice and satisfaction of an occupation depends heavily upon the degree of concordance between the individual's type and his environment.

Holland's theory is complex and sophisticated. He discusses such diverse concepts as the relationship between heredity and environment, and the application of psychoanalytic insights to vocational choice. One important distinction of his theory is that it has been heavily tested and retested by Holland and his associates (Holland, 1973) and is probably the most thoroughly tested of all the vocational theories.

Roe's theory of needs

Anne Roe has put forth a theory of occupational choice and job satisfaction based upon Maslow's ideas of the integrated unity of the individual as a nexus of interacting levels of needs, both conscious and unconscious. "In order to understand the role of the occupation in the life of the individual," Roe (1956) suggests, "we must first have some understanding of the individual and his needs." As she expounds this conceptual understanding of the individual and his needs, she builds a theory of vocational development upon this framework, utilizing both psychoanalytic and empirical methodology for the construction.

One of Roe's more important insights is the relationship between the individual's family background, his upbringing, and his later occupational situation (Roe, 1957). Deficiencies during childhood, she suggests, may be compensated for, by, and through the work that one does. If one did not receive sufficient praise and respect from one's parents, he may attempt to elicit these through his job and consequently seek jobs where such praise and respect would be forthcoming. Likewise, for all the needs that were unmet at earlier stages of development, one turns to one's work to find gratification for these needs.

"In our society," Roe (1956) argues, "there is no single situation which is potentially so capable of giving some satisfaction at all levels of basic needs as is the occupation." She goes on to suggest that Maslow's hierarchy of basic needs (which she lists as "the physiological needs; the safety needs; the need for belongingness and love; the need for importance; respect, self-esteem, independence; the need for information; the need for understanding; the need for beauty; the need for self-actualization") are all satisfied within the job situation. The job, therefore, becomes a primary determinant of one's psychological fulfillment:

In our culture, social and economic status depend more upon the occupation than upon anything else. Sociological as well as psychological studies are practically unanimous on this point, although there are of course exceptions. Feelings of personal esteem are also closely linked to the amount of responsibility the job entails. This is reflected in ratings of the prestige of occupations and in studies of job satisfaction. The degrees of freedom and responsibility in an occupation enter into these evaluations more importantly than do the levels of skills and training, or than do salaries.

People whose life situation is especially difficult may find that the status and prestige conferred by the occupation, or received from fellow workers, are the greatest sources of satisfaction for these needs.... Occupations as a source of need satisfaction are of extreme importance in our culture. It may be that occupations have become so important in our culture just because so many needs are so well satisfied by them. Whether the relation is causal or not, and if so which is cause and which is effect, does not particularly matter.... What is important is that this relationship exists and is an essential aspect of the value of the occupation to the individual. (Roe, 1956, p. 33)

In developing her ideas comprehensively, Roe has attempted to fit her ideas into a matrix-like structure, utilizing groups and levels to explain the occupational phenomena. The eight groups she lists are:

I Service	V Outdoor
II Business contact	VI Science
III Organizations	VII General cultural
IV Technology	VIII Arts and entertainment

The levels range from "professional and managerial" down to "unskilled." Determinations about the personality of the individual can be made from considerations about the group and the level of his occupation and the group and level toward which he strives.

In an important paper written with Marvin Siegelman (1964), Roe discusses the influence of early childhood developmental factors on occupational choice. Display 22.3 shows the relationship between the personality characteristics and the chosen profession (according to groups listed above). The basic core of all the different components—the center of the circle—differentiates between the *warm* and *cold* early home environments. The hypotheses suggested from this model, according to Roe and Siegelman, are:

1 Loving, protecting, and demanding homes would lead to person-orientation in the child and later person-orientation in occupations.
2 Rejecting, neglecting, and casual homes would lead to non-person orientation in occupations.
3 If extreme protecting and extreme demanding conditions were felt by the child to be restricting, he might, in defense, become non-person oriented.
4 Some individuals from rejecting homes might become person-oriented in search for satisfaction.
5 Loving and casual homes might provide a sufficient amount of relatedness that other factors such as abilities would determine interpersonal directions more than personal needs. (pp. 7-8)

As much influence as Roe has had upon subsequent theories of career development and occupational choice, she has suffered her fair share of criticism as

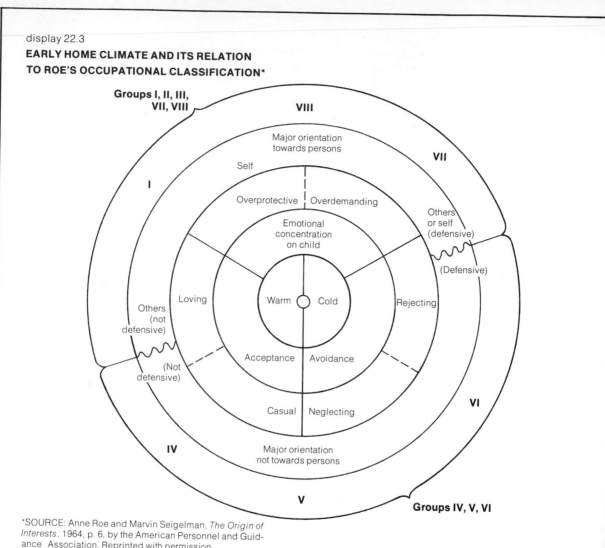

display 22.3

**EARLY HOME CLIMATE AND ITS RELATION
TO ROE'S OCCUPATIONAL CLASSIFICATION***

Groups I, II, III,
VII, VIII

VIII

Major orientation
towards persons

Self

VII

Overprotective | Overdemanding

Others
or self
(defensive)

Emotional
concentration
on child

I

(Defensive)

Others
(not
defensive)

Loving

Warm | Cold

Rejecting

(Not
defensive)

Acceptance | Avoidance

Casual | Neglecting

IV

Major orientation
not towards persons

VI

V

Groups IV, V, VI

*SOURCE: Anne Roe and Marvin Seigelman, *The Origin of
Interests*, 1964, p. 6, by the American Personnel and Guidance Association. Reprinted with permission.

well. Carkhuff, Alexik, and Anderson (1967) give a well-tempered summary of
the weaknesses of Roe's position:

Instead of attempting to generalize her findings into a unique and comprehensive system,
Roe apparently seeks to "rationalize" her results by drawing from analytic theory and
Maslow's postulates to support her findings. She has neither systematically deduced her
hypotheses from these systems nor does she work inductively to these systems.... Roe
neither makes systematic derivations from the theories that she proposes nor is the theory
with which she deals a generalization of her findings, serving to organize the available
evidence and guide the search for better evidence. Rather, she appears to seek entrance to

428

already existing systems. She does not make sufficient attempt to qualify the existing theories in terms of her findings and, thus, provides no unique theory of her own to encompass her results. In summary, then, according to the schema, Roe makes no justifiable generalizations from her data above the level of what has been defined as laws. (p. 337–338)

While these comments do have some validity, there are a number of strong points about Roe's system that should also be mentioned. Her system allows an integrative role to the job function and relates occupational choice to the entire structure of the personality. From a counseling point of view, Roe's insights help the counselor better understand the variety of factors that play a part in the individual's decision to pursue or avoid certain types of jobs and help the counselor understand why a job does or does not meet a client's needs. Moreover, her work sets a foundation from which further empirical research may be conducted to supplement the work that Roe and her associates have already undertaken (Roe et al., 1966; Roe and Siegelman, 1964).

Hoppock's theory

Hoppock (1967) lists the ten major points of his theory:

1 Occupations are chosen to meet needs.
2 The occupation that we choose is the one that we believe will best meet the needs that most concern us.
3 Needs may be intellectually perceived, or they may be only vaguely felt as attractions which draw us in certain directions. In either case, they may influence choices.
4 Vocational development begins when we first become aware that an occupation can help to meet our needs.
5 Vocational development progresses and occupational choice improves as we become better able to anticipate how well a prospective occupation will meet our needs. Our capacity thus to anticipate depends upon our knowledge of ourselves, our knowledge of occupations, and our ability to think clearly.
6 Information about ourselves affects occupational choice by helping us to recognize what we want and by helping us to anticipate whether or not we will be successful in collecting what the contemplated occupation offers to us.
7 Information about occupations affects occupational choice by helping us to discover the occupations that may meet our needs and by helping us to anticipate how well satisfied we may hope to be in one occupation as compared with another.
8 Job satisfaction depends upon the extent to which the job that we hold meets the needs that we feel it should meet. The degree of satisfaction is determined by the ratio between what we have and what we want.
9 Satisfaction can result from a job which meets our needs today or from a job which promises to meet them in the future.
10 Occupational choice is always subject to change when we believe that a change will better meet our needs. (pp. 111–112)

We see how Hoppock's ideas represent a "composite theory," and it is probably for this reason that his writing has enjoyed the wide popularity it has over the years. His ideas are compatible with other theorists, and the concordance between various points of view in vocational counseling attests both to the unity of the discipline and to the integrity of the different systems.

Other theories of career development

In addition to the theories discussed above, there are three other important theories of career development that, because of limitations of space, will be discussed briefly. For a more comprehensive discussion of any of these theories, the reader should direct his attention to the relevant references cited at the end of this chapter.

Eli Ginzberg's (1972) "Theory of Occupational Choice," as it has been reformulated over twenty years, is briefly summarized as follows:

Occupational choice is a process that remains open as long as one makes and expects to make decisions about his work and career. In many instances it is coterminous with his working life.

While the successive decisions that a young person makes during the preparatory period will have a shaping influence on his later career, so will the continuing changes that he undergoes in work and life.

People make decisions about jobs and careers with an aim of optimizing their satisfactions by finding the best possible fit between their priority needs and desires and the opportunities and constraints that they confront in the world of work.

Our reformulated theory is that *occupational choice is a lifelong process of decision-making in which the individual seeks to find the optimal fit between his career preparation and goals and the realities of the world of work.* (p. 172)

This reformulation differs somewhat from the original theory. Because it is more recent and based on more experimentation, it should be considered the definitive statement, supplanting the original formulation.

Tiedeman and O'Hara have developed a system based in part on the constructs of ego psychology. They view vocational development as part of a continuing process of the individual differentiating his ego identity. They describe career development "as the process of fashioning a vocational identity through differentiation and integration of the personality as one confronts the problem of work in living" (Tiedeman and O'Hara, 1963). Heavy on theory and conceptual frameworks, the writing of Tiedeman and O'Hara integrates many of the insights developed by Freud, Erikson, Super, Roe, and Ginzberg. They have attempted over the years to integrate a plethora of new research data into their models, with the result that "their theory cannot emerge beyond the status of a collection of lower-level generalizations. Instead of streamlining and simplifying their theorems, they seem to be moving in the opposite direction—toward encompassing as diverse data as possible, hoping that in the future, out of the midst of chaos, order will emerge" (Carkhuff et al., 1967).

Stefflre (1966) has developed ten propositions, which he calls "exploratory," that summarize many of the insights developed by some of the other theorists we have considered. These propositions are:

430

1 An occupation permits an expression of the individual's public personality which is a special instance of differentiation of function....

2 The occupational persona represents the individual's choice among those masks he would like to wear and those that society will permit him to wear....

3 An occupational role may represent avoidance reaction as well as, or instead of, approach reaction....

4 The importance of the work aspect of the public personality—the occupational persona —varies from being psychologically peripheral to being central. In Havighurst's phraseology, the occupation may vary from being "ego involving" to being "society maintaining." ...

5 The societally limiting forces that determine the occupational persona of any individual vary from the accidental to the essential. If we agree that it is a rare individual who can choose his occupational persona with complete freedom, we must see what sort of limitations he may encounter from society....

6 The expression of the public personality through an occupation—the selection of an occupational persona—must be made on incomplete information.... We cannot possibly know all about ourselves when we move into an occupation, nor can we know all about a particular occupational role until we experience it....

7 The stability of the choice of an occupation after additional information about the work role becomes available varies directly with the psychological commitment to the occupation on the part of the chooser....

8 As further information about the self comes to light, it is more apt to lead to change within the occupation for those who are psychologically committed to the occupation as opposed to change to a different occupation for others.

9 The occupational persona and the self-concept have a symbiotic relationship that moves them toward congruence....

10 The selection of an occupational persona may express any of four relationships between the self and society. The first relationship might be called "fitting." ...A second relationship might be called "permitting." In this situation the self-concept is not completely congruent with the self....

A third relationship might be called "transforming." In this situation the self-concept is congruent with the self but the individual does not wish to display all of his self-concept in an occupation....

The fourth relationship may be thought of as "binding." In this situation the self-concept is congruent with the self and the occupational persona congruent with the self-concept. However, the occupational persona had been selected on the basis of inaccurate occupational role expectations.*

We see from Stefflre's propositions, as well as from the other theories presented, that contemporary models of career development are highly sophisticated theories that account for the psychological as well as the sociological and educational influences on career choices, career satisfaction, and adjustment to career patterns.

---

*From "Vocational Development: Ten Propositions in Search of a Theory" by B. Stefflre, *Personnel and Guidance Journal*, 1966, *44*, 611–616. Copyright 1966 by American Personnel and Guidance Association. Reprinted with permission.

EDUCATIONAL COUNSELING
AND INFORMATIONAL SERVICES

Many of the insights we have seen in the theories of career choice and development apply equally well to educational counseling. Educational counseling may be defined as the total process of helping the client decide upon his educational plans, make sound and appropriate choices, and succeed in all his educational endeavors. Rothney (1972) details nine common problems characteristic of the type that the educational counselor encounters:

1 *Selection among various broad curricular groupings offered by the schools.* Choice of one program from the college preparatory, business, trade, or general groups involves consideration of such matters as a student's post-high school training plans and the generally greater prestige value for parents and students of college preparatory courses.

2 *Selection among electives within or without broad curriculum groupings.* Consideration must be given to such matters as possible vocational and avocational values of courses.... Parents' insistence on certain kinds of training needs consideration....

3 *Arrangement for taking university correspondence courses not offered by a school in order to meet specified requirements or to provide for a student's interests.*

4 *Consideration of students' course loads.* Such factors as health, desire to finish school in less than the usual time, enrichment, opportunity to work for pay, correlation of work in the local vocational school, and participation in work experience programs are given consideration.

5 *Selection of courses designed particularly to prepare for marriage.* Some girls are engaged to be married soon after graduation and want to elect combinations of courses that will prepare for homemaking as well as for the work they plan to do outside the home.

6 *Provision of special help with study habits or with difficulties in particular courses.*

7 *Arrangement of special summer courses or experiences.* These provide enrichment, permit make-up work, or offer special preparation for a planned experience.

8 *Interpretation of educational data.*

9 *Information is given about availability and methods of obtaining scholarships and other aids for post-high school training.** (pp. 11–12)

For each of these situations, the practical counselor may freely apply insights regarding the nature of vocational choice. Why has a student decided to go to college or not go to college? How is the choice of a major subject arrived at? What college has the client selected, and why? Is the client seeking an educational program that is appropriate to his vocational goal?

Much of the counselor's work in educational counseling is of a remedial nature. For the student who is doing poorly in school, who is an underachiever, the counselor can and should play a vital role in helping to maximize the student's potential. The counselor, in addition to exploring the problem with the client,

*John W. M. Rothney, ADAPTIVE COUNSELING IN SCHOOLS, (C) 1972, pp. 11–12. By permission of Prentice-Hall, Inc., Englewood Cliffs, New Jersey.

Mobile units near housing developments provide career counseling.

might be instrumental in arranging tutoring or after-school classes. A comprehensive tutoring program, one that utilizes volunteer tutors, is often helpful in dealing with the underachieving student.

The key point for the counselor to remember in providing educational information is that his job is to make that information meaningful to the student—to help the student put that information into constructive action (Norris, Zeran and Hatch, 1960). "Helping the counselee express his feelings about information and determine its personal meaning are the most important and demanding aspects of the use of information to help the counselee" (Tolbert, 1972). The counselor must avoid the temptation of feeling that, simply having given information, he has adequately discharged his duties. Shertzer and Stone (1971) offer six principles that adequately detail the role, scope, and purpose of the school informational service, be it educational or vocational information.

LEISURE-TIME COUNSELING

In addition to counseling clients in regard to vocational and educational decisions, the practical counselor may also deal with the client's leisure-time activities. This is a particularly important part of *preventive counseling*, since the constructive use of leisure time enables the client to deal more maturely and effectively with his other life decisions. Leisure-time counseling is a new field that has not yet been fully developed but that is being examined quite critically by a number of counseling practitioners.

How does the counselor go about helping the client develop a healthy attitude toward leisure-time activities? It is a three-stage process, involving *exploration, discussion, and integration.*

Exploration

During the course of the normal counseling interview, particularly if it is a vocational counseling interview, the counselor attempts to find out how much leisure time the client presently has available and how he spends that time. The counselor should not be satisfied with ready-made or superficial answers. He must keep in mind that many clients do not know how they spend their leisure time. They have no concept of what leisure time means, and therefore they do not conceptualize ways of spending leisure time. They merely view some segments of time as time without specific obligations, and they may not be consciously aware of how they are spending this time. Some particular questions the counselor may ask to elicit a full analysis of leisure time are: "What hobbies do you have?" "How much time do you spend at this hobby?" "Do you watch much television?" "Do you read?" "Do you have many friends?" "Are you active in sports?" "Do you travel much?"

These types of questions, placed in juxtaposition and examined by the skilled counselor, can reveal to the counselor what type of activities occupy the bulk of the client's free time. Ideally, there should be an interest and an involvement in free-time activities to the extent that these activities contribute productively to the client's life.

Discussion

The dialogue that ensues between the counselor and the client has a twofold purpose. First, it is to help the client identify the use of his leisure time and understand ways in which he may be able to appropriate that time more economically. Second, it is to explore with the client the extent to which he is seriously engaged in meaningful projects during his leisure time. Is he happy to have leisure time or does he suffer from boredom and inactivity? Is there an integration between his leisure-time activities and his need to learn to explore fully different kinds of activities? The discussion phase of the interview is designed to bring these things out into the open and to enable the client to grasp them and to deal with them.

Integration

During this phase, the counselor actively sets out to help the client readjust his leisure-time activities in ways determined through the discussion phase of the interview. Consider, for example, the situation (which is rather typical) in which the client finds himself bored during his leisure time, suffering from feelings of "not having anything to do." This type of boredom may lead to drug abuse, juvenile delinquency, and depression. The counselor, having by this time determined what the client's interests are, may suggest to him certain types of activities that will help him fill his time constructively. A creative counselor may use after-school activities to interest a large number of students in constructive leisure-time activity.

This phase of the interview is called integration because it serves to integrate the leisure-time activity into the counselee's total life style. Leisure-time activity should be an integral, harmonious, constructive part of the client's existence, not something separate and apart from it. The client should learn and grow during his leisure time as he does during other moments of his life.

References

Barnard, C. What do you want to be when you grow up? *Think Magazine* (International Business Machines Corporation), 1972, (Jan./Feb.), 45–48.

Boy, A. V., & Pine, G. J. *Expanding the self: Personal growth for teachers*. Dubuque, Iowa: Wm. C. Brown, 1971.

Carkhuff, R. R., Alexik, M., & Anderson, S. Do we have a theory of vocational choice? *Personnel and Guidance Journal*, 1967, *46*, 335–345.

Foreman, M. E., & James, L. E. Vocational relevance as a factor in counseling. *Journal of Counseling Psychology*, 1973, *20*, 99–103.

Ginzberg, E. Toward a theory of occupational choice. *Vocational Guidance Quarterly*, 1972, *20*, 169–175.

Herr, E. L., & Cramer, S. H. *Vocational guidance and career development in the schools: Toward a systems approach*. Boston: Houghton Mifflin, 1972.

Hewer, V. H. What do theories of vocational choice mean to a counselor? *Journal of Counseling Psychology*, 1963, *10*, 118–125.

Hoffman, D. S. Implications of future shock for vocational counselors. *Vocational Guidance Quarterly*, 1972, *21*, 92–96.

Holland, J. A theory of vocational choice. *Journal of Counseling Psychology*, 1959, *6*, 35–44.

Holland, J. *Some explorations of theory of vocational choice*. Washington, D.C.: Psychological Monographs—American Psychological Association, 1962.

Holland, J. *The psychology of vocational choice*. Waltham, Mass.: Blaisdell, 1966.

Holland, J. *Making vocational choices: A theory of careers*. Englewood Cliffs, N.J.: Prentice-Hall, 1973.

Hoppock, R. *Occupational information* (3rd ed.). New York: McGraw-Hill, 1967.

National Vocational Guid. Assoc. & American Vocational Assoc., *Career development and career guidance*. Washington, D.C.: American Personnel & Guid. Assoc., 1972.

Norris, W., Zeran, F. R., & Hatch, R. N. *The information service in guidance* (1st ed.). Chicago: Rand McNally, 1960.

Roe, A. *The psychology of occupations*. New York: John Wiley & Sons, 1956.

Roe, A. Early determinants of vocational choice. *Journal of Counseling Psychology*, 1957, *4*, 212–217.

Roe, A., Hubbard, W. D., Hutchinson, T., & Batemen, T. Studies of occupational history. Part I: Job changes and the classification of occupations. *Journal of Counseling Psychology*, 1966, *13*, 387–393.

Roe, A., & Siegelman, M. *The origin of interests*. Washington, D.C.: American Personnel and Guidance Association, 1964.

Rothney, J. W. M. *Adaptive counseling schools*. Englewood Cliffs, N.J.: Prentice-Hall, 1972.

Sanderson, H. *Basic concepts in vocational guidance*. New York: McGraw-Hill, 1954.

Shartle, C. L. *Occupational information* (3rd ed.). Englewood Cliffs, N.J.: Prentice-Hall, 1959.

Shertzer, B., & Stone, S. C. *Fundamentals of guidance* (2nd ed.). Boston: Houghton Mifflin, 1971.

Smith, M. Organizing career guidance: A guide to effective program implementation. *New York City Personnel and Guidance Association*, 1973, *1*, 22–23.

Stefflre, B. Vocational development: Ten propositions in search of a theory. *Personnel and Guidance Journal*, 1966, *44*, 611–616.

Stefflre, B., & Grant, H. W. *Theories of counseling* (2nd ed.). New York: McGraw-Hill, 1972.

Super, D. E. A theory of vocational development. *American Psychologist*, 1953, *8*, 185–190.

Super, D. E. *The psychology of careers*. New York: Harper & Row, 1957.

Super, D. E. Vocational development theory: Person, position, and process. *Counseling Psychologist*, 1969, *1*, 2–9.

Tarrier, R. B., et al. Career counseling: Prediction or exploration. Paper presented at the APGA Convention, Atlantic City, New Jersey, April, 1971. (ERIC Document Reproduction Service No. ED 051 510)

Tiedeman, D. V., & O'Hara, R. P. *Career development: Choice and adjustment*. New York: College Entrance Examination Board, 1963.

Tolbert, E. L. *Introduction to counseling* (2nd ed.). New York: McGraw-Hill, 1972.

Tolbert, E. L. *Counseling for career development*. Boston: Houghton Mifflin, 1974.

PART SIX

Those who hide from us also must be reached.

Practical counseling
in the schools
an overview

THE PLACE OF COUNSELING IN EDUCATION

Much of the discussion in these chapters has concerned specific applications of the counseling point of view to school-related problems. We have examined three ways in which the counseling approach contributes to the school environment: (1) by providing enriching, growing experiences that enable the student to develop fully his potentialities; (2) by providing intervening therapeutic forces that militate against those disruptive and counterproductive forces that impede education; (3) by providing a specific group of services for teachers, students, and administrators, including appraisal, information-giving, referral, and the like. Synthesizing these three functions into an integral, organized whole, we begin to understand the rightful place of counseling within the framework of education.

The importance of such an understanding becomes clear when we examine the consequences of misunderstandings. The very limited appropriation of government funds in the area of counselor education and training, as well as in the area of provision for counseling personnel to the public schools, is most likely a result of the failure of legislators to understand that counseling is not a frill of the educational process—not some luxurious adjunct to the core requisites—but an integral, necessary, economically productive part of the educational process.

Under-utilization of the counseling function is another unfortunate consequence of the professional's failure to understand the legion of possibilities that lie hidden in the counseling office. All too often, to the sadness of counselors, the many plans, ideas, and applications that the conscientious counselor has developed lie dormant in his mind or in his filing cabinet, while others on the staff go about their business merrily because they do not recognize the resources available down the corridor. This situation may be the fault of the counselor, too, because of his failure to bring the problem out into the open; but he has been conditioned, by time and experience, to keep a moderately low profile, and he should not have to assume the burden of the blame.

If we try to understand the true, holistic place of counseling within the framework of education, we must look back to the past and try to understand how counseling arose and what purpose it was to serve. Its roots are many and spread far apart. From the beginnings of recorded civilization, men have speculated about their destinies, about their place in the universe, about their motives, character, and ties with other parts of the natural order, particularly the animal kingdom. From this natural inquisitiveness—what Konrad Lorenz calls "curiosity behavior"—man developed a capacity not only to survive in most environments but to master his intellectual, psychological, and philosophical environment as well as his physical environment. His attempts at understanding first took the form of philosophical speculation and analysis. He attempted through the application of his superior mental faculties to come to grips with the problems of his soul. For thousands of years, the philosophy of Western civilization helped shape and clarify the destiny of man.

The advent of scientific studies of the mind—what I call the "Newtonian conception"—transformed the content and substance of these inquiries. Psychoanalysis, built upon the medical model, formulated an image of man based on the idea of an unconscious. A theory of symptomatology was developed, which classified man's diverse emotional differences into groups of psychopathologies, and subsequent psychotherapies, whether they accepted or rejected this classification, had to come to grips with its compelling, scientific logic. It was not until the reaction to this demi-scientific empiricism came to a head that a new "Einsteinian" image of man and his problems, a relativistic position that recognized the integrity and uniqueness of man, came to the fore.

Counseling is the natural, evolutionary synthesis of all these positions with the pragmatic, democratic idealism of guidance that originated in the United States near the beginning of this century. Developed because of a social need for an educational adjunct, the guidance movement slipped gracefully into the scope of education. It is the responsibility of the practical counselor to assure that his integrative counseling and guidance function enjoys the wide acceptance that the guidance function has attained over the years.

A number of writers have suggested ways of doing this. Norman Sprinthall, Carl Rogers, Robert Carkhuff, Leona Tyler, Dugald S. Arbuckle, John W. M. Rothney, have been particularly prominent in this important area. From the writing of these and others, the following four principles have been extracted to clarify the place of counseling in education:

1 Counseling, particularly practical counseling, is never separate from education. The two functions work harmoniously together to achieve a common goal.
2 The counselor does teaching, and the teacher does counseling. Each concentrates on a specific aspect of the growth process, but their functions often overlap.
3 The recognition of two types of growth—intellectual growth and emotional growth—is essential. The development of character should precede the development of intellect, since knowledge and intelligence are formidable tools and should be used wisely.
4 A consistent philosophy underlies both the educative and counseling processes. It is a philosophy that includes a theory of reality, of knowledge, and of values. Every action undertaken by the counselor or by the teacher is explained by the principles of this philosophy. Although the philosophy differs from counselor to counselor, from teacher to teacher, it always emphasizes the dignity and worth of the individual, his uniqueness as a person, his right and his ability to choose freely.

THE COUNSELOR'S WORLD AND WORLD VIEW

The world of the practical counselor is a rich and rewarding world. It is blessed with a wonderful gift, the gift of being able to share with others, of being able to give and to receive, of being able to help others. To appreciate this world, we must understand the work of the counselor, both in its theoretical formulation and in its everyday practice. This is no easy task. For the very nature of the counseling interaction, with its spontaneity and dynamic vitality, its uniqueness, precludes its containment in print, with its linear restrictions. But I shall do my best in this short section to convey the dramatic excitement that infuses the counselor's world and colors with spirit his world view.

"The whole counselor," Carkhuff and Berenson (1967) point out, "trusts his experience of the client more than the client trusts his own experience of himself. The whole counselor trusts his experience more than the client's expression of his" (p. 205). The counselor's experience, therefore, constitutes not only the essential core of his existence, but in an indirect sense also affects the central core of the client's existence as well. If we look at "experience" in the Deweyan sense—as a mutual interaction between the individual and his environment— and if we consider the existence of the client as an important part of the counselor's environment, we can better appreciate the high degree of concordance between the counselor's world, the world of the client, and the process and product of counseling as a function.

In some ways, the very beauty of the counselor's world is fraught with terror. The proximity to pain, the brash confrontation with a myriad of naked others, the precipitous sharpening of human sensitivities, exposes the counselor to what Wrenn (1949) calls "the strain upon the individual of constant contact with human beings." It is at times a difficult strain to endure, thinning as it does the veneer of protective armor with which we have isolated ourselves from the difficulties of reality which compellingly surround us. But the counselor still strives on and sustains himself with the very quality of nurturance that he has voluntarily given to another. The client, in turn, responds; and this mutual interaction provides the dynamic flux of the counselor's world. In this environment of movement, this world of active living, the counselor revivifies himself in the products of his efforts. The counselor is a witness to his own works! He is also an educator. He educates on different levels from those of the teacher. As Berdie (1960) points out,

His greatest role perhaps is to help students apply to their own personal lives those same processes that concern others in the academic enterprise. When students can sense when they have problems and needs, when they can adequately understand the nature of these problems, when they can explore possible solutions and evaluate evidence relevant for these solutions, when they know how to solve personal problems just as they know how to solve more abstract or impersonal problems, then the educational role of the counselor is fulfilled. (p. 463)

Fulfilled—that is the key word. As the counselor carries out his work, as he fulfills his obligation, as he enacts his role, his personal life and sense of importance also lead to a feeling of fulfillment.

But the counselor must also recognize the possibilities of failure. He must develop what May (1967) calls the *"courage of imperfection ... the ability to fail."* For he lives in the real world, not in a fantasy existence, and he must, like any of us, be willing to accept his fallibility. Only by such an acknowledgement can the counselor continue to be strong, to carry out his work in the way that he knows best.

The counselor's world and world view are one. He does as he believes; he lives as he thinks he should live; his life is charged with purpose. He is a minister to the problems of his client; a teacher; a confidant. He is many things, some too subtle for words to express. *But above all he is himself*, doing what he does in his own unique, distinct, personal way.

THE MULTIPLE ROLES OF THE SCHOOL COUNSELOR

The counselor's role is often not clearly defined, and he may well be perceived differently by each of the people with whom he interacts during his typical workday in the school setting. And yet there is a sense of bold definition implicit in everything the counselor does. He defines his role through his actions, in the true existential sense of the word.

Zerface and Cox (1971) discuss the difficulty the counselor experiences in trying to break away from the school's point of view. Counselors are either explicitly or implicitly agents of the school, and they are often caught in conflicts between what they believe they should do and what the school demands of them. As the studies cited in chapter 6 demonstrate, there is a sharp discrepancy between the role of the counselor as he sees it, as it is defined in his training, and as he experiences it in the school situation.

Landy (1963) raises the question, "Who does what in the guidance program?" This is a legitimate question that challenges the coordination of counseling functions and, indirectly, the relationship between the work of the counselor and the work of other school personnel. This must be clarified. Roles should be defined from the beginning, in order to prevent subsequent misunderstandings.

An allied issue, which has been discussed in this text, is the question of the counselor's professionalism. As long as the counselor conducts himself as a professional person working in a highly sensitive and very important position, he is more likely to be able to effect the changes he wishes to effect. In order to be a professional, the counselor has to be sure of himself, of his abilities, and he must also be confident in what his job entails. Arbuckle (1970) discusses this point:

A professional individual, of course, in a school as elsewhere does not ask his employer "What do you want me to do?" It is not a case of the individual being fitted to the job, but rather are the particular skills and capacities of the individual such that he can be effective in a certain task. If they are, he might consider accepting the position, if they are not, he obviously should not accept the position even if it were offered to him. It is difficult for me to believe that any professional school counselor, if asked by a potential employer, "Do you accept the responsibility of utilizing your authority to compel certain students to change their behavior?" would answer any other way than, "No, I do not." On the other hand, it would seem equally logical that a school administrator, if asked the same question, might respond, "Well, I hope we never have to compel a student to do anything, but if his behavior is disruptive, and counter to school policy, then yes, I might have to compel him to change his behavior or leave the institution." (p. 122)

While all counseling efforts must inexorably challenge these difficult predicaments, such challenges are especially important for the practical counselor, whose work stresses fundamental unity of the individual with the school, the school with society, the part with the totality, the theory with the praxis.

The counselor's role definition is a crucial phase of his professional activity because it influences profoundly everything he does. The job of defining his role can be made somewhat simpler if the counselor can communicate to the others with whom he works the multifaceted, integrative approach he is willing to use. He need not and should not emphasize either the therapeutic, the informational, the appraisal, the consultative, or the administrative functions; but he should show the other staff members that he is integrating all these functions together to improve the total service program for the student population as well as for the benefit of the professional staff. Such an integration will not only be appreciated by the others, but it—more than anything the counselor can say—will help them understand the practical application of counseling and the essential role of the practical counselor.

HELPING CLIENTS GROW

We are all one—
born into this rich earth, into the
human experience. We carry
a dream, a special vision inside,
and when the load gets heavy
we can reach for that dream.
Through it life unfolds and we find
strength, faith, love.
　　Yvonne Rankin*

While many writers and practitioners have suggested a variety of different goals for counseling, the key word that characterizes almost all the conceptions is *growth*. "Growth," Cardinal Newman has said, "is the only evidence of life." Counseling promotes life—it is a life-sustaining process—because it contributes to the active nurturing processes of life. As a counseling effort becomes effective in helping the client grow, it can be said to be effective counseling.

But what do we mean by growth? Can we specify growth in a specific direction, or does the term retain a certain vagueness and lack of specificity? If we are compelled to give a single definition of growth that characterizes the type of growth we are speaking about in relation to counseling, I would say that growth is the fulfillment of all the client's potentialities, his self-actualization, his teleological striving toward perfection as an individual. Translated into a practical equivalent, it means that the client is given an opportunity to escape from the prison within himself, which confines him and limits his freedom. Rogers (1969) describes this process poetically:

One thing I have come to look upon as almost universal is that when a person realizes he has been deeply heard, there is a moisture in his eyes. I think in some real sense he is weeping for joy. It is as though he were saying, "Thank God, *somebody* heard me. Someone knows what it's like to be me." In such moments I have had the fantasy of a prisoner in a dungeon tapping out day after day a Morse code message, "Does anybody hear me? Is there anybody there? Can anyone hear me?" And finally one day he hears some faint tappings which spell out "Yes." By that one simple response he is released from his loneliness, he has become a human being again. There are many, many people living in private dungeons today, people who give no evidence of it whatever on the outside, where you have to listen very sharply to hear the faint message from the dungeon. (p. 185)

Within the boundaries of this Rogerian metaphor, growth may be viewed as the individual's release from his self-imposed incarceration. The counselor helps the client grow by helping him become free of these intrapsychic bars of impenetrable steel, hardened by difficult life experiences over the years.

The specific goals of freedom differ from one counseling approach to another. The humanistic approaches view self-actualization as the goal of counseling,

*From record album jacket of "Kenny Rankin—Like a Seed." Reprinted by permission of Little David Records, Inc., and Yvonne Rankin.

since this is the highest level of human development. The psychoanalytic approach emphasizes freedom from repression and an integration of the structures of consciousness—the id, ego, and superego. The existentialist stresses authenticity and the pursuit of meanings in life. "You are what you do," he argues—existence precedes essence—and the existential counselor frees the client by helping him develop and sustain meanings for his life. The behavioral counselor sees growth as the freedom from debilitating symptoms, and he works to free the client from these symptoms of behavioral maladjustment. The rational-emotive counselor, as well as the reality counselor, works toward creating a harmony between the logical, objective reality and the inner-subjective, guiding reality of the client's consciousness. Despite these theoretical differences, the concept that underlies all these positions is growth, change, the dynamic movement of human life.

The counselor helps the client grow through his own personal qualities as well as through his professional expertise. Arbuckle (1970), Carkhuff and Berenson (1967), and others have shown that the counselor's personal and professional characteristics exert a profound influence upon the client's development. Such qualities as empathy, warmth, genuineness, concreteness, positive regard, honesty, sincerity, respect, self-disclosure, confrontation, and immediacy of the relationship are significantly related to the outcome of the treatment. It is not so much the techniques that the counselor uses or the school that he identifies himself with, but what he himself is and what he is willing to give that determines how much the client will be able to grow and consequently how effective the treatment is. "Humanness," Webster (1973) has argued, "is the one essential" for counseling.

Helping clients grow is the goal of all counseling, and the personality of the counselor is the tool. Theories, techniques, and counseling applications are the fine details that explain how the counselor's personal qualities are translated into the specified goals.

References

Arbuckle, D. S. *Counseling: Philosophy, theory, and practice.* Boston: Allyn & Bacon, 1970.

Berdie, R. F. The counselor and his manpower responsibilities. *Personnel and Guidance Journal*, 1960, *38*, 458–463.

Carkhuff, R. R., & Berenson, B. G. *Beyond counseling and therapy.* New York: Holt, Rinehart, & Winston, 1967.

Landy, E. Who does what in the guidance program? *The School Counselor*, 1963, *10*, 112–118.

May, R. *The art of counseling.* Nashville: Abingdon Press, 1967.

Rogers, C. R. *Freedom to learn.* Columbus, Ohio: Charles E. Merrill, 1969.

Webster, S. D. Humanness: The one essential. *Personnel and Guidance Journal*, 1973, *51*, 378–379.

Wrenn, C. G. The fault, dear Brutus. *Educational and Psychological Measurement*, 1949, *9*, 360–378.

Zerface, J. P., & Cox W. H. School counselors, leave home. *Personnel and Guidance Journal*, 1971, *49*, 371–375.

A GLOSSARY OF
DRUG CULTURE TERMINOLOGY*

Acapulco Gold High grade of marijuana; refers to the area of Mexico where it is grown; *see* Marijuana.

Acid LSD, one of the most popular hallucinogens or "psychedelic" drugs; *see* LSD.

Acid Head A person who regularly uses acid (LSD); *see* LSD.

Acid Test Party at which LSD has been added to the punch.

Addict A person addicted or "hooked" to regular use of drugs, especially heroin, morphine, and opium. Also: hophead, hypo, junkie.

Addiction Chronic drug use which involves: (1) a desire or need to take the drug. (2) a tendency to take more and more of the drug. (3) a mental—and sometimes physical—dependence on the drug and its effects.

African Black A grade of marijuana grown in Africa; *see* Marijuana.

Agent Law enforcement officer. Also: buster, fed, fuzz, the heat, the man, plant, sam, uncle, whiskers.

Agonies Withdrawal symptoms, usually in early stages; *see* Withdrawal.

Amphetamine-Barbiturate Combinations *See* French Blue, Greenies.

Amphetamines Stimulants which increase the activity of the nervous system; used medically to relieve depression or to reduce weight; misuse results in tremors, talkativeness. hallucinations, and excitability. Terms and slang names: bennies, co-pilots, dexies, dolls, dominoes, footballs, hearts, jelly babies, jolly beans, lid poppers, methedrine, oranges, peaches, pillhead, roses, speed, truck drivers, ups, wake ups, whites; *see* Methedrine.

Amytal Registered trade name for Amobarbital, a barbiturate; *see* Barbiturates.

Anti-freeze Heroin; *see* Heroin.

Arsenal An addict's or pusher's supply of drugs; *see* Works.

Artillery Equipment (such as hypodermic syringe) used to inject a drug; *see* Works.

Babysit To guide a person through his drug experience; *see* Guide, Guru.

B, Bee A penny match box volume, now a measure of marijuana approximately that size.

Back Track To allow blood to come into the syringe during injection; *see* Flushing.

Bag (1) container of drugs. (2) a problem. (3) a specialty; *see* Dime Bag, Nickel Bag.

Bagman A drug seller: *see* Pusher.

Bale A pound of marijuana.

Bang To inject drugs.

Barbiturates The most commonly abused depressants (sedatives), medically used to produce sleep or to reduce blood pressure; drowsiness, staggering, and slurred speech result when misused. Terms and slang names: blue devils, candy, double trouble, goofballs, nimby, peanuts, pinks, rainbows, red devils, sleepers, tooies, yellow jackets; *see* Amphetamine-Barbiturate Combinations.

Barbs Barbiturates; *see* Barbiturates.

Bennies Capsules or tablets of Benzedrine, a brand of amphetamine; *see* Amphetamines.

Bhang A grade of marijuana found in India; *see* Marijuana.

Big D LSD; *see* LSD.

Big Man Someone high up—or at the top—in a drug selling ring; *see* Pusher.

Bindle A packet of narcotic.

Bit A person's specialty, pastime, or favorite drug; a prison sentence.

Blackbirds Amphetamines; *see* Amphetamines.

Blank Low-grade narcotics.

Blasted Under the influence of—or high on—drugs; *see* Drug Experiences.

Blocked Under the influence of a drug—alone or in combination with alcohol; *see* Drug Experiences.

Blow a Stick To smoke a marijuana cigarette; *see* Marijuana.

Blow Your Mind To experience severe mental effects from a hallucinogenic drug, such as LSD; *see* Drug Experiences.

Boot The temporary elation or thrill experienced by an addict in his early days of using drugs; this experience—like all other claimed "good feelings"—disappears after repeated use; *see* Drug Experiences.

*From "A Handbook of Drug Terms (Revised, 1972)," New York State Drug Abuse Control Commission, formerly Narcotic Addiction Control Commission. Reprinted by permission.

Break the Needle To attempt to break or drop the narcotic habit; *see* Withdrawal.

Brewery A place where drugs are made, bought, or used.

Brick A kilogram (2.2 pounds) of marijuana; *see* Marijuana.

Bridge An alligator clip or other device used to hold a marijuana butt; *see* Crutch, Roach, Roach Clip.

Broker A dealer in drugs; *see* Pusher.

Brought Down Depressed feeling following elation from drug use; *see* Drug Experiences.

Browns Amphetamines; *see* Amphetamines.

Bugged (1) To be irritated by someone or something. (2) To be covered by sores and abscesses caused by repeated injections with unsterile equipment; *see* Drug Experiences.

Bundle A packet or supply of drugs.

Burned To obtain weak or contaminated drugs or a harmless substitute.

Bush Marijuana; *see* Marijuana.

Busted Arrested by the police.

Buster Narcotics agent, usually the Federal Bureau of Narcotics; *see* Agent.

Buttons That part of the peyote cactus containing the hallucinogen mescaline; *see* Mescaline.

Charged Up "High" or under the intoxicating influence of drugs; *see* Drug Experiences.

Chipping Taking small doses of drugs irregularly; *see* Dabble.

Coasting "High" or under the intoxicating influence of drugs; *see* Drug Experiences.

Cocaine A stimulant drug once widely used medically as a local anesthetic; when abused, it results in excitability, talkativeness, and reduction of the feeling of fatigue—and it may result in anxiety, fear, violence, and hallucinations. Also: "C," candy, coke, dust, gold dust, H and C, snow, speedball.

Cocktail Short butt of marijuana cigarette inserted in end of regular cigarette.

Coke Cocaine; *see* Cocaine.

Cold Turkey Withdrawal from physically addicting drugs without medication; the drug user feels chilled and is covered with "goose bumps," looking like a plucked turkey; *see* Withdrawal.

Come Down To lose the drug-induced exhilaration; *see* Drug Experiences.

Congo Mataby African term for marijuana; *see* Marijuana.

Connect To buy drugs (from a "connection").

Connection A drug seller; *see* Pusher.

Contact High The feeling of being "high" on drugs merely by being in contact with someone who is.

Cook Up (1) prepare heroin for injection; *see* Heroin. (2) prepare hashish for inclusion with tobacco by heating in silver paper; *see* Marijuana.

Cooker A spoon, bottle cap, or small cup used to dissolve a narcotic, such as heroin, in water. The solution is "cooked" or heated over a match or candle until the drug-containing powder is dissolved; *see* Works.

Cool A term of approval; drug users feel they are "cool," while non-users are termed "square."

Cop To purchase drugs; to steal.

Crash To collapse from exhaustion, usually while under the influence of drugs; *see* Drug Experiences.

Crutch Device used to hold a marijuana butt.

Cut To dilute or adulterate a narcotic before selling it; heroin is often "cut" with milk sugar so that the seller has more portions or "bags" to sell.

DMT Dimethyltryptamine; a hallucinogen; *see* Hallucinogen.

Dabble To "chip" or take small amounts of drugs irregularly; *see* Chipping.

Dagga South African term for marijuana; *see* Marijuana.

Dealer A drug seller; *see* Pusher.

Deck A small packet of drugs.

Dexies Dexedrine, a brand of amphetamine; *see* Amphetamines.

Dextroamphamine Sulphate An amphetamine; *see* Amphetamines.

Dime Bag A supply of drugs which costs $10.

Dirty Possessing drugs.

Doing To do or take something.

Dollies Dolophine, a brand of the narcotic methadone; *see* Heroin.

Dolls Pills; amphetamines, barbiturates, or a combination of these two drugs.

Double Trouble Tuinal, a brand of barbiturate; *see* Barbiturates.

Down A drug hangover or coming out of a drug-induced state; *see* Drug Experiences.

Drop Out To withdraw from the real world while under LSD or other drugs; *see* Drug Experiences.

Drug Experiences Terms for drug influence; *see* Blasted, Blocked, Blow Your Mind, Boot, Brought Down, Bugged, Charged Up, Coasting, Come Down, Crash, Down, Drop Out, Euphoria, Flake Out, Flattened, Flip Out, Floating, Flying, Freak Out, Gassed, Happening, High, Hopped Up, Horrors, Hung Up, Lift, On a Trip, On the Nod, Out of It, Overcharged, Stoned, Turned On, Up, Up Tight, Wasted.

Euphoria A feeling of well-being or elation sought by drug users and sometimes found the first few times that certain drugs are taken; *see* Drug Experiences.

Flake Out Lose consciousness from misuse of drugs; *see* Drug Experiences.

Flashback The unpredictable phenomenon of undergoing again the effects of LSD weeks or even months after the last use of the drug; *see* LSD.

Flattened An addict in stupor resulting from overdose; *see* Drug Experiences.

Flip Out LSD-induced madness; *see* Drug Experiences.

Floating "High" or under the intoxicating influence of drugs; *see* Drug Experiences.

Flushing Drawing blood back into the syringe during an injection to be sure that a vein has been tapped.

Flying "High" or under the intoxicating influence of drugs; *see* Drug Experiences.

Freak Out To lose contact with reality while on drugs; a bad drug experience; *see* Drug Experiences.

French Blue Amphetamine-barbiturate pill.

Gassed "High" or under intoxicating influence of drugs; *see* Drug Experiences.

Goofballs Barbiturates; large doses make the user sluggish and act "goofy" in the same way as someone who is drunk; *see* Barbiturates.

Grass Marijuana; *see* Marijuana.

Greenies Green, heart-shaped tablets of a barbiturate-amphetamine mixture.

Ground Control Guide/caretaker in an LSD session.

Guide A person who gives guidance or support during a psychedelic drug experience; *see* LSD.

Gum Opium.

Gun Hypodermic needle for "shooting" drugs; *see* Works.

Guru An experienced LSD user who acts as a companion/guide to one who is on a trip.

H Heroin; *see* Heroin.

H and C Hot and Cold, heroin and cocaine mixture; *see* Heroin, Cocaine.

Hallucinogen A drug which causes hallucinations (seeing things which do not exist); distortions of time, space, color, and sound; and rambling speech. Marijuana, LSD, STP, and DMT are the most commonly abused hallucinogens (popularly called "psychedelics").

Happening A psychedelic event or "show"; *see* Drug Experiences.

Hashish A strong form of marijuana; *see* Marijuana.

Head Chronic user of a drug or drugs.

Heroin A strong depressant, the narcotic drug used by nearly all addicts; it is a white powder which is usually dissolved in water and injected into the body. Also: anti-freeze, boy, dollies, dope, H, H and C, hard stuff, horse, junk.

High Under the intoxicating influence of drugs; *see* Drug Experiences.

Hooked Physically addicted to a drug.

Hop Head A narcotic addict; restricted to opiate users in addict usage.

Hopped Up Under the intoxicating influence of drugs; *see* Drug Experiences.

Horrors Terrifying dreams and hallucinations caused by LSD and other hallucinogenic drugs; *see* Drug Experiences.

Horse Heroin; *see* Heroin.

Hot Wanted by the police.

Hot Shot A fatal and usually strong—or even full strength—dose of narcotic or a mixture of a poison and a narcotic given to a troublesome addict or to one who has betrayed sellers to the police.

Hung-up Unable to obtain drugs; depressed, let down, disappointed; *see* Drug Experiences.

Joint A marijuana cigarette; *see* Marijuana.

Joystick Marijuana cigarette; *see* Marijuana.

Kheef Hashish; *see* Hashish.

Kick To stop using drugs; *see* Withdrawal.

Kilo Kilogram, the equivalent of 2.2 pounds; the usual package of marijuana sold in Mexico.

LSD—Lysergic Acid Diethylamide One of the most potent hallucinogens known. Terms and slang names: acid, big D, blue acid, chief, the hawk, instant Zen, sugar; *see also* Acid Head, Blow Your Mind, Flashback, Flip Out, Guide, Horrors, Niacinamide.

Lay-out Equipment for taking drugs.

Leapers Amphetamines; *see* Amphetamines.

Lemonade Poor heroin.

Lid One ounce of marijuana.

Lid Poppers Amphetamines; *see* Amphetamines.

Lift The temporary escape from mental depression given by some drugs; *see* Drug Experiences.

Manicured High-grade marijuana, undiluted by seeds or stems; *see* Marijuana.

Marijuana The most popular hallucinogen, smoked in a cigarette or pipe; made from the resin of the female hemp plant. Also Acapulco gold, cannabis, Congo mataby, dagga, gage, ganga, grass, hash, hashish, hay, hemp, Indian hemp, kief, Mary Jane, Panama red, pot, rope, tea, Texas tea, weed; *see also* Blow a Stick, Brick, Cook Up, Joint, Joystick, Manicured, Pack, Reefer, Roach, Rolling Up, Salt and Pepper, Stick, Stoned, Weed-head.

Mescaline The alkaloid of peyote, a hallucinogen; *see* Hallucinogen, Peyote.

Meth Methedrine, an amphetamine; *see* Methedrine.

Methedrine A powerful amphetamine. Also: meth, speed; *see* Amphetamines.

Narcotic A drug that dulls the senses, relieves pain, and induces sleep; large doses may result in stupor, coma, or convulsions; heroin, morphine, and opium are narcotics.

Niacinamide An antidote for LSD; used to interrupt a bad trip; *see* LSD.

Nickel Bag A five-dollar purchase of narcotics.

O Opium.

O.D. Overdose of drugs, results in coma and/or death.

Off No longer under the influence of drugs; *see* Withdrawal.

On a Trip Under the influence of LSD or another hallucinogen; *see* Drug Experiences.

On the Nod Under the intoxicating influence of drugs, especially the stupor immediately following the injection of a narcotic, such as heroin; *see* Drug Experiences.

Oranges Dexedrine, a brand of amphetamine; *see* Amphetamines.

Orange Sunshine LSD; *see* LSD.

Out of It Not in touch, such as when under the influence of drugs; *see* Drug Experiences.

Overcharged Under the influence of an overdose of narcotics; *see* Drug Experiences.

Pack A pack of marijuana cigarettes; *see* Marijuana.

Peaches Benzedrine, a brand of amphetamine; *see* Amphetamines.

Peanuts Barbiturates; *see* Barbiturates.

Pearly Gates Morning glory seeds; *see* Hallucinogen.

Pentobarbital Sodium A barbiturate; *see* Barbiturates.

Pep Pills Amphetamines; *see* Amphetamines.

Peyote, Peyotl A hallucinogen from the peyote cactus; *see* Hallucinogen.

Pick Up A new customer for drugs; a shot of narcotics usually given another addict as a gift or favor.

Piece A container of drugs; usually an ounce of narcotics.

Pigs Police.

Pill Head Person taking pills, usually amphetamines; *see* Amphetamines.

Pop To inject drugs, especially under the skin.

Pot Marijuana; *see* Marijuana.

Pot Head A chronic user of marijuana.

Psilocybin A hallucinogen obtained from a Mexican mushroom; *see* Hallucinogen.

Psychedelic Anything pertaining to the world of the hallucinogens. Usually vivid, undulating colors; strobe lights; and acid-rock music.

Pusher A person who sells illegal drugs. Also: bag man, big man, broker, connection, dealer, junkie.

Rainbows Tuinal, a brand of barbiturates; *see* Barbiturates.

Rap To talk while under the influence of drugs.

Reader A legitimate prescription for narcotics

used in medicine; morphine is sometimes prescribed.

Red Devils Seconal, a brand of barbiturate; *see* Barbiturates.

Reds and Blues Tuinal; *see* Double Trouble.

Reefer A marijuana cigarette; *see* Marijuana.

Reentry Return from an LSD "trip."

Retinal Circus Visual hallucinations experienced by an LSD user.

Roach A butt of marijuana cigarette; these are saved to make new cigarettes; *see* Marijuana.

Roach Clip Device used to hold a marijuana butt; *see* Bridge, Crutch.

Rolling Up Making a marijuana cigarette; *see* Marijuana.

Salt and Pepper Impure or low-grade marijuana; *see* Marijuana.

Secobarbital Seconal, a barbiturate; *see* Barbiturates.

Shoot To inject drugs.

Shooting Gallery A place where addicts gather to inject drugs.

Skag Heroin; *see* Narcotic.

Skin Cigarette paper.

Skin-popping To inject drugs, particularly narcotics, directly under the skin.

Sleepers Barbiturates in general; *see* Barbiturates.

Smack Heroin; *see* Narcotic.

Snop Marijuana.

Snort To take heroin by sniffing.

Snow Cocaine; *see* Cocaine.

Snowbird Cocaine user.

Spaced Out In a daze, particularly from drug use.

Speed Methedrine, a powerful amphetamine; *see* Amphetamines, Methedrine.

Stick A marijuana cigarette; *see* Marijuana.

Stoned, Stoned Out of Your Mind Being under the influence of marijuana; *see* Drug Experiences, Marijuana.

Strung Out Heavily dependent on, or addicted to, drugs.

Stuff Drug.

Sugar LSD; *see* LSD.

THC Tetrahydrocannabinol, the active chemical in marijuana; *see* Marijuana.

Tabs Drugs in tablet form.

Tar Opium; *see* Narcotic.

Tea Hashish, a strong form of marijuana; *see* Marijuana.

Turned On (1) to alter awareness, with or without drugs. (2) to use drugs.

Up Under the intoxicating influence of drugs; *see* Drug Experiences.

Up Tight Under stress; *see* Drug Experiences.

Ups Amphetamines; *see* Amphetamines.

User Usually refers to user of drugs, one who takes drugs either regularly or irregularly.

Vibrations, Vibes Feeling coming from another or from a situation. May be good or bad vibes.

Viper's Weed Marijuana; *see* Marijuana.

Wake-ups Amphetamines; *see* Amphetamines.

Wasted Under the intoxicating influence of drugs; *see* Drug Experiences.

Wedges Wedge-shaped tablets.

Weed Marijuana; *see* Marijuana.

Weed-head A frequent user of marijuana; *see* Marijuana.

Weekend Habit A small, irregular habit.

Weekend Hippie A person who lives a "normal" life during the week but who lives the part of a hippie—usually including drugs—on the weekend.

Whiskers Narcotic agents or local police.

White Lightning LSD; *see* LSD.

White Stuff Morphine; *see* Narcotic.

Whites White amphetamine tablets; *see* Amphetamines.

Winging High on drugs.

Withdrawal Phenomenon which occurs when an individual who is physically dependent on a drug stops taking that drug. Symptoms include nausea, dizziness, chills, runny nose, and itching. Also: agonies, break the habit, clear up, cold turkey, dried out, kick off, turned off.

Works Equipment for injecting narcotics. Also: arsenal, artillery, canno-, cooker, cotton, equipment, factory, "G," gear, gun, machine, needle, piece, satch cotton, spike.

Yellow Jackets Nembutal, a brand of barbiturate; *see* Barbiturates.

Yen Sleep A drowsy, restless state occurring after LSD use.

Zap Totally destroy.

Zig Zag Brand name of cigarette paper used to roll marijuana cigarettes.

Appendix II

A GLOSSARY OF
TESTING TERMINOLOGY

Ability Test A test designed to measure what a person can do. Ability tests are subdivided into aptitude tests and achievement tests.

Achievement Test A test usually administered at the end of a period of learning to measure growth and progress. The typical classroom test is of this type.

Age Equivalent The age for which a given score is the real or estimated average score.

Age Norms Values or norms that show the typical or average performance for individuals of different age groups on a test.

Anecdotal Record A written report describing an incident of an individual's behavior. Incidents are usually chosen because they appear significant for the understanding of the individual, either as being typical of him or as being unusual and surprising.

Aptitude A combination of abilities and other characteristics, whether native or acquired, known or believed to be indicative of an individual's ability to learn in some particular area. Some exclude motivational factors, including interests, from the concept of "aptitude," but the more comprehensive use seems preferable.

Aptitude Test It may be an intelligence test, achievement test, or personality or interest inventory. Many of our intelligence tests are called "scholastic aptitude tests" because they are used to predict an individual's future school performance.

Arithmetic Mean The sum of a set of scores divided by the number of scores.

Average A general term for the measures of central tendency. The most common averages are the arithmetic mean, the mode, and the median.

Battery A group of tests that are administered at one time to a sampling of a certain population so that the results can be compared. The tests in a battery have typically been planned and developed as a unit, with the objective of providing complete and efficient coverage of some ability or personality.

Ceiling The uppermost limit of an ability or skill measured by a given test.

Converted Score A score expressed in some type of derived unit, such as an age equivalent, grade equivalent, percentile, or standard score.

Correction for Guessing Considered to be of questionable usefulness and validity, this is used by adjusting scores on objective tests such as multiple choice or true and false tests, to counteract the effects of students' guessing the correct answer.

Correlation Coefficient A statistic used to measure the relationship between two sets of variables or data. The most common measurement of correlation is r, named for the founder of the method, Karl Pearson. The correlation may be either positive or negative.

Criterion A standard by which a test may be judged or evaluated; a set of scores, ratings, etc., that a test is designed to predict or to correlate with.

Cross-validation The testing out of a set of items or a system of the weights derived from one sample of individuals upon a new sample, to see to what extent the procedure retains its validity with new and independent data.

Culture-free Test An impossibility, this test is constructed so that any person from any culture has equal opportunity for success. The name has sometimes been changed to culture-fair, designating an equal preparation from different cultures in the test.

Cumulative Frequency A column in a frequency distribution that shows for any given interval all the scores in the distribution that lie below the upper limit of that interval.

Decile Nine points, which divide a distribution of scores into ten equal parts. The first decile is the tenth percentile, the ninth decile the 90th percentile, etc.

Deviation The difference between a score and a certain reference point (the mean, score from another test or norm).

Diagnostic Test A test used to identify certain weaknesses or strengths and their causes, usually a test in spelling, reading, and arithmetic.

Difficulty Index A numerical value used to express the difficulty of a test item, usually the percent getting the item correct.

Discrimination Index A list which designates the differentiation of an item between the more and less able students of a test.

Equivalent Form Two or more forms of a given test that are common in content and difficulty of the items included. They yield approximately the same average scores and measures of variability for a given group, etc.

Error of Measurement An estimation by which an obtained score differs from a hypothetical "true" score since the measurement procedure is never exact.

Face Validity A measuring instrument has face validity when it seems to be valid to the individual being measured, but the measuring instrument itself has no real validity.

Forced-choice (Item) A multiple-choice question in which the examinee *must* choose a statement as most descriptive or least descriptive. All statements in the multiple-choice are prepared so that they are approximately balanced for desirability or acceptability but different in the interpretation of the person taking the test.

Frequency Distribution A distribution of scores from high to low or low to high, usually grouped in intervals of different sizes, designating individuals who fall into each interval or score.

Frequency Polygon A graph representing the frequency distribution. The number of individuals in each score interval are plotted, and the successive points are connected with straight lines.

General Intelligence Test While existing tests are usually abstract intelligence tests, this test measures the ability to deal with problems involving ideas, symbols, and the relationships between them.

Grade Equivalent The grade level for which a given score is the real or estimated average.

Grade Norms The average scores of pupils in different grade levels or the average score of pupils in a given grade.

Histogram A graphic representation of a frequency distribution in which the cases falling in each score category are represented by a bar whose size is proportional to the number of cases. Since each bar is the full width of the score category, the bars make a continuous "pile" showing the form of the frequency distribution.

Intelligence A very difficult term to define, but intelligence in tests is usually abstract, that is, the ability to solve problems involving ideas and symbols.

Intelligence Quotient (IQ) The IQ is measured by taking the score of the test and the age of the examinee. The formula is:

$$IQ = \frac{MA \text{ (Mental age)}}{CA \text{ (Chronological age)}} \text{ (100)}$$

This is useful only with children since mental age does not continue to increase at a constant rate and it eventually ceases in late adolescence or early adulthood. The IQ, therefore, is of little consequence to adults.

Interest A test usually on occupational and educational interests, used to show the examinee's interest or preference in a certain type of activity.

Ipsative Test A test containing multiple scores, but the sum of the scores for all individuals is the same. Therefore, some of the scores of an individual will be high, others low. Rather than expressing the individual's profile in terms of the scores of an outside group, it can be expressed in relation to his own overall average.

Item Analysis A statistical study of test results used to determine the discrimination index of each item, the difficulty of each item, how well each of the distractors is working, and sometimes its correlation with an outside criterion.

Kunder-Richardson Reliability Several formulas are used to determine the reliability of a test. This is done by using the standard deviation of the test, the average score, and difficulty indices for the separate items.

Median The separation of the distribution of scores with 50 percent above the median and 50 percent below the median.

Mental Age The average or normal age of a given score in a test.

Mode The most frequent score or value that occurs in a distribution.

N The representation of a number of cases in a group being studied.

Normal Distribution The bell-shaped distribution of scores or measures on a graph used in much test development work.

Norms Norms are averages, not standards. They are statistics or values describing the performance of various groups on a test. Grade, age, and percentile are the most common types of norms.

Objective Test The results of a test are the same no matter who scores. The test is scored by the use of keys or stencils, and the answers are either right or wrong, never depending on the opinion of the scorer.

Percentile A point (score) below which falls the percent of cases indicated by the given percentile. For example, 20th percentile indicates the score or point below which 20 percent of the scores fall.

Performance Test Rather than using a written test, this test uses such things as mazes, blocks, puzzles, etc. A performance test requires motor responses in which ability is evaluated in terms of something the individual does rather than something he says.

Personality Test A test used to assess the individual's typical way of acting, as distinct from his ability to perform.

Power Test A test with either no time limit or a rather long period of time in which to complete the test, in which the measurement of a person's performance rather than his speed is taken into account.

Proficiency Test A job-oriented skill usually is measured as to the current level of proficiency.

Profile A graphic representation of the results of an individual's performance on a group of tests so that his weaknesses and strengths can be easily seen.

Projective Test In this test, material such as ink blots, pictures, or unfinished sentences are used because the individual can project part of his personality characteristics into his responses, and in turn they can be measured and interpreted to form a basic personality structure.

Quartile One of three points that divide the cases in a distribution into four equal groups. $Q_1 = 25$ percentile, $Q_2 = 50$ percentile, $Q_3 = 75$ percentile, which marks the highest fourth in the distribution.

Random Sample A sample drawn so that every person in the population has an equal opportunity to be included not through the use of selection or bias. This is done so that the sample can be said to be a fair representative of the population, and in turn the sample findings may be generalized.

Range The difference between the highest and lowest scores in a test obtained by some group.

Raw Score The original, untouched result that is obtained from a test or other measuring instrument.

Readiness Test Any test that is used to ascertain whether an individual has attained the maturity necessary to profit from learning. Most commonly associated with reading.

Reliability Usually expressed in terms of correlation coefficients or by use of the standard error of measurement, it is used to show the consistency of measurement in a given test.

Reliability Coefficient The correlation coefficient is acquired by correlating scores obtained from two administrations of the same test, between halves of a test, or between parallel forms of a test.

Semi-interquartile Range (Q) One half the distance between the upper and lower quartiles, used as a measure of variability.

Skewness The tendency for some distributions of scores to pile up at one end and to stretch out at the other end. An easy test would produce this distribution.

Spearman-Brown Prophecy Formula Commonly used in the estimation of reliability of an entire test from the correlation between halves of the test. So long as the reliability of a specific length is known, the estimation of reliability of a test of any length can be established.

Standard Deviation A measure of the variability or dispersion of a set of scores. The more the scores cluster around the mean, the smaller the standard deviation.

Standard Error of Measurement An estimation of the size of the error of measurement in a score, expressed in the same units that were used for the original measurements.

Standard Score A score expressed in terms of standard deviations above or below the arithmetic mean of the group. More complicated types of standard scores may yield distributions differing in shape from the original distribution.

Standardized Test A test that has been given to various samples or groups under standardized conditions and norms established.

Stanine Short for standard-nine, this scale ranges from 1 to 9 and has a mean of 5 and a standard deviation of 2.

Test-retest Reliability A test is given more than once to designate possible changes or inconsistencies of the individual from one occasion to another. The test is not changed at all in each administration.

Validity The extent of effectiveness of the test in the job it is to carry out. The definition of validity depends on the test that is given. For example a test of personality can be valid only if it carries out this task. *Content validity* refers to the faithfulness with which the test represents or reproduces an area of knowledge. *Construct validity* is the accuracy with which a test interprets an individual in terms of some psychological trait or construct. *Criterion-related validity* is the exactitude with which the test scores can predict some criterion variable of educational, job, or life performance.

Variability The span of scores in a set of scores from the average score in the group.

Counseling and values: The counselor rates himself*

Sex-rigid

It is a wife's duty to have intercourse with her husband.

Girls should come to the marriage bed as virgins.

It is bad taste to tell dirty jokes in mixed company.

Men who have sex relations outside of marriage are low and contemptible.

Divorce is never justified.

People should not marry before they are twenty-one.

Sexual intercourse should be had only for the purpose of having children.

The best and truest love is one without sexual thoughts and feelings.

Pulp magazines featuring sexy love stories should be abolished.

Masturbation is a sin.

Sex-free

It's perfectly all right for teen-agers to kiss and neck.

Men ought to have some sexual experience before marriage.

Sexual intercourse provides one of life's most beautiful experiences.

A woman may be justified in having another man if her husband is not satisfying her sexual needs.

Prostitution should be legal.

Unnatural sex acts should not be considered a crime.

Sex-play before intercourse makes it more satisfactory.

Sex education should be taught in public schools.

One should expect one's wife or husband to be attracted to handsome members of the opposite sex.

If young children play with their sex organs, parents need not be worried or concerned.

Antiaggressive

If someone strikes you on one cheek, turn the other.

Using live animals for medical research is wrong.

Judge not lest ye be judged.

One should always try one's best to get along with others.

It is wrong to hate.

Capital punishment is wrong.

If you're angry, count ten and try to let the feeling go away.

Wars are never justified.

The meek shall inherit the earth.

Violence breeds violence.

Aggressive

A man who lives by the sword should die by the sword.

Might makes right.

One should say what one thinks about other people.

If people annoy you, either let them know it or don't bother with them.

Some people are no damn good.

Let the punishment fit the crime: an eye for an eye.

To the victor belong the spoils.

A nation that will not defend its rights or its honor deserves not to survive.

The race is to the swift and the strong.

You have to use brute force to set some matters straight.

Disciplinarian

Labor unions should be strictly regulated.

One should always be busy and keep one's mind occupied.

Children should do as they are told.

Parents act in the best interest of their children.

Parents sacrifice a lot for their children.

"Thou shalt honor thy father and mother" is a commandment which should always be observed.

Everyone should belong to some church.

What our country needs most are great leaders.

A soldier should always obey orders first, ask questions afterward.

Our future lies in the hands of fate.

*From "Changes in Some Moral Values Following Psychotherapy" by David Rosenthal, *Journal of Consulting Psychology*, 1955, 6, 433. Copyright 1955 by the American Psychological Association. Reprinted by permission.

Libertarian

There may be times when one should break the
law.

People should take time out to relax and think
about themselves.

Parents should always tell children why things
should or should not be done.

Many parents do not really love their children.

The trials of parenthood are more than equalled by
its rewards.

Parents often deserve to lose the respect of their
children.

God is created by man in his own image.

Famous leaders owe their greatness to the ones
they lead.

An employee should express his opinion, even when
the boss disagrees.

A person must take responsibility for his own life.

Appendix IV

ETHICAL STANDARDS:
AMERICAN PERSONNEL
AND GUIDANCE ASSOCIATION*

Preamble

The American Personnel and Guidance Association is an educational, scientific, and professional organization dedicated to service to society. This service is committed to profound faith in the worth, dignity, and great potentiality of the individual human being.

The marks of a profession, and therefore of a professional organization, can be stated as follows:

1 Possession of a body of specialized knowledge, skills, and attitudes known and practiced by its members.
2 This body of specialized knowledge, skills, and attitudes is derived through scientific inquiry and scholarly learning.
3 This body of specialized knowledge, skills, and attitudes is acquired through professional preparation, preferably on the graduate level, in a college or university as well as through continuous in-service training and personal growth after completion of formal education.
4 This body of specialized knowledge, skills, and attitudes, is constantly tested and extended through research and scholarly inquiry.
5 A profession has a literature of its own, even though it may, and indeed must, draw portions of its content from other areas of knowledge.
6 A profession exalts service to the individual and society above personal gain. It possesses a philosophy and a code of ethics.
7 A profession through the voluntary association of its members constantly examines and improves the quality of its professional preparation and services to the individual and society.
8 Membership in the professional organization and the practice of the profession must be limited to persons meeting stated standards of preparation and competencies.
9 The profession affords a life career and permanent membership as long as services meet professional standards.

*Reprinted by permission. American Personnel and Guidance Association.

10 The public recognizes, has confidence in, and is willing to compensate the members of the profession for their services.

The Association recognizes that the vocational roles and settings of its members are identified with a wide variety of academic disciplines and levels of academic preparation. This diversity reflects the pervasiveness of the Association's interest and influence. It also poses challenging complexities in efforts to conceptualize:

a the characteristics of members;
b desired or requisite preparation or practice; and
c supporting social, legal and/or ethical controls.

The specification of ethical standards enables the Association to clarify to members, future members, and to those served by members the nature of ethical responsibilities held in common by its members.

The introduction of such standards will inevitably stimulate greater concern by members for practice and preparation for practice. It will also stimulate a general growth and identification with and appreciation for both the common and diverse characteristics of the definable roles within the world of work of Association members.

There are six major areas of professional activity which encompass the work of members of APGA. For each of these areas certain general principles are listed below to serve as guidelines for ethical practice. These are preceded by a general section which includes certain principles germane to the six areas and common to the entire work of the Association members.

General

1 The member exerts what influence he can to foster the development and improvement of the profession and continues his professional growth throughout his career.
2 The member has a responsibility to the institution within which he serves. His acceptance of employment by the institution implies that he is in substantial agreement with the general policies

and principles of the institution. Therefore, his professional activities are also in accord with the objectives of the institution. Within the member's own work setting, if, despite his efforts, he cannot reach agreement as to acceptable ethical standards of conduct with his superiors, he should end his affiliation with them.

3 The member must expect ethical behavior among his professional associates in APGA at all times. He is obligated, in situations where he possesses information raising serious doubt as to the ethical behavior of other members, to attempt to rectify such conditions.

4 The member is obligated to concern himself with the degree to which the personnel functions of non-members with whose work he is acquainted represent competent and ethical performance. Where his information raises serious doubt as to the ethical behavior of such persons, it is his responsibility to attempt to rectify such conditions.

5 The member must not seek self-enhancement through expressing evaluations or comparisons damaging to other ethical professional workers.

6 The member should not claim or imply professional qualifications exceeding those possessed and is responsible for correcting any misrepresentations of his qualifications by others.

7 The member providing services for personal remuneration shall, in establishing fees for such services, take careful account of the charges made for comparable services by other professional persons.

8 The member who provides information to the public or to his subordinates, peers, or superiors has a clear responsibility to see that both the content and the manner of presentation are accurate and appropriate to the situation.

9 The member has an obligation to ensure that evaluative information about such persons as clients, students, and applicants shall be shared only with those persons who will use such information for professional purposes.

10 The member shall offer professional services only through the context of a professional relationship. Thus testing, counseling, and other services

are not to be provided through the mail or by means of newspaper or magazine articles, radio or television programs, or public performances.

Counseling

This section refers to practices involving a counseling relationship with a counselee or client and is not intended to be applicable to practices involving administrative relationships with the persons being helped. A counseling relationship denotes that the person seeking help retain full freedom of choice and decision and that the helping person has no authority or responsibility to approve or disapprove of the choices or decisions of the counselee or client. "Counselee" or "client" is used here to indicate the person (or persons) for whom the member has assumed a professional responsibility. Typically the counselee or client is the individual with whom the member has direct and primary contact. However, at times, "client" may include another person(s) to exercise significant control and direction over the individual being helped in connection with the decisions and plans being considered in counseling.

1 The member's primary obligation is to respect the integrity and promote the welfare of the counselee or client with whom he is working.

2 The counseling relationship and information resulting therefrom must be kept confidential consistent with the obligations of the member as a professional person.

3 Records of the counseling relationship including interview notes, test data, correspondence, tape recordings, and other documents are to be considered professional information for use in counseling, research, and teaching of counselors but always with full protection of the identity of the client and with precaution so that no harm will come to him.

4 The counselee or client should be informed of the conditions under which he may receive counseling assistance at or before the time he enters the counseling relationship. This is particularly true in the event that there exist conditions of which the counselee or client would not likely be aware.

5 The member reserves the right to consult with any other professionally competent person about his counselee client. In choosing his professional consultant the member must avoid placing the consultant in a conflict of interest situation, i.e., the consultant must be free of any other obligatory relation to the member's client that would preclude the consultant being a proper party to the member's efforts to help the counselee or client.

6 The member shall decline to initiate or shall terminate a counseling relationship when he cannot be of professional assistance to the counselee or client either because of lack of competence or personal limitation. In such instances the member shall refer his counselee or client to an appropriate specialist. In the event the counselee or client declines the suggested referral, the member is not obligated to continue the counseling relationship.

7 When the member learns from counseling relationships of conditions which are likely to harm others over whom his institution or agency has responsibility, he is expected to report the condition to the appropriate responsible authority, but in such a manner as not to reveal the identity of his counselee or client.

8 In the event that the counselee or client's condition is such as to require others to assume responsibility for him, or when there is clear and imminent danger to the counselee or client or to others, the member is expected to report this fact to an appropriate responsible authority and/or take such other emergency measures as the situations demands.

9 Should the member be engaged in a work setting which calls for any variation from the above statements, the member is obligated to ascertain that such variations are justifiable under the conditions and that such variations are clearly specified and made known to all concerned with such counseling services.

Testing

1 The primary purpose of psychological testing is to provide objective and comparative measures for use in self-evaluation or evaluation by others of general or specific attributes.

2 Generally, test results constitute only one of a variety of pertinent data for personnel and guidance decisions. It is the member's responsibility to provide adequate orientation or information to the examinee(s) so that the results of testing may be placed in proper perspective with other relevant factors.

3 When making any statements to the public about tests and testing, care must be taken to give accurate information and to avoid any false claims or misconceptions.

4 Different tests demand different levels of competence for administration, scoring, and interpretation. It is therefore the responsibility of the member to recognize the limits of his competence and to perform only those functions which fall within his preparation and competence.

5 In selecting tests for use in a given situation or with a particular client, the member must consider not only general but also specific validity, reliability, and appropriateness of the test(s).

6 Tests should be administered under the same conditions which were established in their standardization. Except for research purposes explicitly stated, any departures from these conditions, as well as unusual behavior or irregularities during the testing session which may affect the interpretation of the test results, must be fully noted and reported. In this connection, unsupervised test-taking or the use of tests through the mails are of questionable value.

7 The value of psychological tests depends in part on the novelty to persons taking them. Any prior information, coaching, or reproduction of test materials tends to invalidate test results. Therefore, test security is one of the professional obligations of the member.

8 The member has the responsibility to inform the examinee(s) as to the purpose of testing. The criteria of examinee's welfare and/or explicit prior understanding with him should determine who the recipients of the test results may be.

9 The member should guard against the appropriation, reproduction, or modifications of published tests or parts thereof without express permission and adequate recognition of the original author or publisher.

Regarding the preparation, publication, and distribution of tests, reference should be made to:

"Test and Diagnostic Techniques"—Report of the Joint Committee of the American Psychological Association, American Educational Research Association, and National Council of Measurements used in Education. Supplement to Psychological Bulletin, 1954, 2, 1-38.

Research and publication

1 In the performance of any research on human subjects, the member must avoid causing any injurious effects or after-effects of the experiment upon his subjects.

2 The member may withhold information or provide misinformation to subjects only when it is essential to the investigation and where he assumes responsibility for corrective action following the investigation.

3 In reporting research results, explicit mention must be made of all variables and conditions known to the investigator which might affect interpretation of the data.

4 The member is responsible for conducting and reporting his investigations so as to minimize the possibility that his findings will be misleading.

5 The member has an obligation to make available original research data to qualified others who may wish to replicate or verify the study.

6 In reporting research results or in making original data available, due care must be taken to disguise the identity of the subjects, in the absence of specific permission from such subjects to do otherwise.

7 In conducting and reporting research, the member should be familiar with, and give recognition to, previous work on the topic.

8 The member has the obligation to give due credit to those who have contributed significantly to his research, in accordance with their contributions.

9 The member has the obligation to honor commitments made to subjects of research in return for their cooperation.

10 The member is expected to communicate to other members the results of any research he judges to be of professional or scientific value.

Consulting and private practice

Consulting refers to a voluntary relationship between a professional helper and help-needing social unit (industry, business, school, college, etc.) in which the consultant is attempting to give help to the client in the solving of some current or potential problem.

1 The member acting as a consultant must have a high degree of self-awareness of his own values and needs in entering a helping relationship which involves change in social unit.

2 There should be understanding and agreement between consultant and client as to directions or goals of the attempted change.

3 The consultant must be reasonably certain that he or his organization have the necessary skills and resources for giving the kind of help which is needed now or that may develop later.

4 The consulting relationship must be one in which client adaptability and growth toward self-direction are encouraged and cultivated. The consultant must consistently maintain his role as a consultant and not become a decision maker for the client.

5 The consultant in announcing his availability for service as a consultant follows professional rather than commercial standards in describing his services with accuracy, dignity, and caution.

6 For private practice in testing, counseling, or consulting, the ethical principles stated in all previous sections of this document are pertinent. In addition, any individual, agency, or institution offering educational and vocational counseling to the public should meet the standards of the American Board on Professional Standards in Vocational Counseling, Inc.

Personnel administration

1 The member is responsible for establishing working agreements with supervisors and with subordinates, especially regarding counseling or clinical relationships, confidentiality, distinction between public and private material, and a mutual respect for the positions of parties involved in such issues.

2 Such working agreements may vary from one institutional setting to another. What should be the case in each instance, however, is that agreements have been specified, made known to those concerned, and whenever possible the agreements reflect institutional policy rather than personal judgment.

3 The member's responsibility to his superiors requires that he keep them aware of conditions affecting the institution, particularly those which may be potentially disrupting or damaging to the institution.

4 The member has a responsibility to select competent persons for assigned responsibilities and to see that his personnel are used maximally for the skills and experience they possess.

5 The member has responsibility for constantly stimulating his staff for their and his own continued growth and improvement. He must see that staff members are adequately supervised as to the quality of their functioning and for purposes of professional development.

6 The member is responsible for seeing that his staff is informed of policies, goals, and programs toward which the department's operations are oriented.

Preparation for personnel work

1 The member in charge of training sets up a strong program of academic study and supervised practice in order to prepare the trainees for their future responsibilities.

2 The training program should aim to develop in the trainee not only skills and knowledge, but also self-understanding.

3 The member should be aware of any manifestations of personal limitations in a student trainee which may influence the latter's provision of competent services and has an obligation to offer assistance to the trainee in securing professional remedial help.

4 The training program should include preparation in research and stimulation for the future personnel worker to do research and add to the knowledge in his field.

5 The training program should make the trainee aware of the ethical responsibilities and standards of the profession he is entering.

6 The program of preparation should aim at inculcating among the trainees, who will later become the practitioners of our profession, the ideal of service to individual and society above personal gain.

Acknowledgments

I am indebted to a number of people for inspiring ideas which were incorporated in the book and for assisting me in the preparation of the manuscript. Professors Philip Phenix and Maxine Greene, both of Teachers College, Columbia University, enriched my background in philosophy and education, which contributed in no small way to the ideas expressed in this book. Professor Greene's most recent work, *Teacher as Stranger*, has had a profound influence on my own thinking, which will be evident to those familiar with her writings. Professor Ruth Skydell, of Long Island University, offered many valuable insights concerning both style and substance. Martin Garfinkle and Alison Belkin (my sister) helped in the labors of research, for which I am grateful. My mother and Lydia Gorski gave up many of their weekends typing the final manuscript. My father provided technical assistance above and beyond the call of paternal duty. All of the people at Wm. C. Brown in Dubuque and at Edit, Inc., in Chicago were of great help during the book's final production. GSB

Credits

Illustrations

Lydia Gorski: 38, 96, 97, 122, 133, 135, 136, 199, 309, 327, 341, 358, 359.

Peter Schwarzburg: i-ii, iv-v, viii, ix, x, 94, 196, 288, 338.

Photographs

Cover: Rosemarie Mazzeo.

The Bettmann Archive, Inc.: 5, 7, 14, 15, 16, 17, 200, 202, 203, 204, 205, 221, 237, 413.

Black Star: Bob Fitch, 3, 46, 181; Rod Hanna, 433; Bruce McAllister, 73.

Albert Ellis: 258.

Frederic Lewis Archives: 234, 342, 343, 348, 383; Steven P. Bloomfield, 345; Dan Coleman, 311; Harold M. Lambert, 375; Anna Kaufman Moon, 370, 378, 379, 389, 406, 409, 436; Alon Reiniger, 373 right; W. L. Riegler, 361; Leo Vals, 352, 373 left.

Historical Pictures Service, Chicago: 269, 273.

Huntsville, Alabama City Schools Adult Education Program, Dr. V. M. Burkett, Superintendent; Dr. James H. Mason, Jr., Adult Education Coordinator: 161.

Rosemarie Mazzeo: ii, iii, 150, 233, 329, 411.

Monkmeyer: 276 bottom; Mimi Forsyth, 246; Hugh Rogers, 276 top.

John H. Murchison, 417.

The New York Times/Sam Falk, 273.

Springer/Bettmann Film Archive, 235.

Teachers College, Columbia University: 271.

Index of Names

Diedrich, R. C., 44
Dilley, J., 111
Dimick, K. M., 42, 68, 109, 274, 302
Dinkmeyer, D., 216, 398
Dollard, J., 85, 273, 282
Downing, L. N., 13
Drasgow, J., 77, 295
Dreikurs, R., 56
Dreyfus, E. A., 241
Durbak, C., 279
Dworkin, A. L., 168
Dworkin, E. P., 168
Dymond, R. F., 290
Ebel, R. I., 395
Eber, H., 99
Egan, G., 319
Egan, J. H., 145
Eidelberg, L., 213
Einhorn, A., 344
Einstein, A., 84
Eisenberg, S., 191
Eitingen, M., 202
Ellis, Albert, 39, 67, 258, 260, 261,
    262, 263, 264, 265, 266, 413
English, R. W., 231
Erikson, E., 347, 386, 387
Esper, E. A., 6, 7
Eysenck, Hans, 270, 274, 290
Ezell, B., 296
Fagan, J., 252
Farrell, B. A., 209
Fazzaro, C. J., 401, 402
Felker, K. R., 189
Felker, S., 301
Ferenczi, S., 202, 211
Fiedler, F. E., 71
Filbeck, R. W., 164
Fischer, E., 344
Fitzgibbons, D. J., 25, 141
Ford, C. S., 362
Foreman, M. E., 190
Foreman, N. J., 329, 333, 418
Forer, B. R., 328
Foulds, M. L., 255
Frank, J. D., 25
Frankena, W. K., 56
Frankl, V., 127, 236, 241, 242, 243
Franklin, A. J., 371
Fredrickson, R. H., 190

Freud, Anna, 206
Freud, S., 4, 5, 6, 7, 16, 17, 18, 67,
    131, 132, 137, 139, 185, 199, 200,
    201, 202, 203, 204, 205, 206, 207,
    208, 209, 210, 211, 219, 224, 248,
    342, 343
Friedersdorf, N. W., 372
Fromm, E., 40, 129, 130
Fromm-Reichmann, F., 22
Fuller, B., 246
Galen, 83
Gannon, W. J., 255
Garrett, H. E., 395
Garris, D., 161
Garvey, W. P., 282
Gazda, G. M., 192, 409
Gellen, M. I., 99
Geller, A., 344
Gelso, C. J., 58
Gendlin, E. T., 315
Gibb, J. R., 313
Gifford, S., 371
Gillespie, J. O., 401, 402
Gimmestad, M. J., 178, 180
Ginzberg, E., 418, 430
Gladstein, G. A., 63, 111
Glasser, William, 257, 258, 259,
    261, 262, 263, 264, 266, 406
Goble, F., 87, 88
Goffman, E., 113, 123
Goldenson, R. M., 248
Goldman, S., 393
Goldsmith, E. B., 178, 180
Goodman, P., 248
Goodwin, F. P., 12
Graffagnino, P. N., 216
Grant, C. W., 159
Grant, H. W., 418
Graver, P. A., 103
Greene, Maxine, 8, 59, 239
Grier, W. H., 371
Gronlund, N. E., 388
Grossberg, J. M., 280
Grummon, D. L., 98
Gust, T., 191
Gustad, J. W., 43
Haettenschwiller, D. L., 155
Hagen, E., 388, 390, 391
Hagenah, T., 396

Halsted, W. S., 343, 344
Hammond, W. A., 343
Hansen, L. S., 383
Harmin, M., 411
Harper, A., 258
Harrington, G. L., 257
Harris, G. A., 190
Hart, D. H., 164
Hatch, R. N., 419, 433
Hawley, P., 373
Healy, W., 12
Heayn, M. H., 384
Hefferline, R., 248
Hegrenes, J. R., 282
Heidegger, 54
Heidegger, M., 233, 234, 236, 237,
    238, 239
Heikkinen, C. A., 99
Heilfron, M., 158
Helpern, J. M. G., 397
Heraclitus, 4
Herbart, 5
Herr, E. L., 418, 422
Herskovits, M. J., 370
Hewer, V. H., 423
Higgins, T. E., 231
Hill, G. E., 175
Hill, J. C., 407
Hiltner, S., 294
Hipple, T. E., 71
Hippocrates, 83
Hobbs, N., 157
Hoffman, D. S., 418
Holland, J., 424-426
Hoopes, M. H., 286
Hoppock, R., 429
Horne, P. S., 407, 408
Horney, K., 205, 206
Howe, L., 412
Hoyt, K. B., 169, 170
Huff, V. E., 42, 68, 109, 274, 302
Hull, C. L., 272, 273
Hume, David, 7
Husserl, E., 237, 238
Hutcheon, W. R., 166
Isaksen, H. L., 170
Island, D., 184
Ivey, A. E., 191
Jackson, M., 101

Index of Subjects